A

TREATISE

ON

THE LAW

OF THE

𝕻rerogatibes of the Crown;

AND THE

RELATIVE DUTIES AND RIGHTS OF THE SUBJECT.

By JOSEPH CHITTY, JUN. Esq.

OF THE MIDDLE TEMPLE.

THE LAWBOOK EXCHANGE, LTD.
Clark, New Jersey

ISBN 9781616190644 (hardcover)
ISBN 9781616190651 (paperback)

Lawbook Exchange edition 2010

The quality of this reprint is equivalent to the quality of the original work.

THE LAWBOOK EXCHANGE, LTD.

33 Terminal Avenue
Clark, New Jersey 07066-1321

*Please see our website for a selection of our other publications
and fine facsimile reprints of classic works of legal history:*
www.lawbookexchange.com

Library of Congress Cataloging-in-Publication Data

Chitty, Joseph, d. 1838.
 A treatise on the law of the prerogatives of the crown, and the
relative duties and rights of the subject / by Joseph Chitty.
   p. cm.
 Originally published: London, J. Butterworth and Son, 1820.
 Includes bibliographical references and index.
 ISBN-13: 978-1-61619-064-4 (hardcover : alk. paper)
 ISBN-10: 1-61619-064-7 (hardcover : alk. paper)
 ISBN-13: 978-1-61619-065-1 (pbk. : alk. paper)
 ISBN-10: 1-61619-065-5 (pbk. : alk. paper)
 1. Prerogative, Royal--Great Britain. I. Title.
KD4435.C45 2010
349.41--dc22
                                    2010012765

Printed in the United States of America on acid-free paper

A

TREATISE

ON

THE LAW

OF THE

𝕻𝖗𝖊𝖗𝖔𝖌𝖆𝖙𝖎𝖛𝖊𝖘 𝖔𝖋 𝖙𝖍𝖊 𝕮𝖗𝖔𝖜𝖓;

AND THE

RELATIVE DUTIES AND RIGHTS OF THE SUBJECT.

———

By JOSEPH CHITTY, JUN. Esq.

OF THE MIDDLE TEMPLE.

———

London:

PRINTED FOR JOSEPH BUTTERWORTH AND SON,

LAW BOOKSELLERS, 43, FLEET STREET;

AND JOHN COOKE, ORMOND QUAY, DUBLIN.

———

1820.

PREFACE.

It may be matter of surprise, that in a country in which the public eye has ever minutely watched the progress of authority, a subject of such interesting importance as the " Prerogatives of the Crown," should not have elicited the most extensive and learned investigation. Whilst under some governments an attempt to discuss the limits of the royal power, would expose the presumptuous subject to the jealous apprehensions of tyranny, English history points out but few instances of periods in which the disclosure would have been dangerous; and the British constitution allows of none: it rather invites than represses the inquiry. For in this country, the relation of sovereign and subject combines reciprocal duties. The prerogative is not the iron tie of unbridled power: it holds the subject in the silken chain of mild subjection, for the general and permanent welfare of society; and as a general principle it affords the sovereign the liberty of restraint, only when the public good is the object in view. As the powers and rights of the King are inseparably connected with the dearest rights and liberties of his people; as their interests and their obligations are

A 2

mutual ; it is incumbent on the subject, desirous of knowing his own duties and rights, to ascertain the exact extent and limits of the duties and prerogatives of his Sovereign. Indeed so intimately, yet beautifully, are they interwoven, that in discussing the latter, the former must necessarily be considered.

That a treatise on this subject is important, both to the public and the profession, needs no comment. That system of jurisprudence on which the prerogative is founded, will be duly appreciated and valued by every one aware of its wisdom and merits ; which will become more apparent, the more they are can-vassed and investigated.

The Author of the following pages has attempted to present a comprehensive and connected, yet com-pressed and logical, view of every prerogative and corresponding right of the subject; but is con-scious of the imperfect manner in which the at-tempt has been executed. If, however, imperfec-tions admit of excuses, the kind, the candid, and the considerate, will find many for the first work on so difficult, so extensive, and so noble a subject. The materials were indiscriminately scattered, or superfici-ally noticed in the law-books, from whence alone the author was able to obtain information. It was frequently necessary to resort to the most antient text-writers, and judicial determinations, and in using such, the idea of overlooking more recent, and, perhaps, dissimilar autho-rities, could not but add the anxiety of being incor-rect, to the labor of discovering and selecting the materials. Nor could the endeavour to form a correct analysis and methodical arrangement of a subject comprising so many considerations, be unattended by difficulties, or free from anxieties.

It seems unnecessary to state, that in the following pages every political disquisition has been avoided, as wholly irrelevant and improper.

The Author is convinced, that every professional inquirer will, on perusing the '*Analysis*,' immediately perceive, that many subjects of high practical utility, and several of daily occurrence in business, are introduced in various parts of the work. And it is hoped, the ' *Index*,' on which the Author has bestowed great pains, will be found to render the work very easy of access.

ANALYSIS.

CHAP. I.

	Page
Origin of Society	1
Legislative and Executive Authorities	2
Principles of the Constitution as to the Royal Power	3
The King's Attributes or Political Power	4
His Prerogative in general	6
Boundaries and restraints	7
Who, in legal contemplation, is entitled to exercise the Prerogatives	9

CHAP. II.

	Page
SECT. 1. Of the King's Right to Allegiance; from whom due	12
2. Of the Nature and Extent of Allegiance, and of taking the Oaths of Allegiance	15
3. Of such Rights of the King over the Persons of his Subjects, as more immediately result from the Allegiance and Submission due from them	18

CHAP. III.

	Page
Where the Prerogatives are exerciseable; and herein of the Prerogative, as it respects the British Colonies	25

CHAP. IV.

Of the Prerogative as it more immediately relates to independent states and foreign matters.

                                            Page

SECT. 1. In general 39

2. As to Ambassadors, &c. . . . 40

3. Of Letters of Marque and Reprisals . . ibid.

4. Of making War and Peace . . . 43

5. Of other Rights incident to the War Prerogative 44

The Militia 45

The Army . . . . ibid.

The Fleet . . . 46

Pressing . . . . ibid,

Of Aliens coming into the Country . . 48

Other Rights 49

CHAP. V.

Of the King as the Head of the National Church.

The Supremacy of the Crown . . . 50

Ecclesiastical Laws; and Powers of the Crown respecting Convocations, or Synods 51

Ecclesiastical Laws under the King's Controul, Protection, &c. 53

Of the King as the *dernier resort* in Ecclesiastical Causes . 55

Prerogative as to the disposal of Church Preferments, &c. . 57

Custody of Temporalities 63

Corodies 65

Tithes, First Fruits, and Tenths, &c. . . . 65, 6

CHAP. VI.

Of the Prerogative with respect to the Houses of Parliament 67

CHAP. VII.

Of the King as the Fountain of Justice and Office, and Administrator of the Laws.

Page

Sect. 1. In general; and as to Public Courts and Offices, and
Officers. 75

2. As to Pardons, Reprieves, &c.

1. In general . . . 88

2. When and how far the King may pardon,
and of Dispensations, *Non Obstantes* and
Reprieves 90

3. Manner of pardoning . . . 98

4. Effect of a Pardon . . . 102

3. As to Gaols 103

4. Of Royal Proclamations.

1. In general; and when they are legal . 104

2. Proclamations, how made . . 106

3. Consequences of disobedience to a Proclamation 107

CHAP. VIII.

Of the King as the Fountain of Honours, Dignities, Privileges, and Franchises; and the nature of them.

Sect. 1. Peerage and grants thereof—Degrees of—How created—Descent of—Precedence, &c.—How extin-
guished--lost, &c.--Other honours.—the Commons,
Privileges, &c. 107

2. Franchises, in general . . . 118

1. Counties Palatine, Cinque Ports, &c. and
Counties Corporate . . . 119

2. Corporations . . . 120

3. Game Franchises; and herein of the King's
Prerogative as to Game and of Forests . 133

4. Free Chases 140

5. Parks . . . . ibid.

		Page
6.	Free Warrens	141
7.	Fisheries and Fish	142
8.	Mines	145
9.	Fairs and Markets	193
10.	Waifs	146
11.	Wrecks	148
12.	Estrays	151
13.	Treasure trove	152
14.	Deodands	153

CHAP. IX.

Of the King as *Parens Patriæ.*

SECT. 1. As to

		Page
1.	Infants	155
2.	Idiots	157
3.	Lunatics	159
2.	As to Charities	161

CHAP. X.

Of the Prerogative as to Commerce.

SECT. 1. Foreign Commerce; Freedom of, and how far under
royal Controul 162
Consuls 170
Dispensations by licences and orders in council from
the effect of war on Commerce, &c. . . ibid.
Prohibition . . . . ibid.
Embargoes 172
Declarations of Contraband . . . ibid.
Sovereignty over the Seas . . . 173
Ports and Havens 174
Beacons and Light-houses . . . 175
SECT. 2. Of the Prerogative with respect to Domestic Commerce or Internal Trade.
1. Monopolies and Patents for Inventions . 176

Page

1. For what inventions Patents may be granted 178
2. Who is to be considered the inventor . 181
3. The description of the Invention in the specification . . . 182
4. How a Patent is obtained . . . 188
5. The Remedies for the Infraction of the Patent Rights 191
6. How the Patent may be vacated . . 193
2. Marts and Fairs . . . . . ibid.
3. Weights and Measures 196
4. As to Money, Coin, &c. . . . . ibid.
   1. The Materials . . . . ibid.
   2. The Impression 197
   3. The Denomination or Value . . ibid.

CHAP. XI.

Of the Prerogatives as to the Revenue.
In general 199

Sect. 1. Ordinary and Inherent . . . 200, 2
   1. Ecclesiastical.
      Custody of the Temporalities of Bishop—
      Corodies —— extra-parochial Tithes —— first
      Fruits and Tenths 202
   2. From immediate Crown Possessions and Rights.
      1. Demesne Lands and Profits thereof . 202
      2. Antient Rights of Seignory . . 211
      3. Forfeitures for Offences.
         1. General Considerations . . 213
         2. With respect to the Offender's Realty 216
         3. His Personalty . . . 222
      4. Escheats 226
      5. Profits from Courts of Justice . . 236
      6. As Guardian of Idiots, &c. . . 237
   3. From Royal Franchises, &c. . . . ibid.
2. As to the extraordinary Revenue of the Crown . ibid.

Page

3. Other Crown Property.
    Antient Jewels, &c.   238
    Prerogative Copyright .   .   .   . ibid.
    Nature of Crown Property   .   .   . 241
    Devise of, &c.   242

CHAP. XII.

Of the Prerogative with respect to Judicial Remedies
   and Proceedings at the Suit of the Crown.
In general   243

SECT. 1. By the usual Common Law Actions   .   . 245
      2. By Inquisitions or Inquest of Office   .   . ibid.
          And herein also of *Extents*
          In general   262

PART I.—*Extents in Chief.*

SECT. 1. Commission to find Debts and Inquisition there-
          on; and herein of Debts due to the Crown . 265
      2. Of the *scire facias* to justify the issuing of the
          Extent in Chief   271
      3. Form.—Teste.—The issuing and return, &c. of
          Extents in Chief   273
      4. When an immediate Extent may issue—Affi-
          davit to obtain it; and Fiat thereon   .   . 277
      5. Execution of Extent in Chief.
          1. In general   280
          2. What may be taken.
              Body 282
              Goods and Sums of Money   . 284
              Lands   293
              Debts and Credits   .   .   . 303
      6. And herein of seizing Debts, Specialties, and
          Credits due to the Crown Debtor: And
          of Extents in Chief, in the second de-
          gree, *i. e.* against Debtors to the Crown
          Debtor, &c.   303

[*Resisting Extents and Proceedings thereon.*—Cʜ. XIII.]

Page

7. *Venditioni exponas*—Order for Sale of defendant's Lands, &c. 307
8. Costs 310
9. Poundage 312

Pᴀʀᴛ II.—*Of Extents in Aid.*

Sᴇᴄᴛ. 1. In general.—The course of proceeding . 317
2. To what degrees Debts may be seized on Extents in Aid 318
3. What Crown Debtor may issue an Extent in
Aid . . . . . ibid.
4. For what sum an Extent in Aid may be issued.—Affidavit, and Fiat . . . 320
5. Form of—What may be taken—Motions—
Pleading—Costs—Poundage, &c. . . 325
Sᴇᴄᴛ. 3. *Scire Facias* to repeal grants, &c. . . 330
4. By Information
1. Of intrusion 332
2. Of debt 335
3. In rem . . . . . ibid.
5. *Quo warranto.* 336
6. *Mandamus* 338

CHAP. XIII.

Of obtaining Redress from the Crown.

In general 339

Sᴇᴄᴛ. 1. Petition of Right . . . 340
2. *Monstrans de droit* . . . 352
3. Traverse of Office . . . 356
And herein of resisting Extents.

		Page
1.	Appearing to Extents, and claiming property	358
2.	Motions to set aside Extents—To pay money, &c.	363
3.	Pleadings on Extents, &c. . .	365
4.	Trial, and proceedings incident thereto	370
5.	Judgment	372
6.	Execution	373
7.	Error	ibid.

CHAP. XIV.

Of the Privileges and Incapacities of the King in several matters 374

CHAP. XV.

What Statutes bind the King . . . 382

CHAP. XVI.

Of Grants from the King.

Sect. 1.	What the King may grant, and what he may not	384
2.	How Grants from, and to, the King are to be effected	389
3.	Construction of	391
	And when void for	
	1. Uncertainty	394
	2. Misrecitals; and herein of false suggestions or deceit . . .	396
4.	Of the Rights and Liabilities of the Grantee .	399
5.	Of revoking or avoiding the Grant . .	400

CHAP. XVII.

Of the King's Family and Councils.

Sect. 1.	The Royal Family	
	1 The Queen	401

Page

1. Queen Regent 401

2. Queen Consort . . . ibid.

3. Queen Dowager 403

2. The eldest Son or Daughter . . ibid.

3. The other Royal Children . . . 405

Sect. 2. The King's Councils.

1. Parliament 408

2. Peers . . . . . ibid.

3. The Judges 409

4. The Privy Council . . . . ibid.

A TREATISE

ON THE

LEGAL PREROGATIVES

OF THE

CROWN.

CHAPTER I.

Origin of Society.—Legislative and Executive Authorities.—Principles of the Constitution as to the Royal Power.—The King's Attributes or Political Character.—His Prerogative in general.—Boundaries and Restraints.—Who, in legal contemplation, is entitled to exercise the Prerogatives.

CONSCIOUS of his infirmities, man has ever been inclined to associate with his fellow-creatures, for the purposes of mutual preservation, comfort, and protection. The social feeling is so firmly rooted in the human heart by nature, and confirmed by an enjoyment of the blessings it imparts, that even the ferocity of the savage is restrained by its dictates. To this sentiment communities or assemblages of men owe their origin. These soon became attached to each other, and to that spot on which they had imbibed their first impressions, and formed their earliest habits. The most barbarous of the human race have their tribes, and exercise within the limits of their own circles, the native affections and good feelings of the heart.

The outlines of society were, however, very imperfect. The earliest assemblages of men were satisfied if their union supplied their immediate necessities, and ensured their personal security. They were regardless, because they were ignorant, of the advantages resulting from civilization, from good order, and good government. As, however, mankind increased,

and

and his intellect expanded, the necessity of establishing a system of laws and subordination, and of placing somewhere the power of commanding and enforcing obedience, became apparent. In the rudeness of his uncultivated sense, man ever adopts the most obvious means. Simple rules of action were adopted; and he whose superior prowess in battle, or address, in their little assemblies, had won their highest estimation, was naturally appointed their leader and governor. Even in its infancy subordination assumed various forms. Time, accident, the progressive increase of mankind, and the diversified extent of the mental feelings and capacities of different nations, have rendered the forms of government more numerous and complicated.

To explain the various merits and demerits of the different forms of government which now exist, is' foreign to the scope and intention of this Treatise. It may, however, be observed, that as on the one hand a despotic monarchical form of government degrades the native freedom and dignity of man; so, on the other hand, the republican system, if it do not expose the people to the worst species of despotism, tends to create endless anarchy and confusion in the State.

The rights of sovereignty, or supreme power, are of a legislative and executive nature, and must, under any form of government, be vested exclusively in a body or bodies, distinct from the people at large. In this country, the legislative and executive authorities are wisely placed in different hands: the power of making laws being allotted to the King, Lords, and Commons, who constitute the Parliament; and the right to administer and execute them being assigned to the King, who in his political capacity of supreme executive magistrate, must in general consider the laws, not his own will, as the criterion of his conduct. That government is arbitrary in which the legislative and executive departments are inseparable; but when firmly and inalienably secured in separate hands, the different branches of government operate as a check on each other, and form that mixed monarchical constitution which has been considered by most writers on political subjects to be best calculated to secure the happiness and liberty of the subject.

The executive power could not exist if the King had no share in the legislative authority; which would in such case

make

make rapid encroachments on, and gradually assume, the reins of government. The King is, therefore, very properly a constituent part of Parliament; in which capacity he possesses the means of preserving inviolate his rights and prerogatives, as supreme executive magistrate, by withholding his assent at pleasure, and without stating any reason, to the enactment of provisions tending to their prejudice. It is, however, only for the purpose of protecting the regal executive authority that the constitution has assigned to the King a share in legislation: this purpose is sufficiently ensured by placing in the Crown the negative power of rejecting suggested laws. The royal legislative right is not of the deliberative kind; the Crown has no power to propound laws; and it would have a dangerous tendency and influence, if the King were allowed to recommend from the throne what laws ought to be passed; as was done by some of our arbitrary Sovereigns, and by the *Roman* Emperors, whose *orationes* were the exact patterns to which the *senatus consulta* were to conform. Important, therefore, as this prerogative of rejection is as a shield against rebellious encroachments, as a preservative of the royal executive function, it is, in other points of view, of a limited and negative nature. Though the King is said to be the *caput, principium, et finis* of Parliament, he is but a part of it, and, *per se*, possesses no legislative power. Though his Majesty alone can call Parliament together, and dissolve its authority, these rights are purely of the executive kind. In a constitutional point of view, however, the legislative power is lodged in the King, subject to the assent of the Houses of Parliament. Laws are said to be enacted " *by the King's Most Excellent Majesty,* by and with the advice and consent of the Lords Spiritual and Temporal and Commons in Parliament assembled."

As supreme executive magistrate, the King possesses, subject to the law of the land, exclusive, deliberative, and more decided, more extensive, and more discretionary rights and powers. These are wisely placed in a single hand by the British constitution, for the sake of unanimity, strength, and dispatch. Were they placed in many hands, they would be subject to many wills; many wills, if disunited, and drawing different ways, create weakness in a government; and, to unite those several wills, and reduce them to one,

is

is a work of more time and delay than the exigencies of State will afford. The King of *England* is therefore not only the chief, but properly the sole, magistrate of the nation; all others acting by commission from, and in due subordination to him. (*a*)

" By the word 'prerogative' we usually understand," observes Sir *William Blackstone* (*b*), " that special pre-eminence which the King hath over and above all other persons, and out of the ordinary course of the common law, in right of his royal dignity. It signifies, in its etymology, (from *præ* and *rogo*) something that is required or demanded before, or in preference to, all others. And hence it follows, that it must be in its nature singular and eccentrical; that it can only be applied to those rights and capacities which the King enjoys alone, in contradistinction to others; and not to those which he enjoys in common with any of his subjects; for if once any one prerogative of the Crown could be held in common with the subject, it would cease to be prerogative any longer. And therefore *Finch* (*c*) lays it down as a maxim, that the prerogative is that law in case of the King, which is law in no case of the subject."

The splendour, rights, and powers of the Crown were attached to it for the benefit of the people (*d*), and not for the private gratification of the sovereign; they form part of, and are, generally speaking, as antient as the law itself, and the statute 17 *Ed.* 2. *st.* 1. *de prerogativa regis* is merely declaratory of the common law. (*e*)

In every community, it is highly important that the greatest reverence towards their sovereign should be instilled into the minds of the governed,—unattended by respect, authority speedily diminishes; and without a due share of authority, it would be impossible for the King to enforce respect to the laws; on the observance of which depend the happiness and security of his subjects. Independently therefore, of the mere trappings and outward magnificence and title (*f*) of royalty, and of the various substantial authorities and powers of the Crown, the constitution has attached to the wearer certain attributes forming his constitutional character and royal dignity.

(*a*) 1 Bla. Com. 250.
(*b*) Ibid. 239.
(*c*) Finch, L. 85.
(*d*) 3 Atk. 171. 4 T. R. 410.

(*e*) 2 Inst. 496. 26°. 10 Co. 64. Bendl. 117.
(*f*) See Com. Dig. tit Roy. B. 1 Bla. C. 190.

These

These attributes are principally *sovereignty* or *pre-eminence*, *perfection*, "the King can do no wrong;" and *perpetuity*, "the King never dies." (*a*)

By the attribute *sovereignty* or *pre-eminence*, and *perfection*, we are not to understand that the King is above the laws, in the unconfined sense of those words, and that every thing he does is lawful; but that his Majesty, individually and person-ally, and in his natural capacity is independent; and is not amenable to any other earthly power or jurisdiction. (*b*)   The inviolability of the King is essential to the existence of his powers as supreme magistrate; and therefore his person is sacred.   The law supposes it impossible that the King him-self can act unlawfully or improperly.   It cannot distrust him whom it has invested with the supreme power: and visits on his advisers and ministers the punishment due to the illegal measures of government.   Hence the legal apophthegm that the King can do no wrong.   As the law provides no redress against the sovereign, it properly attaches the blame of illicit proceedings to those only who are within the reach of punish-ment; for it would be absurd to suppose legal culpability which is dispunishable.   The constitutional signification of the maxim was in former times misrepresented.   It was pretended by some that it meant that every measure of the King was lawful, a doctrine subversive of all the principles of which the con-stitution is compounded.   It is a fundamental general rule, that the King cannot sanction any act forbidden by law: it is in that point of view that his Majesty is under, and not above, the laws; that he is bound by them equally with his subjects. *Ipse autem Rex non debet esse sub homine, sed sub Deo et sub lege, quia Lex facit Regem.   Attribuat igitur Rex legi, quod Lex attri-buat ei, videlicet dominationcm et potestatem; non est cnim Rex, ubi dominatur voluntas, et non Lex.*" (*c*)

The *perpetuity* of the Crown is expressed by the quaint maxim that the King never dies; by which is meant that on the death of the King, the prerogatives and politic capacities of the supreme magistrate, instantly vest, without a moment's *in-terregnum*, in his successor. (*d*)

Having thus considered the attributes constituting the po-

(*a*) 1 Bla. Com. 241.   (*c*) Bract. lib. 1. ch. 8.
(*b*) Ibid.   (*d*) Plowd. 213.   7 Co. R. 10. b.
                                  Post. 11.

litic

litic character and dignity of the King, it will be proper to take a view of his principal and transcendent prerogatives as executive magistrate.

With respect to *foreign states and affairs*, the whole majesty and power of his dominions are placed in the hands of the King, who as representative of his subjects possesses discretionary and unlimited powers. In this capacity his Majesty has the sole right to send ambassadors and other foreign ministers and officers abroad, to dictate their instructions, and prescribe rules of conduct and negotiation. (a) His Majesty alone can legally make treaties, leagues and alliances with foreign states; grant letters of marque and reprisals, and safe conduct; declare war or make peace. As depository of the strength of his subjects, and as manager of their wars, the King is generalissimo of all land and naval forces: his Majesty alone can levy troops, equip fleets, and build fortresses.

The King is also *supreme head of the church :* in which capacity he appoints the archbishops and bishops; convenes, prorogues, restrains, regulates, and dissolves all ecclesiastical synods or convocations; and is the *dernier resort* in all ecclesiastical causes, an appeal lying ultimately to him in chancery from the sentence of every ecclesiastical judge. (b)

With regard to the *Houses of Parliament,* the right to assemble, prorogue, and dissolve them, belongs exclusively to the King as supreme executive magistrate.

As the *fountain of justice,* and administrator of the laws, all judicial power is supposed to be derived from the Crown; and though the King himself possesses none, yet he appoints those by whom it is exercised, and constitutes courts and offices. The pardoning offenders and issuing proclamations, are also ranked among the prerogatives of the Crown.

The King is also the *fountain*, parent, and distributor of *honours, dignities, privileges* and *franchises.*

The *superintendency* and *care* of *commerce*, on the success of which so materially depend the wealth and prosperity of this nation, are also, in various cases, allotted to the King by the constitution.

Though in the exercise of his lawful prerogatives, an unbounded discretion is, generally speaking, left to the King;

(a) 1 Wooddn. 83.   (b) Post. chap. 5.   1 Bla. Com. 279, 280.

and,

and, in using such discretion, his Majesty is irresistible and absolute; (*a*) yet there are certain duties pointed out, with a visible hand, for his observance: and various boundaries and restraints, on the tyrannical and oppressive use of the royal powers, are wisely interwoven into the texture of the constitution.

The *duties* arising from the relation of sovereign and subject are reciprocal. Protection, that is, the security and governance of his dominions according to law, is the duty of the sovereign; and allegiance and subjection, with reference to the same criterion, the constitution and laws of the country, form, in return, the duty of the governed, as will be more fully noticed hereafter. We have already partially mentioned this duty of the sovereign, and have observed that the prerogatives are vested in him for the benefit of his subjects, and that his Majesty is under, and not above, the laws. This doctrine is laid down by several writers; (*b*) and is expressly ratified by the coronation oath, wherein the King swears to govern according to law, to execute judgment in mercy, and to maintain the established religion; and by the statute 12 and 13 *W.* 3. *c.* 2. which declares that " the laws of *England* are the birthright of the people thereof; and all the kings and queens who shall ascend the throne of this realm, ought to administer the government of the same, according to the said laws: and all their officers and ministers ought to serve them respectively according to the same : and therefore all the laws and statutes of this realm, for securing the established religion, and the rights and liberties of the people thereof, and all other laws and statutes of the same now in force, are ratified and confirmed accordingly."

There are also various *boundaries,* which the constitution has set to the royal prerogative. (*c*) These consist in the actual and positive limitation of the powers of the Crown, in certain specified cases. Thus, though the King is supreme head of the church, he can neither legally alter his own, or establish any other, than the national religion ; and must tolerate the dispassionate religious sentiments of others. His

(*a*) 1 Bla. Com. 251,2.

(*b*) Brac. lib. 1. c. 8. lib. 2. c. 16. s. 3. —Year Book, 19 Hen. 6. 63. Fortescue,

c. 9. and 34. 1 Bla. Com. 233,4.

(*c*) See De Lolme on the Constitution of Great Britain, chap. 6.

Majesty

Majesty is invested with the exclusive right to assemble Parliament, but must assemble one at least once in three years: is
the fountain of justice, but has in person no judicial power,
and cannot alter the law, or influence the determinations of his
judges: may pardon offenders, but cannot prejudice civil rights
and remedies: has the management of martial affairs, but cannot, without the consent of Parliament, raise land forces, or
keep them on foot, in time of peace.

The *restraints* on the undue exertion, and the misuse of
even the undoubted powers of the Crown, are also of the
most vital importance; and principally consist in the dependence of the Crown on the people, that is, the House of Commons, for supplies; and in the constitutional responsibility
of the advisers, ministers, and officers of the sovereign. Restraints which are fully sufficient, if unpolluted by the ener-
vating hands of an unconstitutional influence, to deaden and obviate the most strenuous attempts to subvert the constitution.

Unaided by his people, who alone possess the power of
taxing themselves, through the medium of their representatives the Commons House of Parliament, the King has com-
paratively no revenue or resources which he could convert to purposes extensively dangerous: and, as observed by
De Lolme, (a) "In these days when every thing is rated by
pecuniary estimation, when gold is become the great moving
spring of affairs, it may be safely affirmed that he who depends
on the will of other men, with regard to so important an
article, is, whatever his power may be in other respects, in a
state of real dependence." Without money the King can
neither maintain his forces, carry on a war, perform various
treaties with other potentates, or pay the salaries of his officers,
who so materially add to the influence, and consequently to the
power of the Crown.

The constitutional responsibility of the advisers, ministers,
and officers of the Crown, not only operates as an induce-
ment to them to act with caution, but enables the people,
through their representatives the House of Commons, to expose, by an impeachment, to public view, to the eye of the
world, the corrupt, the ill-advised, or impolitic measures of ad-

(a) On the English Constitution, page 72.

ministration;

ministration; an exposure which must tend to the destruction
of ambitious projects, and which the King cannot prevent, the
party impeached not being allowed to plead his Majesty's pardon in bar to the impeachment.

Should a sovereign of *England* again unhappily and personally persist in measures, tending to a dissolution of the principles of the constitution, though the law provide no stated remedy against him, the feelings of mankind point one out, and history furnishes instances of the result of such a conflict. In many
countries tyranny has been confirmed by the struggle: in this,
however melancholy and lengthened the convulsion may sometimes have been, liberty has ever eventually triumphed. And
it is a proud consideration, that in 1688 the Lords and Commons, instead of pretending to a right to form another system, on
Mr. *Locke's* theory, that the constitution was dissolved by the
attempts to destroy it, declared with the profoundest wisdom,
that the constitution still subsisted: and, acting on that solid
principle, they adopted a remedy suited only to the necessity
of the case; adhering to ancient and fundamental doctrines,
so far as circumstances would admit; but at the same time restoring to their original perfection and beauty those principles
which tyranny had endeavoured to sully or subvert.

In considering *who, in legal contemplation, is' entitled to
exercise the prerogatives*, it will naturally be our first inquiry
in whom the Crown is constitutionally vested. It is unnecessary to remark, that by the King alone can the prerogatives
be exercised.

" The Crown is," says Sir *W. Blackstone*, (*a*) " by common law and constitutional custom, hereditary in a manner
peculiar to itself; and, though the right of inheritance may
from time to time be changed, or limited, by Act of Parliament, as was done at the Revolution in 1688, still, under such limitations, the Crown continues hereditary." This
rule is admirably illustrated by Sir *W. Blackstone*, by an Historical Sketch of the Titles of the Kings of *England*.

The rules of inheritance which govern the descent of private estates, are in general equally applicable to the descent
of the Crown. (*b*)   The few differences which exist were in-

(*a*) 1 Bla. Com. 191.
(*b*) 5 Bac. Ab. 591. tit. Prerog. A.   1 Wooldn. V. L. 69.   1 Bla. Com. 193.

troduced

troduced on grounds of political necessity. The general doctrine, that all the daughters of the father, who died seised,
are entitled to his estate, on failure of a male heir (*a*), does
not apply to the descent of the Crown; so that the eldest
daughter of the last King is, under such circumstances, exclusively heiress to the throne. (*b*)   So the rule of *possessio fratris*
does not hold on the descent of the Crown; nor is half-blood
any impediment in such case.   Therefore, if a King has
issue a son and a daughter, by one venter, and a son by
another venter, and die ; on the death of the eldest son
without issue, the younger brother is entitled to the Crown,
to the exclusion of the daughter. (*c*)   Even the doctrine which
antiently prevailed in the law of descents, that when the eldest
son was already provided for, the next brother should take
the rest of their father's inheritance, was never adopted as a
rule of public succession. (*d*)

It should however be remarked, that even a King *de facto*,
or one in the actual exercise of sovereignty, whilst he remains
on the throne, is by law entitled to the royal prerogatives; (*e*)
and is so far King that treason may, legally speaking, be
committed against him. (*f*)   The doctrine is grounded on
the maxim, *protectio trahit subjectionem et subjectio protectionem ;* (*g*) and though it evidently contradicts a very common principle, that no one shall avail himself of his own
wrong, it appears to be in a political point of view highly
reasonable.   It is indeed a political principle instituted for
the safety and benefit of the people, whose loyalty may be
repressed by the overwhelming power of an usurper.   And
Sir M. *Foster* (*h*) speaking of a King *de jure* and *de facto*, and
contending that allegiance is due from the subject to the latter
as well as the former, observes : " He (the subject) hopeth
for protection from the Crown, and he payeth his allegiance
to it, in the person of him whom he seeth in full and peaceable possession of it : he entereth not into the question of

<hr>

(*a*) See Lit. sect. 241.

(*b*) Co. Lit. 15. b. 7 Co. 12. b. 1 Bla.
Com. 194.   1 Wooddn. 69.

(*c*) Plowd. 245. 4 Inst. 206. Co. Lit.
15. b.   1 Wooddn. 69.

(*d*) 1 Bla. Com. 200.

(*e*) Foster, Cr. Law, 188. 399. 402.

See Kelyng, 14. 1 Keb. 315. Bro. Ab.
tit. Charter de pardon, pl. 22. 2 Wooddn.
502, 3.

(*f*) 1 Hawk, P. C. Bk. 1. c. 17. s. 11.
Hal. Hist. P. C. 102.   4 Bla. Com. 77.

(*g*) 7 Rep. 5.

(*h*) Foster, Cr. L. 399.

title,

title, he having neither leisure nor abilities, nor is he at liberty to enter into that question: but he seeth the fountain, from whence the blessings of government, liberty, peace, and plenty flow to him, and there he payeth his allegiance."

The royal rights and powers cannot be vested in two persons at the same time, consequently the King *de jure* is by law disabled from exercising them, whilst the usurper is in the actual possession of the crown. (a) It is even said (b) that the people are legally bound to resist any attempt the King *de jure* may make to assume the royal authority. For the justice of this latter doctrine, but few will contend: and it appears untenable in point of law. Sir *W. Blackstone* satisfactorily refutes the position, and holds that the statute 11 *Hen.* 7. *c.* 1. on which it is attempted to be grounded, does not enforce or command any opposition to a King *de jure*, but merely excuses the obedience paid to a King *de facto.* (c) It must, however, be observed that if the King *de jure* has once had possession of the throne, his subjects cannot legally obey or recognize an usurper of such possession. (d)

Immediately on the demise of the King, his successor is entitled to the prerogatives attached to the Crown: no coronation, no formal recognition of the claim of the successor is necessary to the perfection of his title; he becomes instantly on the dissolution of his ancestor, a King for every purpose. (e) Much inconvenience would occur if the realm were deprived, even for a short period, of a sovereign; without whom no act of legislation however trifling can be perfected, or executive affair, however immaterial, be legally performed. Hence it is a maxim in the *English* law that the King never dies: his political existence is never in abeyance, or suspended. (f)

A titular King, or in other words the husband of a Queen regnant who is in her own right heiress to the crown, has no legal claim to the royal rights; (g) which are in such case vested by the constitution in the Queen. (h) Hence treason,

---

(a) See Bro. Ab. Charter de pardon, 22. 3 Inst. 7. Wood's Inst. 559. Hal. Hist. P. C. 104.

(b) 1 Hawkins, P. C. Bk. 1. c. 17. s. 16. 2 Wooddn. 502, 3.

(c) 4 Bla. Com. 77.

(d) Hal. P. C. 104.

(e) Calvin's Case, 7 Co. R. 12. Plowd.

213. 3 Inst. 7. Hal. P. C. 101. See Fost. R. 189. 1 Bla. Com. 195. 369. 1 Wooddn. 73.

(f) 1 Bla. Com. 249. ante 5.

(g) See 3 Inst. 7, 8. 1 Hawk. P. C. ch. 17. s. 20.

(h) Hal. P. C. 101.

in the legal acceptation of the term, cannot be committed against the husband of a Queen regnant; though it may be committed against the Queen herself. (*a*)   It may safely be advanced that a King who resigns the throne, and whose resignation is confirmed in Parliament, cannot afterwards resume those prerogatives which he has previously renounced by his own voluntary act. (*b*)

By legislative provision (*c*) every person who is reconciled to, or holds communion with, the see or church of *Rome ;* or who professes the popish religion, or marries a papist, cannot inherit or enjoy the crown of this realm, and *Ireland.*   And the King has not the power of subjecting his dominions to the sway of a foreign potentate. (*d*)

It has been practically decided, that in case of a grievous illness depriving the Monarch of the power of exercising the functions of majesty, Parliament may assemble and appoint a Regent, with a general or limited jurisdiction. (*e*)

CHAP. II.

Of the King's Right to Allegiance—from whom due— Nature of it—Of the Oaths of Allegiance.—Rights incident to Allegiance.

Sect. I. — *Of the King's Right to Allegiance—from whom due.*

THE King is entitled, morally as well as legally, to the allegiance of his subjects, in return for the protection and security which his Majesty constitutionally affords them.   The maxim or rule " *Protectio trahit subjectionem, et subjectio protectionem,*" (*f*) has obtained in every age, and in every country ; and extends not only to those who are born within the King's dominions, but also to foreigners who live within them,

---

(*a*) See ibid. 1 Hal. P. C. 106.   4 Bla. Com. 76, 7.

(*b*) And see 2 Hal. P. C. 104.

(*c*) 1 Wm. and M. st. 2. c. 2. s. 9.

(*d*) 2 Rol. Ab. 163. l. 35.   4 Inst. 13. Com. Dig. Roy. A. 3.

(*e*) See Adolphus on the Political State of the British Empire, vol. 1. title King. —Regency Acts 51 Geo. 3. c. 1.   52 Geo. 3. c. 6, 7, 8.   56 Geo. 3. c. 46.

(*f*) Ante, page 10, 7.

though

though their sovereign is at war with this country; (*a*) for they equally enjoy his Majesty's protection. (*b*) It is even stated by Sir *M. Foster*, to have been laid down at a meeting of all the Judges, that if an alien, seeking the protection of the Crown, and having a family and effects here, should, during a war with his native country, go thither, and there adhere to the King's enemies for purposes of hostility, he may be dealt with as a traitor. (*c*) But aliens who in an hostile manner invade the kingdom, whether their King be at war or peace with ours, and whether they come by themselves, or in company with *English* traitors, cannot be punished as traitors, but shall be dealt with by martial law. (*d*) So with respect to any conquered country it is clear that the inhabitants, when once received into the King's protection, become his subjects; and are to be universally considered in that light and not as enemies or aliens; but if the territory be lost by conquest, the after-born inhabitants are to be considered aliens. (*e*)

The mere birth of a person within this country will not constitute him a subject thereof, unless he was also born under the King's obedience and protection; and therefore if foreign enemies should invade the realm, and have children born within it, such children would be aliens. (*f*) But children born here of alien friends are natural born subjects of this country, (*g*) as are in general children born either in his Majesty's colonies, or plantations, or on those parts of the ocean which are reputed the *English* seas. (*h*)

By the common law the children of natural born subjects of this country were aliens if born out of the King's dominions: (*i*) and the only exception allowed was in the case of children of *English* ambassadors. (*k*) But by legislative provision (*l*) all children born out of the King's ligeance, whose fathers (or grandfathers by the father's side) were natural born subjects, are now natural born subjects themselves for

(*a*) 1 Wooddn. V. L. 379.

(*b*) See 7 Rep. 6. Dyer, 145. Hob. 271. 2 Salkd. 630. pl. 2. Statute, 32 Hen. 8, c. 16. 1 Hal. P. C. 59. 1 Bla. Com. 370.

(*c*) Fost. C. L. 185.

(*d*) 1 Hawk. P. C. c. 17. s. 6.

(*e*) Dyer, 224. Vaugh. 281. Cowp. 208. 2 Chalmers' Coll. of Op. 384, 5, &c.

(*f*) 7 Co. R. 18, a. b.

(*g*) Ib. 1 Inst. 8, a. 1 Bla. Com. 373, 374.

(*h*) Molloy, 370.

(*i*) 4 Term R. 308, 310.

(*k*) 7 Rep. 18.

(*l*) 7 Ann. c. 5. 4 G. 2. c. 21. 13 G. 3. c. 21. See 1 Bla. Com. 373. 4 Term R. 309.

every purpose, unless their said fathers at the time of the birth of such children abroad, were either attainted of high treason, or liable to the penalties of high treason, or felony, in case of their returning into *England* or *Ireland*, without the King's licence; or in the actual service of a prince at enmity with *Great Britain.* If, however, an *English* woman, a natural-born subject of this realm, marry an alien abroad, their issue are aliens also, as none of the statutes make any provision for such a case. (*a*)

By various Acts of Parliament, persons not natural born subjects may, in certain cases, become naturalized, as if they were born within the King's territories. Thus every foreign seaman, who in time of war serves two years on board an *English* ship, by virtue of the King's proclamation is, *ipso facto*, naturalized, under the like restrictions as in statute 12 *W.* 3. *c.* 2. (*b*); and all foreign Protestants and Jews, upon their residing seven years in any of the *American* colonies, without being absent above two months at a time; and all foreign Protestants, serving two years in a military capacity there, or being three years employed in the whale fishery, without afterwards absenting themselves from the King's dominions for more than one year, and none of them falling within the incapacities declared by statute 4 *G.* 2. *c.* 21. shall be (upon taking the oaths of allegiance and abjuration, or, in some cases, an affirmation to the same effect) naturalized to all intents and purposes, as if they had been born in this kingdom; except as to sitting in Parliament, or in Privy Council, and holding offices or grants of land, &c. from the Crown, within the kingdoms of *Great Britain* or *Ireland.* (*c*)

Though it has been asserted that the King may nullify for the future, that allegiance which natural born subjects owe him, by ceding a colony in which they live to another potentate; (*d*) yet there can be no doubt that his Majesty is not by law enabled to naturalize an alien. To effect that, an Act of Parliament is necessary, and such act cancels all defects of blood, and has a retrospective energy, so as to enable a son born before the na-

---

(*a*) 4 Term Rep. 300.
(*b*) 13 Geo. 2. c. 3.
(*c*) Stat. 13 Geo. 2. c. 7.
(*d*) See 1 Wooddn. 382. But this is by no means clear: it has been strongly urged that the character and rights of an English born subject are personal, unchangeable, and indelible, and that the King cannot take away this birthright without the aid of Parliament. See several able opinions in Chalmers. See ante 12.

turalization

turalization to inherit, &c.; an effect and power which do not attach to simple denization. (*a*)   His Majesty is, however, entrusted with the important power of making an alien a denizen; which is in a kind of middle state between an alien and natural born subject, and partakes of both of them. (*b*)   Denization enables the alien to purchase, and to transmit lands by descent, &c. but does not qualify him to take any degree of nobility, or to sit in Parliament, be of the Privy Council, or hold any office of trust, civil or military; or take any grant of lands from the Crown. (*c*)   This prerogative cannot be delegated by the Crown to any one (*d*), and should be granted according to the statute 32 *Hen.* 8. *c.* 16. *s.* 7. (*e*) with a proviso in the letters patent, that the denizen shall be obedient to the statutes in force before the making of that statute: but such proviso does not constitute a condition; and therefore the denization is not avoided by the denizen being guilty of a breach of the laws. (*f*)   Denization may be granted for life, or for years; or to the alien born, and the heirs of his body, or to the heirs generally; or for particular purposes and intents, and in certain places, and no further, or upon condition. (*g*)

SECT. II.

Of the Nature and Extent of Allegiance, and of taking the Oaths of Allegiance.

THE well known maxim '*nemo potest exuere patriam*' comprehends the whole doctrine of natural allegiance; (*h*) and is taken in its full extent by the *English* laws. (*i*)   The very existence, and at all events the welfare, of a State would be endangered if its natural born subjects could withdraw, or transfer, with impunity, that natural allegiance which the law of every nation (*k*) has rendered perpetual and unalienable.   To the inseparable and

(*a*) 1 Ventr. 419. Co. Lit. 129. Bac. Ab. Aliens B. 1 Bla. Com. 374. 2 Ib. 249, 250. See post, tit. Escheat as to an alien and denizen inheriting, &c.

(*b*) 1 Bla. Com. 374.

(*c*) Bac. Ab. Aliens B. Molloy, Bk. 3. c. 3. s. 14. 12 W. 3. c. 2.

(*d*) 2 Roll. Abr. 93.   7 Co. 25. b.

(*e*) This act is still in force. 2 Inst. 2. note 7. See 1 Wooddn. V. L. 373.

(*f*) 1 Rol. Ab. 195.   Lane, 58.

(*g*) 2 Rol. Ab. 95. 2 Cro. Jac. 539. 7 Co. 5. b.; 6. 1 Inst. 129. *u.* 1 Wooddn. V. L. 386, 7. Co. Lit. 129. a. 2 Jones, 12.

(*h*) Foster, Cr. L. 184.

(*i*) See 1 Bla. C. 369, &c. 7 Co. 7. 2 P. Wms. 124. Hal. P. C. 59, 61.

(*k*) See Aylif. Civil Law, b. 2. t. 3.

lasting

lasting qualities of this allegiance, which constitute its leading features, we may add, that it is not so much due to the country, as to the sovereign; and is due to him in his natural, more than in his political character. (*a*)   Sir *W. Blackstone* (*b*) terms natural allegiance a debt of gratitude, and we have already seen that it has been considered to be due, in return for that protection which individuals within the King's dominions enjoy from his Majesty. (*c*)

Local allegiance, which is due from an alien or stranger born, whilst he continues within the dominions of the King, (*d*) is implied by law, on the principles we have just considered; but is merely of a temporary nature, and ceases immediately the foreigner withdraws himself from this kingdom. (*e*)

Though the duties of the people towards their sovereign are implied by law; yet, as an oath will most probably impress those duties more strongly on the mind, it has been wisely ordained, that it shall be taken in various cases.

By the common law the oath of allegiance to the King may be tendered either in the court leet, or sheriff's tourn, to all persons above the age of twelve years, whether natives, aliens, or denizens; and whether they hold lands of the King or not: which oath they are by law obliged to take. (*f*)   The oath of fealty, which, during the feudal tyranny, every tenant or vassal was obliged to take to his landlord, generally contained a clause, "*salvâ fide et ligeantiâ domini regis :*" and it was even considered that the lord was liable to be punished if such clause were not inserted. (*g*)

By the oath of allegiance, the person swearing promises to be faithful and bear true allegiance to his Majesty King *George.* (*h*)   The oath of abjuration, which applies to *Ireland,* and all the King's dominions, (*i*) recognizes the right of his Majesty to be King; promises to maintain the succession of the Crown; denies the right of the descendants of the late Pretender, and adjures allegiance to them; it promises and engages, that the person swearing will bear faith and true allegiance to the King, and will defend his Majesty against all trai-

---

(*a*) 1 Ventr. 3.
(*b*) 1 Com. 369.
(*c*) Ante, 12.
(*d*) 1 Bla. C. 370.
(*e*) 7 Rep. 6. 1 Bla. C. 370. 1 Wooddn.
V. L. 379.

(*f*) Spelm. tit. *fidelitas.* 2 Inst. 121.
147. Co. Lit. 85. Finch, L. 241.   1 Hal.
P. C. 64.
(*g*) Ibid.
(*h*) 1 Geo. 1. st. 2. c. 13. s. 1.
(*i*) 6 Geo. 3. c. 53. s. 2.

torous conspiracies and attempts whatsoever against his person, crown or dignity; and disclose and make known to his Majesty and his successors, all treasons and traitorous conspiracies. (*a*) This oath must by the statute be taken by " every person that shall be admitted into any office or shall receive any pay, by reason of any patent or grant from the King or by his authority, or by authority derived from him in England, or in the navy, or in the several Islands of Jersey and Guernsey, or that shall be admitted into any service, office or employment, in the household or family of the King or Queen, or of any of his Majesty's issue, and all ecclesiastical persons, heads or governors, of what denomination soever, and all other members of colleges and halls, within either of the universities, that are or shall be of the foundation, or that do or shall enjoy any exhibition, at the age of eighteen years; and all persons teaching or reading to pupils in either of the universities or elsewhere, and schoolmasters and ushers, and all preachers and teachers of separate congregations, high and chief constables, and every person who shall act as serjeant at law, counsellor at law, barrister, advocate, attorney, solicitor, proctor, clerk or notary, in England. (*b*)

The statute 1 Geo. 1. st. 2. c. 13. s. 10. (*c*) enacts, that "Two or more Justices of Peace, or any other person specially appointed by the King, by order in the Privy Council, or by Commission under the Great Seal, may administer and tender the oaths thereinbefore appointed to be taken, to any person whom they shall suspect to be dangerous or disaffected to his Majesty or his Government; and if any person to whom the said oaths shall be so tendered, shall neglect or refuse to take the same, such Justices, or other person appointed as aforesaid, tendering the said oaths, shall certify the refusal thereof to the next Quarter Sessions of the County, &c. in which such refusal shall be made, and the said refusal shall be recorded amongst the rolls of that sessions, and shall be from thence certified by the Clerk of the Peace of such County, &c. into the Court of Chancery or King's Bench, Court of Sessions, or Court of Justiciary in Scotland, there to be recorded amongst the rolls of the said Courts, in a roll or rolls there to

---

(*a*) 6 Geo. 3. c. 53.

(*b*) Deputy Lieutenants and commissioned officers in the militia are to take the oath, see 42 Geo. 3. c. 90. s. 13; and c. 91. s. 9.

(*c*) And see 6 Geo. 3. c. 53. s. 1.

be

be provided and kept for that purpose only; and that every person so neglecting or refusing to take the said oaths, shall be, from the time of his neglect or refusal, taken, esteemed, and adjudged a popish recusant convict, and as such to forfeit and be proceeded against." (*a*)

The persons who are expressly required to take the oaths, and yet refuse to take them, according to the acts are, *ipso facto*, adjudged incapable and disabled in law to hold or enjoy any of the offices or employments mentioned in the statute 1 Geo. 1. st. 2. c. 13. s. 2.; and if they execute such offices or employments without duly taking the oaths, they are, on conviction thereof, " disabled to sue or use any action or suit, or to be guardian of any child, or executor or administrator of any person, or capable of any legacy, or deed of gift, or to be in any office within the realm of Great Britain, or to vote at any election for members to serve in Parliament, and shall forfeit the sum of five hundred pounds, to be recovered by a common informer, in an action in one of the Courts at Westminster, and by way of summary complaint before the Court of Sessions, or prosecution before the Court of Justiciary in Scotland."

SECT. III.

Of such Rights of the King over the Persons of his Subjects, as more immediately result from the Allegiance and Submission due from them.

THE King has an interest in all his subjects; and is so far entitled to their services, that in case of a sudden invasion or formidable insurrection, his Majesty may legally demand and enforce their personal assistance, though he can on no occasion compel them to leave the country for warlike or other purposes. (*b*) His Majesty may also, on any occasion, employ, and compel his subjects to serve in such offices or functions as the public good and the nature of the constitution require. (*c*) It is a general rule, that where a person is legally

---

(*a*) Persons who refuse to appear before Justices when summoned to take the oaths, &c. are liable to be punished, as if they refused to take them. 1 Geo. 1.

(*b*) Foster, 158. 16 Vin. 169. As to Impressing Seamen, &c. post. ch. 4.

(*c*) Moore, 111. 1 Ld. Ray. 32, 33. and cases cited 5 Bac. Ab. 520. tit. Prerogative, C. 2. 1 Term. Rep. 682.

called

called upon to perform a public duty, he is liable to be punished if he refuse to perform it. (a)   Hence, for instance, a lawyer is bound on pain of punishment to accept the degree of Serjeant at Law, when called thereto by the King's writ; (b) nor can a person duly appointed sheriff legally refuse to execute that office. (c)   This doctrine is not confined to the case of offices immediately under the Crown, nor to officers appointed by his Majesty; for persons named jurymen or parish officers must serve. (d)   Nor can a dignity or honour, as for instance that of knighthood, be legally refused. (e)   There seems also to be no doubt, that a person summoned by the King to the House of Lords, or elected and returned to serve in the House of Commons, is liable to be punished if, being qualified, he refuse to become a member of either assembly. (f)

Various statutes require persons to take the oaths of allegiance and abjuration, and other oaths, before they act in any public office or employment to which they may have been nominated; and provide, that on their neglecting or refusing to take the oaths, they shall be unable to enjoy or possess such offices or employments. (g)   As no one can avail himself of his own wrong, it seems that a person legally called upon and appointed to execute any public office or employment, cannot protect himself from the consequences of his refusal to serve therein, by neglecting to take the oaths required. (h)   It appears, however, to be clear, that a person may legally decline any public function, where sincere religious scruples (which our law does not attempt to disturb or punish, unless they manifestly endanger the peace and welfare of society,) prevent him from conscientiously taking the oaths required. (i)

(a) Per Ld. Ellenborough, 2 M. and Selw. 218.

(b) 2 Inst. 214. 2 M. and Selw. 218.

(c) See Bac. Ab. *ubi supra.*   By 1 Rich. 2. c. 11. no man who has served the office of sheriff for one year is obliged to serve the same within three years after, if there be other sufficient within the county.

(d) See cases cited, 1 Term Rep. 682, 684.

(e) 3 Cruis. Dig. 194, 195.

(f) See 5 Rich. 2. st. 2. c. 4. 6 Hen. 8. c. 16. 4 Inst. 43 and 44. 1 P. Wms. 592. 3 Cruis. Dig. 194, 195, 221.

2 M. and Selw. 218, 220, 222.   2 Bac. Ab. 219. tit. Court of Parliament, C.

(g) See ante. 18.

(h) See 2 M. and Selw. 218. 2 Mod. R. 299. 1 Freem. 327. 1 Ld. Ray. 32, 33. 1 Dougl. on Elections, 283, note. Bac. Ab. Sheriffs, B.

(i) See Ld. Mansfield's most able argument in Cowp. 382, 394. and Harrison v. Evans, Cowp. 393, note, and 535; and see S. C. cited Bac. Ab. Sheriff, B. 2 Burn, Ecc. Law, 185. 6 Bro. P.C.181. Per Ld. Ellenborough, 2 M. and Selw. 218; but see 1 Ld. Raym. 29.

It is a general rule, that the King, as executive magistrate and representative of his people, possesses' the power of exempting individuals from their common law liability to serve in certain public offices and employments, although such offices and employments are not under the immediate controul of the Crown, and the persons who fill them are not appointed by the King. (a) It has,, therefore, been held, that the Crown may exempt a subject from the offices of Sheriff, (b) Alderman of London, (c) Juryman, (d) Constable, and other offices and employments of a similar description. (e) It is, however, an established rule of law, that the King cannot grant an exemption from duties which are imposed by statutes, and which affect the general interest of the realm. (f) Therefore, where a statute enacted, that " The Lord Lieutenants of the several Counties should charge any person with horse and arms for the maintenance of the militia, &c." a charter of exemption from such charge was held invalid. (g) Nor are grants of exemption from the Crown valid where they might occasion a failure of justice, and a public injury; and, consequently, the King cannot exempt a whole county or hundred from serving on juries. (h) And it is a most important limitation of the power of the King in this respect, that his Majesty cannot exempt a person from his liability to be elected a member of, and to serve in Parliament, (i) on account, it should seem, of the nature of the employment. The power of the Crown to grant exemptions from the liability of seamen to be pressed, may be rested on the consideration that

---

(a) 1 Term Rep. 679, 686, &c.

(b) 1 Ld. Raym. 32, 3.   Savil. 43. 2 Co. R. 46. b.   5 Bac. Ab. 520. Prerog. C. 2.

(c) 1 Sid. 287. 5 Bac. Ab. 608. tit. Privilege A.

(d) 2 Rol. Ab. 198. R. 2; 199. l. 5. Sav. 43. Sid. 127. 243. Raym. 113. Hardr. 389. Dougl. 4th ed. 188. It is said in 3 Bac. Ab. 758, 9. that it seems that such exemption does not extend to jurors returned into the King's Bench, unless there be express words including that Court; also, by the better opinion, the Sheriff cannot return such privilege of exemption, but each particular juror must come in and demand it. But such charter of exemption does not extend to the Court of King's Bench, unless particularly named ; nor to any case where the King is concerned, unless it has these words, *licet tangat nos.* And the Sheriff must not return such privilege, but the persons who would have the benefit of it must claim it. 5 Bac. Ab. Privilege A. p. 609. Dougl. 188.

(e) See 6 Com. Dig. 49. tit. Prerogative D. (D. 33.)

(f) 2 Rol. Ab. 198. K. pl. 1, 202. T. pl. 2. Bac. Ab. Privilege A.

(g) 3 Mod. 12.

(h) Bac. Ab. Juries E. 6.

(i) 4 Inst. 49. See 2 M. and Selw. 214.

the right of pressing is vested in the Crown alone. This will be considered hereafter.

Grants of exemptions are construed strictly, and must be clearly made out. (*a*)

The King's right to restrain his subjects from leaving his dominions, and to compel them to return from foreign countries, is also grounded on the interest which his Majesty has in his subjects; but the King has in general no legal power to force any of his subjects out of his dominions, even to carry on a necessary war. (*b*)

By the common law, every one, generally speaking, is at liberty to go out of the kingdom without the leave of the King, (*c*) though some particular classes of persons were it seems always forbidden to do so, without a licence previously obtained. (*d*)

The King's right to keep his subjects within the realm, which exists at common law, (*e*) and is expressly recognized in the great charter of King *John*, (*f*) may be exercised either by laying on an embargo, which, however, can it seems be legally done only in time of enmity, and in case of necessity, &c.; (*g*) or by the common law writ (*h*) of *ne exeat regno;* or, if *Fitzherbert* be correct, by proclamation, because the King may not know where to find his subject so as to direct a writ to him. (*i*)

The writ of *ne exeat regno,* or *de securitate invenienda,* appears from the words used in it, "*quam plurima nobis et coronæ nostræ prejudicialia ibidem prosequi intendis,*" to be a state writ, (*k*) and clearly it was originally used merely as such, principally in cases of attempts, or suspected attempts, prejudicial to the King and nation; in which case the Lord Chancellor granted it on application from any of the principal Secretaries, without shewing cause, or upon such information as his Lordship thought of weight. (*l*) The writ may still be used on similar occasions, and may be obtained in the same manner; and, when it is not issued out of Chancery in aid of

---

(*a*) Cowp. 519. 1 Term Rep. 686.

(*b*) Ante. 18.

(*c*) F. N. B. 85. a. 188. Dyer, 296. a. 165. 3 Inst. 179. 1 Bla. C. 265. 5 Bac. Ab. 522. tit. Prerogative C. 3. Beames, 1, &c.; 14.

(*d*) Ibid. Britton, ch. 123.

(*e*) 3 Mod. 127.

(*f*) 1 Bla. C. 265.

(*g*) Skinner, 335. 3 Lev. 352. 4

Mod. 176. &c. 1 Bla. C. 270, 1. 4 Bac. Ab. 595. tit. Merchant and Merchandize. N.B. See post. ch. 10.

(*h*) 3 Mod. 127.

(*i*) F. N. B. 85. C.

(*k*) 5 Bac. Ab. 520. See Mr. Beames' late work on this writ of *ne exeat regno.*

(*l*) Ld. Bacon's Ordinance, No. 89. Beames, 17.

the debt or demand of a private individual, and in order to prevent the party from evading justice, the King is not restricted to any particular cases; so that the causes of its issuing, and the grounds and motives on which it is granted, are not traversable; and of course, therefore, the King may issue it at pleasure, without any reasons applicable to the party restrained. (*a*)   And it is laid down, that any one upon surmise to the Chancery, may cause this writ to be sued out for the King. (*b*)

But though the writ of *ne exeat regno* is certainly in its nature and origin a state writ, yet it has been gradually introduced into the Court of Chancery, and is now become a common process therein, in order to prevent individuals from going abroad to avoid the payment of their debts. (*c*)   And it may be legally awarded by the Lord Chancellor, not only in aid of a proceeding in the Court of Chancery, but also to prevent a defendant in an Ecclesiastical Court from evading the payment of alimony decreed therein by leaving the kingdom. (*d*) It is, however, permitted to be used in these cases merely on the ground that a failure of justice would otherwise ensue, and debtors would be able boldly to set their creditors at defiance. It is therefore established, that the writ is not issuable out of Chancery at the instance of a creditor, in respect of a demand for which his debtors might be arrested at law. (*e*)

In order to obtain the writ, in respect of an equitable debt, it is necessary that there should be a bill filed in the Court of Chancery, for it is grounded on such proceeding, and till the bill is filed there is no cause before the Court; (*f*) though it was formerly held otherwise. (*g*) The plaintiff must also make a positive affidavit of his debt, and state the amount of it; (*h*) nor will the writ be granted if the debt be of an uncertain nature, (*i*) though it is sufficient if it arise out of cross accounts, and in that case the plaintiff may, it seems, swear that he believes the balance stated to be due to him. (*k*)   Where the demand

(*a*) Dyer, 165, b. 179. Lane, 29. Moor, 109. 3 Inst. 179. Com. 53. 8kin. 166. 12 Mod. 562.

(*b*) F. N. B. 85. F. Com. Dig. Chancery, (4 B.)

(*c*) 5 Bac. Ab. 522.   3 P. W. 312. 7 Ves. 417.

(*d*) 2 Ventr. 345. 1 Ch. R. 715. 2 Atk. 210. Ambl. 76. Beames, 30.

(*e*) 3 P. W. 312. 2 Atk. 410. Ambl. 76. 3 Bro. Ch. R. 218. 427. Beames,

30. Aliter in cases *of account*, Chancery having a concurrent jurisdiction. 8 Ves. 593, 597. Beames, 32, 3. 38.

(*f*) 3 P. Wms. 312.

(*g*) Prec. Ch. 171.

(*h*) 3 Bro. 370. 3 Atk. 501. 2 Vez. 489. 10 Ves. 164. Beames, 36, 7.

(*i*) 1 Atk. 421. 3 Bro. Ch. R. 370. 1 Bro. Ch. R. 376. 8 Ves. 597.

(*k*) 2 Vez. 489. 3 Atk. 501. Beames, 23. See 8 Ves. 597.

is

is against an administrator, &c. the plaintiff should also swear
to his belief of assets come to the defendant's hands (*a*). This
writ may issue against a feme covert executrix, whose husband is out of the jurisdiction. (*b*)

The affidavit must also state, that the plaintiff has reason to
believe' the defendant intends to go out of the kingdom before
the conclusion of the suit, and that in such case the debt might
be lost. (*c*) It should seem on principle to be just and proper,
that the plaintiff should state his reasons for supposing that the
defendant intends to leave the country, in order that the Court
may judge of their sufficiency, (*d*) and it is usual in practice
to do so.

If the defendant has given out that he intends to go abroad,
that will suffice: (*e*) nor need it appear that the defendant intends to leave his Majesty's dominions; it will be a sufficient
cause to detain him, if he purpose to get out of the jurisdiction
of the Court. (*f*)

It was formerly considered, that on the defendant's putting
in a full answer to the bill, the writ should be discharged; but
it is now held that he must give security to abide the order on
hearing, before the Court will discharge the writ. This security is taken by recognizance before a Master in the penalty
of what is sworn to be due; and the Sheriff takes bail accordingly, when he arrests the party thereon; the debt sworn to
being indorsed on the writ as a guide to the Sheriff in taking
bail. (*g*) Indeed as the object of the writ, when applied to
private concerns, is to compel the defendant to abide the event
of the suit; and, as that is effected in substance, as well by
his finding security, as by his being personally within the
jurisdiction of the Court, it is but just that he should be
permitted when taken on the writ to give such security, and
thereupon the writ will be discharged. (*h*)

The writ should be always under the great or privy seal, or
signet; (*i*) and may be directed either to the subject himself;

(*a*) 2 Vez. 489, 3 Atk. 501. 16 Ves.
471.

(*b*) 3 Atk. 409. Ambl. 62. S. C.

(*c*) 5 Bac. Ab. 22. tit. Prerogative
C. 3. Beames, 26 to 28.

(*d*) And see Beames, 25.

(*e*) 77 Ves. 410, 417. 8 Ibid. 597.
11 Ibid. 54. 16 Ibid. 470.

(*f*) See 1 P. Wms. 263. pl 60. Cas.

Temp. Talb. 196. 1 Wooddn. 187. 3
Mod. 127. 11 Ves. 43. Beames, 52.

(*g*) 5 Bac. Ab. tit. Prerogative C. 3.

(*h*) 2 Atk. 409. Ambl. 62. 177. 3
Bro. Ch. R. 218. 1 Ves. Jun. 96.
Beames, 40, 59.

(*i*) F. N. B. 85, a. Lane, 29. 2 Co.
17. 11 Co. 92.

or to the Sheriff, or Justices of the Peace, or both, commanding them that they take sureties of the party *quod ne exeat ;*
and if he refuse to commit him to prison. (*a*)   When used in
aid of a debt the latter course is proper.

As the King may command his subjects to remain in the
country, so he may recal them when abroad by his great or
privy seal; and this prerogative extends over all descriptions
of his Majesty's subjects. (*b*) Various instances in which this
royal right has been exercised and acted upon, are to be met
with in the antient books. (*c*) The contempt is incurred from
the time when the notice by the King's messenger of his Majesty's command is received by the absent subject. (*d*) His
Majesty receives the answer of the subject, and is judge of the
contempt. (*e*)

It is laid down in a book of good authority, that a licence
granted by the Crown to a subject, enabling him to remain
abroad for a certain specified time, cannot be revoked, (*f*)
but this has been denied; (*g*) and it seems more consistent
with legal principles that such licences should be counter-
mandable, as they are merely granted *ex gratiâ*, and circumstances might be discovered or transpire, after the licence is
granted, which would render it dangerous to permit the subject to continue abroad. (*h*)

If the subject to whom the King's command to remain in
or return to this country is directed, disobey it, he is guilty of
a contempt of the royal prerogative, and on proof thereof on
oath, his property may be seized under a commission issued
out of the Exchequer, until he return. (*i*)   In the mean time,
the King has a greater interest in the property seized than a
mere perception of the profits, and may assign or grant the
effects *quamdiu in manibus suis fore contingerint ;* and his Majesty (or his patentee) is it seems entitled to woodfalls, may make
leases and grant copyholds, being *dominus pro tempore.* (*k*)

The King's right is not affected by a fraudulent and pre-

(*a*) F. N. B. 85, 188. B. D. E. See
3 Inst. 179. Beames, 19.

(*b*) 3 Inst. 179, 180. Dy. 128, b.

(*c*) See Dy. 128, b. 176, 375. Lane,
42, 44. 1 Leond. 9. Moor, 109.

(*d*) Lane, 46.

(*e*) Leon. 9.

(*f*) Dy. 177. 3, Com. Dig. Prerog
D. (D. 35.) page 50.

(*g*) Lane, 46.

(*h*) See 16 East, 165, where a protection from impress was held to be revocable. And see post. ch. 16.

(*i*) 1 Bla. Com. 266. 1 Hawk. P. C.
22. 3 Inst. 180. 10 Ves. Jr. 63.

(*k*) Sav. 7, 8. Leon. 9. Dyer, 76,
in marg. 375. Moor, 112; 109.

tended

tended assignment, of the party's property, before he was guilty of disobedience to the King's command. (*a*)   On the return of the offender he is liable to be fined; (*b*) but is entitled to a return of his lands, as a matter of right. (*c*)

CHAP. III.

Where the Prerogatives are exerciseable ; and herein of the Prerogative as it respects the British Colonies.

THOUGH allegiance be due from every one within the territories subject to the British Crown, it is far from being a necessary inference, that *all* the prerogatives which are vested in his Majesty by the English Laws, are therefore exerciseable over individuals within those parts of his Majesty's dominions in which the English Laws do not as such prevail.   Doubtless those fundamental rights and principles on which the King's authority rests, and which are necessary to maintain it, extend even to such of his Majesty's dominions as are governed by their own local and separate laws.   The King would be nominally and not substantially a sovereign over such his dominions, if this were not the case.   But the various prerogatives and rights of the sovereign which are merely local to England, and do not fundamentally sustain the existence of the Crown, or form the pillars on which it is supported, are not it seems *primâ facie* extensible to the colonies or other British dominions which possess a local jurisprudence, distinct from that prevalent in and peculiar to England.   To illustrate this distinction the attributes of the King, sovereignty, perfection and perpetuity, which are inherent in and constitute his Majesty's political capacity, prevail in every part of the territories subject to the English Crown, by whatever peculiar or internal laws they may be governed.   The King is the head of the church(*d*); is possessed of a share of legislation ; and is generalissimo throughout all his dominions: in every part of them his Majesty is alone entitled to make war and peace; but in countries which,

(*a*) See Lane, 42.

(*b*) 1 Bla. Com. 266. 1 Hawk. c. 22.

(*c*) Per Tanfield, C. B.   Lane, 48.

(*d*) 1 Chalmers' Op. 12.

s. 4.

though dependent on the British Crown, have different and local laws for their internal governance, as for instance the plantations or colonies, the minor prerogatives and interests of the Crown must be regulated and governed by the peculiar and established law of the place. Though if such law be silent on the subject it would appear that the prerogative as established by the English law prevails in every respect: subject perhaps to exceptions which the difference between the constitution of this country and that of the dependent dominion may necessarily create. By this principle many difficulties which frequently arise as to the King's foreign prerogative may be readily solved. (a)

This distinction being admitted, it becomes material to consider in what countries dependent on England, the English laws as such prevail. By ascertaining this we shall perceive to what countries the royal prerogative as such extend; and how far they may be exercised therein.

Wales was not completely conquered by England until the reign of Edward the first. That sovereign abolished the line of their antient Princes; constituted his second son Edward Prince of Wales, (b) and reannexed the country by a kind of feudal resumption, to the dominion of the crown of England. (c) Edward the first treated the Welch territory as a conquest; and of his own authority and by virtue of his prerogative, made various regulations for its governance. (d) At last, however, in the reign of Henry 8. it was united to England, and was put and still remains on the same footing with respect to its rights, liberties and laws: (e) and all statutes made in England bind Wales also, though it be not specially named. (f) Therefore as the English laws extend to Wales, all his Majesty's prerogatives equally apply to both countries. (g)

By the 18th article of the Union of England and Scotland,

(a) See further, post. 32, &c.

(b) See Hume.

(c) 1 Bla. Com. 93, 94. Burr. R. 850, 851.

(d) Cowp. R. 210. And see Barrington on the Ancient Statutes, the Statute of Wales 12 Ed. 1. and Tomlin's note to that statute.

(e) 27 Hen. 8. c. 26; see further, 34 and 35 Hen. 8. c. 26. The general rule is, that where one country is united to another in such a manner as that one keeps its government and states, and the other loses them, the latter entirely assimilates with or is melted down in the former, and must adopt its laws and customs. Puff. L. of N. and N. b. 8. c. 12. s. 6.

(f) 1 Bla. Com. 99. Burrow. R. 853.

(g) See Com. Dig. tit. Wales.

which

which was effected in the reign of Queen Ann (a), it is ordained that all the then existing Scotch laws should remain
in force, alterable however by the united Parliament of Great
Britain; so that the municipal or common laws of England,
are generally speaking of no force or validity in Scotland;
though, since the Union, all statutes passed in England bind
and extend to Scotland, though that country be not particularly mentioned. (b)

The *Town of Berwick upon Tweed* was once part of Scotland,
but is now part of England, and governed by English laws;
and statutes made by British Parliament extend to it unless it
be expressly excepted. (c)

The inhabitants of *Ireland* are for the most part, observes
Sir *Wm. Blackstone*, (d) descended from the English; who
planted it as a kind of colony, after the conquest of it by King
Henry the 2d, and the laws of England were then received
and sworn to by the Irish nation assembled at the council of
Lismore. (e) The change made in the antient Irish laws was
not effected by any English Parliament, but by the charters
of Henry the 2d and other subsequent Sovereigns, who considered it as a dependent conquered dominion; and as such,
possessed a legislative right over it. (f) So that it is, generally
speaking, true that the English common law prevails in Ireland: (g) and it is clear that all statutes made in England
before the 10 Hen. 7. were extended to Ireland, and rendered of equal force there, by one of Poyning's laws. (h)
But before the union of the two kingdoms, acts of parliament
made in England since the 10 Hen. 7. in which Ireland was
not expressly comprehended, did not relate to that country.
When that important event took place in the year 1800, and
the two countries were incorporated together, it was expressly
provided, (i) that all laws in force in Ireland at the time of the
Union should remain as by law established, but subject to be
altered by the united Parliament. Since the Union it should
seem that statutes made by the Parliament of the united king-

---

(a) 5 and 6 Ann. ch. 8.
(b) See 2 Burr. R. 853.
(c) See 1 Bla. Com. 99.   2 Burr.
R. 853.
(d) 1 Bla. Com. 100.
(e) Pryn. on 4 Inst. 249.

(f) See Cowp. Rep. 210. post. 29.
(g) Ibid. see 1 Bla. Com. 101.
(h) See 4 Inst. 351. 1 Bla. Com.
103.
(i) 39 and 40 Geo. 3. c. 67. art. 8.

dom

dom extend to Ireland though not specifically mentioned, unless expressly excluded: in the same manner and for the same reasons that Scotland is bound by English statutes since her union with England. (a) The effect of the two unions is to render the different countries inseparably one and the same, with certain exceptions: and as both Scotland and Ireland send representatives to the English Parliament, there seems no reason why a statute made by such united Parliament, without any mention of the places to which it should be applicable, should not bind the whole united kingdom.

With regard to the *other adjacent islands,* which are subject to the Crown of Great Britain, some of them [as the Isle of Wight, of Portland, of Thanet, &c.] are comprized within some neighbouring county, and are therefore to be looked upon as annexed to the mother island, and part of the kingdom of England. But there are others which require a more particular consideration.

The *Isle of Man* is a distinct territory from England, and is not governed by our laws; neither does an Act of Parliament extend to it, unless it be particularly named therein, and then an Act of Parliament is binding there. (b) This isle had generally been vested by royal grant in the hands of English subjects, who exercised a species of royal authority therein, by assenting or dissenting to laws, and exercising an appellate jurisdiction, (c) though an appeal lay from a decree of the lord of the island to the King of Great Britain in council. (d) This island is now vested unalienably in the Crown, by purchase, and subjected to the regulations of the British Excise and Customs. (e)

The islands of *Jersey, Guernsey, Sark, Alderney,* and their appendages, were formerly parcel of the Duchy of Normandy, and were united to the Crown of England by the first Prince of the Norman time. (f) They are governed by their own separate laws, (g) and are not bound by our statutes, unless particularly named; (h) though an appeal lies from the judicial

(a) See ante, 27.

(b) 4 Inst. 284. 2 And. 116. 1 Bla. Com. 105, 6.

(c) See recital of 5 Geo. 3. c. 26. 1 Bla. Com. 105, 6.

(d) 1 P. W. 329.

(e) See 3 Geo. 3. ch. 26. s. 39.

(f) See Hal. Hist. Common Law, 184 to 189. 3 Burr. R. 856, 7.

(g) 1 Bla. Com. 106. Even as to King's debts, 1 Chalmers' Op. 58.

(h) 4 Inst. 286.

decision

decision in the island to the King in council, (*a*) as it does in general from all territories, as the colonies, &c. subject in this manner to the Crown, though they cannot regularly transmit a cause to the King without first giving some judgment in it. (*b*)   If the judicial superintending power over his colonies, &c., by way of appeal, were not vested in the King, the law might be insensibly changed to the destruction of the superiority of the mother country.   The King cannot give a direction to any Court to rehear any cause depending therein ; but rehearings are granted or denied by Courts of Equity, on petition of the parties grieved. (*c*)

Our *plantations or colonies* in America, (*d*) and in other parts of the globe, were of course obtained either by conquest or treaty, or by our taking possession of, and peopling them, when we found them uninhabited.

When a country is obtained by *conquest or treaty*, the King possesses an exclusive prerogative power over it, and may entirely change or new-model the whole, or part of its laws, and political form of government, (*e*) and may govern it by regulations framed by himself.   For instance, ever since the conquest of Gibraltar, in which, besides the garrison, there are inhabitants, property, and trade, the King has made orders and regulations suitable to those who live, &c. or enjoy property in that place. (*f*)   As, however, a country conquered by British arms becomes a dominion of the King in right of his Crown, it is necessarily subject to the legislature of Great Britain; and, consequently, his Majesty's legislative power over it, as conqueror, is subordinate to his own authority in Parliament; so that his Majesty cannot make any new change contrary to fundamental principles, or exempt the inhabitants from the power of Parliament. (*g*)   Nor can the King legally disregard or violate the articles on which the country is surrendered or ceded ; but such articles are sacred and inviolable, according to their true intent and meaning. (*h*)   It is necessary

(*a*) Vaugh. R. 290, 402. 1 Bla: Com. 106. 2 Chalmers' Op. 177, 222, &c.

(*b*) Ld. Raym. 1448.

(*c*) 2 Chalmers' Op. 177.

(*d*) See generally Stokes on the Colonies, ch. 1.

(*e*) Dyer, 224. Vaugh. 281. 7 Rep.

17. The King may *per se* tax a *conquered* country. 2 Chalmers' Opinions, 140, 1.

(*f*) Cowper, 211. See 1 East, 306. See a very clear and able opinion on this subject, 1 Chalmers' Op. 169.

(*g*) Cowper, 209.

(*h*) Ibid. 208, post, 32.

and fit that the conquered country should have some laws; and, therefore, until the laws of the country thus acquired are changed by the new Sovereign, they still continue in force. (*a*) As observed by Lord *Mansfield*, (*b*) the absurd exception as to an infidel country, mentioned in Calvin's case, (*c*) shews the universality and antiquity of the maxim. So, where the laws of the vanquished territory are rejected, without the substitution of other laws, or are silent on any particular subjects, such territory is to be governed according to the rules of natural equity and right. (*d*) The King may preclude himself from the exercise of his prerogative legislative authority in the first instance, over a conquered or ceded country, by promising to vest it in an assembly of the inhabitants, and a governor, or by any other measure of a similar nature, by which the King does not claim or reserve to himself this important prerogative. (*e*)

If an *uninhabited country* be discovered and peopled by English subjects, they are supposed to possess themselves of it for the benefit of their Sovereign, and such of the English laws then in force, as are applicable and necessary to their situation, and the condition of an infant colony; as for instance, laws for the protection of their persons and property, are immediately in force. (*f*) Wherever an Englishman goes he carries with him as much of English law and liberty as the nature of his situation will allow.

Sir *Wm. Blackstone* observes (*g*) on this subject, that "with respect to their interior polity, our *Colonies* are property of three sorts: 1. Provincial establishments, the constitutions of which depend on the respective commissions (*h*) issued by the Crown to the governors, and the instructions which usually accompany those commissions; under the authority of which, provincial assemblies are constituted, with the power of

---

(*a*) 7 Rep. 17. Show. Parl. Cas. 31. 1 Bla. Com. 107, 8. 2 P. W. 75, 6.

(*b*) Cowp. 209.

(*c*) 7 Rep. 17.

(*d*) 2 Salk. 412.

(*e*) Cowp. 204.

(*f*) 2 P. W. 75. 2 Salk. 411. pl. 1. 2 Ld. Raym. 1245. 1 Bla. Com. 107.

(*g*) 1 Bla. Com. 108. And see Stokes on the Constitution of the Colonies, 13. &c. " Provincial establishments are the only species of American governments that now remain to Great Britain." Stokes, 149. 19, 20. Since the 22 G. 3. c. 82. which abolished the Board of Trade, which formerly regulated matters relative to the colonies, the Privy Council is the forum for settling such matters. The Secretary of State is the channel through which the colonial acts are transmitted.

(*h*) See the form of a governor's commission, Stokes, ch. 4.

making

making local ordinances, not repugnant to the laws of England. 2. Proprietary governments, (a) granted out by the Crown to individuals, in the nature of feudatory principalities, with all the inferior regalities and subordinate powers of legislation, which formerly belonged to the owners of counties palatine: yet still with these express conditions, that the ends for which the grant was made be substantially pursued, and that nothing be attempted which may derogate from the sovereignty of the mother country. 3. Charter governments (b) in the nature of civil corporations, with the power of making bye-laws for their own interior regulation, not contrary to the laws of England; and with such rights and authorities as are specially given them in their several charters of incorporation. The form of government in most of them is borrowed from that of England. They have a governor named by the King, (or, in some proprietary colonies, by the proprietor,) who is his representative or deputy. They have courts of justice of their own, from whose decisions an appeal lies to the King and (in) council (c) here in England. Their general assemblies, which are their House of Commons, together with their councils of state, being their upper house, with the concurrence of the King, or his representative the governor, make laws suited to their own emergencies. But it is particularly declared by statute 7 & 8 W. 3. c. 22. that all laws, bye-laws, usages, and customs, which shall be in practice in any of the plantations, repugnant to any law made or to be made in this kingdom relative to the said plantation, shall be utterly void and of none effect. And, because several of the colonies had claimed a sole and exclusive right of imposing taxes upon themselves, the statute 6 G. 3. c. 12. expressly declares, that all his Majesty's colonies and plantations in America have been, are, and of right ought to be, subordinate to, and dependent upon the imperial Crown and Parliament of Great Britain;

(a) Observations on these. Stokes, 19, 20. Governor to be approved by King, 7 and 8 W. 3. c. 22. s. 16.

(b) Stokes, 20.

(c) Ante. 29, 30. post. And see 1 Bla. Com. 231. 1 Vez. sen. 444. " From the decrees of the Courts of Chancery in the Colonies, an appeal lies to the King in Council here in England. And from the judgments of the Courts of Common Law in the Colonies a writ of error lies to the Governor and Council of the Colony; and from their decision an appeal (in the nature of a writ of error) lies to the King in Council here." Stokes on the Col. 26. Proceedings on an Appeal, Ibid. 222 to 231.

who

who have full power and authority to make laws and statutes of sufficient validity to bind the colonies and people of America, subjects of the Crown of Great Britain, in all cases whatsoever. And this authority has been since very forcibly exemplified and carried into effect, by the statute 7 G. 3. c. 59. for suspending the legislation of New-York; and by several subsequent statutes. (*a*) Hence it is clear that, generally speaking, the common law of England does not, as such, hold in the British colonies: (*b*) such colonies are distinct from, though dependent on, England: are subject to the controul of Parliament, though not bound by any Acts of Parliament, unless particularly referred to therein.

With respect to countries which the King does not hold in right of his British crown, as his Majesty's German territories, they have no connection or communication with England or its laws. (*c*)

We have already observed that the King cannot vary from any treaty which he has entered into on the conquest of a country; and may preclude himself from the exercise of his prerogative power of legislation, in the first instance over a conquered or ceded territory, by vesting it in an assembly of the inhabitants or a governor. (*d*) It is indeed a most sound and important principle, that though the King may keep in his own hands the power of regulating and governing the inhabitants; he cannot infringe or depart from the provisions of a charter by which he has, though voluntarily, granted them any liberties or privileges. In every question therefore which arises between the King and his colonies respecting the prerogative, the first consideration is the charter granted to the inhabitants. If that be silent on the subject it cannot be doubted, but that the King's prerogatives in the colony are precisely those prerogatives which he may exercise in the mother country. The prerogative in the colonies, unless where it is

(*a*) By 22 Geo. 3. c. 46. his Majesty was empowered to conclude a truce or peace with the Colonies or Plantations in America; and by his Letters Patent to suspend or repeal any Acts of Parliament which related to those colonies.

(*b*) Of this there can be no doubt. But Mr. Stokes observes, in his work on the Constitution of the Colonies, that the Crown has from time to time esta-blished the common law of England in all the British American Plantations, except Quebec or Canada. See 14 Geo. 3. c. 84. s. 11. establishing the Criminal Law of England in Quebec. Great part of Quebec or Canada has been, it seems, given up to the United States. Stokes, 31.

(*c*) 3 Burr. 856. 1 Bla. Com. 110.
(*d*) Ante, 29.

                                                abridged

abridged by grants, &c. made to the inhabitants, is that power over the subjects considered either separately or collectively, which by the common law of England, abstracted from Acts of Parliament, and grants of liberties, &c. from the Crown to the subject, the King could rightfully exercise in England (*a*). Where the colonial charters afford no criterion, or rule of construction, the common law of England, with respect to the royal prerogative, is the common law of the plantations; and statutes in affirmance of such common law made before the settlement of the colony *primâ facie* bind therein: but clearly Acts of Parliament made in England do not bind the plantations, unless expressly named, or the words "and all other the King's dominions," or similar expressions be used (*b*).

On this distinction it has been considered that if the peculiar laws granted by charter to the colonies do not expressly prevent it, the King may erect courts of justice and exchequer therein (*c*). Indeed the jurisdiction of the colonial judicatories in point of law invariably emanate from the King, under the modifications of the colonial assemblies (*d*). And the Crown may also extend the privilege of sending representatives to the colonial assemblies to new towns (*e*); may order a *nolle prosequi* to be entered on prosecutions in the plantations (*f*); is entitled to present to vacant benefices (*g*), a power which it exercises through the medium of the governor (*h*); and to have royal mines, treasure-trove, escheats, (as ultimate lord of the soil) royal fish, &c. therein (*i*). Nor can any of the colonial assemblies make laws unless empowered by the Crown so to do (*k*); and if when empowered they exceed the prescribed limits, their enactments are void (*l*). There can be no doubt but that the King may alter the constitution of a colony, where such constitution has not been granted by charter, and is not founded on, or fixed by any legal and confirmed act of colonial assembly; but merely by his Majesty's instructions to the governor (*m*).

(*a*) 1 Chalmers' Coll. of Op. 232, 3. ante.

(*b*) Ibid. 194, 5. 1 Bla. Com. 107, 8.

(*c*) 2 Chalmers' Op. 176. 1 Iidd. 182, 3.

(*d*) 2 Ibid. 242.

(*e*) 1 Ibid. 272, 3, &c. 276, 294.

(*f*) 2 Ibid. 178.

(*g*) Stokes, ch. 4. the form of the commission.

(*h*) 1 Chalmers' Op. 18, 23.

(*i*) Ibid. 120, 1. 123, 4. 126, 7. 130. 134.

(*k*) Ibid. 261.

(*l*) Ibid. 28.

(*m*) Ibid. 267, &c.

D

So where peculiar laws and process exist, as in Guernsey or Jersey, the King himself, even in seeking to recover his own debts therein, must resort to such laws for redress (a). And the King cannot tax a colony of English subjects, but through the medium of Parliament or the representative assembly of the plantations (b).

On obtaining a country or colony, the Crown has sometimes thought fit by particular express provisions under the great seal to create and form the several parts of the constitution of a new government; and at other times has only granted general powers to the governor to frame such a constitution as he should think fit, with the advice of a council consisting of a certain number of the most competent inhabitants; subject to the approbation or disallowance of the Crown. In most instances there are three departments forming the colonial government, each of which deserves attention: 1st. The governor who derives his power from, and is substantially a mere servant or deputy of the Crown, appointed by commission under the great seal. The criterion for his rules of conduct are the King's instructions, under the sign manual: 2dly, The colonial councils which derive their authority, both executive and legislative from the King's instructions to the governor (c): 3dly, The representative assemblies chosen by certain classes of the colonial inhabitants. The right of granting this assembly is vested exclusively in the Crown subject to after regulations by the local legislature.

The *governors* of colonies are in general invested with royal authority; they may call, prorogue, (adjourn) (d) and dissolve the colonial assemblies, and exercise other kingly functions: but still they are but the servants or representatives of the King. *Primâ facie* however their acts remain good: and though the King may refuse to confirm, and may revoke the governor's assent to an act of the assembly, it appears that, till revoked, such assent is, generally speaking, effective (e). And there can be no doubt that though the dis-

(a) 1 Chalm. 58.

(b) Ibid. 222, 3.

(c) As to their duty, &c. Stokes, 237. ch. 6.

(d) Post. 35. Stokes, 241, 2. The King cannot adjourn an English Parliament, post. ch. 6.

(e) 1 Chalm. 306, 7. If a governor doubt whether or not a proposed Act of Assembly may prejudice the prerogative, he should not assent till he have received instructions; or should assent, with a clause suspending the operation of the Act, till it be ascertained whether or not the King approve of it. Stokes, 253, 4.

cretion

cretion in passing Acts of Parliament in England is an incommunicable prerogative, it is not so as to acts of assembly, but may be legally communicated to the governor of a colony (*a*). The same as to pardoning offenders in the colonies; though it is usual to except the cases of treason and murder (*b*). Nor can there be any doubt that the King may enable the governor to grant crown lands, franchises, and possessions in the colonies (*c*). The acts of the governor should be under the great seal of the province, unless an usage *è contrà* can be shewn (*d*). His commission may be determined by the demise of the Crown, as other offices under the Crown are: but it seems that his acts done at any time, though after the determination of his office by the demise of the Crown or appointment of a new governor, and before notice thereof, are good (*e*). Nor will the determination of his patent *per se* annihilate the authority of other officers acting independently, though subordinately (*f*).

But the powers of governors of colonies demand a more explicit statement. Every governor of a province, by his commission (*g*) of captain-general and governor in chief, and by his commission of vice-admiral, and the instructions which accompany them, is vested with the following powers:

1. He is captain-general of the forces by sea and land within his province, and where a provincial establishment or King's government joined a charter colony, it was usual to make the governor of the provincial establishment captain-general of the forces by sea and land, within such charter colony. The governor has also the appointment of all militia officers (*h*).

2. As governor in chief, he is one of the constituent parts of the general assembly of his province, and has the sole power of convening, adjourning, proroguing, and dissolving the general assembly; he may also give or refuse his assent to any bill which has passed the council and assembly. The governor has also the disposal of such employments as his Majesty does not dispose of himself (*i*); and with respect to such offices as are

(*a*) 1 Chalm. 316.
(*b*) Ibid. 190.
(*c*) And see Stokes 195.
(*d*) 1 Chalm. 241, 2.
(*e*) 34 Ass. pl. 8. Cro. Car. 97. 1 Vern. 400. 3 P. Wms. 195. 1 Chalm. 313, 4.
(*f*) 1 Chalm. 250.
(*g*) See Stokes, ch. 4, and p. 184.
(*h*) Ibid. 185 to 190.

(*i*) 1 Chalm. 168. Stokes, 23. See the stat. 22 Geo. 3. c. 75, by which offices in the colonies are only to be granted for such time as the grantees shall act personally and behave well therein. By sect. 2. the Governor may remove the officer in case of misbehaviour, &c.; but the latter may appeal to the King in Council.

usually

usually filled by the immediate appointment of his Majesty, if vacancies happen by death or removal, the governor appoints to such offices until they are filled up from home; and the persons appointed by the governor receive all the profits and emoluments of such offices, until they are superseded by the King's appointment of others (*a*).

3. The governor has the custody of the great seal, and is chancellor within his province, with the same powers of judicature that the Lord High Chancellor has in England (*b*).

4. The governor is ordinary within his province; and by virtue of the King's commission, he collates to all vacant benefices: he has also the power of granting probate of wills and administration of intestate's effects, by virtue of his instructions (*c*).

5. The governor presides in the Court of Errors, of which he and the council are judges, to hear and determine all appeals in the nature of writs of error, from the superior courts of common law in the province (*d*).

6. The governor is usually named first in the standing commission, issued under the 11 and 12 Will. 3. c. 7. for the more effectual suppression of piracy (*e*).

7. The governor is also vice-admiral within his province; but he does not sit in the Court of Vice-Admiralty, there being a judge of that Court, who is usually appointed from England. In time of war, commissions to privateers are issued by the judge of the Court of Vice-Admiralty, in consequence of a warrant from the governors (*f*).

With respect to the *colonial assemblies* (*g*), it is most important that any idea that they stand on the same footing as the English House of Commons should be excluded from consideration. The principles on which the English Parliament rests its rights, powers, and privileges, cannot be extended to a provincial assembly. Parliament stands on its own laws, the " *lex et consuetudo parliamenti*" (*h*), which are founded on precedents, and immemorial usage. The plantation assemblies derive their energies from the Crown; and are regulated

---

(*a*) Stokes, 190, 1.
(*b*) Ibid. 191 to 199. Appeal to King in Council, ante.
(*c*) Ibid. 199 to 222.
(*d*) Ibid. 222 to 231.

(*e*) Ibid. 231 to 233.
(*f*) Ibid. 233 to 241.
(*g*) See in general Stokes, 241. ch. 7.
(*h*) 1 Inst. 11. 4 Inst. 50. 2 Ld. Raym. 1114.

by their respective charters and usages, and by the common law of England. The constitutions of the English Parliament and the colonial assemblies necessarily differ: the latter cannot in general even adjourn themselves; this is done by the governor (a), who as representative of the King is the first branch of this subordinate legislature. It is however generally true, that a legal and confirmed act of assembly has the same operation and force in the colonies, that an Act of Parliament has here (b).

Local circumstances, and the necessity of the case, must also create several differences between Parliament and the colonial assemblies with respect to the prerogatives of the King, as their " *caput, principium, et finis.*" So that there can be no doubt that the King may assent to an act of assembly before it meets; or dissent though the session be closed (c). The prerogative of dissenting to colonial acts is so material to the existence of the King's sovereignty, that there can scarcely be imagined a case in which such power could not be exercised.

Though the statute 7 and 8 Wm. 3. c. 15. as to the continuance of Parliament after the demise of the Crown, does not extend to the plantations; several very cogent reasons have been urged in support of the doctrine, that the demise of the Crown does not dissolve a colonial assembly (d). And the death or change of the governor, who is merely the representative of the sovereign, does not, it seems, produce that effect (e).

The dependence of the colonies on the Crown, and the sovereignty of the King over them, are not weakened or affected by the termination of their charters. The King may accept the surrender of a charter granted to the proprietor of a colony, subject to the rights of third persons, previously acquired under the charter (f); and in these cases the Crown may resume the reins of government, and may, by proclamation under the Great Seal, authorize existing magistrates and officers to continue in the exercise of their respective functions (g). So, as the King has a right to govern and protect all his subjects,

---

(a) Stokes, 241, 2. Ante, 34, 35.

(b) 2 Chalm. 1. Stokes, 241, &c. ch. 7.

(c) 1 Chalm. 315, 6.

(d) Ibid. 306, 312, 328, &c.

(e) Ibid. 244. &c. 254, &c. 307.

(f) Ibid. 32, 37.

(g) Ibid. 137, 8. 222.

it seems that even during the existence of a charter the King
may take it away, and grant fresh powers to another, in cases
of positive necessity, and upon an extraordinary exigency, happening through the default or neglect of a proprietor of a colony, or of those appointed by him, or their inability to protect or defend the inhabitants in times of war or imminent
danger; but in such case previous civil rights remain, and
must be respected (*a*). In this case also, and in others where a
charter to a colony is forfeited, an inquisition and *scire facias*
to repeal should regularly be adopted (*b*).

If the King lose a territory acquired by conquest, and recon-
quer it, the former rights of the inhabitants, under charters
granted by the Crown, revive and are restored, *jure postliminii ;*
a conquest by an enemy merely operating as a suspension, not
as an extinguishment, of the rights of former owners (*c*).

In the case of Penn *v.* Lord Baltimore (*d*), it was ingeniously
contended, that a colonial province being a proprietary government and feudal seigniory held of the Crown, which has
the sovereign dominion, the parties holding under charters
from the King have no power to vary or settle the boundaries
by their own act; for such agreement to settle boundaries and
to convey in consequence, amounts to an alienation, which
these lords proprietors cannot do; and that, even supposing
they might alien entirely, they cannot alien a parcel, as that is
dismembering. But Lord Chancellor Hardwicke held otherwise, and considered that the subordinate proprietors might,
bonâ fide, and without fraud, legally agree how they would hold
their rights and settle boundaries between themselves; and
that they, holding in fee, might even alien the lands to natural-born subjects without the royal licence, unless expressly
restrained. His Lordship held, however, that the proprietors
could not dismember their provinces, so as to alter the nature
of the thing granted, and thereby bind the Crown of whom they
held; for the tenure and services would still remain on the
whole, and the Crown might demand the whole services of either.
In this great case it was also laid down, that, though the exclusive and original jurisdiction over questions relative to
boundaries between provinces and the dominion, &c. therein,

(*a*) 1 Chalm. 31. 29. 188, 9.　　　(*c*) Ibid. 108.
(*b*) Ibid. and 108.　　　　　　　　(*d*) 1 Vez. sen. 444.

is in the King in council (*a*), still Chancery may hold cognizance of such question, (the Crown having the option of being
a party, and its right being reserved, if brought before it,) on
an agreement or articles between the proprietors executed in
England, to convey, &c. in pursuance of the boundary to be
established, and the Court accordingly decreed a specific performance; the agreement between the parties having given the
Court a jurisdiction it would not otherwise have possessed.

CHAP. IV.

*Of the Prerogative of the King as it more immediately
relates to independent states and foreign matters.*

SECTION I.—*In general.*

ONE of the chief excellencies of the constitution consists in the
harmony with which it combines all that strength and dispatch
in the executive department of the state, which might be expected only from a despotic government; with every liberty
and right of interference on the part of the subject which is
not inconsistent with the public welfare.

That such strength and dispatch are politically necessary
throughout the whole machine of government, and more especially in that part of it which relates to foreign transactions,
cannot be doubted: and experience has shewn that the
rapidity and secrecy which are generally necessary to the due
execution of public measures, will never be found in large
assemblies of the people.

Wavering with doubts, and distracted by the jealousies and
the animosities of party, such assemblies would be discussing the
propriety of the step after the opportunity and occasion for its
adoption had transpired. It is only by assigning the exclusive
power of managing and executing state measures to one individual, that they can be effectually and properly transacted.

When the rights in question are concentrated in one department of the state, and the power of the realm is wielded

(*a*) Ante.

by one hand, the execution of public measures will inspire the people with confidence, and strike into the enemies of the country that awe, that dread of its activity and power, which it is the constant endeavour of good policy to create.

For these reasons the constitution has made the King the delegate or representative of the people, with regard to foreign affairs; and has invested his Majesty with the supreme exclusive power of managing them (*a*).

SECT. II.

That the King sends Ambassadors, &c. abroad.

THE constitution has vested in the King the sole power of sending ambassadors, consuls (*b*), and other ministers abroad, and receiving ambassadors from foreign states (*c*). These need not be appointed by letters patent or by any other particular instrument, though they universally receive on their appointments some document evidencing their right to fill the situation assigned to them; and a consul is generally, if not always, appointed by a commission directed to him from the King.

SECT. III.

Of Letters of Marque and Reprisals.

THE laws of nature and of nations (*d*), vest in every power a right to make reprisals, and adopt a system of fair retaliation, for the aggressions of another community. Where a nation manifests a general spirit of hostility towards another, by a series of unauthorized attacks, and satisfaction is denied and explanations are evaded, though it be the King's duty as protector of the rights and honour of his dominions, to enable his subjects to retaliate on their oppressors, yet his Majesty being the only constitutional judge of the policy and expedi-

(*a*) 1 Bla. Com. 252.
(*b*) See Chitty on Commerce.
(*c*) 1 Bla. Com. 253.

(*d*) Grotius de jure b. et p. lib. 3. ch. 2. sect. 4 and 5.

ency of commencing hostilities, his subjects cannot legally adopt the *lex talionis* without the royal authority (*a*). As observed by Sir Wm. Blackstone (*b*), the necessity is obvious of calling in the sovereign power to determine when reprisals may be made; else every private sufferer would be a judge in his own cause. The law has therefore wisely ranged the right to grant letters of marque and reprisals, either during war or peace, among the *jura regalia*, and has vested it solely in the King (*c*): so that by the law of the admiralty, the property in a ship taken from the aggressors, without letters of marque and reprisals, vests in the King as a droit to the Crown, not in the suffering or other subject who captured it (*d*). And it has been decided that a subject of the King cannot take goods belonging to the subjects of a prince in amity with the King by virtue of letters of marque, granted by any other sovereign or state (*e*).

It must be remembered that the power which his Majesty grants to his subjects by the letters of marque and reprisals, should be restrained in its operation to the subjects of the offending state; and it has therefore been determined that a clause in a charter which empowers the seizing the goods of every person is illegal and void (*f*). The effect of the grant is to authorize the seizure of the bodies and goods of the subjects of the offending state, which may be detained till satisfaction be made, but no longer (*g*).

The statute 4 Hen. 5. c. 7. declares that " if any subjects of the realm are oppressed in the time of truce by any foreigners, the King will grant marque in due form to all that feel themselves grieved," which form is thus directed to be observed : the sufferer must first apply to the Lord Privy Seal, and he shall make out letters of request under the privy seal; and if after

(*a*) Hal. P. C. 162. 1 Vern. 52. Recital 4 Hen. 5. c. 7.

(*b*) 1 Comm. 259.

(*c*) Ibid. Molloy, 30, b. 1. c. 2. s. 10. 2 Rol. Ab. 175. Chitty's Law of Nat. 73.

(*d*) Vin. Abr. Prerog. N. A. pl. 22. Carth. 399. 2 Wooddn. V. L. 433. 10 Vez. 155.

(*e*) 2 Vern. 592.

(*f*) See Shower, 137. In the case of the *Sacra Familia* it was decided that a vessel cruizing under letters of marque against one state, as for instance, against France, is at liberty, on obtaining notice of hostilities commenced against another, as Spain, to capture a Spanish vessel, with as full advantage to herself as if the prize had been French. 5 Rob. R. 360.

(*g*) Grotius, b. 3. c. 2. 1 Bla. Com. 258. Vattel. b. 2. c. 13. 2 Wooddn. 435 to 440.

such

such request of satisfaction made, the party required do not within convenient time make due satisfaction or restitution to the party grieved, the Lord Chancellor shall make him out letters of marque under the great seal, and by virtue of these he may attack and seize the property of the aggressor nation, without hazard of being condemned as a robber or pirate.

This statute, it will be observed, relates only to injuries during peace, and to the grant of letters of marque and reprisals to the subject who is actually injured by the foreigners. It is said, that the mode of obtaining letters of marque pointed out in the statute has been long disused (a). By various statutes, enacted during every war, the Lord High Admiral, or the Commissioners of the Admiralty, are empowered to grant commissions, or, as they are also called, letters of marque and reprisals, to the owners of ships, enabling them tc attack and take the property of his Majesty's enemies; which statutes contain also various provisions as to the prizes captured (b). These statutes do not, it should seem, affect the royal prerogative in question in the slightest degree.

Letters of marque and reprisals granted by the Crown are liberally construed, but may be vacated in three ways—1st, by express revocation (c), but this is only allowable in the case of letters granted during war; when granted in time of peace and unsatisfied, it is otherwise (d); though, 2dly, even in such case, the cessation of hostilities will defeat the rights granted (e).—3rdly, These letters may be vacated by the misconduct of the grantees, as by cruelty, &c. (f).

In cases of recapture, no letter of marque from the King is required to give to the recaptor the benefit of the same salvage to which he would have been entitled if he had been provided with letters of marque (g).

The King, however, has the right of releasing any prize previously to its condemnation. This, said Lord Ellenborough, in the case of Sterling v. Vaughan (h), is an implied exception in the grant of prize by the Crown.

(a) 1 Bla. Com. 259. Christian's ed. note 8.

(b) See 29 Geo. 2. c. 34. 19 Geo. 3. c. 67. 43 Geo. 3. c. 160. 45 Geo. 3. c. 72. Molloy, ch. 358.

(c) Molloy, lib. 1. c. 2. s. 8. Chitty, L. of Nat. 74, 5.

(d) Ibid.

(e) Ibid. 2 Wooddn. V. L 440. Vern. 54.

(f) 5 Rob. Rep. 9.

(g) 2 Ibid. 224.

(h) 11 East, 619.

By the antient law of nations, debts due to alien enemies might be confiscated by the state; and it seems that in this country the King is entitled to choses in action belonging to an enemy, but that there must be an inquisition to entitle the King; and if a peace be made before the inquisition, the cause of forfeiture is discharged (*a*).

SECT. IV.

Of making War and Peace.

As representative of his people, and executive magistrate, the King possesses, on the principles just mentioned, the exclusive right to make war or peace, either within or out of his dominions (*b*); and the constitution leaves it to the King's discretion to grant or refuse a capitulation or truce to an enemy (*c*). This right may be exercised either partially or absolutely, so that his Majesty may institute a war against part of the subjects of a foreign power, excepting the other part, as was done by William the Third, in a war with France, in which he excepted the French Protestants (*d*). And it is not unusual on declaring war, to qualify it in the proclamation, by permitting the subjects of the enemy resident in this country to continue here so long as they behave peaceably; and there can be no doubt (as observed by Mr. Hargrave) (*e*), that such persons are to be deemed alien friends in effect.

The general rule is, " *ubi bellum non est pax est ;*" and therefore, though no league or articles of peace subsist between this and a foreign state, such state is not to be considered or treated as inimical until the King has denounced war against it (*f*). The King alone has a legal discretion on this subject, under any circumstances which may occur; and though a kingdom which professes to be neutral, should commit the most flagrant acts of aggression and injustice towards this country, and trample on every duty enjoined by the law of nations, still the King alone can legally declare war against it (*g*). " And," says

(*a*) Parker, 267. See per Ld. Alvanley, 3 Bos. and P. 191. Chitty, L. of Nations, 85.

(*b*) Hal. 159. 7 Co. 25. 1 Bla. Com. 257. See per Sir Wm. Scott. 1 Rob. Rep. 196.

(*c*) Cowp. 209.

(*d*) See per Treby, J. Ld. Raym. 283.

(*e*) Co. Lit. 129, b. note 3.

(*f*) Hal. Hist. P. C. 160.

(*g*) 1 M. and Selw. 450.

Brooke, in his Abridgment (a), " if all the people of England would make war with the King of Denmark, and our King will not consent to it, this is not war; but when the peace is broken by ambassadors the league is broken."

The reason which is gven by Grotius (b) why, according to the law of nations, a formal denunciation of war ought always to precede the actual commencement of hostilities, is, not so much that the enemy may be put upon his guard (which is matter rather of magnanimity than right), but that it may be clear that the war is undertaken not by private persons, but the will of the whole community, which, as we have already seen, is, in legal contemplation, transferred to and vested in the King. Blackstone (c) argues, from this reason assigned by Grotius, that in order to make a war completely effectual, it is necessary, by the law of this country, that it be publicly declared, and duly proclaimed by the King's authority, and then all parts of both the contending nations, from the highest to the lowest, are bound by it. Notwithstanding this, it seems that no public declaration, or formal proclamation of war is, by law, absolutely necessary to render it the duty of the King's subjects to consider and treat as an enemy, any foreign power against whom war has in point of fact been resolved upon and commenced by his Majesty (d).

SECT. V.

Of other Rights incident to the War Prerogative.

As the constitution of the country has vested in the King the right to make war or peace, it has necessarily and incidentally assigned to him on the same principles the management of the war; together with various prerogatives which may enable his Majesty to carry it on with effect. Thus the King is at the head of his army and navy, is alone entitled to order their movements, to regulate their internal arrangements, and to diminish, or, during war, increase their numbers, as may

(a) Tit. Denizen, pl. 20.
(b) De jure b. et p. l. 3. c, 3. s. 2.
(c) 1 Vol. 258.

(d) Owen, 45. Cro. El. 142. Freem. 41. Rast. Entr. 605. 4 Rob. Rep. 252. Chitty, L. of Nat. 29,

seem

seem to his Majesty most consistent with political propriety (*a*). On similar grounds the King is solely entitled to erect, fortify, and govern forts and other places of strength, within his dominions (*b*) ; both which prerogatives clearly appertain to the Crown by the fundamental rules of the British constitution, and are expressly recognized as such in the recitals of two statutes passed in the reign of Charles 2 (*c*). " Forasmuch as within all his Majesty's realms and dominions the sole supreme government, command, and disposition of the militia, and of all forces by sea and land, and of all forts and places of strength is, and by the laws of England ever was, the undoubted right of his Majesty and his Royal predecessors, Kings and Queens of England, and that both or either of the Houses of Parliament cannot nor ought to pretend to the same."

With respect to the *militia*, the extent to which they may be employed, and various regulations respecting them, are specially pointed out by a series of legislative provisions (*d*), which do not deny, but admit, the power of the Crown to command them, subject to such provisions. Under these enactments (*e*), the King is enabled in all cases of actual invasion, or upon imminent danger thereof, and in all cases of rebellion or insurrection, the occasion being first communicated to Parliament, if sitting, or if not sitting, declared in Council and notified by Proclamation, to order the militia to be embodied ; and his Majesty may use them, or such proportion of them, and in such manner as his Majesty shall in his wisdom deem necessary, and when drawn out into actual service, they are liable to all the rigours of martial law. But it is expressly enacted by all the statutes on this subject that the militia shall, on no account, be sent out of Great Britain.

With respect to the *regular force* of the kingdom, who are totally unconnected with, and substantially different in their nature and object from the militia, the King is not by law restrained to any particular limits as to the services in which they may be employed against his enemies. They may of course be sent to any place, or employed to any ex-

(*a*) 1 Bla. Com. 262.
(*b*) 2 Inst. 30. 1 Ibid. 5.
(*c*) 13 Car. 2. st. 1. c. 6. 14 Car. 2. c. 3.
(*d*) See 43 Geo. 3. c. 90. which re- duces the preceding statutes into one, and refer to the subsequent statutes. See 1 Bla. Com. 412. Burn, J. tit. Militia.

(*e*) See 43 Geo. 3. c. 96. s. 111.

tent, which his Majesty may think fit. But the constitution has, with the wisest jealousy, ordained that a standing force is not legal in time of peace, unless by consent of Parliament (a). During peace the King has therefore no legal authority or prerogative to keep an army on foot. However, as remarked by Sir Wm. Blackstone, it has for many years past been annually judged necessary by our legislature, for the safety of the kingdom, the defence of the possessions of the Crown of Great Britain, and the preservation of the balance of power in Europe, to maintain even in time of peace a standing body of troops, under the command of the Crown; who are however *ipso facto* disbanded at the expiration of every year, unless continued by Parliament. And it was enacted by statute 10 Wm. 3. c. 1. that not more than twelve thousand regular forces should be kept on foot in Ireland, though paid at the charge of that kingdom; which permission is extended by statute 8 Geo. 3. c. 13. to 16,235 men in time of peace.

The authority and power which the annual Act grants to the King over the forces is extensive. It empowers his Majesty to constitute courts martial, who are to try military offences according to articles framed by his Majesty (b).

The King's power over the *Fleet* in time of war, is as general as that which his Majesty possesses during that period over his armies; except in this respect that the articles of the navy are framed by the legislature, and specify with particularity almost every possible offence and its punishment; thus in effect and in substance depriving his Majesty of a legislative power over his navy (c). As a powerful navy cannot, even during peace, be regarded with the suspicion and distrust which are laudably attached to the existence of a standing army, the King's prerogative over his navy does not by law terminate, nor is it lessened, merely by the cessation of hostilities.

There is also a substantial legal distinction between the mode of raising land and sea forces. Though, as just observed, the King has a right to require the personal service of every man able to bear arms, in case of a sudden invasion or formidable insurrection; and the allegiance due from the sub-

---

(a) Bill of Rights, 1 Wm. and Mary, st. 2. c. 2. Recital in st. 55 Geo. 3. c. 108. and the annual mutiny acts.

(b) See 55 Geo. 3. c. 108. s. 14, 35, &c. 1 Bla. Com. 415.

(c) See 1 Bla. Com. 421.

ject

ject renders it incumbent on him to assist his sovereign on such occasions (*a*); yet except on such emergencies, and at ordinary times his Majesty has no legal power to force any one to enlist in his armies (*b*). With respect however to persons who come within the description of seamen and seafaring men, the King may even in time of peace compel them to re-enter the navy, by forcibly impressing them.

This prerogative of the Crown, which has been much attacked, and is certainly a blot on English freedom, is founded on immemorial usage, recognized, admitted, and sanctioned by various Acts of Parliament (*c*). It is only exerciseable over individuals who have in the first instance voluntarily chosen a seafaring life, and does not extend to landsmen (*d*); fishermen, except in certain cases (*e*); harpooners, line-managers, and boat-steerers employed in the Greenland fisheries (*f*); seamen in the British sugar colonies in the West Indies, or serving in privateers, or trading ships employed in such colonies, except in case of invasion or other emergent necessity (*g*); persons under eighteen years of age or of the age of fifty-five years or upwards; foreigners, whether mariners, seamen or landsmen for the first two years of their going to. sea; or to apprentices not used to the sea for the three first years from the time of their binding themselves to serve at sea (*h*).

The right to impress in particular cases has frequently been discussed in the Courts of law. It has been holden, that a keelman or person employed in navigating rivers (*i*); and carpenters employed on board of ships on a coasting or other trade (*k*); are respectively liable to be impressed. Nor does it appear that the captain or master of a trading vessel is exempted (*l*). And seafaring men are not exempted, because they serve the office of headborough (*m*); or are freeholders (*n*); or because they are freemen, liverymen (*o*), or watermen (*p*), of the City of London.

(*a*) Foster, 158.   11 Hen. 7. ch. 1.
1 Ed. 3. c. 5.   16 and 17 Car. 1. c. 28.

(*b*) See Foster, 157, 175.

(*c*) Ibid. 154. Cowp. 512. 1 Bla. Com. 419. 5 Term Rep. 276.

(*d*) See Foster, 157. Cowp. 519.

(*e*) 5 El. ch. 5. s. 43. 50 Geo. 3. c. 108. s. 2.

(*f*) 11 Geo. 3. c. 38. s. 19.

(*g*) 19 Geo. 2. c. 30. s. 1 and 7.

(*h*) 13 Geo. 2. c. 17. s. 1 and 2.

(*i*) 1 East, 466. 2 and 3 Ph. and M. c. 16. s. 7.

(*k*) 13 East, 459.

(*l*) Ibid. 550, note. 14 Ibid. 346.

(*m*) 5 Term Rep. 276.

(*n*) 5 East, 477.

(*o*) 9 Ibid. 466.

(*p*) Cowp. 512.

It

It seems to have been the opinion of Lord Kenyon, that an exemption from impress cannot be founded on the common law, but only on a legislative provision (*a*). We have, however, in the case of ferrymen, an instance of an exemption grounded merely on the common law (*b*): and the express opinions of Lord Mansfield and Mr. J. Ashhurst, that as the right of pressing is grounded on the common law, an exemption from it may exist on the same foundation (*c*). Of course it is incumbent on the party insisting on the exemption to prove clearly the grounds on which he rests his claim to it (*d*).

There is no doubt that the King may exempt or grant a protection to any particular class of seafaring men from impressment, because, in the Crown alone lies the power of issuing press-warrants. In those warrants instructions are given to the officers not to impress any person protected by the navy, victualling office, &c. Even the officers themselves grant protections; *à fortiori* therefore if the officers, and inferior boards can grant protections, the Crown by its prerogative is entitled to the same privilege. These protections are however revocable at pleasure, though granted for a certain specified time (*e*).

As conductor of a war the King is also entitled to adopt measures to prevent the egress or ingress of his enemies out of or into his Majesty's dominions. Thus his Majesty may promulgate blockades; may during war or threatened hostilities, and on occasions of emergency lay an embargo on all shipping; and thereby prevent any one from leaving the kingdom (*f*). His Majesty may on the other hand permit an enemy to come into the country without molestation, by granting to him letters of safe-conduct (*g*). These letters ought to be under the Great Seal, and inrolled in Chancery (*h*). But passports under the King's sign manual or licences from his ambas-

---

(*a*) 5 Term Rep. 277. and see 1 East, 166.

(*b*) See Sav. 14. 5 Term Rep. 277. per Buller, J.

(*c*) Cowp. 518. 521, 2.

(*d*) Ibid. 519.

(*e*) 16 East, 165. Cowp. 521. See st. 50 Geo. 3. c. 108. ante, ch. 3. as to exemptions in general. Lane, 46. Dyer, 176, 177. So a pardon not under Great Seal but merely under Privy Seal is revocable, Post, tit. Pardons, 1 Chitty, Crim. Law, 770. So of a license to trade.

(*f*) Skinner, 335. 3 Lev. 352. 4 Mod. 176, 177, 179. 1 Bla. Com. 270, 1. 4 Bac. Ab. 595. title Merchant and Merchandize, see further, post. ch. 10.

(*g*) See Ld. Raym. 382. 1 Salk. 46. Lutw. 34, 5.

(*h*) 15 Hen. 6. c. 3. 18 Ibid. c. 8. 20 Ibid. c. 1.

sadors

sadors abroad are now more usually obtained, and are allowed to be of equal validity (*a*).

Alien friends may lawfully come into the country without any licence or protection from the Crown (*b*), though it seems that the Crown, even at common law, and by the law of nations, (and independently of the powers vested in it by the Alien Act, 55 G. 3. c. 54. which extends even to foreign merchants,) possesses a right to order them out of the country, or prevent them from coming into it, whenever his Majesty thinks proper (*c*). The enactment in Magna Charta, c. 30. relates only to foreign *merchants:* " All *merchants,* unless they were openly prohibited before, shall have safe and sure conduct to depart out of England, and to come into England, and to tarry in and go through England, as well by land as by water, *to buy or sell,* without any evil tolls, by the old and rightful customs, except in time of war; and if they be of land at war with us, and if such be found in our land at the beginning of the war, they shall be attached without harm of body or goods, until it be known unto us, or our Chief Justice, how the merchants of our land are entreated who shall be then found in the land at war against us, and if ours be safe there, the others shall be safe in our land." The power of the Crown to dispense with commercial regulations, as to enable an enemy, &c. to trade with this country, will be considered hereafter.

The Alien Act, 55 G. 3. c. 54. was passed for the purpose of vesting extraordinary powers in the King and Magistracy, in order that the country might be protected against aliens; it contains various wholesome provisions for that purpose.

The law has also vested in the King several other rights on similar grounds : Thus, in case of necessity, the King may enter on the lands of his subjects to make fortifications (*d*). His Majesty has a prerogative right in saltpetre and gunpowder (*e*); may, as before remarked, require the personal services of his subjects in this country in case of imminent danger (*f*), and may prohibit the exportation of arms or ammunition, or other articles of that nature, useful in war, called contraband of war,

---

(*a*) 1 Bla. Com. 260.

(*b*) Magna Char. c. 30.   1 Wooddn. 368, 375.

(*c*) 1 Bla. Com. 259, 260. Puffendorff.

See 55 Geo. 3. c. 54. s. 2.

(*d*) 1 Rol. Rep. 152.

(*e*) 5 Bac. Ab. 533.

(*f*) Ante.

out

out of the kingdom (*a*).   But he cannot hinder the building of ships of war for an alien *ami* in this country (*b*).

To finish this part of the subject, in the words of Lord Erskine (*c*), " The King may relax from the utmost rights of war, and from its extreme severities.   What is termed the war prerogative of the King is created by the perils and exigencies of war for the public safety, and by its perils and exigencies is therefore limited.   The King may lay on a general embargo, and may do various acts growing out of sudden emergencies ; but in all these cases the emergency is the avowed cause, and the act done is as temporary as the occasion.   The King cannot change by his prerogative of war, either the law of nations or the law of the land, by general and unlimited regulations."

CHAP. V.

Of the King as the head of the National Church.

The Supremacy of the Crown.—Ecclesiastical Laws and Powers of the Crown respecting Convocations or Synods.—Ecclesiastical Laws under the King's Controul, Protection, &c.—Of the King as the dernier resort *in Ecclesiastical Causes.—Prerogatives as to the disposal of Church Preferments, &c.—Custody of Temporalities.—Corodies.—Tithes, First Fruits and Tenths, &c.*

THE supremacy of the Crown in all matters of an ecclesiastical nature is, as observed by Lord Hale (*d*), a most indubitable right, which may be proved by records of unquestionable truth and authority; and though the Popes made great usurpations and encroachments on this right, they were ever complained of and resisted as illegal (*e*), and were effectually destroyed in the reign of Hen. 8.

(*a*) 12 Car. 2. c. 4. 29 Geo. 2. c. 16. post. ch. 10. as to commerce.

(*b*) Fortescue, R. 388.

(*c*) Speech, Mar. 8, 1808, on the Orders in Council. 10 Cobbett, Parliamentary Debates, 961.

(*d*) Hale, Hist. P. C. 75.   5 Co. 8. 40.   1 Bla. Com. 279.

(*e*) 2 Burn, Ecc. Law, tit. Courts, 35, 36.   Ld. Raym. 25.

By

By the statute 26 H. 8. c. 1. it is declared that " the King shall be taken, accepted, and reputed the only supreme Head on earth of the Church of England, called *Anglicana ecclesia;* and shall have and enjoy, annexed and united to the imperial Crown of this realm, as well the title and style thereof, as all honours, dignities, preeminences, jurisdictions, privileges, authorities, immunities, profits and commodities to the said dignity of supreme Head of the same Church, belonging and appertaining; and that the King shall have full power and authority, from time to time, to visit, repress, redress, reform, order, correct, restrain and amend all such errors, heresies, abuses, offences, contempts, and enormities whatsoever they be, which by any matter, spiritual authority or jurisdiction, ought or may lawfully be reformed, repressed, ordered, redressed, corrected, restrained, or amended, most to the pleasure of Almighty God, the increase of virtue in Christ's religion, and for the conservation of the peace, unity and tranquillity of this realm; any usage, custom, foreign laws, foreign authority, prescription or any other thing or things to the contrary thereof notwithstanding (*a*)."

It need not be observed that the King cannot alter the established religion either in this country or in any other parts of his dominions.

The ecclesiastical law of England is compounded of the civil law, the canon law, the common law, and the statute law (*b*). Before the Conquest, the King, with the assent of the clergy who were assembled by his writ (*c*), made constitutions forming the ecclesiastical law; and after the Conquest, and long before the time of Hen. 8. the right to make canons appertained to the King, through the medium of the Convocations or ecclesiastical Synods or Parliaments, consisting of the archbishops, the bishops, and the representatives of the different dioceses(*d*). By the Act of submission, 25 Hen. 8. c. 19. (after reciting that whereas "the King's humble and obedient subjects, the clergy of the realm of England, have not only acknowledged according to the truth, that the Convocation of the same clergy is, always hath been, and ought to be assembled only by the King's writ; but also submitting themselves to the King's Majesty, have

(*a*) See also 1 El. c. 1, and the Canons. Burn's Eccles. Law, tit. Supremacy.

(*b*) See Pref. to Burn's Eccl. Law.
(*c*) 4 Inst. 322. Godolph. Repert. 99.
(*d*) See 2 Burn, Eccl. Law, 26.

promised

promised *in verbo sacerdotii* that they will never from henceforth presume to attempt, alledge, claim, or put in use, enact,
promulge, or execute any new canons, constitutions, ordinances provincial, or by whatsoever name they shall be called in
the convocation, unless the King's most royal assent and
licence may to them be had, to make, promulge, and execute
the same; and that his Majesty do give his most royal assent
and authority in that behalf;) it is enacted, according to the
said submission, that they nor any of them shall presume to
attempt, alledge, claim, or put in use any constitutions or
ordinances provincial, by whatsoever name or names they
may be called, in their Convocations in time coming (which
always shall be assembled by authority of the King's writ);
unless the same clergy may have the King's most royal
assent and licence to make, promulge, and execute such
canons, constitutions, and ordinances, provincial or synodal
upon pain of every one of the said clergy doing contrary to
this act, and being thereof convict, to suffer imprisonment and
make fine at the King's will." Upon which statute it is observable, 1st, That a Convocation cannot assemble without the
King's consent. 2dly, That after their assembly they cannot
confer to constitute any canons without his licence. And 3dly,
That their canons are imperfect, and cannot be executed without the royal assent (*a*); and that no other assent is requisite
(*b*). The Convocations (for there are two, one for the archbishoprick of Canterbury, and another for the archbishoprick
of York) are usually assembled at the meeting of every new
Parliament; and when assembled, are under the power and
authority of the King (*c*), and are liable to be prorogued,
restrained, regulated and dissolved by his Majesty; a prerogative which was inherent in the Crown long before the time
of Hen. 8. as appears by the statute 8 Hen. 6. c. 1. and the
many authors, both lawyers and historians, vouched by Sir
Edward Coke (*d*). Their jurisdiction is confined to matters of
heresy, schisms, and other mere spiritual and ecclesiastical
causes. They cannot interfere with any matters relating to
the laws of the land, and their canons are void, though

(*a*) 12 Co. 72. Convocations in the
Plantations, 1 Chalmers' Coll. of Op.
12. Consequence of holding without
the royal licence. Ibid.

(*b*) Stra. 1057.
(*c*) Year Book, 25 E. 4, 45, 6.
(*d*) 4 Inst. 322, 3. Wood's Inst. 500.
1 Bla. Com. 279.

assented

assented to by the King, if contrary to the common or statute law, or any custom of the realm (*a*). As the laity are not represented by any portion of the members of the Convocation or Synod, canons are not *proprio vigore*, binding on the laity (*b*). The consent of the people is not included in the royal confirmation of the canons (*c*).

Ecclesiastics, and the ecclesiastical laws, and the execution of them, are peculiarly subject to the royal authority and superintendence, though the King does not execute this prerogative in person. Thus, the King has in general the power of visiting and reforming abuses in the church (*d*), through the medium of the Lord Chancellor, or of Commissioners appointed under the Great Seal. Free chapels, hospitals, and donations of the King's foundation, are visitable only by his Majesty; and where a King and a subject join in a foundation, the King shall visit, for he is founder (*e*).

The right and power of the Crown to dispense with the ecclesiastical law, in matters not repugnant to the law of God, existed before the time of Henry the Eighth (*f*), and still exists, notwithstanding the statute 25 Hen. 8. c. 21. which vests a right to grant dispensations in the Archbishop of Canterbury, for there are no words in the statute expressly depriving the King of his prerogative, who enjoys it concurrently with the Archbishop of Canterbury (*g*). This power is confined to ecclesiastical regulations, and does not apply where any express provisions are pointed out by a statute with which the King cannot dispense (*h*); but in most ecclesiastical affairs the power applies. Thus, the King may grant an exemption from the visitation and jurisdiction of the ordinary (*i*), might enable a bastard to be a priest (*k*), and may grant dispensations in

---

(*a*) 12 Co. 72. 4 Inst. 322. 25 Hen. 8. c. 19. Stra. 1058.

(*b*) Stra. 1056.

(*c*) Ibid. See further as to Convocations or Synods. Burn's Eccl. Law, tit. Convocation.

(*d*) Com. Dig. title Visitor; and see post. 55.

(*e*) Ibid. 2 Inst. 68.

(*f*) Dav. 70, b. and 73. Godb. 108. Com. Dig. Prerogative, D. (D. 29), 6 V. 38. Vin. Ab. Prerogative, K. f. 17 Vol. 255. 2 Burn's Eccl. Law, 164.

(*g*) See Ibid. Hob. 146. Cro. El. 542, 601. Moore, 542. Com. Dig. *ubi supra* D. (D. 19.)

(*h*) See post. ch. 7. And see sect. 6 of the 25 Hen. 8. c. 21. when the Archbishop's dispensations must be confirmed. And Com. Dig. *ubi supra*. D. (D. 19, 20.)

(*i*) Dav. 73, *a*.

(*k*) Hob. R. 147. 17 Vin. Ab. 255. 1 Burn, Eccl. Law, title Benefice, 3, page 156. But now he may be a priest without. 1 Bla. Com. 458, 9.

commendam,

commendam, the nature of which will be considered in a subsequent part of this chapter (*a*). The right of the King to appoint and direct superstitious uses to such uses as are truly charitable (*b*), and to pardon offences against the ecclesiastical laws, flows from the same principle (*c*). So the King may, by proclamation, appoint fasts and days of thanksgiving and humiliation, and issue proclamations for preventing and punishing immorality and profaneness, and enjoin the reading of the same in churches and chapels (*d*).

(*a*) See post. 60.

(*b*) Bac. Ab. Charitable Uses. D.

(*c*) As to this see post. ch. 7.

(*d*) Comp. Incumb. 354. See 10 Ann. c. 7. s. 11. 32 Geo. 3. c. 63. s. 5. as to prayers for the Royal Family. On the occasion of the death of the late Queen, the following appeared in the Gazette:

" *LONDON GAZETTE.*

" SATURDAY, NOVEMBER 21, 1818.

"At the Council-Chamber, *Whitehall,* the 18th of *November,* 1818, present, Archbishop of Canterbury, Lord President, Duke of Montrose, Lord Steward, Earl Bathurst, Earl of Liverpool, Viscount Melville, Viscount Sidmouth, Bishop of London, Lord St. Helens, Sir William Scott, Sir John Nicholl, Mr. Chancellor of the Exchequer, and the Lord Chief Baron.

" Whereas in the Act of Uniformity, which establishes the Liturgy of the Church of England, provision is made for such alterations in the Prayers for the Royal Family, as from time to time shall become necessary, and be directed by lawful authority: it is thereupon this day ordered in Council, that in the Morning and Evening Prayers, in the Litany, and in all other parts of the Public Service, as well in the occasional Offices as in the Book of Common Prayer, where the Royal Family is appointed to be particularly prayed for, the following form and order shall be observed, viz.

" *Their Royal Highnesses George*

Prince of Wales, the Princess of Wales, and all the Royal Family.

" And it is further ordered, that no edition of the Common Prayer be from henceforth printed, but with this amendment; and that in the mean time, till copies of such edition may be had, all Parsons, Vicars, and Curates, within this Realm, do (for preventing of mistakes) with the pen, correct and amend all such prayers in their Church Books, according to the aforegoing direction; and for the better notice hereof, that this Order be forthwith printed and published, and sent to the several Parishes; and that the Right Reverend the Bishops do take care that obedience be paid to the same accordingly.

" CHETWYND.

" In pursuance of an Act passed in the tenth year of Her late Majesty Queen Anne, and of another Act passed in the thirty-second year of His present Majesty, wherein provision is made for praying for the Royal Family in that part of Great Britain called Scotland; it is hereby ordered in Council, that henceforth every Minister and Preacher shall, in his respective Church, Congregation, or Assembly, pray in express words,

" *For His Most Sacred Majesty King George, their Royal Highnesses George Prince of Wales, the Princess of Wales, and all the Royal Family.*

" Of which all persons concerned are hereby required to take notice, and govern themselves accordingly.

" CHETWYND."

On

On the same principles, the King was at common law, and is, the ultimate judge and *dernier resort* in ecclesiastical causes, though he does not exercise this jurisdiction in person (*a*).

By the statute 25 Hen. 8. c. 19. it is declared, that " For lack of justice, at or in any the Courts of the Archbishops of this realm, or in any the King's dominions, it shall be lawful to the parties grieved to appeal to the King's Majesty in the King's Court of Chancery, and that upon every such appeal, a Commission shall be directed under the Great Seal, to such persons as shall be named by the King, like as in case of appeal from the Admiral's Court, to hear and definitively determine such appeals, and the causes concerning the same ; which Commissioners, so by the King to be named or appointed, shall have full power and authority to hear and definitively determine every such appeal with the causes, and all circumstances concerning the same ; and that such judgment and sentence as the said Commissioners shall make and decree in and upon any such appeal, shall be good and effectual, and also definitive ; and no further appeals to be had or made from the said Commissioners for the same."

Upon this statute is considered that the appeal does not lie from a local visitor, nor in any case of a temporal nature (*b*). The Commission is granted on petition, (which may be preferred by a person who is not an original party in the cause, if he be interested) (*c*), to the Lord Chancellor, who appoints the Commissioners or Delegates (*d*). These Commissioners, who may be laymen as well as ecclesiastics (*e*), have power to reverse or affirm the sentence of the inferior Court ; but have no original jurisdiction, that is, a jurisdiction not by way of appeal, as to grant administration, &c (*f*). There are, however, some instances in which the Commissioners appointed by the King seem to possess an original jurisdiction, as where the Archbishop himself is interested, in which case the Commissioners may begin the suit ; or in similar cases (*g*),

(*a*) 1 Wooddn. V. L. 77.   1 Bla. Com. 280.

(*b*) Wats. ch. 6. 4 Inst. 340. Moore, 782.

(*c*) 1 Atk. 298.

(*d*) Bac. Tracts, 294.

(*e*) Comp. Incumb. 56.   1 Burn, Eccl. Law, 61.

(*f*) Latch. 85.   2 Bulstr. 2.

(*g*) 1 Oughton's Ordo Judiciorum, 61.   1 Burn, Ecol. Law, title Appeal, 61.

as where the object is to deprive ecclesiastical persons for offences against the canons (*a*). The proceedings of the Delegates must be according to the ecclesiastical laws; wherefore a suit before them does not abate by the death of either of the parties (*b*); and if they exceed their authority, or proceed in matters not properly within their conusance, they may be prohibited by the Courts of Law (*c*).

The statute 25 Hen. 8. c. 19. s. 4. enacts, it will have been remarked, that the sentence of the Delegates shall be definitive, and that no further appeal shall be had from them, and consequently no appeal lies even to the House of Lords (*d*). It is however settled, that after a sentence of the Delegates, the King may by his prerogative, on petition to him in Council, grant a Commission of Review under the Great Seal, appointing new or adding more to the former judges, to revise, review, and rehear the cause; and such Commissioners may reverse the sentence of the Delegates; for, as observed by Sir Edward Coke (*e*), the statute does not expressly restrain the King in this respect, and after a definitive sentence the Pope used to grant a Commission, *ad revidendum*, and such authority as the Pope had, claiming as supreme head of the Church, of right belongs to the Crown, and is annexed (or rather re-annexed) thereunto, by the statutes 26 Hen. 8. c. 1. and 1 El. c. 1. However, the granting a Commission of Review is matter of discretion and not of right; and if it be a hard case, as where issue might be bastardized, the Chancellor will advise the Crown not to grant it (*f*).

Where the King is interested, an appeal to him in Chancery would be absurd; and therefore the party grieved " may appeal to the spiritual prelates and other abbots and priors of the upper house, assembled and convocate by the King's writ in the convocation being, or next ensuing within the province or provinces where the matter of contention is or shall be

(*a*) 4 Inst. 340. 2 Cro. 37. Mo. 755. St. 1 El. c. 1. s. 18. 1 Wooddn. V. L. 77.

(*b*) Ventr. 133. 2 Lev. 6. Cro. Jac. 483.

(*c*) Moor. 462, 3. Latch. 85, 86, 229. Gibs. 1037.

(*d*) 2 Vern. 118.

(*e*) 4 Inst. 341. Moor. 463, 781. Dyer. 273. Lit. Rep. 232. 1 Burn.

Eccl. Law, tit. Appeal. 2 Bac. Ab. tit. of the Ecclesiastical Courts, A. 10. 3 Bla. Com. 67. There is sometimes a clause in the Commission of Review to admit other allegations and new matter, and to take proofs thereupon, as well on the one part as on the other. 1 Ought. 437.

(*f*) 2 P. Wms. 299. 3 Bla. Com. 67.

begun.

begun, so that every such appeal be taken by the party grieved within fifteen days next after the judgment or sentence thereupon given or to be given: and that whatsoever shall be so done and affirmed, determined, decreed and adjudged by the said prelates, abbots and priors of the upper house of the said convocation, appertaining, concerning or belonging to the King, in any of these said causes of appeals shall stand and be taken for a final decree, sentence, judgment, diffinition and determination, and the same matter so determined never after to come in question and debate, to be examined in any other court or courts (a)."

With respect to appeals from places exempt, the statute 25 Hen. 8. c. 19. s. 6. enacts, " that such appeals shall be made immediately to the King's Majesty of this realm into the Court of Chancery, in like manner and form as they used afore to do to the see of Rome; which appeals and provocations so made shall be definitively determined by authority of the King's commission, in such manner and form as is mentioned in the act; so that no archbishop nor bishop of this realm shall intermit or meddle with any such appeals, otherwise or in any other manner than they might have done afore the making of this act."

The disposal of the principal ecclesiastical preferments belongs also to the King, as the head of the national church.

The statute 25 Hen. 8. c. 20. enacts, that " on every avoidance of every archbishoprick or bishoprick within this realm, or in any other the King's dominions, the King may grant to the prior and convent, or the dean and chapter of the cathedral churches or monasteries where the see of such archbishoprick or bishoprick shall happen to be void; a licence under the great seal, as of old time hath been accustomed, to proceed to election of an archbishop or bishop of the see so being void, with a letter missive, containing the name of the person which they shall elect and choose: by virtue of which licence the said dean and chapter, or prior and convent, to whom any such licence and letters missive shall be directed, shall with all speed and celerity in due form elect and choose the same person named in the said letters missive, to the dig-

---

(a) 24 Hen. 8. c. 12. s. 9. This statute does not appear to have been repealed by the 25th Hen. 8. c. 19. See 1 Wooddn. V. L. 77. 1 Bla. Com. 67.

nity and office of the archbishoprick or bishoprick so being void, and none other: and if they do defer or delay their election above twelve days next after such licence or letters missive to them delivered, that then for every such default the King at his liberty and pleasure shall nominate and present, by his letters patent under his great seal, such a person to the said office and dignity so being void as he shall think able and convenient for the same; and that every such nomination and presentment to be made by the King, if it be to the office and dignity of a bishop, shall be made to the archbishop and metropolitan of the province where the see of the same bishoprick is void, if the see of the said archbishoprick be then full, and not void; and if it be void, then to be made to such archbishop or metropolitan within this realm, or in any the King's dominions, as shall please the King's highness, his heirs or successors: and if any such nomination or presentment shall happen to be made for default of such election to the dignity or office of any archbishop, then the King by his letters patent under his great seal shall nominate and present such person as he will dispose to have the said office and dignity of archbishoprick being void, to one such archbishop and two such bishops, or else to four such bishops within this realm, or in any the King's dominions, as shall be assigned by his Majesty." This statute was afterwards repealed by 1 Edw. 6. c. 2. which enacted, that all bishopricks should be donative as formerly. It states in the preamble, that these elections " are in very deed no elections; but only by a writ of *congé d'elire* have colours, shadows or pretences of election (a)." This is certainly good sense. For the permission to elect where there is no power to reject, can hardly be reconciled with the freedom of election. But this statute was afterwards, repealed by 1 Ma. st. 2. c. 20. and other statutes, and consequently the 25 H. 8. c. 20. was thereby revived (b). But the bishopricks of the new foundation were always donative (c), as also are all the Irish bishopricks by the 2 Eliz. c. 4 (d).

(a) See 1 Burn, Eccl. Law, 202.

(b) 12 Co. 7.

(c) Harg. Co. Litt. 134.

(d) 1 Bla. Com. 379. n. 7. Christian's edition. The proprietor of the Isle of Man was patron of the bishoprick there, but the Archbishop of York did not consecrate him till the broad seal of the King's consent was produced. Johns 29. As to the power of the archbishop to consecrate, &c. bishops in the King's foreign dominions, 26 Geo. 3. c. 84.

Every

Every archbishoprick and bishoprick in England is of the King's foundation (a); and Lord Coke establishes the right of donation in the Crown on that principle (b).

As patron paramount of all the benefices in England, the right and care of filling all such churches as are not regularly filled by other patrons, belongs to the Crown; whether it happen through the neglect of others (as in the case of lapse) or through incapacity to present, as if the patron be attainted or outlawed, or an alien, or have been guilty of simony, or the like (c). Upon which ground the King hath right to present to all dignities and benefices of the advowson of archbishopricks and bishopricks during the vacation of the respective sees. Not only to such as become void after the seizure of the temporalities, but to all such as become void after the death of the bishop; though before actual seizure. And as it is a maxim in law, that the church is not full against the King till induction; therefore though the bishop hath collated, or hath presented, and the clerk is instituted upon that presentation, yet such collation or institution will not avail the clerk, but the right of presenting devolves to the King (d). And it is said, that this privilege which the King possesses of presenting by reason of temporalities of a bishoprick being in his hands, shall be extended unto such preferments, to which the bishop of common right might present, though by his composition he has transferred his power unto others: and therefore when the temporalities of the archbishoprick of York are in the King's hands, the King shall present to the deanry of York, although by composition between the archbishop and the chapter there, the chapter are to elect him; and this because the patronage thereof *de jure* doth belong to the archbishop, and his composition cannot bind the King, who comes in paramount as supreme patron: for of the whole bishoprick the King is supreme patron, although it be dismembered into various branches, as deans and other dignities; and of ancient time all the bishopricks were of the King's gift, but afterwards the King gave leave to the chapters to elect; yet the patronage notwithstanding remains in the King (e).

(a) 2 Inst. 3.
(b) 1 Inst. 134, 344.
(c) Gibs. 763.

(d) Ibid. Wats. c. 9. Co. Lit. 388.
(e) Wats. c. 9. 2 Roll. Abr. 343.

Where

Where the parson of a parish is consecrated (*a*) a bishop, he thereby vacates his benefice and other dignities, and the King who thus occasions the vacancy has the prerogative right of filling all the presentative benefices and dignities thus vacated (*b*). Lord Chief Justice De Grey, speaking of this right (which is in general exerted by the archbishop of Canterbury by the command of the King, but may it seems be exercised by the King himself singly) observes (*c*), that " it appears in Bro. Presentment 61. to be as old as Edward the Third's time. It was exercised under Hen. 8. and Queen Elizabeth. The law concerning it was doubted in Charles the Second's time, and since, but finally determined in favour of the Crown in King William's time, King and Bishop of London (*d*). This is not a right of patronage in the King; nor is it a right of eviction; for it ejects nobody: nor an usurpation; for it is a rightful act. But it is a contingent casual right, arising upon a particular event, the incumbent's becoming a bishop." The patron is not materially prejudiced by this prerogative, as it only occasions the exchange of one life for another.

On a vacancy taking place by the incumbent being made a bishop, the King may also before the title to the bishoprick is complete by the consecration of the bishop, and though the advowson belong to a common person, and without his consent, grant to the bishop a *commendam retinere*, or faculty to retain, thereby committing the vacated benefice to his care and possession to live as before, with the bishoprick (*e*).

Where the benefice, being void (*f*), is in the gift of some other patron than the King, and his Majesty grants the dispensation after the Bishop has been consecrated, the commendam is called not a *commendam retinere*, but a *commendam capere;* and the patron's consent is necessary to the dispensation, and must be given in an authentic manner and mentioned therein (*g*). The rule is, that no commendam can be granted but with the consent of the patron. In granting a *commendam retinere* the King, who is patron by the promotion, signifies

(*a*) 1 Bla. Com. 383.

(*b*) Ld. Raym. 23, and the following note.

(*c*) 2 Bla. R. 773. 2 H. B. 333.

(*d*) Ld. Raym. 23. 4 Mod. 202. 3 Lev. 377, 382, and the case of Saint James's Parish. 3 Lev. 388.

(*e*) See 2 Burn, Eccl. Law, tit. Commendam. Ld. Raym. 23. Com. Dig. tit. Prerogative. D. (D. 18, &c.) Hob. 144. Stra. 1006.

(*f*) Hob. 150.

(*g*) Gibs. 913, 4. Hob. 152.

his consent by his mandate to the Archbishop to grant dispensation.

A commendam may it seems be temporary or perpetual, at his Majesty's pleasure (*a*). When a commendam is limited to a certain time, the King shall present by prerogative at the end of the term, notwithstanding the previous grant of a commendam; unless it happen that the commendatory Bishop die or resign before the expiration of the term; for in such case, the church becoming void not by cession but by death or resignation, the turn of the Crown is served, and the patron, whoever he be, shall present (*b*). It is likewise served, if the commendam was originally unlimited, that is (according to the language of the faculties) during the life of the person and his possession of such see; because this amounts to a presentation, and therefore in this case also the right of the Crown is served, and the patron shall next present (*c*). But if a Bishop who is possessed of a commendam is translated to another see, and so a new title accrues to the Crown by a new promotion, the same commendam may be continued, if the King please; but it must be by a new dispensation, granting it to be held with the new bishoprick (*d*).

Commendam temporary *in retinere* may be renewed and prolonged: that is to say, before the original incumbency ceases by the expiration of the first dispensation, a second dispensation may be granted to prevent the avoidance and continue the incumbency (*e*).

Where the advowson is in common, so that the patrons are to present by turns, the prerogative presentation does not pass for the turn of the otherwise rightful patron; for the prerogative right does not supply, but only suspends or postpones the turn of the patron, and of all the patrons, if more than one, and doth not take away the right of the one, and leave the rest entire; for that would be rank injustice, and this, being

(*a*) Gibs. 914. 2 Burn, Eccl. Law, tit. Commendam, page 6.

(*b*) 4 Mod. 212. Ld. Raym. 23.

(*c*) Gibs, 915.

(*d*) Noy, 94.

(*e*) As to presentments by the King to the prejudice of another's right, see 25 Ed. 3. st. 3. c. 1. By the Lord Chancellor, of Benefices in the King's gift, see 1 Burn, Eccl. Law, tit. Benefice, 143. As to the Law in Ireland with respect to a Bishop's losing, by his translation, benefices which he held before, see Bac. Abr. 530, Prerogative, D. 2. Burn, Eccl. Law, tit. Benefice, 128, and Bishops, 192.

the

the act of law, *nemini facit injuriam* (a). And as the intervention of the prerogative presentation does not satisfy or disap-
point the turn of the otherwise rightful patron, neither does it
destroy the effects of a prior grant of the next presentation by
the owner of the advowson (b). If the incumbent of a donative
is made a Bishop, the King shall not present to the donative,
because such a promotion does not make an avoidance by
cession, for the incumbent is the creature of the founder, and
is not subject to ordinary and episcopal visitation (c).

When the King has in his natural capacity an interest in the
presentation, and the prerogative right happens at the same
time, the interest shall be preferred : as if the King be seized
in fee of an advowson, and create the incumbent Bishop, his
Majesty shall present as patron, that being a title precedent
to that of the prerogative (d).

If a grant be made to the King of the next avoidance of a
living, and a stranger upon the death of the then incumbent
present, and his presentee continue in six months and die, yet
the King may present another, *quia nullum tempus occurrit
regi.* So, if a grant be made to the King of all such presentments as should happen within twenty years, and in the
twenty years there happen ten presentments which are filled
up with a stranger, yet the King shall present to them over
again (e).

If the King be patron of a church, and he omit to present
within six months, the ordinary cannot present for the lapse,
but is only to sequester the profits and serve the cure till the
King thinks proper to present; but if in this case the ordinary
collate his clerk, and afterwards the King present, the clerk
so collated cannot be turned out without a quare impedit (f).

But, though the King may remove the patron's or stranger's
clerk that comes in upon his lapse, yet if such clerk happen
to die incumbent of the church, or if the church become void
by a *bonâ fide* resignation or expiration, before the King presents, the King loses the advantage of the lapse, and shall not

(a) Grocers' Company v. Archbishop
of Canterbury, 2 Bl. R. 770. 3 Wils.
914. S. C.

(b) Cailland v. Troward, 2 H. Bl.
324. judgment affirmed in B. R. 6 Term
R. 439, and afterwards in the House of

Lords, May 16, 1796.

(c) Agreed per Cur. 4 Mod. 213.

(d) Ld. Raym. 26.

(e) Plowd. 243. a.

(f) Bro. tit. Presentment, 24. Comp.
Incumb. 118.

present

present afterwards, or remove the patron's second presentee, because the King is to have but one turn, and that the next; and if the law were otherwise, the King, by suffering many usurpations upon his lapse, might even disinherit, the patron, and the rule *nullum tempus occurrit regi* is not to take place where the King is limited to a time certain (*a*).

Though the King present to a church, and his clerk is admitted and instituted, yet he may, before induction, repeal and revoke his presentation; and it is held in this case, that the presenting another is a repeal in law, without any other notice to the ordinary (*b*). So, where a title by lapse comes to the King, if the King present, and his presentee is instituted, yet the King may revoke his presentation, and so annul the institution at any time before his clerk is inducted; or if his clerk be instituted upon such title, and die before his induction, the King may present another, his turn not being served by the institution only of his clerk (*c*).

All antient deans are elected by the chapter, by *congè d' élire* from the King, and letters missive of recommendation, in the same manner as Bishops (*d*); but in those chapters which were founded by Henry the Eighth, out of the spoils of the dissolved monasteries (*e*), the deanry is donative, and the installation merely by the King's letters patent (*f*). The chapter, consisting of canons or prebendaries, are sometimes elected by each other.

It seems that the King may erect a free chapel, and exempt it from the jurisdiction of the ordinary, or licence a subject so to do (*g*). Churches it seems may be lawfully built by any person, but the Bishop may of course refuse to consecrate them (*h*).

In consequence of his prerogative in church matters, and as founder of archbishopricks and bishopricks, the King is enti-

---

(*a*) 7 Co. 28. Owen, 2. and 148. Cro. Eliz. 44. Cro. Jac. 53. 216. Hetley, 125. Buls. 28. Moor. 269. Fitzg. 30.

(*b*) 7 E. 4, 32. Dyer, 290, 327, 360. But to free the second presentation of all suspicion of being obtained by fraud in deceit of the King, it is proper that it should make express mention of the first presentation, Gibs. 795. Wats. c. 20.

(*c*) Leon. 156. Wright *v.* Bishop of Norwich.

(*d*) Agreed per Cur. 4 Mod. 213.

(*e*) Harg. Co. Litt. 95, note 3.

(*f*) Gibs. Cod. 173.

(*g*) 1 Burn, Eccl. Law, tit. Chapel.

(*h*) 3 Inst. 203. 1. Burn, Eccl. Law, tit. Church I. The new Church Act.

tled

tled to the custody, and is seised of the freehold (*a*) of the temporalities of bishops, (that is, the lay revenues, lands, and
tenements, which belong to an archbishop's or bishop's
see,) (*b*) during the vacancy of the archbishoprick or bishoprick (*c*). This prerogative is of so high a nature, that a subject cannot claim the temporalities during the vacancy, by
grant or prescription (*d*). But now, by statute 14 Ed. 3. st. 4.
c. 4, 5. the King may, after the vacancy, lease the temporalities to the dean and chapter, saving to himself all advowsons,
escheats, and the like. During the vacancy, the Crown has
the right of presenting to such benefices and other preferments as fall within the time of vacation (*e*). And by the
statute 17 Ed. 2. st. 2. c. 14. the King shall have escheats of
lands of the freeholders of archbishops and bishops, when
such tenants be tainted for felony in time of vacation, whilst
their temporalities were in the King's hands, to give at his
pleasure, saving to such prelates the service that thereto is due
and accustomed. Accordingly, the temporalities being in
Queen Elizabeth's hands, a copyhold escheated which was
granted by the Queen, and it was held to be good (*f*). Our
antient Kings, and particularly William Rufus, were not only
remarkable for keeping the bishopricks a long time vacant, for
the sake of enjoying the temporalities, but also committed
horrible waste on the woods and other parts of the estate; and
to crown all, would never, when the see was filled up, restore
to the Bishop his temporalities again, unless he purchased them
at an exorbitant price. To remedy which, King Henry the
First (*g*) granted a charter at the beginning of his reign, promising neither to sell, nor to let to farm, nor take any thing
from the domains of the church, till the successor was
installed (*h*). And it was made one of the articles of the great
charter (*i*), that no waste should be committed in the tem-
póralities of bishopricks, neither should the custody of them
be sold. The same is ordained by the statute of Westminster

(*a*) 1 Wooddn. V. L. 297.
(*b*) Wats. ch. 40. 1 Bla. Com. 282.
(*c*) 1 Burn, Eccl. Law, tit. Bishops,
VI.
(*d*) 2 Inst. 15.
(*e*) 17 Ed. 2. c. 14. F. N. B. 32.
1 Bla. Com. 282. 6 Com. Dig. 45, tit.
Prerogative, D. (D. 23.)

(*f*) Covert's Case. Cro. El. 74.
(*g*) Matt. Paris.
(*h*) But Queen Elizabeth kept the
see of Ely vacant nineteen years, in
order to retain the revenue. Strype, 4
Vol. 351.
(*i*) 9 Hen. 3. c. 5.

the

the first (*a*). And the statute 14 Ed. 3. st. 4. c. 4. (which permits as we have seen a lease to the dean and chapter), is still more explicit in prohibiting the other exactions. It was also a frequent abuse that the King would, for trifling or no causes, seize the temporalities of bishops even during their lives into his own hands; but this is guarded against by statutes 1 Ed. 3. st. 2. c. 2.; 14 Ed. 3. st. 4. c. 3.; 25 Ed. 3. st. 3. c. 6.

This revenue of the King, which was formerly very considerable, is now by a customary indulgence almost reduced to nothing; for at present as soon as the new Bishop is consecrated and confirmed, he usually receives the restitution of his temporalities quite entire and untouched from the King, and at the same time does homage to his Sovereign; and then, and not sooner, he has a fee simple in his bishoprick, and may maintain an action for the profits (*b*).

It seems that for an enormous offence of a Bishop his temporalities may be seized *in manus regis* (*c*).

The King is entitled to a corody, as the law calls it, out of every bishoprick: that is, to send one of his chaplains to be maintained by the Bishop, or to have a pension allowed him till the Bishop promote him to a benefice (*d*). This is also in the nature of an acknowledgment to the King, as founder of the see, since he had formerly the same corody or pension from every abbey or priory of royal foundation. It seems to be now fallen into total disuse, though Sir *Matthew Hale* says (*e*) that it is due of common right, and that no prescription will discharge it.

Under this head may also be mentioned the right of the Crown to the tithes arising in extra-parochial places, which are

(*a*) 3 Ed. 1. c. 21. 1 Bla. Com. 282.

(*b*) 1 Bla. Com. 282, 3. Co. Litt. 67, 341.

(*c*) 2 Roll. Abr. 228. 1. 20. In 6 Com. Dig. 46. tit. Prerogative, D. (D. 25.) the following instances are put: as if he be attainted for trespass *contra pacem ;* for being a prelate, a *capias* does not lie against his person, 2 Rol. 228. 1. 25. or for a contempt, as upon an attachment in prohibition, 2 Rol. 228. 1. 15, 30. or for not admitting a varlet to his corody, 2 Rol. 228. 1. 15 : so if he be found a disturber in a *quare*

non admisit by the king, 2 Rol. 228. l. 17, or be found guilty in a *quare incumbravit,* after a *non admittas* delivered to him, 2 Rol. 228. l. 10 ; or upon the death of a bishop, the king, by his prerogative, shall have his palfrey, bason, and ewer, and kennel of hounds; and process shall issue for them, if not compounded, Sav. 53.; see further, Vin. Abr. tit. Prerogative, 17 V. 242.

(*d*) F. N. B. 230.

(*e*) Notes on F. N. B. above cited. 1 Bla. Com. 283.

vested

vested in him in trust and confidence, that he will distribute them for the general good of the clergy (*a*), but which may be granted by the King to a subject (*b*).

First fruits, primitiæ or *annates*, are the first year's whole profits of a spiritual preferment. *Tenths* or *decimæ*, are the tenth part of the annual profit of each living. These were introduced by, and originated in, papal usurpation; and were ascertained by valuations or rates made during the reigns of Hen. 3. and Edw. 1. This usurpation was long maintained in favour of the Popes, though at times violently resisted; till at length in the reign of H. 8. it was annexed to the Crown by statute 26 H. 8. c. 3. confirmed by 1 Eliz. c. 4. and a new *valor beneficiorum* was then made, by which the clergy are at present rated (*c*). Various equitable discharges, allowances, and exceptions were made and granted in favour of preferments of a trifling value; and Queen Ann " in a spirit of the truest equity," resigned this revenue to the poorer clergy, by applying these superfluities of the larger benefices to make up the deficiencies of the smaller. To this end she granted her royal charter, which was confirmed by the statute 2 Ann, c. 11. whereby all the revenue of first fruits and tenths is vested in trustees for ever, to form a perpetual fund for the augmentation of poor livings. This is usually called Queen Ann's bounty, which has been still farther regulated by subsequent statutes(*d*).

(*a*) 2 Inst. 647. 2 Rep. 44. Cro. El. 512. 1 Bla. Com. 113.

(*b*) Bro. Ab. Patents, pl. 33, cites 22 Ass. 75. 17 Vin. Ab. 88. Prerog. M. b. pl. 15.

(*c*) 1 Bla. Com. 284, 5.

(*d*) Ibid. 5 Ann. c. 24. 6 Ann. c. 27. 1 Geo. 1. st. 2. c. 10. 3 Geo. 1. c. 10. See 2 Burn, Eccl. Law. 46 Geo. 3. c. 133.

CHAP.

CHAP. VI.

Of the Prerogative with respect to the Houses of Parliament.

WE have already viewed the King as a constituent part of the legislature; and it only remains for us to consider in the present chapter the various prerogatives which are more intimately connected with the two Houses of Parliament.

It is in the power of the Crown to add any number of members to the House of Peers, by raising individuals to the English Peerage (a); but it may perhaps be doubtful whether the King has it in his power to increase the number of the members in the lower House of Parliament, by empowering an unrepresented town to elect, and send members to Parliament. It seems clear that from the time of Edward 4, until the reign of Charles 2, both inclusive, our Kings used frequently to assume and exercise this right. The last time it is known to have been exercised was in the 29 Charles 2. who gave this privilege to Newark ; and on the legality of the grant being then questioned for the first time in the House of Commons, it was acknowledged by a majority of 125 members to 73 (b). The reason why it is doubted at the present day is, that by the Scotch and Irish Acts of Union with England, the representatives to be sent by the two former countries to the united Parliament, are limited to a certain specified number; and if the King could add to the number of the English members, the proportion would be unfair in favor of England, to the prejudice of Scotland and Ireland : consequently it is said this prerogative is abrogated (c). But it is submitted that the King cannot be deprived of a prerogative, except by the express words of a statute (d), and the Acts of Union contain no provision on the subject. The argument used against this prerogative of the Crown, seems to prove too much to be

(a) 1 Bla. Com. 157. 1 Wooddn. See post. ch. 8.

(b) Commons Journ. March 1676, 7. Simeon's Law of El. 91, 97. 1 Dougl. on El. 69, 70. 1 Bla. Com. 97, note (6), Christian's edition. See Co. Lit.

109, b. Hargr. note 2. 2 Lord Raym. 951. Power in the Colonies in this respect, ante ch. 3.

(c) See Ibid. Pref. to Glanv. Rep.

(d) See 5 Bac. Ab. 559. title Prerogative, E. 5. post. ch. 15.

tenable.

tenable. Would it not prevent his Majesty from creating or nominating Peers to sit in the upper House? A right which has never been disputed.

The King alone is entitled by the constitution to summon a Parliament, nor can this power be vested in any other department of the State with equal propriety; because, to borrow the words of Sir Wm. Blackstone (a), the King is a single person, whose will may be uniform and steady; the first person in the nation, being superior to both Houses in dignity, and the only branch of legislature that has a separate existence, and is capable of performing any act at a time when no Parliament is in being.

There are indeed two memorable instances on record, in which Parliament have assembled without the authority of the King; and have, when so assembled, effected most momentous revolutions in the government. I allude to the Parliament which restored Charles 2.; and the Parliament of 1688 which disposed of the British Crown to William III. But in both these instances the necessity of the case rendered it necessary for the Parliament to meet as they did, there being no King to call them together, and necessity supersedes all law. Nor is it an exception to this rule, that by some modern statutes (b) on the demise of the King or Queen (which at common law dissolved the Parliament, because it could no longer consult with him who called it) (c), the Parliament then in being or otherwise the last Parliament shall revive or sit, and continue for six months after such demise, unless sooner prorogued or dissolved by the successor: that is, if the Parliament be at the time of the King's death separated by adjournment or prorogation, it shall notwithstanding assemble immediately; or, if no Parliament be then in being, the members of the last Parliament shall assemble and be again a Parliament. For in such case, the revived Parliament must have been originally summoned by the Crown.

By the statute 6 and 7 W. and M. c. 2. s. 1. it is declared and enacted that Parliaments shall be holden once in three years at least; by which we are not to understand that the

(a) 1 Comm. 150. See 1 Chalmers'
Coll. Op. 233, 337.
   (b) 7 and 8 W. 3. c. 15. 6 Ann. c. 7.
1 Bla. Com. 183.

(c) Kelyng R. 19. 1 Chalmers' Coll.
Op. 247. That death of King does not
dissolve colonial assembly, ante ch. 3.

King

King ought to convene within that period a new Parliament, for as the law now stands, Parliaments last for seven years, unless sooner dissolved by royal authority (a).

On a Parliament being called together, every lord, spiritual or temporal, is entitled, *ex debito justitiæ*, to a writ of summons (b). This writ issues out of chancery, and each member should have a distinct one sent to him (c), which, as we have already seen, he is obliged to obey (d).

Upon a general election of members to serve in the House of Commons, writs of summons are issued, and directed to the sheriff of every county, by the clerk of the Crown in the Court of Chancery, in pursuance of a warrant from the Lord Chancellor for that purpose. If a vacancy happen during the sitting of Parliament, the Speaker of the House of Commons, by order of the House, sends this warrant to the clerk of the Crown (e). With regard to a vacancy by death, or the member's becoming a peer, the statute 24 Geo. 3. sess. 2. c. 26. provides that, if during any recess, either by prorogation or adjournment, any two members give notice to the Speaker, by a certificate under their hands, that there is a vacancy by death, or that a writ of summons has issued, under the great seal, to call up any member to the House of Lords, the Speaker shall forthwith give notice of it to be inserted in the gazette; and, at the end of fourteen days after such insertion, he shall issue his warrant to the clerk of the Crown, commanding him to make out a new writ for the election of another member. But this does not extend to any case where there is a petition depending, concerning such vacant seat, or where the writ for the election of the member so vacating, had not been returned fifteen days before the end of the last sitting of the House, or where the new writ cannot issue before the next meeting of the House for the dispatch of business. And, to prevent any impediment in the execution of this Act, by the Speaker's absence from the kingdom, or by the vacancy of his seat, at the beginning of every Parliament he shall appoint any

(a) 1 Geo. 1. st. 2. c. 38.

(b) 4 Inst. 1. For the form of the summons, Cotton's Records, 3, 4. Of the manner of summoning King's counsel, and civilians, masters in Chancery, who have no voices; and how the writ differs from that to a lord of Parliament; vide Reg. 261; F. N. B. 229. 4 Inst. 4.

(c) 4 Inst. 4.

(d) Ante ch. 2. s. 2.

(e) 1 Bla. Com. 177, where see the statutes on this subject cited.

number

number of members, from three to seven inclusive, and shall publish the appointment in the gazette. These members, in the absence of the Speaker, shall have the same authority as is given to him by this statute. These are the only cases provided for by Act of Parliament. So, for any other species of vacancy, no writ can issue during a recess.

It would be irrelevant to consider here the mode of electing and returning members, under the writs of summonses; this does not form any part of the royal authority, but is specifically provided for by various legislative enactments, which are cited and summarily arranged by Sir William Blackstone (*a*), and other subsequent authors (*b*), who have written exclusively on the subject.

The writs of summonses, both in the case of peers and members of the House of Commons, ought to be under the great seal (*c*), and should be issued forty days at least before the sitting of Parliament. This is a provision of the Magna Charta of King John, *faciemus summoneri, &c. ad certum diem, scilicet ad terminum quadraginta dierum, ad minus et ad certum locum.* It is enforced by 7 and 8 Wm. 3. c. 25. which enacts, that there shall be forty days between the teste and the return of the writ of summons; and this time is, by the uniform practice since the Union, extended to fifty days (*d*). This practice was introduced by the 22d article of the Act of Union, which required that time between the teste and the return of the writ of summons, for the first Parliament of Great Britain.

The members of each House being thus duly assembled, the Parliament, of which the King has been termed the *caput, principium, et finis* (*e*), cannot, in point of law, commence but by the presence of his Majesty, either in person or by representation; which representation may be either by a guardian of England, by letters patent under the great seal, when the King is *in remotis* out of the realm, or by commission under the great seal of England, to certain lords of Parliament, representing the person of the King, he being within the realm, in re-

(*a*) 1 Comm. 177, &c.

(*b*) And see 2 Bac. Ab. 120, title Court of Parliament, D.

(*c*) And see 24 Geo. 3. sess. 2. c. 26. s. 2. 1 Chalmers' Op. 234, 6.

(*d*) 2 Hats. 235.

(*e*) 4 Inst. 1, 2. Hale of Parliament 1, ante. See in 1 Chalmers' Coll. of Op. 336, a comment on these words.

spect

spect of some infirmity, or his being engaged in other urgent affairs (*a*).

The two Houses, respectively, possess the exclusive power of *adjourning* themselves, nor can the King exercise it; and an adjournment of one House is not, *ipso facto*, an adjournment of the other (*b*). It appears, however, to have been usual, when the King has signified his pleasure that both or either of the Houses should adjourn themselves to a certain day, to obey the King's pleasure so signified, and to adjourn accordingly. Otherwise, besides the indecorum of a refusal, a prorogation would assuredly follow; which, as it terminates the session (*c*), would occasion great inconvenience to public and private business (*d*). An adjournment may be made by the Houses not only from day to day, but for a fortnight, or a longer period, as is usually done at Christmas or Easter, or upon other particular occasions (*e*); but the King may, by proclamation, call them together at the end of fourteen days from the date thereof, notwithstanding any previous adjournment to a longer and more distant day (*f*).

A *prorogation*, which, as we have just remarked, puts an end to the session, and may be termed a continuation of Parliament from one session to another, can, however, be legally effected only by the authority of the King, expressed either by the Lord Chancellor in his Majesty's presence, or by commission from the Crown, or frequently by Proclamation (*g*). As the obligation of the members to attend arises from writs under the great seal, their discharge from liability to assemble must also flow from the same seal (*h*). It seems clear, notwithstanding the opinion of Lord Coke (*i*) to the contrary, that a prorogation of one House necessarily and tacitly operates as a prorogation of the other (*k*). This prorogation may be legally made even at the return of the writ, and before the meeting of Parliament (*l*). Thus the Parliament after the general election in the year 1790 was prorogued twice by writ, before it

(*a*) 4 Inst. 6.
(*b*) Ibid. 27, 28.
(*c*) Ibid. 27.
(*d*) Ibid. 28. 1 Bla. Com. 186.
(*e*) Ibid.
(*f*) 39 and 40 Geo. 3. c. 14.
(*g*) 1 Bla. Com. 187.

(*h*) 1 Chalm. Coll. Op. 234, 236.
(*i*) 4 Inst. 28.
(*k*) Sir R. Atkins's Argument, 51. cited 2 Bac. Ab. 131, title Court of Parliament, F. 1 Bla. Com. 187.
(*l*) 4 Inst. 7. 1 Chalmers, *ubi supra*.

met (*a*); and the first Parliament in this reign was prorogued four times, by four writs of prorogation (*b*). On the day upon which the writ of summons is returnable, the members of the House of Commons who attend, do not enter·their own House or wait for a message from the Lords, but go immediately up to the House of Lords, where the Chancellor reads the writ of prorogation. And when it is intended that they should meet upon the day to which the Parliament is prorogued for dispatch of business, notice is given by a proclamation (*c*).

His Majesty's assent to a bill during a session (*d*) does not end it (*e*): and it seems that an express prorogation or dissolution is necessary for this purpose (*f*). His Majesty is enabled to call Parliament together at the end of fourteen days from the date of his proclamation for that purpose, notwithstanding any previous prorogation of it to a longer period (*g*).

As the power of convening and proroguing Parliament is vested by the constitution, that is, by the common law, and by the custom of Parliament, in the King, so his Majesty possesses, on similar grounds, the power of dissolving it (*h*). This can only be done in the King's presence, either in person or by representation (*i*). The effect of the demise of the Crown on the continuance of Parliament has been already stated.

With

(*a*) Comm. Journ. 26 Nov. 1790.

(*b*) Ibid. 3 Nov. 1761.

(*c*) 1 Bla. Com. 187, Christian's note. 1 Chalm. Coll. of Op. 234, 6.

(*d*) In point of law, though a Parliament meet and debate, it is no session unless some act be passed or judgment given by the Parliament, 4 Inst. 28. Hal. of P. 48. Hut. 61. Raym. 187. Lev. 442. 2 Keb. 529.

(*e*) 4 Inst. 27. 1 Car. 1. c. 7. Comm. Journ. 21 Nov. 1554.

(*f*) 1 Bla. Com. 187.

(*g*) 39 and 40 Geo. 3. c. 14.

(*h*) 1 Bla. Com 188.

(*i*) 4 Inst. 48. On the subject of dissolving Parliament in person, Mr. Evans, in his " *Parliamentary Debates*," makes the following observations:

" Some Gentlemen thought that the dissolution of Parliament by the Prince Regent in person was ungracious, and that it was intended as a mark of dis-

satisfaction. It certainly appears that, in former times, a dissolution in person was considered an offensive act in the Sovereign. On the 10th of March, 1628, the day to which both Houses were adjourned, King Charles I. came to the House of Lords, and without sending for the Commons, spoke as follows : ' My Lords—I never came here upon so unpleasant an occasion, it being the dissolution of a Parliament ; therefore men may have some cause to wonder why I should rather not choose to do this by commission ; it being rather a general maxim with Kings to leave harsh commands to their Ministers, themselves only executing pleasing things.' And then, after some words, directed the Lord-keeper to dissolve the Parliament. The entry on the Lords' journal is—*Ipse Dominus Rex hoc præsens Parliamentum dissolvit.* On the 28th of March, 1681, King Charles II. suddenly

With respect to their internal arrangements, Parliaments
are, by the constitution of the country, and, indeed, their nature requires that they should be, distinct from, and independent of, the Crown. There are, therefore, but few prerogatives,
except those which have just been considered, legally exerciseable over the two Houses. The King has, however, the

suddenly dissolved the Parliament then
sitting at Oxford. His speech was as
follows:—' My Lords and Gentlemen
—That all the world may see to what a
point we are come, that we are not like
to have a good end, when the divisions
at the beginning are such: therefore,
my Lord Chancellor, do as I have commanded you.' Then the Lord Chancellor said, ' My Lords and Gentlemen—
His Majesty has commanded me to say,
that it is his royal pleasure and will,
that this Parliament be dissolved ; and
this Parliament is dissolved.'--Bishop
Burnet (Hist. of Own Times, V. I. p.
499.) gives the following account of this
dissolution:—' By the steps which the
Commons had taken, the King saw
what might be expected from them ;
so, very suddenly, and not very decent-
ly, he came to the House of Lords, the
Crown being carried between his feet,
in a sedan : and he put on his robes in
haste, without any previous notice, and
called up the Commons, and dissolved
the Parliament ; and went with such
haste to Windsor, that it looked as if
he was afraid of the crowds that this
meeting had brought to Oxford.'

" In these two instances, the dissolution in person was thought indecent and
offensive. It is true that the Parliament of 1660—the Convention Parliament, which restored King Charles II.
—was dissolved by the King in person ;
but then, his Majesty had sent a message to the House of Lords some days
before to signify his intention, which
message was communicated by them to
the Commons, and a conference was
holden upon it. The message was as
follows:—' His Majesty hath expected,
ever since Thursday morning, to be informed that his two Houses of Parlia-

ment had been ready to present such
bills to him as they had prepared for
his royal assent, and hath continued ever
since in the same expectation, and hoped that he might have this day finished
the work. and dissolved them according
to his signification; but, being informed
that there are yet depending in both
Houses some few bills of great importance to his and the public service,
which are not yet ready to be presented
to him ; and being desirous to part with
his two Houses of Parliament, who have
deserved so well of him, in such a manner, that they may not be obliged to
use more expedition in the despatch
than is agreeable to the affairs which
are to be despatched, his Majesty is
graciously pleased to declare, That he
will be ready to pass such bills as are
necessary, in point of time, to be passed, on Monday morning ; and then, that
the Houses adjourn till Thursday, so that
they may have that day and Friday to
put an end to those most public bills
which are not yet finished ; and his
Majesty will, on the next day, being
Saturday the 29th of this month, be
present with them, and dissolve the
Parliament ; and his Majesty desires
both Houses, against that time, to lay
aside all business of private concern-
ment to finish all public bills.'

"Since the Revolution, Parliament
has been always dissolved by proclamation, after having been first prorogued.
The dissolution, therefore, by the Prince
Regent in person was an unusual proceeding ; but it does not appear, from
any thing that was said or done, that it
was meant to be offensive. It was
adopted merely for the sake of dispatch."

undoubted

undoubted right to be present in the House of Lords during the debates, without going in state, or interfering in the proceedings. Charles the Second, and several of his successors, frequently did so; but from the accession of George the First to the present time, the practice has been, and perhaps wisely, discontinued (*a*).

It seems that, in order to make a proxy, which the members of the upper House only can effectually and legally do, the King's licence is in strictness necessary (*b*). Though, it is said, that this is now so much a mere form that the licence may be presumed (*c*).

The Speaker of the House of Lords is the Lord Chancellor, or keeper of the King's great seal, or any other person appointed by the King's commission; and if none be so appointed, the House of Lords, it is said, may elect one (*d*).

The Speaker of the House of Commons is chosen by the House; but must, it seems, be approved by the King (*e*).

The discretionary power of assenting or dissenting to an Act of Parliament is, in England, a high and incommunicable prerogative; though it may be communicated to the governor of a colony, with respect to acts of the colonial assembly (*f*).

The royal assent to a bill (which cannot be given previous to the meeting of Parliament, any more than the dissent can be effectually expressed after the session has ended) (*g*), is proclaimed before the two Houses, assembled in the Lords' House, either by the King in person, or by letters patent under the great seal, signed by his Majesty, and declared and notified in his absence, to the Lords and Commons. Before the assent is given, the titles of the Acts, which have passed both Houses, are read; whereupon, the clerk of the Parliament expresses the assent or dissent. In case of the royal assent to a public bill, the clerk usually declares, " *le roy le veut ;*" to a private bill, " *soit fait comme il est desiré.*" If the King refuse his

---

(*a*) See 1 Adolph. on Political State of the British Empire, 195.

(*b*) Els. ch. 5. 1 Bla. Com. 168. Seld. Baronage, p. 1. ch. 1. And it is laid down in Seld. 3 vol. 2. P. 1476. cited 2 Bac. Ab. 130. tit. Court of Parliament E. that a lord may be summoned with a clause that he do not make a proxy.

(*c*) 1 Bla. Com. 168. Christian's note, 24.

(*d*) 1 Bla. Com. 181. 2 Mounton, 108.

(*e*) Ibid. 2 Hatsell, 154. 1 Wooddn. 57, 59.

(*f*) 1 Chalm. Coll. Op. 316, ante ch. 3.

(*g*) Ibid. 315.

assent,

assent, the words used are " *le roy s'avisera.*"   When a bill of supply is passed, it is carried up and presented to the King, by the Speaker of the House of Commons, and the royal assent is thus expressed, " *le roy remercie ses loyal subjects, accepte lour benevolence, et aussi le veut*—"the King thanks his loyal subjects, accepts their benevolence, and wills it so to be (*a*)."

It is not usual, except in the case of an act of grace, for statutes to originate with the King; but, without doubt, if a bill, with the royal assent, should be sent to the Lords and Commons, and receive their assent also, it would be a perfect law, if even in the form of a charter, as was the case with Magna Charta,

That which constitutes law is the concurring assent of all the branches of the legislature, wheresoever it may originate, whatever may happen to be the form of it (*b*).

CHAP. VII.

Of the King as the Fountain of Justice and Office, and Administrator of the Laws.

Sect. I.—*In general; and as to Public Courts and Offices, and Officers.*

The prerogative of creating courts and offices has been immemorially exercised by the Kings of England, and is founded on the capacities of executive magistrate, and distributor of justice, which the constitution of the country has assigned to the Sovereign (*c*).

Public offices are either *judicial* or *ministerial*.

It seems, that in very early times our Kings, in person, often heard and determined causes between party and party (*d*).   But, by the long and uniform usage of many ages, they have delegated their whole judicial powers to the judges of their several courts; so that, at present, the King cannot

---

(*a*) 1 Bla. Com. 184.
(*b*) Hale, Orig. and Antiq. Parl. Prince's Case, 8 Co. Rep.

(*c*) Finch, L. 162.   See 1 Bla. Com. 266, 272.
(*d*) Ibid.   3 Bla. Com. 41.   1 Bla. Com. 267.

determine

determine any cause or judicial proceeding, but by the mouth of his judges (*a*), whose power is, however, only an emanation of the royal prerogative (*b*). The courts of justice, therefore, though they were originally instituted by royal power, and can only derive their foundation from the crown (*c*), have, respectively, gained a known and stated jurisdiction, and their decisions must be regulated by the certain and established rules of law (*d*). It necessarily follows, that even our Kings themselves cannot, without the express sanction of an Act of Parliament, grant any addition of jurisdiction to such courts (*e*); as, for instance, that the Court of King's Bench may determine a mere real action (*f*), nor authorize any one to hold them in a manner dissimilar to that established either by the common, or statute law of the law of the land (*g*). On this ground it has been determined, that a royal grant of a judicial office for life, which had been always granted only at will, is void (*h*). So, the King cannot grant a mere spiritual jurisdiction, as to ordain, institute, &c. to a lay person, or exercise it himself, but must administer the spiritual law by bishops, as he does the common law by judges (*i*). Nor can his Majesty grant a commission to determine any matter of equity; but it ought to be determined in the Court of Chancery, which has immemorially possessed a jurisdiction in such case (*k*). It is a still more important principle, that the King cannot, legally, authorize any court to proceed contrary to the English laws, or by any other rule (*l*). Therefore, commissions to seize goods, and imprison the bodies of all persons who shall be notoriously suspected of felonies and trespasses, without any indictment or

(*a*) Ibid. 12 Co. 64. Bac. Ab. Courts, A, B. That the King though he may grant, cannot execute offices himself, see 5 Bac. Ab., 180, note in margin. Co. Lit. 3. b. Plowden. 381. 1 Sid. 305. As to taking the judges' opinion, see Fortescue, R. 384 *et subseq.*

(*b*) 1 Bla. Com. 24.

(*c*) 1 Rol. Ab. 361.   2 Bac. Ab. Courts, A, B, page 96. As to Counties, Palatinate, &c. 2 Bac. Ab. 188. 1 Bla. Com. 117. See. Ibid. 267.

(*d*) 3 Hawk. bk. 2, ch. 1. sect. 4. page 2. 2 Bac. Ab. 96.

(*e*) Year Book, 6 Hen. 7. 4, b. 5, a.

2 Inst. 478. 4 Ibid. 125, 127, 163, 200. 1 Wooddn. 97.

(*f*) Ibid.

(*g*) Ibid. 97, 8. 4 Inst. 163, 200, 75. 2 Inst. 478. 3 Hawk. b. 2. c. 1. 37. s. 6.

(*h*) 4 Inst. 87.   1 Sid. 338.

(*i*) See Cro. El. 259, 314.

(*k*) Hob. 63.   12 Co. Rep. 113. See 1 Wooddn. 188 to 190, and 97. Vice-Chancellor's Act, 53 Geo. 3. c. 24.

(*l*) 2 Rol. Ab. 164. 2 Rush. App. 77. 12 Co. 113. 2 Lev. 24. 2 Inst. 73. 2 Ld. Raym. 1344. 3 Hawk. *ubi supra.* 1 Wooddn. 97.

legal

legal process against them (*a*); or to take J. S. a notorious robber, and to seize his lands and goods (*b*), are, respectively, illegal (*c*). Neither can the King grant any new commission which is not warranted by antient precedents, however necessary, or conducive to the public good it may appear to be; and, therefore commissions to assay weights and measures, being of a new invention, were condemned by Parliament (*d*). And Lord Coke asserts (*e*), that the King could not authorize persons to take care of rivers, and the fishery therein, according to the method prescribed by the statute of Westminster the 2nd. ch. 47. before the making of that statute.

Subject, however, to these various restrictions, which are constitutionally just and necessary, the King may, generally speaking, by his prerogative, constitute any number of legal and ordinary courts, for the administration of the general law of the land, and appoint them to be held where his Majesty pleases (*f*), unless, as in the case of the Common Pleas (*g*), the Court must, by law, be holden in any certain place. So the King may issue special commissions, for doing justice according to law, in extraordinary cases, requiring speedy remedy and animadversion; though in ordinary cases, commissioners of Oyer and Terminer can be granted only to the justices of either bench, or the justices in Eyre (*h*). The King, by special commission, may appoint any person to take recognizances, or obligations of record, from one man to another; and such recognizances, duly certified with the commission into Chancery, are binding; and though the commission be so particular as to mention only a recognizance to be taken from A. to B., yet the commissioners have a general power to take a recognizance from any other person (*i*). It seems, that at the present day a palatinate jurisdiction cannot be erected without an Act of Parliament (*k*).

(*a*) 4 Ass. 5. Bro. Ab. Commissions, 9, 15, 16. 12 Co. 30, 31. 2 Inst. 478.

(*b*) 2 Inst. 54.

(*c*) And see 13 Ed. 1. st. 1. c. 29.

(*d*) 18 Ed. 3. st. 2. c. 1 and 4. 4 Inst. 163.

(*e*) 2 Ibid. 478.

(*f*) 1 Wooddn. 97. 3 Bla. Com. 41, 2.

(*g*) Magna Charta, ch. 11. but this was not taken so strictly as to prevent its being adjourned, as well as the King's Bench, and Exchequer, to Reading, on account of the epidemical sickness in the metropolis in Mich. T. 1 Car. 1. See 3 Cro. R. 13.

(*h*) 13 Ed. 1. st. 1. c. 29 and 30. See 1 Wooddn. 97.

(*i*) Bac. Ab. Execution, D.

(*k*) 4 Inst. 204. Cromp. Juris. 139. 2 Bac. Ab. 188. tit. Courts Palatinate.

The

The *Judges* can, generally speaking, derive their authority only from the Crown (*a*), and those who claim a prescriptive right to hold a judicial office, impliedly hold by royal grant (*b*). The Lord Chancellor is appointed by the mere delivery of the King's great seal into his custody (*c*). The Chief Justice of the Court of King's Bench is created by writ (*d*). The Vice-Chancellor (*e*), and the rest of the Judges (*f*), are named by letters patent.

By the policy of the common law, the people choose the Sheriffs, conservators of the peace, and other officers of a similar description, who were concerned in matters that affected the public liberty (*g*).

The right of the people to elect *Sheriffs* was taken from them by the statute 9 Ed. 2. st. 2.; and the custom now is, with reference to various statutes, for the Lord High Chancellor, the Chancellor of the Exchequer, the Judges, several of the Privy Council, and other great officers of state, to assemble in the Exchequer, on the morrow of St. Martin (*h*), in Michaelmas term, when three persons for each county are proposed or selected, out of which three, one is finally appointed by the King (*i*). So that in effect the power of electing Sheriffs is now absolutely in the Crown (*k*): a prerogative by no means unimportant. It has even been laid down that the King may by his prerogative nominate whom he pleases to be Sheriff, whether thus proposed by the Judges and other officers or not (*l*). This assertion is grounded merely on a case peculiarly circumstanced in the reign of Queen Elizabeth, (when, it should be remembered, the doctrine of *non obstantes* was in force (*m*),) in which it was held (*n*), that the Queen's appointment of the Sheriffs, during a time of plague, in consequence of which the

(*a*) 27 Hen. 8. c. 24. Co. Lit. 260. 2 Bac. Ab. 97.

(*b*) 1 Bla. Com. 24.

(*c*) Lamb Archeion, 65. 1 Rol. Ab. 385.

(*d*) 4 Inst. 74, 5.

(*e*) 53 Geo. 3. c. 24.

(*f*) 4 Inst. 74, 75.

(*g*) 2 Inst. 558, 174. 28 Ed. 1. c. 8. Lamb, 15, 16, 17. 1 Bla. Com. 347. 1 Wooddn. 88.

(*h*) 24 Geo. 2. c. 48. s. 12.

(*i*) See statutes 14 Ed. 3. st. 1. c. 7.

23 Hen. 6. c. 8.   12 Rich. 2. c. 2.   34 and 35 Hen. 8. c. 26. s. 61. 1 Bla. Com. 340, 1.   1 Wooddn. 89, 90.   See Christian's note 4, to Bla. Com. where the mode of nominating sheriffs is more particularly stated.   A similar practice in many respects prevails as to Welch sheriffs, 34 and 35 H. 8. c. 26. s. 1.   1 Wm. and M. c. 27. s. 4.

(*k*) See Dav. 60.

(*l*) Jenkins, 229.   Dalt. Sheriff, 6.

(*m*) See post. ch. 7.

(*n*) Dyer, 225.

Judges

Judges and other officers, could not meet as usual in Michaelmas term to appoint them, was valid. This is, however, in
direct contradiction to an unanimous resolution of all the
Judges (a), and the statute 34 & 35 Hen. 8. c. 26. section 61.,
which recognizes the right of appointment by his Majesty only
in case persons have been proposed to him by the assembly in
the Exchequer: and there seems no legal ground for supporting this doctrine at the present day. As the power of electing
Sheriffs was originally in the people, the statutes which vest
the right of appointment in others, must on principle be observed. However the practice of occasionally naming what
are called pocket Sheriffs by the sole authority of the Crown,
has uniformly continued to the reign of his present Majesty (b),
though no compulsory instances have occurred: and if the
point came judicially before the courts of law, it can hardly be
doubted that the legality of the practice would be denied.
Anciently in some counties the Sheriffs were hereditary; as it
seems they were in Scotland till the statute 20 Geo. 2. c. 43.,
and still continue in Westmoreland (c). And the city of London possesses by royal charter the inheritance of the Shrievalty
of Middlesex (d). Sheriffs, by virtue of several old statutes (e),
are to remain in office no longer than one year, and therefore
it seems that the Crown cannot authorize them to remain in
office for a longer period (f).

Coroners are still chosen by all the freeholders in the county
Court (g): and though they are removable by the Lord Chancellor for misbehaviour (h), still the choice of those who are
to supply the place of the delinquents, can be legally made
only by a majority of the freeholders.

The right to name *Justices of the Peace* was vested in the
Crown by statute 1 Ed. 3. c. 16 (i). They are appointed by
the King's commission under the great seal (k); but in selecting individuals to fill this important situation, the Crown must

---

(a) 2 Inst. 559. 1 Bla. Com. 341, 2.

(b) 1 Bla. Com. 342.

(c) Harg. Co. Lit. 326.

(d) 2 Inst. 382. 1 Bla. Com. 339, 340.

(e) 14 Ed. 3. c. 7. 42 Ed. 3. c. 9. 23 Hen. 6. c. 8.

(f) 4 Hawk. bk. 2. c. 37. s. 29. Bac. Ab. Sheriffs, E.; see, however, 1

Bla. Com. 342, 343. 4 Co. R. 32.

(g) 2 Inst. 558. 1 Bla. Com. 347. 1 Wooddn. 103.

(h) 3 Atk. 184. See 25 Geo. 2. c. 19. s. 6.

(i) See Lamb. 15, &c. 20. 4 Ed. 3. c. 2. 18' Ed. 3. st. 2. c. 2. 1 Bla. Com. 350, 1.

(k) Ibid.

ascertain

ascertain whether they are sufficiently qualified according to the several statutes (*a*) on the subject. These magistrates being appointed by the King, his Majesty may determine their commission at his pleasure, either expressly as by writ of discharge under the great seal, or by writ of *supersedeas;* or impliedly, as by making a new commission, and leaving out the former Justices' names (*b*). But where the King constitutes a Mayor, &c. by charter, and by express words (*c*) in the charter enables him to act within certain limits as Justice of the Peace, such Justice is not removeable merely at the pleasure of the Crown (*d*).

With respect to public offices merely of a *ministerial* nature, we may observe that though his Majesty cannot execute them himself (*e*), he has an undoubted prerogative right to appoint officers to fill them, who are removeable at pleasure; as for instance commissioners of the customs, excise, stamps, &c. postmasters, and other persons of that description, whether of a higher or lower degree (*f*). And his Majesty seems to possess a right to constitute even new ministerial offices, and appoint officers to fill them (*g*), subject, however, to various important restrictions, introduced by the laudable jealousy of common law principles. Thus, it is not in the power of the Crown to create any new office inconsistent with the constitution or prejudicial to the subject (*h*). Therefore an office granted by letters patent, for the sole making of all bills, informations, and letters missive in the county of York (*i*), or for registering all strangers within the realm, except merchant strangers, though no fees be attached to it (*k*), is void. So all new offices in which the jurisdiction or authority of the officer is not ascertained and specified in the grant, are on that account merely invalid (*l*).

(*a*) Cited 1 Bla. Com: 352, &c.

(*b*) Dalt. c. 3. Lamb, 67. Moor, 187. 4 Inst. 165. 1 Bla. Com. 353.

(*c*) See 2 Lord Raym. 1030.

(*d*) Dalt. c. 3. See 1 Ld. Raym. 32. Burn's Just. tit. Justice of Peace, 2.

(*e*) Co. Lit. 3. b. ante. 70, note a.

(*f*) 1 Bla. Com. 335, 6. We before considered the King's power to appoint military and maritime officers. As to the appointment of constables, Salk. 150. 1 Bla. Com. 335, 6. Surveyors of the highways, Ibid. 358. And Overseers of the Poor, Ibid. 360. Various offices immediately under the Crown were abolished, by 22 Geo. 3. c. 82.

(*g*) 1 Bla. Com. 272.

(*h*) 2 Inst. 540. 2 Sid. 141. Moor. 808. Rol. Rep. 206. 4 Inst. 200.

(*i*) Jones' Rep. 231.

(*k*) 12 Co. R. 116.

(*l*) 4 Inst. 200. And see Year Book, 9 Ed. 4, 10. 2 Sid. 141. Bac. Ab. Offices, B.

Nor can the King create any new offices with new fees annexed to them, or annex new fees to old offices, for this would be a tax upon the subject, which can only be imposed by Act of Parliament (*a*).

Upon the establishment of the feudal law our Kings frequently granted lands to their subjects, reserving some honorary services to be done by the grantees and their heirs, to the King himself: such as to carry his banner, or his sword, or to be his sewer, carver, or butler at his coronation. This was called tenure by grand serjeanty, and the right of performing these services was considered an office of great honour, many of which still exist and are claimed to be exercised at every coronation (*b*).

There are various inferior offices inseparably annexed to others of a superior nature (*c*), and in this case it is an established rule that the superior office must be granted with all its antient rights, privileges, and appurtenances. The King cannot reserve them to himself, or grant them to another, even though the superior office was vacant at the time (*d*).

An office cannot be granted for any other term than that for which it had immemorially been granted (*e*). There are many offices which may be, and are, inheritable by the lineal descendants of the first grantee of the office (*f*). Various great offices of state have been holden in this manner: as the offices of Steward, Constable, Marshal, great Chamberlain, and

---

(*a*) 2 Inst. 553. 34 Ed. 1. st. 4. c. 1. 1 Bla. Com. 272. See the statute 22 Geo. 3. c. 82. s. 2.

(*b*) Lit. s. 153. 1 Inst. ، b. 107, b. 3 Cruise Dig. 133.

(*c*) The county clerk is appointed ، the sheriff, and his situation is incident thereto, 4 Co. 32, 4, a. Jenk. 216. 4 Mod. 167. The chamberlain of the King's Bench office is named by the marshal, 2 Ld. Raym. 1038. 2 Salk. 439. The Lord Chancellor and chief justices of the King's courts at Westminster, appoint several officers in their respective courts. 3 Cruise Dig. 134. Bac. Ab. Offices, C. They appoint their clerks; the Lord Chancellor appoints cursitors and exigenters: and philazers,

are named by the chief justice of the Common Pleas, Ibid. The justices of assize appoint the clerks of assize, Ibid.

(*d*) Mitton's Case, 4 Co. 32. Dyer, 175, a. pl. 25. 2 Ld. Raym. 1038. Bac. Ab. Offices, C. By the grant of an "office" a house or land belonging thereto impliedly pass. Vaugh. 178. Co. Lit. 49, a.

(*e*) Bac. Ab. Offices, H. What offices may be intailed, 3 Cruise, 147. 1 Inst. 20. a. Collins, 181. 7 Rep. 33, b. 1 Rol. Ab. 838, and are subject to dower and curtesy. 1 Inst. 32, a. 29, a. Plowd. 379. Collins, 5.

(*f*) See 3 Cruise Dig. 141, 2, 2 Bro. Parl. Cas. 167.

Seneschal

Seneschal of England (a) ; and the offices of sheriff, gaoler, park-keeper or forester, steward or bailiff of a manor, have also been legally granted in fee-simple (b). This interest in offices is generally if not universally inapplicable to judicial offices of trust, which are not grantable for a longer estate than for life; because they should be exercised only by persons of skill and capacity, and if grantable for a longer estate than for life, they might become vested in persons wholly unfit to fill them (c). For the same reason they cannot be granted for years (d); nor can a judicial office, or an office partly judicial and partly ministerial, without an express custom, be granted in reversion, for he who at the time of the grant in reversion may be able and sufficient to fill the office, may before it falls, become insufficient (e). But they may be granted for years, determinable on the death of the person to whom they are granted; for in this case they cannot go to executors or administrators (f). Mere ministerial offices are not subject to this rule, and may in general be granted in reversion (g) or for years (h).

Offices may be granted at will, of which there are many instances (i); and it is a general common law rule, upon which, however, various exceptions have been engrafted by statute, that the King may terminate at pleasure the authority of officers employed by his Majesty. The Lord Chancellor holds his high situation only during the King's pleasure (k), and the twelve Judges of the courts of common law formerly held them on the same footing (l); but, by legislative provision, they (m) and the Vice-Chancellor (n) hold their respective situations during their good behaviour, which gives them, in legal contemplation, an estate for life, as their good beha-

(a) 3 Cruis. Dig. 141, 2. Bac. Ab. Offices, H.

(b) Dyer, 285. 7 Co. R. 33. Plowd. 2 ; 379, b ; 381, a. 2 Inst. 382. 2 Rol. Ab. 153. 9 Co. 48, 97. Bac. Ab. Officers, H.

(c) 5 Bac. Ab. tit. Offices, H. 3 Cruis. 142.

(d) 8 Co. 95. See other authorities cited, 5 Bac. Ab. 201, title Offices, H. See 3 Cruis. 144. 2 Show. R. 171.

(e) Co. Lit. 3, b. and note 5. 11 Co. Rep. 2, 4, a. 2 Ventr. 188. Cas. Temp. Talb. 99. 5 Bac. Ab. 202. 3

Cruis. 145 ; but see March. 42. Dyer, 295.

(f) Sutton's Case, 6 Mod. 57.

(g) Bac. Ab. Offices, &c. I.

(h) Ibid. Hardr. 46. 351. See various instances put in 5 Bac. Ab. 201. tit. Offices, H.

(i) See 9 Co. Rep. 91, a. Dyer, 176, a. 5 Bac. Ab. 202.

(k) See 1 Sid. 338. 4 Inst. 87.

(l) 4 Inst. 74, 75, 117.

(m) 12 and 13 W. 3. c. 2.

(n) 53 Geo. 3. c. 24.

viour is presumed by law (a), and of such good behaviour, it seems, Parliament only can judge (b). The Judges do not lose their situations even by the demise of the Crown (c). However, the Vice-Chancellor and the Judges may be, respectively, removed on the address of both Houses of Parliament (d). By the common law, the demise of the crown determined all patents created by royal authority; but by the statutes 7 and 8 Wm. 3. c. 27., and 1 Ann, c. 1., all patented officers are to continue six months after such demise, unless sooner removed by the new King.

Judicial offices cannot be granted to two or more persons, unless there be an immemorial custom to sanction such grant, (for antient offices must be granted as they immemorially have been granted;) though a new judicial office may be granted to more than one person, if there be no statute to the contrary; and it is clear that ministerial offices may be granted to two or more persons jointly (e).

As public offices are instituted, in legal contemplation, for the benefit of the State, and as it is highly important that the various duties attached to them should be properly performed, it has ever been a rule, that such persons only are eligible whose capacities and habits are adapted to the situation to which they are nominated. "If," says Lord Coke (f), " an office, either in the grant of the King or a subject, which concerns the administration, proceeding, or execution of justice, or the King's revenue, or the commonwealth, or the interest, benefit, or safety of the subject, or the like; if they, or any of them, be granted to a man that is unexpert, and hath no skill and science, to exercise or execute the same, the grant is merely void, and the party disabled by law, and incapable to take the same, *pro commodo Regis et populi ;* for only men of skill, knowledge, and ability to exercise the same, are capable of the same, to serve the King and his people."

(a) 1 Rol. Ab. 844. 1 Inst. 42, a. 1 Show. 426, 506.

(b) 1 Wooddn. 88, 121.

(c) 1 Geo. 3. c. 23. See Ld. Raym. 747. Com. Journ. 3 March 1761.

(d) See 5 Bac. Ab. 201.

(e) See 4 Inst. 146. 11 Rep. 3, b. Carth. 213. 4 Mod. 16. 1 Show. R.

289. 2 Salk. 465. 5 Bac. Ab. title Offices, K. See 1 Bla. Com. 40, 41, as to appointing more than four judges to act in K. B.

(f) Co. Lit 3, b. Godb. 391. Hardr. 130. Dyer, 175. Jenk. 121. 3 Cruise Dig. 152. 5 Bac. Ab. 203.

This

This doctrine holds peculiarly strong in the case of offices of a judicial nature, or other offices in which capacity and skill are requisite; and the insufficiency of an individual, to whom such an office is granted, incapacitates him, and avoids the grant, though it be to him " and his assigns," or the office is to be exercised by "a sufficient deputy (*a*)." The insufficiency may arise either from want of mental capacity, or from the party's not having been brought up to, or exercised in, the office to which he is appointed; and there are instances in our books, of persons having been refused admittance into offices in the courts of justice, which had been granted them by the King, on both those grounds of incapacity (*b*).

Ministerial offices may be granted to any persons, and even to women, if they are capable of performing them properly (*c*): but it seems, that even in the case of ministerial offices, an incapacity to execute them with propriety and effect, would form a legal ground of objection (*d*). In this case, however, the objection is obviated, if the grant authorize the exercise of the office by deputy; or contain any other provision by which the deficiency of the immediate grantee is supplied. Therefore, where the office of Registrar to the Bishop of Rochester was granted to J. S., who was an infant of twelve years of age at the time of the grant, to hold after the death of T. D. (who was the Registrar in possession) for his life, to be exercised by him " or his deputy," and afterwards T. D. died, J. S. being at the age of thirty; this was held a good grant at the time of making the office, being to be executed by him " or his deputy (*e*)."

The grant of an office should regularly be under the great seal (*f*). No investiture, or ceremony, is in general necessary to perfect the grantee's title to the office, which becomes vested in him merely by the grant (*g*); though such grant may be ren_

(*a*) Hob. 158. Only ministerial offices can be exercised by deputy. Bac. Ab. Offices, L.

(*b*) See Dyer, 150, b. Bro. Ab. title Office, 48. Cro. Car. 557, 565. 4 Mod. 30. See Bac. Ab. Offices, I.

(*c*) 4 Inst. 311. Cro. Jac. 17. See 3 Cruis. Dig. 153.

(*d*) See Co. Lit. 3, b. note 4.

(*e*) Cro. Car. 279, 556. 2 Rol. Ab.

153. Other cases cited, Bac. Ab., Offices, I. Co. Lit. 3, b. Hargr. note 4.

(*f*) 3 Cruise Dig. 135; see post. ch. 16. s. 2.

(*g*) Mod. 123. 5 Bac. Ab. title Offices, E. page 188. It is said, Leon. 248. Mod. 123; but see Rol. Ab. 154 ; that investiture is necessary in order to make a person created an herald at arms, a complete officer.

dered ineffectual by neglect of the party to take the various oaths before alluded to (*a*).

In creating a new office apt words must be used; therefore in this case the words *erigimus, constituimus,* or other expressions of a similar import are necessary; and the word *concessimus*, &c. will not suffice (*b*).

Offices may be lost; among other means, 1. By misconduct therein: 2. By acceptance of another office incompatible with that the person holds: 3. By the determination of the thing to which the office was annexed (*c*).

We have already extracted from the various rules relating to offices, this important principle, that as they are constituted for the public weal it is expedient that they should be properly executed (*d*). On this principle a condition is tacitly and peremptorily engrafted by law on the grant of all offices, that they be executed by the grantee faithfully, properly, and diligently: on breach of which condition the office is forfeited or liable to be seized (*e*). This principle has ever been admitted: the difficulty has arisen in the application of it. The most methodical and perspicuous mode of stating the cases on this part of the subject, will perhaps be adopted, by considering successively the three causes of forfeiture or seizure of offices, mentioned by Lord Coke, namely, 1st, abuses; 2dly, non-user; 3rdly, refusal (*f*).

Abusing or *misusing* an office is, where the person filling it is guilty of any act contrary to his duty; as if a gaoler is guilty of a voluntary escape (*g*), or is repeatedly guilty of a negligent one (*h*). So, if an officer sell his office illegally (*i*), or if a forester or park-keeper cut down wood, kill deer without authority, or pull down any lodge or house within the park, they respectively forfeit their offices (*k*). And an officer in the courts of justice has been discharged for spoiling records, in violation

(*a*) See ante, ch. 2. s. 2.

(*b*) Bac. Ab. Offices, B. Rol. Ab. 152.

(*c*) 3 Cruis. 165.

(*d*) Ante, 83.

(*e*) Year Book, 11 Ed. 4. 1, b. 2 Rol. Ab. 155. Co. Lit. sect. 378. 233, a.

(*f*) 9 Co. Rep. 50, a.

(*g*) Dyer, 151, b. 2 Rol. Ab. 155.

2 Bulstr. 58, 2 Inst. 43. Bac. Ab. Gaol and Goaler, D. 2.

(*h*) Year Book, 39 Hen. 6. 33. 2 Rol. Ab. 155. N. pl. 2, 3. 2 Vern. 173. Bac. Ab. Offices, M. Burr. 2007.

(*i*) Stat. 5 and 6 Ed. 6. c. 16. Co. Lit. 234, a. As to sale of offices, see Bac. Ab. Offices, F.

(*k*) 9 Co. R. 50, a. Cro. El. 285. Co. Lit. 233, b.

of

of his duty (a). But it seems, that misbehaviour, under an erroneous though conscientious impression, will not of itself create a forfeiture (b), if it do not evince, from being often repeated, a general incapacity to execute the office (c).

By *non-user* (d) must be understood, a general neglect of the proper officer to attend to his duty, at usual, proper, and convenient times and places. A few instances of omitting to attend, when no particular business was expected, and without any particular circumstances, and where the non-attendance was conscientious, do not, it seems, amount to a forfeiture (e). It must appear, that the officer took no manner of care of his office (f), though perhaps one instance, or certainly two instances, of a wilful, voluntary, and determined neglect to attend on a particular occasion, would cause a forfeiture (g), though no inconvenience ensue by such non-attendance (h). Lord Coke (i) takes this distinction, that when the office concerns the administration of public justice, non-user of itself, without any special damage, may occasion a forfeiture, *aliter* as to private offices.

As to *refusal*, that also forms a ground of removal, in cases where the officer refuses, on request, to exercise his office where he ought; as if the steward of a manor refuse to hold a court when requested by the lord (k). The refusal must, however, it should seem on principle, be of a wilful, voluntary, and culpable nature (l).

These conditions, in law, are as strong and binding as express conditions, and an office is lost for ever by the non-observance of them (m). If the tenant in tail of an office commit a forfeiture, this shall bind the issue (n), and the act of the deputy may create a forfeiture of the inheritance (o). But the

(a) Pilkington's Case, 1 Keb. 597.

(b) See 4 Burr. 2003, 4; 1 Ib. 540, 1.

(c) See ante, 84.

(d) 9 Co. 50, a.

(e) See 4 Burr. 2005. 1 Burr. 540, 1.

(f) 1 Hawk. P. C. c. 66. s. 1. p. 167, 8. See Co. Lit. 233, a. and the books referred to by Hawkins: see however Cro. Car. 491. A filazer of C. B. being absent two years, and having farmed out his office from year to year without the license of the court, was discharged by C. B. in open court.

Dy. 114, b. pl. 64. Rol. Ab. 155. S. C.

(g) Ld. Raym. 1237. Burr. 2005, 6. 1 Burr. 540, 1.

(h) Ibid.

(i) Co. Lit. 233, a. 9 Co. 50. 5 Bac. Ab. 210.

(k) 9 Co. 50, a.

(l) See Burr. 2004.

(m) Co. Lit. 233, b. See 5 Bac. Ab. 211, title Offices, M.

(n) 7 Rep. 34, b. 5 Bac. Ab. 212, tit. Offices, M.

(o) Bro. Ab. Deputy, pl. 7. 5 Bac. Ab. 209.

commission

commission of acts amounting to a forfeiture, by an officer who holds for life or for years, does not affect the person entitled to the inheritance in remainder or reversion (a). And if a person having an office of inheritance lease it for life, and the lessee commit a forfeiture, this shall not forfeit the inheritance (b). Where an office is granted to two, and one of them is attainted, the other shall not forfeit (c).

The general rule is, that if an officer, who holds his office by patent, commit an act incurring a forfeiture, he cannot be turned out without a *scire facias,* nor can he be said to be completely ousted or discharged, without a writ of discharge; for his right appearing of record, the same must be defeated by matter of as high a nature (d).

2. A person may also lose an office merely by the acceptance of another office incompatible with that he already holds. Offices are incompatible, and cannot be holden together, when, from the nature or extent of the different duties and businesses attached to them, they cannot be properly and effectually executed by the same person; or when they are subordinate to, or interfere with each other, which creates a legal presumption, that they will not be executed with impartiality and honesty (c). Thus, an admiral commanding on a station loses his right to officiate there, by accepting a command on another station to which he is appointed (f). A Judge of the Court of Common Pleas loses his office by being appointed, and by becoming a Judge of the Court of King's Bench (g). A coroner ceases to be such by being a sheriff (h). Numerous other instances, founded on the principle that a person cannot hold at the same time two offices, one of which is subordinate to, and under the controul of the other, are to be met with (i). The doctrine holds, though the new office accepted by the party is inferior to that which he held before (k). And where the offices are incompatible, the office which the party first

(a) Ibid. 7 Rep. 34, b. Popham, 119. Bac. Ab. Goal and Goaler, D. 2.
(b) 2 Lev. 71. 3 Ibid. 288.
(c) Plowd. 378; 180. 5 Bac. Ab. 212.
(d) See Dyer, 155, 98, 211. 9 Co. 98. Co. Lit. 233. Cro. Car. 60, 1. Sid. 81, 134. 8 Co. 44, b. Rol. Ab.

580. 3 Mod. 335. 3 Lev. 288.
(e) 4 Inst. 100. Bac. Ab. Offices, K.
(f) 1 Hen. Bla. 268.
(g) Dyer, 159. Cro. Car. 12.
(h) Bac. Ab. Offices, K.
(i) See Ibid. Cases cited, 2 T. R. 85, &c.
(k) See 2 T. R. 81.

held

held is impliedly surrendered or vacated, by the acceptance of the new situátion (*a*).

3. An office may be lost by the destruction of the thing to which it is incident (*b*): as if a person grant the office of Parker, and afterwards destroy his park, the office, together with all casual fees annexed to it, is gone (*c*). For the office, being only an accessary, must follow the fate of the principal. For although the grantor of the office could not appoint another person as long as the Park continued, yet when the Park itself was determined and disparked, the office which was appendant thereto, should also be determined. And it was said that if one grant the office of Steward of a Manor, with all profits of courts, and the Manor is afterwards destroyed, the office of Steward, together with the casual profits annexed to it, is determined.

SECT. II.

As to Pardons, Reprieves, &c.

1st. In general. 2dly. When and how far the King may Pardon, and of Dispensations, Non Obstantes, *and Reprieves. 3dly. Manner of Pardoning. 4thly. Effect of a Pardon.*

1st. In general.

THE policy of pardoning public offenders in any case has been questioned by Beccaria (*d*), who contended that clemency should shine forth in the laws, and not in the execution of them. It would certainly be impolitic to remit the punishment attached to an offence very frequently or indiscriminately. Few measures would tend more strongly to embolden offenders; and nothing could more effectually introduce a contemptuous disregard of those laws which were intended to protect society. It should however be remembered that human institutions are fallible, and must in many respects be imperfect. No human faculties can anticipate the various temptations

---

(*a*) 3 Burr. 1616. 2 T. R. 87, 88. (*d*) See Beccaria on Crimes and Pu-
(*b*) 3 Cruise Dig. 169.   nishments, ch. 46.
(*c*) Howard's Case. Cro. Car. 59.

which

which may urge a man to the commission of an offence; or foresee all the shades in the circumstances of a case which may extenuate the guilt of the accused. An offence may be within the letter, but foreign to the general scope and spirit of the law. " If we consider accurately the nature of human punishment, we shall find it attended with unavoidable imperfections. How short is our discernment! The surface of things and actions is alone exposed to our view: the inward thoughts, the habitual temper, which form the greater part of moral conduct, are entirely concealed from us. It is for this reason that laws assign the same name, nature, and penalty to all offences, which bear a conformity in outward resemblance, though intrinsically varying from one another, by a thousand circumstances, known only to the Searcher of hearts (a)."

As, therefore, society cannot sufficiently provide for every possible transgression of its ordinances, and measure by anticipation the degree of guilt which may attach to the offender, it has entrusted the King with the power of extending mercy to him. The coronation oath requires the King to temper justice with mercy; and it was the expression of the unfortunate Lord Strafford, that " the King condemns no man : the great operation of his sceptre is mercy"—a generous principle, which seems to have been sometimes acted upon in this country, even in the worst and more dreary periods of our history.

The King is, in legal contemplation, injured by the commission of public offences; his peace is said to be violated thereby, and the right to pardon cannot be vested more properly than in the Sovereign, who is, from his situation, more likely than any other person to exercise it with impartiality, and to whom good policy requires that the people should look, with submissive respect, as the head of the nation, and supreme guardian of the laws. It seems, that anciently the right of pardoning offences, within certain districts, was claimed by the lords of marches and others, who possessed *jura regalia* (b) ; but the statute 27 Hen. 8. c. 24. s. 1. vests the sole right of pardoning in the King. This right, or rather prerogative, belongs to a King *de facto*, and not to the King *de jure*, during

---

(a) Considerations on the Law of Forfeiture for High Treason, 1748, by the Honourable Mr. York.

(b) Co. Lit. 114. 3 Inst. 235. Bac. Ab. Pardon, A.

the usurpation of the former (*a*). It is an incommunicable prerogative (*b*); except, perhaps, in the colonies, where, by grant from the Crown, it may be exercised by the governor, &c. (*c*). And, by statute 30 Geo. 3. c. 47. the King may, by commission under the great seal, authorize the Governor, &c. of New South Wales, &c. to remit the whole or any part of the term for which offenders may have been transported (*d*).

2dly. When and how far the King may pardon ; and of Dispensations, Non-obstantes, and Reprieves.

The King's right to pardon and remit the consequences of a violation of the law, is confined to cases in which the prosecution is carried on in his Majesty's name, for the commission of some offence affecting the public, and which demands public satisfaction, or for the recovery of a fine or forfeiture, to which his Majesty is entitled. *Non potest rex gratiam facere cum injuriâ et damno aliorum* (*e*). Hence, his Majesty has no legal right to pardon a person found guilty on an appeal of murder, &c. it being a proceeding instituted at the suit, and in the name of a private individual (*f*); though, it seems, that his Majesty may pardon the burning of the hand, which is inflicted by statute on a conviction of manslaughter, on an appeal, such punishment being collateral to the object of the appeal, and intended as a satisfaction to public justice (*g*). Nor can the King's pardon be considered a legal discharge of an attachment for non-payment of costs, or non-performance of an award, &c. (*h*). for though such attachment is carried on in the shape of a criminal process, for a contempt of the court, yet it is in effect, and substantially a civil remedy, or execution for a private injury (*i*). So, where any legal right or benefit is vested in a

(*a*) Bro. Ab. tit. Charter de Pardon, 22.

(*b*) Jenk. 171, pl. 36. Hob. 183. 155. 7 Co. 36. Mo. 764. 27 Hen. 8. c. 24. s. 1.

(*c*) Ante, ch. 3.

(*d*) See 2 B. and Ald. 258.

(*e*) 3 Inst. 236.

(*f*) Ibid. 237. Hawk. bk. 2. c. 37.

s. 33. 4 Bla. Com. 398. 1 Chitty's Crim. Law, 762, 3, 4. See the late Act.

(*g*) 5 Co. Rep. 50, a. 2 Hawk. P. C. c. 37. s. 39. See Cro. El. 682 ; but see Moor. 571. 1 Stra. 529, 30, per Eyre, J.

(*h*) 4 Bla. Com. 285.

(*i*) Ibid. 2 Willes, R. 292, note b. 16 East, 300, 1.

subject,

subject, the King cannot affect it; and, consequently, where a statute gives a right of action to a party grieved, by the commission of an offence, though it be of a public description, his Majesty has no power, by law, to prevent the party aggrieved from bringing his action, even by pardoning the offender before it is commenced (*a*), nor can his Majesty discharge a recognizance to keep the peace towards an individual before it is forfeited, private security being the object of the instrument (*b*). And, though the Crown may legally pardon an offence against a statute, which gives a right of action to a common informer, before the action is begun, and may consequently defeat it (*c*); yet, when the informer has commenced the action, his right to the penalty is, *ipso facto*, irreversibly vested in him, if he succeed, and the King cannot deprive him of it (*d*). In short, the general principle is clear, that the King cannot pardon in cases where no interest is, either in point of fact, or by implication of law, vested in him (*e*).

The right to pardon obtains, however gross and criminal the offence may be, as in the case of a murder, rape, &c.; though certain peculiar forms must in such instances be observed, as will be noticed hereafter.

It is generally laid down in the books, that the Crown cannot pardon a common nuisance while it remains unredressed, and is continuing; so as to prevent an abatement of it, or a prosecution against the offender: though his Majesty might afterwards remit the fine (*f*). As the continuation of a nuisance is, of itself, a fresh offence in point of law (*g*); this doctrine may be supported on the ground that the King cannot, as we shall presently see, dispense with the laws by any previous licence. Besides a prosecution for a nuisance, though technically criminal, is in substance and effect a civil remedy; and the King cannot subject the public to inconvenience by bestowing a favour on an individual or a few persons. There seems, however, to be some reason for the assertion (*h*), that

(*a*) 3 Inst. 238. Plowd. 487. 2 Rol. Ab. 178. Cro. Car. 199. Keilw. 134. Stra. 529, 30; 1272. 2 Term Rep. 569.

(*b*) 3 Inst. 238. 12 Co. 30. Hawk. b. 2. c. 37. s. 34. Dick. Sess. 422.

(*c*) See Ibid.

(*d*) Ibid. 3 Inst. 338. 4 Bla. Com. 398, 9. 2 Stra. 1272.

(*e*) See also Stra. 1272.

(*f*) 12 Co. 30. 2 Hawk. b. 2. c. 37. s. 33. 4 Bla. Com. 398. Bac. Ab. Pardon, B. But now the fine does not belong to the Crown, on indictment for suffering a highway to continue in bad repair, 13 G. 3. c. 78. s. 47. 1 Bla R. 602.

(*g*) See Ld. Raym. 370. 713.

(*h*) 3 Inst. 237. Vaugh. 333. 5 Bac. Ab. 286.

such

the pardon will save the party from any fine to the time when
such pardon was granted: in this case the objection that the
King cannot by previous licence dispense with or suspend the
operation of the laws, does not apply. The Crown may pardon *mala praxis* (*a*).

The King's prerogative right to pardon violations of the
law is not confined to offences punishable at common law by
indictment. His Majesty may by a charter of pardon discharge not only a suit in the spiritual court *ex officio;* but also
any suit in such court *ad instantiam partis pro reformatione
morum* or *salute animæ;* as for defamation, or laying violent
hands on a clerk, &c. (*b*). But the King cannot, by pardoning, discharge any suit in a spiritual (or other) court in which
the plaintiff seeks to recover any property; or in which an
interest is vested in him: as in the case of a suit for tithes or
legacies (*c*).

The King's right to pardon is also taken from him by statute in certain cases, in favour of public liberty. Thus to
commit a subject to prison beyond the realm is by the *Habeas
Corpus* Act made a præmunire which the King cannot pardon (*d*).

So the King's pardon under the great seal is not *pleadable*
in bar of an impeachment by the House of Commons (*e*).
Yet, as remarked by Sir Wm. Blackstone (*f*), " after the impeachment is solemnly heard and determined, it is not understood that the King's royal grace is farther restrained or
abridged; for after the impeachment and attainder of the six
rebel lords in 1715, three of them were from time to time re-
prieved by the Crown, and at length received the benefit of
the King's pardon."

It seems agreed that notwithstanding the King's pardon to
a simonist coming into Church contrary to the purport of
31 Eliz. c. 6.; or to an officer coming into his office by a corrupt bargain contrary to the purport of 5 and 6 E. 6. c. 16.;
may save such clerk or officer from any criminal prosecution

(*a*) Ld. Raym. 214.

(*b*) 2 Hawk. P. C. c. 23. s. 41. 5
Co. 51. Latch. 190.

(*c*) 5 Co. Rep. 51. Cro. Car. 46, 47.
Latch. 100. When the pardon discharges the costs awarded in these cases.
See 5 Bac. Ab. 288. 2 Hawk. c. 37.
s. 41. 2 Rol. Ab. 304.

(*d*) 31 Car. 2. c. 2. s. 12.

(*e*) See 12 and 13 Wm. 3. c. 2. s. 3.

(*f*) 4 Com. 399, 0. And in Fortescue R. 385, 397, the judges agreed that
the King might pardon a party attainted
of high treason, by a bill of attainder
in Parliament.

in respect of the corrupt bargain; yet, shall it not enable the clerk to hold the church, nor the officer to retain the office, because they are absolutely disabled by statute (*a*).

There are some instances which may be here mentioned with propriety, in which offenders are entitled to a pardon as a matter of right; some in which they have a strong equitable claim to it.

Approvement is where a person indicted for a capital crime and arraigned for the same, confesses the fact before plea pleaded, and accuses his accomplices in the same crime, in order to obtain his own pardon. In this case he is called an *approver*, or *prover*, *probator* (*b*). This doctrine of approvement has now fallen entirely in disuse (*c*), but as it is still in force in many instances (*d*), a concise mention of it may not be objectionable; and as Lord Mansfield has admirably summed up the law on this subject, we cannot do better than refer to his expressions for information. " A person" said his lordship (*d*), " desiring to be an approver, must be one indicted of the offence, and in custody on that indictment: he must confess himself guilty of the offence, and desire to accuse his accomplices. He must likewise upon oath discover, not only the particular offence for which he is indicted; but all treasons and felonies which he knows of; and after all this, it is in the discretion of the Court, whether they will assign him a coroner, and admit him to be an approver or not: for if, on his confession it appear, that he is a principal, and tempted the others, the Court may refuse and reject him as an approver. When he is admitted as such it must appear that what he has discovered is true; and that he has discovered the whole truth. For this purpose the coroner puts his appeal into form; and when the prisoner returns into Court, he must repeat his appeal, without any help from the Court, or from any by-stander. And the law is so nice, that if he vary in a single circumstance, the whole falls to the ground, and he is condemned to be hanged, if he fail in essentials. The same consequences follow if he do not discover the whole truth. And in all these cases the approver is convicted on his own confession.

(*a*) Owen, 87. Hetl. 104. Co. Lit. 120. 3 Bulstr. 90, 1. 3 Inst. 154.
(*b*) 4 Bla. Com. 329, 30.
(*c*) 2 Hal. P. C. c. 29. Cowp. 334.

(*d*) Cowp. 335. See further, 2 Hale, P. C. 226 to 236. Staundf. Pl. Crown, lib. 2. c. 52 to c. 58. 3 Inst. 129.

A fur-

A further rigorous circumstance is, that it is necessary to the approver's own safety, that the jury should believe him, for if the partners in his crime are not convicted, the approver himself is executed."

Various statutes have considerably trenched on this antient doctrine and practice of approvement. Persons *out of prison* who have been guilty of robbery, 4 and 5 Wm. and M. c. 8. s. 7.; offences against the coinage acts, 6 and 7 Wm. and M. c. 17. s. 12. 15 G. 2. c. 28. s. 8.; burglary, felonious house-breaking in the day time, horse-stealing, larceny to the value of five shillings, or more, from any shop, warehouse, coach-house or stable, 10 and 11 W. 3. c. 23. s. 5., 5 and 6 Ann. c. 31. s. 4. of destroying fish in private waters, (whether in custody or not) 5 G. 3. c. 11. s. 2.; or destroying locks on navigable rivers, 8 G. 2. c. 20. s. 5.; of using stamps twice contrary to 12 G. 3. c. 48.; or of offences contrary to the statutes against smuggling and resisting custom-house officers, 6 G. 1. c. 21. s. 36., 8 G. 1. c. 18. s. 7., 9 G. 2. c. 35. s. 12. are entitled to the King's pardon thereof; provided they, being out of prison, cause the discovery and conviction of two or more persons guilty of the like crimes. By the statutes 29 G. 2. c. 30. s. 8, 9., 2 G. 3. c. 28. s. 14., 22 G. 3. c. 58. s. 5. a person guilty of stealing metals, &c. and being out of prison, is entitled to the King's pardon, if he discover two or more persons who have illegally bought or received stolen metals, &c. so that they may be convicted thereof. And it is usual in the acts which establish and regulate state lotteries to insert a clause by which accomplices in forging lottery tickets are entitled to a pardon on discovering their associates.

At common law where a person indicted for manslaughter or murder is found by the jury to have killed the deceased in his own defence or by misfortune, he is obliged to crave the King's pardon, to which, however, he is entitled as a matter of right (*a*). It is now usual to avoid expence by directing a general verdict of acquittal.

There is another case in which offenders are entitled as a matter of legal right to a pardon; and that is where the King promises to pardon them, by special proclamation in the Gazette or otherwise (*b*).

(*a*) 1 East, P. C. 221, 2. 1 Chitty, Crim. Law, 765, 6. Hawk. b. 2. c. 37. s. 2.   (*b*) Cowp. 334. 1 Leach, 118.

Accomplices who are, to use a technical expression, admitted to be King's evidence, have no legal claim to a pardon: nor has the magistrate before whom the original examination is taken, any power to promise them one on condition of their becoming witnesses (a). In such case, however, and in others where the party's evidence has been made use of, and he appears to have acted ingenuously, he has an equitable claim to the royal mercy (b); and it is usually extended to him with reference to the old doctrine of approvement.

Where offenders have by any of these means a legal right to a pardon, the Court of King's Bench will bail them, in order to afford them an opportunity of applying for a pardon (c): and even where offenders have merely an equitable claim under the circumstances to the royal mercy, that Court will put off their trials for the same purpose (d).

It may not be amiss briefly to touch upon the antient supposed right of the King to grant suspensions, or dispensations of the laws, *non obstante aliquo statúta in contrarium,* before the commission of an offence; or in other words, suffering a person to commit a breach of the laws with impunity, by rendering him dispunishable (e). This was a prerogative which almost all our antient Kings exercised; it was replete with absurdity, and might be converted to the most dangerous purposes. It was always regarded with jealousy, and being carried by the Judges in the reign of James the Second (f), to an extent which placed the King above the laws; it was enacted by the Bill of Rights, 1 Wm. and Mary, sess. 2. c. 2. that no dispensation by *non obstante,* of or to any *statute,* or any part thereof, shall be allowed, but that the same shall be held void and of no effect, except a dispensation be allowed of in such statute." This provision, we may observe, only relates to dispensations of statutes, and cannot affect dispensations of common law offences. A distinction was formerly drawn between those offences which were *mala in se,* as for instance, murder, stealing, or perjury, and those which were merely *mala prohibita,* or in other words, contrary to Act of Parliament (g). The

(a) Cowp. 336. 1 Leach, 121.
(b) Cowp. 340. 1 Leach, 125. Williams J. Pardon, II.
(c) Cowp. 334. 1 Leach, 119.
(d) Ibid.
(e) Finch. Law, 81, 234. Bacon, Elem. ch. 19. 11 Co. 88. Dyer, 54, pl. 17.
(f) Sir Edward Hale's Case, 2 Show. 475. pl. 440. Comb. 21. Clift. 133.
(g) Vaugh. 330 to 359.

power

power of the Sovereign to dispense with laws relative to offences of the latter description, is' annihilated by the statute; and it is clear that the King cannot exempt any one
from the future operation of a statute expected to be passed,
but not in actual existence (*a*).   It was always held, that his
Majesty had no legal right to dispense with laws respecting
offences which, by an absurd distinction (*b*), were termed *mala
in se ;* or, by previous licence, to render dispunishable offences
which, are indictable at common law, as being contrary to
nature or the public good (*c*).   It was, indeed, decided in the
year books, 3 Hen. 7. 15 pl. 30. that the King's grant to the
Bishop of Salisbury and his successors, having the custody of
a prison, that they should not be liable to be sued for escapes,
was valid.   Serjeant Hawkins (*d*) well observes, that this is a
single instance, and contrary to the general rule.

We have already considered the power of the Crown to
grant exemptions from liability to serve in public offices (*e*),
and dispensations relative to trade and taxes, &c. will be considered hereafter (*f*).

By the common law, the King may annex to his bounty a
condition either precedent or subsequent; on the due performance whereof the validity of the pardon will depend (*g*).
Therefore if a prisoner is pardoned on condition that he find
security for his good behaviour (*h*), and he accordingly enter
into a recognizance, the law tacitly annexes a condition to
such pardon, that if the recognizance be forfeited, the original
judgment remains in force and may be proceeded upon (*i*).

The prerogative may also be partially exercised in pardoning an offender; so that the King may remit part of
the sentence of the law (*k*).   But it does not seem to be established whether he can legally change the mode of punishment by death: that is, substitute a mild for a severe one, by
altering the hanging or burning into beheading, &c.   Both
Lord Coke (*l*) and Sir Matthew Hale (*m*) thought that the

(*a*) Finch, 235. 1 Dyer, 52. 1 Sid.   401. 2 Hawk. P. C. 394. c. 37. s. 45.
6. Hawk. b. 2. c. 37. s. 32.   (*h*) See 5 Wm. 3. c. 13.
(*b*) See 2 Bos. and Pul. 574, 5.   (*i*) Moor. pl. 662.
(*c*) Dav. 75. 5 Co. 35. 12 Co. 29.   (*k*) Fortescue R. 385. 4 Bla. Com.
(*d*) 2 Hawk. P. C. ch. 37. s. 28.   179. 404, 5.
(*e*) Ante, ch. 2. s. 3.   (*l*) 3 Inst. 52.
(*f*) Post. ch. 10.   (*m*) 2 Hal. P. C. 412.
(*g*) Co. Lit. 274, b. 4 Bla. Com.

King

King was not possessed of this prerogative. But the contrary is laid down by other great authorities (*a*). They contend that this prerogative, being founded in mercy and immemorially exercised by the Crown, is part of the common law. As pertinently observed by Sir William Blackstone (*b*): "how far this may fall within the King's power of granting conditional pardon (viz. by remitting a severe kind of death on condition that the criminal submit to a milder) is a matter that may bear consideration." Several instances are also mentioned by Hume and others, in which this latter prerogative has been claimed and exercised by the Crown. As however no judicial determination is to be found, and so great a contrariety of sentiment has prevailed upon the point, there is much difficulty in coming to a satisfactory conclusion respecting it. The better opinion seems to be, that the King is entitled to the prerogative in question; and that as he may pardon a criminal on certain conditions, there is no objection to the condition being the offender's submission to a less severe punishment. The punishment which the law has inflicted is certainly altered by this prerogative: but the power of pardoning or punishing is left by the British constitution very generally with the King.

The term *reprieve* is derived from *reprendre*, to keep back, and signifies the withdrawing of the sentence for an interval of time, and operates in delay of execution (*c*). It is granted either by the favor of his Majesty himself, or the Judge before whom the prisoner is tried, on his behalf; or from the regular operation of law in circumstances which render an immediate execution inconsistent with humanity or justice (*d*).

This temporary mercy may be extended *ex mandato regis*, or from the mere pleasure of the Crown expressed in any way to the Court by whom the execution is to be awarded (*e*). The intention of his Majesty may be signified *ore tenus*, by a verbal message, or by sending his ring in token of his design; but, at the present day, the intimation is usually made by the Privy

---

(*a*) Foster, 270. Fitz. N. B. 244; h. 19. Rym. Fœd. 284. 4 Bla. Com. 404, 5.

(*b*) 4 Comm. 405.

(*c*) 4 Bla. Com. 394. As to reprieves in general, see 1 Hale, 368 to 370. 2

Ibid. 412 to 414. Hawk. b. 2. c. 51. s. 8, 9, 10. Williams's J. Execution and Reprieve.

(*d*) 1 Chitty, Crim. Law, 757.

(*e*) 2 Hale, 412. 1 Ibid. 368. Hawk. b. 2. c. 51. s. 8.

Signet

Signet or the Master of Requests (*a*). On this the Judge of course grants the prisoner a respite, either for a limited time or during the pleasure of his Majesty (*b*).

3dly. *Manner of pardoning.*

A pardon may be effectually granted either by Act of Parliament, or under the great seal, and in general, there seems no other legal mode of obtaining one(*c*). It is settled, that in pleading a pardon it must be averred, that it was granted under the great seal, if it be not granted by statute (*d*); and that a coronation pardon, as it is termed, cannot be taken advantage of, unless it be under that seal(*e*). And, though the King's sign manual, or privy seal(*f*), declaring his Majesty's intention to pardon the prisoner, is a sufficient authority to the Judges to discharge him(*g*); yet such sign manual is revocable, and does not amount to a pardon in legal contemplation(*h*).

The mode of pardoning at the Assizes or Old Bailey, if the Judge think the conviction improper, is, by respiting the execution of the sentence, and sending a memorial or certificate to the King, directed to the Secretary of State's office, stating, that from favorable circumstances appearing on the trial, he is induced to recommend the prisoner to mercy(*i*). If the King agree in the propriety of the suggestion, as is usual, a sign manual issues, signifying his intention to grant either an absolute or a conditional pardon, and directing the Justices of gaol delivery to bail the prisoner, in order to appear and plead the next general pardon that shall come out, which they do accordingly, taking his recognizance to perform the conditions of the pardon, if any are annexed to the indulgence(*k*).

A statute pardon is more beneficial to the prisoner than a

(*a*) 1 Hale, 369. 2 Hale, 412.

(*b*) 1 Chitty, Crim. Law, 757.

(*c*) See 1 Bos. and P. 199. By a late statute, convict not to pay the fees.

(*d*) Ibid.

(*e*) Keble, 707.

(*f*) Under some statutes the King's sign manual actually carried into execution and the conditions performed may amount to a statute pardon, per Lord C. J. Eyre. 1 B. and Pul. 200.

(*g*) 1 Bla. R. 479. 2 Ibid. 797.

(*h*) Ibid. 797, 8. 4 Bla. Com. 400. 5 St. Tri. 166, 173. 1 Leach, 115. 15 East, 463. 2 B. and Ald. 277, 8.

(*i*) Dick. Sess. 432, 3. 4 Bla. Com. 404, n. 1.

(*k*) 1 Bla. Rep. 479. 1 Leach, 74. 15 East, 468. Williams's J. Pardon 3. Dick. Sess. 430,

pardon by the King's charter, under the great seal. The former, if made by a public act, need not be pleaded, but the Court must, *ex officio*, notice it (*a*), which does not hold in the case of a charter of pardon, and it therefore lies upon the prisoner to insist upon and prove it (*b*). Neither can he lose the benefit of the statute pardon by his own *laches* or negligence, or by his omission to plead it at the trial (*c*), as he may of the King's charter of pardon; for if the prisoner plead the general issue, or any other plea, when he might plead the King's charter of pardon, he is considered to have waived it, and cannot afterwards plead it in his defence (*d*). It is, however, clear in general, that if a prisoner avail himself thereof, as soon as by course of law he may, a pardon may be pleaded either upon arraignment, in arrest of judgment, or in bar of execution (*e*).

In order to render the charter valid, it is necessary that it be correct, and sufficiently full in its statement of facts (*f*). It is laid down, as a general rule, that wherever it appears by the charter that the King was misinformed, or not fully apprized of the seriousness of the crime committed by the offender, and of the extent to which legal proceedings have been carried against him, the pardon is void, upon a presumption that it was gained from the King by imposition (*g*). It has, therefore, been determined, that a pardon of a person attainted of felony is ineffectual, unless it mention the attainder, or unless it recite the indictment and conviction, in case he has been convicted by verdict (*h*). The statute 13 Rich. 2. st. 2. c. 1 (*i*). enacts, that no pardon for treason, murder, or rape, shall be allowed, unless the offence be particularly specified therein; and particu-

---

(*a*) Foster, 43.

(*b*) See Cro. El. 153.

(*c*) 1 Wils. 214.   4 Bla. Com. 402. In 1 Wilson Repts. 150, where the prisoner being brought up to receive sentence on an old conviction, pleaded that he was not the same person convicted, which on issue joined was found against him; the Court held that he was not afterwards at liberty to plead an act of grace, or general pardon; observing, that the defendant had been asked what he had to say, &c. and could not be asked twice, and that the plea came too late, he having made his election what to rely upon.

(*d*) Ibid.   4 Bla. Com. 402.   Bac. Ab. Pardon, G. (1.)

(*e*) 4 Bla. Com. 402.

(*f*) The statute 27 Edw. 3. c. 2. enacts, that in every pardon of felony which shall be granted at any man's suggestion, the said suggestion and the name of him that made it, shall be comprized therein, and if the suggestion be untrue, the charter shall be disallowed.

(*g*) Ibid.   3 Inst. 238.   4 Bla. Com. 400.   Bac. Abr. Pardon, D.   4 Hawk. P. C. 336 Bk. 2. c. 37. s. 8.   Post. ch. 16. Grants.

(*h*) Hawk. *ubi supra.*

(*i*) And see 16 Rich. 2. c. 6.

larly

larly in murder, it shall be expressed whether it was committed by lying in wait, assault, or malice prepense. This statute is, it will be observed, confined to cases of treasons, murder, and rape. With respect to other offences, it seems, that if no legal proceedings have been commenced against offenders, they will be protected by a general and indefinite pardon of ' all felonies or misdemeanors by them committed,' although the offences of which they have been guilty be not specifically pointed out, and designated in the charter. Thus, a general pardon of all misprisions, trespasses, offences, and contempts, includes a contempt in making a false return, striking in Westminster Hall, barratry, a premunire, and (it is said) any crime which is not capital (*a*). However, no charter of pardon can be extended beyond its express and clear purport and meaning; and, therefore, a pardon of all felonies will not include such offences as are not strictly such in legal contemplation, as piracies, &c. (*b*). And if the King, after reciting in his charter an attainder of felony, pardon the execution only, his Majesty does not thereby pardon the felony itself, or any other consequence of it, besides the execution (*c*). Where there is any doubt the leaning is, however, in favour of the subject, for whose benefit the pardon was granted (*d*).

The pardon of a principal before conviction necessarily enures to the benefit of the accessary also, by implication of law; because he cannot be arraigned before the conviction of the principal (*e*). A pardon to A. and B. of all offences whereof they are indicted, must be taken severally, from the nature of the thing; because the offences are several, and consequently so is the operation of the pardon (*f*). " The King pardons his loving and obedient subjects:" this extends to aliens, if here at the time, though not made denizens (*g*). The general rule is that if a felony has its commencement, but not its completion, before the pardon is granted, the pardon operates in favor of the prisoner, as it would have done if the felony had been complete before the pardon. By pardoning the act, the consequences of it are pardoned also; though such conse-

(*a*) Lev. 106.   Sid. 211.   5 Mod. 52.
(*b*) See 4 Bla. Com. 400.
(*c*) 6 Co. R. 13.
(*d*) 4 Bla. Com. 400, 1.
(*e*) Cro. El. 30, 1.   5 Bac. Ab. Par-

don, F.
(*f*) Dyer, 34.   Moore, 164.   Lord Raym. 1203.
(*g*) Per Hob. 271.

quences may not have occurred at the time of the pardon: as in the case of pardoning homicide, where the death, occasioned by the wound, transpired after the pardon was granted (*a*). It was however held that if a man gave a blow (which, unless death ensued, was not a capital offence, but merely a misdemeanor by the common law) and a pardon was granted of all misdemeanors, but not of murder, and the party wounded afterwards died, the felony is not pardoned (*b*).

Formerly by the statute 10 Ed. 3. st. 1. c. 3. no pardon of felony by the King's charter could be allowed or was effectual without a writ of allowance, testifying that the prisoner had found six sureties before the Sheriff and Coroners of the county (*c*). This statute of Ed. 3. did not extend to pardons of treason (*d*); and it being found that its operation bore too harshly upon offenders, it was at length entirely repealed by the statute 5 and 6 Wm. 3. c. 13. That statute, however, provides, sect. 2, " that if any charter of pardon be pleaded by any person for any felony, the Justices before whom such pardon shall be pleaded, may, *at their discretion*, remand or commit such person to prison, there to remain until he or she shall enter into a recognizance, with two sufficient sureties, for his or her being of the good behaviour for any time not exceeding seven years. Provided, that if any such charter of pardon be pleaded by a feme covert or infant, such feme covert or infant may find two sufficient sureties, who shall enter into a recognizance for him or her being of the good behaviour as is aforesaid."

The Court in exercising this their discretion, will not require the pardoned offender to find sureties according to the statute, unless it appear that he is a person of ill fame, and one whose general conduct has been suspicious (*e*), and sureties have been rarely required (*f*).

The mode of granting a reprieve has been already mentioned (*g*).

(*a*) Plowd. 401. Hal. P. C. 426. Dyer, 99. pl. 65. Foster, 64.

(*b*) Ibid.

(*c*) See Plowd. 502. Sid. 41. Salk. 499. 4 Bla. Com. 402.

(*d*) Cro. El. 814. Noy, 31.

(*e*) See Rex *v.* Chetwynd, 9 State Tri. 527. Stra. 1203.

(*f*) As to the manner of pleading a pardon, see further Bac. Ab. title Pardon, G. 1 Chitty, Crim. Law, 775.

(*g*) Ante, 97.

The

The law of transportation is founded on several statutes (*a*) which provide generally, that the transportation shall have the effect of a pardon under the great seal, as to the offence for which the offender was transported. By the word transportation, in the statute 8 G. 3. c. 15. is meant not merely the conveying the felon to the place of transportation, but his being so conveyed and remaining there during the term for which he is ordered to be transported; and therefore a felon attainted is not by that statute restored to his civil rights till after the expiration of the term for which he was ordered to be so transported (*b*).

4thly. Effect of a Pardon.

The King's pardon, if general in its purport and sufficient in other respects, obliterates every stain which the law attached to the offender. Generally speaking, it puts him in the same situation as that in which he stood before he committed the pardoned offence; and frees him from the penalties and forfeitures to which the law subjected his person and property (*c*). Though a pardon cannot wash away those doubts with which the evidence of one who has committed a serious offence will be received; yet in point of law, a legal pardon impliedly removes the stigma and restores a man to credit, so as to enable him to be a witness (*d*); and it so far makes him a new man as to entitle him, according to some of our old books, to bring an action against any one who scandalizes him in respect of the crime pardoned (*e*).

When the offender's property and civil rights have once vested in the King they cannot be restored to the offender, nor are they divested from his Majesty by a mere pardon, without a clause of restitution (*f*). It seems however that a

(*a*) 4 G. 1. c. 11.   6 G. 1. c. 23.   8 G. 3. c. 15.   30 G. 3. c. 47. See 2 B. and Ald. 258.

(*b*) Ibid.

(*c*) 4 Bla. Com. 402.   Bac. Ab. Pardon, H.

(*d*) 1 Ventr. 349.   2 Hal. P. C. 278. 4 State Tr. 682. Gully's Case, 1 Leach.

Cro. Cas. 115.

(*e*) See Bac. Ab. Pardon, H.   Hob. 67, 81, 2.

(*f*) 1 Saund. 362, 3.   1 Lev. 120. Bac. Ab. Pardon, H.   2 Mod. 53.   3 Mod. 104. 2 B. and Ald. 277, 8, per Abbott, C. J.

clause

clause of release of all judgments and executions in a general pardon, extends to debts due to the King by forfeiture: and extinguishes or merges the debt in the hands of the debtor (*a*).

A charter of pardon after attainder is not sufficient to restore or purify the corrupted blood of the attainted offender (*b*), and therefore though he may after such pardon purchase and hold lands, yet his descendants who were *in esse* at the time of the attainder, cannot inherit them; nor can he himself inherit as descendant of another (*c*). The King's charter is however sufficient to restore the blood as to all future descendants: consequently a son born after such pardon may inherit (*d*), unless there be in existence an elder brother who was born before the attainder, and who might have inherited had not the attainder taken place; in which case the younger brother cannot inherit, and the land will escheat *pro defectu hæredis* (*e*).

SECT. III.

As to Gaols.

PRISONS being places of a public description, and connected with the execution of justice, are in general the property of the King (*f*). And it seems that by the common law his Majesty is impliedly their governor; though by various statutes (*g*), the custody of gaols, except such as are the legal property or franchise of a subject, is vested in the sheriffs of the different counties (*h*). His Majesty cannot, therefore, now grant the custody of prisoners to private persons (*i*), The formation of a new prison can be legally effected only by the authority of Parliament (*k*).

(*a*) 1 Saund. 362, 3.   1 Lev. 120. Bac. Ab. Pardon, H.   2 Mod. 53.   3 Ibid. 104.   Per C. J. Abbott, 2 B. and Ald. 277, 8.

(*b*) 4 Bla. Com. 402.

(*c*) Co. Lit. 8, a.   Hal. P. C. 358.

(*d*) Ibid.   2 Bla. Com. 254. 4 Ibid. 402.

(*e*) Ibid.   1 Hal. P. C. 358.

(*f*) 2 Inst. 100,   Bac. Ab. Gaol, B.

margin, note a.   8 Term R. 176.

(*g*) 14 Ed. 3.   st. 1.   c. 10.   5 H. 4. c. 10.   19 Hen. 7.   c. 10.   11 and 12 Wm. 3. c. 19. s. 3.   5 Ann. c. 9.

(*h*) See Ibid.   Rol. Ab. 806.   Show. R. 162.

(*i*) And 345.   4 Co. 34, a.   9 Co. 119.   Cro. El. 829, 30.

(*k*) 2 Inst. 705.

SECT. IV.

Of Royal Proclamations.

1st. *In general ; and when they are legal.*

ROYAL proclamations seem to be extremely antient; and, it is most probable, were originally adopted for the purpose of giving additional weight and dignity to the laws.   Proclamations have been frequently made the tools of tyranny and oppression; and by a statute of Henry the 8th (*a*), were in substance set on the same footing as Acts of Parliament (*b*). This statute fortunately existed a very short period (*c*). And it is clear that by the constitution of the country, this prerogative respecting proclamations, merely enables the King as executive magistrate to command and enforce the performance by his subjects of existing laws, and to make or alter regulations over which his Majesty has a peculiar jurisdiction (*d*): and does not entitle him to break through those fundamental principles on which the legislative portion of the government is founded, by commanding the observance of matters not sanctioned by Parliament.   In this point of view, and if thus restricted, the prerogative in question is highly reasonable, and of public advantage ; because, though the making of laws is entirely the work of a distinct part, the legislative branch of the sovereign power, yet the manner, time, and circumstances of putting those laws in execution, must frequently be left to the discretion of the executive magistrate (*e*).   In such case the royal pleasure is usually expressed by a proclamation.

But the people are not to be commanded to observe the laws by any other public mandate than that of his Majesty : and it is an offence punishable by the common law, for a subject to assume and exercise the power of issuing a public proclamation ; even it seems though it respect a private matter wholly

---

(*a*) 31 Hen. 8. c. 8.

(*b*) There was a clause in the statute, that such proclamation should not be prejudicial to any person's inheritances, offices, liberties, goods, chattels, or life ; and see N. Bacon's Hist. 2 part, fol. 215.

(*c*) 1 Ed. 6 c. 12. s. 5.   See 4 Hume Hist. 196, 7.   6 Ibid. 52.

(*d*) See 1 Bla. Com. 270. 5 Bac. Ab. 549, title Prerogative, D. 8.   Instances post. c. 10, as to commerce, &c.   Chitty Law Nat. 259, &c.

(*e*) 1 Bla. Com. 270.

uncon-

unconnected with state affairs (*a*). This is strongly illustrated
by the case of Sir Edward Knightly (*b*), executor of Sir William Spencer, who was fined and imprisoned for making proclamation in certain market towns, publicly and without any
authority, that the creditors of the deceased should come in
by a certain day and prove their debts. However a subject
as a mayor of a town, &c. may by custom, *ratione privilegii,*
possess this right (*c*).

The King may, by proclamation, call or dissolve Parliament, declare war or peace, promulgate blockades, authorize
the Lords of the Admiralty to grant letters of marque and reprisals (*d*); appoint fasts, and days of thanksgiving and humiliation; enjoin the reading of a form of prayer in all churches
and chapels within his Majesty's dominions (*e*); or legitimate
foreign coin, and make it current money of this kingdom, according to the value imposed by such proclamation (*f*). So,
as the King may prohibit any of his subjects from leaving the
kingdom (*g*), a proclamation forbidding this in general for
certain time, by laying an embargo upon all shipping in time
of war, &c. and in case of necessity, is obligatory upon, and
must be attended to by his Majesty's subjects (*h*). But, as the
King cannot restrain trade where the laws do not, a proclamation to lay an embargo in time of peace upon all vessels laden
with wheat (though in the time of a public scarcity), being
contrary to law (*i*), and particularly to the statute 22 Car. 2.
c. 13. the advisers of such a proclamation, and all persons
acting under it, found it necessary to be indemnified by a special Act of Parliament (*k*). So where an act was passed, by
which foreigners were permitted to trade with London, and
Henry the Fourth, by proclamation, prohibited the execution
of the Act, and ordered that it should be suspended, *usque ad
proximum parliamentum,* this was held to be against law (*l*).

(*a*) 12 Co. 75, Bro. Ab. title Proclamation, pl. 1. Crom. Jur. 41. 5
Term R. 442.

(*b*) Bro. Ab. Proclamation, pl. 10.

(*c*) 12 Co. Bro. Ab. Crom. Jur. *ubi
supra.* Wood's Inst. 20.

(*d*) 5 Bac. Ab. 55, title Prerogative,
D. 8.

(*e*) Comp. Incumb. 354.

(*f*) See 3 Inst. 162. 5 Co. 114, b.

Co. Lit. 207. Hal. P. C. 163, 192, 210.
Dav. 21. Post. ch. 10.

(*g*) See ante, ch. 2. s. 3.

(*h*) 4 Mod. 177, 179. See post. ch.
10.

(*i*) See post. ch. 10. 2 Inst. 63.

(*k*) 7 Geo. 3. c. 7.; see 1 Bla. Com.
270, 271. Post. ch. 10.

(*l*) 12 Co. 75.

A pro-

A proclamation for disarming Papists is binding, being only in execution of what the legislature has first ordained; but a proclamation for allowing arms to Papists, or for disarming any Protestant subjects, will not bind; because the first would be to assume a dispensing power, the latter a legislative one, to the vesting of either of which in any single person, the laws of England are absolutely strangers (*a*).

A proclamation is not obligatory or effective, where it restrains his Majesty's subjects in matters on which the laws are silent, though the observance of such matters might be advantageous to the public (*b*); and, therefore, it has been determined that his Majesty cannot, by proclamation or otherwise, prohibit the erection of new buildings in and about London, or forbid the making of starch from wheat (*c*). And the case we have just mentioned, respecting the embargo on wheat, was determined on the same principle.

There are indeed instances to be found of persons who have been sentenced in the Star-chamber upon proclamations against the increase of buildings; and in particular one in Hobart's Reports (*d*), where a person was fined by that Court for building without brick, though upon an old foundation; and it is there laid down that such buildings had an ill effect from the danger of fire, consumption of timber, and difficulty of feeding, cleansing, and governing the city; and that proclamations are just when made *pro bono publico.* But the vague doctrine advanced in this case is so contradictory to every principle and judicial determination on the subject, that we may pass it over with a conviction that it is unfounded, more especially as it was pronounced by an unconstitutional and prejudiced tribunal (*e*).

2dly. *Proclamations, how made.*

A proclamation must be under the great seal, and, if denied, is to be tried by the record thereof (*f*). It is of course necessary that it be published, in order that the people may be ap-

---

(*a*) 1 Bla. Com. 271.

(*b*) 12 East, 296. Chitty L. Nat. 259.

(*c*) 12 Co. R. 74.

(*d*) Armsted's Case, Hob. 251.

(*e*) As to the illegal conduct of the Star-chamber, with respect to Proclamations, see Lord Clarendon's Hist. of Repub. b. 1 and 3.

(*f*) Cro. Car. 180. Rol. R. 172.

prized

prized of its existence, and may be enabled to perform the injunctions it contains.

In the absence of any express authorities on the point, it should seem that if the proclamation be under the great seal, it need not be made by any particular class of individuals, or in particular manner or place : and that it would suffice if it were made by any one, under the King's authority, in the market-place or public streets of each large town. It always appears in the Gazette.

3dly. *Consequences of disobedience to a Proclamation.*

Where the law gives a right, it tacitly affords a remedy for the infraction of it: it would be useless to possess a right unless means were provided to render it efficacious. There can therefore be no doubt that disobedience to a legal proclamation is punishable by fine and imprisonment; and though the matter prohibited be an offence by law before the issuing of the proclamation, yet the disobeying it, when legal, is, of itself, an offence for which the party is liable to be punished (*a*).

CHAP. VIII.

Of the King as the Fountain of Honours, Dignities, Privileges, and Franchises; and the nature of them,

"IT is impossible," says Sir Wm. Blackstone, "that a government can be maintained without a due subordination of rank, that the people may know and distinguish such as are set over them, in order to yield them their due respect and obedience; and also that the officers themselves being encouraged by emulation and the hopes of superiority, may the better discharge their functions : and the law supposes, that no one can be so good a judge of their several merits and services as the King himself who employs them (*b*). The Crown alone there-

(*a*) 12 Co. 74. See Hob. 251.
(*b*) 1 Bla. Com. 271, 396. As to the origin of dignities, 3 Cruise Dig. 171. Seld. Titles of Honour.

fore can create and confer dignities and honours. The King is not only the fountain; but the parent of them. Nor can even an ordinance of the House of Lords confer peerage (*a*).

The titles of nobility now in use are dukes, marquesses, earls, viscounts and barons. These titles were introduced into this country by its Kings at different periods (*b*); and consequently the degrees of nobility are not of equal antiquity. The most exalted in point of rank are not the oldest. Thus the titles of earl and baron, which were the only titles of nobility used before the reign of Edward the 3d (*c*), seem to have existed before the Norman Conquest; at least traces of their existence before that event have been developed; though it appears certain that the exact nature of these titles and the duties which the possessors of them were bound to observe were more clearly ascertained and fixed by the Conqueror (*d*). The dignity of a duke was first conferred on a subject in this country by Edward 3. who created his son the Black Prince, Duke of Cornwall (*e*). This was done with great solemnity in full Parliament at Westminster, March 17, 1337. Many persons were afterwards raised to the like honour. However in the reign of Queen Elizabeth, 1572, the whole order became utterly extinct; but it was revived about 50 years afterwards by her successor, who was remarkably prodigal of honours, in the person of George Villiers, duke of Buckingham. The title of Marquis was afterwards introduced into England by Richard the 2nd (*f*); who conferred it on Robert de Vere, Earl of Oxford: and Henry the 6th introduced that of viscount, by creating John Beaumont a peer, by the name of Viscount Beaumont (*g*).

Various offices and duties were formerly attached to most of these titles (*h*); and there can be no doubt that they were originally territorial, that is, annexed to lands, honours, castles, manors, and the like, the proprietors and possessors of which were (in right of those estates) allowed to be peers of the

(*a*) Wm. Jones, 104.   1 Ld. Raym. 16.

(*b*) See 3 Cruise Dig. 176 to 184.   1 Bla. Com. 396, &c.

(*c*) 1 Ld. Raym. 12.

(*d*) See Cruise Dig. and Bla. Com. *ubi supra.*

(*e*) Hen. Hist. Engl. 8 vol. 135, 8vo. ed.

(*f*) 2 Inst. 5.   Rol. Parl. 3 vol. page 209.

(*g*) Seld. Tit. of Hon. p. 2. ch. 5. s. 31.   2 Inst. 5.

(*h*) See 3 Cruise Dig. 172, 173. 1 Ld. Raym. 12, 13.

realm,

realm, and were summoned to Parliament to do suit and service to their sovereign : and when the land was alienated, the dignity passed with it as appendant. Thus the bishops still sit in the House of Lords in right of succession to certain antient baronies annexed, or supposed to be annexed, to their episcopal lands (*a*): and thus in 11 Hen. 6. the possession of the castle of Arundel was adjudged to confer an earldom on its possessor (*b*). But afterwards when alienations grew to be frequent, the dignity of peerage was confined to the lineage of the party ennobled, and instead of being territorial, became personal. Actual proof of a tenure by barony became no longer necessary to constitute a lord of Parliament; but the record of the writ of summons to him, or his ancestors, was admitted as a sufficient evidence of the tenure (*c*). At the present day therefore, peers may be and frequently are created by the King, though no office or property is annexed to them. It is indeed immaterial whether the place from whence a peer takes his title really existed (*d*).

The *creation* of peers is effected either, 1, by *writ*, or 2, by *patent*, (usually by the latter mode): for those who claim by prescription must suppose either a writ or patent made to their ancestors; though by length of time it is lost (*e*).

1. The *creation* by *writ* (which is more antient than the creation by patent) (*f*), is a summons to attend the house of peers by the style and title of that barony which the King is pleased to confer (*g*): but the writ does not take effect, and the party is not ennobled until he has taken his seat in Parliament by virtue of his Majesty's summons (*h*). Some are of opinion that there must be at least two writs of summons and a sitting in distinct Parliaments to evidence an hereditary barony (*i*).

The King may in his writ of summons restrain the mode in which the dignity is to descend, to males exclusive of fe-

---

(*a*) Glan. l. 7. c. 1.

(*b*) Seld. Tit. of Hon. b. 2. c. 9. s. 5.

(*c*) 1 Bla. Com. 399, 400. 3 Cruis. Dig. 174, 185, &c. 219 Rot. Parl. 4 vol. 441; 5 vol. 148. 1 Dugd. Bar. 322, 323, 361, 363, 365. Collins, 115. 61, 113, 116, 287. Lords' Journ. 1 vol. 516; 2 vol. 345.

(*d*) Ibid. Ld. Raym. 13.

(*e*) 1 Bla. Com. 400. As to a dignity by prescription, see 1 Bulstr. 196.

(*f*) Co. Lit. 16, b.

(*g*) 1 Bla. Com. 400.

(*h*) 12 Co. Rep. 78. Co. Lit. 16, b. 3 Cruise Dig. 194. 1 Bla. Com. 400. The sitting in Parliament must be proved by the records of Parliament. Co. Lit. 16, b. 1 Lord Raym. 14. 3 Cruise Dig. 195.

(*i*) 1 Bla. Com. 400. Whitelock of Parl. c. 114.

males ;

males (*a*); yet it seems clear on principle, and has been accordingly determined, that if no such restraint be made, the dignity created by the sitting in pursuance of the summons, descends to the lineal heirs male and female, of the person first summoned (*b*). Lord Coke, indeed, states that " if one be generally called by writ to the Parliament, he hath a fee-simple in the barony, without any words of inheritance (*c*)," but this is clearly a mistake; for the person summoned has not a fee-simple, but an estate tail general, in the dignity. If he were tenant in fee-simple, the dignity would descend to the heirs general, lineal or collateral, of the person last seised, whereas a dignity of this kind is only inheritable by such of his heirs as are lineally descended from the person first summoned to Parliament, and not to any other of his heirs (*d*)." Lord Coke himself appears to have corrected his mistake in the same page by saying, " and thereby his blood is ennobled to him and his heirs lineal (*e*)." It is frequent to call up the eldest son of a Peer to the House of Lords by writ of summons, in the name of his father's barony: because in that case there is no danger of his children losing the nobility in case he never takes his seat, for they will succeed to their grandfather (*f*). It has been often determined that a writ of summons of this kind to the eldest son of a nobleman, creates a dignity in such son, and renders it hereditary in his blood (*g*). But it must be remembered that where the summons to Parliament is by the title of the father's barony, the son summoned has no other title in the barony than the father has; for the effect of the writ of summons in this case is merely to accelerate and anticipate the son's succession, and therefore in a modern case, where the father's barony was limited by patent to him and the heirs male of his body, and his eldest son was called up to the House of Lords by writ, with the title of this barony, it was held that the writ did not create a fee or a general estate tail, so as to make a female capable of inheriting the title, but

---

(*a*) 1 Inst. 9, b. 7 Co. 33, b.

(*b*) Lords' Journ. 12 vol. 629 ; 15 vol. 442, 458, 552; 17 vol. 81, 91. 3 Cruise Dig. 202. sect. 64. Collins' Append. No. 7.

(*c*) Co. Lit. 16, b.

(*d*) 1 Inst. 15, b. 3 Cruis. Dig. 223,

244, 254.

(*e*) And see 1 Wooddn. 37, note y. 1 Bla. Com. 400, note 6. Christian's ed.

(*f*) 1 Bla. Com. 400.

(*g*) See Lords' Journ. 25 vol. 11, 39, 112, 130. 3 Cruise Dig. 207, &c.

that

that upon the father's death the two titles unite or become one and the same (*a*).

The *creation* by *patent* under the great seal, is a royal grant to a subject of any dignity and degree of peerage (*b*). Antiently a certain corporeal ceremony or investiture was considered necessary to perfect a dignity created by patent, but it has long since been settled otherwise (*c*); and that the creation of the dignity by letters. patent is complete, although the grantee die before he has taken his seat (*d*). The patent must contain apt words to direct the inheritance in the dignity conferred, else it will enure to the grantee for life only, and his descendants will have no claim to it (*e*). We have just seen that the King may restrain the descent of a dignity, and his Majesty may also make either a man or a woman noble for life, but not for years, because then it might go to executors or administrators (*f*). A person may also have a qualified fee in a dignity (*g*), nor can there be any objection to its being limited in remainder (*h*).

Where a person who has a dignity, marries, his wife becomes entitled to the same during her life, unless she afterwards marry a commoner; for as she acquired, so she loses, her dignity by marriage. But where a woman who has a dignity in her own right marries a commoner, she still retains her dignity (*i*), though she communicates no rank or title to her husband (*k*); and it seems that he is not entitled to be tenant by the curtesy of his deceased wife's title, though this latter point is certainly far from being clear (*l*). It is laid down by great authority, that if a Duchess by marriage, marry a Baron, she continues a Duchess still; for all the nobility are *pares,*

(*a*) Case of the claim to the barony of Sydney of Penhurst, disallowed. Dom. Proc. 17 June, 1782; 5 Bro. Cas. in Parl. 509. 3 Cruise Dig. 211, 212.

(*b*) 3 Com. Dig. 215. 1 Bla. Com. 400.

(*c*) 3 Cruise Dig. 218.

(*d*) 1 Inst. 16, b. 12 Rep. 71. Lords' Journ. 21 vol. 682. 3 Cruise Dig. 219. 1 Ld. Raym. 10, 14.

(*e*) Co. Lit. 16, b. 1 Bla. Com. 401. 3 Cruise Dig. 218. See 1 Ld. Raym. 16.

(*f*) 1 Inst. 27, a. 3 Cruise Dig. 222.

It has been supposed that a man may be made noble for the life of another. 52 Hen. 6, 29; by Danby. Co. Lit. 16, b. note 6.

(*g*) 1 Inst. 27, a. 3 Cruise Dig. 222.

(*h*) 3 Cruise Dig. 226. As to entailing a dignity, 3 Cruise 223. s. 101, &c.

(*i*) 1 Inst. 16, b. Dyer, 49. Nobility gained by marriage is to be tried by jury. 6 Co. 53, a. Ld. Raym. 14.

(*k*) Hargr. Co. Lit. 326, b.

(*l*) Co. Lit. 29, b. note 1. 3 Cruise, 227. sect. 106 to 113.

and

and therefore it is no degradation (*a*). The contrary has, however, been asserted (*b*); and on principle the latter opinion seems correct, for though the nobility are, generally speaking, *pares,* yet there are doubtless different gradations of rank among them; nor does there seem any reason why the degradation to the husband's degree should not take place: and Mr. Cruise observes (*c*), that at the coronation of his present Majesty, the Duchess Dowager of Leeds, then the wife of Lord Portmore, claimed to walk as a Duchess, but it was refused.

The King may legally grant to a Scotch Peer a patent of peerage of Great Britain, with all the privileges incident thereto, which was determined by the House of Lords after the unanimous opinion of the Judges to the same effect, in the case of the Duke of Hamilton, who claimed to sit and was accordingly held entitled to sit, as Duke of Brandon (*d*). On the other hand, an English Peer may take a Scotch peerage by descent (*e*).

By the common law, his Majesty might give any nobleman precedence and place in public assemblies, even before others who enjoyed a more antient dignity of the same or a higher degree of nobility (*f*); but this latter prerogative is restrained (*g*) by the statute 31 Hen. 8. c. 10. and 1 W. & M. sess. 1. c. 21. which settle the place and precedence of all the nobility and great officers of state (*h*). The seventh section of the 31 Hen. 8. enacts, " that all Dukes not aforementioned, Marquesses, Earls, Viscounts, and Barons, not having any of the offices therein mentioned, shall sit and be placed after their antienty, as hath been accustomed." As however this statute does not extend to Ireland (*i*), the King still retains this prerogative in that country, without any legal restrictions, except it be by virtue of the 4th article of the 39 and 40 G. 3. c. 67. the Irish Act of Union, which enacts " that as often as three of the Peerages of Ireland, existing at the time of the

---

(*a*) Year Books, 22 Hen. 6, 52. Co. Lit. 16, b. 1 Bla. Com. 401, 2.

(*b*) Owen, 82. Bendl. 37, cited Co. Lit. 16, b. note 6.

(*c*) 3 Vol. Dig. 220.

(*d*) 1 Bla. Com. 97, note. Christian's ed. See Lords' Journ.

(*e*) Ibid. Bla. Com.

(*f*) 4 Inst. 361, 363. Recital, 31 Hen. 8. c. 10.

(*g*) 1 Ld. Raym. 16.

(*h*) As to precedence in general, 4 Inst. 361. Prynn. on 4 Inst. 323. Co. Lit. 16, note 4. 1 Bla. Com. 405, Table of Precedence.

(*i*) See ante, ch. 3.

Union, become extinct, the King may create one Irish Peer; and when the Peers of Ireland are reduced to 100 by extinction or otherwise, exclusive of those who shall hold any Peerage of Great Britain, subsisting at the time of the Union, or created of the United Kingdom since the Union, the King may then create one Peer of Ireland for every Peerage that becomes extinct; or as often as any one of them is created a Peer of the United Kingdom; so that the King may always keep up the number of 100 Irish Peers, over and above those who have an hereditary seat in the House of Lords." The prerogative as to the *number* of *English* Peers does not appear to be thus limited. His Majesty may, by his prerogative, grant rank and precedence to a foreign Prince who intermarries into the royal family, before the greatest officers of state and Peers of the realm, as was done on the marriage of the late Princess Charlotte of Wales (*a*).

We have already considered that the King has an interest in his subjects and a right to command their services, and consequently they cannot with impunity refuse to accept from his Majesty even a mere dignity or honour. So nobility when once acquired cannot be lost or transferred by any other power but that of Parliament, except by death or attainder(*b*). Hence it appears to be now settled, that a Peer cannot be degraded on account of poverty, or for other reasons, even by the King(*c*): and though formerly held otherwise, it is now settled that a dignity or title of honour can neither be effectually aliened by the person in possession of it, though the King's consent is obtained (*d*), or be surrendered to his Majesty(*e*): but in both

(*a*) Tuesday's Gazette, Whitehall, May 8, 1816.—" His royal highness the Prince Regent has been pleased in the name and on the behalf of His Majesty, to declare and ordain that his Serene Highness Leopold George Frederick, Duke of Saxe, Margrave of Meissen, Landgrave of Thuringuen, Prince of Cobourg of Saalfield, Consort of her Royal Highness the Princess Charlotte Augusta, shall take, hold, and enjoy, during the term of his natural life, in all assemblies or meetings whatsoever, the precedence and rank following; that is to say, before the Lord Archbishop of Canterbury, the Lord Chancellor, and all other great officers, and before the Dukes (other than and except the Dukes of the blood royal), and all other Peers of the realm."

(*b*) 7 Rep. 33. 1 Bla. Com. 402.

(*c*) Ibid. 12 Mod. 56. 12 Co. Rep. 107; see 1 Ld. Raym. 16.

(*d*) Lords' Journ. vol. 4, page 150. 3 Cruis. Dig. 230. s. 114. to s. 118.

(*e*) Lords' Journ. 4 vol. 150; 13 vol. 253. Show. Cas. in Parl. 1 ; Lord Purbeck's Case, Coll. 10. 3 Cruise Dig. 232.

these

these cases the heir has a claim, notwithstanding the alienation or surrender.   It is laid down that if a Baron, constituted
by writ of summons, take a grant by patent of the same barony;
this merges or determines his barony by writ (*a*).   But Mr.
Hargrave remarks (*b*), that the doctrine of extinguishing a
barony by writ, by acceptance of a patent barony, seems questionable; for it supposes a right to surrender the barony by
writ, which, as we have seen, cannot be legally done.   Indeed
it was never denied that the barony by writ was not extinguished by the patent barony, in cases where the old barony
by writ was suspended, by the party entitled to it being out of
possession or otherwise (*c*).   And in the case of the barony of
Lord Willoughby de Broke, it was resolved by the House of
Lords, that the grant of a new barony of Willoughby de Broke
to Sir F. Greville, by letters patent, to him and his heirs male,
(he being in possession of the antient barony by writ) did not
destroy such antient barony.   But the same continued and
descended to his sister and sole heir, and so from her to Sir
R. Verney; who was seated in the House of Lords according
to the date of the antient barony.

It is also settled, that if a person possessed of a barony by
writ, which is, consequently, descendible to his heir general, be
created an earl to him and the heirs male of his body, the earldom does not attract the barony, and they are separate and
distinct from each other (*d*), and the barony will descend to the
heir general, although the earldom become extinct (*e*).

Where a dignity or title of honour is descendible to heirs
general, and the person possessed of it dies, leaving only
daughters, or sisters, or coheirs, it falls into abeyance, or rather becomes vested in the Crown, during the continuance of
the coheirship; for a dignity is entire and not divisible, and
no one coheir can in particular sustain a claim to it, and of
course they cannot claim it together (*f*).   But the dignity in
abeyance is not in the power and disposal of the King abso-

(*a*) Hal. M. S.   Co. Lit. 16, b.
note (2).
   (*b*) Ibid.
   (*c*) Ibid. 12 Rep. 1.   Coll. 122,
123.
   (*d*) Collins, 195. 1 Inst. 15, b. note 8.

Lords' Journ. 4 vol. 149.
   (*e*) Collins, 286. 3 Cruise Dig. 237.
tit. Dignity, sect. 131.
   (*f*) Lords' Journ. 3 vol. 535. Collins,
175. 3 Cruise Dig. 245, 248. sect. 149,
&c. Ibid. 266, 7; per C. J. Eyre.

lutely, for his Majesty cannot, by law, extinguish or dispose of it to a mere stranger; and therefore, on the termination of the abeyance, where there remains only one heir, such sole heir becomes entitled to the dignity or title, not as a favour, but as a matter of legal right (a).   It is, however, in the power of the Crown to terminate the abeyance or suspension of the dignity, by nominating any one of the coheirs to it.   Such nomination operates, not as a new creation, but as a revival of the antient dignity, for the nominee becomes entitled to precedence according to the date of the dignity (b).   The abeyance terminates, as a matter of course, whenever there remains, by the death of some of the coheirs, but one heir (c), but the attainder of one of two coheirs does not determine the abeyance (d).

Where the King terminates the abeyance of a dignity in favour of a commoner, he issues a summons to him by the name of the barony which was in abeyance; as, in the cases of Lord Le Despencer, and Lord Botetourt.   But where the person, in whose favour the abeyance is terminated, is already a peer, and has a higher dignity, there the King makes a declaration, under the great seal, confirming the barony to him; and in the case of a female, the abeyance is also terminated by a declaration.   Formerly it was the practice, to confirm the barony to the person, and his or her heirs, but now it is only to the heirs of his or her body (e).

Where an abeyance is terminated by a writ of summons, different opinions have been entertained respecting the extent of the operation of such a writ.   Some eminent persons are said to have held, that where a barony is in abeyance between the descendants of two coheirs, and the King issues his writ of summons to one of the heirs of the body of one of the two coheirs, the abeyance is thereby terminated, not only as to the person summoned, and the heirs of his or her body, but also as to all the heirs of the body of such original coheir; but the

---

(a) 3 Cruise Dig. 254, 5, &c.   See Skin. R. 432, 437.   Dugd. Bar. 2 vol. 363.   Collins, 412; 322.   Lords' Journ. 15 vol. 634, 643, 671; 21 vol. 266, 339.

(b) 3 Cruise Dig. 249.   Lords' Journ. 30 vol. 403, 561, 572; 2 vol. 347; per C. J. Eyre.   3 Cruise Dig. 267, 8.

(c) 3 Cruise, 254.

(d) Stapleton's Case, Printed Cases, Dom. Proc. 1794, 5; cited 3 Cruise Dig. 261. s. 172; 1 ed.

(e) 3 Cruise Dig. 250, 252.

better opinion seems to be, that the effect of a writ of summons in a case of this kind, is only to terminate the abeyance as to the person summoned, and the heirs of his or her body; and that, upon failure of heirs of the body of the person so summoned, the barony will again fall into abeyance, between the remaining heirs of the body of the original coheir, one of whose heirs was so summoned, if any, and the heirs of the body of the other coheir (*a*).

This latter opinion is founded upon a principle of law, that possession does not affect the descent of a dignity, and that a writ of summons to Parliament by an antient title, (as the summons of the eldest son of a peer in the lifetime of his father, by the name of an antient barony then vested in the father,) will not operate, so as to give any title by descent, collateral or lineal, different from the course of descent of the antient barony, and that he who claims a dignity must make himself heir to the person on whom the dignity was originally conferred, not to the person who last enjoyed it (*b*).

Dignities are not within the statute of limitations, and may, consequently, be claimed at any distance of time; and there are instances of claims being recognized after the dignities had been dormant for some centuries (*c*).

If a peer be disturbed in his dignity, the regular course, says Lord Holt (*d*), is to petition the King, and the King indorses it, and sends it into the Chancery or the House of Peers, for the Lords have no power to judge of peerage, unless it be given to them by the King (*e*).

Such persons as are not noble, are, by intendment of law, among the *Commons* (*f*); but even these latter are, by law, divided into several degrees (*g*). We have here only to consider such as are constituted by the royal authority. To borrow Sir Wm. Blackstone's observations (*h*) on this subject, " The first personal dignity after the nobility is a Knight of the Order of

---

(*a*) 3 Cruise Dig. 253.

(*b*) Ibid.

(*c*) Skin. R. 437. Collins, 323. 11 Rep. 1. 4 Inst. 335. 2 Bro. Parl. Cas. 167, 8. 3 Cruise Dig. 274.

(*d*) 1 Ld. Raym. 16.

(*e*) 11 Co. 1. Delaware's Case. W. Jon. 96.

(*f*) Co. Lit. 16, b.

(*g*) 1 Bla. Com. 403.

(*h*) Ibid. 403, 4.

St. George or of the Garter, first instituted by Edward the Third, A. D. 1344 (*a*).   Next (but not till after certain *official* dignities, as Privy Counsellors, the Chancellors of the Exchequer and Duchy of Lancaster. the Chief Justice of the King's Bench, the Master of the Rolls, and the other English Judges,) follows a Knight Banneret, who indeed, by statutes 5 Rich. 2. st. 2. c. 4. and 14 Rich. 2. c. 11. is ranked next after Barons, and his precedence before the younger sons of Viscounts was confirmed to him by order of James the First, in the tenth year of his reign (*b*).   But, in order to entitle himself to this rank, he must have been created by the King in person, in the field, under the royal banners in time of war (*c*), else he ranks after Baronets, who are the next order; which title is a dignity of inheritance, created by letters patent, and usually descendible to the issue male.   It was first instituted by James I. A. D. 1611, in order to raise a competent sum for the reduction of the province of Ulster in Ireland (*d*); for which reason all baronets have the arms of Ulster superadded to their family coat (*e*).   Next follow the Knights of the Bath, an order instituted by Henry 4. and revived by George 1.   They are so called from the ceremony of bathing, the night before their creation.   The last of these inferior nobility are Knights Bachelors, the most antient, though the lowest order of knighthood, amongst us ; for we have an instance (*f*) of King Alfred's conferring this order on his son Athelstan.   The custom of the antient Germans was to give their young men a shield and a lance in the great council; this was equivalent to the *toga virilis* of the Romans.   Before this they were not permitted to bear arms, but were accounted as part of the father's household; after it, as part of the community.   Hence some derive the usage of knighting, which has prevailed all over the western world, since its reduction by colonies from those northern heroes.   Knights are called in Latin *equites aurati: aurati*, from the gilt spurs they wore; and *equites*, because they always served on horseback; for it is observable

(*a*) Seld. tit. of Hon. 2, 5, 41.

(*b*) Ibid. 2, 11, 3.

(*c*) 4 Inst. 6.

(*d*) One hundred gentlemen advanced each one thousand pounds for which this title was conferred upon them, 2 Rep. 185.

(*e*) The arms of Ulster are, a hand gules, or a bloody hand in a field argent.

(*f*) Will. Malmsb. lib. 2.

that

that almost all nations call their knights by some appellation derived from a horse. They are also called in our law *milites*, because they formed a part of the royal army, in virtue of their feudal tenures: one condition of which was, that every one who held a knight's fee immediately under the Crown (which in Edw. 2d's time amounted to 20*l. per annum*) was obliged to be knighted, and attend the King in his wars, or to pay a fine for his non-compliance. The exertion of this prerogative as an expedient to raise money in the reign of Charles 1. gave great offence, though warranted by law and the recent example of Queen Elizabeth; but it was by the statute 16 Car. 1. c. 16. abolished, and this kind of knighthood has since that time fallen into great disregard."

The King possesses also the power of creating Esquires, and therefore if the King by his commission, constituting a subject a magistrate or military officer, &c. term him an Esquire, he *ipso facto* becomes such, and his eldest son is qualified to kill game, &c. (*a*). To the Crown belongs also the prerogative of raising practitioners in the courts of justice to a superior eminence, by constituting them serjeants, &c. or by granting letters patent of precedence to such barristers as his Majesty thinks proper to honour with that mark of distinction, whereby they are entitled to such rank and pre-audience as are assigned in their respective patents (*b*).

As the fountain of *privilege* the King possesses various powers. He may remove personal disabilities by making an alien a denizen(*c*); by enabling a bastard to be a priest, &c.(*d*). And his Majesty may in various instances exempt his subjects from common law liabilities; as for instance, from liability to serve in public employments, offices, &c. (*e*), to be arrested in civil actions, &c. (*f*).

On similar principles is founded the right of the Crown to hold and confer peculiar lucrative powers and franchises. The *jura coronæ* or rights of the Crown, so long as they are attached to the King, are called prerogatives; but when such prerogatives are delegated to a subject, they acquire the appellation

(*a*) See 1 T. R. 44. Chitty, G. L. 55,'6.

(*b*) 3 Bla. Com. 27.

(*c*) Ante, ch. 3.

(*d*) Ante, ch. 5. But now a bastard may be a priest without, 1 Bla. Com. 458, 9.

(*e*) Ante, c. 2 s. 3. And as to the King's power to enable a town to send representatives to Parliament, see ante, ch. 6.

(*f*) See Index, tit. Protection.

of

of franchise; for all franchises are derived from the King (a).
A franchise is defined (b) to be a royal privilege or branch of
the royal prerogative subsisting in the hands of a subject, by
grant from the King. And formerly, grants of royal franchises were so common, that in the Parliament which was
held 21 Edw. 3. (c), there is a petition from the commons to
the King, stating that franchises had been so largely granted
in times past, that almost all the land was enfranchised to the
great *averisement* and *estenysment* of the common law, and in
great oppression of the people; and praying the King to
restrain such grants for the time to come; to which his Majesty answered, that the franchises which should be granted
in future, should be made by good advisement.

In its more extensive sense the term franchise signifies every
description of political right which a freeman may enjoy and
exercise.

Being derived from the Crown, these franchises can in general only arise. and be claimed by royal grant or by prescription which supposes it (d). They may be vested either in natural persons or bodies politic, in one man or in many, but the
same identical franchise that has been before granted to one
cannot be granted to another, for that would prejudice the former grant (e). And it is a clear principle that the King cannot by his mere prerogative diminish or destroy immunities
once conferred and vested in a subject by royal grant.

Franchises are extremely numerous and are of various kinds.
The principal of them will be here mentioned. They are
1. counties palatine, cinque ports, &c. and counties corporate:
2. corporations: 3. game franchises, and herein of the
King's prerogative as to game, and of forests: 4. free chases:
5. parks: 6. free warrens: 7. fisheries and fish: 8. mines:
9. fairs and markets: 10. waifs: 11. wrecks: 12. estrays:
13. treasure trove, and 14. deodands.

1. The *counties palatine,* Chester, Durham and Lancaster,
the royal franchise of Ely, the courts of the cinque ports,

(a) 2 Inst. 281 ; 496. 4 Com. Dig.
244.

(b) Finch, Law, 164. 3 Cruise Dig.
278, 1st ed.

(c) 21 Edw. 3. Rot. Parl. vol. 2. p. 16.

(d) Bract. l. 2. c. 24. f. 55, 56. 2
Bla. Com. 37.

(e) Ibid. 2 Rol. Ab. 191. Keilw.
196.

the Stannary courts, and various courts in cities, boroughs, &c. throughout the kingdom, possessing exclusive and some of them peculiar privileges, may be ranked among royal franchises, as they in general arose from the favor of the Crown to those particular districts wherein we find them erected (*a*).

A court leet is a court of record, having the same jurisdiction within some particular precinct, which the sheriff's torn hath in the county. This Court is not necessarily appendant to a manor, like a court baron, but is derived from the sheriff's torn; being a grant from the King to certain lords, for the ease cf their tenants, and resiants within their manors, that they may administer justice to them in their manors (*b*).

To every court leet is annexed the view of frankpledge; *visus frankplegii,* which means the examination or survey of the frankpledges of which every man, not particularly privileged, was antiently obliged to have nine, who were bound that he should always be forthcoming to answer any complaint.

There are also counties corporate; which are certain cities and towns, some with more, some with less territory annexed to them; to which out of special grace and favour, the Kings of England have granted the privilege to be counties of themselves, and not to be comprized in any other county; but to be governed by their own sheriffs and other magistrates, so that no officers of the county at large have any power to intermeddle therein (*c*). There is no doubt that the Crown possesses the power of granting to any city to have justices of their own within themselves, and may exclude by express words the county justices from intermeddling in the ordinary business of a justice of the peace (*d*).

2. *Corporations.*—Corporations were originally formed for the purpose of promoting the welfare and interests of commerce and the arts; and for the better government of the sub-

---

(*a*) See Bae. Ab. Courts Palatinate, &c. 1 Bla. Com. 116, 7. 3 Ibid. 78, &c. Higher powers formerly exercised by Lords Palatine vested in the Crown, 27 H. 8. c. 24. See Skinn. 604.

(*b*) 2 Inst. 71. 4 Inst. c. 54, 3 Burr. Rep. 1859.

(*c*) 1 Bla. Com. 120. That the King may enable a town, &c. to choose its own sheriff. Vin. Ab. Prerog. M. b. 18 vol. 87.

(*d*) 2 Stra. 1154. 3 T. R. 279. post. 4 T. R. 456.

ject. A consolidation of interests tends to their advantage and
preservation; and ensures a degree of regularity, unanimity,
and strength, which cannot be found in a disjointed and unconnected body. The peculiar properties of a corporation;
its political and indivisible character; and its capability of
transmitting its rights and immunities to its successors to the
remotest period, by operation of law and without any respect
to the individual and personal capacities of its members; are
incompatible with the notion of an unconnected assembly of
persons; without the means of expressing their will, or a hand
exclusively appointed to protect their united rights. Political
governments and sovereign power originated from a common
sense that their existence was necessary on these principles:
and a subdivision of these artificial or political constitutions
naturally and imperceptibly followed.

A corporation may be defined to be a collection of many
individuals, united into one body, under a special denomination, having perpetual succession under an artificial form, and
vested by the policy of the law, with the capacity of acting in
several respects as an individual, particularly of taking and
granting property, of contracting obligations, and of suing and
being sued, of enjoying privileges and immunities in common,
and of exercising a variety of political rights, more or less extensive, according to the design of its institution or the powers
conferred upon it, either at the time of its creation or at any
subsequent period of its existence (a).

Single persons cannot partake of many of the properties of a
corporation, but as they may partake of a few, as for instance,
the capacity of having perpetual succession; our law has divided corporations into two classes, corporations aggregate and
corporations sole (b). Corporations aggregate consist (c) of
many persons united together into one society, and are kept up
by a perpetual succession of members, so as to continue for
ever; of which kind are the mayor and commonalty of a city,
the head and fellows of a college, the dean and chapter of a
cathedral church. Corporations sole consist of one person
only and his successors, in some particular station, who are
incorporated by law, in order to give them some legal capa-

(a) 1 Kyd. 13.   (c) 1 Bla. Com. 469.
(b) Co. Lit. 250. a.

cities

cities and advantages, particularly that of perpetuity, which in their natural persons they could not have had. In this sense the King is a sole corporation (a); so is a bishop; so are some deans and prebendaries, distinct from their several chapters; and so is every parson and vicar.

Corporations, whether sole or aggregate, are also divided into ecclesiastical and lay. The former are composed of spiritual persons, and have for their object the support of religion and the church. The latter are instituted for temporal purposes, and are either civil or eleemosynary. Thus the King is a civil corporation, that the power, the splendour, and the possessions of the Crown may be transmitted to the successor without any *interregnum.* Other civil corporations are established for the maintenance and regulation of some particular object of public policy: such as the corporation of the Trinity House for regulating navigation (b); the Bank and the different Insurance Companies in London. Others for the regulation of trade, manufactures, and commerce: such as the East India Company, and the Companies of Trades in London and other towns. Others for the advancement of science in general or some particular branches of it: such are the College of Physicians and the Company of Surgeons in London, for the improvement of the medical science; the Royal Society for the advancement of natural knowledge; the Society of Antiquarians for promoting the study of antiquities; and the Royal Academy of Arts for cultivating painting and sculpture Some are also instituted for the purpose of local government: as Mayor and Commonalty, Bailiffs and Burgesses of any particular town or district. And some corporations of this kind are not only for local government, but for particular purposes: as Churchwardens for the conservation of the parish goods, &c.; and the Universities are civil corporations (c). Eleemosynary corporations are such as are constituted for the perpetual distribution of the free alms or bounty of the founder of them, to such persons as he has directed; as Hospitals, Colleges, &c. (d).

The exclusive right of the Crown to institute corporations, and the necessity for its express or implied consent to their

---

(a) Co. Lit. 43.　　　　　　(c) 3 Burr. 1656.
(b) Sawyer's Arg. *Quo War.* 9.　　(d) 1 Bla. Com. 471.

existence,

existence is undoubted; and was, so far back as the reign of Edward 3., allowed to have been long settled as clear law (*a*). There are indeed certain corporations which exist solely by force of the common law. Of this sort are the King himself, all bishops, parsons, vicars, churchwardens, and some others, who *virtute officii* are corporations (*b*); the law having affixed to their respective capacities from time immemorial, without any express power from the Crown, certain properties of a corporation. Even in corporations of this description, the King's consent is to be implied, at least as a member of the community (*c*).

A corporation by prescription, is a corporation which has existed from time immemorial, and of which it is impossible to shew the commencement, by any particular charter: as the city of London and many others (*d*). In this case the King's original consent is presumed, and it is supposed that the charter is lost or destroyed, by time or accident.

The King's consent to the formation of a corporation is expressly given in the case of his granting a charter. This need not be done by any particular form of words, the usual expressions are " *creamus, erigimus, fundamus, incorporamus;*" but any equivalent words, as *constituimus,* &c. will suffice (*e*). A grant to a set of men that they may have " *Gildam mercatoriam,*" a mercantile meeting or assembly, is sufficient to incorporate them (*f*). So a gift of land from the King to the burgesses, citizens or commonalty, of such a place, was conceived to be sufficient to incorporate them under such collective name (*g*). And if the King grant to the men of Dale that they may elect a Mayor every year, and that they may plead and be impleaded by the name of Mayor and Commonalty; this seems to be sufficient to incorporate them (*h*). And there are many instances of grants by charter to the inhabitants of a town, " that their town shall be a free borough," and that they shall enjoy various privileges and exemptions, without any

---

(*a*) Bract. lib. 2. c. 24. f. 55, 6. 49 Edw. 3; 3, 4. 49 Ass. p. 8. Bro. Ab. tit. Corpor. 15, Prescription, 15. 10 Co. 33, b. 1 Rol. 512.

(*b*) 1 Bla. Com. 472. 1 Kyd. 39, 40.

(*c*) 1 Kyd. 41.

(*d*) 2 Inst. 330.

(*e*) 2 Rol. Ab. 197. 10 Co. 30. Styles, 198.

(*f*) Ibid. 1 Rol. Ab. 513.

(*g*) 7 Edw. 4. 14 Bro. Corpor. 54.

(*h*) 21 Edw. 4. 56. Bro. Corpor. 65 ; but 21 Edw. 4, 57, b. seems *contra*.

direct

direct clause of incorporation; and yet by virtue of such charter, such towns have been uniformly considered as incorporated(*a*). Nor is it necessary that the charter should expressly confer those powers, without which a collective body of men cannot be a corporation, such as the power of suing and being sued, and to take and grant property; though such powers are in general expressly given (*b*). A grant of incorporation to the citizens or burgesses of such a city or borough, especially an old grant, is good, without the words " their successors (*c*)."

A grant of lands to the men or inhabitants of Dale, *hæredibus et successoribus suis*, rendering rent, makes them a corporation as to these lands (*d*): and if the King grant *hominibus de Islington* to be discharged of toll, this is a good corporation ⌣ this intent but not to purchase (*e*). If the words of the charter be doubtful, they may it seems be explained by contemporaneous usage (*f*): and this, added to the wording of a charter in various respects, may establish a corporation to be a prescriptive corporation, though there be a recent charter containing words of creation only, without words of confirmation (*g*).

But though it is the province of the Crown to constitute corporations, it cannot compel any body to accept its charter. The benefit *primâ facie* conferred by a grant of incorporation, may be counterbalanced by some conditions with which it is accompanied: and it has therefore become an established rule that the grant must be accepted by the voluntary consent of a majority of those men whom it is intended to incorporate, otherwise the grant will be void (*h*). A patent procured by some few persons only shall not bind the rest; nor can a town be incorporated without the consent of the major part of the inhabitants (*i*); nor even then is it compulsory on any one to become a member (*k*). If however a smaller number than a majority of an indefinite part of an existing corporation be sufficient to constitute a lawful assembly for doing corporate

(*a*) Vid. Firm. Burg. c. II. and Madox, Hist. of Exch. 402, the Charter of Dunwich.

(*b*) Vid. 10 Co. 29, b.

(*c*) Brownl. and Goulds. 2nd part, 292.

(*d*) 21, 24. 56, 7 Edw. 4, 3. 2 Hen. 7, 13. Cro. El. 35.

(*e*) 21 Edw. 4, 59.

(*f*) 3 T. R. 279; 288, note. 4 T. R. 421. 4 East, 338. 5 Taunton, 752. See Peak, E. 4th ed. 131.

(*g*) 14 East, 348.

(*h*) Rol. R. 226.

(*i*) 2 Brownl. 100.

(*k*) 1 T. R. 588.

acts, it seems the same number may effectually accept a new charter (*a*). No particular ceremony is necessary to constitute an acceptance of the charter by the grantees: their non objecting for even a short period of time seems to determine their election; and to render the acceptance irrevocable (*b*). And this is a matter to be tried by a jury (*c*).

It is admitted on all hands, that the charter by which a body is incorporated must be accepted, as it is offered: part of its provisions cannot be rejected, and part accepted; and a partial acceptance is, in such case, an acceptance *in toto* (*d*). But there appears to be some doubt whether, if a new charter be given to a corporation already in being, and acting under a former charter, or (which is equivalent thereto) prescriptive usage, such corporation already existing is at liberty to accept the new charter *pro tanto* only, rejecting the remainder. That they may reject the new charter *in toto*, is indubitable; because the King cannot take away, abridge, or alter any liberties or privileges granted by him or his predecessors, without the consent of the individuals holding them (*e*). And in the case of " The King *v.* The Vice-Chancellor, &c. of Cambridge (*f*)," Lord Mansfield said, that " an old corporation is not obliged to accept a new charter *in toto*, and to receive either all or more of it; and that they may act partly under it and partly under their old charter or prescription." That however was a case in which the question rather was as to the acceptance of one of several unconnected and independent statutes or charters to which perhaps there may be no objection. But to hold that a corporation is at liberty to accept parts only of entire and dependent provisions offered them by a charter, would be to permit them, and not the King, to make it. By rejecting part of a consecutive provision, an alteration may be effected in the grant which renders it wholly different from that which the King meant to confer. This distinction seems to have been taken by Mr. J. Buller, in " The King *v.* Amery (*g*)," in which he observed, " that the averment in the plea before him

(*a*) 1 T. R. 588.

(*b*) 4 Mod. 269. 1 Salk. 167. 1 Ld. Raym. 29, 32. 1 T. R. 587. 3 Ibid. 189.

(*c*) Ibid.

(*d*) 3 Burr. 1656.

(*e*) See preceding notes, 1 Kyd. 67.

(*f*) 3 Burr. 1656.

(*g*) 1 Term Rep. 589.

proceeded

proceeded on a mistake, by supposing that a charter may be
accepted in part, and rejected as to the rest. The only instance in which I have ever heard it contended that a charter
could be accepted in part only is, *where the King has granted
two distinct things*, both for the benefit of the grantees : there
I know that some have thought that the grantees may take one
and reject the other. However that may be, it cannot extend
to this case. This corporation must either have accepted *in
toto*, or not at all; if they could have accepted a part only of
the charter, they would have been a corporation created by
themselves, and not by the King. If a charter directed that
the corporation should consist of a mayor, aldermen, and
twenty-four common councilmen, they could not accept the
charter for the mayor and aldermen only, omitting the common councilmen."

The charter should give the corporation a corporate name(*a*):
but it may have a name by implication; as if the King should
incorporate the inhabitants of Dale with power to chuse a
mayor annually, though no name be given, yet it is a good
corporation by the name of mayor and commonalty (*b*) And
corporations may change their names, as they frequently do in
new charters, and they still retain their former rights and privileges (*c*). As it is the King's charter that creates corporations, so his Majesty may by his charter mould and frame them
in the first instance as he thinks fit; and may by the consent
of the corporation afterwards remove or grant additional rules
for their governance, consistently with principles of law (*d*).
In ecclesiastical and eleemosynary foundations, the King or
the founder may give them rules, laws, statutes, and ordinances, which they are bound to observe : but corporations
merely lay, constituted for civil purposes, are subject to no
particular statutes ; but to the common law, and to their own
by-laws, not contrary to the laws of the realm (*e*). And in
such case, without express words the various incidents to
corporations apply (*f*). The constitution of a corporation as
settled by Act of Parliament cannot be varied by the acceptance
of any charter inconsistent with it (*g*). And when it is intended

(*a*) 1 Bla. Com. 474, 5. 10 Rep. 28.   (*e*) Ld. Raym. 8.
(*b*) 1 Salk. 191.   (*f*) See 1 Bla. Com. 475. See Bac.
(*c*) 4 Co. 87. Ld. Raym. 1239.   Abr. Corporations, D.
(*d*) 3 Mod. 13.   (*g*) 6 T. R. 268.

that

that a corporation should be established, vested with powers
or privileges which by the principles of the common law cannot be granted by the King's charter, then recourse must be
had to the aid of an Act of Parliament; as if it be intended
to grant the power of imprisonment, as in the case of the College of Physicians ; or, to confer an exclusive right of trading,
as in the case of the East India Company; or when a court
is erected with a power to proceed in a manner different from
the common law, which is the case of the Vice-Chancellor's
Court in the two Universities (*a*).   But it has been well observed (*b*), that most of those statutes which are usually cited
as having created corporations, either confirm such as have
been previously created by the King; as in the case of the
College of Physicians, which was erected by charter in the
tenth year of Henry the 8th., and afterwards confirmed in Parliament by an Act of the 14th and 15th of the same King (*c*) ;
or they permit the King to erect a corporation *in futuro,*
with such and such powers, as in the case of the Bank of
England (*d*), and the Society of the British Fishery (*e*); so that
the immediate creative act is usually performed by the King
alone, in virtue of his royal prerogative.

Though, as before observed (*f*), the Crown may grant to
any city the privilege of having Justices of their own within
themselves; yet a charter granting jurisdiction to Borough
Magistrates over a district not within the Borough, does not
exclude the County Justices without express words.   And
though such charter contain words of reference to former
charters, in which exclusive jurisdiction is given to the
Borough Justices within the Borough, and add that they
shall have jurisdiction within the new district in *tam amplis
modo et formâ,* &c.; yet if there be in that latter charter a
saving clause of the rights of the Crown, and of all other
persons, the Borough Magistrates have only a concurrent
jurisdiction with the County Justices (*g*).

It is now settled that the King may not only grant to a
subject a power and licence to erect a particular specified

(*a*) Vid. Cro. Car. 73, 87, 88. Jenk.
97, 117.

(*b*) 1 Bla. Com. 473.

(*c*) 14 and 15 Hen. 8. c. 5.   Vid. 8.
Co. 114.

(*d*) 5 and 6 Wm. and M. c. 20.

(*e*) 23 Geo. 2. c. 4.

(*f*) Ante, 120. 2 Stra. 1154.

(*g*) 3 T. R. 279, and 4 Ibid. 456.

corporation; but may give a general power by charter to erect a corporation indefinitely (a). The Chancellor of the University of Oxford has by charter such a right, and has actually often exercised it in the erection of several matriculated companies now subsisting, of tradesmen subservient to the students. His power is most frequently exercised in the case of eleemosynary or charitable corporations, when a licence is granted to a subject to erect such a corporation and to endow it with possessions or revenues, in which case the donor is called the founder. With respect to the mode of erecting such corporations, where there is a subject founder, this difference is to be observed: either the King expresses the words of the incorporation, designs the place, appoints the number, and gives them a constitution and a name by his charter, so that the corporation is complete; and then the founder or donor has nothing more to do than to make dotation, without any instrument comprehending any words of incorporation, for with that in such a case, the common person, who is the founder, has nothing to do; or the King, by his charter, may reserve as well the nomination of the persons, as the name and constitution of the corporation, to the person who is to be the founder; then the latter must name the persons, and declare by what name they shall be incorporated, and what powers they shall exercise; and when he has done this, then they are incorporated by virtue of the King's letters patent, and not by the common person, for he is but an instrument, and it is the King who makes the corporation in such case, in the same manner as if all had been comprehended in the letters patent themselves, according to the maxim that "*qui per alium facit, per se ipsum facere videtur* (b)."

The incorporation ought in fact to precede the dotation, because, before the incorporation, there is no capacity to take as a corporation (c); but it is not necessary that in the letters patent the licence to incorporate and the licence to endow, should be in distinct independent clauses, or that the licence to incorporate should, in the order of expression, precede that

(a) Bro. Ab. tit. Prerog. 53. Vin. Ab. Prerog. 88. pl. 16. 1 Bla. Com. 474.

(b) 38 Edw. 3. 14, b. 22 Edw. 4,

Grant, 30. 2 Hen. 7, 13, a, b. 20 Hen. 7, 7. cited 10 Co. 33, b. 1 Kyd. 51, 2.

(c) Vid. 10 Co. 26, b.

to endow (*a*). Neither is it necessary that the corporation should be actually in existence at the time of the licence to grant to it: it is sufficient that it exist at the time of the grant made (*b*). Nor need all the persons who are to be constituent members of the corporation be named in the letters patent; it is sufficient to give a power of future nomination or election (*c*).

On the principle that the King's consent is necessary to the formation of a society, it is clear that the general corporation of a town, &c. cannot without the King's express authority, and even by subdivisions, &c. create a subordinate and dependent, or independent, corporate body (*d*). And in " the King *v.* the Coopers' Company, Newcastle (*e*)," Lord Kenyon said, " there is a case in Salkeld (*f*) where it is said that a corporation may make a fraternity; but no notice is taken of that point in the other Reports (*g*) of that case. I cannot conceive that they have such a power; it can only be effected by the legislature or by the Crown." But there can, it seems, be no objection to a corporation or any number of persons, forming a mere club or assembly for the purposes of conviviality, &c. though such club or assembly cannot act as a corporation (*h*).

The Parliament, by its absolute and transcendent authority, may perform this or any other act whatsoever: and actually did perform it to a great extent by statute 39 Eliz. c. 5. which incorporated all Hospitals and Houses of Correction, founded by charitable persons, without further trouble; and the same has been done in other cases of charitable foundations. But otherwise it has not formerly been usual thus to intrench upon the prerogative of the Crown, and the King may prevent it when he pleases. And in the particular instance before mentioned, it was done, as Sir Edward Coke observes (*i*), to avoid the charges of incorporation and licences of mortmain in small benefactions, which in his days were grown so great, that they discouraged many men from undertaking these pious and charitable works (*k*).

(*a*) 2 Hen. 7. 13, a, b. cited 10 Co. 27, 8.

(*b*) Ibid. 1 Kyd. 54.

(*c*) 10 Co. 8, b. 31, a.

(*d*) See 49 Ass. p. 8. 49 E. 3, 3, 4. Bro. Corpor. 15, 45 ; Prescription, 15. 10 Co. 33, b. 1 Rol. 512. 1 Sid. 291.

2 Keb. 53.

(*e*) 7 T. R. 548.

(*f*) See page 193. 1 Kyd. 47, &c.

(*g*) See 6 Mod. 128. Holt. R. 433.

(*h*) See Comb. 372, 373.

(*i*) 2 Inst. 722.

(*k*) 1 Bla. Com. 474. 1 Kyd. 57, &c.

The

The powers of the Crown as to visiting of corporations also demand attention. A visitor is a person appointed by law to inspect the proceedings of corporations, and to secure their adherence to the purposes of their institution, and to settle in general, without appeal from his decision(*a*), any disputes respecting their management. The founder of a corporation is naturally its visitor. In the case of eleemosynary or charitable institutions, a private person is in general the visitor as founder. The founder of all corporations in the strictest and original sense is the King alone, for he only can incorporate a society; and in civil incorporations, such as mayor and commonalty, &c. where there are no possessions or endowments given to the body, there is no other founder but the King; but in eleemosynary foundations, such as colleges and hospitals, where there is an endowment of lands, the law distinguishes and makes two species of foundation; the one *fundatio incipiens*, or the incorporation, in which sense the King is the general founder of all colleges and hospitals; the other *fundatio perficiens*, or the dotation of it, in which sense the first gift of the revenues is the foundation, and he who gives them is in law the founder, and it is in this last sense that we generally call a man the founder of a college or hospital (*b*). It is said by Sir Edward Coke, that the foundership is so inseparably incident to the blood of the founder, that it cannot be granted over, and that if a subject founder should grant his foundership to the King by deed inrolled, it would be a void grant (*c*). But here the King has his prerogative: for if the King and a private man join in endowing an eleemosynary foundation, the King alone shall be the founder of it (*d*). And in general the King being the sole founder of all civil corporations, and the endower the perficient founder of all eleemosynary ones, the right of visitation of the former results, according to the rule laid down, to the King; and of the latter to the patron or endower. Where the founder of a college or eleemosynary corporation has appointed no special visitor, if his heirs become extinct, or if they cannot be found, the right of visitation de-

---

(*a*) 1 Burr. 200.

(*b*) 10 Rep. 33. Where no express visitor of a royal endowment is appointed, the Crown is visitor by implication, 2 P. W. 325.

(*c*) 11 Co. 77, a. 78, a.

(*d*) 50 Ass. 6. 1 Rol. 514. 9 Co. 129, b. 2 Inst. 68, cites 44 Edw. 3. 24, 25.

volves to the King, to be exercised by the Chancellor in the same manner as where the King himself is the founder, subject to the regulations of the founder, &c. (*a*).

The King being thus constituted, by the law, visitor of all civil corporations, the law has also appointed the place wherein he shall exercise this jurisdiction, which is the Court of King's Bench; where, and where only, all misbehaviours of this kind of corporations are inquired into and redressed, and all controversies decided.   And this is the meaning of our lawyers, when they say that these civil corporations are liable to no visitation; that is, that the law having, by immemorial usage, appointed them to be visited and inspected by the King, their founder, in his Majesty's Court of King's Bench, according to the rules of the common law, they ought not to be visited elsewhere, or by any other authority (*b*).   And this is so strictly true, that though the King, by his letters patent, had subjected the College of Physicians to the visitation of four very respectable persons, the Lord Chancellor, the two Chief Justices, and the Chief Baron; though the College had accepted this charter with all possible marks of acquiescence, and had acted under it for near a century, yet, in 1753, the authority of this provision coming in dispute, on an appeal preferred to these supposed visitors, they directed the legality of their own appointment to be argued; and as this College was merely a civil and not an eleemosynary foundation, they at length determined, upon several days' solemn debate, that they had no jurisdiction as visitors, and remitted the appellant (if aggrieved) to his regular remedy in his Majesty's Court of King's Bench (*c*).

A licence from the King is necessary to enable a corporation to purchase and hold lands in mortmain (*d*).

(*a*) 4 T. R. 233. 2 Ves. Jun. 609.

(*b*) 1 Bla. Com. 481. This notion is perhaps too refined. The Court of King's Bench (it may be said), from its general superintendent authority where other jurisdictions are deficient, has power to regulate all corporations where no special visitor is appointed. But not in the light of visitor: for as its judgments are liable to be reversed by writs of error, it may be thought to want one of the essential marks of visitorial power. Ib. note (*c*).

(*c*) 1 Bla. Com. 481, 2.

(*d*) Co. Lit. 9. 7 & 8 Wm. 3. c. 3. 1 Bla. Com. 479. 2 Id. 268, &c. 1 Wooddn. 494. A writ of *ad quod damnum* is not usual on granting a licence to alienate in mortmain. Co. Lit. 100, b.; Hargr. n.

It

It is a principle of law, that the King is bound by his own and his ancestors' grants, and cannot therefore, by his mere prerogative, take away vested immunities and privileges (*a*). But a corporation may be dissolved, by surrendering its franchises into the hands of the King (*b*), though legal dissolution is not occasioned thereby, and the charter operates till the surrender be inrolled, because the King can take nothing but by matter of record, and a deed is not of record without enrolment (*c*).

A corporation may also be so far dissolved by the loss of one or more of its integral parts, or by the deficiency of the major part of members necessarily constituting an integral part of the corporation, and which the remainder are not enabled to supply (*d*), as to be incapable of renewing itself, so that the Crown may grant a new charter to the inhabitants of the same place. And yet if the Crown think proper, it may revive and continue the old corporation, by a new grant to the remaining members of the old, dissolved, and dormant corporation, together with the other inhabitants of the place (*e*).

A corporation may be dissolved by misuser or abuser (*f*). But by the statute 11 Geo. 1. c. 4. the neglect to chuse officers on the day appointed by charter or usage, shall not create a dissolution of the corporation.

When a corporation has but an integral part, or is so far reduced, that it cannot continue the succession, it is dissolved without any legal proceeding. " A *scire facias* is proper," says Mr. Justice Ashhurst, " where there is a legal existing body capable of acting, but who have been guilty of an abuse of the power entrusted to them ; for as a delinquency is imputed to them, they ought not to be condemned unheard ; but that does not apply to the case of a non-existing body. A *quo warranto* is necessary where there is a body corporate, *de facto*, who take upon themselves to act as a body corporate, but who, from some defect in their constitution, cannot legally exercise the powers they affect to use." If, in a prosecution against a corporation, the judgment be for the defendants, the form of it

<hr>

(*a*) Admitted in the King *v.* Amery, 2 T. R. 515. post. chap. 16. s. 5.

(*b*) 2 Kyd. 465, 6. 1 Bla. Com. 485.

(*c*) Salk. 191. 12 Mod. 247. 4 East, 327.

(*d*) 4 East, 17.

(*e*) Bac. Ab. Corporation, G. 3 Burr. 1866. 3 T. R. 199; 241. 14 East, 357, note a.

(*f*) Bac. Ab. Corporation, G.

is,

is, "that the liberties be allowed (a);" it it be for the Crown,
and the parties have continued possession of the franchise by
wrong from the beginning, the judgment is, "that they be
ousted;" but if they once had title, and lose it, the judgment
is, "that the liberty be seized into the King's hands (b)." The
prior judgment of seizure is called a judgment "*quousque;*" this
judgment, it hath been thought, would dissolve the corporation, if the parties did not come in and avoid it the same, or at
the farthest, the next term, and that there was no use in a final
judgment, but to shew that the King will take advantage of the
forfeiture, which he may declare by the grant of a new charter (c). But this opinion was over-ruled in the House of
Lords, where it was determined, that the effect of this judgment was merely to lay the King's hands on the franchise of
being a corporation, so that the corporation could not use its
liberties, and the action of its vital powers was suspended; that
in that situation the King might appoint a *custos,* and might
introduce a new corporation by charter, to whom he might
commit the custody; but that the old corporation were entitled
to redeem their liberties, and remove the King's hands, upon
which the power of the new corporation must necessarily cease,
and the letters patent become void (d).

3. Of *Game Franchises,* and herein of the King's Prerogative as to *Game,* and of *Forests.*

Before we consider the right of the King to grant forests,
parks, chases, and warrens; the question whether or not the

(a) Co. Entr. 535, b.

(b) Yelv. 192. Co. Entr. tit. *Quo Warranto.*

(c) Rex v. Amery, 2 T. R. 515.

(d) 4 T. R. 122. Vide the judgment in Rex v. Amery in the House of Lords, in the account of that case in two vols. quarto, and 2 Kyd. 496., &c. 2 Bac. Ab. 31. tit. Corporation, G.—With re-spect to the form of a final judgment, it was determined in Sir James Smith's case, that the corporation of London was not dissolved by the judgment as recited in the act of 2 W. and M. stat. 1. c. 8. which was, "that the liberty, franchise, and privilege of the city of London, being a body politick, &c. should be seized," for the word '*of*' being omitted before the word '*being*', the judgment was not against the corporate existence of the city, but against the franchises it enjoyed: and Holt said, "that a corporation might subsist after its franchises were taken away; for that these were not essential to it, but only a privilege appertaining to it; that the essence of a corporation was to make bye-laws, and govern their members, which a corporation might do, though their franchises were seized." 4 Mod. 52. Skin. 310. Carth. 217. 1 Show. 263.

exclusive

exclusive property in wild animals, or game, is vested in the Crown, is entitled to investigation.

By the law of nature and reason, wild beasts and undomesticated birds, are a species of usufructuary property, as freely the property of the first occupant as the air on which they fly. They form a part, and were formerly a most material part, of those resources which Providence has provided for the sustenance of man. Till an actual seizure of animals, *feræ naturæ*, be made, the property in them remains, by the law of nature, in a species of abeyance (*a*). Game is an object of pursuit; it can only be acquired by exertion, and he who occupies his time, or exercises his ingenuity, in obtaining these animals, ought to possess them. And so it was held by the imperial law, even so late as Justinian's time: " *Feræ igitur bestiæ, et volucres, et omnia animalia quæ mari, cœlo, et terra nascuntur, simul atque ab aliquo capta fuerint, jure gentium statim illius esse incipiunt. Quod enim nullius est, id naturali ratione occupanti conceditur* (*b*)." Before the Norman Conquest, a similar doctrine existed in this country. As observed by Sir William Blackstone (*c*), " every Freeholder had the full liberty of sporting upon his own territories, provided he abstained from the King's forests, as is fully expressed in the laws of Canute, and of Edward the Confessor: " *Sit quilibet homo dignus venatione sua, in sylva, et in agris, sibi propriis, et in dominio suo; et abstineat omnis homo a venariis regiis, ubicumque pacem eis habere voluerit;*" which, indeed, was the antient law of the Scandinavian Continent, from whence Canute probably derived it. " *Cuique enim in proprio fundo quamlibet feram quoquo modo venari permissum.*" The introduction of the feudal system into England at the time of the Conquest, vested in the Crown all the privileges and rights respecting game, which the principles of that system authorized. And it cannot be doubted, that the right of the Sovereign to reserve to himself, and confer on his subjects, certain peculiar and exclusive privileges respecting game, was part of the policy of the feudal constitution, for the purpose of keeping the people in a state of subordination, and preserving, for the exclusive enjoyment of the higher classes, a sport suited to the martial genius of the

---

(*a*) See 2 Bla. Com. 14 and 411.   (*c*) 2 Bla. Com. 415.
(*b*) Inst. 2. 1, 12.

age.

age (a). It became a principle of the English law, that from
the Sovereign alone such exclusive rights can be claimed. It
may even be admitted, that the feudal principles enabled the
King to prohibit the destruction of game by those who did not
possess a royal franchise. But it by no means necessarily follows, that the *sole property* in game vested either in the King
or his grantee. Bracton and Fleta appear, indeed, to have
drawn this inference. The former observes, " *Habet etiam*
(Rex) de jure gentium in manu sua quæ de jure naturali debe-
rent esse communia ; sicut feras bestias, et aves non domesticas (b).''
And Puffendorf, and other writers on general law, lay down
the same principles. Sir William Blackstone subscribed to
the general position, and zealously enforced the doctrine, that
the property of all the game in England is in the King (c),
He observes, that "upon the Norman Conquest a new doctrine
took place, and the right of pursuing and taking all beasts of
chase or venery, and such other animals as were accounted
game, was then held to belong to the King, or to such only as
were authorized under him ; and this, as well upon the principles of the feudal law, that the King is the ultimate proprietor of all the lands in the kingdom, they being all held of him
as the chief lord, or lord paramount of the fee ; and that, therefore, he has the right of the universal soil, to enter thereon,
and to chase and take such creatures at his pleasure : as also,
upon another maxim of the common law, that these animals
are *bona vacantia*, and, having no other owner, belong to
the King by his prerogative. As, therefore, the former
reason was held to vest in the King a right to pursue and
take them any where, the latter was supposed to give the
King, and such as he should authorize, a *sole* and *exclusive*
right."

With respect to the first principle from whence Sir William
Blackstone has deduced this doctrine, it may be observed (as
remarked by Mr. Christian), that it is not evident from the
King's right to the universal soil, that he should have a better
right to such creatures than to any other production of the
soil (d).

The second reason relied upon by Sir Wm. Blackstone,

(a) See 2 Bla. Com. 413, &c.   413, 419 ; 4 vol. 174, 415.
(b) Lib. 2. c. 24. s. 1.   (d) See 2 Bla. Com. 419, note 10.
(c) See 2 Bla. Com. 14, 5 ; 391, 4 ;

that these animals belong to the King as *bona vacantia,* and
as having no other owner, appears also very unsatisfactory.
The general rule seems to be that *bona vacantia* only belong
to the King in *certain instances,* particularly defined by the
common law, and in which certain valuable and distinguished
articles are expressly selected and set apart for the King, as
worthy his acceptance and necessary to support, and especially suitable to his royal dignity : as in the case of swans,
whales and sturgeons, gold and silver mines, treasure trove,
waifs, estrays and wrecks, which will be particularly noticed
hereafter.   In cases in which the royal right to *bona vacantia*
is not particularly pointed out, the first occupant or finder
becomes entitled (*a*).

It is also worthy of remark, that no judicial determination in favour of the King's exclusive property in game is to
be met with : on the contrary there are various *dicta* and decisions sustaining the principle that game is common property (*b*).   So universal a silence on such a point is by no
means a weak argument against this royal claim to an exclusive property : nor is it easily reconciled with the admitted
doctrine that his subjects may acquire an exclusive right to
wild animals by reclaiming them, &c. (*c*).   If the King have
this exclusive property there is no principle for holding that
it may be divested by the wrongful act of a third person, to
which the Crown is not a party.

There seems to be no inconsistency in supposing that though
the King may possess the right to go on his subjects' lands to
kill game, and the power in some cases of enlarging and in
others of restraining the exercise of the natural right to take
it, still the subject may possess *concurrently with the King* the
right of acquisition by reducing game into his possession.
Most of the writers on the law of occupancy find a difficulty
in reconciling the usurped appropriation of wild animals by
any one exclusively, with the general freedom of manucap-
tion, given by the laws of nature, and confirmed by the laws

(*a*) Strange, 505. 1 Bla. Com. 295,
298, 9. 2 Ibid. 259. 4 Burr. 2402. ;
But see Bro. ab Pierog. pl. 12.

(*b*) See the references in 1 Chitty on
Game Laws, 3, note h.   Year Book, 17
Edw. 2. 538. Keilw. 30, 138. Manw.

202. Bro. Ab. tit. Propertie. F. N. B.
197. 11 Co. 87. 4 Inst. 303. 2 Bla.
Com. 419, note 10, by Christian. Hawk.
P. C. c.33. s. 29.

(*c*) See 2 Bla. Com. 391.

of nations and of reason : and therefore, in respect to the exclusive propriety assumed by princes in animals *feræ naturæ,*
they assert that the prince cannot be called the owner of such
animals before he hath actually caught them: so that he who
hunts contrary to a royal prohibition doth not commit theft,
nor take away the goods of another; but only acquires a thing
which another had a primitive or exclusive right of acquiring,
and therefore he may be punished; but as for the thing which
he thus got into his possession, it ought not to be looked on as
a matter of theft, or to be challenged accordingly (*a*).

The better opinion seems therefore to be against Sir William Blackstone's doctrine, that the King has the exclusive
property in game (*b*). He appears to possess it concurrently
with his subjects; though from the civil or feudal laws he
may derive and most certainly possesses the right to grant
game franchises over his own or his grantee's lands. It will
be collected from the limitations of the right of the Crown
to grant such franchises, that little can be argued from the
right in favor of this extended and exclusive property.

A *forest* is defined by Manwood (*c*) to be " a certain territory
or circuit of woody grounds and pastures, known in its bounds
and privileges, for the peaceable being and abiding of wild
beasts and fowls of forest, chase and warren, to be under the
King's protection, for his princely delight, replenished with
beasts of venery and chase, and great coverts of vert, for
succour of the said beasts, for preservation whereof, there are
particulars, laws, privileges, and offices, belonging thereunto."
The commencement of forests may be traced to the Norman
usurpation, which introduced the feudal system; and in consequence thereof the first Kings of the Norman line not only
reserved to themselves the sole and exclusive property of the
antient forests, but also created others of greater extent, particularly the New Forest in Hampshire; and placed them under
the jurisdiction of particular courts, and established a variety

(*a*) Gudelin de jure novissimo, lib. 2. cap. 2. Vinnius Comm. 2. lib. tit. 1. s. 13.

(*b*) See in general, Christian's note to 2 Bla. Com. 415. Selwyn, N. P. 118. tit. Game. Chitty, G. L. And in the recent debates in the House of Commons, (Feb. and March 1819,) the general opinion on this subject seems to have been to this effect.

(*c*) Treat. of the Forest Laws, ed. 1717.

of officers, for the purpose of preserving the game in those forests (*a*).

Numberless oppressive regulations and laws, and amongst other the assumed right of the King to grant forests, over his subjects' lands, were annihilated by the *charta de foresta*, for which our ancestors contended as zealously as they did for *magna charta;* and Lord Coke contends, that the *charta de foresta* was only declaratory of the common law (*b*).

Forests were at first in the hands of the Crown only, but several were gradually conferred by our antient Kings on their great lords and followers as rewards for their services. And at the present day it is clear that forests and other franchises can only be claimed by grant from the Crown, or by prescription which supposes it (*c*). Twenty years' uninterrupted enjoyment of a franchise is presumptive evidence in favor of the claimant (*d*).

The royal grant of a forest or any other game franchise imparts to the grantee various peculiar privileges, with respect to the preservation of game within the districts over which the grant operates; and the legislature has frequently interfered to protect them (*e*). And it is considered that the owner of a forest, chase, park or warren is, as such, independently of any other qualification, entitled to kill game within his franchise; though if he sport out of the limits of his district he will be liable to a penalty, unless otherwise qualified (*f*).

There are various courts and officers incident to a forest: and when a forest is granted by the Crown " *cum omnibus incidentibus et pertinentiis*," the grantee takes it as a forest with courts and officers, except the justice in eyre; and this too may be granted to a subject by express words (*g*). If however those words be omitted, the grantee holds the franchise as a chase only, though the term forest be applied to it in the patent (*h*). And in such case offenders in the forest are punish-

---

(*a*) 1 Inst. 100. See 3 Cruise Dig. 291.

(*b*) 4 Inst. 300.

(*c*) 1 Ibid. 233, a.

(*d*) 1 Chitty's G. L. 22, cites 6 East, 215. 7 Ibid. 199. 11 Ibid. 488. 2 Saund. 175, note 2.

(*e*) See Chitty's Game Laws.

(*f*) 7 Mod. 482. 1 Chitty's Game Laws, 41, 2.

(*g*) Manwood, 159. 4 Inst. 314. Com. Dig. tit. Chase, A. 2.

(*h*) Ibid.

able,

able, not by the forest laws, but by the common law of the land (*a*).

It has recently been decided, that there may be a valid custom in a manor, within the limits of an antient forest belonging to the Crown, for the lord, with the assent of the homage, to grant parcels of the waste to be held in severalty by copy of court-roll, and inclosed, in exclusion of persons having rights of common. And Lord Ellenborough observed, that " He saw no reason why the waste might not legally be granted out in this manner, although part of the manor were within a royal forest. The Crown may still exercise the same rights of forest over it as before. Whether the deer be excluded must depend upon the nature of the inclosures. If the fences erected are higher than are permitted by the laws of the forest, the forest officers may still interfere, and break them down. According to the custom, the grant is only to the exclusion and abolition of rights of common, not of the rights of forest. And his Lordship said, he knew instances in Windsor Forest, in which the Crown has made grants in severalty, reserving the rights of forest, with an advanced rent, while these rights shall not be exercised."

As observed in a recent work (*b*), a *purlieu* (which is derived by Lord Coke (*c*) from *pur*, clear, entire, and exempt, and *lieu*, a place,) is land adjoining to a forest, known by meers immoveable upon record, and which was formerly within the forest, but was disafforested by *charta de foresta* (*d*). The purlieu, however, notwithstanding this statute, still continues a forest, for many purposes relating to game (*e*), and is privileged in the protection of deer by various modern statutes (*f*). The land is disafforested as to the particular owners of it, and for their benefit, and not generally so as to give liberty to every one to hunt; and if animals escape out of the forest into the purlieu, the King has a property in them against every one but the owner of the woods and lands in which they are, and such owners have a special property in them, *ratione loci* (*g*).

(*a*) See Manwood, 49.

(*b*) 1 Chitty's G. L. 16, 17.

(*c*) 4 Inst. 303.

(*d*) Manwood, tit. Purlieu, 242. Com. Dig. tit. Chase I, 1.

(*e*) 4 Inst. 303. Manwood, tit. Purlieu.

(*f*) 3 W. and M. c. 10. 16 Geo. 3. c. 30. 2 Stra. 1119.

(*g*) Manwood, tit. Purlieu.

But Lord Coke (*a*) says, that a man may as lawfully hunt, to
all intents and purposes, within the purlieu in his own grounds,
as any other owner may do in his grounds that never were
afforested.

4. A *Free chase* is a right to hunt and kill game over a certain
district, derivable from a royal grant, or immemorial usage
which supposes it (*b*).   A chase differs from a forest, properly
so called, principally in this respect, that a chase cannot be
subject to the forest laws.   It is an unenclosed place (*c*).   And
a man may have a chase in the ground of another as well as in
his own, and the game therein is protected for his benefit, even
from the owner of the land (*d*).   Not that the King has the
power to grant a chase over the lands of a subject without his
concurrence, or that the subject can, without the King's licence,
make a legal and privileged chase over his own ground (*e*).
The right to a chase over another's land originated from the
grantees of chases selling their estates in antient times, reserving their rights of chase to themselves (*f*).   There can, however, be no doubt, that the King has the prerogative of conferring this franchise over other lands than those of the grantee,
with the consent of the owner; though, as observed by Mr.
Cruise (*g*), it is probable that a chase was never granted over
any grounds but those whereof the grantee was himself seized;
and most of the antient grants of free chase and warren, (of
which an infinite number are mentioned by Dugdale in
his Baronage,) are confined to the demesne lands of the
grantee.

The right to a free chase does not prevent the owner of the
soil from cutting timber and wood growing upon it, though if
he cut so much that there is not sufficient for covert, and to
maintain the game, the King, or his grantee of the free chase,
has his remedy (*h*).

5. A *park* is an enclosed chase, extending only over a man's

(*a*) 4 Inst. 303.
(*b*) 2 Bla. Com. 38.
(*c*) 4 Inst. 317, 8.   Wood's Inst.
219, 20.   2 Bla. Com. 38.
(*d*) Ibid.   Com. Dig. tit. Chase, B.

(*e*) 11 Rep. 87.   2 Inst. 199.
(*f*) 2 Bla. Com. 39.
(*g*) 3 Cruise Dig. 293.
(*h*) See Case of Forest, 12 Rep. 22.
4 Inst. 298.

own ground, to constitute which three things are required (a) : First, a grant or licence from the King, (and there can be no doubt the King may confer the privilege at the present day,) or there must be immemorial prescription; secondly, enclosures by pales, walls, or hedges, though if a legal park, by grant or prescription, has laid open for forty years or more, it may be revived by enclosing it again, &c. (b); thirdly, beasts of the park, such as bucks, does, &c. and, therefore, if there be a grant of a park, " excepting the deer," the exception is void (c). And where all the deer are destroyed, the district shall no more be accounted a park (d).

Manwood says (e), that in many forests there are parks which the owners claim, either by grant from the King, or by prescription. And, if a subject is owner of a forest, he may give licence to another to make and enclose a park within the meers of his forest, and to hold the same as enclosed, with all such venison as the grantee shall put in, to him and his heirs. And this was adjudged a good licence, in a claim made in Eyre; but, if such park is so slightly enclosed and fenced, that the wild beasts of the forest do enter, the lord of the forest may, in such case, enter and hunt them at his pleasure.

Parks as well as chases, are subject to the common law, and are not under the jurisdiction of the forest laws (f).

If any one should erect and assume to possess a privileged park without the King's licence, a *quo warranto* may be granted, and the park destroyed (g).

6. A *Free Warren* is extremely similar to a chase, and is usually united with it, being a place privileged for the keeping of beasts and fowls of warren (h), on certain lands, either of the proprietor of the warren or other person, as in the case of a chase (i). This privilege also can only be claimed from the

---

(a) See 3 Cruise Dig. 294. 1 Chitty, G. L. 18, 19.

(b) Cro. Jac. 755.

(c) 2 Roll's Rep. 276.

(d) Cro. Car. 60.

(e) P. 224.

(f) 4 Inst. 314.

(g) 1 Chitty, G. L. 19.

(h) These are described in Co. Lit.

233, a. Com. Dig. Chase, F. The beasts are hares, conies, and roes; the fowls are either *campestres*, as partridges, rails, and quails; or *sylvestres*, as woodcocks and pheasants; or *aquatiles*, as mallards and herons.

(i) 1 Chitty, G. L. 19, 20. 2 Bla. Com. 38, 9.

Crown (*a*), otherwise, a *quo warranto* may be issued (*b*). As observed by Sir William Blackstone (*c*), " this franchise is now almost fallen into disregard, the name being now chiefly preserved in grounds that are set apart for breeding hares and rabbits." Such place any one may erect and possess; but the royal grant is necessary to confer on it peculiar properties and protection. It will be noticed hereafter how these franchises, forests, chases, parks, and warrens, may be lost.

7. *Fisheries and Fish.*—The King has an undoubted sovereignty and jurisdiction, which he has immemorially exercised through the medium of the Admiralty Courts, over the British seas, that is, the seas which encompass the four sides of the British islands; and other seas, arms of seas, and navigable (but not unnavigable(*d*)) rivers, within and immediately connected with the territories subject to his sway (*e*).

The law of nations and the constitution of the country have clothed the Sovereign with this power, that he may defend his people and protect their commercial interests.

By implication of law the property in the soil under these public waters is also in the King (*f*). But in this, as in most other instances, the prerogative does not counteract or interfere with the natural right of the public to fish in the sea, in arms of the sea, and in creeks and navigable rivers, and to take fish found on the sea-shore between high and low water mark. This is one of the *jura publica* or *communia* (*g*), which never was vested exclusively in the Crown, and of course is not to be considered as a regal franchise.

Notwithstanding this public right of fishery, to which the prerogative of the King is subservient, it appears that the King or one of his subjects may by prescription or immemorial usage (of which twenty years' uninterrupted enjoyment is

---

(*a*) 3 Cruise Dig. 295.

(*b*) Ibid. Com. Dig. tit. Chase, D.

(*c*) 2 Bla. Com. 39.

(*d*) These belong to the owners of the adjacent soil. Hale de jure Mar. p. 1. c. 1. Hargr. Tr. vol. 1. p. 5. Davis's R. 57, a. b. 12 Mod. 510. 4 Burr. 2164. Selw. N. P. tit. Fishery.

(*e*) Seld. Mar. Hale de jure Maris, &c.

(*f*) Post. c. 11. on Revenue.

(*g*) Ibid. Hale de jure Mar. p. 1. c. 4. Hargr. Tr. vol. 1. p. 11. Dav. Rep. 55. 5 Bac. Ab. 498, &c. Willes' R. 265. 2 Bos. and Pul. 476.

evidence

evidence (*a*)), have an exclusive right of fishing in an arm of the sea, or any particular part of a navigable river. For though the prescription or usage derogate from a public right, yet the existence of an exclusive appropriation may be grounded on a supposition that the inhabitants of a particular district might consent to relinquish a general right for some peculiar advantage of a different, though perhaps of an equal or more extensively beneficial nature. This is generally admitted by elementary writers (*b*), and there are several decisions to the same effect (*c*). It seems however that a private right of fishing in the sea cannot be claimed under an existing *grant* from the Crown, for a grant to support it must be as old as the reign of Hen. 2., and therefore beyond the time of legal memory, as the Crown was restrained by King John's Great Charter and by other charters from making fresh grants of exclusive rights of fishery, affecting the public privilege (*d*).

As to the soil or *fundum maris*, there can be no doubt it may be claimed either by charter or prescription, for every prescription respecting a franchise generally supposes a grant, which in this instance could be made by the King, yet it is to be observed that the soil can only be appropriated *sub modo;* for, according to Lord Hale, though the dominion either of franchise or propriety be lodged by prescription or charter in a subject, yet it is charged or effected with that *jus publicum* that belongs to all men (*e*). On the same principles the holder of an exclusive prescriptive right of fishery in public waters enjoys it, subservient to the superior and sacred right of the public to use the arm of the sea or river for the purposes of navigation (*f*).

With respect to private fisheries, the presumption of law is, that the owner of the soil is the owner of the water or fishery;

(*a*) Ante 138.

(*b*) See Co. Lit. 113, a. b. and 114. 2 Bla. Com. 39. Hale de jure Maris, page 1. c. 4. Hargr. Tracts, 1 vol. page 11. Schultes Aqu. Rights, 99, &c. 1 Chitty, G. L. 268 to 272. Selw. N. P. tit. Fishery.

(*c*) Davy's Rep. 55. 1 Mod. Rep. 106. 4 Burr. 2162. 4 T. R. 437. 5 Ibid. 367. 2 Hen. B. 182. 2 Bos. and Pul. 472. 1 Campb. 309. 11 East, 263. That a custom to dry nets on the land of another is good. See 2 Hen. Bla. 395.

(*d*) 2 Bla. Com. 59. 1 Chitty, G. L. 244, 272.

(*e*) Hale de Portibus. See also Craig, lib. 2. dieg. 8. s. 5. 2 Inst. Mag. Ch. cap. 16.

(*f*) Ibid. 1 Campb. 517.

3

nor is the grant or licence of the Crown necessary on a party making a fish-pond (a).

The King has no general property in fish. It would be superfluous to specify and particularly designate Whales and Sturgeons alone, as being royal fish, if all fish were the King's property (b). *Exceptio probat regulam.* With respect however to whales and sturgeons, it was always a doctrine of the common law that they belong to the King (c). And by the statute *de Prerogativa Regis* (d), it is declared that the King shall have whales and sturgeons taken in the sea or elsewhere, within the realm, except in certain places privileged by the King. But to give the Crown a right to such fish they must be taken within the seas parcel of the dominions and Crown of England, or in creeks or arms thereof; for if taken in the wide seas or out of the precinct of the seas subject to the Crown of England, they belong to the taker (e). A subject may possess this royal perquisite: 1st, by grant; 2dly, by prescription within the shore, between the high water and low water mark, or in a certain *districtus maris*, or in a port, creek, or arm of the sea; and this may be had in gross or as appurtenant to an honour, manor or hundred (f).

Under this head may also be mentioned the right of the King to *swans*, being inhabitants of rivers (g). By the statute 22 Edw. 4. c. 6. "no person other than the son of the King shall have any mark or game of swans, except he have lands of freehold to the yearly value of five marks; and if any person not having lands to the said yearly value, shall have any such mark or game, it shall be lawful to any of the King's subjects having lands to the said value, to seize the swans as forfeits, whereof the King shall have one half and he that shall seize the other." A subject may however be entitled to swans: 1st, when they are tame; in which case he has exactly the same property in them as he has in any other tame animal; 2dly, by a grant of swan mark from the King, in which case all the swans marked with such mark shall be the subject's,

(a) 6 Mod. 183. 2 Inst. 199. 1 Chitty, G. L. 278.

(b) See Schultes, 15, 16.

(c) Bracton, 3 lib. ch. 3. s. 5. Britt. 26. b. 7 Co. 16.

(d) 15 Edw. 2. c. 11.

(e) Year Book, 39 Edw. 3; per Belknap. 1 Taunt. 241.

(f) Hale de jure Maris, c. 7. 1 Chalm. Coll. of Op. 131.

(g) 7 Co. 16, 7.

wheresoever

wheresoever they fly; and 3dly, a subject may claim a property in swans *ratione privilegii*, as if the King grant to a subject the game of wild swan in a river (*a*).

8. *Mines*. It is quite clear, that by his prerogative the King is entitled to all mines of gold and silver which may be discovered, not only in his own but even in a subject's lands, within his dominions (*b*).

The danger of rendering a subject too formidable, by vesting in him so immense a treasure as a mine of gold or silver might afford, is the reason assigned for this royal prerogative (*c*). But mines containing baser metal, belong to the subject in whose lands they are discovered (*d*). It was formerly held, that if such mines contained gold or silver, the whole mine belonged to the King; because gold and silver, being the nobler and more valuable metals, should attract the less valuable; and because a subject cannot hold property jointly with the Sovereign, and the King's property, though ever so small, ought not to be lost by mixture with the subject's (*e*). The injustice of such a doctrine called for a remedy; and, accordingly, it was enacted by the statute 1 William and Mary, sess. 1. c. 30. s. 4. " That no mine of copper, tin, iron, or lead, should be adjudged a royal mine, although gold or silver might be extracted out of the same." And it is further provided, by the statute 5 and 6 William and Mary, c. 6. that " the owner of any mine wherein any ore shall be discovered, opened, found, or wrought, and in which there is copper, tin, iron or lead, shall hold and enjoy the same mine and ore, and continue in the possession thereof, and dig and work the said mine or ore, notwithstanding that such mine or ore shall be pretended, or claimed to be a royal mine."

" Provided, that the King, and all claiming any royal mines under him, shall have the ore of any such mine, (other than tin ore in the counties of Devon and Cornwall,) paying to the proprietor or owner of the said mine, wherein such ore shall be found, within thirty days after the said ore is or shall be raised and laid upon the banks of the said mine, and before

(*a*) 7 Co. 16, 17.
(*b*) The case of Mines; Plowd. 315, 6. 5 Bac. Abr. 513. 1 Bla. Com. 295.
(*c*) Plowd. 316.

(*d*) Ibid. 323. 2 Inst. 578. 12 Co. 12.
(*e*) Plowd. 323, 328, 336.

the

the same be removed from thence, the rates following, (that is
to say,) for all ore washt, made clean, and merchantable, wherein is copper, the rate of sixteen pounds per ton; and for all ore
washt, made clean, and merchantable, wherein there is tin,
the rate of forty shillings per ton; and for all ore washt, made
clean, and merchantable, wherein there is iron, the rate of
forty shillings per ton; and for all ore washt, made clean, and
merchantable, where there is lead, the rate of nine pounds per
ton. And in default of payment of such respective sums as
aforesaid, the owner of the said mine, wherein such ore
shall be found, may sell and dispose of the said ore to his own
use."

" Provided always, that nothing contained in this act shall
alter, determine, or make void the charters granted to the tinners of Devon and Cornwall, by any of the Kings and Queens
of this realm, or any of the liberties, privileges, or franchises of
the said tinners, or to alter, determine, or make void the laws,
customs, or constitutions of the stannaries of Devon or Cornwall, or any of them."

By the 55 Geo. 3. c. 134. twenty-five pounds per ton, instead of nine pounds, is the rate at which the King may
exercise the right of preemption of ore in which there is
lead.

The King may legally grant his right to royal mines, and in
the hands of a subject they are a franchise; but such grant
must be in express terms; so that if the King grant to
T. S. certain lands, " and the mines therein contained," and
royal mines are found in them they do not pass to the subject (a).

9. *Fairs and Markets* will be considered in the chapter on
' Commerce.'

10. By *Waifs* are to be understood, stolen goods which are
waived or thrown away by the thief in his flight, for fear of
being apprehended (b). The goods must be *thrown away* by the
thief in his flight; and if he previously hide, or leave them any
where, with intent to resume the possession, so that they were

---

(a) Plowd. 336.   (b) 1 Bla. Com. 296.

not in his possession when he fled, the King's prerogative does not apply, and, the owner is, at all events, entitled to the property (*a*).   But the goods waived need not be the identical property stolen, for if a felon in flight waive his own goods, and the King seize them, they also are a species of waifs, for they are relinquished, and the property is in nobody (*b*).   But these are properly *fugitive's goods*, and not forfeited, till it be found before the coroner, or otherwise of record, that he fled for the felony (*c*).   But waifs vest in the Crown without office found (*d*).   The King acquires no property in the goods waived until they are seized by some one to his use ; and if the owner of the stolen property can seize them first, though at any distance of time, the King shall not have them (*e*).

This prerogative was given to the King, that the owner of the goods might be induced to bring the felon to justice to regain them.   Therefore, though the property is seized and in the hands of the Crown, yet the owner is entitled to restitution, if he used all reasonable diligence in pursuing the thief, or if he bring him to justice by procuring his conviction, or produce evidence which causes it (*f*).   Hence it will be remarked, that this royal prerogative is rather limited, and can only obtain where the party robbed is guilty of that negligence and torpitude, which our law reprehends in every instance, but more especially in those cases where they may occasion the escape of villainy from punishment.

The goods of a foreign merchant, though stolen and thrown away in flight, shall never be waifs (*g*).   " The reason whereof," observes Sir Wm. Blackstone (*h*), " may be not only for the encouragement of trade, but also because there is no wilful default in the foreign merchant's not pursuing the thief, he being generally a stranger to our laws, our usages, and our language."

All waifs are *primâ facie* the property of the Crown, and are not necessarily incident to a leet (*i*), though they are fre-

---

(*a*) 5 Rep. 109. Cro. El. 694. 1 Bla. Com. 296.

(*b*) Bro. Estray, 9. 29 Edw. 3. 19.

(*c*) Hawk. P. C. 481. B. 2. c. 49. s. 14.

(*d*) 5 Co. 109.

(*e*) 21 Edw. 4. 16. Kitchen. 82.

(*f*) Finch L. 212. 1 Bla. Com. 296. st. 21 Hen. 8. c. 11.

(*g*) Fitz. Abr. tit. Estray, 1. 3 Bulstr. 19.

(*h*) 1 Bla. Com. 296.

(*i*) Year Book, 8 Hen. 7. 1. Bro. Estray, 15.

quently

quently franchises in the hands of Lords of manors and others. It is worthy of observation that though the Lord of a manor may have waifs by prescription, yet he cannot have *bona felonum* and *fugitivorum*, although a species of waifs, by prescription, because every prescription must be immemorial, and the goods of felons and fugitives cannot be forfeited without record, which presupposes the memory of that continuance (*a*).

11. By the common law, and as declared by the statute de prerogativa Regis, 17 Edw. 2. statute 2. c. 11. the King is entitled to *wrecks* (*b*). The prevention of the barbarous practice of destroying persons, who in shipwrecks approached the shore, in order to acquire the property shipwrecked, was the object of the law in conferring this prerogative on the King (*c*).

There are four sorts of shipwrecked goods: flotsam, jetsam, ligan, and wreck properly so called (*d*).

Flotsam is when the ship is split, and the goods float upon the water between high and low water mark.

Jetsam is when the ship is in danger of foundering, and for the purpose of saving the ship, the goods are cast into the sea.

Ligan, lagan, or *ligam,* is when heavy goods are thrown into the sea with a buoy, so that the mariners may know where to retake them. These are also the King's if no owner appear to claim them; but if any owner appear he is entitled to recover the possession. For even if they be cast overboard without any mark or buoy, in order to lighten the ship, the owner is not by this act of necessity construed to have renounced his property; much less can things ligan be supposed to be abandoned, since the owner has done all in his power to assert and retain his property (*e*).

Wreck (properly so called) is where goods shipwrecked are cast upon the land; and goods which are termed flotsam, jetsam and ligan, become and are deemed wrecks if they be cast upon the land.

(*a*) Bro. Estray, 13. 5 Co. 109. 43 Edw. 3. 16.
 (*b*) 1 Bla. Com. 290.
 (*c*) Cro. Jur. Belli 117, 132, 141. 2 Inst. 167. Molloy, 237. Moor. 224. Hale de jure Mar. 40.
 (*d*) 1 Bla. Com. 292.
 (*e*) Ibid.

All these species of wreck *primâ facie* belong to, and were originally in, the Crown by virtue of his prerogative (*a*). Being rights of a secondary nature they may belong to a subject by express grant or prescription, and are frequently vested in Lords of manors. If however a subject prescribe or have a grant, for wreck only, he shall not have jetsam, flotsam or ligan (*b*).

The antient common law as to wrecks, was very strict in favour of the King; but as the country became more civilized, mitigations of such severities were gradually introduced; and by the common law as laid down by Bracton, in the reign of Henry 3., neither ships nor goods were considered wrecks if there were any sign or mark designating the right of the owner, who appeared and claimed them (*c*). And by the stat. 3 Edw. 1. c. 4. " concerning wrecks of the sea, it is agreed that where a man, a dog, or a cat escape [quick*] out of the ship, that such ship nor barge, or any thing within them shall not be adjudged a wreck; but the goods shall be saved and kept by view of the sheriff, coroner, [and] the King's bailiff, and delivered into the hands of such as are of the town where the goods were found; so that if any sue for those goods and can prove that they were his, or his lord's, or perished in his keeping, within a year and a day, they shall be restored to him without delay; and if not, they shall remain to the King and be taken by the sheriffs, coroners, [and bailiffs, and shall be delivered to them of the town (*d*)] to answer before the justices of the wreck belonging to the King. And where wreck belongeth to another than to the King, he shall have it in like manner. And he that otherwise doth, and thereof be attainted, shall be awarded to prison and make fine at the King's will, and shall yield damages also. And if a bailiff do so, and be disavowed by his lord, and the lord [will not pretend any title thereunto (*e*),] the bailiff shall answer, if he have whereof; and if he have not whereof, the Lord shall deliver the Bailiff's body to the King." This statute has received a very liberal construction, for it was passed to check the abuse of the royal

---

(*a*) 5 Co. 106. 6 Mod. 149, per cur.
(*b*) 5 Co. 107.
(*c*) 2 Inst. 167. Bracton, lib. 3. fol. 120. 1 Bla. Com. 291, &c
* *i. e.* alive.

(*d*) The translations previous to Pulton read " bailiffs of the town."

(*e*) The translations previous to Pulton, read " will not discharge him thereof."

prerogative to the prejudice of merchants. The act relates as well to flotsam, jetsam, and ligan, as to wreck, properly so called (*a*); and the instance of a dog or cat is only put in the statute by way of example (*b*), and therefore in every case where the owner of the ship or goods can come forward and prove his property, the King has no claim to them. Therefore if a ship be pursued by enemies, and the mariners come on shore and leave the empty floating ship, which comes to land without any person in it, yet if the mariners can prove the property in the ship, the King is not entitled to it (*c*). Notwithstanding the statute, the interest in property shipwrecked vests in the King or his grantee, even before seizure and without office found, against all but the right owner (*d*). The statute only divests this interest in cases where the owner, or his executor or administrator, if he die within the year and day (*e*), pursues the course pointed out by the statute. The owner must therefore apply for the return of his property within a year and a day from the time of the seizure of it, by the persons mentioned in the statute (*f*). But if he sue for its return before the expiration of the year and a day it is sufficient, although the verdict be not given within that time, for the delay of the law must do no man an injury (*g*).

The King is not restricted to the year and day mentioned in the statute, and consequently if the grantee of wrecks take the King's goods as wreck, the King may claim them after that period (*h*).

If goods wrecked be *bona peritura*, the King or Lord may sell them, even before the year and day be past; for the statute shall not be understood to compel them to keep those things which of their own nature cannot be kept (*i*). It should seem, however, that the produce of the articles so sold would be governed in all respects by those rules which would have applied to the articles themselves.

Where the King is entitled to wrecked property, he is entitled to a right of way over any man's grounds to obtain it (*k*).

(*a*) 5 Co. 107.   2 Inst. 167.

(*b*) Ibid.

(*c*) Ibid.   Molloy, 239.

(*d*) 5 Co. 107.

(*e*) 2 Inst. 168.

(*f*) 5 Co. 107.

(*g*) Ibid. 108.

(*h*) 2 Inst. 168.

(*i*) Ibid.   Plowd. Com. 465, 6.   12 Co. R. 73.   Parker's R. 72.   And see same principle, 1 Ventr. 313.

(*k*) 6 Mod. 149. *per Curiam.*

" *Quando*

" *Quando lex aliquid alicui concedit concedere videtur et id sine
quo res ipsa esse non posset.*"

It may also be worthy of observation that the King may by
the statute 27 Geo. 3. st. 2. c. 13. seize goods taken by pirates
where the property is unknown, and detain them until proof
of property is made ; and if they be perishable goods the King
may sell them, and, upon proof, restore the value (*a*).

12. *Estrays* are such valuable animals as are found wan-
dering in any manor or lordship, and no man knoweth the
owner of them ; in which case, says Sir Wm. Blackstone, the
law gives them to the King,. as the general owner and lord
paramount of the soil, in recompence for the damage they
may have done therein (*b*); and they now most commonly belong to Lords of manors by special grant from the Crown.
Animals *feræ naturæ*, and those on which the law sets no value,
cannot be estrays: that term only including, in legal consideration, such beasts as are by nature tame or reclaimable, and in
which there is a valuable property, as sheep, oxen, swine, and
horses, which we generally call cattle (*c*); and with respect to
fowl, only swans may be estrays (*d*).   The reason of which
distinction seems to be, that cattle and swans being of a re-
claimed nature, the owner's property in them is not lost
merely by their temporary escape ; and they also, from their
intrinsic value, are a sufficient pledge for the expense of the
Lord of the franchise in keeping them the year and day (*e*).

In order to vest an absolute property in the King, the
estray must be proclaimed in the church and two market
towns, next adjoining to the place where they are found, and
if no one claim them after proclamation and a year and a day
passed, they belong to the King without redemption (*f*); even
though the owner be a minor, or under any other legal incapacity (*g*).   If the proclamation be irregular, the owner is
entitled to restitution at any distance of time (*h*).   Notwithstanding the proclamation, the King's interest in the estray
does not become vested or indefeasible, until the expiration of

(*a*) 12 Co. 73.   Parker's R. 72.
(*b*) 1 Bla. Com. 296.
(*c*) Ibid. 297.
(*d*) 7 Rep. 17.
(*e*) 1 Bla. Com. 298.

(*f*) Mirror, c. 3. s. 19.   1 Bla. Com.
297.
(*g*) 5 Rep. 108.   Bro. Abr. tit. E-
tray.   Cro. El. 716.
(*h*) 1 Rol. Ab. 879.

the year and day, but his Majesty has a property in it by possession thereof, within the year and day, against all but the right owner (*a*). If however it wander again within that period, and a subject who is entitled to estrays (which he may be either by the royal grant or by prescription, which supposes such grant (*b*),) seize it, the King has no claim (*c*). The right of the subject to seize in such case, clearly proves that the property in the estray was not completely vested in the Sovereign, for it is laid down as clear law that no one can take the King's beasts as estrays (*d*).

The King or his grantee should, so long as the estray is in his possession, feed and preserve it from injury (*e*), and cannot legally use it by way of labour (*f*); though, it seems, that he may milk a cow, which is an estray, or do any act of a similar nature, which tends to the preservation and benefit of the animal, and, consequently, to the advantage of the owner (*g*). If the owner reclaim the estray, he must, it seems, pay the charges of finding, keeping, and proclaiming it (*h*); and though an unreasonable sum, by way of compensation for expenses incurred, be demanded, yet if the owner do not tender sufficient amends, the detainer of the estray is lawful (*i*).

13. *Treasure trove*, is where any gold or silver in coin, plate, or bullion is found concealed in a house, or in the earth, or other private place, the owner thereof being unknown, in which case the treasure belongs to the King or his grantee, having the franchise of treasure trove; but if he that laid it be known or afterwards discovered, the owner and not the King is entitled to it; this prerogative right only applying in the absence of an owner to claim the property (*k*). If the owner, instead of hiding the treasure, casually lost it, or purposely parted with it, in such a manner that it is evident he intended to abandon the property altogether, and did not purpose to re-

(*a*) Yelv. 96.
(*b*) See 44 Edw. 3, 19. 5 Co. 105. Kitch. 80, 2. 5 Bac. Ab. 517.
(*c*) Finch L. 177. 1 Bla. Com. 298.
(*d*) Year Books, 44 Edw. 3. 19. 5 Co. 105. 1 Rol. Abr. 888. Kitch. 80. 5 Bac. Ab. 517. tit. Prerogative, B. 9.
(*e*) 1 Rol. Ab. 889.
(*f*) Cro. Jac. 147.

(*g*) Ibid. 148. Noy. 119.
(*h*) Dalt. Sheriff, 79. 1 Rol. Abr. 879. 1 Bla. Com. 297. See 1 Hen. Bla. 254.
(*i*) 1 Rol. Abr. 879. pl. 5. See Bro. Ab. tit. Estray and Waif, pl. 1. 44 Edw. 3. 14.
(*k*) 3 Inst. 132, 3. Dalt. of Sheriffs, c. 16. 1 Bla. Com. 295.

sume

sume it on another occasion, as if he threw it on the ground, or other public place, or in the sea, the first finder is entitled to the property, as against every one but the owner, and the King's prerogative does not in this respect obtain (*a*). So that it is the hiding, and not the abandonment, of the property that entitles the King to it.

It is the duty of every person who finds any treasure, to make it known to the coroners of the county. The punishment for concealing it is fine and imprisonment (*b*).

14. By *Deodands*, which are also in general a franchise in the hands of lords of manors and others, are to be understood either animals or inanimate things, which occasion the death of a human being, and these are forfeited to the King or his grantee.

The superstition of former times designed them to be used as an expiation for the soul of the deceased, and in later times they were to be applied by his Majesty's almoner to pious uses (*c*). The forfeiture is rational, so far as it strengthens the natural sensations of the mind at the sudden destruction of human life.

The rule is, that *omnia quæ movent ad mortem sunt deodanda :* the forfeiture extends not merely to the article which more immediately occasioned the death, but also to such things as contributed, though remotely, to it, or rendered the wound more dangerous (*d*). Thus, if a cart run over a person and kill him, not only the cart but the luggage, &c. are forfeited, though the wheels were the more immediate cause of the fatal event (*e*). But a thing which in no respect contributed to the death is not forfeited, though annexed to an article which occasioned it ; and, therefore, where a person falls from the wheel of a carriage, which is not in motion, the wheel only is forfeited (*f*). So, if a man fall from the shafts of a waggon on which he was riding, the horses and waggon only are forfeited, and not the loading (*g*). And if a man riding on a horse over a river is

(*a*) Britton, c. 17. Finch L. 171. 1 Bla. Com. 295. See Stra. 505.

(*b*) 3 Inst. 133. 1 Bla. Com. 296.

(*c*) 3 Inst. 57. 5 Co. 110, b. 1 Bla. Com. 299.

(*d*) 1 Bla. Com. 301.

(*e*) Salk. 220.

(*f*) 3 Inst. 58.

(*g*) Ibid.

drowned,

drowned, through the violence of the river, the horse is not forfeited, because, not that but the waters caused his death (*a*); but the horse would be forfeited if it threw its rider into the river (*b*). The forfeiture is incurred in the case of a person falling from any thing standing still; nor is it material whether the owner was to blame or not (*c*). It appears to be now settled, that things fixed to the freehold, as the wheels of a mill, or forge, or bells hanging in a steeple, &c. by becoming entangled or caught in which a man loses his life, cannot be deodands (*d*). And it was always considered, that the forfeiture in these cases takes place at land only, and does not extend to the seas, where accidents are so frequent (*e*); though it is laid down, that a ship, from which a person falls and is drowned in fresh water, is forfeited (*f*).

A forfeiture may take place of an article which occasioned the death of a person within the years of discretion, by running over or falling on him, but not, it seems, in case he falls from any thing not in motion (*g*).

The death of the unfortunate sufferer, within a year and a day from the time he met with the accident, is necessary to vest the deodand in the Crown, or his grantee; and if he die after that period, the law concludes that he died from some other cause, and will not, it should seem, admit evidence to the contrary(*h*). If he happen to die within a year and a day, the article becomes a deodand, by relation back to the time when the wound was received, and no intermediate alienation of it can bar or prejudice the King's claim (*i*). However, nothing is forfeited, or can be legally seized, as a deodand, until it be found by a coroner's jury to have caused a person's death; but after the inquisition, the sheriff is answerable for the value of it, and, therefore, the inquest ought to find the value (*k*);

(*a*) Cro. Jac. 483. 2 Rol. R. 23. Poph. 136.

(*b*) Salk. 220.

(*c*) 1 Bla. Com. 301, 2.

(*d*) 2 Bac. Ab. 293, tit. Deodands. Sid. 204. Lev. 136. Raym. 97. Keb. 723, 744. 6 Mod. 187. 1 Hawk. P. C. 161, &c. B. 1. c. 26. Stra. 61.

(*e*) 3 Inst. 58. Hal. P. C. 423. Staundf. P. C. 20, b. and 21. 1 Bla.

Com. 301, 2.

(*f*) Ibid.

(*g*) See 1 Bla. Com. 500. 2 Bac. Ab. tit. Deodands. 2 Keb. 719, 806. And see Hawk. *ubi supra.* Hal. P. C. tit. Deodands. Sed vide Staundf. P. C. 21.

(*h*) Hawk. *ubi supra.* Bac. Ab. tit. Deodand.

(*i*) Ibid.

(*k*) Ibid. 5 Co. 110, b.

and

and in default of their doing so, the inquisition cannot be taken by the grand jury under their general charge from the Judge of Assize (*a*).   It seems, however, that on the coroner's default, it may be taken by the Justices of Oyer and Terminer, or of the Peace, or of the King's Bench (*b*).   These inquisitions appear to be traversable (*c*).

This forfeiture might, if strictly enforced, be ruinous to an innocent individual, and being founded on the superstition of darker ages, it has been gradually discountenanced.   The coroner's jury usually find the value of the article to be as small as possible, and sometimes find the value of a part only of an entire article occasioning death; a practice which the Court of King's Bench have tacitly sanctioned, by refusing to reform it, on application by the Crown or its grantee (*d*).

CHAP. IX.

Of the King as Parens Patriæ.

Sect. I.—*As to Infants, Idiots, and Lunatics.*

The King is in legal contemplation the guardian of his people; and in that amiable capacity is entitled, (or rather it is his Majesty's duty, in return for the allegiance paid him,) to take care of such of his subjects, as are legally unable, on account of mental incapacity, whether it proceed from 1st. nonage: 2. idiocy: or 3. lunacy: to take proper care of themselves and their property (*e*).

1. This superintending power over *infants* was originally in the King by the common law, and was by his Majesty delegated to the Lord Chancellor, who seems to exercise it as a

---

(*a*) 1 Burr. 17.
(*b*) Ibid.   2 Hale, P. C. 59.
(*c*) Ibid. 19.
(*d*) Foster of Hom. 266. 1 Bla. Com. 302. . 2 Barnardiston's R. 82.

(*e*) Staundf. Prerog. 37.   2 Inst. 14.
4 Co. 12, b.   Bac. Ab. Idiots, C.   1
Bla. Com. 463.   1 Fonbl. Tr. Eq. 3 ed.
52 and 53.   2 Ibid. 223, 227, note (*a*).
3d ed.

branch

branch of his general jurisdiction (*a*); and no separate commission is necessary to legalize the chancellor's jurisdiction in this respect (*b*).

By virtue of this power the chancellor may appoint guardians to such infants as are without them (*c*). And though his lordship cannot remove a testamentary guardian appointed according to the statute, or consider his misconduct a contempt, unless the infant be a ward of court (*d*); yet he may impose restrictions which will prevent such guardian from prejudicing the interests of his award (*e*). And it seems to be admitted that guardians at common law may be removed or be compelled to give security if there appear to be any danger of their abusing either the infant's person or estate (*f*). It is also a general rule that if a person appointed guardian be attainted, or otherwise become incapable, the trust devolves on the great seal, as the general guardian of all infants (*g*). The care of infants is so peculiarly a prerogative of the Crown, delegated to and exercised by the Court of Chancery, that it has also been laid down that the Court may interpose even against that authority and discretion which a father has in general in the education and management of his child (*h*). Though perhaps in this case it is necessary that such child should be a ward of the Court (*i*).

The Chancellor may, generally speaking, cause the performance of any thing essential to the welfare or benefit of infants and their properties (*k*); and will protect their rights. Therefore if a man marry a ward of the Court without the consent of the Court, he shall be committed for such contempt, though it appear that he knew not that she was a ward of the Court (*l*): and there must be a proper settlement made on the

(*a*) See Ibid. 1 Fonbl. 227, 8, note. 10 Ves. 59. See however Co. Lit. 88, b. note (16). Hargr. K. B. has no part of the delegated power over infants. 10 Ves. 59.

(*b*) Ibid.

(*c*) Bac. Ab. Guardians, C. 2 Fonbl. 235, 3rd ed.

(*d*) 2 P. Wms. 561. See next note.

(*e*) 2 Ch. Cas. 237. 1 Vez. 160. 1 Vern. 442. Dick. 88. 2 Fonbl. Tr.

Eq. 230, note (*a*), 3rd ed. and 235, 6.

(*f*). Ibid. 1 Bla. Com. 463.

(*g*) 1 P. Wms. 706.

(*h*) Ibid. 702. Other cases cited, 2 Fonbl. 230, note.

(*i*) See Ibid. 4 Bro. Ch. Rep. 101, 102.

(*k*) See 2 Fonbl. 230, note.

(*l*) Herbert's Case, 3 P. Wms. 116. Butler *v.* Freeman, Ambl. 303. Chassaing *v.* Parsonage, 5 Ves. 15.

wife

wife before such contempt can be cleared (*a*).   So the Court will allot maintenance to infants out of their fortunes suitable to their rank and circumstances (*b*).   But though it is one of the peculiar duties of a Court of Equity to protect the rights of infants, still it will not at any period or under any circumstances act upon such indulgent disposition; and therefore even in equity an infant may be bound by the statute of limitations (*c*).

On the other hand the Court of Chancery will assist guardians in compelling their wards to obey their legal desires. Therefore where an infant went to Oxford contrary to the orders of his guardian, who wished him to go to Cambridge, the Court sent a messenger to carry him from Oxford to Cambridge; and, on his removing to Oxford, another messenger was sent to carry him to Cambridge, and keep him there (*d*).

2. The superintendence of *idiots*, who are persons devoid of understanding from their births, and are presumed never likely to attain any, is also vested in the King, not however it seems by the common law, but by statutes for the benefit of the subject on the party being found an idiot by a jury of twelve men on the old common law writ *de idiota inquirendo* (*e*).

The statute 17 Ed. 2. st. 2. c. 9. provides, that the King shall " have the custody of the lands," (and according to many books, " of the person, goods and chattels" (*f*)), of natural fools; taking the profits of them without waste and destruction (*g*), and shall find them their necessaries, of whose fee soever the lands be holden; and after the death of such idiots his Majesty shall render them to the right heirs, so that by such idiots no alienation shall be made, nor shall their heirs be disinherited.

This statute is not introductive of a new right of the Crown (*h*); though it is certainly doubtful whether the prero-

(*a*) 1 Ves. Jun. 154.

(*b*) See 2 Fonbl. 232. note.

(*c*) Prec. Ch. 518.   1 Fonbl. Tr. Eq. 3rd ed. 159, note.

(*d*) Stra. 167.   3 Atk. 721.

(*e*) F. N. B. 232.   1 Bla. Com. 303. Hume *v.* Burton, T. 1785. 1 Ridgw. P. C. 224; 519, 535.

(*f*) 4 Co. 126, 148.   F. N. B. 232.

(*g*) Which words " waste and destruction" must be construed in their ordinary not their technical sense.   2 Ves. Jun. 71.

(*h*) 4 Co. 126.   Bac. Ab. title Idiots, C.   1 Bla. Com. 303.

gative in question was not obtained by some previous non-existing statute (*a*). It is clear that antiently the custody of idiots and their lands was vested in the lord of the fee (*b*); (and therefore still, by special custom, in some manors the lord shall have the ordering of idiot and lunatic copyholders (*c*);) but by reason of manifold abuses of this power by subjects, it was at last provided by common consent, that it should be given to the King, as the general conservator of his people; in order to prevent the idiot from wasting his estate; and reducing himself and his heirs to poverty and distress (*d*).

This prerogative is generally, but not necessarily, exercised by the person who has the custody of the great seal. It may be delegated to any other person (*e*); and even when granted to the Chancellor, as it almost universally has been, a special authority, under the royal sign manual, seems necessary; for such authority does not appear to form a part of the Chancellor's general jurisdiction (*f*). This warrant confers no *jurisdiction*, but merely a power of *administration;* and if that power be abused, or any erroneous order to be made under it, the appeal is not to the House of Lords, but to the King in Council (*g*).

Where the persons of idiots or lunatics are amenable to the Chancellor's jurisdiction, the circumstance of their property being out of the jurisdiction is not material (*h*); nor is the jurisdiction lost merely by their being abroad (*i*), for the jury may be satisfied of the party's state of mind without an inspection; and a person found a lunatic by a competent jurisdiction abroad, may be considered a lunatic here (*k*). As an idiot's recovery is, in legal contemplation, as well as in point of fact, improbable, the guardian under the King's authority is more than a bailee (*l*), and may make grants from time to time of the idiot's property (*m*). And, though the point has been

---

(*a*) See 2 Inst. 14. Fleta, page 6, sect. 10. Bac. Ab. title Idiots, C.

(*b*) Fleta, l. 1. c. 11. s. 10.

(*c*) Dyer, 302. Hutt. 17. Noy. 27.

(*d*) F. N. B. 232. 1 Bla. Com. 303.

(*e*) 1 Bla. Com. 303, and next note.

(*f*) 3 P. Wms. 108. 2 Atk. 553. 2 Fonbl. Tr. Eq. 228, note, 3d ed. Bac. Ab. title, Idiots, C.

(*g*) Ibid. 2 Ves. Jun. 7, 72. 3 Atk. 635. 6 Bro. P. C. 329. 1 Fonbl. Tr. Eq. 55, note, 3d ed.

(*h*) Ambl. 80.

(*i*) Ibid. 139.

(*k*) Ex parte Gillam, 2 Ves. Jun. 588.

(*l*) 1 Fonbl. Tr. Eq. 3rd. ed. 56, 57.

(*m*) 3 Atk. 635. 1 Fonbl. 55.

　　　　doubted,

doubted (*a*), it seems that the grant of the custody of an idiot and his lands, may be made to extend to the representatives of such grantee (*b*).

3. The King is also guardian of *lunatics ;* and his Majesty's authority in this respect generally is and may be delegated to the Lord Chancellor or other person, in the same manner as that relative to idiots is delegated. An important distinction between the case of a lunatic and that of an idiot, grounded on the consideration that a lunatic's disorder is supposed to be temporary only, should be remarked. Under the expectation that the disorder of the lunatic's mind may be removed, the law constitutes the Crown merely a trustee for the unfortunate persons; to protect their property, and to account to them for all profits received, if they recover, or after their decease to their representatives (*c*). It is therefore declared by the stat. 17 Edw. 2. c. 10. (which is said not to be introductive of any new right of the Crown(*d*)), that the King shall provide for the custody and sustentation of lunatics, and preserve their lands and the profits of them for their use, when they come to their right mind; and the King shall take nothing to his own use. And if the parties die in such estate, the residue shall be distributed for their souls by the advice of the ordinary, and of course (by the subsequent amendments of the law of administration) shall now go to their executors or administrators. On the same principle it has been decided that the King cannot grant the custody of the body and lands of a lunatic to a person to take the profits to his own use (*e*).

The custody of lunatics in private mad-houses is regulated by legislative provisions (*f*), which do not however in any way affect the royal prerogative. Though the King has in general the sole management and superintendence of persons of unsound mind, yet any one may confine or otherwise restrain any madman where it may be necessary (*g*). Where the royal authority for the custody of a lunatic is required, or where the production of a person suspected to be non-compos is enforced

(*a*) 1 Vern. 9.

(*b*) 3 Mod. 43, 4. Skin. 177. pl. 7, 5. 2 Ibid. 171. 3 Bac. Ab. 530, title Idiots, C. 1 Fonbl. Tr. Eq. 55, note.

(*c*) 1 Bla. Com. 304.

(*d*) 2 Ves. Jun. 71. Bac. Ab. title Idiot, C.

(*e*) Moor, 4, pl. 12.

(*f*) 14 Geo. 3. c. 49. 26 Geo. 3. c. 91.

(*g*) 2 Rol. Ab. 546.

by

by the authority of the Court of Chancery (a), the Lord Chancellor, to whom this prerogative is generally entrusted, by special authority from the Crown (b), on petition or information, grants a commission in nature of the writ *de idiota inquirendo*, to inquire into the party's state of mind. If he be found non-compos, his Lordship appoints (c) some friend or relation, not being the next heir of the non-compos, to take care of him (d). An allowance suitable to the circumstances of the unfortunate individual will be granted; and if necessary, the Court will even allow the whole of the yearly value of his property (e). The greatest care is to be taken of the property; and generally speaking, the Court will order any measure conducive to its improvement (f). But the person to whom the care of the lunatic is confided, cannot in general, of his own authority, do any act affecting his property; as he possesses a mere authority without an interest, and is nothing more than a mere bailee (g); nor should any thing be gained by him from the appointment (h).

It is the prerogative of the Crown to avoid, by *scire facias* or information, the engagements and acts of idiots and lunatics, during their incapacities (i). However, the King's right to the mesne profits has relation only to the time when the party was found to be of nonsane mind (k). Any abuse of idiots or lunatics, as, for instance, by taking them out of the custody of the persons appointed to take care of them, or marrying them, is considered a contempt of the Court of Chancery (l).

In general, the Chancellor's guardianship is determined by the death of the idiot or lunatic (m), though his Lordship may, it is held, make an order in their affairs after their deaths (n).

(a) 1 P. W. 721.   2 Ibid. 638.

(b) See ante 158.   3 P. W. 108.

(c) See 1 Fonbl. 56, 7. note, 3rd ed.

(d) 1 Bla. Com. 305.   Co. Lit. 88, b. n. 6.   1 Fonbl. 57, n.

(e) 3 P. W. 110.   2 Ibid. 262.   6 Ves. 8.

(f) Ambl. 706.   1 Fonbl. 59, 60.

(g) Vern. 262.   1 Fonbl. 56, 58 and 59, notes, 3rd ed.   2 Wils. 130, 2.

Bac. Ab. title Idiots, C.

(h) 2 Ch. Cas. 239.   Ambl. 78.

(i) 4 Co. 124.   F. N. B. 232.   1 Fonbl. Tr. Eq. 3rd ed. 55 note.

(k) 8 Co. Rep. 170, a.

(l) Prec. Ch. 203.   Eq. Cas. Ab. 278. ante, 156.

(m) 4 Co. 127, a.

(n) Ambl. 706.   Bro. Ch. R. 138.

SECT. II.

As to Charities.

SIR WILLIAM BLACKSTONE (a) observes, "that the King, as *parens patriæ*, has the general superintendence of all charities, which he now exercises by the keeper of his conscience, the Chancellor. And, therefore, whenever it is necessary, the Attorney-General, at the relation of some informant, (who is usually called the *relator,*) files, *ex-officio*, an information in the Court of Chancery, to have the charity properly established." On this proposition, Mr. Fonblanque (b) remarks, that it is too general, for though it be true, that where a charity is established, and there is no charter to regulate it, as there must be somewhere a power to regulate, the King has, in such case, a general jurisdiction; yet, if there be a charter with proper powers, the charity must be regulated in the manner prescribed by the charter, and there is no ground for the controlling interposition of the Court of Chancery (c). The interposition of the Court, therefore, in those instances in which the charities were founded on charters, or by Act 'of Parliament, and a visitor, or governor, or trustees, appointed, must be referred to the general jurisdiction of the Court, in all cases in which a trust conferred appears to have been abused, and not to an original right to direct the management of the charity, or the conduct of the governors or trustees. A distinction manifested by those cases in which the Court has refused to interpose its opinion against that of the governors of a charity, having a right, by the terms of its foundation, to exercise their discretion in certain particulars (d). It is, however, the general right of the Court of Chancery, derived from the King, to appoint to what charity any gift shall be applied, where the donor does not name any particular charity (e). And, as already mentioned, by statute 1 Edw. 6. c. 14., gifts to certain

---

(a) 3 Com. 427.

(b) 2 Fonbl. Tr. Eq. 206. n. a.

(c) Attorney-General v. Middleton. 2 Ves. 328.

(d) See Attorney-General v. Foundling Hospital. 4 Bro. Ch. Rep. 165.

2 Ves. Jun. 42. Attorney-General v. Middleton: 2 Ves. 327. But see Gower v. Mainwaring. 2 Ves. 89.

(e) 1 Vern. 224. 2 Freem. 261. 1 Bro. Ch. R. 15. Ambl. 712.

super-

superstitious uses therein enumerated, are declared to vest in the Crown; but other gifts, not included within that enumeration, neither vest in the Crown nor in the heir, but shall be appointed to such uses as the King shall order (*a*).

CHAP. X.

Of the Prerogative as to Commerce.

SECT. I.—*Foreign Commerce; Freedom of, and how far under royal Controul.—Consuls.—Dispensations by Licences, and Orders in Council, from the Effect of War on Commerce, &c. —Prohibitions.—Embargoes.—Declarations of Contraband, &c.—Sovereignty over the Seas.—Ports and Havens.—Beacons and Light-houses.*

THE protection of foreign and domestic commerce was, even in the most antient times, a favorite object of the English laws; as is strongly instanced by the provisions in *Magna Charta*, c. 30., and subsequent enactments, respecting the freedom of alien merchants. And in the time of King Athelstan we find a very remarkable law, which says, that any merchant who has made three voyages upon his own account, beyond the British channel, or narrow seas, shall be entitled to the privilege of a thane (*b*): " *et si mercator tamen sit, qui per trans altum mare per facultates proprias abeat, ille postea jure thani sit dignus.*"

It would of course be irrelevant to enter into a detail or explanation of the *lex mercatoria.* Its objects, and the principles and policy on which it is founded, are of a complicated nature; and the numerous regulations respecting trade to be found in our statute books would fill volumes (*c*).

Our foreign commerce is principally regulated by a variety of statutes; and chiefly by the Navigation Act 12 Car. 2. c. 18.;

(*a*) 1 Salk. 162.

(*b*) Wilkins, Angl. Sax. Leg. Judicia Curtatis. Lond. p. 71.

(*c*) See Pope's work; and Chitty, on " Commerce" and " Law of Nations."

the

the object of which was to extend, consolidate, and strengthen the maritime power of the country by confining our foreign trade, as far as was consistent with the extent of it, to the shipping and mariners of this country; and, in order to accomplish that object, to hold out peculiar privileges and immunities to the mariners and shipping of Great Britain; and to prohibit, under severe penalties, the communication of these immunities to the shipping and mariners of foreign states (a).

As these statutes contain comprehensive and positive enactments which bind the Crown (b), it may be laid down as a general rule, that the King does not possess any general common law prerogative with respect to foreign commerce. The King is called by Sir Wm. Blackstone (c), " the arbiter of commerce :" a term which would be somewhat loose, as stated by Mr. Wooddeson (d), if it were applied to general commerce; but which appears to be extremely applicable to the King's authority with respect to *domestic* trade : in which sense only it is used by Sir Wm. Blackstone. A general discretionary power of restraining, regulating and superintending foreign commerce is not assigned by the common law to the King. His prerogatives on this subject are by no means so extensive : for the affairs of general commerce relating to subjects of independent states are regulated by statute law, and by the *lex mercatoria* which the European nations agree to observe.

The freedom of trade and the general inability of the King to restrain it, or to exercise any discretionary power on the liberty of the subject in this respect, by virtue of his common law prerogatives, and independently of any legislative authority, appears to be clear both on sound constitutional principles and from authorities of the first weight and character (e).

In the first place the provision in *Magna Charta,* ch. 30., extending the freedom of trade to foreign merchants, strongly proves that the English had this liberty before : otherwise they

---

(a) 2 Smith, W. N. 212. Beaw. Lex Merc. 16, 17. Chitty, L. of Nat. 200.

(b) 12 East, 296.

(c) 1 Com. 273.

(d) 1 V. L. 80.

[(e) 2 Inst. 57. Hale de Portibus Maris. Pref. to Hargr. Hale, Tracts, vol. 1. p. xxx. Com. Dig. Trade, D. 1, 4 Bac. Ab. Merchant, 595.

would

would not have extended it to aliens, and left themselves without it.

In the s cond place it is declared by many Acts of Parliament; and particularly by the statute 18 Ed. 3. st. 2. c. 3.; " *que le mere soit overt*" " that the sea shall be open to all manner of merchants to pass with their merchandise (where it shall please them)."

" All merchants, strangers and denizens, or any other may sell corn, &c. and every other thing vendible to whom they please, foreigners or denizens, excepting the King's enemies, and any charter, proclamation, allowance, judgment, &c. to the contrary shall be void (*a*)."

Again if it be necessary, the various statutes which have been expressly made for the purpose of preventing the importation or exportation of particular articles, might be used as an argument against this power of the Crown. The embargo which was issued by his Majesty to prevent the exportation of corn in 1766, is noticed by Beawes in his *Lex Mercatoria* (*b*), as having been illegally imposed; such exportation, says he, being allowed by law at the time; and therefore, the preamble to the statute 7 G. 3. c. 7. for indemnifying all persons advising or acting under the order of council, laying an embargo on all ships laden with corn or flour, during the recess of Parliament in 1766, says, " which order could not be justified by law, but was so much for the service of the public, and so necessary for the safety and preservation of his Majesty's subjects, that it ought to be justified by Act of Parliament." This embargo, as was allowed, saved the people from famine; yet it was declared illegal by the above Act of the legislature, including the King himself, who laid it, which was therefore needful to sanction it : and the proprietors of the embargoed ships and cargoes were accordingly indemnified by government. Here there is a legislative declaration what the law is on this subject.

It is on this principle also that embargoes which occasion a suspension of commercial intercourse, are not legal at common law, except when they operate for the public good and

(*a*) 9 Ed. 3. c. 1. 25 Ed. 3. c. 2. 11 Rich. 2. c. 7.
(*b*) Page 276. See Hargr. Law Tracts,

Preface, xxx. Chitty, L. of Nat. 72. See also ante, ch. 7, as to Proclamations.

safety;

safety; being used in time of enmity and threatened hostilities and on an emergency, and not for the private advantage of a particular trader or company (*a*).   Nor can a civil embargo, that is, an embargo which is employed in the case of allies and subjects, be imposed upon British ships in a foreign port, unless by the concurring authority of the state to which that port belongs; for the King has no right to disturb the peace of other nations, by any seizures, however useful to the interests of his own people.   This may be collected from the judgment of Sir William Scott, in the case of the Gertruyda (*b*).

In 1721, on the occasion of ships of war being built by English subjects in England for the Czar, which was complained of by the King of Sweden, the Judges were of opinion that the King could not prohibit the same (*c*).

Lord Hale does indeed in his treatise *de portibus Maris* (*d*) consider this question very cautiously; and, with his usual diffidence on doubtful and important constitutional subjects, avoids giving a decided opinion: but it is tolerably evident what his sentiments were.   He concludes (*e*) by observing, " that upon the whole matter, it will appear from the several Acts of Parliament that have been made for the support and increase of trade, and for the keeping of the sea open to foreign and English merchants and merchandise, that there is now *no other means* for the *restraint* of *exportation* or *importation* of goods and merchandises in times of peace, *but only* when and where *an Act of Parliament* puts any restraint. Several Acts of Parliament having provided, *que la mere soit overt*, it may not be regularly shut against the merchandise of English, or foreigners in amity with this Crown, unless an *Act of Parliament* shut it, as it hath been done in some particular cases, and may be done in others."

The following opinion, upon establishing British manufactures in France, was written in 1718 by Mr. West, then counsel to the Board of Trade, and who died Chancellor of Ireland, in 1726 (*f*).

(*a*) Salk. 32, 335. 3 Lev. 352. 4 Mod. 176. 4 Bac. Ab. 595, title Merchant. Chitty, L. of Nat. 72.

(*b*) 2 Rob. 211.

(*c*) Fortescue R. 388.

(*d*) Hargr. Tr. Pars Secunda, ch. 9.

(*e*) Ibid. ch. 10.

(*f*) 2 Chalmers' Collection of Opinions, 247. 1 ed. Preface, xxxiii.

" To

" To the Right Honourable the Lords Commissioners for
Trade and Plantations.

" My Lords,

" In obedience to your Lordships' commands, signified to
me by Mr. Popple, I have perused and considered the several
letters relating to the establishing several manufactures in
foreign parts by British artificers; but, as the case is not
particularly stated unto me, it will not be possible for me to
give a direct answer to the question proposed. I shall, therefore, beg leave of your Lordships to consider it something at
large, and to lay down some general positions, which I take to
be agreeable to the law of England; a right application of
which, I believe, will in a great measure amount to an answer
to such inquiries as may be made.

" That particular subjects should have an uncontroulable
liberty of all manner of trading, is not only against the policy
of our nation, but of all other governments whatsoever. I do,
therefore, take it to be law, that the Crown may, upon special
occasion, and for reasons of state, restrain the same ; and that
not only in cases of war, plague, or scarcity of any commodity
of more necessary use at home, for the provision of the subject
or the defence of the kingdom, &c. (in which case the King's
prerogative is allowed to be beyond dispute), but even *for the
preservation* of the *balance of trade* : as, suppose a foreign
Prince, though in other respects preserving a fair correspon-
dence and in amity with us, yet will not punctually observe
such treaties of commerce as may have been made between the
two nations; or in case there are *no such treaties* existing,
refuses to enter into such a regulation of trade, as may be for
the mutual advantage and benefit of both dominions : on such
occasion, I am of opinion, that the King, by his prerogative,
may prohibit and restrain all his subjects in general from ex-
porting particular commodities, &c.; or else, generally, from
trading to such a particular country or place : since trade does
not only depend upon the will or laws of the Prince, whose
subjects adventure abroad to carry it on, but also of that
Prince into whose country the commodities are exported, and
with whose subjects commerce is negotiated and contracted;
without such a power it is obvious that the government of
England could not be upon equal terms with the rest of its
neighbours, and since *trade depends principally upon such*
treaties

treaties and alliances as are entered into by the Crown with foreign Princes; and since the power of entering into such treaties is vested absolutely in the Crown, it necessarily follows, that the management and direction of trade, must, in a great measure, belong to the King.

" Things of this nature are not to be considered strictly according to those municipal laws, and those ordinary rules, by which the private property of subjects resident within the kingdom is determined; but a regard must also be had to the laws of nations, to the policy and safety of the kingdom; the particular interest and advantages of private men must, in such cases, give way to the general good; and acting against that, though in a way of commerce, is an offence punishable at the common law.

" Foreign trades carried on by particular subjects, for their private advantage, which are really destructive unto, or else tending to the general disadvantage of the kingdom, are under the power of the Crown to be restrained or totally prohibited. There may be a prohibition of commerce without open enmity, as an actual declaration of war, and particular subjects, who, for private gain, carry on a trade abroad, which causes a general prejudice or loss to the kingdom, considered as an entire body; in doing so, manifestly act against the public good, and ought not only to be prohibited, but punished. Carrying on such trades is in truth (what some Acts of Parliament have declared some trades to be) being guilty of common nuisances, and if the Crown, which in its administration of government, is to regard the advantage of the whole realm, should not be invested with sufficient power to repress and restrain such common mischiefs, it has not a power to do right to all its subjects. If the public mischiefs, from such a way of trading, be plain and evident, there is the same reason for restraining particular persons from carrying on a trade that draws such consequences after it (though it be a trade, that, of itself, is not prohibited by any particular law), as there is that a private subject shall not make such an use of his own house and land (in which he has an absolute propriety and a legal title to it) as will turn to the common annoyance and public detriment of the rest of the kingdom.

" The general trade of the nation, and the maintaining of the customs and duties granted to the Crown for the support

of

of it, are things of so public a concern, that whatsoever has a
direct and evident tendency to the discouragement and disadvantage of the one or to the diminution of the other, is a
crime against the public. As an instance of which, I shall
mention it as a kind of precedent; that raising and spreading
a story, that wool would not be suffered to be exported upon
such a year (probably by some stock-jobbers in those times),
whereby the value of wool was beaten down, though it did not
appear the defendants reaped any particular advantage by the
deceit, was, upon the account of its being an injury to trade,
punished by indictment; and a confederacy, without any further act done, to impoverish the farmers of the excise and lessen
the duty itself, has been held an offence, punishable by information. If, therefore, the consequence of this present undertaking should prove what is apprehended from it, there can be
no doubt but that the Crown has so much interest and concern
for the trade of the nation and its own revenue, as to be able
to put a stop to the carrying on a thing so mischievous to the
one and the other, by the advice and assistance of his Majesty's
own subjects.

" As to the particular subjects so employed abroad, there is
no doubt but that the King, by his prerogative, may restrain
them; it is agreed on all hands, that the statute of fugitives,
is but an affirmance of the common law. That the Crown
may, at its discretion, require the personal presence and attendance of the subject, lest the kingdom should be dis-
furnished of people for its defence, as it is said in some
books; and not only so, but upon a suspicion or jealousy
that he is going abroad. *Ad quam plurima nobis et quam
pluribus de populo nostro prejudicialia et damnosa ibidem
prosequenda* (as the writ, framed upon that occasion, expressed
it). The Crown is, by law, entrusted to judge what things
those are which shall be looked upon to be mischievous and
prejudicial to the Crown and people, and what caution is to be
taken against them; and by that writ it appears it is equally
criminal to do any thing of that kind by any other hand, as to
do it personally himself; and, therefore, after the writ has commanded his not going abroad, it adds, *nec qui quicquam ib.
prosequi attemptes, seu attemptari facias, quod in nostrum seu
dictæ coronæ nostræ prejudicium cedere valeat quo vis modo:
nec aliquem ibidem mittas ex hac causa.*

7

" Upon the very foot of trade itself, it is necessary, that the Crown should have a power over the persons and dealings of their subjects in foreign parts. By the law of nations, a government, if they have no other redress, take goods from any of the same nation, by way of reprisal, for injustice done by one of the nations. So that Englishmen suffered to reside abroad, by their misbehaviour, may endanger more than their own persons and estates. But, as the stating to your Lordships, the power which the Crown has to prohibit the subject from going abroad, when there is reason to suspect, that designs prejudicial to the kingdom are carrying on alone, is not sufficient to answer your Lordships' purpose, I shall beg leave to remind your Lordships of a case parallel to this, which has already had a determination at the Board, *anno* one thousand seven hundred and five : Several English merchants were concerned in a design to set up the manufacturing of tobacco in Russia, to which purpose they had carried over the necessary workmen and instruments; but, upon application to the Board of Trade, the then Lords Commissioners did represent it to the Queen in Council, as their opinion, that the persons who had been already sent to Moscow, might be recalled by letters of privy seal, directed to her Majesty's Envoy, for that purpose; and that the engines and materials of working, should be broken and destroyed in the presence of the said Envoy; and that the persons at home, who were concerned in sending the said workmen over, should be enjoined not to send over any more workmen or materials, &c.

" Upon inquiry, my Lords, I am informed, that the said works and materials were actually destroyed in Russia, and the workmen sent back again by the direction of the Envoy, who took the advantage of the Czar's absence from the place where they were established. What was then done may certainly be repeated. It is not the business of a lawyer to consider, how such a method of proceeding may be relished by a foreign Court; but only to give it, as his opinion, that it may be justified, as against the particular subjects, who are guilty of so high a crime against their country.

" *Dec.* 5, 1718."   " RICH. WEST."

This opinion is written in a most able and plausible manner; but it is conceived, with the greatest diffidence, that many of the propositions and doctrines advanced in it are dangerously incorrect.

It cannot be denied, that as the King alone may make treaties, a treaty made by him with a foreign power, forbidding any particular commercial dealings between the two countries, might have the effect of rendering it illegal for a British subject to enter into such commercial transactions, contrary to such arrangement. Nor will it be disputed that the King, having the absolute discretionary power of recalling his subjects from foreign parts (*a*), may, by virtue of that prerogative, prevent them from personally trading abroad. It is equally true, that by statute (*b*) it is illegal to seduce artificers to go abroad, or to export certain utensils used in trade. But the position that the King may, from mere political motives, and independently of any treaty or legislative provision, prevent his subjects from carrying on, or being concerned in, any particular trade in a foreign country at peace with this, (however prejudicial such trade may be to the interests of this country,) appears to be incorrect.

It is, however, in all cases the peculiar province of the Crown to protect commerce, and there are certainly various instances in which the King has a discretionary right to promulgate commercial regulations, and to grant dispensations in cases of emergency, and where no positive laws exist on the subject, and a discretionary power of interference is necessary; this is, in some cases, by the common law, in others by the statute law of the land.

As the protector of commerce, the King alone possesses the power of appointing Consuls.

During war, trading with an enemy is illegal (*c*); but, as observed by Sir W. Scott (*d*), " it is indubitable. that the King may, if he please, give an enemy liberty to import," (that is, when the navigation, or other statute laws, do not expressly forbid such importation (*e*).) " He may, by his prerogative of declaring war and peace, place the whole of a foreign country in a state of amity, or, *à fortiori*, he may exempt any individual from the operation of a state of war." But the licence

(*a*) Ante, ch. 3.
(*b*) 23 Geo. 2. c. 13.
(*c*) Chitty, Law of Nat. 1, &c.

(*d*) 2 Rob. R. 162. 1 Ibid. 196. 1 East, 486.
(*e*) 12 East, 296.

to enable an enemy to import goods must be express, for an enemy will not be protected by a general licence (*a*), and it has not been usual to grant licences to an enemy (*b*). The right itself is established by the common law (*c*); and in the case of Vandyke *v.* Wintmore (*d*), Lord Kenyon said, " though the King may, at common law, license a trading with an enemy's country, yet he may also qualify this licence, in which case the parties seeking to protect themselves under it, must conform to its regulations."

The most usual mode in which a dispensation is granted to individuals, from the general prohibition upon all traffic with the enemy, is by the grant of licences. The nature of these licences is clearly explained, and certain rules for their construction most ably laid down by the Court, in the case of the Cosmopolite (*e*). In this case, Sir Wm. Scott said, " a licence is a high act of sovereignty; an act immediately proceeding from the sovereign authority of the state, which is alone competent to decide on all the considerations of commercial and political expediency, by which such an exception from the ordinary consequences of war must be controuled. Licences being then acts of sovereignty, they are necessarily *stricti juris*, and must not be carried farther than the intention of the great authority which grants them may be supposed to extend. I do not say that they are to be construed with pedantic accuracy, or that every small deviation should be held to vitiate the fair effect of them."

During the latter part of the late war, numerous questions arose on the construction of licences granted by the Crown. The general leaning in all the Courts was, to give them a comprehensive and liberal construction (*f*).

These licences legalize a trade with the enemy, in every respect fairly falling within their import, and incidental to the subject-matter (*g*). But the King's licence has not

---

(*a*) 1 Acton's Rep. 313, 322, 328. See 16 East, 197. 1 M. and S. 567. 4 Taunt. 605.

(*b*) Philimore, 2d edit. 9, in notes, and Preface, 20, 21.

(*c*) 2 Roll. Ab. 173. pl. 3 ; and 8 T. R. 550. Chitty, L. of Nat. 260.

(*d*) 1 East, 475. And see 12 East, 302.

(*e*) 4 Rob. Rep. 11. 1 Chitty, L. Nat. 261.

(*f*) 3 Taunt. 554. 4 Ibid. 376. See 1 Holt. R. 132, note.

(*g*) 8 East, 273.

the effect of removing the disability of an alien enemy, so as to enable him to sue in his own name (*a*). If, however, the alien reside in this country with the King's permission, he may, in such case, sue in his own name (*b*).

The conclusion of a peace necessarily destroys a licence, it then having no subject-matter to act upon (*c*).

These prerogative dispensations may also be exercised through the medium of orders in council, which are of a more general nature than licences, as they in general contain dispensations, or prohibitions, extending to a whole branch of commerce (*d*).

Though we have seen that the King has not in general, by virtue of his prerogative, a power to dispense with the common law, or any legislative provision (*e*); yet it has been usual, during the war, to give to the King in Council a power of modifying or dispensing with such provisions as it may be found expedient, in particular conjunctures, to alter or suspend; for the interests of commerce being of so variable a nature, and depending so much on circumstances suddenly arising, it would be very difficult, not to say impossible, during war, to make them generally subject to any permanent legislative provision (*f*).

The power to make these orders of council, and to grant licences in pursuance of them being derived from Acts of Parliament, is of a limited nature, and cannot be extended further than the acts themselves permit. The construction of licences granted by virtue of the King's prerogative, will in general be applicable to licences founded on these statutes.

We have also seen, that in cases of positive state necessity, the Crown has the power of laying on a general embargo; and, on the same principle of political emergency and absolute necessity, on which embargoes are justifiable, we may rest the King's power to make *new declarations of contraband*, and to prohibit the trading in articles which are termed contraband of war, as arms, ammunition, horses, timber for ship build-

---

(*a*) 8 East, 273; per Lord Ellenborough.

(*b*) 3 East, 332.

(*c*) 5 Rob. R. 22.

(*d*) Chitty, L. of Nat. 279.

(*e*) Ante, ch. 7. sect. 2. div. 2.

(*f*) See 43 Geo. 3. c. 153. s. 15, 16. 45 Geo. 3. c. 34. 46 Geo. 3. c. 111. 47 Geo. 3. sess. 2. c. 27. 48 Geo. 3. c. 37, 126. 49 Geo. 3. c. 25, 60.

ing, naval stores, provisions, at least when manufactured and fit for consumption, and in general any implements useful in war (*a*).

When, during a war, neutral merchants, &c. assist the enemy with such articles, they are liable to seizure and confiscation (*b*). As observed by Lord Erskine (*c*), " The King having, by his prerogative, the power to promulgate who are his enemies, is bound to watch over the safety of the State; he may, therefore, make new declarations of contraband, when articles come into use, as implements of war, which were before innocent. This is not the exercise of discretion over contraband; the law of nations prohibits contraband, and it is the *usus bellici*, which, shifting from time to time, make the law shift with them."

Under this head it may also be mentioned, that the King possesses the *sovereign dominion* in all the narrow *seas*, that is, the seas which adjoin the coasts of England, and other seas within his dominions (*d*). This prerogative power is vested in the King, as the protector of his people, and guardian of their rights. It is subservient, however, to those *jura communia*, which nature and the principles of the constitution reserve for his Majesty's subjects. It can neither prevent them from trading or fishing.

As a consequence of this prerogative, the King possesses also the power of reforming, preventing, and punishing any nuisances or obstructions in the seas and rivers over which his jurisdiction extends (*e*). And it was held on the same ground, and on the consideration that all matters of a public nature are in a special manner under the King's care and protection, that he might (before any statute made for commissioners of sewers) provide against any inundations, by embankments or other necessary means (*f*). The rights of the Crown, with respect

---

(*a*) Chitty, Law of Nat. 119, &c. 1 Rob. R. 189. 2 Ibid. 182. 4 Ibid. 35. 5 Ibid. 97. 6 Ibid. 93, 126.

(*b*) Ibid. Vatt. b. 3. c. 7. s. 112.

(*c*) Speech, 8 Mar. 1808, on the Orders in Council. 10 Cobbett's Parl. Deb. 958, 9.

(*d*) Seld. Mar. 251, &c. Hale de jure Maris, ch. 4. Rol. Ab. 168, 9. 5 Co. 106. 10 Co. 141. The Court of Admiralty, which is the proper forum for the settling of all maritime affairs, is more especially the King's Court, and derives its jurisdiction immediately from the Crown. 4 Inst. 142. Molloy, 66. See Bac. Ab. tit. Court of Admiralty; and 3 Price's R. 97, as to the jurisdiction, &c. of that Court.

(*e*) Hale de jure Maris, Hargr. Tr. 8.

(*f*) 10 Co. 141.

to the soil under the seas, and to *maritima incrementa*, will be hereafter considered (a).

A *Port* is defined by Lord Hale (b) to be *quid aggregatum*, consisting of something that is natural, viz. an access of the sea, whereby ships may conveniently come safe, a situation against winds, where they may safely lie, and a good shore, where they may well unlade; something that is artificial, as quays and wharfs, and cranes and warehouses, and houses of common receipt; and something that is civil, namely, privileges and franchises, viz. *jus applicandi, jus mercati*, and divers other additaments, given to it by civil authority." It is indisputably established, that the right to erect ports and havens is in general vested exclusively in the Crown (c); and this rule prevails so strictly, that even the lord of a county palatine, though he usually had ports by charter or prescription, cannot erect a common port within his palatine jurisdiction (d); and the exceptions to this rule, viz. that a subject may, by charter from the King, or prescription, erect a port (e), seem strongly to prove it.

The King has not merely the prerogative power of erecting ports and havens, but he possesses *primâ facie* the propriety or ownership in all the ports and havens within his dominions, though the public have a right to use them (f); and even though the right to a port or haven be vested by charter or prescription in a subject, yet he holds it charged or affected with the *jus regium* or royal prerogative, as it relates to ports and havens (g).

The royal right of superintending ports and havens, is a necessary consequence of the prerogative ownership in them (h). Hence the King is entrusted with the care of preventing and reforming public nuisances in ports and havens; the prosecutions for them are in his name, and the fines for the defects or annoyances in them, form part of his revenue (i). But this superintending power does not in general extend so far as to enable the King to open and shut ports and havens for the purpose of prohibiting the importation or

(a) Post, ch. 11.
(b) De portibus Maris, ch. 2.
(c) Ibid. ch. 3.
(d) Ibid.
(e) Ibid.

(f) Ibid. ch. 6. 8 Term R. 606.
(g) Ibid. Hale, ch. 8.
(h) Ibid. ch. 6.
(i) Ibid. ch. 8. Anstr. 603.

exportation

exportation of goods (*a*).   Nor can arbitrary or excessive duties for cranage, wharfage, &c. be taken from the public; but the duties must be reasonable and moderate, though settled by the King's licence or charter (*b*).

As the erection of ports is presumed to be for the advantage of the public, the King in exercising his right to erect them, is not restrained to any particular place, but may erect them in the vicinity but not within the peculiar limits of a former port, though it belong to a subject by charter or prescription ; if by the erection of the new port ships are not excluded from going to the old one (*c*). The King may also prohibit his subjects from bringing their merchandise by sea to any port within a certain distance from one which his Majesty has newly erected, and this prohibition is obligatory, as against every one but the legal owner, or the inhabitants of any port within the specified distance from that newly erected (*d*), although an antient port may lie within the prescribed bounds; but, as already stated, his Majesty cannot erect a port *de novo* within the peculiar precincts or limits which he has by charter previously assigned to a port belonging to one of his subjects (*e*).

The King being entrusted with the safety of navigation, possesses also by the common law, the prerogative right of erecting *beacons* and *lighthouses* in such places as his wisdom may deem most convenient for the preservation of ships and mariners, and the general interests of his subjects (*f*). This royal right is considered so important to the public weal, that it will justify his Majesty in erecting a beacon on the land of a subject without his consent (*g*).

The right of erecting beacons and lighthouses is vested by the common law of the land exclusively in the King; and a subject cannot raise them without the King's permission (*h*). It seems that antiently the power of erecting them was generally vested by the royal letters patent in the Lords of the Admiralty, as it previously appears to have been in the Lord

(*a*) Ante, 165.

(*b*) 8 Term R. 608.

(*c*) Hale de portibus Maris, ch. 5. See 5 Bac. Ab. 502.

(*d*) Ibid. Bac. Ab. 503.

(*e*) Ibid. Hale.

(*f*) 5 Bac. Ab. 510. 1 Bla. Com. 265.

(*g*) See ibid.

(*h*) See ibid. and Carter, 90. 4 Inst. 148.

High Admiral (*a*). At length, by the statute 8 Eliz. c. 13. (*b*), the power was partially vested in the Trinity House at Deptford. That statute provides, " that the Master, Wardens, and Assistants of the Trinity House at Deptford Strond, being a company incorporated as therein mentioned, may, from time to time, at their wills and pleasures, and at their costs, make, erect, and set up such and so many beacons, marks, and signs for the sea, in such place or places of the sea shores, and uplands near the sea coasts, or forelands of the sea, only for sea marks, as to them shall seem most meet, needful, and requisite, whereby the dangers may be avoided and escaped, and ships the better come into their ports without peril."

" And that all such beacons, marks, and signs, so to be by them or their assigns erected, made, and set up, at the costs and charges of the said Master, Wardens, and Assistants, shall and may be continued, renewed, and maintained, from time to time, at the costs and charges of the said Master, Wardens, and Assistants."

This act does not, it will be observed, relate to beacons, sea-marks, or light-houses, which it may be necessary to place in rivers, or other waters, away from the sea, the erection of which must, therefore, be governed by common law rules ; but it seems to extend as well to night light-houses as to beacons or other sea-marks, which may be used in the day-time (*c*).

SECT. II.

The Prerogatives with respect to the Domestic Commerce, or Internal Trade of the Country, may be considered, with reference—1st, To Monopolies and Patents for Inventions.—2dly, Marts and Fairs.—3rdly, Weights and Measures.—4thly, Money, Coin, &c.

THE interests and the freedom of domestic commerce have also been carefully watched and guarded by the English laws.

(*a*) See 4 Inst. 148. 1 Sid. 158.

(*b*) The provisions of this Act were extended to vessels appointed to carry lights, by 48 Geo. 3. c. 104. s. 61. As

to the Edystone, see 4 and 5 Ann. c. 20. And as to the light-house on the Smalls, see 18 Geo. 2. c. 42.

(*c*) See 4 Inst. 149, in margin.

On

On the freedom and careful regulation of the internal trade of a country, materially depend the industry, the wealth, and the comforts of retail dealers, who form by far the greater portion of the mercantile branch of the community, and a very considerable part of society at large; and the welfare of the rest of society are also involved in the immunities of trade. It is, therefore, a settled principle of the common law, that any arrangement which restrains or affects the freedom of trade, or leads to public inconvenience, by raising the price of provisions &c. is invalid (*a*). The law equally restrains the exercise of the highest prerogatives of the Crown, and forbids the most trivial engagement between the lowest of its subjects, when the object or effect may be injurious to the public in this respect. Hence it was, in the most antient times, a rule of the common law, that a monopoly [which may be defined to be an allowance by the King to any person or body of persons, for the sole making or selling, &c., any thing whereby any persons are sought to be restrained of a freedom or liberty they had before, or are hindered in their lawful trade (*b*)], is contrary to law (*c*). These monopolies were granted by Queen Elizabeth, to an intent highly prejudicial to the public, for the purpose of filling her coffers; but the mischief was suppressed by the statute 21 James 1. c. 3. which declares, that all monopolies, &c. are contrary to law, and shall be deemed void and of none effect; and some provisions are made for the prevention of any future grants tending to create a monopoly.

Even at common law, the King had the power of conferring on the *inventor* of any useful manufactory or art, the sole use of it *for a reasonable time* (*d*). This species of monopoly differs widely from that just considered. He who by his ingenuity, his labour, or his skill, has made a discovery essentially beneficial to the public, has in a manner earned an exclusive and temporary right to the profits it may afford. This is but a fair recompence for the benefits he imparts to society, to which justice, and the policy of encouraging talents, and the exercise of skill, evidently entitle him. On this common law principle,

(*a*) See 1 P. Wms. 181. 2 Saund. 157. n. 1. Stra. 739. 5 T. R. 111. 10 East, 22.

(*b*) 3 Inst. 181. 2 Hawk. P. C. 293. bk. 1. c. 79.

(*c*) Ibid. Bac. Ab. tit. Monopoly. Bull. N. P. 76. Bridgm. ed.

(*d*) Noy. 182. 2 Hawk. P. C. bk. 1. c. 79. s. 20.

N

the

the statute of James 1. expressly provides, that no declaration therein contained shall extend " to any letters patents, and grants of privilege, for the term of fourteen years or under, thereafter to be made, of the sole working or making of any manner of *new manufactures* within this realm, to the *true and first inventor* and inventors of such manufactures, which *others* at the time of making such letters patents, and grants, *shall not use*, so as also they be not contrary to the law, nor mischievous to the State, by raising prices of commodities at home, or hurt of trade, or generally inconvenient; the said fourteen years to be accounted from the date of the first letters patents, or grant, of such privilege thereafter to be made, but that the same shall be of such force as they should be, if that act had never been made, and of none other."

In noticing the law, respecting patents for inventions, we will consider—First, for what inventions patents may be granted; secondly, who is to be considered the inventor; thirdly, the description of the invention in the specification; fourthly, how a patent is obtained; fifthly, the remedies for the infraction of the patent right; and, lastly, how the patent may be vacated.

First. It will be observed, that the Act mentions letters patents for the sole working or making of " *new manufactures*" within this realm.

Manufactures are things made by the hands of man, and are reducible to two classes, namely, *machinery* and *substances.* In the former case, the *machine*, in the latter the *substance* produced, forms the manufacture and is consequently the subject of a patent (*a*). As observed by C. J. Eyre (*b*), " the word manufacture is of extensive signification: it applies not only to things made, but to the practice of making; to principles carried into practice. Under things made we may class new compositions of things, such as manufactures in the most ordinary sense of the word; all mechanical inventions, whether made to produce old or new effects, for a new piece of mechanism is certainly a thing made. Under the practice of making, we may class all new artificial manners of operating with the hand, or with instruments in common use, new processes in any art producing effects useful to the public. New methods of manufacturing articles in common use, where the

(*a*) 2 H. B. 481, 2.   (*b*) Ibid. 492.

whole

whole merit and effect produced are the saving of time and expense, and thereby lowering the price of the article, may be said to be new manufactures, in one of the common acceptations of the word, and agreeable to the spirit and meaning of the Act." To the same effect it was observed by Abbott, C. J. in the King v. Wheeler (a), that " the word ' manufactures' has been generally understood, to denote either a thing made, which is useful for its own sake, and vendible as such, as a machine, a stove, a telescope, and many others, or to mean an engine or instrument, or some part of an engine or instrument, to be employed either in the making of some previously known article, or in some other useful purpose, as a stocking-frame, or a steam-engine for raising water from mines, Or it may perhaps extend also to a new process to be carried on by known implements or elements, acting upon known substances, and ultimately producing some other known substance, but producing it in a cheaper and more expeditious manner or of a better and more useful kind." And in Edgeberry v. Stephens (b), the words " new devices" are substituted and used as synonymous with the words " new manufactures."

The novelty of the invention for which the patent is obtained is indispensable to its validity; but the patent is good, though, in inventions through the medium of mechanism, the *materials used be well known,* and have been used before, if the arrangement or combination of them be new, that is, *produce a new effect :* but in such case the patent must be for the compound article, and not for the old materials or ingredients of which it is made (c).

So a material and useful *addition* to, or *improvement* of, an old article is considered as a new manufacture; consequently, also, the subject of a patent (d). And a patent for an improvement of a thing, or for the thing improved, is in substance the same (e). The patent however must not be more extensive than the invention (f): consequently one for an improvement only, must not extend to the whole of the old article, but be

(a) 2 Barnew and Ald. 349.

(b) 2 Salk. 447.

(c) Ibid. 2 H. B. 487. Lord Ellenborough in Huddart v. Grimshaw. Davies on Pat. 267, 8, 9. 2 Marshall, 211.

(d) Lord Mansfield in Morris v. Branson. Bul. Nis. Pri. 76, c. Bridgm. ed.

(e) Mr. Justice Heath, in Boulton and Watt v. Bull. 2 H. B. 481, 2.

(f) Mr. Justice Buller, in the King v. Else. See Bul. Nis. Pri. 76, d. 11 East's R. 109, note.

confined

confined solely to the improvement; as the public have a right to purchase the improvement by itself, without being encumbered with other things (a). Therefore where the invention was of a particular movement in a watch, and the patent was taken out for the whole watch, it was held void (b).

A *mere principle* will not support a patent, because it is the first ground or rule for arts and sciences, or in other words the elements and rudiments of them. A patent must be for some new production from those elements which is vendible; for something of a corporeal and substantial nature, that can be made by man from matters subjected to his art and skill; and not for the elements themselves (c). If, however, a new principle, or method of doing any thing; or using old materials; be reduced into practice; and be so far imbodied or connected with corporeal substances, as to be in a condition to act, and to produce a new result, the patent is sustainable (d). There cannot be a patent for a mere philosophical *principle*, neither organized nor capable of being so; but a patent for a machine improved by a philosophical principle, though the machine existed before, is good. As laid down by C. J. Eyre, in Boulton v. Bull (e). "When the effect produced is no substance or composition of things, the patent can only be for the mechanism, if new mechanism is used, or for the process, if it be a new method of operating, with or without old mechanism, by which the effect is produced. To illustrate this, the effect produced by Mr. David Hartley's invention for securing buildings from fire, is no substance or composition of things: it is a mere negative quality, the absence of fire. This effect is produced, by a new method of disposing iron plates in buildings. In the nature of things the patent could not be for the effect produced. I think it could not be for the making the plates of iron, which, when disposed in a particular manner, produced the effect; for those are things in common use. But the invention consisting in the method of disposing those plates of iron, so as to produce their effect, and that effect being a useful and meritorious one,

(a) Mr. Justice Buller in Boulton and Watt v. Bull. 2 Hen. Bla. Rep. 463.
(b) Jessop's case, cited by Buller, J. in the same cause.

(c) 2 Hen. Bla. 463. 8 T. R. 101. 2 Barnew and Ald. 350.
(d) Ibid.
(e) 2 Hen. Bla. 493.

the patent seems to have been very properly granted to him, for his method of securing buildings from fire." Though a patentee denominate his discovery "a method," or a "principle" only, yet if the thing invented be in fact something substantial, or a new and useful effect produced by a new application of means known before, the verbal inaccuracy will not vitiate the grant (a).

The statute allows of patents for inventions with this qualification, " that they be not contrary to the law, nor mischievous to the State," in these three respects: first, by " raising the prices of commodities at home;" secondly, by being hurtful to trade; or thirdly, by being generally inconvenient. According to the letter of the statute, the saving goes only to the *sole working* and *making ;* the sole *buying, selling* and *using* remain under the general prohibition: and with apparent good reason for so remaining, for the exclusive privilege of *buying, selling* and *using,* could hardly be brought within the qualification of not being contrary to law, and mischievous to the State, in the respects mentioned (b).

The rule that the patent must not be more extensive than the invention will be considered in our observations on the specification.

Subject to these rules the patent and specification ought, it seems, to be liberally construed: there should be no leaning against it; and the patent generally contains an express clause that it shall be taken and construed in the most beneficial sense in favour of the patentee. In Turner *v.* Winter (c), Mr. J. Buller said, " when attempts are made to evade a fair patent, I am strongly inclined in favour of the patentee." Though in Hornblower *v.* Boulton (d), Lord Kenyon remarked, that " he was not one of those who greatly favored patents; for though in many instances the public were benefited by them, yet on striking the balance on this subject he thought that great oppression was practised on inferior mechanics by those who were more opulent."

Secondly, the statute requires that the patent should be

(a) 2 Hen. Bla. 477, per Rooke, J.   (c) 1 T. R. 606.
2 Barnew and Ald. 350.   (d) 8 Ibid. 98.
  (b) 2 Hen. Bla. 492.

granted

granted to *the true* and *first inventor* of a manufacture which
at the time of the grant *has not been used by others.*

The decisions on the wording of this part of the statute,
prove that it is entitled to a liberal interpretation in favour of
new and beneficial discoveries (*a*). The word inventor ("a
finder out of something new (*b*)") has not been restricted to
its literal signification; but has, on fair grounds of political
convenience, been construed to mean the *first publisher* or
introducer of the invention: so that a person in this country
who is in possession of, and introduces a foreign discovery,
may obtain a patent (*c*). And where the patentee was not the
first inventor, though he was the first publisher or introducer,
of a British invention (the first inventor having confined it to
his closet, and the public being unacqainted with it); the patent was considered valid (*d*). In such case the patentee,
though not the inventor, renders a benefit to the public; and
it is the part of good policy to encourage the early production
of the inventions of genius. But when the discovery has *been
used by others* or publicly sold by the patentee himself, only for
a short time, as four months before the time when the patent
is granted, the patentee is unable to confer on the public the
benefit they are entitled to expect, and the patent is void (*e*).
And it seems that if the patentee were informed of the discovery by another person in this country, the patent would be
unfounded (*f*).

Thirdly, Of the *description* of the invention in the *specification.*

Though there be nothing in the Act of James I. requiring a
specification, the patent universally requires, as a condition on
which the validity of the grant depends, that the patentee shall
" *particularly describe* and *ascertain* the *nature* of the *invention,*
and in what *manner the same* is to be *performed,* by an instrument
in writing under his hand and seal ; and cause the same to be

---

(*a*) See post. ch. 16. s. 3 ; as to general rule in construing King's grants.

(*b*) Johnson's Dict.

(*c*) 2 Salk. 447. 2 Hen. Bla. 491.

(*d*) 2 Hen. Bla. 470, 487. And in
Forsyth *v.* Riviere, N. P. K. B. June
4, 1819; C. J. Abbott held that if several simultaneously discover the same

thing, the party who first communicates
it to the public is entitled to the benefit
of it.

(*e*) Tennant's Case, Davies on Patents, 429, &c. and Wood *v.* Zimmer.
1 Holt Rep. N. P. 58.

(*f*) Tennant's Case.

enrolled

enrolled in Chancery within a certain time (usually one calendar month) from the date of the letters patent." The object
of enforcing a full, explicit and precise disclosure of the exact
invention, is to enable the public after the expiration of the
patented term to " work and make" it, as the inventor alone legally could during the fourteen years. The monopoly would substantially be permanent, instead of temporary, if the patentee
were at liberty to conceal either wholly or partially, or were
allowed to state ambiguously the principles on which it is
founded; for in many instances the corporeal substance or
thing forming the subject of the patent, affords no information or clue to a discovery of the mode of making or working
it. In all the cases which are before the public, in which the
specification has formed the subject of discussion, we may trace
the most anxious desire on the part of the Court to act fully
up to this principle. A slight, though inadvertent defect, will
often vitiate the grant. Few specifications have successfully
stood the test of legal scrutiny : a consideration which proves
the necessity of exercising the utmost circumspection and care,
and of calling to the patentee's aid the skill, the experience,
and the unprejudiced judgment of others. He whose mind
and thoughts have long been engrossed with any given subject,
overlooks the ignorance of others, and is apt to forget various
matters which gradually led his mind to the discovery, and
which form a part of the invention.

The general rule with respect to the specification seems to
be this, that it must disclose the nature of the invention, and
the manner in which it is to be performed, so as to enable
mechanical men of common understanding, and a reasonable
degree of skill on the subject, to comprehend and make the
thing by it, without any trial, experiment, invention or addition of their own (a). But it need not explain any thing
respecting the discovery so fully as to enable a person entirely
ignorant of mechanics, and not conversant with the subject,
to understand and act upon the specification without other
assistance (b). Reference must often be necessarily made in
these cases to matters of general science; or the party must

(a) Bul. Nis. Pri. 76, d. Bridgm. ed.   434. 2 Barnew and Ald. 354.
2 Hen. Bla. 484, 496. 11 East, 107, 8.   (b) Ibid.
Davies on Patents, 56, 106, 128, 194,

carry a reasonable knowledge of the subject-matter with him, in order clearly to comprehend specifications of this nature, though fairly intended to be made (a).

In the first place the specification is insufficient if it be *ambiguous*, or give directions which *tend to mislead* the public (b). If articles are put into a specification merely to puzzle, or are not useful for the purpose of the patent, it is void (c). So where the patent was for making a particular sort of yellow, and the patentee directed any sort of fossil salt to be used; when only one sort of it would answer the purpose; the patent was held void (d). An ambiguity may arise from the specification stating as essential parts, any thing which forms a part of a prior invention; for the public are not to be deceived by the patentee holding out as material, those things which in' fact are not so (e). The patentee must, in his claims to novelty, confine himself solely to that which is his invention (f). The patent must not be more extensive than the invention : and where the patent is for an improvement or addition, the patent and specification (g) must not be for the whole machine or manufacture, and the latter must describe precisely in what the alleged improvement consists; so that what is old, may be distinguishable from what is new (h). As observed by Lord Ellenborough (i), " the patentee in his specification ought to inform the person who consults it, what is new, and what is old. He should say, my improvement consists in this, describing it by words if he can, or, if not, by reference to figures. But here the improvement is neither described in words nor by figures, and it would not be in the wit of man, unless he were previously acquainted with the construction of the instrument, to say what was new and what was old. The specification states, that the improved instrument is made in manner following : this is not true, since the description comprises that which is old, as well as that

(a) 11 East, 113.

(b) 1 T. R. 602.

(c) Rex v. Ackwright, Bul. N. P. 77. Davies, 118.

(d) 1 T. R. 602.

(e) See Lord Ellenborough's Observations in Huddart v. Grimshaw, Davies, 279, 294, 5.

(f) 11 East, 109. See per Sir Vic. Gibbs, in Bovill v. Moore, cited Davies, 398.

(g) See Rex v. Ackwright, 1784, cor. Buller, Bul. Nis. Pri. 76, c. Bridgm. ed. 11 East, 109.

(h) 1 Stark. 199. Davies, 411.

(i) 1 Stark. 201.

which

which is new.   Then it is said, that the patentee may put in
aid the figures, but how can it be collected from the whole of
these in what the improvement consists ?   A person ought to
be warned by the specification against the use of the particular
invention, but it would exceed the wit of man to discover from
what he is warned in a case like this."   And if a patentee in
the specification sum up the principle in which his invention
consists; if this principle be not new the patent cannot be
supported, although it appear that the application of the
principle, as described in the specification, be new.   In a late
important case on this subject (*a*), the Court of Common Pleas
held that where a person obtains a patent for a machine consisting of an entirely new combination of parts, though all the
parts may have been used separately, in former machines, the
specification is correct in setting out the whole as the invention of the patentee : but if a combination of a certain number of those parts have previously existed up to a certain point
in former machines, the patentee merely adding other combi-
nations, the specification should only state such improvements;
though the effect produced be different throughout.   But
where the party obtained a patent for a new machine, and
afterwards another patent for improvements in the said machine, in which the grant of the former patent was recited,
it was held that a specification, containing a full description
of the whole machine so improved, but not distinguishing the
new improved parts, or referring to the former specification,
otherwise than as the second patent recited the first, was sufficient (*b*).   And it seems to be unnecessary in stating a specification of a patent for an improvement to designate precisely
all the former known parts of the machine, and then to apply to
these the improvement; but on many occasions it may be sufficient to refer generally to them.   As, in the instance of a
common watch, it may be sufficient for the patentee to say,
take a common watch, and add or alter such or such parts, describing them (*c*).

So the *falsity* of any allegation in the specification will vacate the patent.   As if the patentee say, that by one process he
can produce three things, and he fail in any one ; or if the spe-

---

(*a*) 2 Marshall, R. 211.   (*c*) Ibid. 107.
(*b*) 11 East, 101.

cification direct the thing to be produced several ways, or by several different ingredients, and any one of them fail (*a*). So, if the thing could only be made with two or three ingredients specified, and the patentee has inserted others which will not answer the purpose, that will avoid the patent (*b*). As stated by Sir V. Gibbs, in Bovill *v.* Moore (*c*), " another consideration respecting the specification, which is also a material one, is, whether the patentee has given a full specification of his invention, not only one that will enable a workman to construct a machine answering to the patent, but one that will enable a workman to construct a machine answerable to the patent, to the extent most beneficial within the knowledge of the patentee at the time; for a patentee who has invented a machine useful to the public, and can construct it in one way more extensive in its benefits than in another, and states in his specification only that mode which would be least beneficial, reserving to himself the more beneficial mode of practising it, although he will have so far answered the patent, as to describe in his specification a machine to which the patent extends; yet he will not have satisfied the law, by communicating to the public the most beneficial mode he was then possessed of, for exercising the privilege granted to him." As if the prosecution of a manufacture be assisted in a lace machine, by bending together two of the teeth of the dividers, or making one longer than the rest, if it appear to have been a *subsequent discovery*, it will not break in upon the validity of a patent, it will only shew that the patentee has since found out the means of carrying on his own invention to better effect (*d*); but if at the time when he obtained his patent, he was apprized of this more beneficial mode of working, and did not by his specification communicate this more beneficial mode of working to the public, that will have been a fraudulent concealment from the public, and will render the patent void (*e*). So, if the patentee make the article with cheaper materials than those which he has enumerated, although the latter will answer the purpose equally well, the patent is void, because he does not put the public in possession of his invention, or enable them to derive

(*a*) 1 T. R. 602.

(*b*) 1 Ibid. 607.

(*c*) At N. P. Davies, 400. In C. P. 2 Marshall, 211.

(*d*) Davies on Patents, 381. Sir V. Gibbs in Bovill *v.* Moore.

(*e*) Ibid. 401.

the

the same benefit which he himself does (*a*).   In a case before Lord Mansfield, for infringing a patent for steel trusses, it appeared, that the patentee in tempering the steel, rubbed it with tallow, which was of some use in the operation, and because this was omitted, the specification was held to be insufficient, and the patent was avoided (*b*).   And in a recent case, the wilful omission to state an article, which, though it was not necessary to the composition of the manufacture, produced it more expeditiously, was held to vacate the grant (*c*).   In short, the exact nature, and the mode of conducting the processes, and the times they are to be continued, should be accurately stated, and specifically pointed out (*d*).

It is not necessary to set forth a model or drawing, illustrative of the invention described in the specification (*e*) : but it is usual and perhaps advisable so to do.   It should be drawn on a scale, especially where relative sizes or distances are important (*f*).   The general rule however seems to be, that the specification must contain *within itself* the necessary information, and should not refer to other distinct instruments or books, &c. for particulars (*g*).   But in Harmar *v.* Playne (*h*), a patent for improvements upon a former machine was held good, although the specification described the whole machine, without distinguishing the improvements from the part of the whole machine or referring to the former specification, otherwise than as the second patent recited the first.

Care must also be taken that the denomination or title of the invention in the patent is not more or less extensive, and does not vary from that mentioned in the specification.   The language of the patent as was observed in a late case (*i*), may be explained and reduced to a certainty by the specification; but the patent should not represent the party to be the inventor of one thing, and the specification shew him to be the inventor of another; because, perhaps, if he had represented himself as the inventor of that other, it might have been well known that the thing was of no use, or was in common use,

---

(*a*) 1 Term R. 607. and 1 Holt, R. N. P. 60.

(*b*) 1 Term, 608.

(*c*) Holt's Rep. N. P. 58.

(*d*) 2 Barnew and Ald. 345.

(*e*) See 2 Hen. Bla. 463.

(*f*) Hands on Patents, 11.

(*g*) Harmar *v.* Playne, 11 East, 112, 3. 1 Ves. and B. 67.

(*h*) 11 East, 101.

(*i*) 3 Barnew and Ald. 350. 1.

and he might not have obtained a grant as the inventor of it. We have already considered that patents for improvements must be taken out accordingly (*a*). In Hornblower *v.* Boulton (*b*), the patent was obtained " for a method of lessening the consumption of steam and fuel in fire engines." This was effected by improvements of an old machine, and the patent was held good. Grose J. observed, " I consider the patent and specification so connected together as to make a part of each other; and that to learn what the patent is I may read the specification, and consider it as incorporated in the patent. Whether the patent call the manufacture by its name, or style it an invention, a mode, or method, or in any other manner, it signifies nothing; for the specification describing the thing as required by the patent must be resorted to, and may fairly be deemed a part of the patent itself." But in a subsequent case, a patent "for an improved mode of lighting cities, towns, and villages," was held not to be supported by a specification describing an improved lamp. The patent should have been obtained "for an improved lamp (*c*)." And a patent for a " tapering brush" will not support a patent for a brush, differing from a common brush in no other respect, than in the circumstance that the hair or bristles are purposely made of unequal lengths (*d*). Nor will a patent "for a new or improved method of drying and preparing malt" be sustained by a specification for heating, &c. ready made malt (*e*).

Particular care should be taken that the specification is acknowledged and lodged in the inrollment office before the expiration of the specified time, as the legislature only can give relief afterwards (*f*). A proviso that a specification shall be enrolled within one calendar month then next after the date, which is the 10th of May, is satisfied by an inrolment on the 10th of June (*g*).

Fourthly. How a patent is obtained.

To obtain a patent, a petition for it must be prepared, together with an affidavit of the inventor in support of the petition. These are then taken to the office of the Secretary

---

(*a*) Ante, 184.
(*b*) 8 T. R. 95. 2 Barnew and Ald. 350.
(*c*) 1 Stark. 205.
(*d*) 2 Stark. Rep. 249.
(*e*) 2 Barnew and Ald. 350.
(*f*) 6 Ves. Jun. 599.
(*g*) 2 Campb. 294.

of State for the Home Department, where they are lodged. A, few days after, the answer to the petition may commonly be had, containing a reference of it to the attorney or solicitor-general, which must be taken to either of their chambers for the report thereon; and in a few days afterwards the clerk will deliver it out. The report is then to be taken to the Secretary of State's office for the King's warrant, and the clerk will inform the person leaving it when it may be called for. The warrant is directed to the attorney or solicitor-general, and is to be taken to their patent office for the bill. When the bill is prepared, it is taken to the Secretary of State's office, for the King's sign manual to the bill. As soon as this is obtained, it is carried to the signet office to be passed there, when the clerk prepares a warrant for the Lord Keeper of the privy seal, whereupon the clerk of the privy seal prepares his warrant to the Lord Chancellor. This warrant is then to be taken to the Lord Chancellor's patent office, where the patent itself is prepared and will be delivered out as soon as it is sealed. The specification should then be prepared, acknowledged, and lodged at the enrollment office, to have the usual certificate of the enrollment indorsed on it; this is commonly done in about a week or fortnight afterwards, and then the patent is in every respect complete. For Ireland and Scotland there must be distinct patents (a).

With respect to a *caveat*, Mr. Davies in his work on this subject makes the following useful remarks: " It now only remains that we should say a few words upon the nature and effect of a caveat, which during our practice we have frequently found to be very much misunderstood. It has been thought by many inventors, that upon entering a caveat they secured the right to themselves of obtaining a patent, notwithstanding the invention might be brought into use prior to their having done so; in short, that it was a kind of minor patent, giving them every privilege for one year which the patent itself would do for fourteen, or that it would operate as a proof of their being the first and true inventors, and that upon their afterwards obtaining a patent, they would be able to maintain it against any person, who, in the mean time, might have made

(a) See Hands, 12, &c.

use of the invention. In order to obviate such erroneous ideas, it is necessary to explain the nature and effect of a caveat.

" A caveat is merely a desire that if any person should apply for a patent for any particular invention, notice of such application should be given to the party. This caveat is usually entered at the offices of the attorney and solicitor-general, and upon an application to either of them for his report upon a petition to the King for a patent for any discovery of the same nature as that described in the caveat, notice is given to the person who has taken this precaution, which gives him an opportunity, if he thinks the inventions interfere with each other, of opposing the application. If it is meant to oppose, the attorney or solicitor-general before he makes his report will give a separate audience to each party, and examine the nature of the two inventions, and according to his opinion of their similarity, will make his report or not: if he is of opinion that there is a material coincidence, he will not report in favour of the application; but if otherwise, he makes his report, and the patent proceeds in its regular course. If however the party entering the caveat is not satisfied with the decision of the attorney or solicitor-general, he has another opportunity of opposing, by entering a caveat at the great seal, when the Lord Chancellor will himself give a similar audience and examine the pretensions of the parties. This practice is not often recurred to, as it is attended with much expense, and the Chancellor usually orders all costs to be paid by the party opposing, if he does not succeed, as he is averse to the caveat in so late a stage of the business, after great part of the expense of the patent has been incurred (a).

" The caveat remains upon the books for one year, and may be renewed from year to year as long as may be considered requisite.

" If it is thought necessary to enter a caveat, it is proper to use general expressions, rather than to express the precise invention, as by that means the inventor would receive notice of any application for a patent, connected with the subject of the invention mentioned in the caveat, which might not be the case if the particular invention or improvement should be ex-

---

(a) In ex parte Fox, 1 Ves. and B. 67. the Lord Chancellor held that no costs   shall be allowed where the *caveat* is not unreasonable.

                                        actly

actly identified.   Another reason for general expressions is, to guard against the opposite party obtaining a knowledge of the invention, as he might be able to affect the validity of the patent, by publishing the invention before the patent is sealed, which would have the effect of throwing the invention open to the public.   But it will sometimes happen, that two ingenious persons may, without any improper communication, make a discovery of a similar invention, in which case, upon the similarity of the invention appearing to the attorney or solicitor-general, it is usually recommended that the parties should unite interests, and take out a patent in their joint names, which seems to be the most prudent plan for both parties, as priority of invention would be of no avail, if the other party should be inclined to publish the invention, so as to affect the patent.   We cannot, however, too much reprobate a practice, which has of late grown into use by some speculative persons, of keeping a list of caveats upon general principles entered in the books, without any idea of obtaining patents themselves, but with the sole view of being acquainted with every improvement that is going on, whereby they gain an opportunity of coming to a compromise with the real inventors, and sometimes have obtained large sums of money from them, to withdraw their opposition."

It will have been collected from the cases cited before (*a*), that great care must be observed in stating for what the patent is taken out, and that an error in this respect may be fatal.

By provisoes in the patent, the grant becomes void if the patent right become vested in five different persons at the same time, or if the specification be not enrolled within the time.

The term for which the patent is granted can only be prolonged by Act of Parliament.

Fifthly, Of the *remedies* for the infraction of the patent right.

The exclusive right of the patentee " to work and make" the subject-matter of the grant, is infringed by any other person copying any part of the invention.   And though the machine, &c. made by the defendant be *in form* different from the

(*a*) Ante, 184, 188.

patentee's, still, if the defendant has availed himself *substantially* of the new *idea* of the plaintiff, however ingeniously the exterior of the production may have been worked up into a different shape, the remedy seems clear (*a*). The law will not suffer an individual to do indirectly that which it directly forbids. And in *ex-parte* Fox (*b*), the Lord Chancellor observed, " If the petitioners have invented certain improvements upon an engine for which a patent had been granted, and those improvements could not be used without the original engine, at the end of fourteen years the petitioners could make use of a patent taken out upon their improvements, though, before that period expired, they would have no right to make use of the others' *substratum*."

The remedies are by action at law for damages, or by proceedings in Chancery. Perhaps it is in general advisable as a matter of course to commence proceedings in Chancery with all possible expedition, for an account of the profits made from the illegal use of the invention. An injunction may thereby also be obtained to restrain the party from the further use of the patent right (*c*); but there must be separate bills upon every distinct invasion of the patent (*d*). An action at law to try the validity of the patent is almost invariably directed by the Lord Chancellor.

On the trial of the action, the plaintiff must give some general or slight evidence, shewing the nature of the invention and that it produced the effect specified. It is in strictness incumbent on the defendant to falsify the specification (*e*); but it is advisable that the plaintiff should be prepared with the strongest possible evidence in support of the merits of the discovery, and the sufficiency of the specification. Letters patent being under the great seal are matters of record (*f*), and are therefore read without proof: and by statutes 3 and 4 Ed. 6. c. 4. and 13 El. c. 6. patentees and all claiming under them, may make title by shewing the exemplification or constat of the roll. These statutes have been held to extend to all the

(*a*) See per Rooke, J. in Boulton *v.* Bull, 2 H. B. 477. Sir V. Gibbs, C. J. Bovill *v.* Moore, Davies, 405.

(*b*) 1 Ves. and B. 67.

(*c*) See Mitf. Chancery Pleadings, 124.

(*d*) 2 Ves. Jun. 486.

(*e*) 1 Term R. 602.

(*f*) 2 Bla. Com. 346. Dr. and Student, book 1. dial. 8. Phillips's Evid. 173, 4. See Bull. N. P. 227.

King's patents, which concern lands, privilege, or other thing granted to a subject, corporation, or any other (*a*).

Sixthly, The mode of *vacating* the patent by *scire facias* will be considered hereafter. Besides which its defects may be exposed and established by the verdict of the jury against the patentee, in an action for infringing his right: or in answer to his suit in equity for an account and injunction to prevent the further use of it. The statute of monopolies, 21 Jac. 1. c. 3. s. 2. declares that monopolies, letters patent, &c. and their force and validity, " ought to be and shall be examined, heard, tried, and determined by and according to the common laws of this realm, and not otherwise."

2. *Marts and Fairs* were originally instituted for the benefit of the public, and the better regulation of trade. As protector of commerce, the King alone possesses the power of creating markets and fairs; nor can any one claim them but by grant from the Crown or by prescription, which supposes such grant (*b*); though they may exist by way of royal ordinance, without being granted to any one in particular (*c*). It was observed by Lord Mansfield (*d*), that the reason why a fair or market cannot be holden without a grant, is not merely for the sake of promoting traffic and commerce, but also for the like reason, as in the Roman law, for the preservation of order and prevention of irregular behaviour; " *ubi est multitudo ibi debet esse Rector*."

The King is also the sole judge where markets and fairs should be kept; and therefore it has been laid down, that if he grant a market, to be holden in any particular place, which happens to be inconvenient for the public, yet it must be holden in the place appointed by the King (*e*). If no place be specified in the grant on which the market or fair is to be holden, the grantee may keep it where he pleases, so that he do not prejudice the rights of other grantees or create a nuisance to the public. Where the grant states that the fair or market shall be holden in any particular town, &c. it may be held in any part of it; and though the grantee hold it for up-

<hr>

(*a*) Page's Case, 5 Co. Rep. 53.

(*b*) 2 Inst. 220.

(*c*) Hob. 22. 17 Vin. Ab. 145, Prerog. H. C.

(*d*) 3 Burr. 1817.

(*e*) 3 Mod. 127. 2 Rol. Ab. 140. Bac. Ab. Fairs, B.

wards

wards of twenty years in one spot, he may remove to another within the precinct of the grant. And where a market is granted generally to a corporation, they may remove it to any place within the limits of their jurisdiction, though immemorially holden in a certain place (*a*). By the statute 13 Edw. I. c. 5. no fairs or markets shall be kept in churchyards.

It is most important to remember that the King does not grant a market or fair without a writ of *ad quod damnum* being previously executed (*b*). Even if that be done (*c*), the Crown cannot enable a subject to erect a market or fair so near that of another person as to affect his interests therein, though the new market or fair be holden on a different day, or which occasions a damage in any respect to the public (*d*). Nor can the King grant that a shop shall be a market overt (*e*). The mode of avoiding grants from the Crown will be considered hereafter (*f*). It may not be irrelevant to remark, that if the grantee of a market under letters patent from the Crown, suffer another person to erect a market in his neighbourhood, and use it for the space of twenty-three years without interruption, he is by such user barred of his action on the case, for disturbance of his market; but this presumptive bar does not it seems apply against the King (*g*).

By the general grant of a market or fair, the grantee is authorized to hold, without any express words to that effect, a court of record, called the court of *pie powders*, as incident to the market or fair, and for the advancement of justice therein (*h*). But toll is not incident of common right to a fair or market; therefore, if the King do not expressly authorize the grantee to take it, he cannot legally do so, though the grant contain the words 'with all its appurtenances,' and in such case the market or fair is free (*i*). Where, however, an old market or fair, in respect whereof toll was due by prescription, comes

(*a*) 3 Mod. 108. 3 East, 538. 1 Selw. and B. 67.

(*b*) Bac. Ab. Fairs, A. Burr. 1818.

(*c*) 2 Ventr. 344.

(*d*) 2 Saund. 174, n. 2. 2 Inst. 406. Com. Dig. Market, C.

(*e*) Mo. 625. See 4 Taunt. 524.

(*f*) See post. ch. 12. s. 3 ; ch. 16. s. 5. See also Burr. 1812, as to a *Quo Warranto* for setting up a market without authority.

(*g*) 1 Bos. and P. 400. 2 Saund. 175, note. 3 East, 298. 6 Ibid. 456. See post. ch. 14. as to the Crown being barred.

(*h*) 2 Inst. 220. 4 Ibid. 272. Bac. Ab. Fairs, C. 4 Taunt. 533. Nature of it, Com. Dig. Market, G.

(*i*) 2 Inst. 220. 2 Lutw. 1336. Palmer's R. 78. Wood's Inst. 222. 6 East, 438, note. Stra. 1171.

to the King, and he grants the market *cum partimentiis*, the toll passes (*a*). The King may clearly enable the grantee to take a reasonable toll; and, it seems, the exact toll to be taken need not be specified in the patent (*b*), and that usage may fix the identical charges (*c*). However, apt and certain words must be used in the grant, if it profess to point out what toll is to be taken; and, therefore, a grant of such toll to be taken at two bridges, as is used to be taken, ' *ibi et alibi infra regnum Angliæ*, has been held uncertain and void (*d*). The King may, after he has granted the fair or market, grant to the patentee the right to take toll in respect thereof; but in such case there must be a *quid pro quo*, some proportionable benefit to the public (*e*).

If an unreasonable toll be granted, the patent is void as to the toll, *in toto*, and the market or fair becomes free (*f*). So, if the patentee of a market or fair take outrageous toll, (the reasonableness of which, under all the circumstances, is a question determinable at law (*g*)), he forfeits the whole toll *in futuro ;* and the King may, on office found (*h*), seize the market or fair into his own hands till it be redeemed (*i*). But the market or fair itself is not forfeited in such case (*k*). Toll cannot be taken for goods not brought to a market, or sold therein by sample only (*l*).

The King is not liable to pay toll (*m*), nor is he bound by a sale in market overt (*n*). He may grant an exemption from tolls due to himself, or which may thereafter become due in respect of a subsequently granted fair or market, but not from toll due on account of an old fair or market (*o*).

As just observed, a market or fair is not absolutely forfeited

(*a*) Palmer's R. 78.

(*b*) See Ibid. 86. This was the opinion of three judges. See also the Register, p. 103. But Montague, C. J. held the contrary; and in Palm. 79, said that it was agreed by Popham in Heddy's Case, (see Heddy *v.* Wheelhouse, Cro. El. 558; and 591.) that the King ought to determine the *quantum* of toll, Moore, 474, S. C. In Osbuston *v.* James and others, 2 Lutw. 1377, the same objection was taken; but judgment was given on another point.

(*c*) 5 East, 2.

(*d*) Cro. Jac. 421.

(*e*) 2 Inst. 220. Cro. El. 558 ; 591. Moore, 474. 4 Taunt. 519, 520.

(*f*) 2 Inst. 220. 2 Lutw. 1336.

(*g*) 2 Inst. 222.

(*h*) 2 Ibid. 221.

(*i*) Ibid. Pal. 82. Com. Dig. Market, I.

(*k*) Ibid.

(*l*) 4 Taunt. 520.

(*m*) 2 Inst. 221, 2 Rol. Ab. 198.

(*n*) 2 Inst. 713.

(*o*) Ibid. 221. Bac. Ab. Fairs, D. 2.

by the grant of unreasonable toll, or by the owner taking such
toll.   It seems also, that it is not forfeited by the owner holding it longer than the time allowed by the patent, the statute
2 Edw. 3. c. 15. merely providing, that the King may in such
case (on office bound (*a*)), " seize the fair into his own hands,
there to remain till the owner pay a fine, &c." which implies,
a seizure and not a forfeiture (*b*).   It appears, however, that if
a market or fair be holden on a different day, and not at all on
the day allowed, or if there be any abuse in a matter by law,
incident to a market or fair, as in the court of *pie powders*, an
absolute forfeiture is incurred (*c*).

3. The regulation of *weights* and *measures*, is ranked by Sir
William Blackstone among the rights of the Crown (*d*); but,
(as observed by Mr. Christian,) with some degree of impro-
priety; for, from Magna Charta to the present time, there are
above twenty Acts of Parliament to fix and establish the standard and uniformity of weights and measures (*e*).

4. *As to Money, Coin, &c.*—As the regulator and protector
of commerce, of which money is the medium, the King alone
is entrusted with the right to coin money, to fix its denomination or value, and to render it current (*f*).   His Majesty may
legitimate foreign coin, and make it current here, declaring at
what value it shall be taken in payment (*g*), and may, at any
time, decry any coin of the kingdom, and make it no longer
current.

This prerogative may be considered with reference—1st, to
the materials; 2dly, the impression; and, 3dly, the denomination or value of coin.

1. Sir Edward Coke asserts (*h*) that the money of England
must consist either of gold or silver, and none other was ever

(*a*) 2 Inst. 222.
(*b*) Ibid. See Com. Dig. Market, I.
2 Rol. Ab. 124.   A similar construction
has been also applied to the statute
Westminster 1. c. 31. as to taking excessive toll.   Ante, 195.
(*c*) Ibid. Palmer's R. 82.
(*d*) 1 Bla. Com. 274.
(*e*) Ibid. 276, note 16. See Magna

Charta, ch. 25, and the statutes cited
3 Bac. Ab. 113, title Fairs, C.
(*f*) 5 Co. 114. Dav. 19. 2 Rol.
Ab. 166. Plowd. Com. 316. 1 Bla.
Com. 276. Hal. Hist. P. C. 188.
(*g*) 1 Hal. P. C. 197. 1 Bla. Com.
278, see 1 March 6. 5 El. c. 11. 18
El. c. 1. 43 Geo. 3. c. 139. s. 3.
(*h*) 2 Inst. 577.

issued

issued till 1672, when copper farthings and halfpence were coined by Charles 2. and ordered by proclamation to be current in all payments under the value of sixpence, and nòt otherwise.   But this copper coin is nòt upon the same footing with the other in many respects, particularly with regard to the offence of counterfeiting it (a).   It seems therefore that the King may make money of other materials than gold, silver or copper, though such money would not in various respects be protected by laws which relate to other coin.

2. As to the impression, the stamping thereof is the unquestionable prerogative of the Crown; for though divers bishops and monasteries had formerly the privilege of coining money, yet, as Sir Matthew Hale observes (b), this was usually done by special grant from the King, or by prescription, which supposes one; and therefore was derived from and not in derogation of the royal prerogative.   Besides that, they had only the profit of the coinage, and not the power of instituting either the impression or denomination; but had usually the stamp sent from the Exchequer.

3. The denomination or value for which the coin is to pass current, is likewise in the breast of the King; and if any unusual pieces are coined, that value must be ascertained by proclamation.   In order to fix the value, the weight and the fineness of the metal are to be taken into consideration together.   When a given weight of gold or silver is of a given fineness, it is then of the true standard, and called esterling or sterling metal (c).

Whether the King can legally change the established weight or alloy of money, without an Act of Parliament, seems not to be quite clear.   By the statute 25 Ed. 3. st. 5. c. 13. it is " accorded and established that the money of gold and silver which now runneth, shall not be impaired in weight nor in alloy; but as soon as a good way may be found that the same be put in the antient state as in the sterling." Lord Coke (d), in his comment of *articuli super cartas*, ch. 20, 21. cites, among other acts and records, this statute of the 25 Edw. 3. and the Mirror of Justices, ch. 1. s. 3. (" *Ordein fuit que nul roy de ce*

(a) 1 Bla. Com. 277.

(b) 1 Hist. P. C. 191.   1 Bla. Com. 277.

(c) Ibid. 278, and see Ibid. note 10. Folkes on English Coins.

(d) 2 Inst. 575, 577.

realme

realme ne poit changer sa money ne impayre ne amender ne antre money faire que de or ou d'argent, sans assent de touts ses counties,") in support of his opinion against the King's right to alter money in weight or alloy. Lord C. J. Hale (*a*) differs with Lord Coke, and relies 1st upon the ' *case of mixt monies* (*b*);' 2dly, on the practice of enhancing the coin in point of value and denomination, which he observes has nearly the same effect as an embasement of the coin in the species; and lastly, on the attempts which have been made to restrain the change of coin without consent of Parliament. In the case reported by Sir John Davis, it appears that Queen Elizabeth sent into Ireland some mixed money, and declared by proclamation that it should be current and lawful Irish money. This money was certainly held to be legal coin of Ireland ; but it is most probable that as the case was in Ireland, the statute of 25 Edw. 3. and the other Acts cited by Lord Coke, were not considered in discussing it; as it is clear from one of Poyning's laws (*c*) they might have been. And it is a fair presumption that those statutes were not brought before the Court, no mention being made of them, though Sir M. Hale himself admits that the statute of Edw. 3. is against his opinion. As to the practice mentioned by Lord Hale of enhancing the coin in point of value and denomination, that seems very distinguishable from altering the species or material of coin, by changing its weight or alloy. Even admitting the existence of a practice to imbase coin in the alloy, still little importance will be attached to it, when it is remembered how frequently some Kings have endeavoured to extend the limits of their prerogatives. The attempts which have been made to restrain the change of coin without consent of Parliament, prove but little in favor of Lord Hale's opinion; for those attempts might have been so made in order to restrain the exercise of a prerogative which was denied, and it does not appear that they were made in order to overturn a prerogative, the legal existence of which was admitted. The authority of Sir Wm. Blackstone may perhaps turn the scale in favor of Lord Coke's opinion, if that opinion required it. He observes (*d*), "that the King's

---

(*a*) 1 Hal. P. C. 192.   22. 1 Bla. Com. 103. 4 Inst. 351.
(*b*) Davis's Rep. 18.   8 State Tr. 343.
(*c*) See Irish Statute, 10 Hen. 7. c.   (*d*) 1 Bla. Com. 278.

prerogative

prerogative seemeth not to extend to the debasing or enhancing
the value of the coin below or above the sterling value, though
Sir Matthew Hale appears to be of another opinion." It need
only be added, that the statute 14 Geo. 3. ch. 92. seems to
furnish an inference that the standard weight of the gold and
silver coin of the kingdom is unalterable, but by Act of Parliament. If Lord Coke's opinion be correct, it seems, as laid
down by Sir Wm. Blackstone (*a*), that the King must fix the
value of foreign money, rendered current in this country, by
comparison with the standard of our own coin; otherwise the
consent of Parliament will be necessary.

No proclamation seems necessary to the legitimation of
money coined by the royal authority in this country (*b*), unless
unusual pieces be coined (*c*); but such proclamation is essential to the legitimation of foreign coin made current here.

CHAP. XI.

Of the Prerogative as to the Revenue.

THE power of a state must greatly depend on the income it
possesses (*d*). If it enjoy a considerable and unencumbered
revenue, it can employ a larger proportion of its subjects to
carry on war, or may cultivate to more advantage the arts of
peace, when unembarrassed with hostilities : whereas, with a
small income, it can neither reward the services, nor encourage
the exertions, of its people ; and it must principally trust, both
for its improvement and protection, to the natural activity of
mankind, or to the voluntary and disinterested zeal of public-
spirited individuals.

But, however numerous the advantages of a great revenue,
they are dearly purchased if they cannot be procured without
oppression. A certain share of his annual income no indivi-

(*a*) 1 Bla. Com. 278.

(*b*) 1 Hal. P. C. 196, 7, 8.   See vide
Davis's Rep. 19.

(*c*) 1 Bla. Com. 278.

(*d*) See Sir John Sinclair's excellent
work on the Revenue of Great Britain,
vol. 1. ch. 1. page 1.   *Thesaurus Regis
est fundamentum belli et firmamentum pacis.* Co. Lit. 131, b.

dual. can refuse to contribute, for the general purposes of the State. Sometimes, also, a slight additional burden may prove an incentive to labour, and a spur to greater diligence and activity. But if the load become too heavy, either in consequence of the greatness of the amount, or the impolitic mode of laying it on, the industry of a nation diminishes, its wealth necessarily disappears, the number of its people decreases, and the greater the occasion it has for resources, the fewer it will actually enjoy.

The constitution has vested a revenue in the King, in order to support his dignity, and maintain his power; being a portion which each subject resigns of his property in order to secure the remainder (*a*).

This revenue is either—1st, ordinary, that is inherent in the Crown; or, 2dly, extraordinary.

Before the Revolution, the wants of government were principally supplied by various ordinary lucrative prerogatives inherent in the Crown, and which had existed time out of mind. After that event, which introduced England to an expensive continental warfare, it was discovered that such resources were very inadequate to the expenditure of the country, not so much on account of the decay which had befallen them, arising either from the profusion of the Court, the rapacity of favorites, or the negligence or treachery of officers; as from the unexampled magnitude of the wars, and the gigantic extent of the views and attempts of the government. A complicated system of taxation and finance was commenced, to which our ancestors were strangers, and which has been gradually, and perhaps necessarily, carried to an extent which may be considered alarming, unless wisdom and prudence regulate its progress, and a continued peace prevent its increase, and gradually ameliorate the burthens it imposes. If that can be effected, it is a consolation to reflect, that the inhabitants of England have no great reason to regret (especially since the repeal of the income tax) the change which has taken place in the system and mode of supplying the exigencies of the State. History furnishes a most painful account of the endless, oppressive, and cruel hardships borne by the subject, in consequence of the military tenures, the grinding extortions of tyrannical adminis-

(*a*) 1 Bla. Com. 281.

trations, and the disgusting exactions of papal authority. Some of these were partly founded in law; but the grand defect of the system was, that it afforded excuses for the oppressions of tyranny, and was grounded on principles inconsistent with the freedom of the constitution. It is true, observes Sir John Sinclair (a), that these burdens did not exist at once, and that sometimes one mode of exaction prevailed, which in process of time was abandoned in favor of another. But, whatever the *landatores temporis acti* may say, it must be evident to every impartial person, that our ancestors had great reason to be dissatisfied with their political situation, even in the article of taxation; and perhaps the present *æra* is, in that as well as in many other respects, as desirable a period to live in as any that can be pointed out in the history of this country; our additional weight of taxes being fully compensated by a more extended commerce, by improvements in every branch of science and of art, and by great accessions to our wealth, our security, and our freedom. Though complaints have sometimes been made of the increase of the civil list, yet, if we consider the sums that have been formerly granted, the limited extent under which it is now established, the revenues and prerogatives given up in lieu of it by the Crown (b), the numerous branches of the present royal family, and (above all) the diminution of the value of money compared with what it was worth in the last century, we must acknowledge these complaints to be void of any rational foundation, and that it is impossible to support that dignity which a King of Great Britain should maintain, with an income in any degree less than what is now established by Parliament.

It is observable, that a portion of the revenue is exclusively devoted to the support of the King, and his personal establishment and dignity; the rest is appropriated to the public service. The civil list is indeed properly the whole of the King's revenue in his own distinct capacity; the rest being rather the revenue of the public, or its creditors, though collected and distributed again, in the name and by the officers of the Crown, it now standing in the same place as the hereditary income did formerly; and, as that has gradually diminished, the par-

---

(a) 1 Ves. 57.   (b) 1 Bla. Com. 333.

liamentary

liamentary appointments have increased (a). It is a most important principle of law that the King has no prerogative power of taxing his people : that can only be affected by Act of Parliament.

SECT. I.

I. The first four of the King's ordinary revenues, viz. the *custody* of the *temporalities* of bishops, *corodies*, *tithes* of *extra parochial places* and *first fruits and tenths* (the last of which no longer exist as a Crown revenue), are of an ecclesiastical nature, and have been already considered.

II. In considering the ordinary and inherent resources arising from immediate Crown possessions, and rights peculiar to the Crown, we may mention,

1. The profits accruing from the *demesne lands* of the Crown. The demesne lands, *terræ dominicales regis*, of the Anglo Saxon monarchs were very great : a circumstance not difficult to be accounted for. The kingdoms of the Heptarchy were founded by chieftains, who commanded troops attached to them by the ties of consanguinity, who were born with an hereditary regard for the family they represented, cr were led to join in the incursion, from the high idea they entertained of their courage, character and good conduct. In other words, they were the heads of clans or little tribes, such as now exist among the Tartars, and some vestiges of which still remain in the mountains of Scotland. Such commanders, it is probable, would claim a considerable share of the territory that was conquered; and as, besides the plausibility of their original pretensions, it was discovered, in the course of the war, that many advantages resulted from subordination on the one hand, and pre-eminence on the other, it was natural to suppose, that a considerable portion of the new acquisition would be given to the leader, not only to preserve so useful a pre-eminence,

---

(a) 1 Bla. Com. 332.

but

but also to support the dignity of his office, and to reward his valour in the field.   Thus each petty monarch of the Heptárchy came to be possessed of a landed estate of great value and extent; and when all the domains of these different kingdoms united to enrich one Sovereign, the whole must have yielded a very considerable revenue.   Considerable additions must have arisen from the extensive confiscations of manors and lordships, &c. which subsequently took place in times of civil commotion and rebellion (*a*).

But whatever might be the original value and extent of the landed property of the Crown, and however great the accessions which it might receive, and though the strictest laws were enacted to prevent its alienation, and to check encroachments, yet the royal domains of England have shared the same fate with those of other countries, and hardly a vestige now remains of the extensive property which William I. and some of his successors were possessed of; in consequence of the numerous royal grants; arising from the generosity, the weakness, or profusion of the Crown (*b*).   This frequently occasioned the interference of Parliament, and particularly in the reign of Queen Ann (*c*); after William 3d. had greatly impoverished the Crown; an Act passed to restrain the alienation of the Crown lands, and subsequent provisions have been made for the same purpose.   By the statute of Ann, grants, leases, or other assurances from the Crown, of any tenements, except advowsons of churches and vicarages, " in England, Wales or Berwick upon Tweed," belonging to the Crown, " whether in right of the Crown of England, or as part of the principality of Wales (*d*), or of the duchy or county palatine of Lancaster (*e*), or otherwise howsoever", for any longer term than thirty-one years, or three lives, are declared to be void: and no reversionary lease can be made, so as to exceed, together with the estate in being, the same term of three lives or thirty-one years; that is, where there is a subsisting lease, of which there are twenty years still to come, the King cannot grant a future interest, to commence after the expiration of the for-

(*a*) See 1 Sinclair 19, and 1 Bla. Com. 286.

(*b*) Recital, 1 Ann. st. 1. c. 7. s. 5. 1 Sinclair, 26.

(*c*) 1 Ann. st. 1. c. 7. s. 5.

(*d*) See 54 Geo. 3. c. 70. s. 8.

(*e*) 34 Geo. 3. c. 75, s. 20. 47 Geô, 3. sess. 2. c. 24.

mer, for any longer term than eleven years (*a*). The tenant must also be made liable to be punished for committing waste; and a fair and reasonable rent must be reserved (*b*). The 8th section of the Act excepts its operation in the cases of grants, &c. in the duchy of Cornwall, according to statute 12 and 13 Wm. 3. c. 13. of grants and restorations of forfeited estates; of grants, &c. of lands seized on outlawry or Crown process; of grants and admittances which of right or custom ought to be made of copyholds, parcel of Crown manors; and in the case of trustees for sale of fee-farm and other rents according to certain statutes (*c*). By the 34 Geo. 3. c. 75. the King may grant lands for building for any term not exceeding ninety-nine years or three lives at certain fines and rents, and on certain terms(*d*): and Crown leases are not to be renewed, till within a certain number of years prior to their expiration (*e*).

The statutes do not however prevent an exchange of Crown lands for lands of equal value (*f*). And by the 39 and 40 Geo. 3. c. 88. exceptions are made to these statutable provisions and restrictions, in the case of lands and tenements purchased by the Crown out of the privy purse, or other monies not appropriated to any public service; or which come to the King or his successors, &c. by the gift or devise of, or by descent, or otherwise, from his ancestors or private persons. These his Majesty may grant, sell, give or devise, as his subjects may their property: but if not entirely disposed of by grant, will or otherwise, the same, or the estate therein undisposed of, shall, on the demise of the Crown, descend, as if the Act were not made, and subject to the restrictions in the statute

(*a*) 1 Bla. Com. 286, 7.

(*b*) 34 Geo. 3. c. 75. s. 4.

(*c*) As 22 Car. 2. c. 6. 23 Car. 2. c. 24. See 19 Geo. 3. c. 45.

(*d*) See other cases of charitable institutions, &c. in which the King may grant leases, reserve rent, &c. 46 Geo. 3. c. 151. As to ascertaining rent where houses to be rebuilt, 48 Geo. 3. c. 73. s. 23. And as to leases of property as uncertain in its produce, see 48 Geo. 3. c. 73. s. 21. By 26 Geo. 3. c. 87. amended by 50 Geo. 3. c. 50. Commissioners were appointed to inquire

into the state and condition of the woods, forests, and land revenues of the Crown, and to sell fee-farm and other inimprovable rents. And see 34 Geo. 3. c. 75. See grant of palace, &c. in Greenwich Park, 47 Geo. 3. sess. 1. c. 52. s. 2. Forest of Brecknock, 55 Geo. 3. c. 190. see further 57 Geo. 3. c. 24.

(*e*) Crown leases for gardens, &c. how renewable, 48 Geo 3. c. 73. s. 4. Purchase and surrender of Crown leases, 55 Geo. 3. c. 55.

(*f*) 1 Bla. Com. 287, n. (52.) Archb. ed. cites Vin. Ab.

of 1 Ann, &c.   And the 6th section subjects such lands, &c.
to taxes, whilst they belong to the Crown, &c. Copyholds and
leaseholds which thus come to and are vested in the Crown,
are by section 2. vested in trustees appointed by the Crown (*a*).

Even at common law, the leaning and endeavour seems
always to have been to preserve entire and to keep in the
possession of the Crown its demesne lards and possessions, as
materially conducive to its dignity and honour.   Various exceptions in favor of the King's grants of lands from common
law rules, are occasionally to be met with (*b*); and Sir Wm.
Blackstone regrets that the legislative restrictions on the alienation of Crown lands were made " too late, and after almost
every valuable possession of the Crown had been granted away
for ever, or else upon very long leases ; but such restrictions
may be of some benefit to posterity when those leases come to
expire (*c.*)"

The King has two capacities, the one natural and the other
politic ; and the general rule seems to be that the latter shall
prevail, so that lands given to the King and his heirs shall
descend, as if they were given to him and his successors (*d*).
Even at common law, the rule seems to have been, that lands
and possessions whereof he was seized *jure coronæ ;* (as purchases made after assumption of the Crown, tenements which
have usually been annexed to the Crown, acquisitions by conquest, &c.) shall *secundum jus coronæ* attend upon and follow
the Crown.   Therefore to whomsoever the Crown descends,
these lands and possessions descend also, and not to another,
who might otherwise be heir at law to the King in his natural
capacity; the lands and the Crown being *concomitantia* (*e*).
Hence if an usurper purchase lands, and the right heir resume
the Crown, he shall have the purchase : *et e converso,* an usurper
shall have the purchases made by a rightful King, so long as
he has the Crown(*f*). So if lands in gavelkind descend to the
King and his brother, the King shall take one moiety and his
brother the other ; but when the King dies, his moiety shall

(*a*) See 56 Geo. 3. c. 16. which regulates offices for the receipt of Crown
rents.

(*b*) See Co. Lit. 21, b. 5 Bac. Ab.
553, tit. Prerogative, F. 3, &c.

(*c*) 1 Bla. Com. 287.
(*d*) 1 Kyd. 74.
(*e*) Co. Litt. 15, b. and n. 4; 16, a.
7 Co. 10, 12. 9 Co. 123. Plowd. 212.
(*f*) Co. Lit. 15, b. note 4.

descend

descend to his eldest son, and not according to the rules of descent in gavelkind; for the King was seized of his moiety *jure coronæ*, therefore it shall attend the Crown, and consequently go to the eldest son (*a*). As observed by Lord Holt, " the King can have nothing in his natural capacity, unless in right of his duchy or an estate-tail, by the statute *de donis*, and duchy lands would now be in the Crown, if not kept separate by (*b*) Act of Parliament (*c*)." It was laid down by Lord Hale (*d*), that "purchases made before accession of the Crown, or descents from collateral ancestors after descent of the Crown, vest in a natural capacity; and that therefore in the re-ademption of the Crown by Edward 4. there was a special Act to give to the King all the possessions of Hen. 6. But such lands are qualified and affected differently from those of other persons. They will pass by letters patent only and without livery; and the grants of them shall not be effected by nonage, *et similiter*." We have just seen, that though lands purchased out of the private monies of the Crown, or which came to the Crown by descent, &c. may be granted and devised, &c.; still if no such grant or devise be made, they descend with the Crown on the decease of the King, and the restrictions which in general obtain, in whatever capacity the Crown lands are holden, then apply. As Crown lands in general descend in the same manner as, and with the Crown, it will be sufficient to refer to the first chapter for information on the subject.

We have already mentioned the sovereignty of the Crown over the seas and navigable rivers within his dominions. The King is also by his prerogative, on principles of expediency or as lord paramount of the soil, the owner of such lands as are covered by the narrow seas adjoining the English coasts, or by arms of the seas or navigable rivers, within his dominions (*e*); and is therefore entitled to *maritima incrementa*, or lands which increase by the casting up of sand and earth from the sea. If

(*a*) Plowd. 205, a. Co. Lit. 15, b.

(*b*) The statute of 1 Hen. 4, provides, that when the duchy lands come to the King, they shall not be under such government and regulatious as the demesnes and possessions belonging to the Crown, for the Act says, *Quod taliter et*

tali modo et per tales officiarios et ministros gubernentur et si ac ' culmen dignitatis' regiæ assumpti minime fuissent. Raym. 90.

(*c*) 7 Mod. 78.

(*d*) Co. Lit. 15, b. note 4.

(*e*) Ante, ch. 8. s. 2. div. 7. Fisheries.

indeed

indeed such increase be so insensible that it cannot be by any means ascertained that the sea was there, the King has no claim to land so increased, and the owner of the adjacent property is entitled thereto (*a*).

So the King by his prerogative is entitled to such lands as become *derelict* by the sudden desertion of the sea, or a river where there is a flow of the sea; and such lands belong immediately to the King, because they never were apportioned out to any of his subjects (*b*). But the King is not entitled to lands left dry by a river in which there is no tide; for such lands are supposed to have been distributed out as other lands, and therefore belong to the owners of the soil on both sides (*c*). Nor can the King claim such lands as are *regained* from the sea after having been covered by it several years, if the former owner can recognize the land which belonged to him, before his land was covered by the water; for in this case an owner being found, the King's title which depended on the want of such owner, is excluded (*d*). As to the islands arising *de novo* in the King's seas, or the King's arms thereof (that is called an arm of the sea where the tide flows and reflows, and that only (*e*)), these *primâ facie* and of common right also belong to the King, for they are part of that soil of the sea that belonged before in point of propriety to the King; for when islands *de novo* arise, it is either by the recess or sinking of the water, or by the exaggeration of sand and slab, which in process of time grow firm land environed with water; and thus some places have arisen, and their original recorded, as about Ravesend in Yorkshire (*f*).

The King is also, by his prerogative, the *primâ facie* owner of the shores, (that is the land which lies been high and low water mark, in ordinary tides (*g*)), of the seas and navigable rivers, and arms of the seas, within his dominions (*h*). A subject

ject

(*a*) Hale de jure Maris, c. 4.

(*b*) 2 Rol. Ab. 170. Dyer, 326. Hale de jure Maris, c. 4.

(*c*) 2 Rol. Ab. 170.

(*d*) 8 Co. Sir Francis Barrington's Case.

(*e*) 29 Ass. 93.

(*f*) Hale de jure Maris, c. 4.

(*g*) Ibid.

(*h*) Ibid. The shore may not only belong to a subject in gross, which possibly may suppose a grant before time of memory, but it may be parcel of a manor. And the evidences to prove this fact are commonly these; constant and usual fetching gravel and sea-weed, and sea-sand, between the high-water and low-water mark, and licensing others to do

ject may by custom or prescription, be entitled to ground
added to his land by sand and earth from the sea; but custom
cannot entitle a subject to lands deserted by the sea, or an arm
thereof (a). The reason assigned for this distinction is, that in
the former instance, the accession or addition of the land by
the sea to the dry land gradually, is a kind of perquisite;
whereas, in the latter case, the land, as it belongs to the King
when covered with water, cannot become the property of the
subject, merely because the water has left it, though this
reason for the distinction is not perhaps very satisfactory.
Where the interest in a creek, arm of the sea, or *districtus maris*, is, by charter or prescription, vested in a subject, he is entitled to claim all those rights which the King is entitled to,
as owner thereof; and, therefore, such prescription does not
merely give a liberty or profit, *apprendre*, within such creek,
&c.; but the party prescribing will be entitled to lands forsaken
by the water, or islands arising therein (b).

The King is a sole corporation, capable of taking mere chattel interests in succession (c). Consequently, a fee passes on a
grant to the King without the word ' successors (d);' and a grant
by the King, without mentioning successors, binds them (e).

The Crown possesses peculiar prerogative privileges, with
respect to *distresses* for rent due from its tenants. At the common law, if a grant of land or rent were made to the King, he
can distrain without attornment by virtue of his prerogative (f). And he may distrain for a rent-service, fee-farm,
rent-charge, or even a rent-seek, though it vest in him not by
grant, but by escheat upon attainder, not only on lands out of
which such rent is reserved, but on all other the lands of
the tenant, although held of other lords; provided the lands
distrained upon be in the actual possession of his tenant,

---

do so; inclosing and imbanking against
the sea; and enjoyment of what is so
inned; enjoyment of wrecks happening
upon the sand; presentment and punishment of purprestures there, in the
Court of a manor and such like. Ibid.
So agreed in Sir Henry Constable's case,
5 Co. 107. 5 E. 3. 3 Dyer, 326, b.
So in the Exchequer Chamber, P. 16.
Car. inter l'Attorney Generall et Sir
Samuel Rolls, Sir Richard Buller, and

Sir Thomas Arundel, per omnes ba-
rones. 5 Bac. Ab. 499.

(a) Hal de jure Maris, c. 6.
(b) Ibid.
(c) Co. Lit. 90, a. 11 Co. 92, a.
(d) Co. Lit. 9. Plowd. 250. Jenk.
209, 271.
(e) Plowd. 176. Yelv. 13.
(f) Co. Lit. 809. May distrain for an
amerciament in a Court Baron. Cro.
El. 748.

for, if they be underlet for years or at will, the under-tenant's effects are not liable to the King (*a*). The King may, however, distrain on lands so underlet *after* his rent distrained for accrued due (*b*). And the King may distrain in the highway (*c*).

In general, this prerogative is peculiar to the Crown, and its grantee cannot exercise it (*d*). But even at common law, if the King granted to a subject a reversion or services, the estate passed immediately without attornment, and the grantee might distrain (*e*), unless in the case of lands held of the Duchy of Lancaster, and not situate within the county palatine (*f*). And by force of the statute 22 Car. 2. c. 6. for the sale of Crown fee-farm rents (*g*), the vendees of such rents may distrain on all the lands of the original grantor. And, it seems, that either the King or his vendees, may make such a distress, although the lands distrained upon be under a sequestration out of Chancery (*h*).

It seems that the tenant may replevy on the Crown distress for rent (*i*), though a replevy on a distress for a fee-farm rent or other duty to the Crown (*k*), or on a seizure in order to condemnation (*l*), is not, it appears, allowable.

As the King may distrain on all his tenants' lands, he may reserve rent out of inheritances which are incorporeal, as commons, tithes, fairs, &c. (*m*). So the King may, contrary to the general rule, reserve rent payable to a stranger (*n*). But where the King made a lease of his house, belonging to his house-keeper, of Whitehall, reserving a rent to the house-keeper for

---

(*a*) Bro. Prerog. pl. 68, 77. 2 Inst. 132. 4 Ibid. 119. 3 Leon. 124. 4 Rep. 56. Plowd. 227. 16 Vin. Ab. 513, 4. tit. Prerog. F. Bac. Ab. Prerog. R. 3. 2 Vernon, 714.

(*b*) 1 Rol. Ab. 670. Bradby on Distr. 92.

(*c*) 2 Inst. 131.

(*d*) Bro. tit. Prerog. 68. Vin. *ubi supra.*

(*e*) 1 Rol. Ab. 291. Bradby Distr. 93.

(*f*) Co. Lit. 314, b. Plowd. 221. 4 Inst. 209.

(*g*) And see 26 Geo. 3. c. 87. 30 Geo. 3. c. 50. 34 Geo. 3. c. 75. But not entitled to process of extent. 22 Car. 2. c. 6. s. 8.

(*h*) 2 Vern. 713. 1 P. Wms. 306.

(*i*) Bro. tit. Repl. pl. 51. per Hide to the Lords. 3 Rush. 1361. Bac. Ab. Replevin, C.

(*k*) Bunb. R. 14.

(*l*) Anstr. 212.

(*m*) Ibid. Co. Lit. 47, a. n. 1.

(*n*) Moor, 162. Co. Lit. 143, b. 2 Rol. Ab. 447.

P

the

the time being, it was held an ill reservation; for though the King may reserve rent to a stranger, he cannot reserve it to an officer who is removeable at his will (*a*).

If the King make a lease reserving rent, with a clause of re-entry for nonpayment, he is not bound to make any demand previous to his re-entry, but the tenant is obliged to pay the rent for the preservation of his estate; because it is beneath the royal dignity to attend a subject to demand the rent; but the law, for the support of that dignity, obliges every private person to attend the King with the services due to him (*b*).

But if the King, in cases where he need not make a demand, assign over the reversion, the patentee cannot enter for non-payment without making the regular previous demand; because, this privilege being inseparably annexed to the person of the King, for the support of his royal dignity, shall not be extended to cases where the King is no way concerned (*c*).

So, if a prebendary make a lease rendering rent, and it be provided that if the rent be in arrear and be demanded, it shall be lawful for the prebendary to re-enter; if the reversion in this case come to the King, he must demand the rent as in common cases, though he shall by his prerogative be excused from an implied demand; for the implied demand is the act of the law, the other the express agreement of the parties, which the King's prerogative shall not defeat; and therefore even in the case of the King, if he make a lease reserving rent, with a proviso that if the rent be in arrear for such time (being lawfully demanded, or demanded in due form), that then the lease shall be void: it seems that not only the patentee of the reversion in this case, but also the King himself, whilst he continues the reversion in his own hands, is obliged to make an actual demand, as in ordinary instances, by reason of the express agreement for that purpose (*d*).

If land be given to the King and a subject, to have and to hold to them and their heirs, yet they are tenants in common

(*a*) Lord Raym. 36.

(*b*) 2 H. 7, 8. Bro. Prerog. pl. 101. Co. Lit. 201, b. But this prerogative is not to be extended to the duchy lands. Moor, 149, 154, 161.

(*c*) 4 Co. 73. Moor, 104. Cro. Eliz. 462. Dyer, 87. And, R. 304. Co. Lit. 201, b.

(*d*) Moor, 210. Dyer, 87. See 2 Maul. and S. 528.

and

and not joint tenants, as they take in different capacities; and the King cannot be a joint tenant with a subject (*a*).

2. The King's ordinary revenue arose also from *antient rights of seigniory;* as military tenures; from *purveyance* and *pre-emption,* and *wine licences.* These are now abolished, but still require some slight notice.

The feudal system was adopted in England at the time of the Conquest, and in consequence of its introduction it became a fundamental maxim and necessary principle (though in reality a mere fiction) of our English tenures. " That the King is the universal lord and original proprietor of all the lands in his kingdom (*b*); and that no man doth or can possess any part of it, but what has mediately or immediately been derived as a gift from him, to be held upon feudal services." The intention of this fiction was to enable the King, by his royal prerogative, to put the kingdom in a state of defence whenever it might be necessary; and every holder of land, was thus obliged to maintain the King's title and to defend his territories, with equal vigour and fealty, as if he had received his estate upon that express condition (*c*)." But this system, originally intended for the public protection and security, was afterwards made a pretext to introduce a plan of tyranny and oppression, hardly to be equalled in history.

For in the first place, the proprietor of every estate in the kingdom, in proportion to its extent, was burthened with military services; for which, in process of time, a certain sum of money was taken, by way of fine and commutation, called *escuage.* 2. He was also subject to certain annual payments or *rents* in money, laid on as a mark of the lord's pre-eminence, and in order to keep the vassal in perpetual remembrance of his feudal subordination. 3. He was obliged, under the name of *aids,* to give pecuniary assistance when necessary, to ransom the King's person if taken prisoner, to furnish a portion to his daughter, and to contribute to the expense incurred on making his eldest son a knight. 4. It was supposed upon the death of the feudal possessor, that the estate ought to revert into the hands of the

(*a*) Co. Lit. 190, a. 1 Saund. 319, n. 4. Bac. Ab. Joint Tenants, B. 2 Bla. Com. 184.

(*b*) Montesq. Sp. L. b. 31. c. 1. See 12 East, 96, as to the presumption of

law, that on the death of the tenant last seised without heirs, the King is entitled.

(*c*) 1 Bla. Com. 51.

superior lord, and under that pretence it was contended, that the new vassal ought to make him a present of a suit of armour (which in antient times was reckoned peculiarly valuable), or to pay a fine under the name of *relief;* to which, in process of time, an addition was made, called *primer seisin,* entitling the King to demand from the heir of any of his tenants *in capite,* who died seised of a Knight's fee, one year's profit upon his being put in possession of the estate. 5. If the heir was under age at the death of his predecessor, the King was entrusted with the *wardship,* or the custody both of his person and estate; and enjoyed the income which it yielded till he arrived at the age of twenty-one years, and consequently was able to perform the services stipulated for his feud. If the heir was a female, she came of age at sixteen years, being then supposed capable of marrying a husband who might act in her stead. 6. If the possessors of feudal estates had the power of entering into matrimonial connections during their minority, according to their own fancy and humour, they might introduce into the joint possession of the *fief,* an enemy of the lord; perhaps one descended from a family with whom he had an hereditary variance (*a*). Upon this ground, the feudal superior was invested with some degree of control over the ward's marriage, and at length the right of selling the ward in marriage, or of receiving the price or value of the match, was confirmed by an express act of the legislature. 7. It was asserted by the feudal lawyers, that when the King gave an estate to be holden of himself and his successors, it was a gift to a chosen and selected individual, which no other person ought to be put in possession of, without his privity and consent; and that any attempt to infringe upon this essential stipulation, by alienating the lands to a stranger, ought to be attended with the forfeiture of the grant (*b*). This right was exercised with great severity during several reigns in the earlier part of the English history, until at last it was provided by statute Edward 3. c. 12. that one third of the yearly value of the lands should be paid by way of *fine,* for a licence of *alienation;* but if the tenants presumed to aliene without a licence, that they should be liable to a full year's rent of the

(*a*) Dalrymple on Feud. Prop. ch. 2.   (*b*) Bacon's Works, fol. edit. vol. 3.
sect. 2. page 38, 4th edit.   p. 551.

estate. 8. *Escheat* was the last fruit or incident resulting from the feudal system. It was a species of confiscation (*a*) by which the feud reverted to the sovereign, either from the delinquency of the vassal (who held it under the implied condition that he should not prove guilty of any act of felony or treason), or in consequence of his dying without an heir, either fit to perform the stipulated services, or entitled, by the original grant, to succeed to the feud (*b*).

It was imagined that the King would often find it necessary, with a view of examining into the real state and circumstances of the country, to make a personal progress throughout his dominions; and as the removal of the Court would occasion an unusual demand at the places to which it went, for every species of provisions, it was thought requisite to give the Crown a right of purchasing necessaries for the maintenance of the royal household, at an appraised valuation, in preference to all other persons, and even to force the sale or the hire of any thing peculiarly wanted, without the owner's consent (*c*). This prerogative, which obtained the names of *purveyance* and *pre-emption,* was afterwards extended to every spot where the royal family resided. But the powers vested in the purveyors, or officers appointed for that purpose, being greatly abused, and indeed becoming every day less requisite, in consequence of the great increase of cultivation and improvement, and of the abundance which necessarily followed, the whole right was abolished, at the same time with the harsh and obnoxious system of military tenures; and by 12 Car. 2. c. 24. the hereditary excise, and a duty on wine licences, were settled on the Crown in its stead (*d*). The duty on wine licences was abolished by statute 30 Geo. 2. c. 19. and an annual sum of upwards of 7000*l.* per annum, issuing out of the new stamp duties imposed on wine licences, was settled on the Crown in its stead.

3. *Of forfeitures for offences,* which afford another ordinary resource for the exigencies of the state.

" The true reason and only substantial ground of any forfeiture for crimes consist," says Sir Wm. Blackstone (*e*), " in

(*a*) See Wright on Tenures, p. 117, note 10.

(*b*) See 1 Bla. Com. 63, &c. 1 Sinclair, 29, &c.

(*c*) 5 Hume's Hist. 365, 490, 547.

(*d*) 4 Inst. 273. 1 Sinclair, 36. 1 Bla. Com. 287, S.

(*e*) Ibid. 299.

this, that all property is derived from society, being one of those civil rights which are conferred upon individuals, in exchange for that degree of natural liberty which every man must sacrifice when he enters into social communities. If, therefore, a member of any national community violate the fundamental contract of this association, by transgressing the municipal law, he forfeits his right to such privileges as he claims by that contract, and the state may very justly resume that portion of property, or any part of it, which the laws have before assigned him. Hence, in every offence of an atrocious kind, the laws of England have exacted a total confiscation of the moveables or personal estate, and in many cases a perpetual, in others only a temporary, loss of the offender's immoveables or landed property, and have vested them both in the King, who is the person supposed to be offended, being the one visible magistrate in whom the majesty of the public resides (a)."

In some instances, the punishment by forfeiture of inheritances, is politically necessary to the preservation of the state. It is in the case of high treason, a safeguard with which every well regulated state, whether built on maxims of monarchy or freedom, has ever been provided; and without which it were liable to perpetual disorder from the desperate sallies of resentment, or the daring projects of ambition. Here too, our own constitution preserves its usual excellence; and, being framed with much wisdom and equity as to the crime of treason, it seems difficult to account for the conduct of those, who, in the Parliament of the 7th of Queen Anne, were for abolishing that punishment of the crime, which has subsisted for ages past, is interwoven with the first principles, and intimately connected with the foundations of, our policy (b). To visit the consequences of a crime on the innocent posterity of the offender, by depriving them of his property, may seem unjust; but investigation will establish the wisdom of making the natural and social affections a controul upon irregular and selfish passions. And it is observable, that the right of inheritance being, it seems, rather a matter of civil regulation and policy, than exclusively conferred by the law of nature (c), it is not injustice to inter-

(a) Forfeitures in counties palatine, 1 Bla. Com. 118.

(b) See Considerations on the Law of Forfeiture, said to be written by the Honourable Mr. York, page 5.

(c) See Ibid. 2 Bla. Com. 11.

weave with those regulations such as manifestly tend to confirm the bonds of society, however unhappy and lamentable
the effect may be on the criminal's posterity. Nor is any
thing a punishment which does not affect a right strictly so
called (a).

However, life and liberty are the gifts of nature, and should
never be taken away because of the parent's offence; nor
should a subject be made incapable of employments without
some crime committed by himself. Such severities are unwise,
as well as unequitable. A difference, therefore, must be observed between the natural rights and common liberties which
are annexed to the person of every subject, and the peculiar
distinctions of society, such as riches and honours. These last
are merely contingent, and, if hoped for in the course of succession, depend on the conduct of those ancestors from whom
we would derive them. And it is not to be said, men are punished when those contingent advantages, which themselves neither
acquired nor merited, having, by reason of the "civil qualification of their blood," (as a great lawyer of our own has expressed it,) been brought into view by the desert of one ancestor, are intercepted by the crimes of another.

There is a very important distinction between the prerogative right to forfeitures and the right of the Crown, as lord of
the fee by escheat, which will be more particularly mentioned
in the next section. The law of forfeiture was the doctrine of
the old Saxon law (b), and formed a part of the antient Scandinavian constitution (c), as a punishment for the offence, and
does not at all relate to the feudal system, nor is the consequence of any seigniory or lordship paramount (d). But, being a prerogative vested in the Crown, was neither superseded
nor diminished by the introduction of the Norman tenures, a
fruit and consequence of which escheats must undoubtedly be

(a) "Every thing," says Puffendorf,
"which causes a sorrow or loss, is not
properly punishment. It is a misfortune to be reduced to poverty by a
crime, which caused the magistrate to
set a large fine upon the father of a
family; but not a punishment. How
many are there who come into the

world without the expectation of a pa-
trimony ? How many who lose all they
have by war, fire, or shipwreck ? L. VIII.
c. 3. s. 30.

(b) L. L. Alfred 4. L. L. Canute, c. 54.

(c) Stiernh. de jure Goth. l. 2. c. 6.
and l. 3. c. 3.

(d) 2 Inst. 64. Salk. 85.

reckoned.

reckoned. Escheat, therefore, operates in subordination to this more antient and superior law of forfeiture (*a*).

Forfeitures for offences may be considered 1st, with respect to the *realty;* 2dly, with regard to the *personalty* of the offender.

With respect to the *real property* he may possess, a person attainted of *high treason* forfeits for ever (*b*), to the Crown, though the lands are holden of another original proprietor or lord (*c*):

1st. His lands and tenements of inheritance, whether fee simple or fee tail (*d*), and the King shall be entitled and adjudged in possession of them without any inquisition or office found (*e*).

2dly. All hereditaments whether they lie in tenure or not, as fairs, markets, warrens, rents, advowsons, commons or corrodies certain(*f*), or whether they are of the tenure of gavelkind (*g*): but copyhold escheats revert to the lord of the manor, not to the King (*h*), and such inheritances as be purely in privity appropriate to the person, as a foundership or corrody uncertain, are neither forfeitable at common law, or by any statute (*i*).

3dly. Rights of entry into lands, whether the possessor be in merely by usurpation or abatement, or by title; but in such case there must be an inquisition and seizure on an office not to entitle the King to the right of entry, but to bring him into actual possession of the land (*k*). But if the traitor only possessed when he committed the treason a right of action touch-

---

(*a*) 2 Bla. Com. 251, 2. and 4 Ibid. 383.

(*b*) 7 Ann. ch. 21. 17 Geo. 2. e. 39. 37 Geo. 8. c. 39.

(*c*) 1 Hal. P. C. 360. See post. tit. Escheats. As to forfeitures in counties palatine, see 1 Bla. Com. 118.

(*d*) 26 Hen. 8. c. 13. s. 5. 33 Hen. 8. c. 20. See the cause of making this Act of 33 Hen. 8. 3 Co. 10. b, 5 and 6 Edw. 6. c. 11. s. 9. These statutes are not repealed by the statute 1 Mary, sess. 1. c. 1. See Staundf. P. C. 307. 3 Inst. 19. 1 Hal. P. C. 240, 1. Bac.

Ab. Forfeiture, A. C. 1 Chitty, Crim. Law, 727.

(*e*) Ibid.

(*f*) 3 Inst. 19, 21. 1 Hal. P. C. 253. Bac. Ab. Forfeiture, A. As to forfeiture of offices, see ante, ch. 7. s. 1.

(*g*) Somner, 53. Wright's Ten. 118. 1 Hal. P. C. 360. 2 Bla. Com. 252.

(*h*) 1 Cruise, 361. 2 Bac. Forfeiture, A. 1 Hal. P. C. 360. 1 Chitty, Crim. Law, 728, 9.

(*i*) 1 Hal. P. C. 253.

(*k*) Ibid. 241.

ing

ing any lands, or a right to reserve a judgment given against him by writ of error, or a right to bring a formedon or writ of entry, but had no right of entry without a recovery by action, the King is not entitled to the exercise of such respective rights. This was determined in Dowby's case (a), though Sir M. Hale cites two cases which, he says, tread hard upon the heels of the judgment in that case (b).

4thly. The benefit of all conditions of re-entry and powers of revocation, by virtue of which the offender could have reduced any land into possession (c). But it seems, that the King is not entitled to the benefit of conditions, the performance whereof is strictly and substantially restrained to the person attainted (d), and cannot execute a power, the execution of which is to be attended with circumstances inseparably annexed to the person of him to whom the power is given (e).

5thly. All lands holden by another in trust for the offender (f).

6thly. It seems any property which the traitor may hold as trustee for another; and in this case it appears the party for whose use the lands were holden loses them entirely (g), for the legal estate is forfeited by the attainder to the King, and his Majesty cannot be compelled to, though as will be fully mentioned hereafter (h), he may execute the trusts (i). It is held that in case of the attainder of a mortgagor the mortgagee shall hold till the Crown think fit to redeem, for the Court will not decree a foreclosure against his Majesty (k).

7thly. If a husband be seised of lands of inheritance in right of his wife, and be attainted of treason, the King hath

(a) 3 Co. 3, a. 10, b.

(b) 1 Hal. P. C. 242.

(c) 33 Hen. 8. c. 20. 1 Hal. P. C. 243, 4. 3 Co. 10, b. Gilb. Uses, 146.

(d) 1 Hal. P. C. 244, 5, 6. 7 Co. 13, a. 4 Leond. 135. 2 Keb. 564, 608, 763, 772. 1 Mod. 16, 38. See Latch. 25, 69, 102. Sir Wm. Jon. 134. Bac. Ab. Forfeiture, A.

(e) Ibid.

(f) 21 Rich. 2. c. 3. 33 Hen. 8. c. 20. 1 Hal. P. C. 247, 8. Cro. Jac. 512. Hob. 214.

(g) Lane, 54. Jenkins, 190, case 92.

Hard. 466. Bro. Feoffment al. Uses. pl. 31. Vin. Ab. tit. Uses, pl. 4,-noté. 1 Fonbl. Tr. Eq. 3rd ed. 168, 9. note, book 2. c. 7. s. 1. 1 Hal. 249. 1 Cruise, 500. 1 Chitty, Crim. Law, 728. Post. tit. Escheats; but see Com. Dig. Forfeiture, B. 1 Carter, 67. Prec. Ch. 202.

(h) Post. Fil Escheats.

(i) 1 Cruise Dig. 550. See 39 and 40 Geo. 3. c. 88. s. 12.

(k) Bridg. Index, ' Treason,' ' Prerogative.' 2 Atk. 223. Hardr. 465. 2 Ves. 286. 1 Chitty, Crim. L. 728.

the

the freehold during the coverture, and if the attainted husband be possessed of a term in right of his wife, the King shall have it. So if tenant for life be attainted of treason the King hath the freehold during the life of the party attainted, or his interest if he have a term for years only (*a*). It may be added, that the wife of a traitor forfeits her dower by the attainder of her husband for high or petit treason (*b*), but not her jointured lands (*c*); and he shall be tenant by the curtesy, though she be attainted (*d*); if there were issue before the treason committed (*e*).

8thly. With respect to corporations, it may be observed, that in the case of a corporation aggregate, as dean and chapter, mayor and commonalty, where the possessions are in common in the aggregate corporation, nothing is forfeited by the attainder of the head of the corporation, as the dean, mayor, &c. (*f*). By the common law a sole corporation, as an abbot, bishop, dean, prebendary, parson, or vicar, by attainder of treason forfeited to the King the profits of his abbey, bishoprick or prebend during his incumbency; but their successors were not bound by that forfeiture, for though the profits as they arose belonged to their persons, yet the inheritance was in right of their church (*g*). The statute 26 Hen. 8. c. 13. s. 5. altered the common law in this respect, for by that statute the rights of others are saved and preserved to them, excepting only the traitor, his heirs " and successors" (*h*). Sir M. Hale however asserts, that the statute 5 and 6 Edw. 6. c. 11. s. 5. restores and preserves the common law right of the successors of the sole corporation, because it saves the rights of all others on a forfeiture for high treason, except the offender, " and his heirs" (omitting the word " successors") (*i*).

It is laid down by Sir M. Hale (*k*), that where lands come

(*a*) 1 Hale, P. C. 251, 252.

(*b*) 5 and 6 Edw. 6. c. 11. 1 Hal. P. C. 359. There are some exceptions by special legislative provision, as upon the statute of 5 El. c. 11. for clipping money; 18 El. c. 1. for impairing money; 5 El. c. 1. for refusing the oath of supremacy the second time, and some others.

(*c*) 4 Bla. Com. 381,

(*d*) Ibid. 382.

(*e*) 1 Hal. P. C. 359. Co. Lit. s. 35.

(*f*) 1 Hal. P. C. 252.

(*g*) Ibid.

(*h*) See Ibid. Hale. Dyer, 289. 27 Hen. 8. c. 28. 31 Hen. 8. c. 13.

(*i*) See 1 Hale, P. C. 252, 3. 6 Bac. Ab. Statutes, D. &c. as to a statute operating as a repeal of a former statute.

(*k*) 1 P. C. 253.

to the Crown by attainder of treason, he does not take by way
of escheat, and all mesne tenures of common persons are extinct, and the King takes *jure coronæ* or *prerogativæ regalis.*
But the King is not entitled in general to a larger interest or
more extensive degree of property in the lands or tenements
forfeited, than the person attainted himself enjoyed; so that
his Majesty cannot lawfully eject from the forfeited premises a
person legally in possession as tenant; or do any other act
which the law would not have permitted the traitor to commit
with impunity, the statute expressly saving to others, (except
the offender and his heirs and assigns, and every of them, and
all and every other person and persons claiming by them or
any of them, or to their uses, or to the uses of any of them,
after the said treasons committed) all such right, title, use,
possession, entry, reversions, remainders, interests, conditions,
fees, offices, rents, annuities, commons, leases, and all other
commodities, profits and hereditaments whatsoever they or any
of them should, might, or ought to have had, if this act had
never been had or made (*a*). The Crown or its grantee on
forfeiture will take the estate, subject to all charges binding on
the party though voluntary, if no fraud, but not subject to
debts at large; and they have the same equity to be relieved
against a conveyance as the party had for fraud on him (*b*).
We shall hereafter see when an inquisition is necessary to entitle the King.

By an attainder of *petit treason* or *felony* the offender forfeits (*c*) to the Crown all his chattel interests absolutely, and
the profits of all estates of freehold, whether held by him in
his own or his wife's right (*d*), during his life, and, after his
death; all his lands and tenements in fee simple (but not those
in tail) to the Crown, for a very short period of time; for the
King shall have them only for a year and day, and may commit therein during that period what waste he pleases; which is
called the King's "year day and waste" (*e*). The person entitled to the lands on the death of the offender, whether the

---

(*a*) 3 Bac. Ab. 269. See 26 Hen. 8.
c. 13. s. 5.   33 Hen. 8. c. 20. s. 2.   1
and 2 Ph. and M. c. 10. s. 7.

(*b*) 2 Ves. 116; 228.   3 Price's R.
122.

(*e*) See 4 Bla. Com. 385.   2 Inst. 37.

Bac. Ab. Forfeiture A.   3 Inst. 19.
  (*d*) 3 Inst. 19.   Fitz. Assize, 166.
Forfeiture, 23, 4.   Ass. Pl. 4.
  (*c*) 2 Inst. 37.   4 Bla. Com. 385.
Staundf. Prerog. Regis, c. 16.

wife

wife of the offender, issue in tail, or a reversioner, cannot enter
on them, until it appear by due process, that the King has
enjoyed this prerogative (a): but an office is it seems necessary
to entitle the King to it (b): and if he do not seize within a
year and day after office found, he ought it is said to have a
scire facias before seizure (c).

It is most probable that antiently the sovereign was only
entitled to commit waste on the freehold property of the
attainted felon, and that it being discovered that this destruction tended to the detriment of agriculture (d) and otherwise
to the prejudice of the public, possession of the lands was given
to his Majesty for a year and day in lieu of his right to destroy
them. This appears to have first prevailed in the reign of
Henry 1 (e). Magna Charta 9 Hen. 3. c. 22. does not mention waste, and merely provides that the King shall not hold
the lands of those who may be convicted of felony, but for one
year and one day; and Sir Edw. Coke (f) was of opinion that
the commission of waste where the King also held the lands,
was an encroachment, though a very antient one, of the royal
prerogative. However the statute *de prerogativa Regis*, 17
Edw. 2. st. 2. c. 16. appears to recognize the right of the
King to hold the lands, and also to commit any destruction
therein. That statute provides that if a felon attainted have a
freehold, it shall be forthwith taken into the King's hands,
and the King shall have all the issues thereof, for one year
and one day; and the land shall be wasted and destroyed in
the houses and gardens, woods, and in all manner of things
belonging to the same land. At the present day therefore
this year day and waste regularly belong to the Crown, but are
usually compounded for (g); and this is the more expedient as
this prerogative cannot be granted to a subject by the King (h).
We have seen that after the expiration of the year day and
waste on an attainder of felony, the lands of the party escheated,
in consequence of the corruption of his blood, to the lord of
the fee; but the 54 Geo. 3. c. 45. has abolished both the

(a) Staundf. P. C. 191. 2 Hawk. P.
C. c. 49. s. 3. 1 Hal. P. C. 360.
(b) Staundf. Prerog. Regis, 55, b.
53, b.
(c) Ibid. 54, b.
(d) See Co. Lit. 85, b.
(e) Mirr. c. 4. s. 16. Flet. l. 1. c. 28.

4 Bla. Com. 385, 6.
(f) 2 Inst. 37. And see Mirr. c. 5.
s. 2. 4 Bla. Com. 385, 6.
(g) Ibid. 386,
(h) Bro. Ab. Prerog. pl. 104. Jenk.
307. pl. 83.

corruption

corruption of blood and the forfeiture of lands after death, in every case except *treason, petit treason,* and *murder,* which still remain as at common law. So that at the present day on attainder of ordinary felony, except for murder, the criminal forfeits only his goods and chattels, and choses in action, and the profits of land during life, while his real estate comes in the ordinary channel of descent to his heir, who is thus also restored to a full capacity to inherit (*a*).

The forfeitures with which the crime of high treason, petit treason and felony are punishable, are not in legal contemplation incurred until the attaint takes place: that is, till judgment of death be passed upon him, and therefore if the offender die before judgment be pronounced, or is killed in open rebellion, or is hanged by martial law, it works no forfeiture of his lands, for he never was attainted (*b*). A judgment of outlawry for treason or other capital crime, is however equivalent to an attainder (*c*), and if the Chief Justice of England in person, upon view of the body of one killed in open rebellion, record it, and return the record into his own Court, both lands and goods shall be forfeited (*d*).

Where on outlawry the offender's lands are seized, the King has no estate in the lands, but only a pernancy of the profits. He cannot manure or sow the ground, and his Majesty's interest continues no longer than the offender had an estate in the lands, and determines with the death of the latter, or by the reversing or superseding of the outlawry (*e*).

Although the forfeitures of *lands* above-mentioned do not take place until the attaint of the offender is effected (*f*), yet when that has been done, the forfeiture relates back to the time when the treason or felony was committed (*g*), so as to avoid all sales, incumbrances, or other acts relative to the property, which may have transpired since that period (*h*). But no attainder whatsoever has any relation as to the mesne profits of the lands of the person attainted, but from the time of the attainder (*i*).

(*a*) 1 Chitty, Crim. L. 735.

(*b*) Co. Lit. 13, 391, a. 3 Inst. 455. 4 Bla. Com. 381.

(*c*) Ibid. See Bac. Ab. Outlawry, D. 1, 2, 3.

(*d*) 4 Co. Rep. 57.

(*e*) Bac. Ab. Outlawry, D. 2.

(*f*) See ante, 216.

(*g*) 3 Inst. 211. 4 Bla. Com. 386, 7. Bac. Ab. Forfeiture, D.

(*h*) Ibid.

(*i*) 8 Co. 170. Plowd. 488. 1 Chitty, Crim. L. 735.

If

If the proof as to the time when the offence was committed, vary from the time mentioned in the indictment, and the jury find the offender guilty generally, the forfeiture relates to the time laid, until the verdict be falsified by the party interested, as it may be in this respect, though not as to the point of the offence (*a*). But if the jury specially find the offender guilty on the day on which the fact is proved to have been committed, whether before or after the day laid in the indictment; in such case the forfeiture relates to the day so found (*b*).

If an alien purchase land in this country for his own use, the King is entitled to them by way of forfeiture, but the vendor is not affected thereby (*c*). This will be considered in the next section on escheats.

Forfeiture of Personalty.—The forfeiture of goods and chattels to the Crown accrues in every one of the higher kinds of offences, in high treason or misprision thereof, petit treason, felonies of all sorts, whether clergyable or not, self-murder, petit larceny, standing mute, and, among other offences, that of striking in Westminster-hall, or drawing a weapon upon a Judge sitting in one of the King's courts of justice there (*d*). And where a man, being accused of the commission of treason, felony, or even petit larceny, flies from the inquiries of justice, and the jury find the flight (which they seldom or never do), he forfeits all his goods and chattels to the King, although he be acquitted on the trial of the offence imputed to him (*e*). If, however, in this case the indictment be insufficient (*f*), or the flight be disproved on a traverse of the finding of the jury (*g*), the forfeiture is saved. It seems to have been formerly considered, that a coroner's inquest finding the flight, could not be traversed, so as to save the forfeiture (*h*); but the injustice and hardship of subjecting a man to so severe a punishment as the confiscation of all his personalty, by a finding which took place in his absence, and most probably without giving him an op-

---

(*a*) 1 Hal. P. C. 361. 3 Inst. 230.

(*b*) Kely. 16. Hal. P. C. 361. 2 Inst. 318. 3 Ibid. 230.

(*c*) Co. Lit. 2. 1 Bla. Com. 372.

(*d*) 4 Ibid. 386. Bac. Ab. Forfeiture, B. 5 Co. 109.

(*e*) 4 Bla. Com. 387. Bac. Ab. For-

feiture, B.

(*f*) Bac. Ab. Ibid.

(*g*) Bac. Ab. Ibid. Keilw. 68. 5 Co. 110. Staundf. 184.

(*h*) 13 Hen. 4. 13. pl. 6. 5 Co. 109. Dyer, 238. 2 Inst. 147. 3 Keb. 366, 564. 2 Lev. 141.

portunity

portunity of shewing his innocence, together with the circumstance of less weight having been of late years attached to the verdict of a coroner's jury than antiently, it was considered as entitled to (*a*), appear to justify the assertion, that at the present day a party might legally traverse the finding of the coroner's inquest, in order to obviate the consequences of the flight of which he is accused (*b*). But this matter is not of much practical importance, as the flight is never found.

On an outlawry, whether in a criminal or civil case, the party forfeits his personal property to the Crown (*c*). In this case, however, the forfeiture may be obviated by a reversal of the award of the exigent, either for error in fact or law (*d*). But it seems, that if a person accused even of petit larceny only, makes default till the award of the exigent, his goods are forfeited, and though he is entitled to them on a reversal of the outlawry, yet he cannot claim a return of them, merely because he is acquitted at the trial of the offence for which he is indicted (*e*).

Every thing which comes within the description of personal property is forfeited, without office found, in the above instances; and even choses in action or debts, whether due on specialty or simple contract, and whether acquired before or after the attainder (*f*). And, it seems, that trusts of personalty stand in this respect on the same footing as trusts of realty (*g*). It is, however, clear, that such property as the offender holds as executor or administrator, is not forfeitable to the Crown (*h*). Where the party is joint obligee of a bond with another, it seems, the King shall have the whole (*i*), because the demand is indivisible. And, on the same ground, if another were also interested in a horse or ox with the defendant, the King shall still have the whole (*k*).

We have already seen, that lands are only forfeited upon at-

(*a*) See 2 Hawk. P. C. c. 9. s. 53, 55. Bac. Ab. Coroners, B.

(*b*) And see 1 Bac. Ab. 755. 2 Hawk. P. C. c. 9. s. 54; but see 1 Chitty, Crim. L. 731.

(*c*) Bac. Ab. Outlawry, D. 2.

(*d*) Ibid.

(*e*) Ibid. 5 Co. 110. Cro. Jac. 464. 1 Chitty, Crim. L. 731, 2.

(*f*) Bac. Ab. Forfeiture, B. 3 vol.

966. Hawk. P. C. b. 2. c. 49. s. 9. Bullock *v.* Dodds, 2 B. and Ald. 259.

(*g*) See Ibid. Cro. Jac. 312. Hob. 214.

(*h*) Cro. Car. 566. 2 Leon. 5 and 6. Moor, 100. Dyer, 309, 10. Cro. El. 575, 851. 2 Rol. Ab. 806.

(*i*) 1 Wightw. 51, 2.

(*k*) Plowd. 243, 323. Post. s. 3.

tainder; personalty is, however, forfeited upon the offender's being convicted, or, in other words, found guilty by the jury (*a*); and although in outlawries for treason, or felony, lands are forfeited only by the judgment, yet the personal property of the offender is forfeited, by his being first put in the exigent without staying till he is *quinto exactus*, or finally outlawed; for the secreting himself so long from justice is construed a flight in law (*b*).

There is a further material distinction between the forfeiture of real and personal property; for the forfeiture of the former has relation to the time when the offence was committed, so as to avoid all subsequent sales and incumbrances; but the forfeiture of personalty has no relation backwards, so that those only which the offender had at the time of the conviction shall be forfeited; and, therefore, a traitor or felon may sell any of his personal property for the sustenance of himself and family, between the fact and conviction (*c*). And in the great prisage case, in Bulstrode's Reports (*d*), this point is put, " A termor is distrained for rent behind; afterwards he is attainted for felony, done before the distress taken; *Per Curiam.* " The King shall not have this distress as a forfeiture, unless he do satisfy the party who distrained, for this was lawfully taken *tempore captionis.*" If, however, the property be parted with collusively, and in order to defraud the King, his Majesty will be entitled to it (*e*).

As laid down in a recent work (*f*), " By the 1 Rich. 3. c. 3. the sheriff and other officers are precluded from seizing the goods of a party arrested or imprisoned for treason, or felony, until his attainder or conviction. This Act is said to be only in affirmance of the common law (*g*), and extends to money as well as specific chattels (*h*). It seems, however, that the goods may be appraised, or inventoried, after indictment found, in order that no sequestration or collusive transfer may defeat

(*a*) Co. Lit. 391, a. 1 Hale, 362. 4 Bla. Com. 387.

(*b*) 3 Inst. 232.

(*c*) 8 Co. 171. 4 Bla. Com. 387. 3 Price, R. 121.

(*d*) 3 Bulstr. 17.

(*e*) Skin. 357. pl. 4. 13 El. c. 5. 4 Bla. Com. 388.

(*f*) Chitty, Crim. L. 736.

(*g*) Hard. 97. 3 Inst. 229. Com. Dig. Forfeiture, B. 4. Ibid. Justices, Z. Hawk. b. 2. c. 49. s. 39.

(*h*) Sir Thomas Bay. 414. Hawk. b. 2. c. 49. s. 39. Com. Dig. Forfeiture, B. 4. Ibid. Justices, Z.

the

the Crown of the forfeiture (*a*). This, indeed, does not extend to a removal; and it is clear, as just observed, that the party indicted may sell any of them for his support in prison, or that of his family, or to assist him in preparing for his defence on the trial (*b*). But a fraudulent conveyance, without consideration, as a bill of sale to a felon's son, will be void; because, as the owner might, if acquitted, have recovered them back himself, so, if convicted, the transfer will not avail against his Majesty (*c*). And though the property cannot be touched before, it is certain that it may be seized as soon as the forfeiture is completed (*d*). It seems, too, the whole township is answerable to the King for their production, and are, therefore, empowered to seize them wherever they may be conveyed (*e*). And, at common law, they could exonerate themselves from responsibility, by shewing that they delivered the goods to an individual by whom they were secreted (*f*). But by the 31 Edw. 3. c. 3. they are admitted to excuse themselves, by throwing the blame on the party actually culpable. The Crown seems to take them free from liability to the previous debts of the convict, though it should seem that, in some cases, the Crown will allow the creditors to reap benefit from them (*g*)."

The King's pardon will effectually remit and prevent such forfeitures as accrue to the Crown, but not vested escheats to a subject who may be lord of the fee. The power of the Crown to regrant forfeitures, &c. will be mentioned in the next section, on escheats (*h*).

To consider the various cases in which the right of the Crown to goods forfeited for breaches of the revenue law, obtains, would lead one into a detail of the revenue laws; a subject principally founded on the positive enactments of the

---

(*a*) 1 Hale, 367. 3 Inst. 228. Hawk. b. 2. c. 49. s. 35. Bro. Abr. Forfeiture, 10, Burn's J. Forfeiture, J. Williams's J. Seizure of Felon's Goods.

(*b*) 4 Bla. Com. 387, 8. 8 Co. 171. Skin. 357, 8. 1 Hale, 361. Hawk. b. 2. c. 49. s. 33. Com. Dig. Justices, Z. Bac. Ab. Forfeiture, E. Williams's J. Seizure of Felon's Goods.

(*c*) Ibid.

(*d*) Co. Lit. 391, a. Hawk. b. 2. c. 49. s. 40.

(*e*) Staundf. Prerog. 47. Bro. Ab. Charge, 45. Hawk. b. 2. c. 49. s. 40. Bac. Ab. Forfeiture, E.

(*f*) Hawk. Ibid. s. 41. Bac. Ab. Ibid.

(*g*) Dougl. 542. See form of commission, to inquire of lands forfeited on outlawry, &c. 1 Lil. Ent. 304.

(*h*) Post, 235.

legislature.

legislature. It may, however, be remarked, that when forfeitures of this description are incurred, they accrue instantly
to the Crown, and will not be divested by a subsequent *seizure*
of the same article, as a droit of admiralty, or otherwise (*a*);
though, as the Admiralty Court proceeds *in rem*, a *judicial sale*
of a vessel, &c. as a derelict, without fraud, is available against
the Crown's right of seizure for a previous forfeiture under the
revenue laws; although the Crown was not a party to the proceeding in the Admiralty Court, other than by the King's Pro-
curator-General claiming the vessel as an Admiralty droit; and
although no decision of droit, or no droit, was awarded, and
the sale took place, *pendente lite*, under an interlocutory order (*b*).

4. We may mention *Escheats* as constituting another, and
by no means an unimportant part, of the ordinary and inherent revenue of the Crown.

As before observed, the doctrine of escheats is a consequence
of tenure in chivalry, according to the antient feudal system.
Escheat is (*c*) the determination of the tenure, or dissolution of
the mutual bond between the lord and tenant, from the extinction of the blood of the latter, by either natural or civil
means; if he died without heirs of his blood, or if his blood
was corrupted and stained by commission of treason or felony,
whereby every inheritable quality was entirely blotted out and
abolished. In such cases the land escheated, or fell back, to
the lord of the fee; that is, the tenure was determined by
breach of the original condition expressed or implied in the
feudal donation. In the one case, there were no heirs subsisting of the blood of the first feudatory or purchaser, to which
heirs alone the grant of the feud extended; in the other, the
tenant by perpetrating an atrocious crime, shewed that he was
no longer to be trusted as a vassal, having forgotten his duty
as a subject, and therefore forfeited his feud, which he held
under the implied condition that he should not be a traitor or
a felon. The consequence of which in both cases was, that the
gift being determined, resulted back to the lord who gave

(*a*) Parker, 273. Observations on (*b*) 3 Price, 97.
this case, 3 Price, 134.   (*c*) 2 Bla. Com. 72. Co. Lit. 13.

it.

it (*a*). It is in this point of view that Bracton (*b*) terms an escheat a species of reversion.

Wherever lands escheat, they become the property of the lord of the seignory, or person of whom they were held. Now by the statute 12 Cha. 2. s. 24. for changing all the antient tenures into free and common socage, the rents and services (among which fealty is occasionally due) are preserved to the lord ; of him therefore the lands are still holden, and to him they may escheat. But if all these badges of tenure have been neglected to be preserved, and it be no longer known of whom the lands are mediately holden ; then the King, as the great and chief lord, shall have them by escheat ; for to him fealty belongs, and of him they are certainly holden by presumption of law, and without the necessity of proof (*c*). At the present day therefore the King is almost universally though not necessarily the lord of the seignory, and as such entitled on the escheat of inheritances. The case of a copyhold, which escheats to the lord of the manor, as the person of whom they were held, seems to form the only general exception. It will not therefore be a digression to enter rather fully into the law of escheats.

An escheat may, says Lord Coke (*d*), happen 1st, *aut per defectum sanguinis* (that is) for the default of an heir ; 2dly, *aut per defectum tenentis.*

1. To state fully all the particular instances in which an escheat may occur, in consequence of a party dying without relations who can inherit, it would be necessary to enter into the principles and niceties of the law of descents. It will suffice to observe in this place, that escheats arising from a deficiency of blood, whereby the descent is at an end, take place, 1st, where the tenant dies without any relations on the part of any of his

(*a*) Feud. l. 2. t. 86. 2 Bla. Com. 72, and 244. Co. Lit. 13. Wright's Ten. 115. 2 Inst. 64. 1 Bla. Rep. 133.

(*b*) 23, a.

(*c*) Booth's Real Act, 135. Cro. Eliz. 120. 3 Cruise Dig. 496. 2 Bla. Com. 245. Sed qu. whether at common law upon the death of the tenant last seised of the land without heirs, the right and possession must be *presumed* to be immediately in the Crown *without office,* as though the person last seised were the King's immediate tenant ; the King's title not appearing by any matter of record, and the possession not having been vacant from the death of the tenant last seised. *See* 12 East, 96, 109, 110.

(*d*) 1 Inst. 13, a. 92.

ancestors ;

ancestors; 2dly, where he dies without any relations on the part of those ancestors from whom the estate descended; and 3dly, where he dies without any relations of the whole blood. In all these cases the lands escheat, because there is no one capable of inheriting them (*a*).

An extinguishment of inheritable blood takes place, and the doctrine of escheat to be lord of the fee also obtains, if there be no other heir to the party who died seised but a *monster*, which has not the shape of mankind, and in any part evidently bears the resemblance of the brute creation, for such monster cannot inherit (*b*). And the same doctrine applies where the only claimant is *illegitimate* (*c*). And as bastards cannot be heirs themselves, so neither can they have any heirs but those of their own bodies. For as all collateral kindred consists in being derived from the same common ancestor, and as a bastard has no legal ancestors, he can have no collateral kindred; and, consequently, can have no legal heirs, but such as claim by a lineal descent from himself. And therefore if a bastard purchase land, and die seised thereof without issue, and intestate, the land shall escheat to the lord of the fee (*d*).

There is another case in which lands may escheat to the lord *propter defectum sanguinis*, and that is where a man leaves no other relations but *aliens* (the persons falling within which denomination have been already considered); for it is a rule of law, founded as much on political as feudal principles, that aliens cannot take by descent, and are incapable of inheriting (*e*). In every country restraints have been laid upon aliens: in England the disabilities to which they are subject are not imposed on them as penalties and forfeitures, but are founded on the necessary policy of the state (*f*).

Aliens have no inheritable blood to transmit, and consequently can have no heirs (*g*), unless made denizens by the King, or naturalized by Act of Parliament. In the first case

(*a*) 3 Cruise Dig. 382, and 492.

(*b*) Co. Lit. 7, 8.   1 Bla. Com. 247.

(*c*) Ibid. 1 Inst. 7, b. 244, b. 245. a. n. 1.   Finch, L. 117.

(*d*) 2 Bla. C. 249. and 3 Cruise Dig. 374.   See Bract. l. 2. c. 7.   Co. Lit. 244.

(*e*) Co. Lit. 8.   Bac. Ab. Aliens, C.

2 Bla. Com. 249.

(*f*) It has therefore been adjudged in Equity, that an alien cannot demur to a discovery of any circumstances necessary to prove the fact of alienage. Parker, 144.   5 Bro. P. C. 91.

(*g*) Ibid.   Co. Lit. 2.   1 Lev. 59.

children

children born after the denization may inherit, in the latter they may whether born before or after (*a*).

It may not perhaps be irrelevant to consider in this place the rights of the Crown on an alien purchasing lands. Aliens are by law incapable of holding lands by purchase (*b*): but their purchases stand good (*c*), and as every person resident in the country is *primâ facie* a natural born subject, the freehold remains in them (*d*), till on office or inquisition the same are divested and seised to the King's use (*e*); for on office found the King by his prerogative is entitled to such lands of whomsoever they are holden (*f*). But if an alien who can have no heir purchase land and die, the freehold is cast upon and is in the King without office found (*g*): unless after the purchase he has been made a denizen and hath issue; for in such case the son has a plausible, though not a legal (*h*) claim, which should be investigated and disproved only on office found (*i*). In general if a denizen purchase a fee, and die without issue, the lord of the fee shall have the escheat, and not the King, the effect of denization being to enable the party to purchase (*k*). It should be remarked, that though an alien may hold under a purchase, that is, till office found, and the land then enures for the benefit of the Crown, yet he cannot, even for the benefit of the King, take by act of law, as by descent, &c. (*l*). And if he purchase in the name of J. S. in trust, &c. the legal estate being in the latter, it is held the Crown must sue in Chancery to have the trust executed

(*a*) 1 Bla. C. 374. 2 Ibid. 250.

(*b*) Co. Lit. 2.

(*c*) 1 Bla. Com. 372.

(*d*) And therefore on a covenant to stand seised an use will arise for an alien, Godb. 275. Feoffment to an alien, &c. Dyer, 283, b.

(*e*) Co. Lit. 2, a. 5 Co. 52, b. 1 Bac. Ab. 133. Before office recovery by an alien tenant in tail will bar remainder, Gouldst. 102. 4 Leon. 84. But even before office found the King is so far entitled to the property as to have a right to the assistance of a Court of Equity to enforce a discovery of the fact of alienage. Park. 144.

(*f*) If an alien purchase a copyhold, it is said that it shall escheat to the lord. Dyer, 2, b. and 303, a. in marg. But see 1 Mod. 17; and All. 14. Hargr. n. 4, and Co. Lit. 2, b.

(*g*) Ibid. Co. Lit. 2, b. See in Plowd. 229, several cases, in which, for a like reason, the King is entitled without office. See 12 East, 96, and post. c. 12. s. 2. Offices.

(*h*) See ante, 228.

(*i*) Ibid. Bac. Ab. 133, tit. Aliens, C.

(*k*) Co. Lit. 2, b.

(*l*) 7 Co. 25, a. 1 Ventr. 417. Co. Lit. 2, b. n. 1.

for

for his benefit (*a*). The King is it seems entitled to a lease for years taken by an alien contrary to 32 Hen. 8. c. 16. s. 13 (*b*).

2. On the same principles of the feudal system is founded the doctrine of escheats to the lord of the fee *propter delictum tenentis.* The blood of the tenant being corrupted and rendered no longer inheritable by an attainder, the original denomination of the feud is altered and determined: it being always granted to the vassal on the implied condition of *dum bene se gesserit* (*c*). It is in this point of view that escheats to the lord, and forfeitures of lands to the Crown, which have sometimes been confounded together, essentially differ; for forfeitures were, as before observed, used and inflicted as punishments by the old Saxon law without the least relation to the feudal system, and they differ in other material respects (*d*).

At common law the blood was corrupted by an attainder (but not till the attainder) of high treason, or any species of felony. In the former case it still obtains, except in the instance of treasons respecting the coin (*e*). But by a late statute 54 G. 3. c. 145. the corruption of blood and a forfeiture of lands after death is taken away in all cases, except high and petit treason and murder, so that no attainder for any other felony "shall extend to the disinheriting of any heir, nor to the prejudice of the right or title of any person other than the right or title of the offender during his natural life only; and that it shall be lawful to every person to whom the right or interest of any lands or hereditaments after the death of any such offender should or might have appertained if no such attainder had been, to enter into the same."

We have already seen to whom escheats revert, that is, to the lord of the fee, who is almost universally the King. In the case of attainder of high treason, the superior law of for-

---

(*a*) 1 Bla. Rep. 144; and 1 Bac. Ab. 134, cites Rol. Ab. 194. Hob. 214. Cro. Jac. 512. Allen, 14. Style, 20, 21, 76. Parker, 156. See 13 Geo. 3. c. 14. which enables aliens to lend money on West India Land.

(*b*) Co. Lit. 2, b, and n. 6. See notes,

Ibid.

(*c*) 1 Inst. 8, a. 391, b. 2 Bla. Com, 252.

(*d*) 1 Bla. Rep. 143.

(*e*) 5 El. c. 11. s. 2. 18 El. c. 1. s. 2. 8 and 9 W. 3. c. 26. s. 8. 15 Geo. 2. c. 28. s. 4.

feiture

feiture intervenes, and renders the doctrine of escheat irrelevant; for by such attainder lands of inheritance, though
holden of another lord, are forfeited to the Crown, there being
an exception in the oath of fealty which saves the tenant's allegiance to the King (a).   In case of petit treason and murder
no absolute *forfeiture* of lands is incurred : and in these cases
the 54 G. 3. does not take away the corruption of blood ; and
therefore in such instances the law of *escheats* is still important
and applicable.

Though the land escheat to another lord the King is entitled,
before such lord enter, to his year day and waste which has
been already considered.

The corruption of the offender's blood by an attainder of
high treason, petit treason, or murder (which alone can now
occasion it), renders him ignoble, and annihilates his honours
and dignities (b).   Unlike the case of mere forfeiture for offences,
it not only causes all he has to escheat from him, but renders
him incapable of inheriting any thing in future (c); so that
property subsequently acquired escheats to the Crown(d).   And
if therefore a father be seised in fee, and the son commit treason and is attainted, and then the father die; here the lands
escheat to the lord; because the son, by the corruption of his
blood, is incapable to be heir, and there can be no other heir
during his life; but nothing shall be forfeited to the King, for
the son never had any interest in the lands to forfeit (e).   In
this case the escheat operates, and not the forfeiture ; but in
the following instance the forfeiture works, and not the escheat.   As where a new felony is created by Act of Parliament, and it is provided (as is frequently the case), that it shall
not extend to corruption of blood ; here the lands of the felon
shall not escheat to the lord, but yet the profits of them shall
be forfeited to the King for a year and a day, and so long after
as the offender lives (f).

The corruption of blood affects also the posterity of the
offender.   His blood being corrupted and rendered imper-

(a) 1 Hale, P. C. 360.   Bac. Ab. Forfeiture, A. and Prerogative, B. 2. ante,
ch. 2. s. 2.
(b) Co. Lit. 8, 41.   3 Inst. 211
Hawk. b. 2. c. 4. s. 47.
(c) 2 Bla. Com. 253.
(d) Co. Lit. 2, b.
(e) Co. Lit. 13.
(f) 3 Inst. 47.   2 Bla. Com. 253.

vious, he is not only unable to transmit his own property by
heirship, but obstructs the descent of lands to his heirs, in all
cases where they are obliged to derive their title through him
from any remoter ancestor (*a*).   Therefore, the son of an attainted traitor cannot inherit his grandfather's lands, but they
escheat to the Crown (*b*); and where there were two brothers,
and the youngest had issue a son, and was attainted of treason,
and executed, it was held, that the son of the youngest brother
could not inherit from his uncle, because he must derive his
descent through his father (*c*).   It is, however, a clear rule,
that the corruption of blood does not affect the succession of
collateral issue; so that if a person whose blood is corrupted
has sons, one of whom acquires an estate of his own, and dies
without issue, his brother will inherit, because there is no necessity in such a case to make any mention of the father (*d*).
And it is a general rule, that where there is no necessity to
name the individual attainted in a title, his corruption of blood
will not vitiate, though the ancestor be ever so distant (*e*).
Thus, for example, if there be a father and two sons, and the
eldest is attainted in the lifetime of the father, and dies without
issue, the younger son will succeed to those estates which
otherwise would have descended to his brother; but if the elder
son, who was attainted, survive the father but a day, so as to
have been placed in his room, the lands must escheat, and the
succession be for ever defeated (*f*).   A person may, however,
inherit from one of his parents, though the other should be attainted of treason, or felony, for *duplicatus sanguis* is not necessary in descents.   Therefore, if an attainted person marry an
heiress, and have issue by her, that issue shall inherit, for
the marriage was lawful, and he claims only from the mother (*g*).

All lands and tenements held in socage, whether of the King
or of a subject, are liable to the law of escheats; as are copyhold lands, on attainder, which, however, revert to the lord of

(*a*) Hal. P. C. 356.

(*b*) Ibid.

(*c*) Grey's Case. Dyer, 274. Cro.
Car. 543. 3 Cruise Dig. 379.

(*d*) Co. Lit. 8, a. 1 Hale, 357. Hawk.
b. 2. c. 49. s. 49. 1 Chitty, Crim. L.

740.

(*e*) Hawk. b. 2. c. 49. s. 49. Bac. Ab.
Forfeiture, G.

(*f*) 1 Chitty, Crim. L. 741.

(*g*) Jenk. Cent. 1. ca. 2. Cent. 5.
ca. 27. Noy. 168. 3 Cruise Dig. 378.

the

the manor (*a*). But gavel-kind lands (*b*), and estates tail (*c*), do not escheat, though they are forfeitable for treason. And no species of real property, which does not lie in tenure, as a rent-charge, right of common, or free warren, is subject to escheat (*d*). So, if lands be given to a corporation, on the dissolution thereof, the donor, or his heirs, shall have them again in reversion, and not the lord by escheat, which is a very peculiar case (*e*).

Even the King, when he is lord, cannot claim by escheat contrary to the terms and conditions under which the tenant held (*f*). His Majesty's right, by escheat, stands on the same ground as every other legal right ; it arises out of the seizin (*f*), and is, in general, governed by the same rules as govern escheats to the subject (*g*). Wherever, therefore, there be a tenant to perform the services (*h*), the Crown, though the lord of the fee, cannot claim by escheat, more than any other lord ; as if *cestui que trust*, or a mortgagor, die without heirs, or be attainted of petit treason or murder, which seems to make no difference. The trustee in the one case, and the mortgagee in the other, and not the King, shall have the inheritance (*i*).

(*a*) Co. Cop. s. 28. 2 Ves. jun. 170. 1 Chitty, Crim. L. 728, 9. But the homage ought to present the death of the party without heirs, and proclamation ought to be made requiring claimants, if any, to appear, &c. Ibid. It has been holden, that if a surrender of a copyhold be made to a party who is executed before admittance, the land will not escheat to the lord, but return to the surrenderor and descend to his successors, 1 Wils. 13.

(*b*) Rob. Gav. 226. 2 Bla. Com. 252.

(*c*) 3 Co. R. 10, b. Cro. El. 28. 3 Cruise Dig. 473, 4,

(*d*) 3 Inst. 21. As to forfeiture thereof, ante, s. 1.

(*e*) 2 Bla. Com. 256.

(*f*) 1 Bla. Rep. 165.

(*g*) To what incumbrances the lord taking by escheat is liable in general, 3 Cruise, 496. 1 Bla. R. 134; may distrain for rent, 1 Inst. 215, 6 ; and entitled to all charters, &c. Bro. tit. Chart. pl. 59. 3 Cruise, 499.

(*h*) As to this, see 1 Bla. Rep. 175. 3 Cruise Dig. 493, 515; what alienation prevents an escheat, 3 Cruise Dig. 495.

(*i*) 1 Bla. Rep. 123. Ld. Mansfield, Diss. And this was somewhat doubted by Lord Thurlow; see 1 Bro. Ch. Cas. 204. But the law seems clearly to be so on the ground above stated. And I have MSS. opinions of Mr. Serjeant Hill, Mr. Serjeant Heywood, and Mr. Hughes, to the same effect ; on the ground that there can be no want of a tenant to perform the services, in which case only an escheat takes place where there is a person seised of a legal estate in fee, capable of performing such services. On which ground also they thought there was no escheat in the case of a mortgagor's death, &c. ; but that the mortgagee was the tenant according to the opinions expressed by the Lord Keeper and the Master of the Rolls, in the case in Bla. Rep. see Ibid. 149, 170, 184. See Jenk. 190. Hardr. 495. Sid. 403.

But

But where a mortgagor of freehold property was attainted of high treason, the Court would not decree a foreclosure against the Crown, but directed that the mortgagee should hold and enjoy the mortgaged premises, till the Crown thought fit to redeem the estate (a). It has been held, that where the character of land is not imperatively and definitively fixed upon money, by the terms of a will, or other instrument, a Court of Equity will not order it to be laid out in land, in order to let in the Crown, claiming by escheat (b). It seems, however, to be a general rule, that the Crown, when it takes by escheat, is free from equitable claims (c), as if a trustee die without heirs, the King is not subject to the trusts (d). And where the inheritance escheats, and there is an outstanding term which is attendant thereon, the lord, by escheat, will be entitled to such term (e). But it is said, that mortgaged lands escheat on the death of the mortgagee in fee, without heirs, subject to the mortgage (f).

The King's pardon does not prevent the escheat to the lord when vested (g); and though a pardon will enable the party to transmit after acquired property to his children, yet an Act of Parliament reversing the attainder is necessary, to remove the stain or corruption of blood entirely (h).

The mode by which the Crown obtains property to which it is entitled by escheat, will be considered hereafter. But it may be observed in this place that an office or inquisition is in general unnecessary (i); though an entry should, it seems, be made on the part of the Crown, for the failure and neglect to claim or the doing any act which amounts to an implied waiver of the right of the claimant by escheat, (as accepting homage, or in some instances, rent of a stranger, who usurps the possession, &c.) may at all events, in the case of a subject, effectually bar the title by escheat (k).

(a) 2 Atk. 223,

(b) 2 Ves. jun. 170.

(c) 1 Bla. Rep. 143,

(d) 3 Cruise Dig. 497, 8.

(e) 1 Vern. 340.

(f) 1 Bla. Rep. 170.

(g) 1 Chitty, Crim. L. 742. Owen, 87. 2 Bla. Com. 254.

(h) Ibid. ante, c. 7. s. 2. div. 4. 1 Hale, 358. 3 Inst. 240, 1.

(i) 5 Bac. Ab. 566, ante 22?. When necessary in the case of an alien purchasing land, ibid.

(k) See Co. Lit. 268. 2 Bla. Com. 244, 5. 5 Bac. Ab. 497, tit. Prerogative. 3 Cruise Dig. 494. However no laches is imputable to the King: but a recognition of another's title by express acts is another consideration.

The

The exercise of the right of the Crown by escheat, to the prejudice of the relatives of a party who died without heirs, or attainted, or in the case of purchases by aliens, &c. would in many cases be harsh. It has therefore been the practice for the Crown on a petition disclosing the facts, to grant the lands to parties who might otherwise lose them; and to direct the execution of trusts, to which the property may be liable, &c. In furtherance of this liberal practice, it is enacted by the statute 47 G. 3. sess. 2. c. 24. " that in all cases in which his Majesty, his heirs or successors, hath or shall, in right of his Crown or of his Duchy of Lancaster, become entitled to any freehold or copyhold manors, messuages, lands, tenements, or hereditaments, either by escheat for want of heirs, or by reason of any forfeitures, or by reason that the same had been purchased by or for the use of or in trust for any alien or aliens, it shall be lawful for his Majesty, his heirs and successors, by warrant under his or their sign manual, or under the seal of the duchy or county palatine of Lancaster, according to the nature of the title to such manors, messuages, lands, tenements, or hereditaments respectively, to direct the execution of any trusts or purposes to which the same may have been directed to be applied, and to make grants of such manors, messuages, lands, tenements or hereditaments, or of any rents or profits then due and in arrear to his Majesty in respect thereof respectively, to any trustee or trustees, or otherwise, for the execution of any such trusts or purposes, or to any person or persons for the purpose of restoring the same to any of the family of the person or persons whose estates the same had been, or of carrying into effect any intended grant, conveyance, or devise of any such person or persons in relation thereto, or of rewarding any person or persons making discovery of such escheat, or of his Majesty's right and title thereto, as to his Majesty, his heirs or successors respectively, shall seem fit."

In a modern case, Lord Eldon said, it is perfectly familiar, that where there is an escheat for want of heirs, and the fact is not communicated, it is usual to petition the King, stating that there is such an interest, and praying some reward upon the ground of the discovery, if it can be made out; and the ordinary rule upon an escheat is, for the Crown to give a lease,

as

as good a lease as it can give, to the person making the discovery (a).

5. The profits arising from the King's ordinary Courts of Justice form another branch of his ordinary and inherent revenue. And these consist, according to Sir Wm. Blackstone (b), not only in fines imposed upon offenders, except in the case of a fine on an indictment for not repairing a highway (c), forfeitures of recognizances, and amercements levied upon defaulters; but also in certain fees due to the Crown in a variety of legal matters, as for setting the great seal to charters, original writs, and other forensic proceedings, and for permitting fines to be levied of lands in order to bar entails, or otherwise to ensure their title. As none of these can be done without the immediate intervention of the King, by himself or his officers, the law allows him certain perquisites and profits, as a recompense for the trouble he undertakes for the public. These in process of time have been almost all granted out to private persons, or else appropriated to certain particular uses; so that though our law proceedings are still loaded

(a) 7 Ves. jun. 71. The following is a sketch of the form of a " Warrant under the Sign Manual," for granting a freehold, &c. (forfeited by alienage) upon trust for sale, for the benefit of the alien and his wife. It recited that the Commissioners of the treasury had represented, that by inquisition before four commissioners, before a jury of twelve men that the alien had purchased by deed, &c. certain premises (describing them); that the premises devolved to the Crown by prerogative; and the Commissioners had accordingly seized the same into the King's hands; that the alien by memorial had represented and discovered the circumstances and the King's right, to the Commissioners of the Treasury; and prayed them to intercede for a grant from the Crown, and for relief; that the Treasury had so done; it then granted the premises to trustees, their heirs, &c. upon trust, to carry into effect any contract by the alien for the sale of them, and to sell, &c.; that the Trustees' receipts should be a discharge to purchasers, &c.; that the surplus of the purchase-money should be paid to alien, after paying costs therein mentioned, for his own use; that the trustees should stand possessed of the rents and profits till sale, upon trust, to be applied in the manner therein directed. It then contained provisions for appointing new trustees, and for their indemnity in the usual way. " Given at the Court, &c. —— day of —————— in the 56th year of the reign, &c."

(b) 1 Bla. Com. 289.

(c) 3 Salk. 32. 13 Geo. 3. c. 78. s. 47. 1 Bla. Rep. 602. Where an Act of Parliament directs a fine at the will of the King, it means at the constitutional discretion of the Judges, 3 Salk. 33. 4 Inst. 71. As to mitigating and remitting fines, 1 Chitty, on Crim. L. 809, 811. K. B. may give part to prosecutor, Ibid. 810. Bac. Ab. Indictment, A.

with

with their payment, very little of them is now returned into the King's exchequer, for a part of whose royal maintenance they were originally intended.   All future grants of many of these fines, &c. are, however, by the statute 1 Ann, st. 1. c. 7. s. 7. to endure for no longer time than the Prince's life who grants them, and if otherwise granted, the grant shall be void without a *scire facias* or inquisition, &c.

6. The prerogatives as to the *custody of idiots and lunatics,* which constitute another branch of the King's ordinary revenue, has been already considered (*a*).

III. With respect to the third and last branch of the ordinary revenue of the Crown, arising from profits from certain royal *privileges or franchises,* which are sometimes in the hands of subjects, and are frequently annexed to manors, &c. (as forests, mines, fish and fisheries, waifs, wrecks, estrays, treasure-trove, and deodands) it will be remembered that we have already fully treated of them (*b*), and consequently any further mention of them in this place is unnecessary.

SECT. II.

As to the Extraordinary Revenue of the Crown.

WE have already before pointed out the change which occurred about the period of the Revolution, in 1688, in the mode of supplying the wants of the Government (*c*).   The King's ordinary or inherent revenues having been gradually reduced to a very narrow compass, it became necessary to resort to a fresh system of parliamentary taxation and finance, which was antiently but little known.   The present taxation is principally founded on the positive regulations of various statutes, which it is hardly relevant to consider in this work.   The revenue, though under the superintendence of Government, being at the present day peculiarly the revenue of the public, and its creditors, and the civil list alone being properly the King's revenue,

(*a*) Ante, ch. 9. s. 1.   (*c*) Ante, s. 1.
(*b*) Ante, ch. 8. s. 2.

in his own distinct capacity (*a*), it may, however, be observed, that the following are the chief parts of the extraordinary revenues of the Crown, viz.—The land-tax and malt-tax; the customs or duties on goods; the excise duties; the salt duties; the post-office duties; the stamp duties; the duties on houses and windows, on servants and hackney-coaches, and numerous other taxes might be mentioned (*b*)—" a list," to use the words of Sir Wm. Blackstone (*c*), " which no friend to his country would wish to see further increased."

SECT. III.

Other Crown Property.

As the antient jewels and treasure of the Crown are necessary to support the splendor and dignity of the Sovereign for the time being, they are considered heir-looms, and descend to the successor to the Throne, and not to the executor of the last Monarch (*d*), and, consequently, they are not devisable. But it is said (*e*), that the King may dispose of them in his lifetime, by letters patent.

With respect to *prerogative copyright*, we may refer to the admirable remarks (*f*) of Lord Erskine, at the bar of the House of Commons, as counsel of Carnan, the bookseller, who resisted the monopoly of almanacks, obtained under a supposed prerogative copyright in those publications:

" On the first introduction of printing, it was considered, as well in England as in other countries, to be a matter of state. The quick and extensive circulation of sentiments and opinions which that invaluable art introduced, could not but fall under the gripe of Government, whose principal strength was built upon the ignorance of the people who were to submit to them. The press was, therefore, wholly under the coercion of

---

(*a*) Ante, s. 1.

(*b*) See 1 Bla. Com. 308, and Sinclair on Revenue, for information on this subject.

(*c*) 1 Bla. Com. 326.

(*d*) Co. Lit. 18, b. 11 Co. 92. 2

Rol. Ab. 211. 1 Bla. Com. 428.

(*e*) Cro. Car. 344.

(*f*) 1 Vol. of the Collection of Ld. Erskine's Speeches, page 40, 1, 2. by Ridgw.

the

the Crown, and *all printing,* not only of public books, containing ordinances, religious or civil, but every species of publication whatsoever, was regulated by the King's proclamations, prohibitions, charters of privilege, and, finally, by the decrees of the Star Chamber.

" After the demolition of that odious jurisdiction, the Long Parliament, on its rupture with Charles the First, assumed the same power, which had before been in the Crown. After the Restoration, the same restrictions were re-enacted, and re-annexed to the prerogative, by the statute of the 13th and 14th of Charles the Second, and continued down by subsequent Acts till after the Revolution. In what manner they expired at last, in the time of King William, I need not state in this House. Their happy abolition, and the vain attempts to revive them in the end of that reign, stand recorded on your own journals, I trust, as perpetual monuments of your wisdom and virtue. It is sufficient to say, that the expiration of these disgraceful statutes, by the refusal of Parliament to continue them any longer, formed the great æra of the liberty of the press in this country, and stripped the Crown of every prerogative over it, except that which, upon just and rational principles of government, must ever belong to the executive magistrate in all countries, namely, the exclusive right to publish religious or civil constitutions—in a word, to promulgate every ordinance by which the subject is to live, and be governed. These always did, and from the very nature of civil government always ought, to belong to the Sovereign, and hence have gained the title of prerogative copies."

It is, therefore, on grounds of political and public convenience, that the prerogative copyright exists, and its applicability must be restrained to the reasons for its existence. The law reprobates monopolies, and even in the case of the Crown, they are only allowed to subsist when necessity requires it. It is—1. As *executive magistrate,* that the Crown has the right of promulgating to the people all acts of state and government. This gives the King the exclusive privilege of printing, at his own press, or that of his grantees, all Acts of Parliament, proclamations, and orders of council (a). 2. As *supreme*

(a) 1 Bla. Rep. 105. 2 Burr. 661. tit. Prerogative, F. 5. Generally, Millar
2 Bla. Com. 410. And see 5 Bac. Ab. *v.* Taylor. 4 Burr. 2305.

head

head of the church, he hath a right to the publication of all liturgies, and books of divine service, &c. (*a*). 3. He is also said to have a right, *by purchase*, to the copies of such law books, grammars, and other compositions, as were compiled or translated at the expense of the Crown (*b*). And upon these two last principles combined, the exclusive right of printing the translation of the bible is founded (*c*). There are, however, very forcible objections against any prerogative monopoly in bibles, *bonâ fide* published with annotations, prints, and explanations. And in the case of Grierson, the King's printer at Dublin, *v.* Jackson, which originated upon an application for an injunction to prevent the defendant from printing an edition of the bible in numbers with prints and notes; Lord Clare asked, if the validity of such a patent as the King's printer enjoyed, had ever been established at law? and said, that he did not know that the Crown had a right to grant a monopoly of that kind. He further added, " I can conceive the King, as head of the church, may say, that there shall be but one man who shall print bibles and books of common prayer, for the use of churches, and for particular purposes; but I cannot conceive that the King has any prerogative to grant a monopoly as to bibles for the instruction of mankind in revealed religion. If ever there was a time which called aloud for the dissemination of religious knowledge, it is this; and, therefore, I should, with great reluctance, decide in favor of such a monopoly as this, which must necessarily confine the circulation of the book. As to very particular purposes, I have no doubt that the patentee has an exclusive right to print bibles and prayer-books; but 'unless I am bound very strictly, I will not determine upon motion that no man but the King's printer has a right to print such works as these." The Crown has no prerogative copyright in almanacks (*d*).

But the King has no prerogative property in the art of printing, nor can he restrain the press on account of the subject-matter upon which the author writes, or his mode of treating it. He has no controul over the press, but what

(*a*) 1 Bla. Rep. 105. 2 Burr. 661. 2 Bla. Com. 410. And see 5 Bac. Ab. tit. Prerogative, F. 5. Generally Millar *v.* Taylor. 4 Burr. 2305.

(*b*) 2 Bla. Com. 410.

(*c*) Ibid.

(*d*) 2 Bla. Rep. 1004. 21 Geo. 3. c. 56. s. 10. And see Ld. Erskine's Speech, in 1 vol. Coll. of his Speeches, p. 42, &c.

arises

arises from his property in his copy (a). So the King cannot, by law, grant an exclusive privilege to print any book which does not belong to himself. If there be no certain author, the property is not in the King, but is common and crown-copies are, as in the case of an author, civil property; which is deduced, as in the case of an author, from the King's right of original publication. The kind of property in the Crown, or a patentee from the Crown, is just the same, incorporeal, incapable of violation, but by a civil injury, and only to be vindicated by the same remedy, an action upon the case, or a bill in equity. The King's copyright continues after publication (b).

The rights of the Crown as to lands (c) and franchises (d), and as to *bona vacantia*, as general occupant (e), have been already considered.

There is this peculiar quality attached to the mode of acquiring property by prerogative, that the King cannot have a *joint* property with any person in one *entire* chattel, or such a one *as is not capable of division* or *separation;* but where the titles of the King and a subject concur, the King shall have the whole; in like manner as the King cannot, either by grant or contract, become a joint-tenant of a chattel real with another person (f); but by such grant or contract shall become entitled to the whole in severalty. Thus, if a horse be given to the King and a private person, the King shall have the sole property: if a bond be made to the King and a subject, the King shall have the whole penalty, the debt or duty being one single chattel (g). And so, if two persons have the property of a horse between them, or have a joint debt owing them on bond, and one of them assigns his part to the King or is attainted, whereby his moiety is forfeited to the Crown, the King shall have the entire horse and entire debt (h); for as it is not consistent with the dignity of the Crown to be partner with a subject, so neither does the King ever lose his right in any instance; but where they interfere, his is always preferred

(a) 4 Burr. 2332. 2401.
(b) Ibid. 2401. 5 Bac. Ab. 598.
(c) Ante, ch. 11. s. 1.
(d) Ante, ch. 8. s. 2, &c.
(e) Ante, ch. 8. s. 2. div. 3.
(f) 2 Bla. Com. 184, 409.

(g) Fitzh. Abr. t. dette, 38. Plowd. 243.
(h) Cro. Eliz. 263. Plowd 323. Finch, Law, 178. 10 Mod. 245. See 1 Wightw. 50.

R

to that of another person (*a*); from which two principles it is
a necessary consequence that the innocent, though the unfortunate partner, must lose his share in both the debt and
the horse, or any chattel in the same circumstances (*b*). However in favor of commercial interests, it has been recently
holden, that on an extent against one of several partners, only
the interest of that one can be taken (*c*). And as the prerogative works no wrong, the general rule seems to be in the cases
of real estates, that if by descent, &c. a share of land come to
the King, though his Majesty cannot be joint-tenant with the
other proprietor, he shall not have the whole, but only his
portion (*d*). And the King and a subject may be tenants in
common (*e*).

Grants from the Crown will be considered hereafter (*f*), but
some important provisions in a late Act may be here stated
with propriety. By the 39 and 40 Geo. 3. c. 88. s. 10. after
reciting that it was his Majesty's most gracious desire that all
such personal estate and effects, as his Majesty shall be possessed of or entitled to at the time of his demise, and over
which he shall have the full and absolute power of disposition,
by his last will and testament, should be subject and liable to
the payment of all such debts of his Majesty as shall, during
his lifetime, be properly payable out of his privy purse: and
that it is reasonable that all such personal estate and effects as
any of his Majesty's successors, Kings or Queens of this realm,
shall be possessed of or entitled to in like manner, should also
be subject and liable to the like charge; and it is expedient to
fix and regulate what personal estate and effects of his Majesty
and his successors are subject to such testamentary disposition,
and in what form such disposition shall be made. It is enacted
and declared, that all such personal estate of his Majesty and
his successors respectively, as shall consist of monies which
may be issued or applied for the use of his or their privy purse,
or monies not appropriated to any public service, or goods,
chattels or effects, which have not or shall not come to his
Majesty, or shall not come to his successors respectively, with

(*a*) Co. Lit. 30.
(*b*) 2 Bla. Com. 409.
(*c*) 1 Wightw. 50.
(*d*) Plowd. 247, a. So if an alien and
natural born subject buy land, King
shall only have alien's moiety. 1 Inst.
180, b. n. 2. 186, a. And see 2 Cruise
Dig. 507, 8.
(*e*) Bro. Ab. Prerog. pl. 105.
(*f*) Post. ch. 16.

or in right of the Crown of this realm, shall be deemed and taken to be personal estate and effects of his Majesty and his successors respectively, subject to disposition by last will and testament; and that such last will and testament shall be in writing, under the sign manual of his Majesty and his successors respectively, or otherwise shall not be valid; and all and singular the personal estate and effects whereof or whereto his Majesty or any of his successors shall be possessed or entitled at the time of his and their respective demises, subject to such testamentary disposition as aforesaid, shall be liable to the payment of all such debts as shall be properly payable out of his or their privy purse; and that, subject thereto, the same personal estate and effects of his Majesty and his successors respectively, or so much thereof respectively as shall not be given or bequeathed, or disposed of as aforesaid, shall go in such and the same manner on the demise of his Majesty and his successors respectively, as the same would have gone if this Act had not been made.

CHAP. XII.

Of the Prerogative with respect to judicial Remedies and Proceedings at the Suit of the Crown.

THOUGH justice flows from the King, as its fountain, he cannot administer it personally, or authorize any deviation from the laws. The first principles of equity forbid that any one should be judge in his own cause; which may be one reason that the constitution has, by an indiscriminate dictate, deprived the Crown of the power of personally interfering with the administration of justice. If this were not the case, the prerogative, instead of being in fact subservient to, would be above the laws, and the property of the subject would be defenceless.

There are certain substantial and important peculiarities in favor of the King, with respect to legal proceedings, which will be here mentioned; others, of less importance, will be incidentally stated in the course of this and the following chap-

ter.

ter. Extraordinary remedies are assigned to the King, because, as Lord Coke observes, ' *Thesaurus Regis est fundamentum belli et firmamentum pacis* (*a*).'

In the first place, though his subjects are, in many instances, under the necessity of suing in particular courts, the King has the undoubted privilege of suing in any court he pleases (*b*). He may bring a *Quare Impedit*, or writ of right, or of escheat, in B. R., and may have a *Quare Impedit* in B. R., though there have been a recovery in C. B. (*c*). The Crown possesses also the power of causing suits in other courts to be removed into the Court of Exchequer, where the revenue is concerned in the event of the proceeding, or the action touches the profit of the King, however remotely, and though the King be not a party thereto (*d*). And an account with the King can only be enforced in this his court of revenue (*e*). There can, however, be no doubt that the King may waive this prerogative, and suffer his rights and interests to be discussed in actions between third parties, out of the Exchequer (*f*). It seems, also, that where a mere equitable question is raised, Chancery is the better forum to entertain it, though the King be interested (*g*). Though it has been truly said (*h*), that "for any thing which toucheth the King, and may turn to his advantage to hasten the King's business, the Exchequer hath jurisdiction over it, were it a thing spiritual or temporal." Wherever also the King's title be clearly elicited, even in actions between third parties, the Court may, *ex-officio*, give judgment for the Crown thereon (*i*). And the Attorney-General, or other proper officer of the Crown, is always made a party in any cause in Chancery, &c. in which the King's rights are or may be called in question (*k*).

The King is also supposed to be always present in court,

(*a*) Co. Lit. 131, b.

(*b*) 4 Inst. 17. Plowd. 243. Rol. R. 290. Finch, L. 84. Fortescue, R. 101.

(*c*) 1 Bla. Rep. 131, 2.

(*d*) Parker, 143. Anstr. 205, 214. 1 Bla. R. 131. 1 Chitty's R. 440. See the excellent and luminous judgment of the Court, in Anstr. See further Manning's Pr. 161. Semb. Exchequer may revise judgments in B. R. or C. B. if King interested therein. Ibid. 624.

(*e*) 2 Atk. 56. 2 Sch. and Lef. 618.

(*f*) 1 Bla. Rep. 132.

(*g*) Hardr. 488. 2 Vez. sen. 448, per Ld. Hardwicke. 1 Bla. Rep. 131. 3 Atk. 171.

(*h*) Godb. 291. 16 Vin. Ab. 520.

(*i*) 2 Manning's Pr. 619. 5 Bac. Ab. 570.

(*k*) Ridgw. Cas. Temp. Hardw. 322. 2 Vez. sen. 445, 448. 2 Sch. and Lef. 618. In the Admiralty; 3 Price's R. 97.

and, therefore, cannot be nonsuit, though the Attorney-General may enter a *non vult prosequi* (a); and his Majesty is not said to appear by his Attorney (b).

The modes of redress which the Crown may adopt against a subject are—1st, by the usual *common law actions;* 2, by *Inquisition,* or *Inquest of Office,* and under this head, we will consider *extents* in chief and in aid, and the writ of *diem clausit extremum;* 3, by *scire facias,* to repeal grants, &c.; 4, by *information* of intrusion or debt and *in rem;* 5, by *quo warranto;* 6, by *mandamus.*

1. The general rule is, that the King may waive his prerogative remedies, and adopt such as are assigned to his subjects. He may maintain the usual common law actions, as trespass *quare clausum fregit,* or for taking his goods (c). The only exception seems to be in the case of actions, which suppose an eviction or disseisin, as an assize, or, it seems, an action of ejectment (d). The King cannot maintain such actions, they being inconsistent with his royal dignity, and contradictory to the fiction of law, that the King cannot be dispossessed of property once vested in him (e). But the King may maintain a *quare impedit,* which supposes the claimant's possession (f), and might also maintain a writ of ravishment of ward (g). And though the King chuse a common law action, he may, by virtue of the prerogative we have just noticed, commence it in any court (h).

Where the King proceeds by suit at common law, and another person is interested with him, it seems, that the action may be brought in the name of the King and such common person; as, " if A. is bound by a written obligation in 100*l.* to the King ' and his customers,' if the 100*l.* be not paid, the King and the customers ought to bring their action upon the said obligation jointly, in the name of the King and the customers:

(a) Co. Lit. 139. Finch, L. 81, 2. 2 Atk. 302. On prosecutions in the colonies, ante, ch. 3.

(b) Finch, L. 81. 1 Bla. Com. 270.

(c) Thel. Dig. l. 1. c. 3. 1 Rol. Ab. 373. Bro. Ab. tit. Prerogative, pl. 130. F. N. B. 90. 16 Vin. Ab. 537. tit. Prerogative, Q. pl. 8. As to a *distress* at the suit of the King; see ante, ch. 11, s. 1.

(d) Bro. Ab. tit. Prerogative, pl. 89. Staundf. Prærog. Regis, 56, b. ch. 18. Anstr. R. 215. 10 East, 106, 7. Ejectment on the demise of the Crown, 12 East, 96.

(e) 3 Bla. Com. 257.

(f) F. N. B. 32.

(g) Staundf. Prærog. Regis, 56, b. ch. 18.

(h) 3 Bla. Com. 257.

By all the Justices in the Exchequer, *lecta quæ scripto nititur a scripto variare non debet* (a)." And this distinction has been drawn, that where the King has part of a thing, *ratione prærogativæ*, there, if it be entire, he shall have the whole; as if one of several obligees be *felo de se*, or outlawed, the King or his assignee shall have the action sole; but if he has title to a parcel or part, by *another*, there the King may join, as if an obligation be made to a customer for customs, &c. there the King and the customer shall join (b). And, it seems, that the King and a subject may join in a presentment, or *quare impedit* (c). Instances of the King and a subject joining are to be met with (d); and in one case the King and his chaplain joined in an action for trespass and contempt done in the King's palace, and in presence of him and his justices (e). In cases of this nature the writ may also abate for the subject, and stand for the King (f).

The law having provided more efficacious and peculiar remedies in favor of the Crown, it is very unusual for it to proceed by the usual common law actions.

2. Proceedings under an *inquisition* or *inquest of office*, or an *office*, as it is termed in the old books, is a peculiar prerogative remedy for the benefit of the Crown, which was formerly much in use, and is still resorted to on many occasions. It is an inquiry made (through the medium of an indefinite number of jurors summoned by the sheriff (g)) ; by the King's officer, his sheriff, coroner, or escheator, *virtute officii*, or by writ to them sent for that purpose, or by commissioners specially appointed, concerning any matter that entitles the King to the possession of lands or tenements, goods or chattels (h).

(a) Jenk. Cent. 65, pl. 22. Fitzh. Ab. tit. Joinder in Action, 3. Vin. Ab. tit. Prerogative, Q. 2.

(b) 8 Edw. 4. 4, a. 246. 19 Hen. 6. 47, a. 10 Hen. 4. 3. Dyer, 95. F. N. B. 32. note (c).

(c) F. N. B. 32. 16 Vin. Ab. 535. tit. Prerogative, Q. 3.

(d) Ibid. .

(e) Bro. Abr. tit. Joinder in Action, pl. 56. tit. Prerog. pl. 48 : cites 27 Ass. 49.

(f) Bro. Abr. tit. Prerog. pl. 100 :

cites 35 Edw. 3. and Fitzh. Ab. Briefs, 729.

(g) Finch, L. 323, 4, 5. Com. Dig. Viscount, C. 5. Prerogative, D. 55. Gilb. Excheq. 109. But in the Addenda, 2 Manning's Pr. 635, is the following note : " *Inquisitio evacuata in comitatu Linsolniæ quia fuerunt tantum* 11 *Juratores, Recorda, Hil.* 13. *H.* 6. *Jones,* IER *Memoranda, tit. Inquisitio.*" There should be several inquests of lands in different counties, &c. Staundf. Præ. Regis, cap. 176. fol. 51.

(h) Ibid.

These

These offices are of two sorts, one of *entitling* and another of *instruction*. The former issued out of Chancery in cases where an office is necessary to ENTITLE the King; and is under the great seal, as the King cannot take but by the matter of record: the latter issued out of the Exchequer Court under its seal; or if the land were under 5*l*. in value, was taken by the King's escheator, &c. of his own accord and *virtute officii;* in cases where an office was not necessary to *entitle* the King, for the better instruction of the officer before seizure, and in favor of the subject that hasty measures might not be adopted (*a*). This inquiry is an office or presentment: an office which finds matter to entitle the King to some possession, for an office is a title for the King (*b*). This is an admirably constructed barrier between the Crown and the subject: the object evidently is to support that fundamental principle of English law, that the King may not enter upon or seize any man's possessions upon bare surmises, without the intervention of a jury (*c*). And the object is attained by the opportunity afforded the subject of interpleading with the Crown by *traversing* its title, or setting up a better in a *monstrans de droit* or *petition of right*, which will be considered in the next chapter. For in cases where an office is a necessary preliminary, the King and his officers cannot seize the property without it, nor has the King a title for many purposes (*d*). At present our inquiry will be, 1st, as to offices with respect to *real property;* and 2dly, with respect to *goods* and *debts;* under which head also will be considered the law of *extents*, and some general observations on the law of offices will be submitted to the reader's attention.

1. With respect to *lands*, inquests of office were more frequently in practice than at present, during the continuance of the military tenures amongst us: when, upon the death of every one of the King's tenants, an inquest of office was held called an *inquisitio post mortem*, to inquire of what lands he died seised, who was his heir, and of what age, in order to entitle the King to his marriage, wardship, relief, primer

---

(*a*) Gilb. Excheq. 109, 13, 4. 16 Vin. Ab. 79. Office, B. 12 East, 102.

(*b*) Finch, L. 324. That is a finding or evidence of a title which enables him to sue. An inquisition of attainder is only to inform, and does not enti-

tle the Crown to any right. 2 Atk. 399. post, 252.

(*c*) Magna Chart. 9 Hen. 3. 29. 2 Inst. 46. Gilb. Excheq. 132. Hob. 347. 1 Bla. Rep. 130. 3 Bla. Com. 259.

(*d*) 12 East, 96.

seisin,

seisin, or other advantages, as the circumstances of the case might turn out. To superintend and regulate these inquiries, the court of wards and liveries was instituted, by statute 32 Hen. 8. c. 46. which was abolished at the restoration of King Charles 2. together with the oppressive tenures upon which it was founded (a). Latterly the inquiries are whether the King's tenant for life died seised, whereby the reversion accrues to the King? whether A. who held immediately of the Crown, died without heirs, in which case the lands belong to the King by escheat (b)? whether B. be attainted of treason(c), whereby his estate is forfeited to the Crown? whether C. who has purchased lands, be an alien, which is another cause of forfeiture? whether D. be an idiot *a nativitate*, and therefore, together with his lands, appertains to the custody of the King? and other questions of like import, concerning both the circumstances of the tenant, and the value or identity of the lands (d).

The principal rule with respect to offices is, that they are not necessary when the King's title already appears *in any shape* of record (e).

" Therefore if the King's tenant alien without licence, which alienation appeareth by fine, or other matter of record, in this case if there be another record found that proveth the lands to be holden of the King *in capite*, upon these two records together, process shall be made against the party by *scire facias*, to come and shew why he should not make a fine for the alienation. Like law, it is where there is a record to prove that he that aliened is but tenant in tail of the King's gift, and he pretending to be tenant in fee simple, doth purchase a licence of alienation, and alieneth; and after dyeth without issue, which death is found by office, but nothing of this estate tail or licence appeareth in the said office, yet upon these records laid together, the King shall have a *scire facias* against the alienees, to shew why the land should not be seized into his hands, and his Highness answered of the profits since the death of the tenant in tail; for when he was but tenant in tail

(a) 3 Bla. Com. 258.
(b) 12 East, 96.
(c) Post, 249.
(d) 3 Bla. Com. 258.
(e) Staundf. Prerog. 56, a. Staund-

ford was frequently referred to and recognised in 12 East, 96, both by the Counsel and the Court. Not that the book is without its inaccuracies.

it appeareth that the licence was purchased upon a false suggestion, and so void, and then the lands ought to revert to the King, because his reversion could not be discontinued (*a*).

" Like law hath been used where his Highness is to seize lands of priors, aliens within this realm *ratione guerre,* his Highness doth it without any office, for in both these cases the King's *title is notorious enough although it appear not of record.* But yet in these cases his Highness must seize ere he can have any interest in his lands, because they be penal towards the party (*b*)."

So (*c*) if possession in law or a freehold, be cast upon the King, as it may be on a common person, there as the freehold ought not to be in suspense, the King is entitled and may seize without any office, as in the case of a descent in remainder or reverter; or of an escheat, if, as seems necessary in such a case, the deceased tenant held *in capite* or the King's title otherwise appear of record (*d*). Nor is an office necessary where the Crown claims the temporalities of a Bishop during the vacation of the see (*e*), or an estate under a devise from a subject (*f*), or the lands of an alien deceased; but " if the alien be living an office is necessary; and if he obtain a charter of denization and die, there, if the alien heir enter, since he was freeman of the charter, an office is necessary to defeat the estate (*g*)."

And by the statute 33 Hen. 8. c. 20. in case of attainder of high treason, the King shall have the forfeiture instantly, without any inquisition of office (*h*). In the case of other attainders, it seems to have been considered that an office is necessary to entitle the King, unless in the case of the attainder and death together of the party (*i*).

With respect to the necessity of having an office, the rule is, that in all cases where a common person cannot have a possession, neither in deed nor in law, without an entry, the King cannot have it without an office, or other record (*k*). As, if

(*a*) Staundf. Prærog. Regis, 56, a.

(*b*) Ibid. 4 Term R. 734.

(*c*) Staundf. 54, a.

(*d*) See per Lord Ellenborough, 12 East, 109, 110. See Ibid. 99, and 103.

(*e*) 4 Co. 58. Savile, 7. 9 Co. 95, b. Staundf. Prærog. Regis, 54, a. Gilb. Hist. Excheq. 108.

(*f*) Bro. Ab. Prerog. pl. 143.

(*g*) Gilb. Hist. Exchcq. 109. Co. Lit. 2, b.

(*h*) Staundf. Prærog. Regis, 53, a. 4 T. R. 730, 734. post, 250.

(*i*) Staundf. 53, b.

(*k*) Staundf. Prærog. Regis, 55. 6 Com. Dig. Prerog. D. 67.

the

the King's tenant alien in mortmain, or without licence (*a*), or his Majesty claim upon a forfeiture (*b*), or a condition broken (*c*), an office is necessary. With respect to forfeitures and the right of the Crown, to enter without office under a proviso of re-entry in a Crown lease, on non-payment of rent, &c. the distinction seems to be, whether or not such forfeiture appear of record. If the rent, in such case, be made payable at the Exchequer, an office seems necessary; because, " if the rent had been paid, the payment would have been entered of record, and not being so, the default appears of record (*d*);" *aliter* if the rent be not so payable (*e*).

So, if the King claim the land of an idiot, lunatic, &c. the person ought to be found an idiot, &c. by office (*f*).

So, if he claim the year, day, and waste, of a felon attainted, or the temporalities of a bishop (*g*), or a freehold, or inheritance, as forfeited for a contempt (*h*).

So if he claim, as forfeited to the Crown, *choses in action*, which belonged to an alien enemy; and in such case, a peace, before the inquisition taken, discharges the forfeiture (*i*). And an office seems necessary to entitle the King to a bond forfeited by one of two joint obligees committing suicide (*k*).

There are some cases in which the King is not considered as entitled till an actual seizure, or *scire facias*, even after the office found.

As before observed (*l*), though an office be unnecessary in the case of lands of aliens forfeited, *ratione guerre*, an actual seizure is requisite. And in the case of an attainder of high treason, Mr. Justice Buller appears to have considered that an actual seizure is proper; though, as between the party attainted and a wrong doer, it would not be necessary that the Crown should actually seize the property of the former, in order to divest him of it (*m*).

(*a*) Staundf. Prerog. 55, b.

(*b*) Sembl. Lev. 1. Cro. Car. 100, 173. Sir W. Jon. 78, 217.

(*c*) Sav. 70. 2 Rol. 215, l. 15.

(*d*) 2 Leon. 134, 139. Poph. 25, 28, 53. 12 East, 113.

(*e*) Ibid. Cro. Car. 200.

(*f*) Staundf. 55.

(*g*) Ibid.

(*h*) Sav. 8.

(*i*) Parker, 267.

(*k*) Bro. Ab. Forfeiture, pl. 58.

(*l*) Ante, 249.

(*m*) 3 Term R. 730, 734. See Dyer, 145, 6. 12 East, 114. And see post, 254, and note (*d*), whether the King could grant in such case, before office found.

" The

" The possession of the King," says Staundford (*a*), " is of two sorts, in law and in deed; in law merely by force of law; in deed, by actual taking by an officer, though without office found.

" An office that entitleth the King to possession is sufficient by itself, without any seizure or entry of the escheator, to make a possession in deed in the King, if it be so that the possession were vacant when the office was found. But if the possession were not vacant, but another than he in whose right the King seizeth, was tenant thereof at the time of the finding of the office, then must the King enter or seize by his officer, before the possession in deed shall be judged in him. And if his Highness seize not by the space of a year and a day after the finding of the office, then may he not seize without a *scire facias*, to be pursued against him that is tenant thereof. But hereupon is there a distinction to be made, whether that the King is entitled unto by office, be it a thing manual, and whereof profit may be taken forthwith, after the finding of the office, or not. For if it be such a thing as is not manual, and whereof there is no profit to be taken forthwith, until such time it falleth, in that case, although the King be in possession of the right of the thing, yet is he not in possession of the profit thereof, until such time as his Highness actually by his officer, when it falleth, taketh and perceiveth the said profit. As for example, the thing the King is entitled to is no land, but advowson, rent, or a common, although that the King by this office be patron of the advowson, or owner of the rent, or common, and thereby when the benefice becometh void may present, or when the rent becometh, may receive the rent, or when the common is to be taken, may use the said common; yet, if the office that entitleth his Highness be false, and he that was in possession at the time of the office taketh the profit, whether it falleth before the King's officer do take it, in this case this taking is no intrusion upon the King's possession, for he was never seized in deed : wherefore, being driven to his action, if his Highness bring his *quare impedit*, or action of trespass, the defendant may traverse the office with him in the said actions, keeping still his possession, and need not to sue in the Chan-

(*a*) Prærog. Regis, 54, b. ch. 18. nised in Finch, Law, 325. 9 Co. 95, b.
And see the doctrine of Staundf. recog- Com. Dig. tit. Prerogative, D. 68, 69.

cery

cery for the traversing of the same. Thus you may see a difference between a thing that is manual and a thing that is not manual. And the reason is, that when a stranger is tenant at the time of the office, finding the office maketh no possession in deed in the King before an entry or seizure, and then whether the King's officer taketh not the profits when it falleth, but suffereth him that was in possession to take it, then was the King never seised, but he still remains in possession that was possessed at the time of the finding of the office until such time as seizure be made for the King, which cannot be done at all times, as it may be of land, but only at such times as the profit thereof to be taken; that is to say, when it falleth, and that is now past for this time, seeing it is already taken, and, therefore, the King in that case is driven to his action. But query, whether his Highness may be brought in possession in these cases by a claim, or not?

" Like law is it, where an office is found, which doth not entitle the King to the possession by entry, but only by action, as where it is found that the King's tenant, for term of life or years, or the grantee of a forest, hath done waste (*a*), or made a feoffment by collusion, contrary to the statute of Marlebridge, or such like. For it is a general rule, that in all cases where a common person cannot enter, but is driven to his action, there the King cannot have the possession but by like action, or else by a *scire facias*, after office found, in nature of the action; for the office in this case entitleth the King to no other thing but only to the action (*b*). But query, of a feoffment that is found to be made by collusion, contrary to the statute 34 and 35 Hen. 8. c. 5. for in that case, it seems, his Highness may enter without *scire facias*, because the said statute appoints no action to be sued in the case. And note, that in all these cases before, where the King is driven to his *scire facias*, or other action, if the office be false the party may traverse the office, with the King keeping still his possession, whether it be in the Chan-

---

(*a*) 9 Co. 96, b. Sav. 1. So, if the King's title appears by two distinct records, the King shall not be in possession before a *scire facias*, though a common person in such case might enter without action, except in special cases; as if an office finds that the manor of D. is held of the King, and it appears by a fine, that the manor of D. is aliened in *mortmain*, the King ought to have a *scire facias* before seizure; for it is possible that there are two manors of D. 9 Co. 96, a.

(*b*) Ante, 247.

cery or any other court, and need not sue any *ouster le main*, if it be found for him, because he never was out of possession."

As the King takes by matter of record, so, generally, his estate shall not be divested, without office, or other matter of record. As if land be given to the King by deed inrolled, upon a condition; the grantor cannot enter for the condition broken, without office (*a*).

But where the King's estate depends upon the estate of another, if the former be defeated, the remainder to the King shall be divested, without office; as if land be granted to *A.* for life, with power of revocation, remainder to the King; if the uses are revoked, the King's remainder is divested without more (*b*).

So if an estate be demised to *A.* for life, remainder to the King, upon condition, that if the lessor pays to *A.* 10*l.* he shall re-enter; if he pays, he may re-enter, and divest the remainder in the King without office (*c*).

Here also should be noticed the restraints imposed by the legislature on *grants* by the Crown, of lands seized, *before office found*, and *returned*.

By the common law the subject was exposed to much inconvenience, and his rights were endangered, by the Crown being enabled to grant or convey lands seized under inquisitions, to third persons, before the claimant had an opportunity of putting in his claim, that is before the return of the inquisition (*d*). To remedy this grievance the statute 8 Hen. 6. c. 16. provides that no lands nor tenements, seized into the King's hands upon inquest before escheators or commissioners, be in anywise let or granted to farm by the chancellor or treasurer of England, or any the King's officers, until the same inquests and verdicts be fully returned into the chancery or exchequer; but all such lands and tenements shall entirely and continually remain in the King's hands, until the said inquests and verdicts be returned, and by a month after the same return; unless the party grieved come into Chancery (*e*), and proffer to tra-

---

(*a*) 6 Com. Dig. tit. Prerogative, D. 89.

(*b*) 2 Rol. Ab. 215. l. 45.

(*c*) Ibid. l. 35. Mo. 546.

(*d*) See further how this was at common law. Staundf. 68, b.

(*e*) This was because, where an office was necessary to entitle the King, the commission must issue out of Chancery. 5 Rep. 52, a.

verse

verse the inquest, and offer to take the same lands and tenements to farm; and if he do, then the lands shall be committed to him upon certain terms, till the traverse is decided: and if any letters patent of any lands and tenements be made to the contrary, or if they be let to farm within the said month, they shall be holden for none.

The statute 18 Hen. 6. c. 6. recites the above provisions, and states that, to evade it, divers persons had sued to obtain gifts, grants and farms by patent, before any inquisition or title found for the King; pretending such gifts or grants were not comprised or remedied by the former Act, though they are within the same mischief; and therefore provides that no letters patent shall be made to any person of any lands or tenements before inquisition of the King's title in the same be found in the chancery, or in his exchequer returned, if the King's title in the same be not found of record, nor within the month after the same return; if it be not to him or them which tender their traverses as before mentioned: and if any letters patent be made to the contrary, they shall be void and holden for none.

In a recent case on this abstruse subject (a), Lord Ellenborough remarked, "that the object of the legislature plainly was, according to the words of the Acts, that in all cases in which the King's title did not appear upon record, (" if the King's title in the same be not found of record") the possession should be open to whoever could claim against the King, till the final decision of the right; and that any grant to obstruct him should be void: and the authorities correspond with this object." The statutes being passed to redress a grievance are entitled to a liberal construction (b): and they relate not only to all cases of seizure of lands on inquisitions; but even it seems to cases where the King, *not having a title of record,* yet has a possession in law without office, and does not claim by inquisition, as in the cases of an escheat, &c. (c); and the other instances of a freehold falling on the King as in a descent remainder reverter (d). Though in such cases offices would, generally speaking,

(a) 12 East, 111, 12.
(b) Co. Lit. 77, b.
(c) 12 East, 96, 112.
(d) Ante, 249. 12 East, 96, 112, 13,

105. Though on an attainder for high treason, the actual possession and seisin of the land are by statute 33 Hen. 8. c. 20. s. 2. in the King before office; yet

speaking, be unnecessary to entitle to the Crown for other purposes, and the seisin in law still remains in the King as before (*a*), these statutes restrain him from prejudicing the claims of his subjects by a premature grant of the property. To enable the King to make a valid grant an office would therefore be requisite in such cases; and, as the King's grant would be void without it, neither can a plaintiff in ejectment recover upon a demise of the Crown in the same circumstances. And in cases within the Act an office found and returned afterwards will not make an intermediate lease or grant good by relation (*b*). But the statutes do not apply where an office is unnecessary, *and the King has a title of record;* as for instance if the King lease; the rent to be paid in the exchequer, with a proviso of re-entry on non-payment; here as the non-payment and forfeiture would by reference to the records in the exchequer appear of record (*c*), the King may grant, &c. this not being within these statutes of Hen. 6. (*d*). It will also be remarked the statutes do not extend to grants of personalty (*e*).

By these statutes of Hen. 6. the claimant or traverser, &c. of the claims of the Crown, is entitled to a lease of the lands in dispute under and in pursuance of the statute 36 Ed. 3. c. 13. by which if any come before the Chancellor, (&c.) and shew his right, by any shewing by good evidences of his right, the Chancellor (&c.) by his discretion shall *let* the lands seized to the party "yielding to the King the value, if it is adjudged for the King, in manner as he and other Chancellors have done before him by their good discretions:" so that he to whom it shall be letten, find security to do no waste or destruction "till judgment thereon (*f*)." "By the words of the statute,"

---

yet until office found and returned or something equivalent, it does not seem clear that a grant by the King, of the forfeited lands, is not within the prohibition of the statute, 18 Hen. 6. See Dyer, 145, 6. 12 East, 105, 114.

(*a*) Staundf. 54. 12 East, 104.

(*b*) Savile, R. 70.

(*c*) Ante, 250.

(*d*) 12 East, 113, 14.

(*e*) Staundf. Præ. Regis, 54. a. 69, a.

(*f*) The wording of the statutes, 8 Hen. 6. c. 16. and 18 Hen. 8. c. 16. are substantially the same as to letting the lands to the claimant; the former has it "to hold, till the issue be taken and determined for the King or the party:" the latter says, "to hold till the issue taken be found and discussed for the King or the party." And other officers besides the Chancellor have this power of letting. See also ante, 253. note (*e*).

says

says Staundford (*a*), " it should appear that the Chancellors
before this time, by their discretions, had used to let the lands
to the party to farm; and that is true, for the King used so to
do upon a petition, which was made to him by the order of the
common law, instead of a traverse now used.   And therefore I
think he may do so at this day, both upon a petition and a *monstrans de droit*, although the statute makes no mention thereof,
for so it was used to do by order of the common law."   " And it
is to be noted," continues Staundford(*b*), " that the *shewing of
the evidence* is only rehearsed to the letting of the lands to farm
and not to the traverse.   For he may traverse without shewing
any evidence, but not have the lands to farm.   Also by these
statutes he is not bound to any certain time for taking of his
traverse, but only for the taking of the lands to farm; for he
may tender his traverse when he will, so he desires not the
farm of the lands.   But if he will have them to farm he must
tender his traverse within one month; and now by the statute
of 1 Hen. 8. c. 16. he has three months liberty to do it.   Also
note the things that he must find surety for: that is to say, to
sue with effect, to pay the rent after the traverse be discussed,
and to do no waste or destruction.   For in this word rent is implied all the rent that shall accrue between the taking of the
farm and the discussing of the traverse (*c*); and yet it is not so
expressed.   And the lease that is made to him that tenders the
traverse is not of any term certain, but only by these words
donec discussum fuerit; for the words of the statute are so.
And therefore as soon as the traverse is found against him that
tendereth it, by and by the lease he had in the land by force
of the statute is void, without any further process.   Howbeit
forasmuch as the words be to hold till the issue upon the said
traverse taken be found and discussed for the King or for the
party, I would learn if the party be nonsuit (*d*) upon his
traverse, or that the traverse be adjudged against him upon a
demurrer in law, whether the lease should be void or not, like
as it shall be upon the issue found.   And it seems it shall be,
by the words comprised in the said statute of 36 Edw. 3. but
not by any words comprised in the said statute of 8 Hen. 6.
for the words of the 36 Edw. 3. are " till it be adjudged."

(*a*) Præ. Regis, 67, b. &c.   (*d*) See as to nonsuit on a *Monstrans*
(*b*) Ibid. 68, a.   *de droit*, or *Traverse*, post.
(*c*) See Bunb. R. 25.

The

The rights of the Crown to the *mesne* or *intermediate profits* of tenements to which it is entitled, are also of a peculiar nature. " If," says Staundford (*a*), " the King have a title, right or interest to any lands or tenements, his Highness when he seiseth, shall be answered of all the mesne issues and profits from the time when his said title, right or interest accrued; and whether it be a right of entry or title of entry, it makes no difference in the King's case. As for example, the King enters for a condition broken, he shall be answered of all the issues and profits since the condition broken; and in that case a common person shall not have the issues and profits but from the time of his entry. Like law is it if the King's tenant alien in mortmain, and the King enters; but it is otherwise if he enters for mortmain in lands not holden of him, upon a title which accrues to him in default of other lords. The law is the same where the King is entitled to seize, for that the lands are of his foundation and aliened contrary to the statute of Westminster, 2. c. 41. In this case he shall be answered of all the mesne issues accrued from the time of the alienation. And note also, that if the King make any grant which is not sufficient in the law, or is deceived in the making of the same, by reason of its being made upon a false suggestion; in this case if he resumes this grant and annuls it *jure regis,* as he may, he shall then be answered of all the mesne issues and profits which were lost by means of the said insufficient grant: but if the King be entitled to any lands *nomine districtionis,* there he shall not be answered of the profits but from the finding of the title, as in case where the King's tenant in chief aliens without licence, and an office is thereof found, in this case he shall not be answered of the profits from the time of that alienation, but only from the time of the finding of the office, or from the time of a *scire facias* returned, where the alienation is of record. And note that where the King is to be answered of the mesne issues and profits perceived and taken of any lands which have come to sundry hands, since the King's title first accrued to the same, there every one of those who have severally so perceived and taken the profits, shall answer for his own time, and not one for all."

By the statute *de escheatoribus,* 29 Edw. 1. if the escheator, by

---

(*a*) Prærog. Regis, c. 27, fol. 84, b.

writ out of the Chancery, seize land into the King's hand, and after upon inquisition, no title is for the King to have the custody, an *ouster le main* shall be awarded for the party out of the Chancery. Provided, that if any thing afterwards may be found in the Chancery, Exchequer, or King's Bench, for the King, a *scire facias* shall go out against the party. And if the King have right, it shall be answered of all the issues from the time of the escheator's first seizing of the land.

The requisites of the office, in point of form, will be considered hereafter. But a very important provision in the statute 2 and 3 Edw. 6. c. 8. may be here noticed. By the 8th section of that Act (*a*) it is provided, that " where *any* (*b*) inquisition or office shall be found by these words, or the like, ' *Quod de quo vel de quibus tenementa prædicta tenentur juratores prædicti ignorant,*' or else found holden of the King, ' *per quæ servitia juratores ignorant,*' it shall not be taken for any immediate tenure of the King in chief; but in such case a *melius inquirendum* shall be awarded, as hath been accustomed of old time (*c*)." Under this statute it was considered, in a recent case (*d*), that an office or inquisition not finding of whom the lands are holden, is in substance the same as one finding the ignorance expressly; for, in favor of the omission to find as directed, it must be presumed that the jurors did not know, rather than that they knew, and would not return the fact; and that in either case, the award of a *melius inquirendum* would be necessary.

If the office be found against the King, a *melius inquirendum,* or further inquiry under the former commission, may be awarded for the King. But in good discretion, no *melius inquirendum* shall be awarded in such case, without sight of some record, or other pregnant matter for the King, to shew the former was mistaken. And by pregnant matter for the King is meant, matter pregnant with evidence of the King's right (*e*).

But,

(*a*) See Ld. Coke's comments on this section, Co. Lit. 77, b.

(*b*) The statute is not confined to the inquisitions mentioned in the previous and other sections of the Act ; but relates to all inquisitions as to lands. 12 East, 96.

(*c*) See Co. Lit. 77, b.

(*d*) 12 East, 96, 115.

(*e*) 8 Co. 168. 2 Ves. 555. The *melius inquirendum* is grantable only on the part of the Crown, and is given because the Crown cannot traverse as the subject can. 3 Atk. 6. No *melius inquirendum*

But, if the *melius inquirendum* be found against the King, he is thereby precluded from having another *melius inquirendum ;* for if this were allowed, it would lead to infinity, for by the same reason that he might have a second, he might have them without end. However, if the first writ of *melius inquirendum* were repugnant in itself, if it did not give authority to find such an office as was found ; as, where the writ was to inquire, whether at the time of the death of a person who died in the reign of Queen Elizabeth, the manor of O. was holden of the lord the King that now is, another writ of *melius inquirendum* may be awarded (a).

2dly, As to *Personalty,* the general rule seems to be, that the King is entitled, without office or other matter of record : as in the case of goods and choses in action of felons, wreck of the sea, treasure trove, or the profits of lands of clerks, &c. convicted of felony, or of persons outlawed in a personal action (b). So, in the case of Simony, the King shall present without office, and it is unnecessary, on the nomination of the Crown to an office void by the statute 5 and 6 Edw. 6. c. 16 (c).

On this subject Sir Wm. Blackstone remarks (d), that "with regard to other matters, the inquests of office still remain in force, and are taken upon proper occasions ; being extended not only to lands, but also to goods and chattels personal, as in the case of wreck, treasure trove, and the like, and especially as to forfeitures for offences. For every jury which tries a man for treason or felony, every coroner's inquest that sits upon a *felo de se,* or one killed by a chance-medley, is not only with regard to chattels, but also as to real interests, in all respects an inquest of office ; and if they find the treason or felony, or even the flight of the party accused (though innocent), the King is thereupon, by virtue of this office found, entitled to have his forfeitures ; and also in the case of chance-medley, he or his grantee are entitled to such things, by way of deodand, as have moved to the death of a party."

By the statute 1 Hen. 8. c. 8. the escheators were to sit in

---

rendum on an insufficient office taken by an escheator *virtute officii* and of his own accord, and not by virtue of a writ : but such office shall be deemed void. F. N. B. 255.

(a) 8 Co. 163.

(b) Staundf. Prærog. Regis, 56, a. Sav. 8. 2 Ventr. 270. 2 Barnew and Alder. R. 258. 2 Manning Pr. Exch. 523.

(c) Ibid. Com. Dig. Prerog. D. 70.

(d) 3 Com. 259.

open

open places, and the sheriffs were to return jurors, and the inquisition was to be taken by indenture, whereof one part was to remain with the foreman of the jury, and the other part was to be returned into the Chancery or Exchequer, within one month; and from the Chancery it was to be transcribed into the Exchequer. The reason why it was returned into Chancery was, because that was a Court that was always open, since the Chancellor was always an itinerant with the Prince (a).

On a fine imposed by K. B. for an offence, the amount becomes, by the record of judgment, a debt due to the King *instanter* (b), and process may either issue out of that Court, or the fine may be estreated into the Exchequer, and proceedings taken therein. The process is by *capias pro fine* (c), or by *levari facias*, which, as we shall presently see, is abolished on extents for the King's debts. A *levari facias* may also be issued after conviction, on an indictment for not repairing (d). If the King is willing to remit the fine, the Attorney-General must acknowledge satisfaction by an entry to that effect on the record (e); but it should seem, that the defendant is not entitled to his discharge from imprisonment in respect of such fine, on the ground of his being an insolvent debtor, as it is not a debt, but a punishment for a crime (f). And in a late important case, Rex *v.* Woolf and others (g), it was held, on the authority of an old case (h), that in the case of a judgment for a misdemeanor, that the party convicted be imprisoned for two years, and pay a certain fine, and be further imprisoned till the fine be paid, a *levari facias* may issue for the fine before the expiration of the two years. The Court considered the party in confinement as a punishment for the offence; but appeared to hold that the Crown has the power of taking body and property for its debts. This will be more fully noticed under the head of extents.

(a) Gilb. Excheq. 110. and Finch, L. 326.

(b) 3 Salk. 32.

(c) 1 Ibid. 56, a.

(d) Com. Dig. Execution.

(e) Bunb. 40. Trem. P. C. 303. See form of entry of satisfaction. Trem. P. C. 303. 4 Hargr. St. Tr. 760.

(f) 2 M. and S. 201. ac. 4 Burr. 2142. 13 East, 190.

(g) 1 Chitty's Rep. 432. And this was acted upon in the subsequent cases of Carlile the bookseller, convicted of publishing several libels; and of Sir M. Lopes, convicted of bribery.

(h) Rex *v.* Webb, 2 Show. 173. Skinner, 12. Sir T. Jones, 185.

In the case of an outlawry in a personal action, a *levari fa-cias* is the process to be issued: and, on proper application, the proceeds which in point of law belong to the King, may be paid over to the plaintiff in the action (*a*).

On a *levari* the cattle of strangers levant and couchant on the defendant's property may be taken, for they are considered issues thereof (*b*). And by Lord Holt (*c*): " if *A*. being outlawed, makes a feoffment during the outlawry, the feoffor puts in his cattle, doubtless these are issues, because the feoffee takes the land in the same plight as the feoffor had it, but the feoffment notwithstanding is good (*d*). But the interest of the King to take the profits continues notwithstanding the feoffment, though the opinion in 21 Hen. VII. 7. a. is contrary. If issues be returned upon a juror, they shall be levied upon the feoffee. If *A*. be outlawed, and aliens his land before inquisition taken, the alienation prevents the King from taking the profits, otherwise if the alienation were after the inquisition found; and this is the constant course of the exchequer."

For the recovery of *debts* and *penalties*, and other monies due to the Crown, the usual remedy is by the prerogative writ of *extent* which will be considered under the following arrangement:

In general.

PART I.—*Extents in chief.*

SECT. 1. Commission to find debts and inquisition thereon: and herein of debts due to the Crown.

2. Of the *scire facias*, to justify the issuing of the extent in chief.

3. Form.—Teste.—The issuing and return, &c. of extents in chief.

4. When an immediate extent may issue.—Affidavit to obtain it and trial thereon.

(*a*) Tidd's Practice, 5th ed. 139, 40. 6th ed. 138.
(*b*) Ld. Raym. 306. 16 Vin. Ab. 519.
(*c*) Ld. Raym. 307.
(*d*) 21 Hen. 7. 7, a.

5. Execution of extent in chief.
In general.
What may be taken.
Body.
Goods and sums of money.
Lands.
Debts and credits, and herein,
6. Of seizing debts, specialties, and credits due to the Crown Debtor : and herein of extents in chief in the several degree, *i. e.* against debtors to the Crown Debtor, &c.
[Resisting extents and proceedings thereon, Ch. XIII.]
7. Venditioni exponas.—Order for sale of defendant's lands, &c.
8. Costs.
9. Poundage.

Part II.—*Extents in aid.*

Sect. 1. In general. The course of proceeding, &c.
2. To what degrees debts may be seized on extents in aid.
3. What Crown Debtor may issue an extent in aid.
4. For what sum an extent in aid may be issued. Affidavit and fiat.
5. Form of.—What may be taken.—Motions.—Pleading.—Costs.—Poundage, &c.

Of Extents in general.

It was ever a principle of law, that the Crown might seize in execution consecutively the body, lands, and goods of its debtor and even debts due to him ; but the right to take them all at once, was not it seems vested in the Crown at common law (a), but was confined to executions by *extendi facias* against

(a) Gilb. Excheq. 7.

the

the conusor on a statute merchant or statute staple, which were instruments having peculiar properties in favour of trade (a). The writ of extent as a Crown process, appears to be founded on the statute of 35 Hen. 8. c. 39 (b). By the 55th section of that statute, it is enacted, " that all and every suit and suits, which thereafter should be had, made, or taken of, for or upon any debt or duties, which thereafter should grow or be due to the King, in the several offices and courts of his Exchequer, duchy of Lancaster, augmentations of the revenues of his Crown, surveyors general of his manors, lands and tenements, master of the wards and liveries, and courts of the first fruits and tenths, or in any of them, or by reason or authority of any of them, should be severally sued in such one of the said courts and offices, in the which court and office, or by reason of the which court and office, the same debt or duty should grow or become due, or in the which office or court the recognizance, obligation or specialty should be or remain; and that every such several suit and suits should be made in every of the said several offices and courts, under the several seals of the said several courts, by *capias, extendi facias, subpœna,* attachments and proclamations of allegiance, *if need should require,* or any of them, *or otherwise, as unto the said several courts should be thought by their discretions expedient for the speedy recovery of* the King's debts. And that the said Court of Exchequer, and all and every of the said Courts, should have whole and full authority and power, to hear and determine all and every such suit and suits, as thereafter should be taken, commenced and pursued for the intent above specified; and thereupon to award, make and do execution by and upon the body, lands and goods of the party or parties that should be so condemned accordingly."

Statutes merchant, statutes staple, and recognizances in the nature of statute staple, are now out of use. But the powers and energies of those instruments are still in force in favour of

(a) Hob. 60. 2 Rol. Ab. 475, 2 Wms. Saund. 70, b.

(b) See Bunb. 233. West. 332, 3, &c. 2 Manning, Pr. 513. 4 T. R. 412. per Ashhurst, J. As to this statute in general. See 2 Bla. Rep. 1295. The reader will observe, on perusing the following pages on this difficult subject, that the author derived considerable assistance from Mr. West's work on extents.

the

the Crown. And since the statute of Hen. 8. the writ of *extendi facias* or extent, by which the sheriff is authorized in one writ to take person, goods, lands and debts, has been the constant execution at the suit of the Crown, against its own immediate debtor.

The writ of extent, as a prerogative process, is of two descriptions: one, called an extent in chief, issues for the benefit of the Crown against the Crown debtor, or his debtor, on the principle that the King is entitled to the debts due to his debtor; the other is called an extent in aid, and is issued against the debtors of the Crown debtor, at the instance and for the benefit of the latter.

Extents *in chief* are also of two descriptions: the one is called an *immediate* extent, that is, an extent which issues without the intervention of a *scire facias*, on an affidavit that the Crown debt is in danger; the other is an extent, which is the ultimate process of execution on a Crown judgment, obtained on a *scire facias* or other action, there being no affidavit that the Crown debt is in danger. The immediate extent is founded on the words in the 33 Hen. 8. which give the Court of Exchequer power to issue an extent, &c. " if (as is established by the affidavit of the debt being in danger) *need shall require*, or otherwise as to the court shall be thought, by its *discretion* (*a*), expedient (which discretion is evinced and expressed by the fiat of the Court or a Baron) for the *speedy* recovery of the King's debts."

Extents in chief are either issued against the immediate Crown debtor or against the debtor to such debtor. In the latter case the extent is called an extent in chief in the second degree. An extent is first sued out against the Crown's immediate debtor; on that extent an inquisition is held, under which debts due to the Crown debtor are found and seised into the Crown's hands. A second extent then issues on that finding against the debtor to the Crown debtor, under which second extent also an inquisition is taken, by which the debts

(*a*) " As to the statute 33 Hen. 8, I think that does not leave it to our discretion to alter the course and nature of proceedings, or to do a thing that was never done before, and may be of mischievous consequence." Per Baron Comyns, Stra. 760.

due

due to that debtor are found and seised into the Crown's hands. A third extent then issues against the party so found to be a debtor by the preceding inquisition, and so on to the fourth degree, &c.

PART I.—*Extents in chief.*

SECT. I.—*Commission to find Debts, and Inquisition thereon and herein of Debts due to the Crown.*

IT would be contrary to the first principles of law and justice, to issue process of execution before it is ascertained what debt is due to the Crown, and such debt become a debt on record. It may, therefore, be laid down, as a general rule, that till the debt, not being *per se* of record, be ascertained, and become a record by a commission and proceeding thereon, the Crown is not entitled to process of execution, unless in cases of danger, or insolvency, when an immediate extent may be issued, subject to the rules which will be mentioned. The Crown has no election on this subject. It is bound strictly by this principle.

With respect to the question, what is a debt of record? it seems, that at common law, there is no exception in the case of a Crown debt from the general rules prevalent on this subject in common cases. There are, however, some few exceptions by statute.

By the statute 33 Hen. 8. c. 39. s. 50. it is enacted, " That all obligations and specialties, which shall be made for any cause or causes touching, or in anywise concerning, the King's most royal Majesty, or his heirs, or to his or their use, commodity, or behoof, shall be made to his Highness, and to his heirs, Kings, in his or their name or names, by these words, *Domino regi*, and to none other person or persons, to his use, and to be paid to his Highness by these words, *solvend.* ' *eidem Domino regi, hæred.*' *vel executoribus suis*, with other words used and accustomed in common obligations ; and that all such obligations and specialties so to be made, shall be good and effectual in the law to all purposes and intents, and shall be of the same *nature, kind, quality, force and effect*, to all intents and purposes *as the writings obligatory* taken and
acknowledged

acknowledged according to the *statute* of the *staple* at Westminster had, at any time before the making of that Act, been taken, used, exercised, and executed against any lay person."

This statute, it will be remarked, gives the effect of records to those bonds only which are made for any cause concerning the King, and in the form therein prescribed; and it is, therefore, doubtful whether an obligation to the King, not saying ' *hæred.' vel exec. 'suis,'* is within the statute (*a*). It is, however, held, that a bond to the King, to be paid " to his heirs or *successors,"* or conditioned " to account for monies received either on account of the excise, *or on the private account of the obligee,"* or with a condition for causes touching the King, without shewing by what particular authority, or officer of the Crown, it was taken, is within the statute (*b*). And where the bond is within the statute, the remedy by extent is given to the King, though the bond be made not to him, but to another for his use (*c*)

Debts due from *tax-collectors* have, in certain cases, the effect of debts of record, it being enacted, by the statute 43 Geo. 3. c. 99. s. 41. that " whenever any money of the duties therein mentioned shall be detained in the hands of any collector, and the same or any part thereof cannot be recovered by or under the warrant or authority of the respective commissioners, or the said respective commissioners shall neglect to issue such warrant, then such part thereof which cannot be so recovered, which shall have arisen from the said duties, shall be *recoverable* as *a debt upon record* to the King's Majesty, his heirs and successors, with all costs and charges attending the same."

With respect, however, to simple contract debts, and bonds, and other specialties, not within the statute of 33 Hen. 8. the first step towards rendering such debts and bonds, records, on which an extent may be issued, is the issuing a commission, (which seems to be necessary as well by the equity of the sta-

(a) Moore, 193. 1 Anderson, 129. Com. Dig. Dette, 9.

(b) Bunb. 58. 2 Brown, Parl. Cases, 575. Lill. Ent. 423. West's Appendix, 323. It is a *quære* whether a bond to the King, with condition to answer and pay the revenues of the duchy of Cornwall to the Prince, is within this statute ?

(c) 4 T. R. 413, 4. Bonds given by governors of proprietary colonies, for observing acts of trade, should be given in pursuance of the statute of Hen. 8. 1 Chalmers' Coll. Op. 259.

tute

tute of Westminster (a), as by express authority (b),) under which an inquisition is held to find the debt, and when returned, such inquisition becomes matter of record (c).

The commission is issued by the clerk in Court of the Crown, and is directed to two commissioners, whom it empowers to inquire, as well on the oaths of good and lawful men, &c. as by the testimony on oath of any other credible persons, (and as some of the precedents, &c. run, "by all other ways, means, and methods, whatsoever,") whether the defendant be not indebted to his Majesty in any and what sums of money, and to return the inquisition taken thereon at the return of the commission; and it also commands the sheriff (of Middlesex), in his character of sheriff, to cause a jury to attend before the commissioners; and it empowers the commissioners to summon before them witnesses, and it concludes " by warrant indorsed, and by the Barons (d)."

The " warrant indorsed," at the conclusion of the commission, is an indorsement of his name on the commission by a Baron, or the Chancellor of the Exchequer, and is the fiat or authority for its issuing. And although in practice, it seems, that the commission is not taken to the Baron to be indorsed, till after the inquisition has been taken on it, when the commission is taken to him for his indorsement, and the extent and affidavit for his fiat at the same time (e); still, if no application has been made for the warrant, and none has been obtained, the proceedings are irregular (f). The commission is vested in the name of the Chief Baron, and signed by the King's remembrancer, and sealed with the Exchequer seal. It may be issued and tested in the vacation, but must be returnable in Term (g).

The defendant is not entitled to notice of the execution of the commission on the extent; but, it seems, the Court will, on application, make an order that reasonable notice be given (h).

The usual, if not universal, practice is, to adduce no evi-

(a) 13 Edw. 1. st. 1. c. 18.
(b) Cro. Jac. 569. Brown, Pr. Ex. 364.
(c) See West on Extents, c. 4.
(d) Ibid. On occasions of importance inquisitions have been taken before a

judge. Dyer, 228, marg. 2 Mauning, Pr. 235, b.
(e) Ibid.
(f) 3 Price, 278.
(g) West, 22.
(h) 1 Ves. 269.

dence of the debt before the jury, except the affidavit, which is prepared for the purpose of obtaining the immediate extent. On this affidavit, and this affidavit alone, usually, if not universally, the jury find the debt (*a*). If witnesses duly summoned refuse to attend, or to answer proper questions, the Court will grant an attachment (*b*).

The statute 1 Hen. 8. c. 8. s. 2. (*c*) enacts " that every escheator and commissioner shall sit in convenient and open places, according to the statutes theretofore made. And that the said escheators and commissioners shall suffer every person to give evidence openly in their presence, to such inquest as shall be taken before any of them, upon pain of forty pounds." Upon this provision, which seems to be confirmatory of the common law, it is considered that the inquisition is irregular, if secretly and clandestinely taken, and that on the taking of the inquisition on the extent, a stranger has a right to prove his property in the goods seized (*d*). The Crown cannot be a sufferer by this doctrine, as a *melius inquirendum* may issue if the finding of the jury be dissatisfactory. At all events, persons interested may appear on the execution of the writ and cross-examine the Crown witnesses : and as observed by C. B. Thomson, " it would be hard to put the parties to the expense and trouble of traversing the inquisition ; and irreparable injury may be done, when, if the evidence had been suffered to proceed, and had the question proposed been allowed to be put, the truth of the matter would have been shewn (*e*)."

Simple contract debts, and specialties, not included in the

(*a*) West, 22.

(*b*) Parker, 269. Witness cannot refuse to answer a question which might render him liable to the Crown civilly for a debt, 46 Geo. 3. c. 37.

(*c*) That the statute applies to inquisitions before sheriffs. 4 Co. 58, a.

(*d*) Bunb. 233. This doubted in 3 Price, 454. As to the testimony of the claimant himself, 1 Fowl. 160. 6 Bac. Ab. 129, 30.

(*e*) The King *v.* Bickley, Exch. Sittings, after M. T. 1816. The facts of this case are reported in West on Extents, p. 69, and the judgment in the Appendix, p. 330. S. C. in 3 Price 454. It appears that the Court did not decide on the express point in Bunbury, but held the inquisition irregular specifically on the ground that the under-sheriff had refused to suffer a *cross-examination* of one of the *Crown's* witnesses, on a question which related not only to the property in the goods seized being in a stranger, but brought under consideration the character in which the defendants had the goods and related to their possession of them. But C. B. Thomson seemed to approve of the decision in Bunbury. See S. C. 3 Price's R. 463.

statute

statute 33 Hen. 8. should be found by the inquisition; and should it seems be stated and explained therein with some degree of legal form and certainty (*a*). The inquisition, being an office not of *information* but of *entitling* (*b*), is bad if argumentative, or if it be not direct and positive, so that no certain traverse can be taken on it (*c*); as where the inquisition stated that a manor was holden, &c. " *as it appeareth by,* &c. (*d*)," and facts, not evidence, should be found (*e*). The inquisition may however find a particular estate, without tracing its origin, so that the precision of a plea is not necessary in these cases (*f*). And on the rule *utile per inutile non vitiatur,* if the necessary facts be properly stated, the finding of a mere matter of law, may be rejected as surplusage (*g*). As the inquisition is engrafted on, and becomes part of the record, it may for defects of this nature on the face of it, be demurred to, or set aside on motion to the Court. Where a part of the debt on which the inquisition is founded is invalid, the inquisition may be set aside *pro tanto* only (*h*). And the quashing an inquisition will not it seems preclude the Crown from taking an inquisition on a new writ of extent of the teste of that quashed (*i*).

With respect to the nature of the debts to be found under the inquisition, the general criterion seems to be whether the demand is of such a nature that an action might be maintained against the debtor, were the debt due to a subject (*k*).

It being now held that an action is sustainable for monies which lie in account, and though there be complicated cross accounts (*l*), it seems that such monies may be found, as debts under the inquisition. So that the antient Crown proceeding by a *distringas ad computandum,* on the finding of the jury, is disused (*m*).

(*a*) West, ch. 5. 3 Price, 269.

(*b*) See ante, this ch.

(*c*) See 3 Price, 269, 274.

(*d*) 13 Co. 72. Inquisition set aside for not saying in what county taken; for saying *diversa messuagia,* without naming them ; for not stating in what county lands lie. Jones IER *Memoranda, tit. Inquisitio.*

(*e*) 3 Price, 269.

(*f*) 2 Manning, 535, notes (*c*) and (*d*).

(*g*) 2 Manning, 535. Com. Dig. Pleader, S. 28.

(*h*) 1 Anstr. 192. Hughes, 178.

(*i*) 3 Price, 464. A new writ necessary, if former returned. Ibid. 269.

(*k*) 2 Manning, 525, 6.

(*l*) See 5 Taunton, 431.

(*m*) 2 Manning, Pr. 527, 530, 541. West, 26, 33. Whether the defendant can have credit given him depends on the right to set off against the Crown, as to which see post, ch. 13. s. 3. div. 3.

With

With respect to a receiver of the King's money, the rights of the Crown are in some respects of a more peculiar nature. The general rule is, that if a man receive the King's money (as a collector of taxes, &c.), knowing it to be so, he may be treated as an accountant or debtor to the King, though he received the money *bonâ fide* without any, or under an insufficient, appointment from the Crown : otherwise if he do not know it to be the King's money (*a*).

The leaning is against constructive receipts of the King's money, therefore where A. being the receiver of the King's money, drew a bill on B. payable to the excise, expressing that it was the King's money, and remitted to B., who accepted the bill, an indiscriminate mass of bills and cash, not to answer the bill in question in particular, but upon a general running account between A. and B. it was determined that B. could not be considered a receiver of the specific money of the King (*b*).

In general, debts due from a receiver of the King's money, are on the footing of simple contract debts only, and are not records ; but in the case of collectors of taxes, debts due from them are, as before observed (*c*), sometimes to be considered as of record.

In cases where bonds, bills of exchange or promissory notes, have been given to the Crown or its agents, it is frequently a most important matter of investigation whether or not either of the parties to such instruments can be considered a receiver of the specific money of the King, for the Crown never relinquishes its claims on such receiver, and may issue an extent against him before the bill or note (and it seems before a bond (*d*), whether given immediately to the Crown or not) has become due (*e*). This claim on the actual receiver of its money is however peculiar, and where the Crown holds bonds, bills or notes against parties who cannot be considered receivers of the specific money of the Crown, it is clear that such parties are not liable to proceedings by extent, &c. till the instrument be due (*f*). And in a late case (*g*) it was held that

(*a*) 11 Co. 92, a.   Cro. El. 545. 1 Leon. 32.   Lane, 23.   Bingham on Executions, 206, &c. Stra. 978.

(*b*) Bebb's Case, reported by Hughes.

(*c*) Ante, 226.

(*d*) West, 45, 6 ; 271.

(*e*) See Bebb's Case, by Hughes; and West, c. 6.   3 Price, 75.

(*f*) See Ibid.

(*g*) 1 Wightw. 32.

a plea

a plea to an extent in aid, stating that the defendant had accepted a bill drawn upon him by the original debtor, and which did not become due till the day after the inquisition was taken, is good, although the defendant had refused payment, and the original debtor to the Crown had been obliged to take it up. It would be rank injustice to permit the Crown by a prerogative anticipation of the forfeiture of a bond, or maturity of an acceptance, or note, to fall suddenly on a party, who, having no public money in his hands, had no reason to expect summary proceedings, and who naturally deferred providing funds to answer demands then only in abeyance, till the time for payment arrived. Where the receiver is the drawer or acceptor of a bill which is not due, the extent is against him in his character of receiver, and not of drawer or acceptor.

As an unsettled balance between partners will not support an action by one against the other, such an interest cannot be seised as a debt, or returned under an inquisition to find debts (*a*).

If the Crown be dissatisfied with the finding of the jury, as to the defendant's property in the goods seised under the extent, a *melius inquirendum* or further inquiry, under the same commission, may be issued (*b*).

SECT. II.

Of the Scire Facias *to justify the issuing of the Extent in chief.*

THE general rule is, that an extent being process of execution, cannot issue without a *scire facias* (founded on the inquisition which renders the debt a debt of record), to bring the defendant into Court and afford him an opportunity of pleading any defence he may have. And the Crown has no election in this respect, so that unless in case of insolvency, justifying an immediate extent, a *scire facias* is absolutely necessary; and where the defendant becomes insolvent, pending the proceeding by *scire facias*, it is usual to abandon the extent and resort to a *scire facias* (*c*). This, and not the revival of the suit, is the

(*a*) 2 Manning, 527, 548.   (*c*) 3 Price, R. 292, 296.
(*b*) 2 Ves. 555. 8 Rep. 168. Ante, 258.

ground

ground on which a *scire facias* is in general necessary, previous
to the issuing of extents. As no time runs against the King,
a *scire facias* is, generally speaking, unnecessary to revive
proceedings at his Majesty's suit (*a*). When bonds for the
performance of covenants are assigned to the King, a *scire
facias* is necessary as the first process (*b*). There is an exception under the statute 33 Hen. 8. as we have already seen, if
the debt be in danger of being lost and that fact be verified by
affidavit. In such case an immediate extent, which is in the
nature not of an action but of an execution, may be issued ;
but if no such affidavit can be made, a *scire facias* must be
issued, the Crown debt being of record either as a judgment
or recognizance, or as a bond within the 33' Hen. 8. or as
any other specialty or a simple contract debt, recorded by
inquisition under a commission.

The *scire facias* is under the seal of the Court of Exchequer,
and signed by the King's Remembrancer, and tested by the
Lord Chief Baron. It recites the inquisition, or the bond, or
recognizance, &c. and commands the sheriff to warn the defendant to appear before the Barons on a day certain, to shew
cause why the debt should not be levied. The *scire facias,*
though it may be sued out in vacation, must be tested in term.
And therefore a *scire facias* cannot be sued out in vacation, on
an inquisition taken under an extent which has been sued out, and
is consequently tested in that vacation ; because as the *scire
facias,* if sued out in vacation, must be tested as of the antecedent term, and must recite the inquisition in such case as the
foundation of it, it would appear in such case that the *scire
facias* was sued out before the inquisition on which it was
founded, was taken. And the Court quashed such a *scire
facias* on motion (*c*), and ruled that the objection could not be
got rid of by a special memorandum upon the record, shewing
the day on which the *scire facias* was really issued.

If the sheriff warn the defendant, he returns *scire feci* (*d*).
If he do not warn him, he returns *nihil* (*e*), in which last case
a second *scire facias* issues. On the return of *scire feci* or of
two *nihils,* a four-day rule is given on the writ for the defend-

(*a*) 2 Salk. 603. 1 Price, 295.   (*d*) Tremaine, 609. West, 317.
(*b*), 2 Leond. 55, 77. Owen, 46.   (*e*) Tremaine, 609.
(*c*) 3 Price. R. 258.

ant to appear and plead thereto, or an extent to issue. If the defendant appear, then another four-day rule is given for him to plead, or an extent to issue; but if the defendant do not appear on the first rule, or appearing does not plead on the second rule, process of extent issues without any judgment on the *scire facias*. But judgments have been entered up for the King, on the defendant's default in not appearing, or in not pleading after appearance (*a*). And it is an indulgence in the court, that they do not enter up judgment; for if the judgment were entered, then the Court would be concluded, though perhaps the defendant had no notice of the debt (*b*). Where the *scire facias* is returnable on the last day of term, a rule may be given to appear by the sealing day after such term; and, in default thereof, proceedings may be had as where there are days in term for giving such rules (*c*).

The defendant may obtain six weeks' further time to plead after the expiration of the four days, on a motion of course on the signature of counsel; and may, on affidavit of special circumstances, obtain further time after the expiration of the six weeks, by motion in court, on affidavit of special circumstances (*d*).

SECT. III.

Form, Teste, Issuing, and Return, &c.

Of Extents in chief.

THE extent, after reciting the bond, or the finding of the simple contract debt by the inquisition, taken by virtue of the commissioners, directs the sheriff (*e*) to omit not, &c., but to enter, &c., and take the defendant, and to inquire, on the oaths of good and lawful men, &c. what lands and tenements, and of what yearly values, the said defendant now hath, (if the extent be on a simple contract debt,) or had (if the extent be on a bond) on

(*a*) Parker, 94. Gilbert's Exch. 169. West, 318.

(*b*) Gilbert's Exch. 170.

(*c*) West, 318.

(*d*) Ibid.

(*e*) It is directed to the coroners, or in London, to the lord mayor, if the sheriff be the extendee, 2 Manning, 531.

T   the

the day of ——, (the date of the bond before recited,) or at any time since; and what goods and chattels, and of what sorts and prices, and what debts, credits, specialties, and sums of money, the said defendant, or any person or persons to his use, or in trust for him, hath in his bailiwick, and to appraise and extend all and singular the said goods and chattels, lands and tene-ments, &c. and to take and seize the same into the King's hands (*a*).

It then directs the sheriff to summon witnesses, and to re-turn the writ. Then follows a proviso, that the sheriff should not sell the goods and chattels till he should be otherwise com-manded; and it concludes (if on a simple contract), " by the said commission and inquisition, by warrant of Mr. Baron ———, by the said Act of Parliament, made in the 33d year of the reign of the late King Hen. 8. and by the Ba-rons (*a*)."

If the extent be on a bond, it concludes, " by the writing obligatory aforesaid, by the aforesaid Act of Parliament, &c. by warrant of Mr. Baron ———, and by the Barons."

The extent is tested by the Chief Baron, signed by the King's Remembrancer, and sealed with the Exchequer seal (*b*).

If the extent be on a bond, it is not necessary (whatever may be the decision with respect to the question of issuing an extent against the obligor, in a bond to the Crown, before the bond be payable,) to set out any breach of the condition of the bond in the extent. It is sufficient in the extent, as it is in a declaration, or *sci. fa.*, to set out the penal part of the bond, and the defendant must shew the condition in his defence, and all the forms are so (*c*). Where the debtor is already in cus-tody, the extent may contain a clause of *habeas corpus cum causâ* (*d*).

The writ of extent may be tested in vacation, for it issues out of the equity side of the Exchequer, which is always open; but cannot be tested before, though it may be tested on the day of the date of the Baron's fiat, which is the authority on which it issues, the fiat being in effect an award of execution (*e*). It

(*a*) West, 55.

(*b*) This is directed by statute 33 Hen. 8.

(*c*) See Tremaine, 637. Brown, 416. Tidd's Appendix. West, 57, and Ap-pendix, 18.

(*d*) Dyer, 197, a. 2 Manning, 517, 533.

(*e*) Stra. 749. Bunb. 164. 8 Rep. 171.

must be returnable on a general return day in Term; and, at least when the *capias* clause is introduced, is irregular if a Term intervene between the teste and the return (*a*). A mistake in the teste may be rectified, it appears, by the Baron's fiat (*b*).

The writ may be issued in vacation, and before the commission, when necessary is returnable, though not, it seems, before it is actually returned and filed (*c*).

Any number of extents may issue into different counties at the same time. Before or after the return of the first extent, any number of extents may issue with the same teste as the first extent, *i. e.* of the date of the fiat. If they issue before the return of the first extent, they may issue as a matter of course ; if they do not issue till after the return of the first extent, a motion must be made in Court, on affidavit, of special circumstances (*d*), before they can issue. It seems, that the affidavit ought at least to state, that the effects seized under the first extent are insufficient to pay the debt.

If the teste be prior to the death of the defendant, the extent may, like any other execution (*e*), be issued against his effects after his death, on the ground that the fiat, with reference to which the teste is generally, if not invariably, inserted, binds his effects from the day on which it is dated (*f*). And, as we shall hereafter observe, even an *action* at the suit of the Crown, does not abate by the death of the defendant (*g*).

If an extent be set aside for any irregularity, which does not effect the fiat, a new extent, tested as of the date of the fiat, may be issued (*h*). And from this it appears, that it is generally useless for the defendant to move to set aside an extent for any formal defect in it subsequent to the fiat, since a new extent of the same teste as the first may be issued, even if the defendant succeed in setting the first aside. But this observation does not apply to the case where a stranger moves to set aside an extent, under which his property has been improperly taken (*i*).

(*a*) 2 Manning, 530. 7 Mod. 17.

(*b*) West, 58.

(*c*) 3 Price, 288.

(*d*) Parker, 35, 176, 282. And see West, 59. 3 Price, 369.

(*e*) See 1 Ld. Raym. 695. 2 Ibid. 850. 7 T. R. 20. 1 B. and P. 571. 6 T. R. 368.

(*f*) West, 60.

(*g*) 2 Cro. 481. Post, 280.

(*h*) West, 60, note f. 3 Price, 269. Parker, 271, 35, 176, 282. As to inquisition being set aside, post, ch. 13. s. 2. Ante, this ch.

(*i*) West, 60 and 333.

It

It appears to have been recently decided, that an extent may be issued on an inquisition and fiat of eight years' old, and that no new affidavit or fiat is requisite, nor is any proceeding by *scire facias,* or otherwise, necessary to revive such extent (a). As, however, the Court of Exchequer possess a discretionary power in these cases, and extreme hardship must generally ensue from this doctrine, it might perhaps have been as well to require at least a fresh affidavit of the continued insolvency of the defendant, and that an application should be made to the Court for leave to issue the extent by analogy to the case of executions, on old warrants of attorney(b). The ground of the decision, namely, that from the moment of the return of the inquisition, the debt becomes a debt of record, against which no time runs, and that where the King is a party a *scire facias* is not necessary to revive the record, is however indisputably true, though this application of it may perhaps be doubtful. And, as before observed, a *scire facias* seems necessary before seizure, if a year and a day have elapsed after office found (c). After that period, a presumption of payment might fairly be made.

Where a joint debt has been found, the death of one of the defendants, in the interval between the fiat and extent, does not vitiate the proceedings (d).

Though the sheriff need not file his return in the King's Remembrancer's office until the *quarto die post* of the return day, his power is determined on the actual return day (e). For a false return the remedy is, by information in the Exchequer, in the name of the Attorney-General (f).

(a) 1 Price, R. 395.
(b) See Bunb. 62.
(c) Ante, this ch. tit. Inquisition.
(d) 1 Price, 395.
(e) Manning, Pr. 16. See further,

as to the sheriffs' return, and of the writ of *Idemptitate nominis,* where a wrong person is molested under prerogative process. 2 Ibid. 552.

(f) 2 Manning, Pr. 632, 3.

SECT. IV.

When Immediate Extent may issue.—Affidavit to obtain it ; and
fiat thereon.

THE rule is, that simple contract debts and specialties, not
included in the statute of Hen. 8. being rendered records by
the return of the inquisition ; and bonds within that statute,
and certain other debts, being of themselves on the footing of
records ; the Crown may (without issuing a *scire facias)* on
the wording of the statute 33 Hen. 8. c. 39. s. 55. issue an *imme-*
diate extent, on an *affidavit* of the debt, and that it is in danger of
being lost, in consequence of the insolvency or needy circumstances of the debtor, and on the *fiat* of a Baron (*a*).   The
immediate extent is founded on the presumption that the
Crown would be prejudiced by the delay attending the ordinary proceeding by *scire facias.*

We have already considered in what cases an extent may be
issued, especially with reference to the instances of a receiver
of the Crown debt, and of the demand being grounded on a
bond or bill of exchange not yet due (*b*).

It seems originally to have been held, that on a bond or
recognizance to the King, for the performance of covenants,
or other collateral things, a *scire facias* should always first
issue, and not an immediate extent.   But it was afterwards
decided, and seems to be law, that on an affidavit of danger,
and that the condition of the bond is broken, an immediate
extent may issue in every case, as well where the bond is for
the payment of a sum certain, as where it is for the performance of covenants or other collateral acts (*c*).

The commission to find simple contract debts is always, as
before observed, returnable in term ; but the immediate extent
for a simple contract debt, which extent is founded on the
inquisition taken under that commission, may, and constantly

(*a*) Ante, Extents in general, and
sect. 1.   This is different from the
writ of extent, as a final process, or
process of execution, after a *judgment*
in favor of the Crown, either in a
scire facias or other action ; or on a

judgment for a penalty, when, and not
before, an extent, as final process issues
without any affidavit. 2 Manning, 517,
521, 526, n. g. 574.
    (*b*) Ante, s. 1.
    (*c*) West, 47, 8.

does,

does, issue in vacation before the commission is returnable; though it seems that the commission ought to be actually returned into the office and filed before the extent issues (a).

The affidavit for the immediate extent must disclose the nature and ground of the debt, and state its existence with some degree of certainty and particularity. As observed by Mr. West (b), " as to the statement of the debt, there seems no reason why the same rules that are laid down in civil actions, in affidavits to hold to bail, should not be adopted in affidavits for immediate extents; as the latter process, by which body, lands and goods are taken, and on which no bail is allowed, would seem to require regulations at least as strict as the former; under which the body only is taken and bail is allowed. But the affidavits have not generally been so particular for extents."

The statement of the debt in the commission and inquisition taken thereupon, and in the affidavit for the immediate extent, is nearly the same; except that the commission does not generally state the debt so fully; in fact, the language of the commission and inquisition is taken from the affidavit, which is the foundation of the whole proceeding (c).

The affidavit must also contain not only a general allegation that the defendant is in insolvent circumstances and that the debt is likely to be lost, but must also disclose the reason for the deponent's thinking so, by alleging some fact or instance of insolvency, from which the Court or a Baron may, in the exercise of the *discretion* mentioned in the statute of Hen. 8. form an opinion whether the debt really is in danger; as, " that he has stopped payment," " has absconded," " a docquet has been struck against him," " he has committed an act of bankruptcy," or the like (d). For it would be unjust to leave to the determination of a party interested, so complicated a fact as insolvency. There are many creditors who are but too willing to construe an ambiguous act into a sign of instability, though consequences fatal to future credit and prosperity are the probable result.

An affidavit which merely stated that " the defendant was in

(a) Ibid. 3 Price, 288.

(b) West, 51.

(c) Ibid. 52.

(d) West, 52. What is insolvency in general, 1 M. and Selw. 338, 350, 3.

suspicious

suspicious circumstances, and that the debt was in danger of being lost," was held insufficient (a): but it is sufficient to state, that " the defendant is likely to become insolvent, having told deponent he could not pay the debt, nor give security, and was selling off his effects in order to withdraw himself (b)."

As the Court will not permit the defendant to deny the insolvency by a counter affidavit, and he cannot traverse, or demur to, the statement of insolvency in the affidavit, it being no part of the record, it is very properly allowed him to apply to the Court to set it aside, if it be defective (c).

The affidavit may be sworn either before a Baron of the Exchequer in town, or a commissioner of the court in the country (d).

The authority for issuing the extent is the fiat of the Chancellor of the Exchequer, or of one of the Barons of the Exchequer. This fiat may be obtained at any time, either in vacation or in term, by application to the Chancellor of the Exchequer, or one of the Barons. Nor is any motion in court necessary for it now in term time. The commission and inquisition thereupon (if the debt be by simple contract) and the affidavit, are taken to the Chancellor of the Exchequer, or the Baron, after the execution of the commission, and he signs his name on the back of the commission (which, as before observed, is the warrant for the issuing of the commission), and at the same time signs the fiat for an extent at the foot of the affidavit; which fiat runs thus : " 1st of January, 1816 (or whatever the day may be). Upon reading this affidavit and also a commission and inquisition taken thereupon, whereby the above-named C. D. is found indebted to his Majesty in the sum of £ —, let a writ or writs of immediate extent issue against the said C. D. for the recovery thereof, with the usual proviso (e).

" G. WOOD."

If the debt to the Crown be by bond, the bond itself is usually brought to the Baron, and then the fiat is, " Upon reading this affidavit and the bond of the said C. D. let a writ or writs, &c."

(a) Bunb. 360.   (d) Ibid. 54.
(b) Ibid. 134.   (e) West, 49.
(c) West, 180.

If

If the bond, as is sometimes the case, according to the present practice, is not taken to the Baron, &c. the fiat is, " Upon reading this affidavit, let a writ or writs, &c. (*a*)."

SECT. V.

Execution of Extents in chief.

1. *In general.*

THE mode of taking the inquisition under the commission, and the proceedings thereon, have been already noticed.

The extent always contains the usual *non omittas* clause, and the sheriff may enter into any liberty for the purpose of executing it (*b*). He may also break open outer doors, having previously signified his authority, and requested admittance (*c*). But the process cannot, it seems, be executed on a Sunday (*d*).

Under the writ of extent, the sheriff may take the body, lands, and goods, &c. of the defendant at once; and where there are several defendants, the operation of the writ is several, and separate property of each respectively is liable. Nor, as just observed, will the death of one of two defendants, found to be jointly indebted to the Crown, in the interval between the fiat and extent, prejudice the proceedings (*e*).

The extent directs the sheriff to take all and singular the goods and chattels, lands and tenements, debts, credits, specialties, and sums of money, &c. and the jurors in the inquisition say, that the defendant hath not any other or more goods, chattels, lands and tenements, debts, credits, specialties, or sums of money, in the sheriff's bailiwick, to the knowledge of the jurors, which can be seized. It appears to be clear, that the sheriff may, by virtue of the statute 33 Hen. 8. c. 39. which vests in

(*a*) Ibid. West, 50. Semb. that the production of the bond may be dispensed with, 2 Price, 164. But see West, 50, note.

(*b*) Bro. Prerogative, pl. 109, cites 41 Ass. 17. See 16 Vin. Abr. tit. Prerog. Q. 6. Extent does not lie to Guernsey or Jersey, ante, ch. 3. To whom extent directed, ante, 273.

(*c*) 5 Rep. 91, b. 93, a. Sir T. Jones, 234. 4 Leon. 41. pl. 11. Goulds. 679. pl. 114.

(*d*) 29 Car. 2. c. 7.

(*e*) 1 Price, R. 395. ante, 275.

the

the Crown the rights of a party under a writ of execution, on a statute merchant, or statute staple (*a*), legally seize all the defendant's goods, though considerably more than sufficient to satisfy the debt; but it does not appear that the sheriff could be prejudiced by his taking only sufficient to pay the demand. And under an extent *in aid*, it would be improper to levy more than the sum mentioned in the *fiat*, in pursuance of the late Act, 57 Geo. 3. c. 117.

By Magna Charta, 9 Hen. 3. c. 8. it is provided, that the Crown " shall not seize any land, nor rent, for any debt, as long as the chattels of the debtor forthcoming suffice to pay the debt, and the debtor himself be ready to satisfy therefore." Notwithstanding Lord Coke's opinion (*b*), it seems, from the words of the writ, and the return which is invariably made to it, and from the statute 33 Hen. 8. c. 39. above alluded to, that the Crown may, since that statute, seize the defendant's lands, though his goods are sufficient to satisfy the debt (*c*), but they cannot in such case be sold (*d*).

The extent is an execution, and the Crown is not bound by the statute of bail-bonds, 23 Hen. 6. c. 9. and consequently the defendant is not bailable.

The sheriff may take any thing leviable on a *fieri facias,* and in many respects more extensive powers are attached to the writ of extent, as will be seen hereafter. The sheriff is only to seize and not to sell the goods under the writ of extent; and the seizure of lands and debts under the extent, is effected by the finding of the jury, and is merely nominal. Actual seizure is unnecessary (*e*). The inquest finding the office, vests the property in the Crown, and it immediately becomes free from liability to be distrained on for any cause (*f*). The practice is, for the sheriff to keep the specialties seized, till called upon to deliver them to the solicitor for the Crown (*g*).

Extents in chief take place *inter se*, according to their teste (*h*). An extent in chief, finding the same goods found

(*a*) See ante, Extents in general. Vin. Ab. St. Merchant, West, 75, 6. And see the former statutes, 51 Hen. 3. c. 4. and 28 El. c. 12. 2 Manning, Pr. 549.

(*b*) 2 Inst. 19.

(*c*) See Gilbert, Hist. Excheq. 127. West, 74 to 79. 2 Manning, 549.

(*d*) Post, sect. 7.

(*e*) See 2 Manning, Pr. 550, n. y.

(*f*) Ibid. 551. Officina Brev. 301. Jenk. 112. pl. 18. Plowd. 242.

(*g*) West, 74. See post, 293. title Seizure of Lands, as to mode of finding lands on inquisition.

(*h*) Parker, 281.

upon

upon a former extent in aid, shall be preferred and paid before it (*a*). If an extent in aid issue, and goods be found and seized, and upon a *venditioni exponas*, the sheriff return that he has the money, and an extent in chief then comes, which also finds the goods first extended, the King shall have the money (*i. e.* on the extent in chief), but not if the money had been delivered over (*b*). If goods are found on an extent in aid, and then an extent in chief comes, on which goods are found, but not the same that were found on the extent in aid, as to which no evidence is offered, nor is it insisted that they should be found, and then another extent in chief comes, and the party prosecuting it offers to find what was seized in aid, and is refused, the Court will order a new extent of the like teste, as the second extent in chief, and refuse it to the first extent in chief (*c*). Where the same goods as are found under one extent are also seized under a second, it should be mentioned in the second inquisition, that these goods are subject to the first extent. And where the two extents are executed at the same time, as the sheriff may have some doubt about their priority, it would seem to be the safest way to mention in the inquisition, under each extent, that the goods are seized under the other extent (*d*).

2. *What may be taken.*

Body.

By the common law (*e*), and the statute of extents, the Crown in all suits for debts due to it may take the body of its debtor; who cannot as just observed be admitted to bail. The capias clause is in almost every case inserted in the writ, though it appears not to be customary to take the defendant (*f*). If, however, he be arrested, he can obtain his discharge only on a special application to the Court, or a baron in vacation, when security is sometimes required (*g*).

With respect to the King's interest in his debtor's body, he was by the common law, and, under certain restrictions still is, possessed of the power of protecting his debtor from the

---

(*a*) Parker, 281.
(*b*) Ibid. 282.
(*c*) Ibid. 283.
(*d*) West, 118.

(*e*) 3 Rep. 12.
(*f*) 2 Price, R. 153. 3 Ibid. 94.
(*g*) 3 Ibid. 536.

proceedings

proceedings of other creditors, till the Crown debt be satisfied (a). This was effected by a writ of protection, and antiently this prerogative was carried so far that the executor of the King's debtor could not take out probate or intermeddle without the King's permission (b). Great inconvenience, says Lord Coke (c), arose out of these protections; for to delay other men of their suits the King's debts were the more slowly paid: and therefore by the 25 Edw. 3. st. 5. c. 15. " Forasmuch as our Lord the King hath made, before this time, protections to divers people which were bounden to him in some manner of debt; that they should not be impleaded of the debts which they owed to other till they had made satisfaction to our Lord the King of that which to him was due by them by reason of his prerogative; and so during such protections no man hath dared to implead such debtors: it is accorded and assented, that notwithstanding such protections, the parties which have action against their debtors shall be answered in the King's Court by their debtors, and if judgment be thereupon given for the plaintiff or demandant, the execution of the same judgment shall be put in suspence (d), till satisfaction be made to the King of his debt. And if the creditors will undertake for the King's debt, they shall be thereunto received, and moreover shall have execution against their debtors of the debt due to them; and also shall recover against them as much as they shall pay to the King for them." So that since this statute the Crown can only delay the *execution*, not the *suit* of its *subjects:* and the statute only applies where a writ of protection is actually granted (e). Protections are now obsolete though the power of the Crown to grant them remains entire (f). Consequently in the King v. Cotton (g), the King sent his writ out of Chancery to the justices of C. B. commanding them to surcease *execution* in a suit between subject and subject, the defendant being his debtor till the debt should be satisfied; and this was considered so much a matter of course, that the plaintiff asked no more of the Court than that the cause should be kept on foot in Court by continuance on

(a) F. N. B. 28, B.   Co. Lit. 131, b.
Godb. 290.   2 Rol. R. 294.

(b) 16 East, 261, 281.

(c) Co. Lit. 131, b.

(d) This was done in 41 Edw. 3. See

Fitz. Abr. Execution, pl. 38, cited in Rex v. Cotton, Parker, 123.

(e) Cro. Car. 389.

(f) Co. Lit. 131, b. and note 206.

(g) Parker, 123.

the

the roll in order that when the King's debt should be satisfied there should be an award of execution for him.

So in respect of a subject being engaged in the King's service out of the realm, the King may, by his writ of protection, privilege such subject from all personal and many real suits for one year (*a*).

It seems at the present day to be clear that the subject may have an interest in his debtor's body, *simul et semel* with the Crown (*b*); for, as observed by Lord Hobart, " the body is all to all," and the Crown cannot be prejudiced by the subjects having an interest in common with him in the body of its debtor. This doctrine holds it should seem though the party be first taken by the Crown (*c*). The Crown has however the prerogative right of choosing the custody in which its prisoner is to be kept; and no subject can without the consent of the Crown remove the party from such custody for the purpose of charging him with a declaration, charging him in execution, or surrendering him in discharge of his bail, &c. (*d*)

As the bankrupt (*e*) and insolvent laws do not bind the Crown, a bankrupt's certificate and insolvent's discharge will not entitle the party to be released from confinement on an extent. And it seems to have been held that a bankrupt may be arrested for a Crown debt when under examination *eundo et redeundo* (*f*).

Goods and Sums of Money.

The goods and monies of the defendant are also to be seized under the extent.

An extent binds the defendant's goods, whatever the nature of the debt may be, only from the award of execution, that is

---

(*a*) Co. Lit. 130, 1. 3 Bla. Com. 289.

(*b*) See Cro. Car. 389, 390. Savile, R. 29. Hob. 115. and the following notes, vide Dyer, 297. pl. 24,

(*c*) Ibid. But see Godb. 298.

(*d*) 5 Taunt. 503. and cases there cited. In this case the defendant having given bail to the action and being in custody of the sheriffs of London under an extent of the Crown, the Court of C. P. held, that they could not grant his bail, a habeas corpus to bring him up, and render him in their discharge to the fleet without the consent of the Crown. See further on this subject, 3 Manning, 533. In Criminal Cases, &c. Chitty, Crim. Law, 811, 812.

(*e*) Bunb. 202. 1 Atk. 262.

(*f*) Bla. Rep. 1142. 1 Montague, Bankrupt Laws, 664.

in

in strictness the fiat (*a*); but as it is the sheriff's duty, as appears from the form of the writ, merely to take the property the defendant had at the time the writ is tested, it is the invariable practice to teste the writ as of the date of the fiat, and it cannot be tested before. No difficulties can therefore arise in this respect as to the teste and fiat, and the distinction between them is nominal. The King is not named in, and consequently is not bound by, the statute of frauds, 29 Car. 2. c. 3. which directs that goods shall be bound only from the delivery of writs of execution to the sheriff (*b*).

The sheriff may seize all the defendant's goods in his own possession or in the hands of another as his trustee (*c*), except things necessary *pro victu* of himself and family: and except also *averia carucæ*, if in the latter case there be other chattels sufficient (*d*). The King is not bound by a sale in market overt (*e*); or by the custom of London for the pledgee to retain goods against the real owner (*f*).

The general rule is, that a stranger insisting that a seizure under an extent is invalid, must claim a *property* in the goods taken (*g*).

It will be proper to consider the effect of an extent: 1st, Where a stranger claims a special or other property in the goods. 2dly, Where he claims an interest without a property.

First, in the case of a claim of a *special property* in the goods, as contra-distinguished from the general property in them, the rule is, that if such claim arose prior to the fiat or teste of the writ, the extent shall not operate. As if the goods were *bonâ fide* and not fraudulently assigned in trust for creditors, &c. though such assignment amount to an act of bankruptcy (*h*), or were pawned, demised, &c. to another, for a term certain, so as to vest a special property in them in the pawnee or

---

(*a*) 8 Rep. 171. Gilb. Excheq. 90. Stra. 754. Warrant from Commissioners of Taxes, Ibid. 982.

(*b*) See 7 Viner, 105. 2 Bac. Ab. 365, K. Gilb. Excheq. 90.

(*c*) 12 Rep. 2.

(*d*) 2 Rol. Abr. 160. pl. 8. Com. Dig. Dette, G. 3. 16 Vin. Ab. 520. tit. Prerog. I. pl. 8.

(*e*) 2 Inst. 713.

(*f*) Plowd. 243. Bro. Prerog. 5. If a Tortfeasor hold defendant's goods the inquisition should find the fact to ground process of withernam or an information in the nature of trover or detinue against him, 1 Manning, Pr. 544, 5. 1 Mod. 90. pl. 58.

(*g*) See post, ch. 13. s. 3. div. 1.

(*h*) West. 115. Tidd, 5th ed. 992. 3 M. and S. 371.

bailee.

bailee (*a*). It seems however that goods pawned before the teste of the extent, may be taken as against the pawnee, on satisfaction of the pledge (*b*), or taken and sold, subject to the pawnee's right (*c*).

As however the Crown is not bound, by the bankrupt statutes not being named in them, and relations which are but fictions of law, cannot bind the King (*d*), the extent operates on the defendant's goods, though a commission of bankrupt has issued against him, if the assignment of his effects be not executed before the fiat or teste of the writ; but the Crown cannot take the effects if actually assigned before the fiat or teste, and a provisional assignment is sufficient for this purpose (*e*). If the assignment of the bankrupt's effects and the teste of the extent be on the same day, the King's prerogative shall prevail (*f*). But an extent issued out of term cannot be ante-dated, so as to over-reach the assignment (*g*).

It has been asserted (*h*), that if husband and wife are joint tenants of a term, demised to them during the coverture, and the husband become indebted to the Crown, the King may have execution of this term against the wife, after the husband's death, because the taking the lease was the husband's act, and he had power of the term at the time of his death, and the wife came to it without valuable consideration, and *quodammodo* continued in of the interest of her husband. Rolle however says he does not see how this doctrine can be law ' *entant que l' execution ne relate* (*i*);' and it seems to be unfounded, if there be no fraud. On the death of the husband

---

(*a*) Bro. Abr. tit. Barre, 121; Plowd. 487. Pledges, 28; Trespass, 92. 7 T. R. 112. So the Crown or its grantee takes by forfeiture, subject to previous *bonâ fide* charges, *though voluntary.* 2 Vez. 116.

(*b*) Bro. Ab. tit. Pledges, pl. 28, 31.

(*c*) 8 East, 467.

(*d*) Hob. 339.

(*e*) Parker, 126. 7 Vin. Ab. 104. 1 Atk. 95. 4 Term R. 411. Stra. 749, 979. 1 East, 363. 5 Ves. Jun. 297. 14 Vez. 87. 1 Montag. Bkpt. Laws, 663. 16 East, 279.

(*f*) 2 Vez. 295. Stra. 749. Parker, 126. Bunb. 33

(*g*) Stra. 749. It is said the Crown cannot prove under a commission. Ibid. 752.

(*h*) In Sir G. Fleetwood's Case, 8 Rep. 171; and the authority cited for the position is 50 Ass. pl. 5. See 1 Wightw. 37.

(*i*) 2 Rol. Ab. 157, Prerog. F. pl. 5. And see 16 Vin. Ab. 521. If a party purchase or convey lands to himself and his wife (for her jointure), and to his heirs, and then becomes indebted to the King, and dies so, no execution having issued during his life, the land cannot be charged during the life of his wife. Ibid. 156. Post, 300.

the

the chattle real vests, by operation of law, absolutely in the wife, as survivor, he having omitted to dispose of it during her life (a); and there is no principle of law in favour of a relation back further than the teste of the writ. And dower is free from the claims of the Crown against the deceased husband (b).

Under an extent against one partner, the Crown may *seize* partnership goods, but it can *sell* only the interest of the partner against whom the extent issues; which is his share of the surplus, after payment of the partnership debts (c).

The invariable form of the writ shews, that under an extent against several, the separate goods of each may be taken.

Secondly, where a stranger claims an *interest*, without a property in the goods, the general rule seems to be, that though such interest arose prior to the fiat or teste of the writ, the prerogative shall prevail. Therefore where goods are *distrained*, but not sold, before the fiat or teste, they may be taken, because till the sale the property in them remains in the defendant (d). Nor is the landlord in such case entitled to a year's rent, under the statute 8 Ann, c. 14 (e). So the effects of a bankrupt are subject to the extent, if not actually assigned before the fiat or teste, though the creditors have an interest therein (f). But goods holden by the defendant in his representative capacity of executor or administrator, cannot be taken (g). And if the defendant be a member of a corporation which has been fined, the goods of which he is possessed in *jure proprio*, shall not be seized for the fine (h). Nor is an executor or administrator liable, even at the suit of the Crown, for the testator's or intestate's debts, if there be no assets (i).

It seems that the cattle of a stranger, levant and couchant, on the debtor's property, cannot be taken on an extent (k), though they may be on a *levari facias*. It is even said that if the King's debtor suffer *A.* to manure his land, the goods of *A.* may be

(a) Bac. Ab. Baron and Feme, C. 2. D. Co. Lit. 351. a note.

(b) Co. Lit. 31, a. post, 300.

(c) 1 Wightw. 50.   See 3 Bos. and P. 288, 9.   See ante, ch. 11. s. 3.

(d) Parker, 112, 121.   4 T. R. 211. 16 East, 279.

(e) See sect. 8.   So on extents in aid. 2 Price, 17.

(f) Ante, 286.

(g) Rol. Ab. Prerogative, 159, 1. 49. 2 Ibid. 806. Com. Dig. Debt, G. 7. 4 Term R. 628.   17 Vez. 152.

(h) 2 Rol. Ab. 159.

(i) 33 H. 8. c. 39. s. 77.

(k) 2 Rol. Ab. 159. 16 Vin. Ab. 519. 1 Ld. Raym. 307.   12 Mod. 178.

seized on a *levari* by the King for the debt(*a*). But in the case of tenants in common, the cattle of one going upon the land cannot be taken for the Crown debt due from the other (*b*).

With respect to the powers of the extent, in case the defendant's goods have been already taken or seized in execution on a *fieri facias*, &c. at the suit of a subject, the statute 33 Hen. 8. c. 39. s. 74. enacts, that "if any suit be commenced or taken, or any process be hereafter *awarded* for the King, for the recovery of any of the King's debts, that then the same suit and process shall be preferred before the suit of any person or persons : and that our said Sovereign Lord, his heirs and successors, shall have first execution against any defendant or defendants, of and for his said debts, before any other person or persons, so always that the King's said suit be taken and commenced, or process awarded, for the said debt at the suit of our said Sovereign Lord the King, his heirs or successors, before judgment given for the said other person or persons."

The general common law rule is, that even a prior seizure under a *fieri facias*, does not operate or render the execution complete against an extent; though a *sale* previous to the fiat or teste of the extent, will secure the subject's right (*c*). Notwithstanding the above section, it is clear therefore that if the Crown suit be commenced or the fiat for the extent be made, before judgment be given for the subject, the Crown process shall be preferred (*d*). And the word "debt," in the above section, includes a "penalty" due to the Crown. Therefore in Butler *v.* Butler(*e*), it was decided that process sued out by the Crown against a defendant to recover penalties, upon which judgment for the Crown is afterwards obtained, entitles the King's execution to have priority within the statute, before the execution of a subject, whose execution had issued and been commenced on a judgment recovered against the same defendant prior to the King's judgment, but subsequent to the commencement of the King's process: the King's writ of execution having been delivered to the sheriff

(*a*) Lane, 91. 16 Vin. Ab. 519, tit. Prerogative, I.

(*b*) Ibid. 2 Rol. Abr. 457. Lord Raym. 308.

(*c*) Dyer, 67, b. margin. Parker, 125. Gilb. Excheq. 90. 16 East, 264, 5.

(*d*) 1 East, 338.

(*e*) Ibid.

before the actual sale of the defendant's goods, under the plaintiff's execution.

But since the statute, it has become a dubious question whether or not the Crown suit is to be preferred where the subject's judgment is prior to the commencement of the Crown suit, or the award of the Crown process, and where the subject's writ is also delivered to the sheriff before the extent. The Courts of Common Pleas (a) and King's Bench (b) have unanimously decided in favor of the subject on this point, but the Court of Exchequer have subsequently and recently held otherwise (c). As the authorities are contradictory, the subject demands investigation.

That

(a) Uppom v. Summer, 2 Bla. Rep. 1294.

(b) Rorke v. Dayrell, 4 Term Rep. 402.

(c) The King v. Allnut, cited 16 East, 278, notes. See the argument in Thurston v. Mills, ibid. 254. confirmed in the King v. Sloper and Allen, Exchequer, Saturday, November 14, 1818. The following is the report of that case in the Times newspaper. "The Attorney-General on a former day obtained a rule calling on the sheriff to pay over to the Crown a certain sum of money which he had in his hands, the property of the defendants, in satisfaction of a debt due from them to his Majesty.

" Sir William Owen, on the part of Messrs. Morlands, bankers, opposed the motion. It appeared that Messrs. Morlands had obtained a verdict against the defendants, and had entered up judgment, sued out execution, and placed it in the hands of the sheriff, who had levied under it. Three days after the levy was made, and before the goods were sold, his Majesty came in with his writ of extent. The sheriff however, on the part of Messrs. Morlands, retained the money which was the proceeds of the goods, on the ground

that they having obtained their judgment and execution before his Majesty's writ came down, the Crown was ousted.

The Attorney-General, on the other side, contended, that the taking of the goods by the sheriff did not at all divest Sloper and Allen of their property in them. They were still their goods, and only in the legal custody or possession of the sheriff, for a purpose to be afterwards carried into effect, namely, for sale, in order that the proceeds might be applied to payment of a debt due from the defendant to Messrs. Morlands. The King's writ came down before that circumstance took place; and therefore the rule applied laid down in the King and Allnut, in which case the judges held, that up to the change of property actually taking place, the King's writ should have precedence of all others. Had the sale taken place only one minute before the King's writ arrived, he was ready to acknowledge the King would have been ousted; but as it was, he contended his motion was well founded.

" The Court after hearing the argument, decided that the Attorney-General was entitled to his rule. The case of the King and Allnut was decided fourteen years ago; the Court had acted on it ever since; and until it was impeached,

That the Crown is entitled at common law to a preference, till the subject's execution is *complete*, is not denied. The general common law doctrine, that the prerogative must prevail where it stands in competition with a subject's rights, arising concurrently with those of the Crown, and that consequently the prior part of the 74th section is merely declaratory of the old common law, is also admitted. But it is contended on the part of the subject, that the statute confers various benefits and advantages to the Crown, as by putting bonds to the King on the footing of statutes staple, by giving to the King the prerogative execution by extent, &c. and therefore he can only avail himself of it, by taking it subject to the express and clear exception in favor of the subject, in case his judgment be obtained before the King's suit be commenced or his process awarded : and that the latter part of the clause is restrictive and imposes a condition on the prerogative. But the chief ground of Lord Kenyon's opinion in Rorke *v.* Dayrell, namely, that the property of the goods was altered by the delivery of the writ to the Sheriff, is now given up, it being admitted that the property of the goods is in the defendant till sale (*a*).

On the other hand, the prior claim of the Crown is contended for principally on these grounds :

First, It is urged, that the case falls within the general common law principle, exemplified in the case of a distress for the same goods, or the bankruptcy of the defendant, that if the King's execution bear teste before the property in the goods is actually *altered*, they are bound by the extent, and that until the sale under a *fieri facias* the property remains, as is admitted on the other side, in the defendant. That however the case may be between subject and subject, a superior obligation, by force of the Crown process, may intervene before a sale, and overpower it.

To obviate the construction put on the 74th section, in favor of the subject, it is contended on the part of the Crown, that if the words " so that the King's suit or process be before the subject's judgment," be literally construed, the Crown

peached, by some motion for its reconsideration, the Court would not depart from the rule there laid down.

" The rule, calling on the sheriff to pay over the money, was made absolute."

(*a*) 16 East, 267, 282.

would

would be placed in a worse condition than a subject, as the subject's prior judgment would prevail against the extent, though the execution on the judgment were after the extent. That the priority of the judgment never was a criterion by which the preference of execution could be determined. That express words are necessary to abridge or take away a prerogative, and if any other construction can be reasonably applied to the words of the 74th section, it should be adopted. That the history of this branch of the prerogative will prove that the statute was meant to give the subject a benefit, and restrain the Crown in a distinct and irrelevant case. " By the antient prerogative of the Crown (it is ingeniously argued (a)), as it stood at common law, the King was to be paid first, and was entitled to stay the suit of other creditors against the King's debtor, until the King's debt was paid, and the means by which that was effected was, to grant a protection to the debtor (b). The first alteration that was made by statute in the King's prerogative was by 25 Edw. 3. stat. 5. c. 19. which narrowed the prerogative, by allowing the suits of other creditors to proceed to judgment, notwithstanding such protections; but the execution was to be suspended, unless the creditor should undertake for the King's debt. The next alteration was by the statute now under discussion, 33 Hen. 8., which is very obscurely worded; for it would appear to one not conversant with the law, as it then stood, from a view of this clause of the statute, as if it gave to the King something which he had not before, but at the same time gave it with qualifications; whereas, it is quite clear, from the above considerations, that although worded in the form of a gift, it gives nothing to the Crown, nor enables it to do any thing which it might not have done before. But it imposes conditions, and, therefore, must be considered as a restraining clause. Now the rule is, that the p erogative of the Crown shall not be taken away, except by clear and unambiguous words. According to that rule, the statute must be taken to have worked this restraint, and no farther, viz. that the King shall not prevent the subject from taking out execution upon a judgment obtained against the King's debtor; unless, before the time when the

(a) 16 East, 260, &c. 281, 2.   (b) See Bac. Abr. Statute, I. 4.

subject

subject shall have obtained such judgment, the King shall have commenced his suit, or instituted process for the recovery of his debt. This will be an abridgment of the prerogative, (for under 25 Edw. 3. it has been shewn, that the King might have prevented the subject's execution, although the King's suit was not commenced before the subject had obtained judgment,) and will satisfy the words of the statute, and also conform to all the authorities prior to Uppom *v.* Sumner. The words of the statute cannot possibly be taken in their literal sense; for then, if the subject's judgment were first he would have precedence, although his execution were last, which is not the case, even between subject and subject. That sense, therefore, must prevail, which the words will best admit of, upon a reference to the law as it stood before the act. The substance of the enactment is this, that the King's suit and process (which is intended of mesne process), and the King's execution, are to be preferred to that of the subject, which is so far the same as at common law; but he is only to have first execution, *i. e.* a right to prevent the subject from issuing execution until the King's debt be satisfied in the case there provided for. But the statute was never intended to be applied to concurrent executions."

It may be observed upon this most important question, that this mode of construing the statute seems reasonable, and it does not appear that any positive objection to this explanation of it has been offered. The leaning and construction should, it seems, be rather in favor of the Crown, in the case of an enactment apparently abridging its prerogatives; and in order to discover the scope and meaning of a statute, especially if it be ambiguous, it is perfectly consistent with legal principles to regard the common law as it existed at the period when the act was passed (*a*). And it appears on the whole highly probable that the question, if it arose again, would be finally settled, in conformity with the very recent decision in the Exchequer, in favor of the Crown (*b*).

If the facts are returned specially by the jury, which appears to be the usual and most advisable course, they must be stated

---

(*a*) See Bac. Abr. Statute, I. 4.   See however Mr. West's observations,
(*b*) Ante, 289.   West on Extents, 107 to 112.

and found with a precision and certainty which will enable the parties to traverse, and take a clear issue on them (*a*).

The Court possesses, in many instances, a discretionary power to protect its officers, when, without any fault on their parts, they are placed in a dilemma in consequence of any doubtful point of law. If, therefore, the sheriff have a *fieri facias* and an extent in his hands against the same party, and the operation of each be not clear, he should not proceed with the former, unless the plaintiff will indemnify him; and if the plaintiff refuse to do so, the Court will enlarge the time for making his return to the *fieri facias*, on an affidavit of the circumstances (*b*).

By the 28 Geo. 3. c. 37. s. 21. the Crown has a lien on goods and articles used in trades subject to the excise (*c*). And by the 43 Geo. 3. c. 99. s. 37. the goods of persons assessed to and owing the taxes therein mentioned, cannot be taken in execution, or assigned, &c. (though they may be seized for rent), unless the plaintiff in the execution, or the assignee, shall, before the sale or removal of the goods, pay the duties due for the year.

Lands.

The Crown has at common law, and by the statute 33 H. 8. c. 39. s. 55. a right to take in execution the lands of its debtor or accountant (*d*). As already observed (*e*), it seems that the sheriff may *seize* the defendant's lands under the extent, though his goods be sufficient to satisfy the debt.

With respect to the time from which the lands of the debtor are bound by the Crown debt, the general criterion and rule at common law seems to be, that the lien or claim obtains only from the time when the debt becomes of record, and is thereby presumed to be of public notoriety.

Debts of record always bound the land from the date of the record (*f*). The statute 33 H. 8. (*g*) puts bonds taken in the form thereby prescribed on the footing of statutes staple, and consequently *such* bonds so taken, bind the obligor's lands by

(*a*) West on Extents, 114. note *c*.

(*b*) 7 T. R. 174. 1 Taunt, 120. 16 East, 263.

(*c*) See Dougl. 416. 6 T. R. 437; Decisions on this statute.

(*d*) 3 Rep. 12. 4 Taunt. 334.

(*e*) Ante, 281.

(*f*) Gilb. Excheq. 88.

(*g*) c. 39. s. 50.

virtue of that statute, from the time they are executed (*a*).
But *other* bonds and specialties only bind the party's lands, as
at common law, from the time they become of record, under
the inquisition on a commission. The same doctrine obtained
at common law, and in general still holds with respect to
simple contract debts (*b*). However, even at common law, debts
due from certain known public officers and accountants to the
Crown, though not of record, bound the debtor's lands from
the time they accrued due (*c*). And the statute 13 Eliz. c. 4.
s. 1. extends this common law exception, by providing that
debts due from the officers, collectors and receivers, &c. mentioned therein, shall bind their lands from the time when they
entered into the offices.

By that statute " for the better security of the Queen's Majesty, her heirs and successors, against such as shall have the
receipt and charge of the money and treasure of her Highness,
her heirs and successors, it is declared and enacted, that all
lands, tenements, profits, commodities and hereditaments,
which any treasurer or receiver, in or belonging to any of the
Queen's Majesty's Courts of the Exchequer, Wards and Liveries, or duchy of Lancaster, Treasurer of the Chamber,
Cofferer of the Household to the Queen's Majesty, her heirs
or successors, Treasurer for the Wars, Treasurer of any fort,
town or castle, where any garrison is or shall be kept, Treasurer of the Admiralty or Navy, Treasurer, under Treasurer,
or other person accomptable to the Queen's Majesty, her heirs
or successors, for any office or charge, of or within the Mint,
Treasurer or Receiver of any sums of money imprest, or otherwise, for the use of the Queen's Majesty, her heirs or successors, or for provisions of victual, or for fortifications, buildings,
or works, or for any other provisions to be used in any of the
offices of the Queen's Majesty's ordnance and artillery,
armoury, wardrobe, tents and pavilions, or revels, customer,
collector, farmer of customs, subsidies, imposts or other duties
within any port of the realm, Collector of the tenths of the
clergy, Collector of any subsidy or fifteen, Receiver-General

---

(*a*) 8 Rep. 171. 2 Rol. Ab. 156, 7.   Lane, 65.
The King's execution on a bond assigned   (*b*) 1 Wightw. 84.
to him, relates only to the date of the   (*c*) See the cases cited, 1 Wightw.
assignment. Lit. 124, 5. Savil. 11.   36, &c.

of

of the revenues of any county or counties answerable in the receipt of the Exchequer, or in the Court of Wards and Liveries (*a*), or the duchy of Lancaster, Clerk of the Hamper, now hath, or at any time hereafter shall have, within the time whilst he or they or any of them shall remain accountable, shall for the payment and satisfaction unto the Queen's Majesty, her heirs and successors, of his or their arrearages, at any time hereafter to be lawfully, according to the laws of this realm, adjudged and determined upon his or their account (all his due and reasonable petitions being allowed) be liable to the payment thereof, and be put and had in execution for the payment of such arrearages or debts to be so adjudged and determined upon, any such Treasurer, Receiver, Teller, Customer, Collector, Farmer, Officer or Accountant, as is before named, *in like and in as large and beneficial manner*, to all intents and purposes, as if the same Treasurer, Receiver, Teller, Customer, Farmer or Collector, upon whom any such arrearages or debts shall be so adjudged or determined, *had the day he became first officer or accountant stood bound by writing obligatory*, having *the effect* of a *statute of the staple, to her Majesty*, her heirs or successors, for the true answering and payment of the same arrearages or debts."

With respect therefore to debts due from the officers enumerated in this statute, they bind the land (if incurred at any time during the continuance of the office (*b*)) from the time of entering into the office (*c*), since the writing obligatory *having the effect of a statute staple*, mentioned in the statute, binds the land from the time it is entered into.

The enumeration of officers and receivers, &c. in the statute, is, it will be observed, very general. The words "treasurer or receiver of any sums of money imprest or otherwise," are particularly so, but they do not mean any person who gets the King's money into his hands. Being introduced in the enumeration of certain known public officers, they must be confined to that class of persons; and therefore where it appeared that the party had received the King's money from the paymaster-general of the forces, and not in any specific public character of

---

(*a*) Court of Wards and Liveries taken away, 12 Car. 2. c. 24. s. 1.
(*b*) 10 Rep. 55. West. 128.

(*c*) 1 Wightw. 34. 2 Leon. 90. West, 128, 9.

his own, he was held not to be within the meaning of the statute, and consequently that a *bonâ fide* purchaser without notice, after he received the money and before the inquisition, was protected (*a*). The general rule, therefore, clearly is, that debts due from persons not within the enumeration in the statute of Elizabeth, remain as at common law. It would be a serious hardship on purchasers, if an individual holding no office known to the public, to be an accountable office, might by casually receiving part of the King's treasure bind his land in the hands of a *bonâ fide* vendee without notice.

Mr. West observes (*b*), that simple contract debts are recorded by the inquisition under the commission. But whether they date of record from the finding of the inquisition or from the actual return of it into the Exchequer (whether before or after the day appointed for the return), or from the appointed return day, if then returned, does not seem to be decided." It appears that the debt would be of record from the time when the inquisition is returned and filed.

The Crown may take not only the legal estate, but estates, held by another in trust for the defendant, or an equity of redemption, to which he is entitled, even though the legal estate had never vested in the defendant, the mortgagor, but had been conveyed to the mortgagee by the trustees, in whom it had been vested in trust for him; but the mortgagee will be protected (*c*). This was the common law doctrine, and, in confirmation of it, the statute 13 Eliz. c. 4. s. 5. enacts, that " If any person or persons, accountant or indebted as is aforesaid, shall at any time after he or they shall become accountant or chargeable, as is aforesaid, purchase and buy, or cause to be purchased and bought, any lands, tenements, or hereditaments, and cause the assurance thereof to be made in the name of any other person or persons, where the same is indeed meant or intended to the use, profit, or behoof of such person, accountant or indebted, or of any other person or persons, and that the

---

(*a*) Wightw. 44.

(*b*) On Extents, 129.

(*c*) Godb. 289. Hardr. 495. Forest's Rep. 162. 1 Price's R. 207. Rex v. Smith, in Sugden, V. and P. See post.

298. Order for sale of Lands; that Court will protect mortgagee and how ; and 1 Price, 207. Cannot be taken in execution at the suit of a subject, 8 East, 467.

same

same manner of purchasing, and secret uses, profits, or behoof, shall be found by office or inquisition, that then all and every lands, tenements, and hereditaments, so to be bought or pur-chased, or caused to be purchased, (as is before mentioned in this last proviso,) shall, by virtue of this Act, be taken, secured, and used for the satisfaction of the arrearages and debt of eve-ry such accountant or debtor, as is above mentioned, to all in-tents and purposes, as though the person or persons indebted, upon his or their account or farm, were thereof actually seised of such estate, that was conveyed to any person or persons, by any such accountant or debtor, or by his means, as is afore-said; and that all sales to be thereof made by the Queen's Ma-jesty, her heirs or successors, for satisfaction of such debt, or arrearages, as shall be found, as is aforesaid, to be due and ow-ing to our said sovereign lady the Queen, her heirs and suc-cessors, shall be of the like effect, and be used and done in such like manner and form as is before expressed."

Rents-service (a) and rents-charge (b), and tithes in the hands of lay impropriators, or leased for life, or for years (c), may be extended as part of the realty; but tithes in the hands of ecclesiastical persons, cannot be seized under the extent, though on the sheriff's return that the defendant is a beneficed clerk, process to the ordinary, or a *levari facias* to the bishop, may be issued (d).

It should also be observed, that copyhold lands, and leases of copyholds, cannot be taken in execution, even at the suit of the Crown (e). And though a term for years be extended as land, instead of being appraised as a chattel, as it may be, it is bound as a chattel only, from the award of execution, against a *bonâ fide* purchaser before that period (f).

It will now be proper to consider the effect of the extent, where a stranger claims—1st, an interest and property in the lands of the debtor; or, 2dly, has a lien or claim on them, by virtue of a judgment, or other debt of record, or an execu-tion.

(a) H. 13 H. 4. Fitz. Avowry, 237.

(b) 7 Co. 37. The previous arrears form of course part of the debts seized. Ibid.

(c) 3 Price, 223. 2 Manning, 541.

(d) 2 Manning, 540, 1. See Tidd's Pr. Index, tit. *Fieri facias.*

(e) Hardr. 432. Kitch. 123. Parker, 135. 1 Rol. Abr. 888. pl. 3. *Quære,* As to customary freeholds, 2 Manning, Pr. 541, 2.

(f) 8 Rep. 171. 2 Rol. Ab. 156, 7.

1. Of

1. Of course, even *bonâ fide* alienation and charges, do not in general bind the King, if they be made after the period from which the lands of the Crown debtor are bound (*a*); for the King's debt is in the nature of an original charge on the land itself, and, therefore, must subject and bind every one that claims under it. And it has been held, that a term of years, created out of an estate, prior to the right of the Crown attaching on the estate, and assigned to a trustee, in trust for a purchaser, would not protect such purchaser against Crown debts, though he purchased *bonâ fide*, and without notice (*b*). But it is still a common law rule, that alienations and charges, as sales, legal mortgages, &c. and even, it seems (*c*), voluntary charges, if *bonâ fide* created before the claim of the Crown on the land commenced, are valid (*d*). And we have just observed, that a term for years *bonâ fide* purchased from the defendant, shall be bound as against a purchaser, as a chattel only, from the award of execution (*e*).

The general common law doctrine is, however qualified by, and must be carefully regarded, with reference to the 75th section of the statute of extents, 33 H. 8. c. 39. which vests in the Crown a continuing claim *in certain cases* on estates, after the *death* of the Crown debtor. Fee simple lands might it seems be followed, but at common law, if a tenant in tail became indebted to the King in any manner and died, the King could not extend the land in the seisin of the issue in tail, because the King was bound by the statute *de donis conditionalibus* (*f*). To remedy this, the statute of Hen. 8. enacted, that all manors, lands, tenements, possessions and heredita-ments, " the which now be, or that hereafter shall come or be, in or to the hands, possession, occupation or seisin of any person or persons, to whom the same manors, lands, tenements or hereditaments, have heretofore or hereafter shall *descend, revert* or *remain* in *fee simple or in fee tail, general or special,*

(*a*) 7 Rep. 21; 3rd Resolution.

(*b*) Rex *v.* Smith, Sugd. V. and P. App. &c. See however Mr. Sugden's observations on this point.

(*c*) At least this is so when the Crown claims by forfeiture. 2 Vez. 116.

(*d*) Gilb. Excheq. 91. Moore, 12, 126. 2 Mod. 247. 1 Price, 207. 1

Wightw. 34. Per Cur. in Rex *v.* Smith, Sugd. V. and P. Equitable mortgage and mere agreement *to* sell, will not, it seems, be available. Post, 303. 1 Price, 216, 220, notes.

(*e*) Ante, 297. 8 Rep. 171.

(*f*) 7 Rep. 21. Plowd. Ld. Berkeley's Case.

by,

by, from or after the death of any his or their ancestor or ancestors *as heir*, or *by gift of his ancestors whose heir he is*, which said ancestor or ancestors was, is or shall be indebted to the King, or to any other person or persons to his use, *by judgment, recognizance, obligation or other specialty*, the debt whereof is or shall not be contented and paid : that then in every such case the same manors, lands, tenements, possessions and hereditaments shall be and stand, by authority of this Act, from henceforth charged and chargeable to and for the payment of the same debt, and of every part thereof." And by the same section, the heir is made liable, though not mentioned in the specialty (*a*).

The debts of the ancestor mentioned in the statute are not confined to such as accrued before the conveyance : and consequently the heir who claims by the gift of his ancestor, whether in fee simple or in fee tail, shall be bound to pay the King's debt, whether due before or after the gift (*b*). It will however be remarked that the statute mentions only four species of debts from the ancestor, viz. " by judgment, recognizance, obligation or other specialty," and is confined to debts " to the King or to any other person or persons to his use." Consequently other debts than those by judgment, recognizance, obligation or other specialty, remain as at common law: and the statute does not apply where the debt, of whatever nature it be, was not *originally* due to the King but to a subject, and accrued to the King by reason of an attainder, outlawry, forfeiture, gift of the party, or by any other collateral way or means. In neither of such cases is the land in the possession of the heir in tail, chargeable for the Crown debt(*c*). And it has been resolved on the statute, that if a tenant in tail become indebted to the King by one of the four ways mentioned therein and die, and before any process or extent, the issue in tail *boná fide* alien the land in tail, it shall not be extended by force of the statute, for it only renders liable the land in the possession or seisin of the heir in tail, against the issue in tail, and not the alienee (*d*). Lands in fee simple were extendible at common law, in the hands of any person;

(*a*) See 1 Inst. 386, a. Wood's Inst. 20.

(*b*) 7 Rep. 19 ; 6th Resolution.

(*c*) Ibid. 21 ; 2d and 4th Resolution.

(*d*) Ibid. 3rd Resolution.

and therefore as to them the statute was *declarativum antiqui juris,* and the alienee of such fee simple lands, from the heir of the Crown debtor, would not, it seems, be protected; but as to estates tail, the statute was *introductivum novi juris,* against the issue in tail. It seems also that a conveyance in consideration of marriage, is not a gift within the meaning of the statute (*a*).

It has been observed by C. B. Manwood (*b*), that the heir of a Crown debtor shall not be charged if his executor have assets; nor the feoffee who comes in by purchase, if the heir have assets; for the heir comes to the land *gratis,* and therefore with reason ought to be charged. On the death of the King's debtor, process shall issue against the executors, the heir and terretenants jointly at once (*c*).

It seems that lands held by the Crown debtor when alive, as joint-tenant with another person who survives him cannot be extended after the debtor's death in the hands of the survivor, they being his by survivorship (*d*). And if a party purchase or convey lands to himself and his wife (for her jointure), and to his heirs, and then become indebted to the King and die so, no execution having issued during his life, the land cannot be charged during the life of his wife (*e*). And the wife's dower is free from debts due from the deceased husband to the Crown (*f*).

Commissioners of bankrupts have but a power and the assignment from them to the assignees of the bankrupt's lands by bargain and sale is not complete till enrolment (*g*): and consequently the Crown may take the lands though the teste of the writ be subsequent to the bargain and sale if it be prior to the enrolment (*h*).

2. As to the effect of the extent, where a subject has a lien or claim on the defendant's lands by virtue of a judgment or other debt of record or an execution, &c.

Where the subject has a lien on the land by judgment prior

(*a*) 2 Leon. 90. 7 Rep. 19. Moore, 126.

(*b*) Dyer, 67, b.

(*c*) Savil. 52.

(*d*) Co. Lit. 185, a.

(*e*) 2 Rol. Ab. 156. 1 Wightw. 39, 40.

(*f*) Co. Lit. 31, a. See F. N. B. 150, 1. Bro. Distress, 72.

(*g*) 13 El. c. 7. s. 2. Sir T. Jones, 196. Montag. Bkpt. Laws, 465. West, 149.

(*h*) Ibid.

to the King's debt of record or the entry into office, &c. or to
the commencement of the Crown suit, and has perfected his
execution before the issuing of the extent at the suit of the
Crown, the subject shall retain the lands against the Crown's
extent (*a*). But it appears that if the Crown suit be commenced
prior to the subject's judgment being obtained, the Crown process shall at all events prevail.

It seems to have been clear at common law, that though a
subject has a judgment prior to the King's debt or before office
entered into under the statute of Elizabeth, yet the King might
by an extent issued before execution commenced, or even after
it was commenced if before it was perfected (*b*) by the subject,
take the defendant's lands and thereby oust the subject's execution (*c*). Chief Baron Gilbert observes, " if the subject's debt
be by statute staple on judgment, and prior to the King's debt;
and the King extend the lands first; the subject shall not, by
any after extent, take them out of his hands. But if such
judgment be extended, and the subject has the possession delivered to him by a *liberate*, he shall hold it discharged from
the King's debt; but if the King's extent come before the possession by *liberate*, the King's extent shall be preferred, and
the subject wait till the King's debt be satisfied. The reason
of the difference is, because the King's debt is in nature of a
feudal charge; which if it comes on the lands before the property of them is altered, it seizes them as it might have done
for the original service at first imposed; but if there had been
a lawful alienation before such debt, there is not the feud of
the tenant, and therefore such charge cannot affect it; therefore if there was a precedent judgment or statute staple, and
a *liberate* pursuant, before the King's extent comes down, there
it cannot charge the lands; because the property is altered by
the extent of the subject, which relates to the time that the
judgment was first given, or statute staple acknowledged; because such extent and *liberate* of the subject was only executing such judgment or statute on the land, and the execution
was relative to that judgment, which was prior to the King's
charge; and so there was a complete alteration of property

(*a*) Gilb. Exch. 91, &c. 3 Leon. 239.   (*c*) Gilb. Exch. 91. 3 Leon. 240.
Hardr. 23. West, 160.   Cases in Parl. 72. Hardr. 106. 1 East,
(*b*) 1 East, 338.   338. 16 East, 279.

prior to the King's charge, before his extent came down: but if the King's extent had come before the *liberate,* he had charged' the land whilst it was in the hands of his debtor, and then his charge would be satisfied, as if it had been in the first feudal donation; for nothing can hinder the King's charge, (which comes on the land as if it had been settled in the first feudal donation,) but what amounts to a precedent alienation; for so far as there is a precedent alienation, they are not the lands of his debtor, and the feudal charge is only laid on the lands of his debtor; and if such lands were not his debtor's lands, they are not subject to that charge; and a *liberate* in pursuance to a preceding judgment, amounts to an alienation of the land itself, before it became charged to the King."

" Note also, the lien upon lands by the subject's debt came in by the statute West. 2.; for before that, the judgment did not bind the lands; but the King's debt bound the land before that statute. But that statute does not touch the King's prerogative, and therefore the King has a power to levy upon the lands notwithstanding the preceding lien by judgment; and therefore the King may seize lands that are bound by a preceding judgment, whilst the lands are in the custody of the law on the elegit or extent, and before they are actually delivered out to the creditor by the *liberate,* as a satisfaction of his debt; but when they were actually delivered out to the creditor by the *liberate,* they then no longer belonged to the debtor; since the King's writ had delivered them over for satisfaction of a debt that was precedent to the King's: for the creditor did not take them under the burthen of the King's debt, because his lien was antecedent to the King's debt; and it were repugnant to construe him to take the land *sub onere* of the King's debt, when he took it in satisfaction of a debt precedent."

It will be observed that C. B. Gilbert does not notice the provisions of the statute 33 Hen. 8. c. 39. s. 74. which certainly render the above doctrine doubtful in cases where the Crown process is issued for debts not due on outlawries, &c.; but for debts originally due to the King, and where the subject's judgment has been obtained, and execution commenced before the Crown suit has commenced, or its process been awarded. This has been already considered (*a*).

(*a*) Ante, 289 to 292.

The

The extent prevails in favour of the Crown against a mere previous agreement with a third person, for the sale of the defendant's estate, though part of the purchase-money has been paid, because the conveyance not having been executed, the fee still remained in him (*a*).   It seems also to be a general rule, that an equitable mortgage by deposit of title deeds will not hold against an extent (*b*).   It will not at all events if such deposit be made by an accountant of the Crown in the hands of one who has an opportunity of knowing that the depositor is or may become a debtor of the Crown (*c*).

Debts and Credits.

The sheriff is also to seize debts and credits due to the defendant, and specialties his property, which leads us to the 6th Section.

SECT. VI.

*Of seizing the Debts, Specialties, and Credits of the Crown Debtor,
and herein of Extents in Chief, in the second degree,* i. e. *against
Debtors to the Crown Debtor.*

UNDER the extent, it is the duty of the jury to inquire respecting the debts due from third persons to the Crown debtor, and his credits and specialties.   The jury should in their inquisition find, and state, any special matter respecting such property, and such finding vests the debtor's rights and interests in the Crown; and though the seizure be nominal, the King is thereupon entitled to adopt measures against the defendant's debtors.   And though extents in aid are properly limited in this respect, it seems, that the Crown may proceed against the debtors to those against whom the extent is issued, for its benefit, *in infinitum,* that is, to the remotest degree (*d*).

It seems, that debts due to the defendant are bound as goods are from the fiat or teste of the extent, and not merely

---

(*a*) Rex *v.* Snow, 1 Price, R. 220,
note (*b*).

(*b*) Rex *v.* Benson, Ibid. note (*c*).

(*c*) Ibid. 216.

(*d*) Hardr. 404. Com. Dig. tit. Dette,
G. 15. Gilb. Hist. Excheq. 178.

from the caption of the inquisition under which they are found. This at least has been decided in a case where the defendant had become a bankrupt, and the debt had been assigned by the commissioners to the assignees, between the teste of the writ and caption of the inquisition (*a*). It has been subsequently held, that inquisitions are bad which merely state that the debt was due to the Crown debtor, on the teste of the writ, omitting " *necnon die captionis inquisitionis* (*b*)." Mr. West observes (*c*), that the distinction to be collected from these two cases seems to be this : " That payment of a debt to the Crown debtor, after the issuing of the extent, and before the caption of the inquisition, will discharge a party paying without notice of the Crown process ; and, therefore, it is necessary that the inquisition should state that the party was indebted at both periods. But a mere *assignment* of the debt to the assignees of a bankrupt between the teste of the extent and caption of the inquisition, will not discharge the debtor as against the Crown." It is, however, apprehended, that if the debt is in one case bound from the fiat or teste of the writ, it would be in the other, and that the extent would over-reach even a *bonâ fide* payment, after the teste and before the caption, as it does *bonâ fide* alienations and sales of goods during that period. At least the contrary does not seem to be proved by the decisions, that the inquisition must state that the debt is due on the day of the finding. That statement may be necessary, in order to shew, that the debt is not destroyed by the operation of other circumstances than payment, and it is easy to conceive that there may be other events transpiring after the teste, which would destroy the debt, even as against the Crown. It should seem, that though the defendant has been paid the money, yet as that payment would, if the general effect here attached to the former decision be correct, be effectless, at least as against the Crown, the inquisition might correctly state, that the money was still due. No substantial legal reason can be assigned why debts should not be bound from the teste of the writ, as well as goods. In either case hardships may occur. And if the Crown can be bound by a subsequent payment of the debts, it seems

(*a*) 7 Vin. Ab. 104.   1 Atk. 262.   163 and 329.
Bingham, 216. West, 327.   (*c*) West, 164.
(*b*) Bunb. 265. 2 Price, 396. West,

difficult

difficult to prove why it should not equally be bound by an actual assignment of it, under a commission of bankrupt; for the Crown, as already observed, is in general bound by an actual assignment under a commission of bankrupt, if such assignment be executed before the teste of the writ.

It is clear at the present day, that debts due to the Crown debtor on simple contract, may be seized under the extent (*a*); and the general rule seems to be, that any debt or credit due to the Crown debtor, for which the latter might maintain debt, covenant or *indebitatus assumpsit*, and which would support proceedings at the suit of the Crown against its immediate debtor if due from him, may be seized under the inquisition; as sums due on, and which lay in, account (*b*): and a liability, *in futuro*, on a bond, bill, or note, &c. then in existence, may be found on the inquisition (*c*); but process cannot, in general, be issued thereon, till the instrument be due (*d*). Nor can it issue at all, unless the debt be found and seized on the inquisition, upon the first extent (*e*). If the debtor to the Crown debtor have accepted a bill for the debt, drawn by the latter in favor of a third person, or payable to the Crown debtor, and which he has indorsed over; or have drawn a bill on a third person, for the debt in favor of the crown debtor, which has been accepted by the drawee, and such bills are not due at the time of the inquisition, the debt cannot be found under it (*f*). On the same principle, that which the defendant could not alien, cannot be taken on the extent; as an annuity created in favour of the defendant, but subject to be suspended, in case of any act done to change or alien (*g*).

Under an extent against one, the whole of the debts due to that one and another may be seized, but the other creditor seems to have a remedy, by proceedings in equity against the Crown for an account (*h*). The form of the extent shews that under an extent against several, the debts due to any one may

---

(*a*) Lane, 23.　4 Rep. 95.　See Plowd. Com. 441, as to taking rents in arrear: 2 B. and Ald. 258.

(*b*) Ante, s. 1.

(*c*) Hughes, 106, 118, 19.

(*d*) See ante, sect. 1. and post. part 2. s. 5. Pleadings, as to the best mode of finding a liability on bills and notes. See West, 165.

(*e*) Bingham, 216, note (*r*).

(*f*) 1 Wightw. 32.　Rex *v.* Cust, Hughes, 186.　Rex *v.* Heath, Hughes, 155. See further post. pt. 2. s. 5. Extents in Aid and Pleadings thereto.

(*g*) 1 Wightw. 386.　2 Manning, Pr. 548.

(*h*) See MSS. cases cited, West, Ext. 170.　See 1 Wightw. 50, 52.

be

be seized. So if one of the obligees in a bond be outlawed, the duty being intire is vested in the Crown, and the King cannot have a partner with him (a). But in favor of commerce, under an extent against one of several partners, only the interest and share of that one can be taken (b).

Under the extent against the Crown debtor, the debts due to him are merely found by the inquisition, which amounts to a seizure in law. The sheriff cannot compel payment; that is effected by a *scire facias* or immediate extent, which are issued in the same manner and subject to the same rules, as are applicable in the case of an extent against the immediate Crown debtor.

When the debts due to the Crown debtor are seized, that is, are found under the inquisition taken on the extent against the Crown debtor, they become debts to the Crown; and, if due (c), the same process may issue against the person owing them, as against the original debtor to the Crown, and the debtor to the King's debtor stands in the same situation.

The ordinary mode of proceeding also for debts due to the King's debtor, is by " *scire facias* (d) ;" and where the debts are small, the Court may order a receiver to collect them, and pay them to the Deputy Remembrancer (e). But if, on an extent against the King's debtor, the inquisition find that *B.* is indebted to him, on return of the inquisition *and affidavit made*, that the money in *B.*'s hands is in danger, an immediate extent shall issue against B. (f); even though there be reason to suppose that the King's debtor became so with intent to strip the rest of *B.*'s creditors.

So if it be found by inquisition against a Receiver-General, that he has paid money over to *A.*, an immediate extent may issue against *A.*, for this is the King's money (g).

It is held, that upon affidavit of debt and a Baron's fiat, an immediate extent may issue against the debtors to the Crown debtor, before the extent under which they are found to be debtors to the Crown debtor, is returnable (h); though it must

(a) Ibid. Bro. Joint Ten. 34, 39. Oblig. 50; Forfeiture, 16. Plowd. 243, 259, 323.
(b) Wightw. 50. ante, ch. 11. s. 3.
(c) Ante, 305.
(d) As to which see ante, sect. 2.

(e) Bunb. 293.
(f) Ibid. 24. 3 Price, 299.
(g) Bunb. 123.
(h) Rex v. Pearson, 3 Price, 299. West, 242.

be actually returned (*a*) before the second extent can issue. As soon as this debt due from the debtor to the Crown debtor, is recorded by the return of the inquisition under which it is found, the proceedings for the recovery of such debt are substantially the same as for the recovery of the debt to the Crown from its original debtor.

SECT. VII.

Venditioni exponas.—*Order for Sale of Defendant's Lands, &c.*

If in pursuance of the rule which will be mentioned in the ensuing chapter, and in which the mode of resisting extents, will be considered, no one appear and defend, a *venditioni exponas* issues; and under it all the defendant's goods, against which alone it is directed, may be sold, though their value far exceed the amount of the debt; unless the writ be indorsed to sell the amount of the debt only, as it sometimes is (*b*). No motion need be made to the Court to authorize the issuing of the writ, but the defendant is entitled to notice of the intended sale (*c*). The sheriff is to sell for the best price he can, and at least for that price at which the goods were appraised, and to have the proceeds of the sale before the Barons to be paid to them to the use of the Crown (*d*). If the sheriff cannot sell the goods for the appraised price, he should return that fact; and then a *venditioni exponas* issues for him to sell *pro optimo pretio*, without reference to the appraisement. The sheriff must make a return of the whole sum produced by the sale, when the Court will order it to be paid over, deducting poundage; and he must move the Court for any *extra* allowance to which he may be entitled (*e*).

The sale of lands seized under an extent at the suit of the Crown, is, at the present day, regulated by the statute 25 Geo. 3. c. 35. which abolished the common law proceeding by a *levari facias*, concerning which much is to be found in the old

---

(*a*) Rex *v.* Pearson, 3 Price, 299. West, 242.

(*b*) West, 219, 220. 2 Manning, Pr. 553, 4. As to sale on extents *in aid*, see post, pt. 2. s. 5.

(*c*) Ibid. 2 Price's R. 155.

(*d*) See Brown, page 486.

(*e*) Price's R. 205. West, 220.

books,

books, and under which only the rents and growing profits of the lands were levied, and the prolix and inconvenient remedies given by the statute of Eliz. (*a*). The 25 Geo. 3. enacts, that it shall and may be lawful to and for his Majesty's Court of Exchequer, and the same Court is thereby authorized, on the application of his Majesty's attorney-general, in a summary way, by motion to the same Court, to order that the right, title, estate and interest of any debtor to his Majesty, his heirs and successors; and the right, title, estate and interest of the heirs and assigns of such debtor, in any lands, tenements or hereditaments which have been or shall hereafter be extended under and by virtue of any such writ of extent or *diem clausit extremum* as aforesaid, or so much thereof as shall be sufficient to satisfy the debt for which the same shall have been so extended, shall be sold in such manner as the said Court shall direct; and that when a purchaser or purchasers shall be found, the conveyance of the lands, tenements or hereditaments so decreed to be sold, shall be made to the purchaser or purchasers, by his Majesty's Remembrancer, in the said Court of Exchequer, or his deputy, under the direction of the said Court, by a deed of bargain and sale, to be inrolled in the same Court; and that from and after the making of such conveyance, and the inrolment thereof as aforesaid, the bargainee or bargainees in such conveyance, and his or their heirs, executors, administrators and assigns, shall have, hold and enjoy the lands, tenements and hereditaments therein comprised, for his and their own respective use and benefit, not only against the extent of the Crown, but also against such debtor of the Crown, or the surety or sureties for such debtor, and all persons claiming under such debtor, or the surety or sureties, unless by a title paramount to, and available in law against such extent as aforesaid: and all monies which shall become payable from any such purchaser or purchasers as aforesaid, shall be paid, accounted for and applied towards discharge of the debt due to the Crown, and of all *costs* and *expenses* which shall be incurred by the Crown in enforcing the payment of such debt, in such manner as the said Court of Exchequer shall from time to time order and appoint; and if, after payment of the whole debt to the Crown, and of all costs and

(*a*) See 13 Eliz. c. 4. s. 2.   27 Eliz. c. 3. s. 2.   39 Eliz. c. 7.

expenses

expenses incurred in enforcing the payment thereof, there shall be any *surplus* of the monies arising from any such sale, the said surplus shall belong to the same person or persons as would be entitled to the lands, tenements or hereditaments sold, if there had not been a sale thereof, and shall accordingly be paid to such person or persons, under the order and direction of the said Court of Exchequer, upon motion or petition to the said Court, to be made upon such notice to the Crown, and to be supported by such affidavits or other proofs, as to the said Court shall from time to time seem just and reasonable." And by the 2d sect. the Court of Exchequer is enabled to order the production of title deeds.

By virtue of this statute the express leave of the Court must be obtained before the defendant's lands can be sold, and the Court seems to possess a species of legal discretion in granting this leave. The lands are to be sold " in such manner" as the Court shall direct, and the Court will not make an order for the sale, if goods sufficient to pay the debt have been seized under the extent (a).

It is observable also, that the party's lands are to be sold only to the amount of the debt.

As before observed an equity of redemption may be taken under the extent (b), but the Court will protect the interests of the mortgagee. The mortgagor's interest alone should be disposed of, and the mortgagee is entitled to notice of the motion, on an order to sell it (c). If the whole estate be sold and the proceeds of the sale paid into Court, the Crown will not be allowed on motion to satisfy the mortgagee, but the Court will order a reference to the deputy remembrancer to ascertain what is due on the mortgage (d). So in the case of a claim of dower (e): or where it is necessary and just that the exact sum due to the Crown for principal and interest, &c. should be ascertained (f).

(a) 3 Price, 40.   S. C. in West, 177. 225.

(b) Ante, sect. 5, Lands.

(c) 1 Price, 207. 2 Price, 67.

(d) Ibid.

(e) Ibid. 71.

(f) Ibid,

SECT. VIII.

Costs.

With respect to costs, the general rule is, as observed by Sir Wm. Blackstone (a), that " the King (and any person suing to his use (b)), shall neither pay nor receive costs; for, besides that he is not included under the general words of the statutes relative to costs, as it is his prerogative not to pay them to a subject, so it is beneath his dignity to receive them." It seems that the statute 43 Geo. 3. c. 46. s. 5. which enacts, " that in every action in which the plaintiff shall be entitled to levy under an execution against the goods of any defendant, such plaintiff may also levy the poundage fees and expenses of the execution, over and above the sum recovered by the judgment," does not extend to the Crown. For none of the many statutes respecting costs and poundage have ever been held to extend to the Crown, where it has not been specially named; and this statute has no words which would embrace the Crown more than the several statutes anterior to this: and besides, the extent is not an action, but an execution (c).

Some exceptions to the general common law rule, that the Crown is not entitled to costs, have however been justly introduced by the legislature; and it would be but reasonable that the Crown should in all cases be entitled to its expenses, which sometimes exceed the amount of the debt.

1. The statute of extents, 33 Hen. 8. c. 39. s. 54. enacts, that " the King in all suits hereafter to be taken in or upon any *obligation* or *specialties* made or thereafter to be made *to the King*, or any *to his use*, shall have and recover his just debts, *costs* and *damages*, as other common persons use to do in suits and pursuits for their debts."

This statute does not it will be perceived relate to simple contract debtors; even when their debts are rendered records by the inquisition on the commission to find debts: but is con-

(a) 3 Bla. Com. 400. 1 Anstr. 50.   (b) Stat. 24 Hen. 8. c. 8.
7 T. R. 367. Costs on *Quo Warranto.*   (c) See 7 T. R. 367. West, 238.
9 Ann. c. 20. s. 5. 1 Burr. 402, 407, 8.

fined

fined to debts by bond or other specialty *originally* made to the King or to any one to his use (*a*).

2. In all cases where lands are sold by virtue of the 25 Geo. 3. c. 35. the monies produced by the sale are as we have just seen " to be applied towards discharge of the debt due to the Crown, and of all *costs and expenses* which shall be incurred by the Crown in enforcing the payment of such debt." It is frequently therefore important for the Crown that the defendant's lands should be seized and sold under the extent, and, as before observed, if the defendant apply to pay the debt into Court, he must pay costs too, if, under the circumstances, the Crown would on succeeding be entitled to sell the party's lands. But the Court will not compel him to pay costs into Court with the debt, if the goods seized, on the sale whereof no costs are in general allowable, be sufficient, though there be lands also; because it is a rule that the defendant's lands shall not be sold if the goods are sufficient, and the Court will not make an exception to this rule merely that the Crown may get its costs (*b*). It seems that the Crown may, by extending its debtor's lands only, secure its costs, though the defendant is amply supplied with goods.

On the sale of lands under an extent, the sheriff is not entitled to poundage (*c*), and therefore it cannot constitute an item of costs payable by the defendant to the Crown.

3. By the statute 43 Geo. 3. c. 99. s. 41. collectors of taxes are in certain cases liable to costs in proceedings at the suit of the Crown.

A Crown solicitor's bill of costs may be taxed (*d*), by the deputy remembrancer (*e*). If costs are levied when not due, the Court will on motion order them to be refunded (*f*).

(*a*) 1 Price, 434. But when the Court grant any indulgence, they sometimes make it a condition that costs shall be paid. Hardr. 136.

(*b*) Ante, 309.

(*c*) Post, 312, 314.
(*d*) West, 230.
(*e*) 3 Price, 280.
(*f*) 1 Price, P. 448.

SECT.

SECT. IX.

Poundage.

AT common law, poundage was not due on an extent. But it is enacted, by the 3 Geo. 1. c. 15. s. 3. that " All sheriffs who shall levy any debts, duties, or sums of money, whatsoever, except post fines, due or thereafter to become due to the King's Majesty, his heirs or successors, by process to them directed, upon the summons of the pipe or green wax, or by *levari facias*, out of the Court of Exchequer, shall from time to time, for their care, pains, and charges, and for their encouragement therein, have an allowance upon their accounts, of *twelve-pence* out of every *twenty shillings*, for any sum not exceeding one *hundred pounds*, so by them levied or collected; and the sum of *sixpence* only for every twenty shillings, *over* and above the *first one hundred pounds;* and for all debts, duties, and sums of money, except post fines, due or to become due to his Majesty, his heirs and successors, by process on *fieri facias* and extent, issuing out of any of the offices of the Court of Exchequer, the sum of one shilling and sixpence out of every twenty shillings, for any sum not exceeding one hundred pounds, so by them levied or collected; and the sum of twelve pence only for every twenty shillings over and above the first one hundred pounds. Provided always, such sheriff shall duly answer the same upon this account, by the general sealing day of such Term, in which he ought to be dismissed the Court, or in such time to which he shall have a day granted, to finish his said accounts, by warrant signed by the Lord Chief Baron, or one of the Barons of the coif of the said Court for the time being, and not otherwise."

And by section 13, " For preventing of oppressions and injuries, which may happen to his Majesty's subjects, by the abuse of sheriffs, bailiffs, and others, employed in levying and collecting any debts, duties, or sums of money, due or thereafter to become due to his Majesty, his heirs or successors, by process of the Court of Exchequer;" it is enacted, that " No sheriff, under-sheriff, bailiff, or other person, employed in levying or collecting any of the said debts, duties, or sums of money, shall take, ask, or receive any fee, gratuity, or reward, whatso-

ever,

ever, of the person or persons liable to pay the said debts, duties, or sums of money, or of any other person, for or upon pretence of such levying or collecting, except the sum of four pence only for an acquittance of such sum as shall be so levied or collected; which acquittance such officer is thereby required to give and deliver to the person upon or from whom such debt shall be levied, collected, or received; and the bailiff, or other person, receiving such debt or sum of money, shall, from time to time, answer and account for the same to the sheriff or his deputy, and may require an acquittance also from such sheriff or his deputy, for such sum, who are hereby required to give the same without any fee or reward; and of and from such debts or sums of money so levied, collected, or received as aforesaid, the said sheriffs, and every of them, shall effectually discharge the said debtors and persons respectively, by telling and answering the same to his Majesty, his heirs and successors, upon their respective accounts, in the Exchequer.   And in case any sheriff, under-sheriff, or deputy-sheriff, shall nichil, or not duly answer to the Crown any debt or sum of money so levied, collected, or received, such sheriff, under-sheriff, or deputy-sheriff, for every such offence, shall forfeit treble damages to the party aggrieved, and double the sum so nichilled, or not duly answered as aforesaid; which said damages and penalty shall be ordered, decreed, and given to the person aggrieved, by the Court of Exchequer, upon complaint and proof of such abuse as aforesaid, made and exhibited before the Barons of the said Court, in such short and summary way and method as to them shall seem meet; and in case any sheriff, under-sheriff, deputy-sheriff, bailiff, or other person, shall presume to demand, take, or receive any sum or sums of money whatsoever, be the same more or less, of any person whatsoever, from whom any debt or sum of money is or shall be due and payable to the Crown, by process out of the Court of Exchequer, for or in respect, or upon pretence, of executing the said process, or for or in respect, or upon pretence, of fees due to them, or any of them, for collecting or receiving the same, contrary to the true intent and meaning of this Act; or if any of the officers, or persons aforesaid, shall demand, take, and receive, any sum or sums of money whatsoever, for not levying, or forbearing to levy, any debts, duties, or sums of money, due to his Majesty, his heirs and successors, and written out to

them,

them, or any of them, by the process aforesaid; in all and every
such case, every person so offending, and being thereof lawfully convicted, shall be adjudged, deemed, and taken to be guilty
of extortion, injustice, and oppression; and all and every such
person and persons, being thereof lawfully convicted, shall
forfeit, for every such offence, treble damages and costs to the
party aggrieved, and double the sum so extorted. All which
damages and penalties shall be ordered, decreed, and given, by
the Barons of the Court of Exchequer, upon complaint and
proof of such extortion, made and exhibited before them, in
such short and summary way and method as to them shall seem
meet as aforesaid; provided such conviction be had and made
within two years after such offence committed, and not otherwise."

Provided, by section 14, "that nothing in this Act contained
shall be construed to deprive any sheriff of such poundage or
allowance as is allowed and given to them by virtue of this
Act; or of such poundage, allowance or reward, as may hereafter be made, allowed and given to them, or any of them, by
warrant or order from the Lord High Treasurer or Commissioners of the Treasury, Chancellor of the Exchequer or
Barons of the Court of Exchequer for the time being, for or
in respect of any *extraordinary service* to the Crown that may
happen to be performed by them, or any of them; but that
the said sheriffs shall and may enjoy the full benefit and advantage of such poundage, allowance and reward, without any
impeachment or molestation whatsoever; any thing in this Act
contained to the contrary thereof in anywise notwithstanding."

It will be observed that under this statute, which relates to a
seizure under an extent in aid, as well as on an extent in
chief (*a*), the poundage is claimable from, or falls on, the
Crown or other prosecutor of the extent, and not the defendant, because the nett debt merely is to be levied; and as the
poundage is not to be levied in addition thereto, it is payable
out of the sum levied. If however the debt be secured by a
penalty, poundage may be levied in addition to the debt, so
that the levy do not exceed the penalty (*b*): and wherever the
Crown is entitled to levy its costs and charges, as mentioned
in the preceding section, and is bound by the statute 3 Geo. I.

(*a*) Parker, 180.   (*b*) 2 Anstr. 369.

to allow the sheriff poundage; in such case poundage may be levied by the Crown as an item of such costs and charges (*a*). The statute 3 Geo. 1. does not however relate to the sale of land under an order of the Court, in pursuance of the 25 Geo. 3. and consequently the sheriff, not being entitled to poundage, the Crown cannot claim poundage as an item of its costs and charges, as against the defendant (*b*).

The poundage is claimable, though after the levy and before the *venditioni exponas*, the debt be paid to the prosecutor of the extent, or to the sheriff for him (*c*). But it seems from the wording of the statute, section 3, that though the whole debt be paid to the extent holder, the sheriff is entitled to poundage only on the amount *levied*.

With respect to the apportionment of poundage between different sheriffs, the 9th section of the statute (after reciting " that it frequently happens that the process issuing out of the Court of Exchequer, for levying debts and duties due to the Crown, may be in part executed by a sheriff before he be superseded, and afterwards in part by the subsequent sheriff: and that no provision had been made for settling and adjusting the distribution of the fees and poundage, claimed and demanded by them in such cases:) enacts, that when and so often as any sheriff shall, by process out of the Court of Exchequer, seize or extend any goods, chattles or personal estate, into the hands of his Majesty, his heirs or successors, for any debts or duties due to the Crown, and shall die or be superseded before a writ of *venditioni exponas* be awarded to him for sale of the same, or before such sheriff hath made actual sale thereof; and a writ shall afterwards be awarded to a subsequent sheriff, who by virtue thereof shall make sale or disposition of such goods, chattels and personal estate, so seized and extended by such preceding sheriff as aforesaid, in such case the Barons of the Court of Exchequer, if then sitting, and if not sitting the said Barons, or any one of them, being of the degree of the coif, shall order, settle and apportion the fees or poundage, due for such seizure and sale, between such preceding and subsequent sheriffs, in such manner and proportions as to him or them

(*a*) 3 Price, 280.
(*b*) West, 237.

(*c*) Parker, 180. 3 Anstr. 718, notes.
5 T. R. 470.

shall

shall seem meet, with regard to the expense and trouble each respective sheriff hath had, or shall have, in the execution of the said process."

Where two extents issue into different counties for the same debt, and both sheriffs seize goods, and the debt is paid to one of the sheriffs before a *venditioni exponas* to either, that sheriff to whom the money is paid shall have full poundage (*a*). But in such case where the debt is paid to the officers of the Crown immediately, the poundage shall be apportioned between the sheriffs (*b*).

Under the statute 3 Geo. 1. the sheriff may retain his poundage out of the sum levied under the extent, and need not wait for the allowance of it on his account (*c*). When, however, he makes his return to the *venditioni exponas*, it must be of the whole sum produced by the sale, when the Court will order it to be paid over, deducting poundage (*d*). And if the sheriff have paid over the money levied to the prosecutor of the extent, without having deducted poundage, he may obtain it by motion to the Court (*e*).

By statute 3 Geo. 1. c. 15. s. 14. as before observed, the Lord High Treasurer or Commissioners of the Treasury, Chancellor of the Exchequer or Barons, may give the sheriff any additional allowance or reward, in respect of any extraordinary service to the Crown. But the sheriff cannot deduct any extra expenses, but must apply to the Court on a rule *nisi*, for a reference to the deputy remembrancer for an allowance (*f*). And if poundage be improperly taken, the Court will on motion order it to be refunded.

(*a*) 1 Anstr. 279. 3 Anstr. 717. 1 Wightwick, 117.
(*b*) 3 Anstr. 718, note. West, 240, 1.
(*c*) Parker, 180.
(*d*) 1 Price, 205.
(*e*) Parker, 180.
(*f*) 1 Price, 206. 4 Ibid. 131.

PART II.—*Of Extents in aid.*

SECT. I.—*In general.*—*The Course of Proceeding.*

IT has been before observed, that extents in aid owe their origin to the statute of extents 33 Hen. 8. c. 39., and are grounded on the principle, that the King is entitled to the debts due to its debtor. The main distinction between extents in chief and extents in aid is this, that the former issue at the suit of the Crown, the latter at the suit and instance of the Crown debtor, against his debtor. The prerogative process is called an extent in aid when the subject, being indebted to the Crown, avails himself of such process against his debtors.

In this case the writ is founded on a fiction. The fiction of an extent issuing against the Crown debtor at the suit of the Crown. The Crown debtor himself privately and *pro formâ*, procures his debt, if by simple contract, to be put upon record by means of a commission, and the inquisition taken under it. If the debt to the Crown be by bond, this first step is of course unnecessary. The Crown debtor then sues out an extent against himself, omitting all the words which direct the sheriff to seize his body, goods, and lands, leaving the words merely which direct the sheriff to seize his debts, specialties, and sums of money. Under this extent the debts due to the Crown debtor are found and seized into the Crown's hands; and on such finding an extent issues as in the other case against the debtor to the Crown debtor (*a*). By the 57 Geo. 3. c. 117. s. 1. the produce of the extent is by order of the Court to be paid over to his Majesty's use; but it seems the Crown debtor may procure the consent of the Crown to the sheriff's paying it over to himself.

(*a*) West, 264. 2 Manning, 568. Extents in aid may also be issued by the Crown debtor on an adverse extent, at the suit of the Crown against himself. Ibid.

SECT. II.

To what degrees Debts may be seized on Extents in aid.

It seems from the older authorities that the King may, on process of extent prosecuted at his instance, and for his benefit, seize the debts due to his debtor, &c. *in infinitum,* i. e. to the remotest degree (*a*). It is not, however, so clear to what degree the Crown debtor may use the process by extent. According to the antient books, debts cannot in such case be seized beyond the third degree, counting the Crown debtor as one of them (*b*); and consequently only the debtor of the debtor to the Crown debtor could in such case be reached. But in the King *v.* Lushington (*c*), the Court of Exchequer held, that the Crown debtor is not to be counted as one of the degrees, and therefore the process may be used even to the fourth degree, counting him, or to the third, omitting him. In that case Austen and Co. were the original Crown debtors, Boldero and Co. were indebted to Austen and Co., the Lushingtons to Boldero and Co., and Miss Dehany to the Lushingtons; and on an extent against the Lushingtons, which had issued after extents against Austen and Co. and Boldero and Co., the debt due from Miss Dehany to the Lushingtons had been seized; and the Court held that this debt had been properly seized, and that on the ground that the Crown debtor was not to be counted in reckoning the degrees.

SECT. III.

What Crown Debtor may issue an Extent in aid.

Before the statute 57 Geo. 3. c. 117., the doctrine of extents in aid for the benefit of the Crown debtor, had been carried to an almost unqualified length, and there were but few Crown debtors who were not entitled to convert to their own private

(*a*) Hardr. 405. Com. Dig. tit. Dette, G. 15.

(*b*) Lane, 111, 12. Parker, 16, 259.
(*c*) 1 Price, R. 95.

benefit

benefit, a species of execution which should be confined to the Crown. The unjust effect this frequently had on the funds of a debtor by affording an undue preference called loudly for a remedy, which was accordingly provided by the legislature.

By the above-mentioned statute, it is enacted, (Section 4.), " that from and after the passing thereof it shall not be lawful for any person or persons, companies or societies of persons, corporate or not corporate, who shall or may be indebted to his Majesty by simple contract only; nor for any such person or persons, companies or societies, who shall or may be indebted to his Majesty by bond for answering, accounting for, and paying any particular duty or duties, or sum or sums of money, which shall arise or become due and payable to his Majesty from such person or persons, companies or societies respectively, for and in respect, and in the course of his or their particular trades, manufactories, professions, businesses or callings; nor for any sub-distributor of stamps who shall have given bond to his Majesty; nor for any person who shall have given bond to his Majesty, either jointly or separately, as a surety only for some other debtor to his Majesty, until such surety shall have made proof of a demand having been made upon him on behalf of his Majesty, in consequence of the non-performance of the conditions of the bond by the principal, and then only to the amount of the said demand; to sue out and prosecute any extent or extents in aid, by reason or on account of any such debt or debts to his Majesty respectively, for the recovery of any debt or debts due to such person or persons, companies or societies, or to such sub-distributor of stamps or surety as aforesaid; and that all and every commissioner and commissioners to find debts, extent and extents in aid, and other proceedings which shall be so issued or instituted at the instance of or for such simple contract or bond debtor or debtors respectively, and all proceedings thereupon shall be null and void: Provided always, that nothing herein contained shall extend or be construed to extend to preclude or prevent any persons who shall or may become debtor or debtors to his Majesty by simple contract only, by the collection or receipt of any money arising from his Majesty's revenue for his Majesty's use, from applying for and suing out any commission or commissions, extent or extents in aid, in case one or more of such persons shall be bound to

his

his Majesty by bond or specialty of record in the said Court of Exchequer, for answering, securing, paying over or accounting for to his Majesty, the particular duties or sums of money which shall constitute the debt that may be so then due, from such person or persons to his Majesty (a); any thing hereinbefore contained to the contrary notwithstanding.

" Provided, nevertheless, and be it further enacted, that no extent in aid shall be issued on any bond given by any person or persons as a surety or sureties for the paying or accounting for any duties which may become due to his Majesty from any body or society, whether incorporated or otherwise, carrying on the business of insurance, against any risques either of fire or of any other kind whatever (b)."

SECT. IV.

For what Sum an Extent in aid may be issued.—Affidavit and Fiat.

THE 57 Geo. 3. c. 117. s. 1. after reciting that extents in aid have, in many cases, been issued for the levying and recovering of larger sums of money than were due to his Majesty, by the debtors on whose behalf such extents were issued, and that it was expedient to prevent such practice in future, enacts, " That upon the issuing of every extent in aid, on behalf of any debtor to his Majesty, after the passing of the Act, his Majesty's Court of Exchequer at Westminster, or the Chancellor of his Majesty's Exchequer, or Lord Chief Baron, or other Baron of the said Court, granting the fiat for the issuing of such extent in aid, shall cause the amount of the debt, or sum of money, due or claimed to be due to his Majesty, to be stated and specified in the said fiat; and that in all cases in which the debt or debts found due to the debtor of his Majesty, shall be equal to or exceed the debt stated and specified in the said fiat as afore-

---

(a) It should seem, that since this Act, the bond to the Crown must be forfeited before the extent in aid can be issued by the obligor. See 1 Price, 202.

(b) As to extents in aid of *sureties* in general. See 2 Manning, Pr. 565, &c. 1 Wightw. 1.

said,

said, the amount of the debt so stated and specified in the said fiat, shall be indorsed upon the writ, and the writ so indorsed shall be deemed to be, and be, the authority and direction to the sheriff or other officer who shall execute such writ, in making his levy and executing the same, as to the amount to be levied and taken under the said writ; and that in all cases in which the debt or debts found due to the debtor to his Majesty, shall be of less amount than the debt stated and specified in the said fiat as aforesaid, the amount of such debt or debts found due to such debtor to his Majesty, shall be indorsed upon the writ, and the writ so indorsed shall be deemed to be, and be, the authority and direction to the sheriff, or other officer, who shall execute the said writ, in making his levy and executing the same, as to the amount to be levied and taken under the said writ; and that the money levied, taken, recovered, or received, under or by virtue of every such extent in aid so prosecuted and issued, shall be, by order of the said Court, paid over to and for his Majesty's use, towards satisfaction of the debt so due to his Majesty as aforesaid."

There is some difference between the affidavit for an extent in aid, and the affidavit for the extent against the original debtor to the Crown, which we have already considered (a). In the affidavit for an extent against the original debtor to the Crown, it is necessary to swear to the fact of the debt being due, as the affidavit is the only evidence of that fact; no evidence of the debt being laid before the jury, on finding the commission, according to the present practice, but the affidavit. But on the taking of the inquisition under the first extent, on which the debt due to the Crown debtor is found, evidence of that debt is always laid before the jury; and, therefore, all that is necessary to swear in the affidavit for the extent in chief in the second degree is, that the defendant was found indebted under the inquisition, (which is, in fact, merely identifying the defendant with the party found to be indebted under the inquisition,) and that he is insolvent. As to the allegation of insolvency, the observations made on that part of the affidavit for the extent in the first degree, will of course apply here, and to every affidavit for an extent (b).

The affidavit which is necessary to obtain an extent in aid

(a) Ante, 277.   (b) West, 245.

states—1st, The debt due to the Crown from the Crown
debtor, who is the prosecutor of the extent in aid. 2dly, It
states the debt due to the Crown debtor from his debtor, who
is the defendant under the extent in aid. 3rdly, That such
debt is in danger of being lost from the insolvency of the defendant. 4thly, That the debt due to him is a debt originally
and *bonâ fide* due to him without trust. 5thly, That it has not
been put in suit in any other Court. And, 6thly, That the
Crown debtor is thereby less able to pay the debt due to the
Crown. If the debt be by bond, it sets out the penal part of
the bond; and, as has been before mentioned, usually proceeds
to state, that the obligor has received money, for which the
party is accountable by the condition of the bond (*a*).

1. The necessity of the allegation of the debt due to the
Crown, from the prosecutor of the extent, which allegation is
not required in the affidavit for an extent, in the second or other
degree, for the benefit of the Crown, is apparent, from this consideration, that on the latter extent there has been already an
affidavit of the debt due to the Crown, in order to obtain the
first extent; but on the extent in aid, for the benefit of the
Crown debtor, there is no affidavit or proof of the debt
to the Crown, till the affidavit is made for the extent in aid.

2 & 3. With respect to the allegation of the debt from the
defendant to the Crown debtor, and the danger of its being
lost, the observations which have been before made on those
points, as to the extent in chief, will apply to this affidavit for
an extent in aid (*b*).

4 & 5. The allegations that the debt due to the Crown
debtor is a just debt, *originally* and *bonâ fide* due and without
trust, and that it has not been put in suit in any other Court,
are rendered necessary by the rules of the 15 Car. I. by one of
which it is ordered, " that no debts be assigned to the King,
nor found by inquisition for the King's debtors or accomptants
in aid, save such as are originally due to them *bonâ fide*, without any manner of trust, and according to the directions and
instructions hereafter following, viz. he who desireth any debt
or debts to be found by the inquisition in his aid, shall
take this oath: the said *B.* maketh oath the day and year above
written, that he is justly indebted unto *A.* one of the farmers of

(*a*) West, 275, 6.   2 Manning, 575.   (*b*) Ante, 277.

his

his Majesty's customs, &c. and that the same debt is a just and true debt, originally due to the said *A.*, *bonâ fide* without any manner of trust, and that the said debt hath not been put in suit in any other Court, and that he hath not received the same nor any part thereof, except so much, &c.; and that *C.* is justly indebted to him the said *B.*, originally and *bonâ fide* without trust; and that *C.* is much decayed in his estate, so that unless a speedy course be taken against the said *C.*, the said debt by him owing is in great danger to be lost."

And though these rules have been said by the Court in some instances to be obsolete, yet that observation must be confined to such of these rules as do not appear to have been acted upon; but where the practice shews that they have been adhered to, in those points they are still considered as binding. And as far as respects the allegations at present under consideration, all the affidavits for extents in aid, prove that these rules have been adhered to, and these allegations considered necessary ingredients on the affidavit (*a*).

With respect to the allegation in the affidavit, that the debt to the Crown debtor is due " originally and *bonâ fide* and without trust," it is said to have been decided in the case of the King *v.* Mainwaring (*b*), that this express allegation is not indispensable; but it seems that this decision is only applicable to cases in which it is evident that the debt could not be a trust debt, or not originally due to the prosecutor of the extent, and is not applicable to cases where the debt might been a trust debt, and not originally due to the prosecutor of the extent (*c*). It has been the uniform practice to insert this allegation in the affidavit, and the practice of inserting the other allegation, viz. that the debt had not been put in suit, was, in the case of the King *v.* Boyes (*d*), considered to be decisive of the necessity of such allegation. And it seems perfectly clear that an extent in aid cannot be maintained for a debt which is not originally *bonâ fide* due to the prosecutor of the extent, but which has been assigned to him for the purpose of enabling him to use the Crown process for the recovery of it (*e*).

(*a*) West, 278.
(*b*) 1 Price's R. 202.
(*c*) West, 278.
(*d*) See Ibid. 282.
(*e*) Bunb. 225. West, 280, 1. Noy,

154. 1 Anstr. 190. But a debt due to the prosecutor *jure uxoris* is sufficient. 2 Cro. 524. Breadman *v.* Coles, Hob. 253. Parker, 271, 2.

With

With respect to the allegation in the affidavit that the debt has not been put in suit, it may be observed, that it is doubtful on the rule of Court whether that allegation applies to the debt which is sought to be recovered by the extent in aid. However, it has always been usual in affidavits for extents in aid, to state that the debt for which the extent in aid issues, has not been put in suit; and the practice is the best interpreter of the rule. And accordingly in two different cases lately, the Court of Exchequer has held, that if a debt has before been sued for either, by proceeding in equity, or by attachment in the Lord Mayor's Court, an extent in aid should not issue for it (*a*).

6. As to the allegation, that the prosecutor of the extent is less able to satisfy his Majesty, it is apprehended that the omission of this allegation would not be material. For the words themselves seem to have no more meaning than that which must necessarily follow from the facts stated in the affidavit, viz. that the prosecutor of the extent is indebted to the Crown, and the defendant to the prosecutor of the extent (*b*).

In order to procure the fiat for the extent in aid, for the benefit of the subject, the course of proceeding at present in practice, is this (*c*): a commission and inquisition in the case of a simple contract debt to the Crown are engrossed; the statement of the debt to the Crown from the prosecutors being taken in each of these proceedings from the affidavit; an extent *pro formâ* against the Crown debtor, and inquisition thereon, are also engrossed, the statement of which is likewise taken from the affidavit; the commission and inquisition thereon, the extent *pro formâ* and the inquisition thereon, are then laid before the jury, together with the affidavit; and on that affidavit, which is the only evidence, they find the inquisitions as before engrossed. The commission and inquisition thereon, and the extent *pro formâ*, and the inquisition thereon, with the affidavit, are then taken to a Baron of the Court or the Chancellor of the Exchequer; and he indorses his initials

(*a*) 2 Price, 379. West, 282, &c. But may abandon *scire facias* and proceed by immediate extent if insolvency, 3 Price, 288.

(*b*) See Phillips *v.* Shaw, 8 Ves. Jun. 241.

(*c*) West, 288.

on the commission, which, as before-mentioned, is the warrant for its issuing, and signs his fiat for the extent in aid at the foot of the affidavit, at the same time.

If the Crown debtor be a debtor by bond, then of course no commission issues; but the affidavit and extent *pro formâ*, and the inquisition thereon merely, are laid before the jury, on which affidavit, as the only evidence, the jury find the facts already stated in the inquisition. For the extent in aid for the Crown, there is usually but one fiat, namely that for the extent in aid, which is the second extent, it not being very usual to grant a fiat for the first extent, i. e. the extent *pro formâ*, though that is sometimes done.

It has been the practice of late for the Barons to grant fiats for extents in aid of bond debtors to the Crown, on the affidavit merely, without the production of the bond. The rule of Court 3 W. and M. by which " it was ordered that one of the Barons of the Court be attended with the bond, wherein the party is indebted to the King, before any extent do issue to find debts in aid, without specialty in the vacation time; and that no extents do issue in the term time to find any debts in aid without specialty, but by motion in open Court," being one of those rules which has been considered as obsolete. But some of the Barons have lately signified that the bond should be produced (*a*).

No motion in Court is now necessary in term time, in order to procure an extent in aid for any debts, whether by simple contract or otherwise, though the 5th of the rules 15 Car. and the rule 3 W. and M. formerly required a motion in Court for an extent in aid, for a simple contract debt (*b*).

SECT. V.

Form of. — What may be taken. — Motions. — Pleading. — Costs. — Poundage, &c.

THE *form* of an extent in aid is the same as that against the Crown debtor, with the exception of the recital of the debt.

Under an extent in aid, the sheriff is to *take* the body, goods,

(*a*) West, 290.   (*b*) Ibid. 291.   2 Price, 15.

lands,

lands, debts, credits, specialties, and sums of money, of the defendant, in the same manner as under an extent against the Crown's first debtor; the goods, debts, &c. of the debtor of the Crown debtor, being bound in the same manner as the goods, debts, &c. of the Crown debtor, on the first extent; and all the observations before made in this particular, with respect to the first extent in chief, will apply to the extent in the second degree. But with respect to the lands of the Crown debtor's debtor, which the sheriff is directed to seize, under the extent in chief in the second degree, they, of course, are bound merely from the recording of the debt from the Crown's debtor's debtor to the Crown debtor under the inquisition; unless, indeed, the debt due to the Crown debtor be by judgment or recognizance, in which cases the Crown of course takes the lien of the plaintiff in the judgment, or conusee in the recognizance, on the land of the defendant or the conusor, which they had at the time of the judgment entered, or recognizance acknowledged. But by 57 Geo. 3. c. 117. s. 1. before cited, the officer is to seize only to the amount of the debt due to the Crown debtor. The defendant's body may be taken under an extent in aid; but the 57 Geo. 3. c. 117. s. 6. affords such defendant relief, by enabling him to apply to the Court of Exchequer for his discharge, on giving a month's notice to his creditor, and making a true disclosure of his property, and the Court has a discretion to discharge him *quoad* such his imprisonment.

Besides the *motions* which may be made against an extent for the benefit of the Crown, and which will be considered in the next chapter, the defendant on an extent in aid may, it seems, move to set it aside, on the ground that no debt was due to the Crown from the alleged Crown debtor. It may also be moved, to set it aside the extent in aid, on the ground of the insufficiency of the affidavit on which it is founded, or that the party fraudulently procured himself to become a debtor to the Crown, for the purpose of using the Crown process (*a*), or that the prosecutor of the extent in aid sued it in breach of good faith, &c. (*b*).

The Court will not (*c*), in exercise of its equitable jurisdiction over extents, grant a writ of *amoveas manus*, to release property seized under an extent in aid against a debtor in a more

(*a*) West, 295, 6.   (*c*) 1 Price, R. 96.
(*b*) West, 297.

remote

remote degree, on the ground that the debt which had been found on the original commission to be due to the King's debtor has been subsequently satisfied, by the payment of bills of exchange deposited with him for the securing that debt; if it appear that those bills were not the *bonâ fide* property of the person depositing them, who thereby committed a breach of trust; because the Court will consider, that the real proprietors of the bills have a paramount claim on the person with whom they had been so deposited, if he has been satisfied his debt by other means.

It is provided by the 57 Geo. 3. c. 117. s. 2. that if on an extent in aid on behalf of the Crown debtor, there be levied and produced more than the sum due to the Crown debtor, the overplus shall be paid into the Court of Exchequer, with the principal sum indorsed on the writ, and the Court may, on summary application, make such order for the return, disposal, or distribution, of any such surplus, or any part thereof, as shall appear proper.

In *pleading* to an extent in aid (*a*), it is apprehended that the defendant may plead any matter which would be a good defence, as against his creditor, *i. e.* the Crown debtor, and which would shew, that on the day on which the inquisition was taken no debt was due to the latter from him. As that the debt due to the Crown debtor is, in respect of bonds, bills, or notes, not yet arrived at maturity (*b*); or that the defendant on the extent in aid, gave the Crown debtor a bill for the debt which became due after the day on which the inquisition was taken, though it has been subsequently taken up by the Crown debtor (*c*). So, in the King *v.* Copland (*d*), it was held, that on an extent in aid, the defendant might plead a set-off of sums due from the Crown debtor to himself. And the Chief Baron there said, " as to the set-off, it is true, you cannot set-off as against the Crown; but qu. if this is so. It is a mistake in terms so to call it. He (*i. e.* the Crown debtor) is to collect his own debt, and that is the balance. It is a debt due between subject and subject." It would seem (*e*), both upon principle and

(*a*) As to pleadings and subsequent proceedings on extents in general, see next chapter.

(*b*) Bebb's Case, by Hughes. **Ante,** 305.

(*c*) 1 Wightw. 32.

(*d*) Appendix to Hughes's Case of Bebb, page 204.

(*c*) West, 249.

7   upon

upon the authority of this case, that the statute of limitations or bankruptcy, &c. might be pleaded as against a debt due to the Crown debtor, seized under an extent. The defendant, too, sometimes traverses the debt alleged to be due from the Crown debtor to the Crown.

The technical rules as to pleadings and other proceedings in the case of the Crown will be fully considered in the next chapter. With respect to *costs* and *poundage*, &c. the observations before made as they relate to the extent in chief, may be here referred to (*a*).

Equity does not in general afford any remedy to the defendant on an extent in aid against the prosecutor of the extent on the ground that he has sufficient assets to pay the Crown without resorting to the writ, &c. (*b*). And as between debtors to the Crown in different degrees no one of them has an equitable claim to be relieved from any part of the debt which must consequently fall on some of the others (*c*). But if the King's debt be levied on his debtors' tenants, of course, the rents are satisfied by such levy, and the matter may be specially shewn in an avowry (*d*).

There is a peculiar or special writ of *extendi facias* which is issued in the event of the *death* of the Crown debtor, and is called a *diem clausit extremum ;* as it recites the death of the party.

By the writ of *diem clausit extremum*, the sheriff is commanded to inquire, by means of a jury, when and where the Crown debtor died; and what goods and chattels, debts, credits, specialties, and sums of money, and what lands (*e*), the said debtor had at the time of his death, &c. and to take and seize them into the King's hands, &c. (*f*). It will be observed that the form of the writ is in substance like that of the extent in ordinary cases; and the *diem clausit extremum* and the ordinary extent are governed in general by the same rules (*g*).

It seems that the *diem clausit extremum* is founded on the

(*a*) Ante, 310 and 312.

(*b*) 8 Ves. Jun. 241.

(*c*) 1 Price's Rep. 96.

(*d*) 16 Vin. Ab. 520. tit. Prerogative, I.

(*e*) As to the sale of them, see ante, 307.

(*f*) West, on Extents. Appendix, 129. See as to the old writ of *diem. cl. extr.* Staundf. Prær. Regis, 51. c. 17.

(*g*) 2 Manning, Pr. 519. 3 Price, 295. If not issued within a year after the death. Ibid. F. N. B. 233, C. Staundf. *ubi supra.*

common

common law prerogative right of the Crown to priority (a). However that may be, it is provided by *Magna Charta*, c. 18. that "if any one holding of us lay-fee, die, and our sheriff or bailiff do shew our letters patent of our summons for a debt which the dead man did owe to us; it shall be lawful to our sheriff or bailiff to attach and inventory all the goods and chattels of the dead, being found in the lay-fee, to the value of the same debt, by the view of lawful men; yet so that nothing thereof shall be taken away, until there be paid unto us the debt clearly made to appear; and the residue shall be left to the executors to perform the testament of the dead; and if nothing be owing unto us by him, all the chattels shall go to the use of the dead, saving to his wife and his children their reasonable parts."

Upon this statute the *diem clausit extremum* may be issued (without waiting for an executor or administrator (b)) against the deceased debtor's estate, in every case in which an extent might have issued against him if he were alive (c). But in order to support the writ the deceased must have *died indebted* to the King (d); and before the writ issues such debt must be of record (e): but it is sufficient if, having died indebted to the King by simple contract, the debt due from the deceased be found by inquisition after his death (f). In order however to maintain this writ against the property of a deceased debtor of the Crown debtor, it is necessary, on the wording of *Magna Charta*, that the debt from the deceased be found by inquisition in his life-time (g).

An executor in administering the assets must first discharge the King's debt (h); nor can he retain even for his own bond debt against the Crown's simple contract debt (i). But a payment by an executor or administrator of a bond debt is good against a Crown debt not of record, of which the personal

---

(a) Vin. Ab. Prerogative, H.
(b) 16 East, 281.
(c) Bunb. 119.
(d) Parker, 100.
(e) Ibid. 98.
(f) Ibid. 95, 100.
(g) Ibid. 16. 2 Price, 380. S. P. Exchequer, A. D. 1816; Rex v. Sidle:

Hanson, Chancery Lane, Attorney.
(h) 2 Inst. 32. 1 Chalmers' Coll. of Opinions, 28. By 9 H. 3. c. 18. the King's debtors dying, the King shall be served before the executor.
(i) Attorney-General v. Barnett, Hil. 1681, in Sccio: Bingham on Execution, 219, note (c).

repre-

representative was not aware (*a*). And it seems funeral charges, expenses of probate, or taking out letters of administration, shall be first defrayed (*b*).

The remedy by *ouster le main* if the *diem clausit extremum* be unfounded will be considered in the next chapter (*c*).

<hr>

SECT. III.

Scire Facias, to repeal Grants, &c.

THE *scire facias* to *repeal*, or revoke, unfounded or improvident grants of the Crown (*d*), is another prerogative process which requires consideration. The King is, generally speaking, bound by his grants; but this is only when they are not contrary to law either in themselves; or void for uncertainty or deception; or unjust as injurious to the rights and interests of third persons (*e*). In these cases the King *jure regio*, for the advancement of justice and right, may repeal his own grant (*f*). As if the King grant what by law he is restrained from granting (*g*): or the grant be obtained by fraud or a false suggestion (*h*): or be uncertain (*i*). So if an officer be guilty of acts which create a forfeiture of his office (*k*).

(*a*) 3 Price, R. 122. 1 Rol. Ab. 926. S. pl. 1. Per Choke, if the King's debt, in such case, be not of record, then it cannot be pleaded in bar; *aliter*, if it is. 21 E. 4. fol. 21. pl. 2. 1 Anderson, 129. But see Moor, 193. A judgment recovered against the testator, shall be preferred by the executor to a bond assigned to the King after testator's death. Lane, 65, *aliter*, if the judgment had been recovered against the executor. Attorney-General *v.* Hart, Trin. 1686, in Sccio. MSS. Bingham on Execution, 212, note. Where, after the death of *B*, a bond entered into by him to *A*, the Crown creditor is seized under an extent against the obligee, the executor of *B*. may pay a judgment creditor of his testator in preference to the Crown debt; the latter not being of record before testator's death, Anon. 2 Rol. Ab. 159. And see Parker, 260.

(*b*) 1 Rol. Ab. 926, S. pl. 1.

(*c*) Post, 348.

(*d*) Ante, 250, as to *scire facias* on inquests of office in general: and ante, 271, as to *scire facias* on extents.

(*e*) See post, ch. 16. s. 1 and 3.

(*f*) 4 Inst. 88.

(*g*) Ibid. 3 Bla. Com. 260. Though if the patent be void in itself, *non concessit* may it seems be pleaded without a *scire facias*. 2 Rol. Ab. 191, S. pl. 2.

(*h*) Ibid. Bro. Patent, 14; Petition, 11. 11 Rep. 74, b. 2 Rol. Ab. 191, T. Dyer, 197.

(*i*) 5 Bac. Ab. Prerogative, 602.

(*k*) Dyer, 197, b; 198, a; 210, 211. Ante, 85. as to forfeitures of offices.

If

If a Crown grant prejudice and affect the rights of third persons, the King is by law bound on proper petition to him, to allow a subject to use his royal name, to repeal it in a *scire facias* (a). And it is said that in such case the party prejudiced may, upon the inrolment of the grant in Chancery, have a *scire facias* to repeal it, as well as the King (b); as in the instance of an unfounded patent for an invention, or where the specification is incorrect (c). So in the case of a grant of a mart or fair, &c. whereby another antient mart or fair is prejudiced (d). Where the same thing is granted twice the first patentee is entitled to a *scire facias* to repeal the subsequent grant(e): but the second patentee is not, though his right be superior (f).

The *scire facias* may be prosecuted in the Petty Bag Office in Chancery, for the patent is a record there (g). So it may be in the King's Bench (h). A memorial is presented to the Crown for a *scire facias*, whereupon his Majesty's warrant is obtained to the attorney-general to sue it, and the attorney-general grants his fiat thereon (i).

On the *scire facias* the defendant is summoned to appear, which affords him an opportunity of so doing, and of pleading any defence he may have, or of demurring (k) if the matter alleged be insufficient to repeal the grant; on which proceedings are taken, as in ordinary instances of that description, at the suit of the Crown (l). If no defence be set up, the judgment (which, if it be for the King, is that the letters patent and the inrolment be revoked, vacated, &c.) may be either by confession or by default, if the defendant be returned warned, or upon two *nihils* (m). No costs are payable to the Crown or prosecutor on a *scire facias* to repeal letters patent (n).

(a) Bro. Ab. tit. Scire Facias, 69, 185. 2 Ventr. 344. 3 Bla. C. 260, 1.

(b) 6 Mod. 229. 2 Saund. 72. q.

(c) See ante, 193. as to patents.

(d) Dyer, 276, b. 3 Lev. 220. 2 Ventr. 344.

(e) 4 Inst. 88. Dyer, 137, b. 198, a. 2 Rol. Ab. 191, U. pl. 2.

(f) Dyer, 276, b. 277, a. 2 Saund. 72, p.

(g) Ibid. 4 Inst. 88. 3 Lev. 223.

(h) 4 Inst. 72. As to the form, &c. 2 Saund. 72, q. Tidd's Appendix.

(i) 2 Rich. Prac. C. P. 391, and 398. Hands on Patents.

(k) 3 Lev. 221.

(l) See post, ch. 13.

(m) Dyer, 197, b. 198, a. 2 Rol Ab. 192, X. pl. 1.

(n) 7 Term Rep. 367. Ante, 310; as to costs in general at the suit of the Crown.

SECT.

SECT. IV.

Information.

ANOTHER prerogative process is by *information*, filed in the Exchequer, at the instance of the King's attorney-general. This is wholly different from the criminal proceeding by information in the King's Bench, in which the object is the punishment of some public offence. The prerogative remedy here treated of, is in the nature of a civil action at the suit of the Crown, and is instituted for the purpose of obtaining satisfaction in damages for some injury to Crown possessions, or to recover money due to, or goods claimed by, the King. The information is not founded on any writ, but merely on the intimation of the attorney-general; upon which the party is put to answer, and trial is had as in ordinary cases (*a*).

Informations are, generally speaking, of three descriptions. 1. Informations of *intrusion.* 2. Of *debt.* 3. *In rem.*

An information of *intrusion* is in the nature of an action of trespass, *quare clausum fregit* (*b*), and is usually brought against the tortfeasor, or if dead, his executor (*c*), for trespass committed on the lands of the King (*d*); as by entering thereon without title, holding over after a Crown lease is determined, taking the profits, cutting down timber, and the like (*e*).

The information of intrusion into land states (*f*), that the attorney-general gives the Court to " understand and be informed" that certain land (the particular species or quality of which need not be described (*g*)), ought to be in the hands and possession of the King, in right of his Crown of England, &c. Nevertheless the defendant contriving the disinherison of his Majesty with force and arms to in and upon his possession, entered, intruded and made ingress, and with cattle depastured, &c. Wherefore the said atttorney-general of our said lord the King (who for our said lord the King in this behalf prosecuted), for our said lord the King, prays the con-

(*a*) 3 Bla. Com. 261.
(*b*) Sav. 48.
(*c*) Sav. 40.
(*d*) Cro. Jac. 212. 1 Leon. 48.

(*e*) 3 Bla. Com. 261.
(*f*) See Co. Entr. 372, b. F. N. B. 90, I. Plowd. Com. 547.
(*g*) Sav. 48.

sideration

sideration of the Court here in the premises, and that due process of law (that is a writ to the sheriff upon which defendant may appear and defend (*a*)) may be awarded against the defendant in his behalf, to make him answer to our said Lord the King, touching the premises aforesaid."

The King may lay his venue in what county he pleases; and may try a question as to lands lying in any county, in the Court of Exchequer (*b*).

At common law, the Crown has the prerogative right on an information of intrusion, of putting the defendant on shewing his title specially, and the defendant could not rely merely on his possession (*c*), which in ordinary cases is sufficient title for a defendant (*f*). If not guilty (*e*), or *non intrusit* (*d*) generally, be pleaded, (and the defendant cannot plead double (*g*),) nothing but the mere fact of an intrusion having been committed is put in issue, and the defendant in possession would be immediately evicted from it; for a title for the King appears upon the information, if no title appear upon record for the defendant (*h*). This has, however, been remedied by the statute 21 Jac. 1. c. 14. in certain cases. By that statute, whensoever the King, and such from or under whom the King claimeth, and all others claiming under the same title under which the King claimeth, shall have been out of possession by the space of twenty years, or shall not have taken the profits of any lands, tenements, or hereditaments, within the space of twenty years, before any information of intrusion brought, or to be brought, to recover the same, that in every such case the defendant may plead the general issue, if he so think fit, and shall not be pressed to plead specially; and that in such cases the defendant shall retain the possession he had at the time of such information exhibited, until the title be tried, found, or adjudged for the King.

(*a*) In 6 Com. Dig. 65, tit. Prerog. D. 73, it is laid down that the process upon an information shall be a *venire distringas*, afterwards a writ out of Chancery directed to the treasurer and barons. 4 Inst. 110.

(*b*) 1 Ventr. 17. Sav. 10. Com. Dig. Prerog. D. 85. 2 Price, 113.

(*c*) Dyer, 238, b. 4 Inst. 166. How this is on a traverse of office, post, ch. 13. s. 3. div. 3.

(*d*) See 1 East, 244.

(*e*) Sav. 66.

(*f*) Sav. 4.

(*g*) Parker, R. 1, 16.

(*h*) 4 Inst. 116.

" And

" And be it further enacted, That where an information of intrusion may fitly and aptly be brought on the King's behalf, that no *scire facias* shall be brought, whereunto the subject shall be forced to a special pleading, and be deprived of the grace intended by this Act."

It is, in general, sufficient for the defendant to shew a mere legal title to possession only; and it will suffice if he shew a right to possession concurrently with the King, as where the defendant pleaded that she had a jointure of a third, without answering to the residue (*a*). The defendant must, of course, plead a sufficient *legal* title (*b*); otherwise, the Attorney-General may demur: though it is said, that if instead of so doing, he take issue on a fact stated in the plea, which is found against the King, the defect cannot afterwards be taken advantage of (*c*).

The King may traverse all the different facts stated in the defendant's plea (*d*); and if the plea allege a title, which avoids the possession in the King supposed by the information, the King need not, at least where he is entitled by matter of record, maintain the information, but may traverse the title alleged by the plea (*e*).

The Crown has the privilege of waiving his count, and declaring *de novo*, even after plea or demurrer; but only, it seems, during the Term in which the original declaration was made (*f*), though the King may amend at any time, paying costs (*g*).

The judgment for the King in an information for intrusion is, that the defendant be amoved from the possession; and for damages, in case damages be found, for any particular trespasses committed by the defendant, as cutting trees, &c. (*h*).

After

(*a*) Mo. 370, 376.　5 Bac. Ab. 567, Prerogative, E. 7.

(*b*) Sav. 34, 48.　Dyer, 238.

(*c*) Dyer, 238, b.

(*d*) Sav. 19.

(*e*) Ibid. 61.　Vaugh. 64.　16 Vin. 538.　6 Com. Dig. 74.　See post, ch. 13. s. 3. div. 3. Traverse of office; Pleadings on Extents.

(*f*) Bro. Ab. Prerog. pl. 13, 15; Variance, pl. 79.　Vin. Ab. Prerog. 25. Vaugh. 62, &c.

(*g*) Ibid. Vin. Ab.　10 Mod. 200.　3 Anstr. 714.

(*h*) Sav. 35, 49.　In Hardr. 460, 462, it is also said " that the judgment shall be *quod capiatur pro fine*, and thereupon there shall be an injunction for the possession;

After judgment in an information for intrusion, execution shall be sometimes by injunction, or it may be by *amoveas manum ;* and, thereupon every party to the information, or claiming under him, shall be removed from the possession. But a stranger to the information shall not be debarred of his entry, for no judgment of seisin is given, nor does an *habere facias seisinam* go (*a*).

2. The *Information* of *debt* is in effect and substance the King's action of debt, and is usually brought in the case of forfeitures to the Crown, upon the breach of a penal statute, enacted for the support of the revenue (*b*). For monies due to the Crown on contract, process of extent is the usual remedy.

Where the King is entitled to any part of a penalty, for which a *qui tam* action is brought, the defendant cannot obtain leave to compound till the consent of the law officers of the Crown be given, in whatever stage of the cause the application to compound is made (*c*). It appears, that by a standing privy seal, the Commissioners of the Treasury, High Treasurer, Chancellor, Under-Treasurer, Chief Baron, Barons of the Coif, and Attorney-General, were respectively empowered to give licence to compound (*d*). And the Court, in the exercise of their discretion to grant leave to compound, will refuse the indulgences in cases of collusive attempts to defraud the Crown (*e*). Where leave is given to compound a penal action, the moiety of the Crown is to be paid into the hands of the Master (*f*), and this is usually done before the rule is drawn up (*g*).

3. The *Information in rem* is, where any goods are supposed to become the property of the Crown, as derelict, and no man appears to claim them, or to dispute the title of the King; or where goods are forfeited for non-payment of customs, &c. (*h*).

possession ; for the King is supposed in possession." And see 6 Com. Dig. 67. tit. Prerogative, D. (D.) 77.

　(*a*) Sav. 35. Hardr. 450, 462.

　(*b*) 3 Bla. Com. 261.

　(*c*) 1 Taunt. 102. 2 Ibid. 213. 5 Ibid. 268.

　(*d*) Gilb. Excheq. 137. See further

on this subject, Ibid.

　(*e*) 2 Bla. R. 1157.

　(*f*) 4 Burr. 1929.

　(*g*) 1 Manning, P. E. 229. When Crown shall have half the costs the plaintiff agreed to take. 2 Taunt. 215.

　(*h*) 3 Bla. Com. 262. Gilb. Excheq. 180.

The

The 13th chapter of Chief Baron Gilbert's " Treatise on the Court of Exchequer," contains so able and so ample an explanation of this subject, that no apology need be offered for referring the reader to it for information (a).

SECT. V.

Quo Warranto.

THE writ of *quo warranto* is an antient and high prerogative remedy, in the nature of a writ of right for the King, against him who usurps or claims (b) any franchises or liberties (c), to say by what authority he claims them (d). It is also sustainable where any new jurisdiction or a public (e) trust is executed without authority; though it is no usurpation on a franchise of the Crown (f). Nor is it material that the franchise is of such a nature that it cannot be seized into the King's hands or held by him, though judgment be given for his Majesty, because the defendant may

(a) And see Parker's Rep. 57, 69, 196, 7. The Court of Admiralty, like the Exchequer, proceeds *in rem:* and the Crown may be bound by a judicial sale therein. See 3 Price, 37.

(b) There must be an *user* as well as a claim of a franchise. 5 T. R. 85. 4 East, 337.

(c) As waifs and estrays. Co. Entr. 528, 541, 544. Goods and chattels of felons, and deodands, Ibid. 529, 549. Fines, amerciaments, and issues, Ibid. 551, b. 561, a. A park, warren, &c. Ibid. 561. Wreck, 2 Rol. Ab. 205, l. 35. For taking lastage or ballotage of ships, 1 Sid. 86. So it lies for franchises, which cannot be seized into the King's hands; for the party may be ousted of them; as for a Court Baron, *Quo Warranto.* 14 Treby's argument. Yel. 190. A Court Leet, or Borough Court. Co. Entr. 527, b. 544. A fair, market, toll, &c. Co. Entr. 527, b. 544, 561, a. Information in the nature

of *quo warranto* lies against any one claiming an exclusive ferry over a public river, but not for taking money of passengers. Stra. 1161. So it lies for claiming to be a corporation. Co. Entr. 537, b. To choose bailiffs or other officers, Ibid. 527, b. 537, b. Coroner, constable, clerk of a market, justice, &c. Ibid. 528, a. 537, b. 551, b. For exercising the office of steward of a Court Leet, but not of a Court Baron. Stra. 621. It lies for the office of constable, Ibid. 1213. So it lies upon a claim of exemptions; as to be exempt from the government of the mayor, justices, &c. Co. Entr. 528, a. Proceedings against the City of London, in the time of Charles 2. See 2 Burnett's Hist. 925. ed. 1725. 2 Selw. N. P. tit. *Quo War.* 2 W. and M. sess. 1. c. 8.

(d) 2 Inst. 282. 9 Co. 28, a. Yelv. 191. Com. Dig. tit. *Quo War.* A.

(e) See 6 Com. Dig. tit. *Quo War.* B.

(f) Stra. 299, 836. Ld. Raym. 1559.

still

still be ousted (*a*). It also lies in the case of a forfeiture of an office by abuser, &c. (*b*).

In case of judgment for the defendant, he shall (*c*) have an allowance of his franchise; but in case of judgment for the King, for that the party is entitled to no such franchise, or hath disused or abused it, the franchise is either seized into the King's hands, to be granted out again to whomsoever he shall please; or if it be not such a franchise as may subsist in the hands of the Crown, there is merely judgment of ouster, to turn out the party who usurped it (*d*). There is also judgment of *capiatur pro fine*, though the fine is nominal.

This writ which must be brought before the King's Justices at Westminster (*e*), has now fallen into disuse, principally on account of the length and complicated nature of the process (*f*), and the circumstance of the judgment on the writ being final and conclusive, even against the Crown (*g*). In its place has been substituted *the information in the nature of a writ of quo warranto*, which is filed in the King's Bench by the attorney-general (*h*); and lies also in the Exchequer (*i*); and wherein the proceedings are more speedy and less conclusive (*k*). The Court, however, will not extend this remedy beyond the limits prescribed to the old writ; and as that could only be prosecuted for an usurpation on the rights or prerogatives of the Crown, so an information in the nature of *quo warranto*, can only be granted in such cases (*l*); and upon this principle, the Court refused to grant an information to try the validity of an election to the office of church-warden. The *quo warranto*

(*a*) Ante, 335, note (*i*).

(*b*) 2 Inst. 486. 3 Bla. Com. 262. Ibid. 263.

(*c*) 3 Bla. Com. 263.

(*d*) Cro. Jac. 259. 1 Show. 280. Co. Entr. 530, 539, a. Rast. Entr. 540, b. 3 Bla. Com. 263.

(*e*) 3 Bla. Com. 263. Com. Dig. *Quo Warranto*, A.

(*f*) See Com. Dig. tit. *Quo Warranto*, C. 2. The proper course in the Exchequer seems to be, to issue a writ to the sheriff, directing him generally to inquire into usurpations of franchises ; upon which the sheriff takes an inqui-

sition, finding the particular usurpation intended to be drawn in question. The defendant traverses or demurs to the inquisition, and proceeds as in other cases. 2 Manning, Pr. 510. Defendant cannot plead not guilty, or *non usurpavit*, but must justify or disclaim, 12 Mod. R. 225. 10 Ibid. 296.

(*g*) 1 Sid. 86. 2 Show. 47. 12 Mod. 225.

(*h*) See 3 Burr. 1812. 1 Bla. Rep. 579.

(*i*) 2 Manning's P. Exch. 509, 10.

(*k*) 3 Bla. Com. 263.

(*l*) 4 T. R. 381. Stra. 1196.

z   information

information is now considered merely in the nature of a civil
proceeding (*a*), and is the usual remedy in the case of corporation disputes between party and party, without the intervention of the prerogative, but by leave of the Court, in
pursuance of the statute (*b*), which permits an information in
nature of *quo warranto* to be brought with leave of the Court,
at the relation of any person desiring to prosecute the same
(who is then styled the relator) against any person usurping,
intruding into or unlawfully holding any franchise or office in
any city, borough or town corporate; provides for its speedy
determination, and directs that if the defendant be convicted,
judgment of ouster (as well as a fine) may be given against
him, and that the relator shall pay or receive costs, according
to the event of the suit (*c*).

SECT. VI.

Mandamus.

THE writ of *mandamus* (*d*) is another high prerogative
writ, issuing out of the Court of King's Bench, as the peculiar superintendent of inferior jurisdictions and authorities,
directed to any person, corporation or inferior Court of judicature, requiring them in the King's name, to do some particular
thing therein specified, which appertains to their office, situation or duty, and which is consistent with right and justice (*e*).
The object of the writ is not to supersede legal remedies, but
only to supply the defect of them. The only proper ground

(*a*) 2 T. R. 484.

(*b*) 9 Ann. c. 20. See 4 and 5 W.
3. c. 18. Selw. N. P. 3rd and 4th ed.
tit. *Quo Warranto.*

(*c*) This statute, with regard to costs,
extends only to cases where the title of
a person to be a corporate officer, as
mayor, bailiff, or freeman, is in question; but an information to try the

right of holding a court is not within it,
but stands upon the common law only,
and being a prosecution in the name of
the King, no costs are given. 1 Burr.
402.

(*d*) See the points on this subject ably
collected in Selw. N. P. tit. Mandamus.

(*e*) 3 Bla. Com. 110.

of

of the writ is a defect of justice. It is the absence or want of
a specific legal remedy, which gives the Court jurisdiction (*a*).
There must however be a specific legal right, as well as the
want of a specific legal remedy, in order to form an application
for a mandamus (*b*). The writ is grounded on the oath of the
party injured shewing his right, and the denial of justice below,
whereupon the party complained of is directed to shew why
the writ should not issue (*c*). This being substantially a civil
remedy for the subject, and the King's name being only nominally used, no further mention of it will be here made.

CHAP. XIII.

Of obtaining Redress from the Crown.

The principle or maxim, that the King can do no wrong has
been before explained (*d*). It does not mean that the subject is
without remedy for every act of the Crown. The King is not
indeed personally chargeable, nor can he be subjected to the
usual common law proceedings, which may be instituted
between subject and subject. For all judicial proceedings and
writs must be in the King's name as the fountain of justice:
and it would be absurd that the King should command or require another to command himself: independently of its being
contrary to the constitutional idea of the King, to imagine that
he is subject to the controul and command of any of his own
courts. Whatever therefore may have formerly been considered on this subject, there can be no doubt that at all events
since the reign of Edward 1. the Crown has been free from
any action at the suit of its subjects (*e*): and on this principle

---

(*a*) Per Ld. Ellenborough, 2 Selw.
N. P. tit. Mandamus, 1.
(*b*) 8 East, 219.
(*c*) See 3 Bla. Com. 112, 264.

(*d*) Ante, 5.
(*e*) 1 Bla. Com. 255. 4 Co. 55, a.
Com. Dig. Prerog. (D.) 78; Action,
(C.) 1. Staundf. Prerog. 42, a.

it is that no one can vouch for the King, for that is in the nature of an action; and that if a fine be levied by the King of lands, it should be by render and not by writ of covenant (*a*).

With respect to *personal* injuries, the inviolability of the sovereign, and the improbability that any injuries of that nature should be committed by the King, have combined to establish it as a clear maxim in law, that he cannot be guilty of them. The law will presume that the subject cannot have sustained any such personal wrong from the Crown, because it cannot afford any adequate remedy: and want of right and want of remedy are the same thing in law (*b*). With respect however to injuries to the rights of *property*, as such injuries may be, and generally are, committed through the medium of the King's agents, and by misinformation or inadvertence, the law has furnished the subject with a decent and respectful mode of removing the invasion by informing the King of the true state of the matter in dispute: and, as it presumes that to know of any injury and to redress it are inseparable in the royal breast, it then issues as of course in the King's own name, his orders to his judges to do justice to the party aggrieved (*c*).

The modes of proceeding against the Crown to recover lands or personal property are of three descriptions: 1. by *petition*: 2. by *monstrans de droit, manifestation,* or *plea of right*: 3. by *traverse* of *office.*

Sect. 1.—The *petition de droit,* or petition of right, is an antient common law remedy for the subject against the Crown and is said to owe its origin to Ed. 1. (*d*).

This mode of proceeding is peculiarly suited to the dignity of the sovereign; and being instituted for the purpose of pre-

(*a*) H. 9. H. 6, 3 and 4.

(*b*) See Bac. Ab. Actions, B. *Quod Remedio destituitur ipsa re valet si culpa adsit.* 6 Co. Rep. 68. If the King were to command a third person to commit an injury on a subject, of course such third person would be liable to an action, and could not plead the invalid command of the King. Bac. Ab. Prerogative, E. 1. Same principle as to lands. See post, 342.

(*c*) 3 Bla. Com. 255.

(*d*) Bro. Ab. tit. Prerog. 2. Fitz Ab. Error, 8. 3 Bla. Com. 256.

serving

serving entire the respect and submission due to the King, can be adopted only against him, and does not lie in the case of the Queen, or the Prince (*a*).   But where the King is concerned, and a petition is the proper remedy, it is immaterial whether his Majesty be seized of the property in question in his own or another person's right (*b*).

It will be material to consider, 1st, when a *petition* is the *proper remedy*, and 2ndly, the *mode of proceeding* upon it.

1. Antiently a petition was the necessary course of proceeding in numerous cases: but the delay and expense attending the proceeding induced the legislature to afford the subject a much more summary method of interpleading with the Crown.   This was effected by extending and rendering almost universal, the remedies by '*monstrans de droit*' and '*traverse of office*' which will be considered in the ensuing sections.   Whenever therefore either of such remedies can be adopted, that by petition, though it be sustainable (*c*), would not be adopted and is irrelevant (*d*).   In every case however in which the subject hath a right against the Crown, and yet no *monstrans de droit* or traverse of office lies, a petition is the birth-right of the subject, and is sustainable at common law (*e*), and this not only in the case of real property, but of chattels real or personal (*f*), or unliquidated damages (*g*).

In the case of inquisitions or offices finding that property belongs to the King (*h*), either the *monstrans de droit*, or *traverse* of office, may in almost every instance be adopted; and a petition would not be the better remedy.   And here we may notice the wise precaution of requiring that matter of record shall in general be necessary to pass property from the subject to the King; the consequence being that claimants are thereby in most instances let in at once to traverse such matter of record, without being driven to circuitous and expensive proceedings (*i*).

(*a*) 1 H. 4. f. 7. Staundf. Prerog. 75, b.

(*b*) Ibid. and 10 H. 7. fol. 4.

(*c*) Bro. Ab. Travers, D. Office, pl. 18.

(*d*) Staundf. Præ. 74, a.

(*e*) Ibid. Com. Dig. Prerog. D. 78.

(*f*) Staundf. Prærog. 72, b.

(*g*) Year Book, 22 Ed. 3, 5.

(*h*) Ante, 246.

(*i*) See 2 Manning, Pr. 579.

" To

" To declare specially," says Staundford (*a*), "where a petition lieth and where not, it were a long matter to intreat of. But generally and by general rules, a man may briefly declare it; that is to say, in all cases where the party hath a right against the King, and yet no *traverse* or *monstrans de droit* will serve, there he is driven to his petition : as for an example, where the King is entitled by double matter of record (*b*). Like law it is, where the King is entitled by a record not traversable, as take the case: the King recovered by assent and without title, a stranger that hath good title shall not falsify his recovery by a traverse or *monstrans de droit*, but is driven to his petition. So it is where the King recovereth by erroneous process, the party shall not have a writ of error (*c*) until he have sued by petition for it. So likewise it is if lands are holden of me by knight's service, a stranger brings a *præcipe in capite* of those lands against my tenant and recovereth by default, although by this recovery I am not put out of possession of my seignory, but that the tenant holdeth of me as he did before, and also of the King by collusion; yet in this case if the recoverer die, his heir within age, and the King seizeth the ward, I am driven now to my petition for the ward, for this is another thing than ever I was seized of. Also it is a general rule, that where a stranger that hath title cannot enter upon a common person, but is driven to his action, there he can have no remedy against the King, but only a petition. As take the case to be : it is found by office the King's tenant in chief died seized, his heir within age, where indeed the said tenant had nothing but by disseisin done to me, and I suffered him to die seized without any claim made; in this case I get no remedy by *monstrans de droit* or *traverse*, but am driven to my petition. And so in all cases like where mine entry should be tolled if the lands were in the hands of a common person. Also where the King doth enter upon me, having no title by matter of record or otherwise, and put me out and detain the possession from me, that I cannot have it again by entry without suit, I have then no remedy but only by petition. But if I be

in the case in 12 East, 96.

(*b*) See now 2 and 3 Ed. 6. c. 8. s. 7. Post, 352.

(*c*) Post, s. 3. div. 7 ; as to a writ of error against the King.

suffered

suffered to enter, mine entry is lawful, and no intrusion; or if
the King grant over the lands to a stranger, then is my petition
determined, and I may now enter or have my assize by order
of the common law, against the said stranger, being the King's
patentee (*a*).   And a great difference is between this case and
the case where the King is entitled by double matter of record (*b*)
or such like; for in these (*qu.* 'latter') cases, notwithstanding the
grant made over by his Highness of the lands to another, yet
am I driven still to my petition to the King, and have no other
remedy: but it is not so in this case (that is, when the King
having no right, has granted away the property).   And the
reason of this diversity is, because that when his Highness
seizeth by his absolute power, contrary to the order of his
laws, although I have no remedy against him for it but by
petition, for the dignity's sake of his person; yet, when the
cause is removed, and a common person hath the possession,
then is my assize (*c*) renewed; for now the patentee entered
by his own wrong and intrusion, and not by any title that the
King giveth him, for the King had never title or possession
to give in that case, and therefore not like the other cases before, where the King hath the lands by the order of his laws:
that is to say, by double matter of record, or such other like.
Like law it is if I have a rent charge out of certain land, and
the tenant of the land enfeoffeth the King by deed inrolled;
now during the King's possession, I must sue by petition, but
if his Highness enfeoff a stranger, I may distrain for my rent
on the stranger; and so it is in all the cases before, where a
man may have his *traverse* or *monstrans de droit*, if the lands
be once *out of the King's hands, the party then may have*
his remedy that the common law giveth him: for in all these
cases the petition did lie only for the dignity of the King's
person, and not for the right that his Majesty had to the possession of the thing.   But if the King purchaseth lands holden
of me, learn what remedy I may have for my seignory during
the King's possession; for Wilby saith (*d*) that I have no remedy in that case, and if his Highness make a feoffment of
these lands to hold of himself, yet I cannot distrain for my

(*a*) 4 Ed. 4. f. 22.   24 Ed. 3. f. 65.
10 Ed. 3. f. 2.   See ante, 339, note (*e*);
that a wrong-doer cannot justify under
the King's unfounded claim or com-

mand.
(*b*) See ante, 341, note (*b*).
(*c*) Ejectment.
(*d*) Assize, 124; 20 Ed. 3.

seignory

seignory like as I might do in the case of the rent charge
before, because there cannot be two seignories of the same
land, but am driven to my petition in this case; for the King
upon this feoffment, by order of his laws, should have renewed
the seignory in me: that is to say, to have made the feoffee to
hold of me of whom it was held before. And so it hath been
used always where his Highness hath lands by forfeiture of
treason (*a*), holden of a common person, if he make a feoffment
of those lands it must be to be holden of those that they were
holden of before. And so it is where the time is devolved to
his Highness for a mortmain; but that is given by the statute
de religiosis. Also if the King disseise my tenant during this
possession, I have no remedy for my seignory but only by petition: and if the King enfeoff my tenant to hold of his Highness, yet have I no remedy for my seignory (*b*) but only by
petition. But if one hold certain lands of me which are *falsely
found by office* to be holden of the King *in capite,* and the King
seizeth them, and enfeoffeth my tenant thereof to hold of his
Highness; in this case I may now distrain for my seignory
and am not out of possession. And the reason of the diversity
is this, because that in the last case my seignory was never
suspended, but evermore had its being, and that notwithstanding the office; for it did not appertain to me to traverse the
office and discharge the tenure: but that matter was left to my
tenant to do, and seeing he did not, he hath charged himself
of a tenure by way of *collusion* to the King as well as to me:
but it is not so in the other case. Also it is to be noted that
if the King seize lands by title of wardship and make a feoffment thereof, in this case the heir need not sue his petition,
but may have a *scire facias* to repeal the said letters patent,
because the King was deceived in his grant. For there the
King himself is in possession still till livery be made; so the
heir there hath no cause to sue by petition, and the King is
bound to deliver it unto him in whose right he seized."

A petition seems also to be the only remedy where the King
does not pay a debt, as an annuity or wages, &c. due from

(*a*) Where an estate is forfeited to
the King by attainder, &c. none can
sue to the King by petition before office
found, for till office-found the estate is
not vested in the King. Sir W. Jones, 78.

(*b*) That is as against the King only
in this case, *quære.* See ante, 342, and
note (*a*).

him

him (a), or in the case of unliquidated damages, occasioned by
any breach of contract with the King himself; or in case the
King, without any office, take or detain a subject's goods.   A
quare impedit against the King must also be by petition (b);
and it seems to be the only legal remedy on the reversal of an
outlawry, or an extent, &c. on error, where the monies have
been accounted for in the Exchequer, and have reached the
hands of the Crown, if the Court cannot interfere (c).

2dly. As to the *mode of proceeding.*—It is the very essence
of the 'petition' that it should contain nothing of a mandatory
nature.   The petition is, however, substantially, as well as nominally, a petition *of right,* as the prayer of it is grantable,
ex debito justitiæ; and *Magna Charta* says, " *nulli vendemus,*
nulli negabimus, aut differemus justitiam vel rectum (d)."
The petition must be carefully drawn up, and must state the
whole of the title or titles, or claim of the Crown, " for if it be
found by the writ of search, that any title of the King be omitted, the petition shall abate; and the reason of it is, because
that if on this suit of petition the King take an issue with the
party which is found against him, his highness then shall be
concluded for evermore to claim by any of the points contained in the said petition (e)."   And of course the plaintiff
or suppliant must state his own title at length.   Thus if a disseisor of lands, which are holden of the Crown, dies seized
without any heirs, whereby the King is *primâ facie* entitled to
the lands (f), and the possession is cast on him either by inquest of office, or by act of law without any office found; now
the disseisee shall have remedy by petition of right, suggest-
ing the title of the Crown, and his own superior right before
the disseisin made (g).
The petition may be to the King in Parliament, or in any

(a) Lord Somers, Arg. 11 St. Trial
81, 85.   Com. Dig. Prerog. D. 78.

(b) 43 Ass. 272. pl. 21.   H. 8. H. 4.
fol. 21.   2 Manning's Pr. 579.

(c) See Staundf. Prærog. Regis, 75,
b. 76, a.   Year Book, T. 34 H. 6. fol.
51.   2 Manning, Pr. 624. *sed vide* 1 H.
7. fol. 3.

(d) See 2 Manning, 578.   That

Magna Charta binds the Crown, see
Vin. Ab. Statutes, E.

(e) Per Settle, J.   Year Book, 9 Ed.
4. fol. 51.   Staundf. Prerog. 73. b.
Finch L. 256.   3 Bla. Com. 256.

(f) See however 12 East, 96.

(g) Bro. Abr. tit. Petition, 20. 4
Rep. 58.   Post, 352.

of the King's Courts of Record (*a*), and is usually in the treasurer's remembrancer's office (*b*).

When the petition is sued in parliament, "it may, says Staundford (*c*), be enacted, and pass as an Act of Parliament, or else to be ordered in like manner as a petition that is sued out of the parliament which is in this manner. First, after the petition is indorsed it shall be delivered to the Chancellor of England, and then shall there be a commission (*d*) awarded out of the Chancery, to find the right or title of him that sueth the petition; which being found by inquest then he may interplead with the King and not before. And if upon the commission no title be found for the party but only for the King, yet the petition shall not abate, but the party shall have a new commission in that case, for the petition is but as void until the party's title be found by office, and is not to be said depending until that time (*e*). And note that when the petition is indorsed the party must follow and pursue the same according to the indorsement, or otherwise his suit is void; because the indorsement is his warrant therein. And therefore some petitions be indorsed and sent into K. B. or C. P. and not into Chancery, and that groweth upon a special conclusion in his petition, and a special indorsement upon the same, for the general conclusion is " *que le roy ley face droit et reason*" which is as much as if he had prayed restitution of that that he sueth for: and there, upon such a general conclusion, the indorsement is " *soit droit fait al partie* (*f*)", which ever is delivered unto the Chancellor as is declared. But if the conclusion in the petition be special, and the indorsement special, then they shall proceed according to the said special indorsement; as for an example, the King recovereth in a *quare impedit*, by default against one that was never sum-

(*a*) Staundf. Prærog. Regis, 72, b. Com. Dig. Prerogative, D. 80.

(*b*) 2 Manning, Pr. 578, n. m. Ibid. Appendix, 253. Jones, IER, *Memoranda*, tit. Error.

(*c*) Prærog. Regis, ch 22. fol. 72, b. to 74, a. And see Bro. Ab. tit. Petition. Fitz. tit. Traverse. 11 St. Tr. 149. 5 Bac. Ab. 572. tit. Prerog. E. 7. Com. Dig. Prerog. D. 80.

(*d*) Rast. Entr. 461. The Commission is not necessary if the Attorney-General confess the suggestion, Skinner, R. 608. Where office is found to entitle the Crown, the party may sue a petition without any inquisition for him Com. Dig. *ubi supra.* Moore, 639.

(*e*) M. 3 H. 7. fol. 13.

(*f*) This is now the usual indorsement. Lord Somers, Arg. 11 St. Tr. 149.

moned.

moned.   In this case the party that lost cannot have a writ of deceit until such time as he have sued the King by petition for the said writ; and if in his petition he conclude and pray that the King do him right generally, now the justices upon whom the recovery was had, cannot examine the deceit without an original writ directed unto them for that purpose; and yet before he obtained that writ his right shall be inquired of by commission: but if he conclude specially in his petition, that is to say, please his Highness to command the justices to proceed to the examination; which petition is endorsed accordingly, then may they do it without any such writ or commission to be sued (*a*).   So ever the following and pursuing of the thing must be according to the indorsement; for however the conclusion in the petition be, the indorsement may be always as it shall please the King; and according to that the party must pursue it.   And note that in every petition where the King hath granted the land over to another, a *scire facias* must be awarded against the patentee, like as it shall be where a traverse or *monstrans de droit* is tendered, which patentee if he have not the whole fee simple, but that there is a reversion in the King, or that the King is bound to warrant when he appeareth upon the *scire facias*, he may have a writ of search (*b*) to be awarded into the treasury, to search what they can find for the King's title (*c*).   But query, if search shall be granted upon a *traverse* or *monstrans de droit*, because the statute of 14 E. 3. c. 13., that concerneth search, doth speak only but of a petition.   But to that it may be said, that at the time of making of the statute there was no traverse given (*d*).   And Skrene sayeth, that search shall not be granted

---

(*a*) M. 10 H. 4. fol. 4.

(*b*) See 2 and 3 Ed. 6. c. 8. s. 13. Where a petition disaffirms the King's possession, there ought to be four writs of search directed to the treasurer and chamberlain of the Exchequer; but writs of search are not necessary, where the petition affirms the King's possession : as, upon a petition of a right of dower. Moor, R. 639. Co. Lit. 77, b.   The writs of search issue upon the suggestion of the Attorney-General, that there are in the Treasury several records, charters, deeds, muniments, &c.

touching the King's right to the estate in question.   Rast. Entr. 462, a. Ld. Coke says, " Upon the petition there be four writs of search, and every one must have forty days before the serving." Co. Lit. 77, b.

(*c*) H. 9 Ed. 4. fol. 51.

(*d*) By the 2 and 3 Ed. 6. c. 8. s. 13. upon every traverse under that Act in lieu of the petition to which the party was put at common law, there shall be two writs of search instead of four, as on a petition. See Co. Lit. 77. b.

but

but when one sueth by petition. And note also, that in every petition whether it be sued in the parliament or elsewhere, or whether the lands remain in the King's hands, or not in the King's hands, but be granted over, yet writs of search shall be awarded to search the King's title ere the party shall interplead with the King. Also it appears (a), that upon a petition the King's patentee had aid of the King : it also appears that if the King be not entitled by any matter of record, but without any title do enter into my land whereby I sue by petition unto his Highness; that in this case no search shall be granted, because no title can be intended for the King in such case."

On the return of the inquisition, the Attorney-General may plead in bar or demur: and an issue of fact or law being joined, the merits may be discussed and determined by a jury (b), or the Court, as in ordinary cases between subject and subject.

If the subject recover lands, &c. the *judgment* follows as a matter of course; and the party need not sue to the King for the same (c). It is that " the hands of the Crown be removed, and possession restored to the petitioners :" whereby the King is immediately, by operation of law, out of possession (d). Indeed the *amoveas manus* or *ouster le main* is the end of every suit where a man comes to interplead with the King, for without that judgment the land will still remain in the King's possession (e). But in all judgments or decrees in equity against the King or respecting his rights and claims the clause " *salvo jure domini regis*" is always inserted, and is expressly required by the statute 2 and 3 E. 6. c. 8. s. 14. (f). But as the Admiralty Court proceeds *in rem*, the Crown is bound by a judicial sale of a vessel by order of that Court, though it had a prior title by forfeiture which was not discussed (g). If on the petition money be recovered, the writ of execution for the subject is directed to the treasurer and chamberlains (h). And it is said they are personally liable if

(a) 16 E. 4. f. 3. And see Rex v. Smith, Assig. Whiteball, Jones, IER, Addenda, tit. Excise, 2 Manning. Pr. 579, note s.

(b) As to the Venire, see post, 348, and sec. 3. div. 4.

(c) Staundf. Prerog. 82, b.

(d) 2 Inst. 695. Rast. Entr. 463. Finch, 459. 3 Bla. Com. 257.

(e) Keilw. 158, a. post, 349.

(f) Finch, L. 459, 460.

(g) 3 Price, R. 97.

(h) Vid. Reg. Brev. 193. Plowd. 382, 459. 2 Manning, Pr. 579.

they

they do not satisfy the suppliant's demand out of the first monies that come to their hands by virtue of their office (*a*).

The suppliant may be nonsuited though a verdict be pressed for (*b*). It has been said that this suit being as it were in the nature of a writ of right the subject cannot have a fresh petition if he be nonsuited (*c*); but the law seems otherwise on this point (*d*).

On the subject of the judgment of ' *ouster le main*,' ' *amoveas manus*,' or ' that the King's hands be amoved,' Staundford (*e*) has the following observations. " *Ouster le main* is the judgment that is given for him that tendereth a traverse, or sueth a *monstrans de droit*, or petition; for when it appeareth upon the matter discussed, that the King hath no right or title to the thing he seized, then judgment shall be given in the Chancery, that the King's hands be amoved : and thereupon *amoveas manum* shall be awarded to the escheator, which countervails as much as if the judgment were given that he should have his lands. And this judgment sometimes is given in the King's Bench, and not in the Chancery ; and that is in case where the parties descend to an issue, then for the trial thereof, they of the Chancery must award a *venire facias* returnable in the King's Bench at a certain day, at which day notwithstanding that the sheriff return not the writ yet the *alias venire facias* shall not be awarded out of the Chancery, but of the King's Bench : for there and no where else it is recorded *quod vicecomes non misit breve*. And when the issue is found for the party they of the King's Bench shall give judgment and award an *ouster le main* without suing for the same in the Chancery. Also note that sometimes there goeth an *ouster le main* as well to the King's patentee as to the escheator ; and that is where the King hath granted the thing that be seized to any other. But notwithstanding that there go such writs of *amoveas manum* both to the escheator and to the party ; yet the King is out of possession as soon as judgment is given in the Chancery; not

(*a*) Vid. Reg. Brev. 193. Plowd. 382, 459. 2 Manning, Pr. 579. F. N. B. 121.

(*b*) 11 Hen. 4. 52. pl. 30. Fitz. Petition, 2, 11, 17

(*c*) H. 11 Hen. 4. fol. 52. and M. 3 Hen. 7. fol. 14. Staundf. Prærog. Regis, 76, a. Semb. also a nonsuit on a

monstrans de droit is peremptory. 4 Hen. 6. 12. pl. 9.

(*d*) See 4 Hen. 6. 13. pl. 9. Bro. Ab. Nonsuit, 12. And see Fitz. Petition, 11, 16, 17. M. 17 H. 7. fol. 13. pl. 19. cited 2 Manning, 579. 1 Vez. 454, 5.

(*e*) Prærog. Regis, c. 24. fol. 77, b.

forcing

forcing whether any of these writs be awarded or not, either
to the escheator or to the party: and thereupon the party for
whom judgment is given may ouster forthwith into the lands
and shall be said no intruder (a). And the reason of it is because the judgment tieth not the King to the delivery of the
possession, but only to leave his hands of the possession. And
note, that if a *diem clausit* (b) come to the escheator, he by
virtue of that writ, before he make any inquiry, may seize the
land for the King's behoof; which after he hath once seized,
if after by office no title be found for the King, then the party
that ought to have again the land may sue for the same in
Chancery where the office is returned: and then *amoveas
manum* shall be awarded." "In times past (c), men have sued
ouster le main upon a seisin made for the King, although the
office found afterwards did not entitle his Highness. Howbeit
at this day it is not so used, for the escheator will not seize,
unless there be an office found, although he might lawfully
do it by the words of the writ *diem clausit,* which usage I do
nothing dislike considering the great trouble it avoideth, that
might else ensue to the King's subjects. And note, that in all
cases where the King is seized, or in possession of the land
by office or any other matter of record, his highness' seizin
cannot be delivered out of him until such time as an *ouster le
main* be sued (d). As if the King be seized by office of the
land of any idiots, or for year day and waste of lands of a
person attainted; in these cases he that should have these lands
after the King's title determined, must sue an *ouster le main;*
otherwise it is where the King is not seized of the land but
only entitled to the *profits:* as of the lands of him that is outlawed in a personal action, or a clerk convicted, or such like;
there need no *ouster le main* to be sued. And if the lands
which are seized into the King's hands be holden jointly by
many, yet every one of these by himself may sue his *ouster le
main* of his own part without his companions."

Where the *ouster le main* or proceedings thereon, are used
by the subject recovering against the Crown, unduly, and contrary to law, or upon an office which in point of law is insuffi-

(a) And see post, sec. 3. div. 5 and 6.   (c) Staundf. Prerog. 78, b.
Judgment and *Execution* on extent, &c.   (d) Ante, 347.
(b) Ante, 328.

                                                                              cient

cient for the party to have *ouster le main*, the King may *reseize* the lands without suing any process against the party; and is entitled to all the intermediate or mesne issues and profits (*a*). The subject who adopted such proceedings is also in that case to be treated and considered as an intruder upon the King's possession after office (*b*). But if the *ouster le main* is at the time on due process, and the King's title, though it existed before, did not appear till after the proceedings had by the subject, a *scire facias* is necessary to turn the subject out (*c*).

Before the statute 2 and 3 Ed. 6. c. 8. persons were still liable to be precluded of their rights, by the untrue finding of offices. As, for instance, persons holding terms for years or by copy of Court-roll, were often put out of their possession by reason of inquisitions, or offices found before escheators, commissioners and others, entitling the King to the wardship or custody of lands, or upon attainders for treason, felony or otherwise; and this, because such terms for years, and interests in copyhold were not found: after which they had no remedy, during the King's possession, either by *traverse* or *monstrans de droit*, or otherwise; because such interests were only chattels in customary hold, and not freehold. In like manner persons having any rent, common, office, fee or other profit *apprendre,* if such interest were not found in the office entitling the King, they had no remedy by traverse or other speedy means, without great and excessive charges, during the King's right therein. To redress these hardships on the subject, it is declared by the statute 2 and 3 E. 6. c. 8. that all persons in the above cases shall enjoy their rights and interests, the same as if no office or inquisition had been found, or as they might if their interest had been regularly found at the same time in such inquisition or office (*d*). Lord Coke observes (*e*) that " this being a beneficial law, the estates of tenant by statute staple, merchant or *elegit,* and executors that hold lands for

---

(*a*) Staundf. Prerog. c. 26. fol. 80, b. &c.

(*b*) Ibid.

(*c*) Ibid. 81. a. St. de Escheatoribus, 29. Ed. 1.

(*d*) See Com. Dig. Prerog. D. 84. Staundf. Præ. 62, b. that a traverse is in this case the proper remedy. And

in what other instance parties interested may claim, &c. see post, sec. 3. div. 1 ; resisting extents. That it is a general rule, that the prerogative does not overreach claims and rights of third persons acquired before the Crown's title first accrued. Ibid. ante, 298.

(*e*) Co. Lit. 77, b.

payment

payment of debts, are taken to be within the benefit of the clause."

The law respecting grants by the Crown of lands seized, before office found, and the right of the claimant to have a lease of such lands, have already been noticed (*a*).

SECT. 2.—The *monstrans de droit, manifestation* or *plea of right,* is another medium of redress for the subject against the Crown. As before observed, the ' petition' to the King appears to be the only *common law* remedy against him; and, though the contrary has been asserted (*b*), there can be little doubt that neither the *monstrans de droit* or the *traverse of office* (as to lands), was sustainable till the statute 36 Edw. 3. c. 13. (*c*).

By that statute (*d*) it is provided, that if there be any man that maketh claim or challenge to the lands seized, the escheator do send the inquest into the Chancery within the month after the land so seized, and that a writ be delivered to him to certify the cause of his seisin into the Chancery, and there shall the cause be heard without delay to traverse the office, or otherwise to *shew his right,* and from thence sent before the King to make a final discussion, without attending other commandments. And in case that any come before the Chancellor and shew his right, he shall have a lease of the lands, &c. (*e*).

The *monstrans de droit,* which, in cases where it lies, supersedes the proceeding by petition, may be brought either in the Petty Bag Office in Chancery (*f*), or in the Office of Pleas in the Exchequer (*g*); except in particular cases, as in Lady Broughton's case (*h*), where the *monstrans de droit* was brought

---

(*a*) Ante, 253.

(*b*) H. 9 E. 4. fol. 52. 13 E. 4. fol. 8. 4 Co. 55, a. Skin. 609. Com. Dig. Prerog. D. 81. 3 Bla. Com. 256.

(*c*) See Staundf. Prærog. Regis, 70, b. 60, a. 1 Anders. 181. 11 St. Tr. 154. 5 Bac. Ab. 571. Prerog. E. 7.

(*d*) And see 14 E. 3. st. 1. c. 13. 8 H. 6. c. 10.

(*e*) See note (*a*).

(*f*) In such case it seems the proceedings are not enrolled as in other

Courts, but remain upon files in the office. Co. Entr. 405. If there be a *monstrans de droit* upon an inquisition in Chancery, and upon that the Attorney-General demurs, there it shall be delivered into B. R. by the hands of the Chancellor, and there determined. Salk. 448.

(*g*) 4 Co. R. 57, a. Godb. 300. pl. 417. Skin. 609. Com. Dig. Prerog. D. (D. 82.) 3 Bla. Com. 256.

(*h*) 1 Skin. 610.

in

in B. R. because the record of the conviction and seizure were there. The bill of manifestation of right or *monstrans de droit* recites the inquisition found for the King, and then shews the right of the party, which it offers to verify : and concludes with praying judgment and an *amoveas manus*, and restitution of the lands and tenements, and of the profits from the time of taking the inquisition (*a*).

With respect to the instances in which this is the proper remedy, the most important rule appears to be this, that it is not maintainable where the subject's title is inconsistent with that found for the King by the inquisition (in which event a *traverse* is the proper course :) but only in cases in which the party in shewing his right is able to confess the *primâ facie* title found for the King and yet to avoid it (*b*). As in the case before put (*c*) of a disseisor of lands holden of the Crown dying seized without issue, there on such *primâ facie* title being found, and specially recited in an office for the King, the party really entitled may, though his title be not found (*d*), on confessing such *primâ facie* claim of the King shew his superior right before the wrongful eviction by the deceased disseisor (*e*). So that this is the peculiar remedy where the King is entitled by office or other matter of record (which indeed is always necessary to entitle the subject to his *monstrans de droit*) that is traversable ; but being true cannot be traversed (*f*).

It is in all cases necessary for the subject to shew a title in himself : and, if he do not, it is immaterial that the King has no title (*g*).

At common law the subject could not in general have had a *monstrans de droit* if the King were entitled by double matter of record ; that is, by two distinct records, each finding matter entitling the King to lands : as for instance in the case of an *office* finding an *attaint*, and that the offender was seized of lands ; here the office and the attainder form two records (*h*). But even at common law the subject had his *monstrans de droit* in such case, if there were no such attainder in point of law,

(*a*) Co. Entr. 402.
(*b*) Staundf. 71, a. Co. Entr. 405, 6. 2 Manning, 583.
(*c*) Ante, 344.
(*d*) H. 9 E. 4. Staundf. Prerog. R. 72, a.
(*e*) And see other instances, Staundf.

Prerog. 72, a. Com. Dig. Prerog. D. 82.
(*f*) Ibid.
(*g*) 2 Salk. 448.
(*h*) Staundf. Prær. Regis, fol. 71, b. Ante, 341.

or his title appeared by any record (*a*). And by the statute 2 and 3 Ed. 6. c. 8. s. 7. it is enacted, "that where it is untruly founden by office or inquisition, that any person attainted of treason, felony or *præmunire*, is or shall be seised of any lands at the time of such treason, felony or offence committed or done, or any time after, whereunto any other person hath any just title or interest of any estate of freehold, that then in every such case every person grieved thereby shall have his or their traverse, or *monstrance de droit* to the same, without being driven to any petition of right, and like remedy and restitution upon his title found or judged for him therein, as hath been accustomed and used in other cases of traverse, although the King be in such case entitled to any such lands, by double matter of record."

If the Attorney-General confess the title of the party, or if he reply and afterwards confess, or if it be found for the party by verdict or upon demurrer, the judgment is *quod manus domini regis amoveantur* (*b*), and that the party be restored to the possession of the premises with the appurtenances, together with the mesne profits from the time of the caption of the inquisition not answered to the Crown, *salvo jure domini regis* (*c*).

There is some contradiction in the books whether or not the subject on a *monstrans de droit*, or *traverse of office*, is to be considered in the nature of a plaintiff or defendant. The older books consider him in the nature of a plaintiff (*d*): and consequently that the Crown may plead in disability of his person (*e*), and that he may be nonsuited (*f*). This doctrine is however rendered extremely doubtful by subsequent authori-

---

(*a*) Staundf. Præ. Regis, fol. 71, b. and 72, a. b.

(*b*) As to which and proceedings thereon, &c. see ante, 347, 8.

(*c*) Ante, 347. Co. Entr. 404, 406, b. Finch L. 459, 460. 2 Inst. 695.

(*d*) 4 H. 6. 11. 4 Co. 57, a. 2 Salk. 448. Bull. N. P. 216. One reason is, that the suppliant on a petition is a plaintiff, (and he appears to be so,) and consequently, the party in a *monstrans de droit* or traverse, is so; such

remedies being given in lieu of the petition.

(*e*) Ibid. Y. B. 26 H. 8. 1.

(*f*) Ibid. Staundf. Præ. R. 68, b. 2 Manning, 581. where it is also laid down, "that the nonsuit is peremptory, 4 H. 6. 12. pl. 9. at least where issue has been joined. Semb. M. 7 H. 7. fol. 13. pl. 19. But after a nonsuit in a manifestation of right or traverse of office, the subject may sue by petition of right, 4 H. 6. 13."

ties, and the reasons urged therein (a) against it. The party assumes, and acts throughout on the face of the proceedings in the character of a defendant : he shews his right in the shape of a plea: the Attorney-General replies, and the subject when he takes the issue *ponit se super patriam,* as on the other hand the Attorney-General in that case *petit quod inquiratur per patriam.* And Lord Somers in his argument on this sub-ject (b) observed, " I take it to be generally true, that in all cases where the subject is in the nature of a plaintiff, to recover any thing from the King, his only remedy at common law, is to sue by petition to the person of the King. I say, when the subject comes as a plaintiff. For, when upon a title found for the King by office, the subject comes in to traverse the King's title, or to shew his own right, he comes in in the nature of a defendant; and is admitted to interplead in that case with the King in defence of his title, which otherwise would be defeated by finding the office." And in another part he said explicitly : " in this sort of proceeding (*viz. a monstrans de droit*), the subject is in the nature of a defendant, and comes in and pleads to a title found for the King." The decision in Rex *v.* Roberts (c) is also to the same effect. In that case Roberts having traversed an inquisition whereby he was found a lunatic, the Attorney-General filed the common replication, and the proceedings being sent from the petty bag office to the King's Bench, the prosecutor of the commis-sion made up the record and carried it down to trial. Upon which it was objected that the supposed lunatic was in the na-ture of a plaintiff; and therefore had the right to carry down the record. And his traverse is in the nature of a *monstrans de droit* (d). " To which it was answered and resolved by the Court, that he was properly considered as a defendant oppo-sing the title found for the Crown, without setting up any title in himself; as he might do in a petition of right. And indeed it would be absurd to construe the liberty of traversing to give a power of delaying the Crown, which must be if the party is considered as having the common right of a plaintiff. It was

(a) 5 Bac. Ab. 574. And see Tre-main Entr. 628, 652. Co. Entr. 404. 4 H. 6. 13. a. Vaugh. R. 62. Bro. Ab. Traverse, D. Office, 54.

(b) 11 St. Tr. 154.
(c) 2 Stra. 1208.
(d) Query, a Traverse, 2 and 3 Ed. 6. c. 8. s. 6.

therefore held that the record was well made up and carried down by the prosecutor of the commission."

SECT. 3.—Of *traverse of office*, and herein of *resisting extents.*

The traverse of office (*a*) was at common law a very contracted remedy. It only lay in the case of goods and chattels (*b*), or where the office did not give a seisin or possession of land to the King, but merely entitled him to an action (*c*) for the recovery of land; as for instance, in the case of an office finding that the King's tenant had done waste or collusively conveyed, &c. (*d*). It was not sustainable at common law, where the King was entitled to lands by office or by other matter of record, judicial or ministerial, however untrue (*e*). And it was a still more mischievous hardship on the subject, that at common law, only offices of instruction (*f*) could be traversed (*g*). All these mischiefs are now however removed by several statutes (*h*), which gave a traverse (or *monstrans de droit*) in lieu of the proceeding by petition (*i*). So that at the present day, offices (*k*) may be traversed by any subject (*l*) claiming property seized by the Crown, whether the object be to recover land or not, and though the office be untrue; or the traverser have no record shewing his right, or in some cases, though the King be entitled by double matter of record, and the subject be not put out of possession by the escheator (*m*).

Between subject and subject, mere prior possession is in general sufficient against a wrong-doer or person who cannot shew a better title (*n*). But in the case of a seizure of land by

(*a*) As to offices or inquisitions, ante, 246.

(*b*) Staundf. Prerog. 60, a. 67. a. though the King be entitled by double matter of record. Ibid.

(*c*) Ante, 250, &c.

(*d*) 4 Co. 56, b.

(*e*) Ibid.

(*f*) Ante, 247.

(*g*) Sav. 130.

(*h*) 34 Ed. 3. c. 14. 36 Ed. 3. c. 13. 2 and 3 Ed. 6. c. 8. s. 6. Ld. Coke calls the latter statute a " right profitable one," and points out the several

common-law hardships it was intended to remedy and redress, in favour of various parties. Co. Lit. 77, b.

(*i*) Ante, 340.

(*k*) Traversable offices. Staundf. Pr. 67, a.

(*l*) See ante, 340, the statute 2 and 3 Ed. 6. c. 8. protecting copyhold terms, rent, &c. out of premises, though not mentioned in the office.

(*m*) And see Staundf. Pre. 63, a. et subseq. Com. Dig. Prerog. D. 83, 84.

(*n*) 1 East, 244. See Mr. Adams's able work on Ejectments, Index, *Title*.

the

the Crown, it is not sufficient for the subject traversing the office to rely on his own title or possession, however strong'; but he must answer the King's title, as found by the office, and though the King have none and the office be untrue, yet if the traverser cannot shew a legal title, his prior possession will not avail, and the King may retain against him (*a*). But it seems an estate by disseisin is sufficient (*b*). The party traversing must also establish his title as stated in the traverse: if he cannot, it will not avail that he has in fact a good title (*c*).

" Also," says Staundford (*d*), " it is not sufficient to traverse one of the King's titles, but he must traverse them all: for though the King's title that he is seised by be found not good, yet if there be any other record, that makes the King a title, whereby he may retain the lands; the party must avoid also that title or else he gets no *ouster le main*. But learn if there be no such record *in esse* or being, at the time of the traverse tendered; and hanging the plea upon the traverse, a new record, that is to say, an office is found, which entitleth the King, whether in this case the party shall be driven to traverse this office or not, ere he have his *ouster le main*. And it seems he shall not, for so he might be delayed of his possession infinitely by finding one office after another; wherefore this office found hanging the traverse, shall be accounted in law as though it had been found after the party had had his *ouster le main ;* in which case then the party upon the first traverse found for him, shall be restrained to his possession by an *ouster le main ;* and then after upon a *scire facias*, sued against him to shew why the land should not be reseised, upon this new office found for the King, he shall be received in that *scire facias* to traverse this new office. Howbeit this advantage he wins hereby, he then traverses with the King, keeping still his possession, where else he should traverse being still out of possession (*e*). Thus may ye see, when a man traverseth with the King, he may traverse all the King's titles that have then their being by matter of record, and is not bounden any further to answer for that time."

(*a*) Staundf. Præ. 63, a. 64, *a*.
(*b*) Hardr. 230, 251, 2, 3. 2 Saunders, 3.
(*c*) Staundf. 63, a. 64, *a*.

(*d*) Prærog. Regis, 64, b.
(*e*) T. 11 Hen. 4. f. 80. 13 H. 4. f. 8.

We

We have already noticed the point whether or not the traverser is to be considered in the nature of a plaintiff or defendant (*a*): and the judgment on a traverse (*b*); the granting the lands to the traverser, &c. (*c*); together with the protection afforded to persons holding inferior interests and claims on lands, to which the King is entitled by office (*d*), have also been explained.

Pleadings, and other proceedings on ordinary occasions, in the case of the Crown, and in particular in the event of a traverse of an office, will be now considered in noticing the *mode of resisting extents* upon inquisitions or offices.

Extents (*e*) are founded on offices under which the Crown claims certain property. There is nothing peculiar to traverses to offices on extents; and the law respecting such traverses is equally applicable in the case of traverses to other offices. " If," says Gilbert (*f*), " any will plead in discharge of the extent, or of the debts, he must traverse upon a particular roll, the whole matter of charge to which he pleadeth; and upon plea put in, the party who prosecutes for the King, must procure the attorney-general to demur or reply, as the case requireth. This traversing of offices upon extent, seems to come in by 34 Edw. 3. c. 14. and 36 Edw. 3. c. 13. (*g*)."

The mode of resisting extents and proceedings thereon, may be considered in the following order : 1. *Appearing* to extents and *claiming* property. 2. *Motions* to set aside extents, to pay money, &c. 3. *Pleadings* on extents, &c. 4. *Trial* and *proceedings* incident thereto. 5. *Judgment*. 6. *Execution*. 7. *Error*.

1. *Appearing to Extents and claiming Property*.

It is a principle of law that no one can traverse the King's title without shewing title in himself (*h*). Wherefore it has always been a rule in the Court of Exchequer, that no one shall be allowed to plead to an extent, that is to traverse the inquisition, or can have a *locus standi* in Court, till he has claimed property.

(*a*) Ante, 354, 5.
(*b*) Ante, 347.
(*c*) Ante, 253.
(*d*) Ante, 340.

(*e*) Ante, 261.
(*f*) Excheq. 171.
(*g*) Ante, 356.
(*h*) Staundford, Prerog. 63, a.

On

On the return day of the extent, the following rule to appear and claim is indorsed on the back of the extent (*a*).

——— day of ——— 181—.

" It is this day ordered by the Court, that if no one shall appear and claim the property of the several goods and chattels, lands and tenements, debts, credits, specialties and sums of money, particularly mentioned and described in the inquisition, and several schedules hereto annexed," (varying the description according to the property seized) " on or before this day se'nnight, a writ of *venditioni exponas* do issue to sell the same."

" Fowler."

If the extent should not be actually returned till after the return day, the rule, it should seem, cannot be given till the writ is actually returned. This rule is always drawn up for " this day se'nnight," *i. e.* it is a six day rule, not accounting Sunday, whether intervening or at the end. If there should not be time to give this rule in term, it is given for the sealing-day, or seal-day, as it is indifferently called after term (*b*).

The general seal-day, which for the purposes of sealing and issuing the King's process, and for filing and delivering over informations in matters of revenue, is considered as the fictitious last day of term, is always appointed, at the discretion of the Court, on the last day of every term. In the issuable terms, from the increase of the revenue business, the seal-day has been appointed on the Friday month after the term. In Michaelmas Term it is appointed within a day or two of Christmas day, and in Easter Term it is appointed on the Friday before Whitsunday; but for the precise days on which the general seal-day is appointed, reference must be had to the minute book of the register, in which it is always noted the last day of every term (*c*).

If the defendant mean to dispute the debt, or a third person wish to claim the property, he must (*d*) appear and claim before the expiration of this rule and enter his appearance and claim

---

(*a*) West, 174. 2 Manning, 553.

(*b*) R. T. 2 Jac. 2. West, Appendix, 128. Manning, App. 232.

(*c*) Fowler's Equity Practice of the

Exchequer, vol. 2. p. 4. West, 175.

(*d*) See West, 175, 6. Otherwise the owner of the goods is bound. 3 Price, 127.

on the back of the writ, either in his own name or in the name of one of the sworn clerks of the King's remembrancer's office in which the return is filed (*a*). The form usually is " *A. B.* appears and claims all and singular the goods and chattels, lands and tenements, debts, credits, specialties, and sums of money," (varying the description according to the property claimed,) " taken and seized under and by virtue of a writ of immediate extent issued against ———— for the sum of ———— ".

The 36 E. 3. c. 13. (*b*), upon which the traverse upon extents is founded, directs that the claimant be heard without delay. It seems also that the subject as a matter of right may enter his claim at any time (*c*): though a strict adherence to the rule may be necessary to prevent a sale, unless the Court interpose (*d*), and as before observed (*e*), the claimant cannot insist on a lease of the land unless he claim within a month. At all events however, if a party do not appear and put in his claim within the time limited by the rule, the Court will it seems admit him to appear and claim afterwards, on an affidavit of special circumstances. Accordingly in a late case (*f*) where the claim had been entered in the name of the assignee the Court on motion that a claim might be entered in the name of the bankrupt for the purpose of avoiding the necessity and expence of proving the bankruptcy and proceedings thereon, granted a rule to shew cause which was afterwards made absolute, no cause being shewn. So where the clerk in court accidentally omitted to enter the claim in due time (*g*).

Of course the party against whom the extent issued may appear for the purpose of denying the debt: and there are few, if any instances in which others claiming any property or interest in the lands or chattels seized, and having a legal (*h*) title may not come in and interplead with the Crown. The statute 2 and 3 E. 6. c. 8. protecting the interests of others in lands, has been already mentioned (*i*). So a mortgagee though

---

(*a*) 2 Manning, 585, 590. Ibid. Appendix, 282, 6, 7.

(*b*) Ante, 356, and note (h).

(*c*) Y. B. 13 Ed. 4. 8.

(*d*) And see Manning, 586.

(*e*) Ante, 255, 6. 56 Ed. 3. c. 13. See Bunb. 25; What security usually

taken.

(*f*) Rex v. Aspinall, H. T. 57 Geo. 3. West, 178.

(*g*) 3 Price, R. 38, note.

(*h*) Ante, 303.

(*i*) Ante, 350.

he

he has not had possession (*a*), or a party holding a statute merchant and possessed of the land by virtue thereof (*b*); or a party with whom the extendee has contracted (*c*); or whose goods he has wrongfully taken (*d*); may appear and claim. The interest claimed by a stranger must however be distinct from that of the party against whom the extent issues; it must be a property and interest to which he may be restored (*e*). When a term is extended the reversioner, having no interest during the existence of the prior chattel interest seized, cannot claim (*f*): nor can a creditor suing the extendee move to set aside the extent if it cannot delay the creditor's execution, he not having obtained judgment (*g*).

In cases where a common (*h*) or profit *apprendre* in the lands of the extendee is claimed by a stranger under the 2 and 3 Ed. 6. c. 8 (*i*). and such interest is not found by the inquisition, as it is better to effect if possible, a traverse is under that statute the proper course of proceeding.

Different parties may appear and claim different parts, or the same parts, of the property seized (*k*): and one joint tenant may sue without his companion (*l*). Where there are various conflicting claims, the Crown has the prerogative power of deferring the establishment of its title till the parties have interpleaded among each other, when perhaps the Crown claim may be rendered more evident (*m*).

(*a*) Bunb. 104. pl. 163. Stone *v.* Evans, Woodff. 5th ed. and 7 East, 340, 1. note. 3 Campb. 394. 1 B. and A. 593.

(*b*) Bunb. 123. Where, on an inquisition, a man was found possessed of a term *jure uxoris*, and after his death it was sold on a *venditioni exponas*, the widow was permitted to plead to the inquisition, though she had defended an ejectment brought by the purchaser, and filed a bill in Chancery. Bunb. 220.

(*c*) 7 Ves. 261.

(*d*) 2 Manning, 588.

(*e*) P. 15 H. 7. fol. 6, b.

(*f*) 50 Ass. 324, pl. 5. Fitz. Traverse, 33. 2 Manning, 587.

(*g*) See 2 Price, R. 156.

(*h*) In Ld. Raym. 308, it is said that if *A* hath land, in which *B.* hath common of pasture for sheep; *A.* is outlawed, and the title of *B.* is not found upon the inquisition; his cattle may be taken upon a *levari facias*, until he hath pleaded his title in the Exchequer, and hath it allowed; *contra*, if his title had been found upon the inquisition.

(*i*) Ante, 340.

(*k*) West, 176.

(*l*) 2 Manning, 588.

(*m*) See Ibid. See Staundf. Pre. R. ch. 19, on Interpleader, between heirs, where there are several offices and different grantees of the Crown, &c. As to the remedy of the party who succeeds, 2 Manning, 589.

2. *Motions to set aside extents ;—to pay money, &c.*

These motions may be made either in term time on any day except Monday or Thursday (Fridays and Saturdays are the usual days (*a*)); or they may be made at the sittings after term (now usually held in Gray's Inn Hall), which are always appointed by the Court on the last day of every term, except Easter term, when, on account of the shortness of the vacation, the Thursday next after the last day of that term is always fixed as a day for motions only (*b*).

It is usual to give (to the clerks in Court, not to the solicitors immediately employed (*c*)) two days previous notice of a motion to set aside an extent (*d*): and it is highly reasonable that the opposite party should be provided with the means of resisting the application. But on pressing occasions, towards the end of the term, the Court will sometimes direct that short notice of motion for the next day be accepted (*e*). And no notice is necessary where the party moves for a rule to shew cause merely (*f*). And the writ ought to be brought into Court by the officer of the Court before the motion is made, where the objection arises upon the face of the extent (*g*).

1. Even such of the proceedings as do not form a part of the record, as the affidavit of the debt and insolvency, may be set aside on motion for any insufficiency apparent on the face of them. It is highly reasonable that this remedy should be open to the defendant, as of course only such statements as constitute a part of the record can be traversed or demurred to. This summary remedy by motion to the Court, is also allowed the defendant where the proceedings on record are on the face of them defective : as where a sufficient debt is not stated, or the inquisition is argumentative, &c. (*h*). For, though a demurrer on account of such defects in the record is decidedly sustainable, and where the point is doubtful, the Court will

---

(*a*) 2 Manning, 610.

(*b*) 1 Fowler's Eq. Pr. Excheq. 284. West, 179.

(*c*) 1 Price, 385.

(*d*) Ibid. 2 Manning, 610.

(*e*) 1 Price, 117. Questions of irregularity settled by deputy remembrancer, who may give costs. Manning, App.

233. 2 V. 606.

(*f*) Rex *v.* Collingbridge. Dec. 17, 1816. West, 179. S. C. but not S. P. 3 Price, 280.

(*g*) 1 Price, R. 395.

(*h*) 3 Price, 288. See ante, 268. as to the validity of the inquisition.

leave the defendant to that remedy (*a*): still it would be unjust to deny him a mode of taking advantage of the irregularity, by which considerable expense and delay are avoided. Where either course of proceeding is open to the defendant, it is in general advisable to move in the first instance, instead of demurring, because if the motion be decided against the claimant, he may still plead; whereas after argument on demurrer, the judgment is usually final (*b*).

2. Irregularities not apparent on the face of the record, generally arise out of the proceedings before the sheriff and jury, on the taking of the inquisition under the commission, or of that under the extent; as that insufficient evidence was considered by them sufficient. As in these cases the defect cannot be pointed out by a demurrer, it not being apparent on the face of the proceedings, the defendant may, and if he mean to take the objection must (*c*), indeed apply to the Court by motion, which should however be supported by an affidavit of the circumstances. If the Court entertain doubts respecting the facts on either side, they will in some cases direct a feigned issue to ascertain them (*d*). Where a stranger is the party moving on account of some extraneous defect, he must it seems shew his title to the property seized by affidavit (*e*); but it appears that any man may as *amicus curiæ*, and without an affidavit, move to set aside extents to which there are obvious objections (*f*).

It seems that a motion to set aside an extent should be made as early as possible, the general rule being that an irregularity in practice is waived by the party being knowingly so inactive as to lead his opponent to suppose that he does not mean to take advantage of it, by which he is or might be induced to proceed (*g*). The motion comes too late after the party has obtained time to plead (*h*). But it may be made before the appearance and claim are entered, and the assignees of a bank-

---

(*a*) Bunb. 33.

(*b*) West, 182. Tidd, 6th ed.

(*c*) 4 Price, R. 11. In which case the prerogative process was not maintainable according to the practice of the Court.

(*d*) 2 Manning, 609.

(*e*) West, 183.

(*f*) Hardr. 85, 99. 2 Manning, 607, 9.

(*g*) 2 Manning, 606. 1 East, 77. Tidd, 6th ed. 954. 6 Taunton, 7. 1 Marsh, R. 403. S. C. 2 Smith, 391.

(*h*) 3 Price, 38 But still he may demur if the objections appear on the face of the record.

rupt

rupt have been allowed to move to set aside an extent, even after a *venditioni exponas* has issued, no claim having been entered, and it appearing that there had not been an unreasonable delay (*a*). It seems also that objections to the process itself, but not informalities in the execution of it, may be taken advantage of by motion after appearance (*b*). In every case it is a question for the discretion of the Court, under the peculiar circumstances, whether a reasonable degree of diligence has been exercised, and whether the opposite party has been prejudiced by the delay.

The Court will not in general try a matter of fact on affidavits (*c*), and therefore the only case in which the defendant would be allowed to deny the debt on affidavit, seems to be where the question is as to the legal effect of facts which neither party disputes (*d*).

The inquisition may be set aside *pro tanto* only, as for a part of the debt, the residue of the inquisition and extent remaining effective (*e*). A new writ may be resorted to (*f*).

There are other motions besides those to set aside the proceedings which the defendant or claimant on the extent may sometimes have occasion to make, as that debts collected by the sheriff under the extent (the payment of which he has not the power to enforce (*g*),) be paid by him into the hands of the deputy remembrancer, to be laid out *pendente lite* in the funds or in Exchequer bills, or in such manner as the Court shall direct, as the money would otherwise be likely to lie unproductive for some time (*h*). It seems, that the right of the Crown to the money when disputed, remains in abeyance till judgment, and consequently, that the consent of the Crown to the object of the motion is unnecessary (*i*).

The party, too, sometimes moves to pay the debt, for which the extent issued, into the receipt of the Exchequer; or that the sheriff, who has levied money, shall pay the debt out of the money in his hands into the receipt of the Exchequer, and that on such payment an *amoveas manus* do issue; and it would seem, that this may be done at any period of the currency of

(*a*) West, 184.
(*b*) 3 Price, 288, 290. 2 Manning, 401.
(*c*) See Tidd, 5th ed. 187.
(*d*) West, 184, 5. 2 Manning, 605.

(*e*) 1 Anstr. 192. Hughes, Ext. 178.
(*f*) Ante, 258, 271. 3 Price, 269.
(*g*) Ante, 306.
(*h*) 1 Price, R. 301.
(*i*) West, 186.

the

the extent, and the Court will permit this to be done, provided the Crown is not placed in a worse situation by such payment than that in which it would be on recovering judgment. Therefore, where goods and lands were seized under an extent, and the goods, according to the appraised value in the extent, were more than sufficient to pay the debt, the Court allowed the party to pay the debt into the receipt of the Exchequer, without costs, because the Crown, if it succeeded, could not have recovered costs on the sale of the goods, and as they were sufficient to satisfy the debt, the sale of the lands on which costs are in general attainable could not have been allowed (*a*). On the same principle, however, if lands only are seized, the defendant must also pay costs into Court; but in such case poundage is not an item of costs, it not being due on the sale of lands (*b*).

If a greater sum than is due be levied under an extent, or if costs or poundage be levied where they are not payable, the Court will on motion order them to be refunded (*c*).

3. *Pleadings on Extents, &c.*

The appearance and claim being entered, a four-day rule to plead is given on the back of the writ. Further time (usually six weeks) to plead may be obtained on a motion of course under counsel's hand; and, on affidavit of special circumstances, further additional time may on motion be gained, at the expiration of the period allowed in the first instance.

Pleas to extents are either—1st, By the *party against whom the extent issued,* whether he be the original Crown debtor, or a debtor in the second degree (*d*), and by persons claiming in some *representative character* under them; or, 2dly, By *strangers* claiming a property in the effects seized, without objecting to the debt.

In the *former* case, the statute 33 Hen. 8. c. 39. s. 79. seems to afford a very extensive and just remedy for the subject, and has on that account been called the statute of equity. It pro-

(*a*) 3 Price, R. 40. As to costs, ante, 310. If doubt as to amount of debt, a summons may it seems be obtained for the particulars of it. 2 Man-

ning, 607, 8. note *q.*
(*b*) Ante, 311.
(*c*) 1 Price, R. 448.
(*d*) Ante, 303.

vides,

vides, "that if any person, of whom any such (*a*) debt or duty shall be demanded or required (*b*), allege, plead, declare or shew, in any of the said Courts, good, perfect, and sufficient cause, and matter in law, reason, or good conscience, in bar or discharge of the said debt or duty; or why such person ought not to be charged or chargeable to or with the same; and the same cause or matter so alleged, pleaded, declared or shewed, sufficiently proved in such one of the said Courts as he shall be impleaded, sued, vexed, or troubled for the same, that then the said Courts, and every of them, shall have full power and authority to accept, adjudge, and allow the same proof, and wholly and clearly to acquit and discharge every person that shall be so impleaded, sued, vexed, or troubled for the same."

With respect to the subject-matter (*c*) of defence to the debt on which the extent is founded, there is nothing very peculiar in the case of pleading to Crown process. The defendant's inability to plead the statute of limitation, a set off (*d*), bankruptcy (*e*), insolvency (*f*), *solvit post diem* (*g*), the statute of frauds, or any other defence given by statutes, by which the King, not being named, is not bound (*h*), forms substantially the only exception from the general law of pleading defences to debts between subject and subject. The defendant in the case of an extent, may plead *non est factum*, or performance (*i*), if the Crown claim a debt on a specialty; and, in the case of a simple contract debt, though it become a record by the inquisition (*k*), the defendant, under the general issue, *non indebitatus modo et forma* (*l*), may dispute the debt, or give in evidence any defence, except those above mentioned. Nor could the Crown, before the statute 58 Geo. 3. c. 93. (*m*), enforce the

(*a*) It relates to all debts due to the Crown. 7 Co. R. 19.

(*b*) It will be observed, that the clause only extends to pleadings by Crown debtor, not to pleadings by a stranger claiming property and not disputing the debt.

(*c*) Form of pleading, see the Entries, and West, 194, &c. Tidd's App. tit. Extent.

(*d*) Rex *v.* Copland, Hughes, 204.

1 Price, 23. West, 199. Post. 368, n. (*c*)

(*e*) Ante, 284.

(*f*) Ibid.

(*g*) 1 Price, 23.

(*h*) By what statutes the King is bound, post, ch. 382 to 384.

(*i*) Trem. 584, 608.

(*k*) West, 200.

(*l*) Ibid. 199. Trem. Pl. Cr. 583.

(*m*) See 4 Price, 50.

payment

payment of a bill of exchange, tainted with usury in its original formation.

The effects being seized as the property of the defendant, it is of course unnecessary for him to claim in his pleadings any property in them. He merely disputes the Crown debt; if that be unfounded, his right to the pro₁ erty remains or reverts to him as a matter of course. But where third persons claim in a representative capacity, under the defendant, as assignees of the defendant, a bankrupt, they must deduce title from him; and in such case the assignees must shew, separately, every fact entitling them to maintain the character they assume (*a*).

It is however highly worthy of observation, that where the extent is not against the immediate Crown debtor, but against his debtor, or other debtor in the third or other degree, such debtor in the second, third or other degree, may, in disputing the debt due from him (the party pleading) to the Crown debtor, set up any defence, whether given by statute or not, which he might have insisted upon if he were sued by his immediate creditor, the Crown debtor (*b*). As in the case of an extent by the Crown against *B.* who owed money to *A.*, the Crown debtor, *B.* may plead a set off, &c. to the debt due from him (*B.*) to *A.* And the reason is, that the Crown in seizing the debts due to its debtor, cannot be in a better situation with respect to the right to such debt, than the Crown debtor himself; a better remedy only, not a better right, is claimed by the King (*c*). The debtor in the second or third degree may also contest the right of the Crown to issue an extent, on the debt alleged to be due from the Crown debtor.

In no case can a defendant plead double or several matters in the case of the Crown, under the statute 4 and 5 Ann, c. 16. (*d*). But he may plead separately to distinct parts of the inquisition; or plead as to one part, and demur to another distinct and independent matter (*e*). And where the Crown claims by two or more distinct titles, each must be traversed (*f*): otherwise where there are two inquisitions finding the same title (*g*).

(*a*) West, 196. See Ibid. 177, 8, 197; where the best mode of proceeding in such case is clearly pointed out.

(*b*) Ante, 305, 327.

(*c*) 2 Manning, 593.

(*d*) Parker, 13. Forrest's R. 57. 1

Price, 23.

(*e*) Trem. Pl. 582. 2 Manning, 598, 9.

(*f*) Ibid. and 601, 2. Ante, 357.

(*g*) Ibid. 2 Manning, 601, 2.

It will have been remarked that the statute of Hen. 8. before mentioned (*a*), allows the debtor to allege, plead, declare or shew any sufficient matter in law, " reason or good conscience," in discharge of the debt.

Several old cases (*b*) are to be met with, in which parties have been relieved under equitable circumstances, in pursuance of the provisions of this enactment; though it is difficult to lay down any precise rule or criterion on this point (*c*). The claim to relief may be brought forward either by pleading to the extent (*d*), or by bill in the Exchequer (*e*), or by motion to the Court of Exchequer, who possess an equitable jurisdiction over extents (*f*).

2. In the case of pleadings by *strangers* claiming title paramount the interest of the Crown, the debt due from the Crown debtor cannot be disputed. The pleadings or traverse in this case are not founded on the statute of Hen. 8. (*g*). Their foundation has been already mentioned (*h*). In this case the party must, as before observed (*i*), not only shew his own title, but traverse that of the Crown, i. e. of the party against whom the extent issued, or confess and avoid it.

If a bad title be found for the Crown on the face of the inquisition, the party may, it seems, demur without traversing or shewing title (*k*). If found against the claimant, it seems to be peremptory (*l*). But it seems he may afterwards have a petition (*m*).

As to the *replication* or *demurrer*, on the part of the Crown, it will be remembered that the Crown cannot be non-prossed (*n*); and consequently a rule to plead would be ineffectual and cannot be given. But the Court in the exercise of their legal and equitable jurisdiction in cases of this nature, will order judgment to be entered for the defendant, as if his plea were

---

(*a*) Ante, 365, 6.

(*b*) 7 Rep. 20. Lane, 51. Hardr. 176, 502. cited West, 201 to 208.

(*c*) See 1 Price, 216. Query, whether a set off be within the statute. 2 Manning, P. E. 592. note *i*.

(*d*) See note a.

(*e*) Ch. Pre. 153.

(*f*) 1 Price, R. 96. note x.

(*g*) Ante, 365, 6.

(*h*) Ante, 356, 360. See 2 Manning, 506.

(*i*) Ante, 357.

(*k*) 50 Ass. 322. pl. 1. Bro. Demurrer in Ley. 25. Hardr. 176. Sed vide West, 215.

(*l*) Staundf. Prerog. 65, b. Post.

(*m*) Ante, 354, note (*f*).

(*n*) 3 Anstr. 753. See Ante, 244, 5.

confessed

confessed, if the attorney-general will not on application enter a *nolle prosequi*, or proceed within a reasonable time (*a*).

The Crown has various prerogatives in replying to its defendant's traverse or plea (*b*). In cases where the right of property is in dispute, the claimant, as we have just seen, must not only state his own title, but should traverse that of the Crown. In this case the Crown has the option of maintaining its own title, without noticing the defendant's: or, without noticing the defendant's traverse of the Crown title, the King may merely dispute the title set up by the claimant (*c*). And it appears that the King may in a manner reply double, by maintaining not only his own title, but disputing also that set up by the traverser; and it is also usual for the Crown to confess and avoid, and traverse also (*d*). So if the plea allege several facts, the King may traverse all of them (*e*): and if several of the King's titles be traversed, he need not maintain all of them (*f*). And though no estoppel can exist against the Crown (*g*), the traverser may be concluded by the King replying matter of estoppel (*h*).

During the term in which issue has been joined with the Crown, but not in a subsequent term, the Crown may waive the issue and take another, or demur (*i*). But the defendant cannot waive his plea, and plead the general issue without the consent of the attorney-general (*k*); though he may enter a

---

(*a*) Parker, 50. On extents in aid judgment is moved for if the Crown does not reply before the end of the third entire term. 2 Manning, 603.

(*b*) As to replying in *abatement*, 2 Manning, 600.

(*c*) Bro. Prerog. pl. 65, 78. Staundf. Pre. 65, a. Vin. Ab. Prerog. Q. 5. Com. Dig. Prerog. D. 75, 85. Sav. 67. 2 Cro. 481. Sav. 64. 2 Vez. 541. Ante, 357. But it seems necessary for the Crown to reply to the fresh matter set up in bar by the defendant, where the Crown title is not on record by office, &c. as in the case of an information for a penalty, &c. Vaugh. 64. 16 Vin. Ab. 538. 6 Com. Dig. 74. And in Vaugh. 62. it is on this ground laid down: " that where the King's title appears to be no more than a bare

suggestion, (that is, not material,) the King can, no more than a common person, (and for the same reasons,) forsake his own title, and endeavour only the destroying of the defendant's title; for the weakening of the defendant's title without more, can no more make a good title to the King than it can to a common person." See 2 Vez. 541.

(*d*) See 2 Manning, 601, cites Keilw. 175, b. pl. 3. 9 H. 4. 6. pl. 20.

(*e*) Com. Dig. Prerog. D. 75. Savil. 19.

(*f*) Staundf. Prerog. 65, a.

(*g*) 1 Co. R. 43. Hob. 339.

(*h*) Com. Dig. Estoppel, D.

(*i*) Staundf. Prerog. 65, u, b. Vaugh. 65. Com. Dig. Prerog. D. 85. Not after verdict, Hardr. 455.

(*k*) Cro. Car. 347. 2 Rol. 41.

retraxit

retraxit generally, even after the replication (*a*). The Crown cannot depart from an issue actually joined on its own title, to' traverse the party's title (*b*). If issue has not been joined, the Crown may, even in a subsequent term, waive his replication or demurrer (*c*), and may amend at any time, on paying costs (*d*).

By not demurring to collateral and formal objections to the traverse, and taking an issue in fact, which is found against the King, the Crown waives its right to take advantage of them (*e*).

The replication is bad if it amount substantially to a departure from the extent or inquisition, instead of supporting it according to the ordinary rules of pleading (*f*).

It is usual for the Attorney-General to confess the plea where it is evidently true: affidavit of the facts being sometimes previously made (*g*). A confession by the Attorney-General in a matter of fact binds the King, but not it seems in the case of a confession of a matter of law, the traverse being bad in law (*h*).

The replication is always signed by the Attorney-General: during the vacancy of that office by the Solicitor-General (*i*).

The rule to rejoin is, like the rule to plead (*k*), entered on the back of the extent; and is a four day rule. Further time to rejoin may be obtained if necessary.

4. *Trial; and Proceedings incident thereto.*

Issue being joined, the next step is for the Crown to issue a *venire* (*l*) to try it by a jury. This process may be issued into any county by the prerogative of the King who may try an issue where he pleases (*m*). But issues on extents are always tried in Westminster (*n*).

(*a*) Brown, P. E. 541.

(*b*) Ante, 369, note (*c*).

(*c*) 2 Rol. R. 41. Cro. Car. 347. Vaugh. 65. Hardr. 455. Pl. Com. 322, a. Sir T. Jones, 9, 10.

(*d*) 3 Anstr. 714. ante, 310. As to waiving the count in an information of intrusion, &c. ante, 334.

(*e*) Dyer, 223, b. The Court will not direct a second argument in a cause argued during the absence of the Solicitor-General, merely to hear him. 2

Price, 5.

(*f*) Trem. P. C. 594.

(*g*) See Bunb. 102. pl. 62.

(*h*) Hardr. 170. Com. Dig. Prerog. D. 85.

(*i*) 4 Burr. 2572.

(*k*) Ante, 365.

(*l*) See Tidd's Append. tit. Extents.

(*m*) 1 Sid. 412. 1 Ventr. 17. Parker, 189. 2 Price, 113.

(*n*) West, 216.

If

If the defendant live at a distance, or 40 miles from town, 10 days' notice of trial is proper: otherwise 6 days (*a*).

If the Crown will not proceed to trial, the defendant after waiting has no other remedy (*b*) than by application to the equitable jurisdiction of the Court (*c*); and the Court will give judgment for the defendant or claimant if the Crown will not on application proceed in a reasonable time (*d*). On extraordinary occasions of delay the Court will order the Crown officers to shew cause why the effects should not be returned to the party (*e*). But though there is in strictness no positive mode of compelling the Crown to proceed to trial, it appears to be the better opinion that after a *distringas* and jury returned upon it, the Attorney-General cannot stay the trial (*f*).

Notice of trial having been duly given, the Crown enters the record, and the cause is called on as usual (*g*).

The Crown has the privilege of trying its causes at *nisi prius*, or in bank. Trial at *nisi prius* shall not be granted, unless the Attorney-General consent (*h*): and it shall be there and not in bank if he require it, even upon an indictment removed by *certiorari* (*i*).

Where there are distinct issues by different defendants in fact and in law, the Crown may try which it chooses before the other (*k*).

Whether or not the traverser may be nonsuited has been doubted (*l*). On demurrer being found against him it is peremptory (*m*): though he still has his petition (*n*).

The verdict is as in ordinary cases (*o*). It may be general or special. And, as in verdicts between subject and subject, a verdict in the case of the Crown may aid a case defectively stated.

The postea being returned a four day (*p*) rule for judgment

(*a*) West, 216. 2 Manning, 612.

(*b*) Ibid.

(*c*) As in the event of the Crown delaying to reply, ante, 368, 9.

(*d*) Parker, 51.

(*e*) 3 Anstr. 753.

(*f*) 4 Leon. 32. cited Com. Dig. Prerog. D. 85. 5 Bac. Ab. 571; Prerog. E. 7.

(*g*) 2 Manning, 613.

(*h*) Savil. 2. 2 Inst. 424. 2 Hawk.

P. C. 411. c. 42. s. 2.

(*i*) Cro. Car. 348.

(*k*) 1 Str. 266.

(*l*) See ante, 354. 2 Manning, 613. Staundf. Prerog. 65, b.

(*m*) Ibid.

(*n*) 2 Manning, 581, 613, 14.

(*o*) See as to demurrers to evidence by the Crown. Ibid. 613. Plowd. 4, 8.

(*p*) 2 Manning, 615.

is given to allow the traverser to move in arrest of judgment, &c. as in other cases. The party has also the privilege of pleading (in lieu of the remedy by *auditâ querelâ*, which is not maintainable against the Crown (a)), any matter as a release, &c. arising after verdict and between the award of execution (b).

5. Judgment.

If the King succeed either upon verdict or nonsuit (c), the judgment (which need not however be drawn up unless error be brought, as the King is already in possession under the extent), is that the subject take nothing by his traverse (d).

The judgment for the traverser against the King is universally, that the King's hands be amoved and the party be restored, &c. (e).

A peculiar prerogative of the King may here be noticed, namely, that if in any suit between subject and subject a clear title in the King appear, (that is, it seems, be admitted between the parties (f),) the Court may *ex officio* (g) give judgment for him on such title; though the Crown were not a party to the suit (h). And the Crown may interpose to take an issue for the purpose of eliciting a title (i). Nor will Chancery decree against the Crown on a title apparent on the record, though not insisted on at the hearing (k). But if only a presumption of title appear for the Crown, the Court will in some cases proceed to give judgment in the action, but will suspend execution until the party has interpleaded with the King (l).

(a) 2 Manning, 378, 578.

(b) Ibid. 615. Bro. Ab. Prerog. pl. 46. See further as to motions for new trials. *Venire de novo*, &c. 2 Manning, 616, 7.

(c) Ante, 354.

(d) 2 Manning, 618.

(e) Ante, 348.

(f) Bro. Ab. Prerog. pl. 16.

(g) " The Judges *ex officio*, and every one else in his station ought to assist the king in his rights, and the judges are bound *ex officio* to take notice of every statute which concerns the King."

Jenk. 303. pl. 67. See post, ch. 16. that the judges are one of the King's councils.

(h) Jenk. 25. pl. 47 ; 219. pl. 65. F. N. B. 38. Cro. Car. 590. Plowd. 243. 5 Bac. Ab. 570. Ante, 244. 2 Barn. and Ald. 269, 70 ; *arg.*

(i) Cro. Car. 589. Hob. 126. 1 Anderson, 53. pl. 131.

(k) 3 Ves. 424. In Admiralty, 3 Price R. 97.

(l) Trin. 29 Edw. 1. Memoranda in Scaccario, 42, 3. Adam Penreth's Case.

6. *Execution.*

It rarely happens that any process of execution, actually issues either for the Crown or the subject: the former being in general already in possession of the property; and the latter being at liberty to enter merely by virtue of the award of an *amoveas manus,* which has been fully considered (*a*). The award is of itself a transfer of possession in point of law, and is necessary to divest the interest acquired by the King under the office; as without it the subject has no legal possessory right, and cannot sue trespassers, &c. (*b*).

The party is also entitled to restitution of his property, without deductions of poundage or expenses (*c*).

7. *Error.*

By several statutes (*d*), a writ of error lies on a judgment on an extent, &c., into the Exchequer Chamber. It seems, however, that the consent of the Attorney-General is previously necessary (*e*): but such consent will not be withheld if any point really arguable can be raised (*f*). After the termination of the writ of error in the Exchequer Chamber the case may be taken into the House of Lords (*g*).

A *scire facias* is unnecessary, on a writ of error against the King (*h*). The writ does not preclude the subject from taking possession on his judgment of *amoveas manus* (*i*). And where a judgment for the King is reversed, the subject is entitled to be restored to his property and all intermediate issues (*k*), though he is, it seems, driven to his petition for monies actually paid over and received into the King's hands (*l*).

(*a*) Ante, 348.
(*b*) Staundf Prerog. 78, a. 1 Rol. Ab. 738. Plowd. 546, 559. Hardr. 422.
(*c*) West, 217. Costs, &c. ante, 310.
(*d*) 31 Ed. 3. c. 12. 31 El. c. 1. s. 1. 16 Car. 2 s. 2 and 3.
(*e*) M. 24 E. 3. f. 35. pl. 43. F. N. B. 21. H. (*a*). Savile, 131. pl. 203.
But see 2 Leon, 194. pl. 244. cited 2 Manning, 621.
(*f*) 1 Price, 209.
(*g*) 2 Brown, P. C. 375.
(*h*) F. N. B. 21. H. Sav. 10, pl, 26.
(*i*) 2 Manning, 496, 621.
(*k*) See the cases, &c. Ibid. 624.
(*l*) Ante, 345.

CHAP. XIV.

Of the Privileges and Incapacities of the King in several matters.

THE more important privileges of the King have already been fully and separately noticed. There are also various royal immunities of minor importance, which require consideration. These principally relate to the person and private property of the King, and are no less just and politic than those weighty prerogatives which are inherent in his Majesty for the benefit of his people.

The dignity of the sovereign and the safety of the state, necessarily free the person of the King from liability to be arrested on any occasion (*a*). Neither can he be amerced or nonsuited (*b*). And in order that the King may not be exposed to inconvenience, and as a mark of that respect towards him which the law invariably inculcates, on sound principles of public policy, none of his Majesty's household or menial servants or officers, *bonâ fide* substantially and continually employed, or liable to be permanently employed, in waiting or attending on the royal person, can be arrested or taken in execution in civil actions (*c*), without notice first given to, and leave obtained from, the Lord Chamberlain of his Majesty's household (*d*). This is the prerogative of the King: it is an important freedom from the full operation of the laws, which was instituted, not for the benefit of the servant, but for the convenience of the sovereign. The reason assigned by Lord Coke (*e*) for this privilege, is thus put by him: " concerning those that serve the King in his household, *their continual service and attendance upon the royal person is necessary.*" To cases falling within the reason and groundwork of this immunity, must the privilege be restrained. Where the party is a domestic and menial servant of the King, as for instance,

(*a*) 2 Inst. 50.

(*b*) Bro. Ab. Prerogative, pl. 100. Vin. Ab. Prerog. T. 2.

(*c*) 5 T. R. 686. and cases there cited. Qu. on a *capias utlagatum.* Ibid.

687.

(*d*) T. Raym. 152. 2 Keb. 3, 485. Tidd, 6th ed. 197.

(*e*) 2 Inst. 631.

a clerk

a clerk or junior clerk of the King's kitchen (*a*), or his Majesty's coachman in ordinary (*b*), there can be no doubt of his privilege. But difficulties may frequently arise, and it is by no means an easy task to point out distinctly what particular officers fall within this doctrine. Attention must be paid to the nature of the duties required by the office holden by the party claiming the privilege. If he be merely a nominal officer without fee, assisting only on certain grand and peculiar occasions, as coronations, royal funerals, &c.; and neither acts as a servant in ordinary in the royal household, nor is a continual attendant on his Majesty's person, there seems no legal foundation for the privilege (*c*). And it appears that a gentleman of the privy chamber is not therefore privileged from arrest (*d*). On the accession of his present Majesty to the throne, a proclamation was issued (*e*), whereby (after reciting that his Majesty's predecessors had signified their pleasure that the royal servants should have and enjoy all antient privileges) his Majesty, thinking it reasonable that all his *servants in ordinary with fee should, in regard of their constant attendance upon his Majesty's person,* enjoy the like privileges with those of his predecessors, ordered that the Lord Chamberlain and other officers therein mentioned, should signify to all mayors, sheriffs, &c. of corporations and counties, that his servants should have their antient privileges, and that thenceforward none of the *servants in ordinary with fee,* should bear any public offices, serve on juries or inquests, watch or ward." This proclamation does not mention the privilege from arrest, as the antient proclamations on these occasions used to do. In a recent case, Abbott, C. J. observed (*f*), that "the form of the proclamation shews that the privileges there enumerated are confined to his Majesty's servants in ordinary *with fee.* And that though the proclamation was not applicable in all its terms to the case then before the Court, it furnishes a ground for a distinction, which may be taken between servants with and without fee."

It should seem that if a servant of the King be clearly pri-

(*a*) 5 T. R. 686.
(*b*) 2 Taunt. 167.
(*c*) 2 B. and Ald. 234, 7, 8, &c.
(*d*) Ibid.
(*e*) Pegg's Curialia, Dissertation on

the original nature and duty of the gentlemen of the Privy Chamber, p. 77; cited 2 B. and Ald. 236 and 239, note.
(*f*) Ibid. 237.

vileged from the nature of his employment, the privilege will not be affected by the circumstance of the King not residing personally, at the time, in the palace in which the servant is employed; such palace being still privileged as such (*a*). And it has been decided that a servant of the King is privileged from arrest, though he publicly carry on trade, and the debt was contracted in the course of his trade (*b*).

Where the privilege is clear, the Court will discharge the party on motion; where it is doubtful they will leave him to his writ of privilege (*c*).

On the same principles, no arrest can properly be made in the King's presence, or within the verge of the royal palace (*d*), except by an order of the Board of Green Cloth, or unless the process issue out of the Palace Court (*e*). And all the royal palaces are sanctuaries for persons liable to be arrested; and no species of judicial process can be executed therein; if any thing in the shape of possession and royal appearance be kept up, though the King do not at the time personally reside there (*f*). Nor can a distress be made on lands in the King's possession (*g*).

As the law cannot presume indiscretion or imbecility in the King, however young, his being under 21 years of age does not avoid his acts (*h*), and his non-age does in no case operate as a disability.

The King's goods are also exempt from various liabilities, which affect the personalty of his subjects. Even if a subject succeed in a petition against the King, his Majesty's goods are not liable to be taken in execution (*i*). The King is not liable

---

(*a*) See 10 East, 578.

(*b*) 2 Taunt. 167.

(*c*) 2 B. and Ald. 234.

(*d*) 3 Bla. Com. 289. 4 Ibid. 276. Tidd, 6th ed. 222. By 28 H. 8. c. 12. the verge of the palace of Westminster extends from Charing Cross to Westminster Hall. But an arrest within the verge of the palace is no ground for discharging the defendant out of custody. 7 Taunt. 311.

(*e*) 3 Term R. 735.

(*f*) 10 East, 578. 1 Campb. 475, note. So of ecclesiastical process. 3 Inst. 141. Wood's Inst. 19. 8th ed.

(*g*) Jenk. 112. pl. 18. Plowd. C. 242, b.

(*h*) See Co. Lit. 43. Bac. Ab. Infancy, B. "If the King alien lands parcel of his Dutchy of Lancaster, within age there, he may avoid it for his non-age; for he has the dutchy as Duke not as King; otherwise of land which he has as king, for the King cannot be disabled by non-age, as a common person may be." Bro. Ab. tit. Prerog. pl. 132.

(*i*) See the remedy, ante, 348, 9.

to pay taxes (*a*), toll (*b*), pontage, passage (*c*), custom (*d*), or poor rates (*e*); nor is his personal property subject to the laws, relative to wreck, estrays, waifs (*f*), sale in market overt (*g*), distress damage feasant (*h*), or the like. It is, indeed, generally laid down, that " no custom which goes to the person, or goods, of the King shall bind him (*i*)." But the King is not, it seems, by virtue of his prerogative, discharged of tithes for the antient demesne lands of the Crown; but his Majesty being *persona mixta*, is capable of a discharge *de non decimando*, by prescription, which in effect operates as a general discharge from tithes (*k*). But this privilege does not extend to the King's grantee (*l*); and by the alienation the prescription is destroyed for ever, and will not revive, even though the lands subsequently come to the Crown (*m*).

The privileges and prerogative rights of the Crown in judicial remedies and proceedings (*n*), and various peculiarities respecting the Crown lands (*o*), have been already mentioned. We may here add, as disabilities arising from the royal dignity, that the King cannot personally execute any office, judicial or ministerial (*p*), or arrest in person (*q*). For the same reason, and also on the ground that even the King shall not give evidence in his own cause, it is clear that his Majesty's testimony is not admissible in cases of treason or felony (*r*). Whether or not his Majesty's certificate, under his sign manual or the great seal, as to facts within his knowledge, can be admitted as evidence in a civil cause between subject and sub-

(*n*) See 39 and 40 Geo. 3. c. 88. s. 6. Crown lands, when bought by private funds of the King, &c. liable to parliamentary and parochial taxes.

(*b*) Palmer, 85. Com. Dig. Toll, G. 1.

(*c*) Jenk. 83. pl. 62. Vin. Ab. Prerog. T. 2.

(*d*) Ibid. Bro. Ab. Prerog. pl. 112. Fitz. Ab. Tolle, 5.

(*e*) 2 T. R. 372. 3 Ibid. 519. See 39 and 40 Geo. 3. c. 88. s. 6. ante, note (*a*).

(*f*) Vin. Ab. Prerog. T. 2.

(*g*) 2 Inst. 713. Plowd. C. 243, b.

(*h*) 2 Manning, P. E. 551.

(*i*) Vin. Ab. Prerog. T. 2.

(*k*) Hardr. 315. Sir W. Jones, R. 387. 2 Bla. Com. 31. " Forest land is not titheable, provided it is in the hands of the King, or of his lessee; but

if the forest be disafforested, and be within any parish, then it becomes titheable. 3 Cruise, 66.

(*l*) Ib. Hotham *v.* Foster, 3 Gwill. 869.

(*m*) Hardr. 315.

(*n*) Ante, 245, &c.

(*o*) Ante, 203 ; 209 to 211.

(*p*) Ante, 75, 6; 80. Bro. Prerog. 125. Co. Lit. 3, b. 8 Co. 55. 2 Ventr. 270. But still an office may be granted to him, as he may execute it by deputy 17 Vin. Ab. 168.

(*q*) 2 Inst. 187. " The King cannot arrest any one on suspicion of felony or treason, though the subject may ; for if the King do wrong there is no remedy against him." Per Markham, C. J. 1 H. 7. 4.

(*r*) 2 Hal. P. C. 282.

ject,

ject, may admit of some doubt.   Rolle, in his Abridgment (*a*), says, that " *it seems* that the King cannot be a witness in a cause by his letters under his sign manual."   No reason is, however, assigned, or authority cited, for the proposition; and Rolle admits, that the case of Lord Abignye *v.* Lord Clifton, in Chancery (*b*), is to the contrary.   In that case, King James's certificate, under his sign manual, of promises made by Lord Clifton, was allowed upon the hearing as a proof and exception for so much.   So, in 10 Jac. 1. the King's certificate was admitted and acted upon as proof (*c*), and clearly the King's testimonial, under the great seal, was antiently allowed in the case of an essoin *de servitio regis* (*d*).

Also, on account of the dignity of the King, he is not bound to offer an acquittance to any man; but the subject who pays to the King ought to bring with him acquittance, and demand it of the King (*e*).   Nor can the King be a copyholder; and, therefore, where a person who holds a copyhold estate becomes King, the copyhold is suspended; for it would be beneath the dignity of a King to perform such services as those to which copyholds are subject.   But after his decease, the next person who becomes entitled to it, (not being a King), shall hold by copy in the usual manner, and the tenure be revived (*f*).   Indeed, the general rule is, that the King cannot be tenant to, or hold by any services of, his subjects (*g*).   The King may however, it seems, hold as a trustee of lands, though he cannot be compelled to execute the trust (*h*).   And as observed by Lord Bacon (*i*), " the King may be a *cestui que use*, but it behoveth both the declaration of the use and the conveyance itself to be matter of record, because the King's title is compounded of both."   And as the King cannot in law be seised to a use, he cannot convey by bargain and sale (*k*), by covenant to stand seized (*l*), or by lease and release (*m*).   The King

(*a*) Tit. Testimonies, H. pl. 1.

(*b*) Hob. R. 213.

(*c*) Godb. 198, 9.

(*d*) F. N. B. 17.   2 Hal. P. C. 282. The author has been favoured with a sight of a MS. of Ld. Chancellor Finch, in which Rolle's opinion is decidedly contradicted, and it is clearly laid down, " that in a civil Court, between party and party, the King may testify his knowledge."

(*e*) Bro. Ab. Prerog. pl. 11. cites 2 H. 7, 8.   See Vin. Ab. Prerog. T. 2.

pl. 13.

(*f*) 2 Sid. 82.   And see Bac. Ab. Prerog. E. 1.

(*g*) Ibid.

(*h*) See Ibid. Bac.   Lane, 54. 1 Ves. 453.   1 Cruise, Dig. 1 ed. 407, 422, 488 ; Index, title King.   See ante, 217, 235.   39 and 40 Geo. 3. c. 88. s. 12.

(*i*) Read. 60.

(*k*) 4 Cruise, Dig. 173, 1 ed.

(*l*) Ibid. 187.

(*m*) Ibid. 198.

may also be appointed an executor; but, as it cannot be presumed that he has sufficient time and leisure to engage in a private concern, the law allows him to nominate such persons as he shall think proper to take upon them the execution of the trust, against whom all persons may bring their actions; also, the King may appoint others to take the accounts of such executors (*a*).

The King may levy a fine by grant and render (*b*), and bar his estates tail thereby (*c*). So he may devise lands (*d*); and reversions, and remainders vested in him are not barrable by recovery (*e*). So the King may declare the uses of a fine or recovery (*f*). But his Majesty cannot suffer a common recovery (*g*), and is bound by the statute *de donis* (*h*); and by the statute 32 Hen. 8. c. 28. s. 4.; so that if a husband alone levy a fine of his wife's lands to the King, still the wife may enter after the death of her husband (*i*).

Between subject and subject the rule is, *vigilantibus et non dormientibus jura subveniunt* (*k*). So that in many instances rights may be lost merely by the neglect of the party to enforce them. From the earliest periods of English law, it has, however, been a maxim that *nullum tempus occurrit Regi* (*l*); a maxim grounded on the principle that no laches can be imputed to the sovereign, whose time and attention are supposed to be occupied by the cares of government, (*ardua regni pro bono publico* (*m*);) " nor is there any reason that the King should suffer by the negligence of his officers, or by their compacts or combination with the adverse party (*n*)."

Numberless decisions in the Books have proceeded entirely on this principle (*o*). Thus the King cannot be barred by a fine to which he is not a party, and five years' non

(*a*) 4 Inst. 335. Godolph. Repert. 76.

(*b*) Dugd. Orig. Jur. 93. Maddox. No. 394. 7 Rep. 32.

(*c*) Ibid. and 52, a. Plowd. 227.

(*d*) Ante, 204.

(*e*) 5 Cruise, Dig. 502, 1 ed. Tit. 36. c. 13. s. 20, &c.

(*f*) 4 Cruise, Dig. 221, 1 ed.

(*g*) Cro. Car. 96, 7. Pigot, 74, 5.

(*h*) 7 Rep. 52, a. Plowd. 227.

(*i*) 1 Inst. 681.

(*k*) Hob. 347. 2 Bos. and Pul. 412.

(*l*) Staundf. 32, 3. Plowd. Com. 243, a. 263, b. Com. Dig. Prerog. D. 86. Godb. 297.

(*m*) Godb. 295.

(*n*) Hob. 347.

(*o*) See 5 Bac. Ab. 562. tit. Prerog. E. 6. It is on this ground that King's goods shall not be wreok, strays, waifs. How this rule affects presentation to benefices, &c. ante, 62.

claim.

claim (*a*).   Nor can there be a tenant at sufferance against the King; for as no laches can be imputed to his Majesty for not entering, if the King's tenant hold over he will be considered as an intruder (*b*).   So no man by entry can at common law gain himself a title against the King (*c*), nor will any descents toll his entry (*d*).   So the statute of limitations does not bind the King (*e*).   And it seems, that if a bill of exchange or promissory note come into the hands of the Crown before it be due, the non-presentment of it when, due, and omission to give notice of dishonour, are not material (*f*).

Even at common law, however, a prescription may be good against the King, as in the case of waifs (*g*); and in many cases the Crown, by deferring a seizure, &c. may have a less efficacious remedy (*h*); and " custom upon the land, as borough English, gavelkind, &c. shall bind the King (*i*)."

And by the *nullum tempus* Act, 9 Geo. 3. c. 16. (*k*), the King shall not sue, &c. any person, &c. for any lands, &c. (except liberties and franchises), or any title which has not first accrued within sixty years before the commencement of such suit, unless he has been answered the rents within that time, or they have been in charge, or stood *insuper* of record, and the subject shall quietly enjoy against the King, and all claiming under him, by patent, &c.   This extends not to estates in reversion or remainder, or limited estates.   These lands shall be held on the usual tenures, &c.   Usual fee-farm rents confirmed.   Putting in charge, standing *insuper*, &c. good only when on verdict.   Demurrer or hearing, the lands, &c. have been given, adjudged, or decreed to the King.   And prescription is now pleadable against the Crown, even in the case of franchises and offices; for by statute 32 Geo. 3. c. 58. six years'

(*a*) 5 Cruise, 1 ed. 208. ch. 13. s. 2.

(*b*) 1 Inst. 57, b.   2 Leon. 143.   Bro. Ab. tit. Disseisin, 4.   Hob. 322.   Rol. Ab. 659.

(*c*) Co. Lit. 41, b.

(*d*) 2 Leon. 31. pl. 37. Plowd. 243, a. Vin. Ab. Prerog. T. 2.

(*e*) Ante, 366.

(*f*) Chitty on Bills, 5th ed. 257, 319. cites West on Extents, 28, 29, 30.

(*g*) Staundf. Prærog. Regis, 32, a. b.

(*h*) Ibid. ante, 251.   And see further exceptions to the rule *nullum*, &c.   Co. Lit. 119, a. note 1.

(*i*) Vin. Ab. Prerog. T. 2.   If land, which ought to pay a fine at the alienation, be aliened to the King, he shall not pay fine.   Per Priscott, Bro. Ab. Customs, pl. 5, cites Y. B. 35 H. 6, 25.

(*k*) Act on this subject relative to Ireland, 48 Geo. 3. c. 47.

possession

possession of a corporate office gives the corporator a prescriptive title upon an information in the nature of a *quo warranto*, exhibited by the Attorney-General, or other officer, on the behalf of the Crown, by virtue of any royal prerogative, or otherwise. Neither is it competent to the Crown to question any derivative title, where the person from whom it is derived was in exercise, *de facto*, of the office or franchise, in virtue of which he communicated the title for a like period of six years.

The King is not bound by fictions or relations of law (*a*); or by estoppels (*b*), even though such estoppels would affect the party through whom the Crown claims (*c*). But this does not prevent the King from taking advantage of estoppels, though they ought in general to be mutual (*d*).

It is also an established principle, that where the King's right and that of a subject meet at one and the same time, the King's shall be preferred (*e*). *Detur digniori* is the rule in the case of a concurrence of titles between the King and subject (*f*). This rule has been already explained, as it regards debts and remedies in the case of the King (*g*); and there are several cases in the books on the same doctrine (*h*).

(*a*) Jenk. 287. pl. 21.

(*b*) Godb. 299. 1 Co. R. 43. Hob. 339.

(*c*) Staundf. Prerog. 64, *a.* Godb. 391.

(*d*) Co. Lit. 352, a. b.

(*e*) Co. Lit. 30, b. 4 Co. 55. 9 Co. 129. Hardr. 24. 3 Leon. 251. 16 Vin. 566, 7.

(*f*) 2 Ventr. 268.

(*g*) Ante, 288, &c..

(*h*) See 5 Bac. Ab. 558. Prerog. E. 4. 16 Vin. Ab. 566, tit. Prerog. T. 2. pl. 23. "Hence it is said, that if there be a lord mesne and tenant, and the tenant pay the rent at the day to the mesne, before noon; and after on the same day, the mesne die, his heir within age, the tenant shall pay it over again to the King." 3 Leon. 251. If a woman marry and hath issue, and lands descend to the wife, and the husband enters, and after the wife is found an idiot by office, the lands shall be seized for the King; according to this maxim, that when the title of the King and a common person begin at one instant, the title of the King shall be preferred. Co. Lit. 30, b. So, if the woman had been the King's nief, and one had married her without the King's license, &c. and lands had descended before or after issue, yet the King, upon office found. shall have them. Co. Lit. 30, b. 4 Co. 55. Baron and feme joint purchasers of a term for years, the husband drowns himself, the lease is forfeited, and wife surviving shall not hold it against the King or his almoner; because the title of the King and a common person coming together, the King's shall be preferred. Dyer, 108. Plowd. 260. Dame Hale's Case.

On

On the same principle, the King cannot be a joint tenant, &c. with a subject (*a*).

CHAP. XV.

What Statutes bind the King.

THE general rule clearly is, that though the King may avail himself of the provisions of any Acts of Parliament (*b*), he is not bound by such as do not particularly and expressly mention him (*c*).

To this rule, however, there is a most important exception, namely, that the King is impliedly bound by statutes passed for the public good; the relief of the poor; the general advancement of learning, religion and justice; or to prevent fraud, injury or wrong (*d*). Therefore the King, though not named, is bound by the statute *de donis* to prevent wrongful alienation (*e*); the statute of H. 8. against discontinuances or alienations by husbands of their wives' estates (*f*); and the statutes of Eliz. against leases of ecclesiastical lands (*g*), simony (*h*), and fraudulent conveyances to defraud purchasers, &c. (*i*). So the King is bound by the statute of Marlbridge (*k*) against distraining tenants to answer without writ (*l*), and other similar statutes (*m*). So by the statute Westm. 1. (3 Ed. 1.) c. 5. that none shall disturb elections upon pain of great forfeitures (*n*); and by the statute of additions, 1 Hen. 5. c. 5. (*o*).

So where an Act of Parliament gives a new estate or right to the King, it shall bind him as to the manner of enjoying and

---

(*a*) Ante, 241, 2.

(*b*) 11 Co. 68, b. Leon. 150.

(*c*) 19 Vin. Ab. Statutes, E. 10. Bac. Ab. Prerog. E. 5. 2 Hawk. P. C. c. 42. s. 3.

(*d*) Ibid. Plowd. 136, 7. 11 Co. 68, b.

(*e*) Ante, 379.

(*f*) Ibid.

(*g*) 11 Co. 75. Rol. R. 151.

(*h*) Co. Lit. 120.

(*i*) 11 Co. 74. b.

(*k*) 52 H. 3. cap. 22.

(*l*) 2 Inst. 124, 169.

(*m*) Bac. Ab. Prerog. E. 4.

(*n*) 2 Inst. 169. 4 Mod. 207.

(*o*) Bro. Ab. Parliament, pl. 47, cites 5 Ed. 4, 32.

using

using the right, as well as a subject (*a*). And though upon the construction of a statute, nothing " shall be taken by equity," (or relaxed construction,) against the King (*b*); yet it has been observed by J. Doderidge (*c*), that " where the subject has authority to do a thing by the express letter of a statute, this shall not be taken away by any strained construction, though it be for the benefit of the King." And the Crown, though not named, is bound by the general words of statutes which tend to perform the will of a founder or donor (*d*).

But Acts of Parliament which would divest or abridge the King of his prerogatives, his interests or his remedies, in the slightest degree, do not in general extend to, or bind the King, unless there be express words to that effect (*e*). There-fore the statutes of limitation, bankruptcy, insolvency, set-off, &c. (*f*) are irrelevant in the case of the King; nor does the statute of frauds (*g*) relate to him (*h*). So on the statute *quia emptores*, that none shall alien lands in fee to hold of himself (*i*), and Magna Charta, that common pleas shall be holden in some certain place (*k*): and other instances might be mentioned (*l*).

And in mere indifferent statutes, directing that certain mat-ters shall be performed as therein pointed out, the King is not

---

(*a*) 4 Mod. 207. Show. R. 208. Crooke's Case. By an Act of Parlia-ment, 22 Car. 2. c. 11. the parishes of St. Michael, Wood Street, and St. Mary Staining, in London, were united and established as one parish church; and it was provided, that the first pre-sentation should be made by the patron of such of the said churches, the en-dowments whereof were of the greatest value; the King was patron of St. Mary Staining (of far less value), and a com-mon person patron of St. Michael, Wood Street, who presented Mr. Crooke; on a *caveat* entered against the institution, it was determined by civi-lians, by the advice of lawyers, at Doc-tors' Commons, that this statute, though in the affirmative, and without any ne-gative words, extended to, and so far bound the King, as to deprive him of any preference he might have by his prerogative, as in cases where his inter-est is intermixed with others; and that the Act of Parliament, giving a new estate to the King, and prescribing the manner of enjoyment, the method li-mited must take place of the King's prerogative.

(*b*) Godb. 308, *arg.* cites Plowd. 233, 4.

(*c*) Rol. R. 67. See 10 Rep. 84.

(*d*) Vin. Ab. Statutes, E. 10. pl. 11. cites 11 Rep. 72, b. 73, a.

(*e*) 19 Vin. Ab. Statutes, E. 10. Bac. Ab. Prerog. E. 5.

(*f*) Ante, 366.

(*g*) 29 Car. 2. c. 3.

(*h*) 1 Salk. 162. This doctrine as to the statute of frauds, doubted by Lord Hardwicke. 3 Atk. 154.

(*i*) Lit. s. 140. Co. Lit. 98. Plowd. 240. 11 Co. 68, b.

(*k*) Plowd. 240, b. 244, a. ante, 77.

(*l*) See Bac. Ab. Prerog. E. 4.

thereby

thereby in many instances prevented from adopting a different course, in pursuance of his prerogative. " There are also statutes (says Lord Hobart (a)) which were made to put things in an orderly form, and to ease a sovereign of labour ; but not to deprive him of power which cannot be said to bind the King." Thus though the 25 H. 8. c. 21. s. 3. directing the manner of granting dispensations, licences, &c. in ecclesiastical cases, provides that dispensations shall not otherwise be granted, the King may grant them as before (b). And though the statute 27 H. 8. c. 27. enacted, that all grants concerning the Court of Augmentations, should be under the seal of that Court, grants under the great seal have been held valid (c).

CHAP. XVI.

Of Grants from the King.

Sect. I.—*What the King may grant and what he may not.*

There are certain supreme powers and prerogatives inherent in, and inseparably annexed to the royal character. These form the political capacity of the King, and are incommunicable ; the constitution having entrusted the King alone with the discretion and power of exercising them. So that for instance his Majesty cannot grant to another the prerogatives (d) of assenting to Acts of Parliament (e); of pardoning offenders, unless perhaps abroad and on sudden occasions, as during the King's absence, &c. (f); or of making Judges, &c. (g), or de-

---

(a) Hob. R. 126.

(b) Ante, 53.

(c) Dyer, 50, a.

(d) " The King cannot grant his prerogative," Bro. Ab. Patents, pl. 13. cites 14 H. 4. 9. Bro. Ab. Prerog. pl. 18, 60. " Though the King grant *jura regalia*, yet it shall not exclude the King himself," per Heath, J. Mar. 165. See the statute 27 H. 8. c. 24. for re-annexing to the Crown several powers and authorities theretofore exercised by owners of the Counties palatine. Re-

straint on aliening hundreds. Skinner, 604.

(e) Ante, 74. Qu. in the colonies, ante, 34, 5.

(f) Jenk. 171. pl. 36. Hob. 155. 7 Co. R. 36. Mo. 764. 27 H. 8. c. 24. s. 1. In the colonies, ante, 35. Power of Governor of New South Wales, &c. to remit sentence of transportation. Ante, 89, 90. 30 Geo. 3. c. 47.

(g) Bro. Patents, pl. 45, 111. 17 Vin. Ab. 89. Prerog. m. b. pl. 21. Statute 27 H. 8. c. 24. s. 2. 5.

nizens.

nizens (*a*). Nor can the King grant a trust reposed in himself as sovereign, as a lapse (*b*). Nor could he grant his dispensing power (*c*); or purveyance; butlerage, &c. (*d*): and he is restrained from transferring his prerogative in saltpetre (*e*); the year day and waste (*f*); and the power of prosecution upon and carrying into effect, a penal or other statute or law (*g*).

The King's grants are also void whenever they tend to prejudice the course and benefit of public *justice*. Thus the King cannot grant an exemption from the jurisdiction of any Court, if he do not erect another jurisdiction of the same nature, for that would create a failure of justice: so that he cannot exempt a town from the Admiralty jurisdiction, if he do not grant a power to have another jurisdiction there (*h*). Nor can the King exempt any one from civil responsibilities to a fellow subject (*i*); or from liability to be punished for offences he may commit (*k*). And both at common law (*l*), and by statute (*m*), grants or promises of fines or forfeitures before the conviction of, or judgment against, the party on whom they are to be levied, are void.

Nor can the King by grant create a forfeiture of goods, &c. On this ground the charter of Hen. 6. to the corporation of dyers within London, granting them power to search, &c. and if they found any cloth dyed with logwood, that the cloth should be forfeited, was held void (*n*). It is also a clear general principle that the King cannot by grant or otherwise impose new, or enhance old, charges, impositions or taxes on any of his subjects (*o*). Therefore grants by the King that a merchant shall pay so much for searching or measuring his goods (*p*); that he shall not import wine without paying so much (*q*); that a merchant who imports wine at any other port

---

(*a*) Bro. Patents, pl. 45. 111.   17 Vin. Ab. 89. Prerog. m. b. pl. 21.   Statute 27 H. 8. c. 24. s. 2, 5.

(*b*) Hob. 208.   That the King may empower a subject to grant or erect a corporation, ante, 127, 8.

(*c*) 7 Co. 36, b.   21 Jac. 1. c. 3. s. 1.

(*d*) 2 Rol. Ab. 187. 1. 35.

(*e*) 12 Rep. 13.

(*f*) Jenk. 307, pl. 83.   Bro. Ab. Prerog. pl. 104. Ante, 220.

(*g*) Jenk. 190, pl. 93.   7 Co. 37, a.

(*h*) 2 Rol. Ab. 201. 1. 45.

(*i*) Ante, 90, 1.; &c.

(*k*) 2 Rol. Ab. 192. 32, 35.   Vin. Ab. Prerog. Y. b.

(*l*) Ibid.

(*m*) 21 Jac. 1. c. 3. s. 1.   1 W. and M. st. 2. c. 2. s. 1.

(*n*) 2 Inst. 47.   Sid. 441. Ventr. 47.

(*o*) 2 Inst. 58, 60.   Com. Dig. Prerog. D. (D. 48.)

(*p*) 2 Inst. 62.

(*q*) Ibid. 63.

than

than the port of *S.* shall pay treble customs (*a*), are respectively unfounded.   And merchants are not, it seems, bound by their voluntary grant to the King of a tax on their goods; as that would induce them to sell at higher prices (*b*).   But in certain cases where there is a substantial *quid pro quo,* a real benefit to the subject of which he can and does avail himself; the King may by grant impose a reasonable charge on his subjects for a limited or other period.   Therefore the King may grant a market, fair, ferry, &c. with liberty to take toll (*c*): and by prescription, a subject may claim pontage, for building and keeping a bridge; or murage, for erecting and keeping a wall for defence, &c. (*d*); or toll thorough, that is, toll for passing a highway kept in repair, &c. by the claimant, there being a good consideration and benefit moving to the subject (*e*).   The writ of *ad quod damnum* (*f*), which is in general issued previous to the grant of a fair, &c. shews how zealously the law has consulted the common weal in these cases.   So a grant from the Crown, in derogation of the common law, as that one should hold a court of equity, &c. (*g*); or that an estate should descend contrary to the common law, as according to the custom of gavelkind, &c. (*h*); or contravening the statute law, as the Navigation Act, &c. (*i*), is void; for the King cannot make law or custom by his grant.   And if penalties are given by Acts of Parliament for relief of the poor, the King cannot dispose of them otherwise (*k*).

It is scarcely necessary to mention that the King's grants are invalid, when they destroy and derogate from rights previously vested in another subject by grant, &c. (*l*).

Having thus mentioned the principal cases in which the King is *restrained* in his grants, it will naturally be our next subject of inquiry, in what instances no such restraint exists.

(*a*) 2 Inst. 61.

(*b*) 2 Rol. Ab. 173. 1. 20, 25.

(*c*) Ante, 194, 5. 2 Rol. Ab. 171. 1. 30; 202. 1. 42. Bro. Patents, pl. 12. Com. Dig. Prerog. D. 48, and tit. Toll. 18 Vin. Ab. Prerog. *M.* b. pl. 19.

(*d*) Ibid. Bro. Ab. Contempts, pl. 4. Noy. 176.

(*e*) 1 Wils. 299. 1 T. R. 660. 4 Taunt. 520.

(*f*) F. N. B. 220.

(*g*) 2 Rol. 192. 1. 37. Hob. 63.

Ante, 76.

(*h*) 2 Rol. Ab. 164. 18 Vin. Ab. Prerog. *M.* b. pl. 23. Bro. Ab. Patents, pl. 25, 41, 100. Ibid. Prerog. pl. 53 and 103.   But it seems the King may convey in fee, with a condition restraining the grantee from alienating. Bro. Ab. Prerog. pl. 102.

(*i*) 12 East, 296. Ante, 163.

(*k*) Jenk. 307, pl. 83. 7 Co. 36, b.

(*l*) See ante, 193, 4. 119, 125, 132. post. 400.

The

The King's power to grant letters of marque and reprisals (*a*), courts and offices (*b*), franchises (*c*), patents for inventions (*d*), Crown lands and possessions (*e*), the sole liberty of printing certain works (*f*), protections (*g*), and lands seized under offices (*h*), have been already considered at large, and various other rights of the King, as to grants, have also been incidentally noticed.

Grants of the revenue were formerly unlimited (*i*), but are now very properly restrained. Formerly, every branch of the revenue was in the disposal of the Crown, and might be granted; but since the Revolution, and the introduction of the funding system, this has been altered, and a particular portion only of the public revenue, viz. the civil list, is the property of the King, and vested in him for the maintenance of his dignity (*k*). Still, however, the power of the Crown over such civil list remained without limits; and, therefore, as well to secure the Crown as the subject, the legislature introduced several provisions, restraining and regulating the grants of pensions out of the civil list (*l*) And Parliament had long before confined and regulated the alienation of Crown lands (*m*). Still, however, the right of the King to transfer to a subject franchises, which are termed flowers of the Crown, and formerly constituted an important part of the revenue; and forfeitures; fines for offences, &c. (*n*), remains unchanged.

Between subject and subject, choses in action, or rights of action, are not assignable, so as to vest in the assignee the power of suing at law in his own name against the debtor (*o*): but this doctrine does not extend to the King, who, by virtue of his prerogative, may effectually take by assignment, or, by express and special words (*p*), transfer to another, a right of, or

---

(*a*) Ante, 40.

(*b*) Ante, 75, &c.

(*c*) Ante, 118 to 155.

(*d*) Ante, 176 to 193.

(*e*) Ante, 203, &c.

(*f*) Ante, 238 to 241.

(*g*) Ante, 282 to 284.

(*h*) Ante, 253, &c.

(*i*) Plowd. 236. Vaugh. 62. Co. Lit. 19. 7 Co. 12. See the banker's case, 5 Mod. 46. Comb. 270. Skin. 601, pl. 11. 11 St. Tr. 136.

(*k*) Ante, 201, 2.

(*l*) 22 G. 3. c. 82. s. 17. 25 G. 3. c. 61. Pension list rated to Land Tax, 29 G. 3. c. 6. s. 78. 35 G. 3. c. 2. s. 71. Pensions to persons who have served abroad. 50 G. 3. c. 117. s. 13, 14. Accumulation of arrears prevented. 44 G. 3. c. 80. s. 2.

(*m*) Ante, 203, &c.

(*n*) Ld. Raym. 213, 14.

(*o*) Co. Lit. 214, a. Chitty on B. 5th ed. 7, 8.

(*p*) 3 Lev. 135. 12 Rep. 2.

chose

chose in, action against a third person (*a*).   But this rule appears to relate only to causes of action for debt and things certain; not to a right of action for trespass or uncertain damages (*b*).   And it may be doubtful whether it relates to *choses real*, as rights of action, &c. relative to land, so as to vest them at law in the grantee (*c*).   It seems, also, part of a debt cannot be assigned to the King (*d*).

But the assignment of debts to the Crown having been greatly abused, it was enacted, by the statute 7 Jac. 1. c. 15. (*e*), that " no debt shall be assigned to the King, by or from any debtor or accountant to his Majesty, other than such debts as did before grow due originally to the King's debtor or accountant *bonâ fide ;* and that all grants and assignments of debts to the King, which shall be had or made contrary to the true intent of that Act, shall be void."   And even at common law, the assignee of a chose in action from the Crown has not the power of assigning it to another subject, so as to enable the latter to sue in his own name (*f*).

The King may also, in general, grant a condition in future, a matter depending on a contingency, *quando acciderit*, or a mere possibility (*g*); or convey in fee, with a condition against alienation, by the grantee (*h*).   But the King cannot grant land ' when it shall escheat (*i*);' or the next lapse of the church of *D.* (before it happens) 'when it shall happen (*k*).'   But his Majesty may, in some cases, discharge a subject of liabilities not yet accrued (*l*).   So that he may grant that a spiritual man shall be discharged of tenths, " when they shall be granted" by the

---

(*a*) Y. B. 31 H. 7. 19. Bro. Ab. Prerog. 40.   Co. Lit. 232. b. n. 1. 1 Dyer, 1. pl. 7. 30. b. pl. 208.   Cro. Jac. 17, 82.   17 Vin. Ab. 88. Prerog. *M.* b.

(*b*) Vin. Ab. *ubi supra*.   Bro. Ab. Chose in Action, pl. 11.

(*c*) Vin. Ab. Bro. Ab. Patents, pl. 98. Chose in Action, pl. 14.   11 Co. R. 12. See Leon. 21. 3 Leon. 198. 17 Vin. Ab. 79. tit. Prerog. G. b. 3. in which it is said, that the King may, by special words, grant a right of entry and a real action.

(*d*) Owen. R. 2.

(*e*) See Hob. 258.   And as to the remedy, &c. see ante, 322; Extents.

(*f*) Cro. Jac. 180.   Skin. 6, 26.

(*g*) Jenk. 210.   See the cases, Com. Dig. Grant, G. 1. and Assignment, D. 17 Vin. Ab. 145. Prerog. I. c. 2. and Ibid. 83. *M.* b. 3.   Bac. Ab. Prerog. F. 3.

(*h*) Ante, 386, note (*h*).

(*i*) T. Raym. 241. 1 Chalmers' Collection of Op. 131. 2 Lev. 171. Or forfeited property before forfeiture. Ante, 385.

(*k*) Hob. R. 208.   See ante, 253, &c. as to grants of property seized under offices.

(*l*) Bro. Ab. Patents, pl. 53.   Y. B. 6 H. 7. 4.

clergy;

clergy (*a*); or that the grantee shall not be impeached of a certain recognizance he may subsequently enter into (*b*).

The King cannot, it is said, grant an annuity, for his person is not chargeable; but he may if it be charged on any of his Majesty's possessions (*c*).

Grants of exemptions having been treated of in a previous chapter (*d*), it may be sufficient to add in this place, that the King may by grant exempt a subject from tolls in his Majesty's markets (*e*), and from impositions and charges due personally to himself; but not, it seems, from charges imposed by Act of Parliament for the general interests of the country (*f*).

SECT. II.

How Grants from and to the King are to be effected.

It is a clear rule, that, as well for the protection of the King as the security of the subject, and on account of the high consideration entertained by the law towards his Majesty (*g*), no freehold interest, franchise (*h*), or liberty, &c. can be transferred from the Crown but by matter of record *i* . This is effected by letters patent under the great seal, which is a record

(*a*) Bro. Ab. Patents, pl. 53. Y. B. 6 H. 7. 4. 9 H. 6. 62. For this, it is added, sounds in covenant, and against the King no writ of covenant lies, and therefore the grant is good.

(*b*) 19 H. 6. 64. Vin. Ab. Prerog. I. c. See ante, 91, that the King cannot discharge a recognizance for the security of a subject.

(*c*) Salk. 58. pl. 1. Freem. 331.

(*d*) Ante, 20.

(*e*) Sir W. Jones, 119. Com. Dig. Prerog. D. 33. Ante, 195.

(*f*) Ibid. Ante, 20. 17 Vin. Ab. 150, 1. Prerog. K. c., L. c. 2 Rol. Ab. 199. Vaugh. R. 161. Sav. 52.

(*g*) Dr. and Stud. 61, d. 8.

(*h*) Even within the Duchy of Lancaster, and notwithstanding the statute 3 H. 5. and 27 H. 8. c. 40, which only relate to possessions, &c. as lands therein; not to franchises created *de novo*. 2 Lutw. 1233, 1237. 17 Vin. 73. Com. Dig. Patent, C. 4.

(*i*) 2 Co. 16, b. 17 Vin. Ab. 70. Prerog. C. b. Com. Dig. tit. Patent. 2 Bla. Com. 346. Pardon must be under Great Seal. 1 B. and Pul. 199. Cannot convey by bargain and sale, covenant to stand seized or by lease and release, ante, 378. Grants of offices, ante, 78.

and

and evidence *per se,* without further proof (*a*); and that such seal may not be affixed without due caution and consideration several preliminary steps are requisite. Grants or letters patent must first pass by bill (*b*), which is prepared by the Attorney and Solicitor-General, in consequence of a warrant from the Crown (*c*), and is then signed, that is, subscribed at the top, with the King's own *sign manual,* and sealed with his *privy signet,* which is always in the custody of the principal secretary of state; and then sometimes it immediately passes under the great seal, in which case the patent is subscribed in these words, *per ipsum regem,* by the " King himself (*d*)." Otherwise, the course is to carry an extract of the bill to the keeper of the *privy seal,* who makes out a writ or warrant thereupon to the Chancery, so that the sign manual is the warrant to the privy seal, and the privy seal is the warrant to the great seal, and in this last case the patent is subscribed, *per breve de privato sigillo,* "by writ of privy seal (*e*)." But there are some grants which only pass through certain offices, as the Admiralty or Treasury, in consequence of a *sign manual,* without the confirmation of either the *signet,* the *great,* or the *privy* seal (*f*).

It also appears (*g*), that chattels real can in general only pass from the Crown under the great seal. But it is a general rule, that personal things, as goods or *choses in action,* or the discharge of a debt, need not be granted by the Crown under the great seal, but may be legally transferred under the privy seal (*h*). Various other matters of small importance may also be done without the great seal (*i*); and, it seems, that land may,

---

(*a*) See 3 and 4 Ed. 6. c. 4. and 13 El. c. 6. Peake, Ev. 4th ed. 31, note c. Phillips, Ev. 1 ed. 173, 4. There are three seals of which the law takes notice, the Great Seal, the Privy Seal, and the Signet. 2 Inst. 554.

(*b*) See ante, 188, 9 ; grants of patents for inventions.

(*c*) No officer which the King has, nor altogether, may, *ex officio,* dispose of the King's treasure, though it be for the honour or profit of the King himself, 11 Co. 91. b. " They cannot without the King's own warrant." Ibid.

92.

(*d*) 9 Rep. 18.

(*e*) Ibid. 2 Inst. 555.

(*f*) 2 Bla. Com. 346, 7.

(*g*) Per Coke, Attorney-General, Mo. 476. pl. 681. cited 17 Vin. Ab. 74. Prerog. F. b. *sed qu.* Cro. Jac. 109. Com. Dig. Patent, C. 3. and 2.

(*h*) Ibid. Rol. R. 7. Com. Dig. Patent, C. 5. 2*u.* if without writing. Bro. Abr. Prerog. pl. 61.

(*i*) Instances, Ibid. Vin. Ab. *ubi supra.* 2 Inst. 555. cap. 6.

by

by the course of the Court, be granted or leased under the Exchequer seal (*a*).

Money, says Gilbert (*b*), was never issued on the great or privy seal; and antiently there were no writs of *liberate* for the payment of money on any debt due from the Crown, or any grants made of any sums, but afterwards they were wont to grant patents or privy seals to the Treasurer, giving him authority to issue warrants for the money. The writs were antiently directed to the Treasurer and Chancellor, and, therefore, the warrants are at present signed by the Treasurer and Chancellor, and mention the authority of the broad seal by which he issues them.

Nor can the King take any freehold interest, or even a term, for years (*c*), or surrender, &c. without matter of record, as a deed inrolled, &c. (*d*). But, it seems, that the surrender of a copyhold to the King, as lord of a manor, in pursuance of the custom of the manor, is good (*e*). And the Crown may take goods and choses in action without matter of record, either by way of grant or testamentary bequest (*f*).

SECT. III.

Construction of :—And when void for, 1. *Uncertainty ;* 2. *Misrecitals ; and herein of false Suggestions, or Deceit.*

In ordinary cases between subject and subject, the principle is, that the grant shall be construed, if the meaning be doubtful, most strongly against the grantor, who is presumed to use the most cautious words for his own advantage and security. But in the case of the King, whose grants chiefly flow from his royal bounty and grace, the rule is otherwise; and Crown

---

(*a*) Cro. Jac. 109. See Com. Dig. tit. Patent, C. 3. 12 East, 98.

(*b*) Hist. Excheq. 143.

(*c*) Lane, 60.

(*d*) Plowd. Com. 213, b. 484, b. 105. Bro. Prerog. pl. 41, 56, 93. 17 Vin. Ab. 171, 173. tit. Prerog. Z. c. B. D. What is matter of record for this purpose,

Ibid. Vin. A. d. Subsequent enrolment has relation back, Bro. Prerog. pl. 57.

(*e*) Keblc, 720.

(*f*) 40 Ass. 38. Vin. Ab. *ubi supra.* Bro. Ab. Prerog. pl. 36, 40, 50, 145. and Ibid. tit. 'Done.' pl. 16. tit. Chose in Action, pl. 4. cites Y. B. 21 H. 7, 19.

grants have at all times been construed most favorably for the King, where a fair doubt exists as to the real meaning of the instrument, as well in the instance of grants from his Majesty, as in the case of transfers to him (*a*). As if the King grant a manor purchased by him, with all franchises belonging, &c. the franchises in the hands of the feoffer, and which became merged in, or re-annexed to, the Crown, by the King's purchase, do not pass (*b*). So, if the King grant a manor with all lands accepted or reputed as parcel, nothing passes which is not parcel in truth and of right, and which had not immemorially been so (*c*). Nor will a grant of ' mines, amerciaments, and escheats,' pass royal franchises of that description (*d*); or a grant of *bona et catalla sua*, pass specialties (*e*); or a grant of *bona felonum* pass the goods of a suicide (*f*). " Because general words in the King's grant never extend to a grant of things which belong to the King by virtue of his prerogative, for such ought to be expressly mentioned (*g*)." In other words, if under a general name a grant comprehends things of a royal and of a base nature, the base only shall pass (*h*).

It is indeed expressly provided by the statute *de prerogativa regis*, 17 Ed. 2. st. 2. c. 15. (*i*), that " when our Lord the King giveth or granteth to any, a manor or land with the appurtenances, unless he make express mention in his deed in writing, of knight's fees, *advowsons* of churches and *dowers*, when they happen, belonging to such manor or land, then at this day the

---

(*a*) 2 Co. R. 24. 5 Ibid. 56. Plowd. 243. 11, a. 17 Vin. Ab. Prerog. O. c. and O. c. 2 ; Y. c. 5. Com. Dig. Grant, G. 12. 5 Bac. Ab. 602. Prerog. F. 2. 2 Bla. Com. 347: 2 Rol. R. 219. As to explaining an old charter by contemporaneous usage, 3 T. R. 279, 288. n. 4 Ibid. 421. 4 East, 338. 5 Taunt. 752. Peak. Ev. 4th ed. 331.

(*b*) 2 Rol. Ab. 184. 1. 50. 193. 1. 30. The King granted to a ranger of a forest " all manner of wood blown or thrown down by the wind, and all dead wood, and the boughs and branches of trees and wood in the forest, cut off or thrown down ; and house-bote and fire-bote, for himself and the foresters and keepers." It was adjudged, that under

these words, branches cut from trees felled for his Majesty's use did not pass. Anstr. R. 592.

(*c*) 2 Rol. Ab. 186. 1. 25, 30. But if the King grant a messuage and all lands ' *spectantes aut cum eo dimissas ;*' lands enjoyed with it for a convenient time pass. Cro. Car. 169.

(*d*) Plowd. 336. Dav. 17, 57.

(*e*) 2 Rol. 195. 1. 20. See Vin. Ab. Prerog. E. c. See 1 Bla. Rep. 120.

(*f*) 17 Vin. Ab. 130. tit. Prerog. C. c.

(*g*) Ibid. Rol. Ab. 195, E. Com. Dig. Grant, G. 7.

(*h*) 1 Bla. R. 118.

(*i*) See 17 Vin. Ab. 131, 2. Prerog. C. c. 10 Co. 64.

King

King reserveth to himself such fees, advowsons and dowers, albeit that among other persons it hath been observed otherwise."

It is also a branch of this rule, that though in the case of a subject's grant, many incidental matters are presumptively admitted, (as if a feoffment of land were made by a lord to his villein, this operated as a manumission (a)); still in the case of a Crown grant it shall not enure to any other intent than that specified in the grant : so that if the thing granted cannot pass without implying something not granted, it shall be void rather than operate to two intents not noticed in the grant (b). As if the King grant land to an alien, it operates nothing; for such grant shall not also enure to make him a denizen, so that he may be capable of taking by grant (c). Nor shall a grant of lands to a felon amount to an implied pardon (d). But if the King grant a messuage and all lands *spectantes aut cum eo dimissas*, lands enjoyed with it for a convenient time pass (e).

But the rule that grants shall be construed most favorably for the King, is subject to many limitations and exceptions.

In the first place, no strained or extravagant construction is to be made in favor of the King. If the intention be obvious, royal grants are to receive a fair and liberal interpretation accordingly (f). And, though the general words of a grant may be qualified by the recital (g); yet if the intent of the Crown be

---

(a) Lit. s. 206.

(b) 3 Leon. 243. 17 Vin. Ab. 142. Prerog. G. c. 2 Bla. Com. 347. 1 Bla. R. 118. The King's grant shall not enure (to his special prejudice) to two intents, viz. to a demise of the land, and also to a suspension of his condition by which he may defeat the estate for life, and other estates, as it should be in the case of a common person ; or to a demise in respect of his present estate *per auter vie*, and also to a confirmation of his condition by which otherwise he might defeat all, as it should be in the case of a common person ; for the grant of the King shall be taken according to his express intention comprehended in his grant; and shall

not extend to any other thing by construction or implication, which does not appear by his grant; and therefore in such cases the King ought to be truly informed, and he ought to make special and particular grant, which by express words may enure to all such several intents as are desired. 7 Rep. 14, a. So where the King has two rights in him, he cannot exclude himself of both without special words. Ibid. 14, b.

(c) Finch, L. 110. Bro. Ab. tit. Patents, 62. 5 Rep. 56.

(d) Ibid. 1 Bla. Rep. 118.

(e) Ante, 392, note (c).

(f) 2 Inst. 496, 7.

(g) 4 Taunt. 593. 2 M. and Selw. 18.

plainly

plainly expressed in the granting part, it shall enure accordingly, and shall not be restrained by the recital (*a*).

In the second place, the construction and leaning shall be in favor of the subject, if the grant shew that it was not made at the solicitation of the grantee, but *ex speciali gratiâ, certâ scientiâ, et mero motu regis* (*b*). Though these words do not of themselves protect the grantee against false recitals, &c. (*c*).

In the third place, if the King's grants are upon a valuable consideration, they shall be construed strictly for the patentee for the honor of the King (*d*).

So where the King's grant is capable of two constructions, by the one of which it will be valid and by the other void, it shall receive that interpretation which will give it effect (*e*); " for that will be more for the benefit of the subject and the honor of the King, which ought to be more regarded than his profit (*f*)." As if there be a grant to discharge one from the collection of tithes granted *per clerum Angliæ*, he shall be discharged if the grant be *per clerum provinciæ Cantuariensis* (*g*); for it is not usual to have a grant by both provinces together (*h*).

In considering the cases in which a royal grant may be ineffectual on account of mistakes, deceit, &c. it may be proper to divide the subject into the following branches: 1. *Uncertainties.* 2. *Misrecitals;* and herein of false suggestions and deceit.

1. A decided *uncertainty* will avoid a grant from the Crown, not only as against the patentee, but also as against the King, because it raises a presumption of deceit (*i*). As if the King grant a piece of land, parcel of a waste, &c. without designating what piece (*k*); or grant land or a rent, in which there may be various interests (*l*), without limiting or specifying any particular

(*a*) 10 Co. 112.

(*b*) Finch L. 100. 1 Rep. 40. 10 Rep. 112. Com. Dig. Grant, G. 12. Vin. Ab. Prerog. E. c. 3.

(*c*) 10 Co. Rep. 112. 3 Leon. 249. 2 Salk. 561.

(*d*) 2 Inst. 446, 7. 6 Co. 6, a. 10 Co. 65. 5 Bac. Ab. 604.

(*e*) 9 Co. 131, a. 10 Co. 67, b. 6 Co. 6.

(*f*) Com. Dig. Grant, G. 12.

(*g*) Y. B. 21 Ed. 4. 48, b. 2 R. 2, 4.

(*h*) Ibid.

(*i*) Bulstr. 10. 17 Vin. Ab. 140. Prerog. F. c. 6 Bac. Ab. 602. Prerog. F. 2. Co. Entr. 384.

(*k*) Leon. 30, pl. 36. 12 Rep. 86.

(*l*) Because if the thing granted be such of which divers estates cannot be limited, but one estate only is incident thereto,

cular estate in the gift; and in this case the patentee takes no interest whatever (*a*). So in the case of a grant of debts which have accrued to the Crown, to the amount of a certain sum, within a limited period, without saying what debts (*b*); of a grant of the custody of all the King's houses, not saying which (*c*); of a grant of *bona felonum*, not stating in what manor or county (*d*); and of a grant that T. S. shall not be sheriff without saying " of what county" or " of any county in England (*e*)." And in granting tolls, the amount intended to be granted must not be left a matter of doubt and uncertainty (*f*).

But the rule *id certum est quod certum reddi potest* obtains, even in the case of the Crown; and therefore if the grant refer, or has relation, to that which is certain, though it be not matter of record but mere matter of fact or *in pais*, it is sufficient (*g*). As if the King grant to a city all the liberties, which London has (*h*): or grant a manor *habend'* to the grantee and his heirs ' *adeo plenè et integre*, as it came into the hands of the King by the attainder of T. S.;' or ' as is contained in such letters patent (*i*);' or 'with such privileges and franchises as the Dean and Chapter of Saint Paul's, &c. formerly enjoyed therein (*k*);' or ' as belonged to the manor when purchased (*l*).' And though, as before observed, advowsons, &c. do not pass under a grant of a manor *cum pertinentiis* (*m*) ; yet advowsons appendant, &c. may pass without express words if there be any words of relation (*n*). Many other instances of this rule are to be met with in the old books (*o*).

thereto, which the law limits without any limitation made by the grantor, of such thing the grant of the King cannot be doubtful or uncertain, nor can the King be deceived, nor can he err ; for *error est in bivio*, and no error can be where there is only one way to be taken. Dav. Rep. 45, a.

(*a*) Ibid. Rol. Ab. 845. Dav. 35, 45. 1 Bla. R. 118.

(*b*) 12 Rep. 86.

(*c*) Jones, R. 293.

(*d*) Com. Dig. Grant, G. 6.

(*e*) Y. B. 2 R. 3. 7. Bro. Ab. Patents, pl. 92. But a grant of the stew-

ardship of several matters by name, without mentioning in what county, is good. 9 Co. 42, 47. a. 4 Mod. 279.

(*f*) Ante, 195.

(*g*) Com. Dig. Grant, G. 5. Vin. Ab. Prerog. R. c.

(*h*) Y. B. 20. H. 7. 7. b.

(*i*) 10 Co. R. 63.

(*k*) Cro. El. 512, 13.

(*l*) 2 Rol. Ab. 184. 1. 54.

(*m*) Ante, 392, 3.

(*n*) 10 Co. 64. Plowd. 251. Com. Dig. Grant, G. 5.

(*o*) Com. Dig. Grant, G. 5.

Where a particular certainty precedes, it shall not be destroyed by an uncertainty or a mistake coming after *(a)*.

2. With respect to *mis-recitals* and *false suggestions* or *deceit,* these also will, in certain cases, invalidate a grant from the Crown *(b)*.

And here it may be noticed, that to prevent deceits, it is in general necessary that a grant by the Crown of any reversion should recite the particular previous term estate or interest, still *in esse,* and which is of record *(c)*. And even if the King (by matter of record, as is necessary), lease land to *B.,* and afterwards grant him a new lease, without reciting the first, the last charter is void, without regard to the effect it may have on the first *(d)*. But the grant of a copyhold need not recite that it is a copyhold *(e)*. And if the King lease strictly at will, a second lease at will to another need not recite the first *(f)*. So if he lease part of a manor, and afterwards lease the manor to another, it seems the first grant need not be recited *(g)*. So in the case of a second grant of a mere charge or trust, without fee or profit *(h)*. And the recital, when necessary, need not specifically designate the previous charter, or mention its date, but may notice it by general expressions; nor is a mistake in the recital of the date of the first grant fatal *(i)*. And if the King grant land, which is in lease of record, without recital of the first grant, but with these words " notwithstanding that it be in lease for life or years, of record or otherwise," or other equivalent expression, this is a good grant, and will pass the reversion; for many inconveniences might arise, if the necessity of reciting previous interests could in no shape be obviated *(k)*. And, on the same ground, if land be in lease of record, and the King, without reciting the lease, grant the land, and further grant ' the reversion thereof, expectant on any estate for life or for years,' this is good *(l)*.

(a) Cro. El. 34, 48. Yelv. 42. 3 Leon. 162, 148. 2 Godb. 423. 10 Co. 112.

(b) 2 Bla. Com. 348.

(c) 17 Vin. Ab. 108, Prerog. Q. b. 2. Com. Dig. Grant, G. 10.

(d) Cro. El. 231.

(e) 2 Sid. 139.

(f) Bro. Patent, 2.

(g) 1 And. 46.

(h) Bro. Ab. Patent, 2.

(i) 17 Vin. Ab. 110, Prerog. R. b.

(k) 4 Co. 35, b.

(l) Ibid.

The

The general rule appears to be that the grant need not recite the King's title (a): and it seems that if after reciting certain facts a charter draw as a conclusion that the King has a certain estate, which is neither correct in law or fact, this false conclusion, not being any part of the consideration of the grant, and not having arisen from the misinformation or fault of the grantee, but being the surmise and mistake of the King, shall not avoid the charter (b). So if the King mistakenly surmise in his grant that he holds by escheat, whereas the lands are his inheritance; or grant in consideration of supposed services (c); or call the grantee a knight, he not being one (d); such grants are good notwithstanding these mistakes. But it seems that royal grants are always void where the King evidently mistakes his title in a material point to the prejudice of his tenure or profit (e).

So if the recital of a thing in a patent which sounds to the King's benefit be false, the grant will be void; for the King is in point of law deceived (f). As if the patent recite a grant of a reversion which was void, and the grant be to commence after it (g): if it recite an inquisition of his presentation; and he then confirm it; where the presentation was repealed (h): or if the King lease for twenty-one years after a former lease to *A.* determines; which was before surrendered (i). So if the King grant a greater or different estate than he could effectually transfer (k). And if the false recital, &c. arise from the suggestion of the party applying for the grant, such grant will be void. As if the grant be founded on a false suggestion, that the land be of less value than it is (l); or that the King had it by escheat when he had not (m). And if any thing men-

(a) 1 Co. 45, b. 51, a.   Mo. 318, 20.

(b) 6 Co. 55, a.

(c) Plowd. 455.

(d) Ld. Raym. 292.   Skinner, 651.

(e) 5 Bac. Ab. 603. Prerog. F. 2.

(f) 2 Co. 54.   1 Co. 43, a.   Dyer, 352, a.   11 Co. 90.   2 Rol. Ab. 188. l. 12.

(g) 11 Co. 4, b.   2 Rol. Ab. 188. l. 32.

(h) 2 Rol. Ab. 188. l. 45.

(i) 3 Leon. 5, 6.

(k) See the Instances, Com. Dig.

Grant, G. 8.   2 Bla. Com. 348.

(l) 2 Rol. Ab. 188. l. 15.   Yelv. 18. See Lord Hardwicke's observation on Lord Baltimore's information to the Crown, that certain lands in the plantations were uncultivated and possessed by barbarians, previous to his obtaining a charter, whereby the King might be involved in disputes, the land being possessed by Dutchmen and Swedes, &c. 1 Ves. sen. 451.

(m) 2 Rol. Ab. 188. l. 20.

tioned as the consideration of the grant, or which sounds for the benefit of the King, (be it executed or executory, matter of record or *in pais,*) be false, the King is deceived, and the grant will be void (*a*). As if the King grant in consideration of the surrender of a prior interest or estate; when the surrender was only in appearance (*b*); or conditional (*c*); or the whole was not surrendered (*d*). So if his Majesty grant, " in consideration of a grant or surrender by an husband and wife;" for the wife could not surrender (*e*): " in consideration of a surrender;" when part was leased to another (*f*): " in consideration of an antient rent of 5*l.* 16*s.* 8*d.*" when the rent was 6*l.* but 3*s.* 4*d.* allowed for payment at the exchequer; for the rent here is the consideration (*g*): or " in consideration of the surrender of a lease;" and the lease was void (*h*). But it is said, that if the King in consideration of 20*l.* paid, grant; it is sufficient without shewing that it was paid: for it is a personal thing executed, and accepted by the King (*i*). Or, in consideration that the grantee shall repair; if the grantee does not repair, the grant is not void, for the King may have covenant (*k*). So if the King grant, in consideration of a surrender; it is sufficient, though the surrender was not inrolled till after the grant; for the surrender was good, though not completed (*l*). So, if the King be misinformed, but not deceived, it will be good: as, if he let land, which is recited to be 10*l. per annum,* when it was 20*l.* rendering 20*l. per annum* (*m*): if he recite land to be concealed, when it was not: where it appears that he intends a grant of the land, though not concealed (*n*): if he grant the manor of *B. quod manerium fuit seisitum in manus nostras, &c.* though it was not so (*o*): or, the office of parker of *B. quod H. habuit ;* for it was added for the more certainty(*p*): or the manor of *D. quod fuit in tenura de B.* when it was not (*q*): or, a manor and advowson, *adeo plene*

(*a*) 5 Co. 94, a. 2 Rol. Ab. 188. l. 25. 199. l. 30, 50. Lane, 75, 109.

(*b*) Dyer, 352.

(*c*) 2 Rol. Ab. 409. l. 52.

(*d*) Dyer, 352. 5 Co. 94, a. 2 Rol. 189. l. 35. Ibid. l. 26. 45.

(*e*) Hob. 223. 2 Rol. Ab. 199. l. 45.

(*f*) 2 Rol. 188. l. 25. Lane, 75, 109.

(*g*) Yel. 43, 48.

(*h*) 5 Co. 94, a.

(*i*) 10 Ibid. 67, b. 2 Rol. Ab. 200. l. 10.

(*k*) Ibid. l. 5.

(*l*) Hob. 221.

(*m*) Yel. 48.

(*n*) Sal. 561.

(*o*) 10 Co. 113, a.

(*p*) Ibid.

(*q*) Ibid.

as

as we by any means had it *cuidam archiepiscopo dudum spectan';* where the archbishop had the manor, but not the advowson (a): or, if he grant lands, all which are of such a value; though the value be misrecited, if there be a *non obstante* of the misrecital of the value (b).

SECT. IV.

4. *Of the Rights and Liabilities of the Grantee.*

IN the case of lands the grantee does not by taking them from the Crown acquire any particular privileges. He is not thereby protected against the common law remedies and rights which others may possess in respect of the property, however such remedies and rights might be impeded whilst the King held it (c): nor shall he take advantage of the maxim *nullum tempus occurrit regi* (d). The right of the grantee of crown lands to distrain, and to use crown process, has been already noticed (e).

The assignee of a chose in action granted by the Crown (f), may either sue in his own name, or use the King's name, and the prerogative process; though the assignment contain no words expressly enabling the grantee so to do (g).

If the King grant wrecks his privilege of going over another man's land to take them passes to the grantee (h).

The right of a grantee to a *scire facias* to repeal grants, injurious to his own, has been already mentioned (i).

(a) 2 Mod. 1.
(b) Hardr. 232.
(c) Ante, 340, and note (b). 342.
(d) Poph. 26.
(e) Ante, 209.
(f) Ante, 387.
(g) Owen, 113. Cro. Jac. 82, 179.

Dyer 30, and 1 pl. 7, 8. Sav. 2, 133.
1 P. Wms. 252. 17 Vin. Ab. 96. tit.
Prerog. M. 69. 5 Bac. Ab. 606. Prerog. F. 3.
(h) 6 Mod. 149.
(i) Ante, 331.

SECT. V.

Of revoking or avoiding the Grant.

WHEN royal grants are void, a *scire facias* is in general requisite (*a*): but by statute 1 Ann. st. 1. c. 7: s. 7. for restraining grants of the lands and revenues of the Crown, . grants contrary to that act shall be void without any inquisition, or *scire facias*, or other proceeding.

The grants of the King when valid in general bind him, though without consideration, as subjects are bound by their grants (*b*): except in cases where a mere authority, licence or exemption is given without an interest; as in the case of a licence to go abroad when the party is recalled; or the grant of an exemption from impress (*c*). And, though the grant of a mere licence or authority from the Crown (*d*), or a grant " during the King's will (*e*)," is determined by the demise of the Crown; it is clear that in other cases where an interest only is transferred by the Crown, the King's successors are bound by it, though they be not mentioned in the grant (*f*): and this even on a grant to a college to be discharged of toll (*g*).

(*a*) See as to this, Index, tit. Scire facias. Ante, 330. 250. 38.

(*b*) Ld. Raym.32. Ante,119. 125. 132.

(*c*) Ante, 24. 48. 5 Bac. Ab. 526. 16 East, 165.

(*d*) Hardr. 442. But not an authority coupled with an interest, Freem. 331. 17 Vin. Ab. 90.

(*e*) Mo. 176. Com. Dig. Grant, G. 3.

(*f*) Ibid. 1 Sid. 6. Hardr. 443, 4.

(*g*) Yelv. R. 15.

CHAP. XVII.

Of the King's Family and Councils.

THE Queen of England is either—1. Queen *regent, regnant,* or *sovereign,* that is, the Queen reigning in her own right, and holding the Crown as her own inheritance, whether married or not. 2. The *Queen consort,* that is, the wife of the reigning King; or, 3. The *Queen dowager,* in other words, the King's widow (*a*).

1. A Queen *regent* stands in all respects in the same situation as a King of England, is entitled to the same rights and prerogatives, and subject to the same duties (*b*). Her marriage does not diminish her powers in the slightest degree; even her husband would be her subject, and might be guilty of high treason against her as his sovereign (*c*).

2. The King's *consort* possesses of course no share of the kingly authority; and as the various duties, responsibilities, and cares of government, are fully sufficient to occupy the time and attention of the King, the law, as a further comment on the principle, that the royal functions should be unembarrassed by minute considerations, has wisely freed his Majesty from the necessity of interfering with the management of the domestic affairs of his consort; by rendering her in legal contemplation a *feme sole,* by absolving her from the many, and indeed almost universal, restraints and incapacities to which other married women are by their marriage exposed (*d*). She may have a separate property either in lands or goods, and may purchase, sell, lease, or devise them (*e*). She may even take lands or debts

---

(*a*) 1 Bla. Com. 218.

(*b*) Ibid. 190. 1 Mar. st. 3. c. 1.

(*c*) 1 Hal. P. C. 101, 106. Ante, 11, 12.

(*d*) Finch, L, 86. 17´Vin. Ab. 204, tit. Prerog. B. C. Com. Dig. Roy. F. Fortesc. R. 412. 1 Bla. Com. 217, 18.

(*e*) Ibid. And see recital of 39° and

40 G. 3. c. 88. s. 8, 9. By that statute to prevent doubts on this subject it is expressly enacted, that any queen, consort, may during the King's life by deed under her hand and seal attested by two or more witnesses; or by will attested by three witnesses; grant, give, dispose of, or devise any tenements her property:

debts (*a*) by grant from the King (*b*); or give a bond or other specialty (*c*). And her pre-eminence and distinctness of character hold in all legal proceedings : so that her Majesty may sue or be sued alone (*d*) ; and has her separate offices and officers, and legal advisers (*e*); and, it appears, that a grant of the King to be a servant or officer to the Queen is void (*f*).

The life and honour of the Queen are peculiarly regarded and protected by the law. It is high treason to compass her death, or violate or defile her person ; and she is a participator in this high offence, and the consequent punishment, if she consent to the illicit connexion (*g*).

So, in respect of the high importance of the Queen, Acts of Parliament relating to her are to be deemed public Acts, and to be noticed accordingly (*h*).

In general, the Queen consort is not exempted from laws operating on other subjects of the King (*i*) ; but in many instances the law has expressly granted her several immunities. Thus the Queen consort pays no toll (*k*) ; and cannot be amerced (*l*), or arrested ; nor is she obliged to find pledges *de prosequendo* (*m*); or bound by the statute of Marlebridge, for driving a distress into another county (*n*). But the servants of the Queen consort or Queen dowager are not privileged from arrest (*o*).

There are also several antient revenues and perquisites of the

property : and may by her will bequeath her personalty, as if she were unmarried. Proviso as to disposal of palaces, &c. of the King in right of the Crown vested in the queen consort, for her life as a jointure or otherwise. In Wood's Inst. 22. ; 8th ed. it is said, " both the real and personal property of the queen consort go to the King after her decease, if she do not in her life-time dispose of them, or bequeath them away by will."

(*a*) 17 Vin. Ab. 205. tit. Prerog. B. *e*. pl. 11.

(*b*) Ibid. 1 Bla. Com. 219.

(*c*) 2 Rol. Ab. 213. l. 25.

(*d*) Com. Dig. Action, B. 2. Co. Lit. 133. Form of proceedings by and against the Queen. See 2 Chitty on Pl. 25, 3rd ed. She shall not be sued by petition as the King is, ante, 341. 1 H.

4. f. 7. Bro. Ab. Nonability, pl. 60. Staundf. Præ. 75, b. 2*u*. whether the King may by grant give her the prerogative remedies to recover her debts. Mod. 247. Com. Dig. Roy. F. 1.

(*e*) 1 Bla. Com. 219.

(*f*) See 2 Rol. Ab. 213. l. 42. Com. Dig. Roy, F. 1.

(*g*) 1 Bla. Com. 222.

(*h*) Finch L. 86. 8 Rep. 28.

(*i*) The Queen is a sole person by the common law, but not to all intents, per Brian. Bro. Ab. Aid, Del. Roy. pl. 96, cites 3 H. 7. 14.

(*k*) Co. Lit. 133.

(*l*) Finch, L. 185.

(*m*) Co. Lit. 133, a.

(*n*) Ibid. 133, b.

(*o*) 1 Keb. 842, 877.

Queen, as *aurum reginæ*, or Queen's gold, being a portion of monies voluntarily paid to the King by any subject, by way of offering or fine for any franchise or liberty granted him, &c. (*a*); rents or reservations out of the demesne lands of the Crown (*b*); and (though the addition may be deemed ludicrous) her Majesty's share (that is, the tails) of whales, but not of sturgeons, taken on the coasts (*c*). But as these sources of emolument have long since fallen into decay, it will not be necessary to make any further mention of them.

8. Notwithstanding the death of the King, his consort, who thereby becomes the *Queen Dowager*, retains most of her privileges (*d*). But it is no longer high treason to conspire her death, or to violate her chastity, as the purity of the royal succession cannot be tainted thereby. She does not lose her royal rank by marrying (*e*) a commoner (*f*); and is entitled to dower though an alien born (*g*).

With respect to the King's *children*, the *eldest son* or heir apparent and *his consort*, and the King's eldest daughter, who alone would inherit on failure of male issue, particularly claim our attention. That the succession may be less open to doubt and danger, it is high treason to conspire the death of either of these high personages; or to defile the persons of either of the latter (*h*).

The eldest son or heir apparent of the King, has, since the time of Edward I., who conquered Wales, been titular Prince or Princess of Wales. But this title, and that of Earl of Chester, which has also been usually granted to the heir

---

(*a*) 12 Co. 22. Com. Dig. Roy. F. 2. Fortesc. R. 398. 1 Bla. Com. 219, &c.

(*b*) Ibid.

(*c*) Ibid. 222.

(*d*) 1 Bla. Com. 223. The hospital of Saint Katharine was founded by Eleanor, dowager of King Hen. 3. with reservation of the patronage, *sibi, &c. et reginis succedentibus*; wherefore the Queen dowager shall always have the nomination of a master, when there is not a Queen consort *in esse*. Ca. Ch. 215. Skin. 15. So though there be a Queen

consort. Per Hale, Ca. Ch. 215. So if a Queen consort grants, it is not determined when she becomes dowager. Skin. 15.

(*e*) Whether she can marry without licence of the King seems questionable, see 1 Bla. Com. 223. cites 2 Inst. 16. Riley's Plac. Parl. 72. See Co. Lit. 133. Hargr. note. Fortesc. R. 418.

(*f*) 2 Inst. 50. 1 Bla. Com. 223.

(*g*) Ibid. Fortesc. R. 420.

(*h*) 1 Bla. Com. 223,

apparent,

apparent, do not necessarily vest in him as such, but arise from special creation and investiture under the great seal (a).

The title of Duke of Cornwall, and the inheritance of the duchy of Cornwall, were first created and vested in Edward the Black Prince, by a grant in the eleventh year of the reign of Edw. 3. This grant has been held to be an Act of the legislature, or a charter confirmed by Parliament, and is consequently good, though it alter the established course of descent which the King's charter cannot do (b). Consequently the King's eldest son, being heir apparent, is always by inheritance Duke of Cornwall, without a new creation (c). On the death of the eldest son, the eldest surviving takes the inheritance : a peculiar descent founded on the legislative grant (d). But it seems that as the Duke of Cornwall must be not only the eldest son, but the heir apparent, the second surviving son would not succeed to the dukedom, if his eldest brother left issue, who would be heir apparent, but that it would in such case revert to the Crown (e). There are authorities, that the disabilities of minority do not hold against a Duke of Cornwall, with respect to the duchy rights and possessions (f). The general rule is, that till a Prince be born, the King is seized of all the possessions (g); but when born, the Prince is immediately seized in fee; and leases, &c. by the King may be determined by the Prince (h), and he may have a *scire facias* for that purpose (i).

The Prince has no other specific privileges over the rest of the royal children, but he is regarded in law as partaking in some measure of the royal dignity. " *Coruscat radiis regis patris et censetur una persona cum ipso rege* (k)." And the in-

(a) 4 Inst. 243. 1 Bul. 133. 1 Bla. Com. 224.

(b) The Prince's case, 8 Co. Rep. 1. By the charter the Black Prince was created Duke of Cornwall, ' *habend*' *eidem duci et ipsius et hæredum suorum regum Angliæ filiis primogenitis et dicti loci ducibus in regno Angliæ hæreditarie successuris.*' Ibid.

(c) Ibid. His wife shall be endowed. Ibid. 7.

(d) 1 Vez. 294. Collins, Proceed. on

Bar. 148. 1 Bla. Com. 224. n. 10, by Christian.

(e) Ibid. Christian's note 10.

(f) Ibid. Christian's note. Ante, 376, and note (h). Bro. Ab. Prerog. pl. 132.

(g) Com. Dig. Roy, G.

(h) Ibid. Ca. Ch. 215. *aliter,* if the King present to an advowson, his clerk shall continue. Ibid.

(i) 5 Com. Dig. 280, 1.

(k) The Prince's Case, 8 Co. 28. R. and see Hob. R. 226.

troduction

troduction to a patent in the time of Hen. 6. runs, " *Ut ipsum qui reputatione juris censetur eadem persona nobiscum digno preveniamus honore, &c.*" On this ground, an Act of Parliament, (as the Act respecting the duchy of Cornwall), which relates to the Prince, has been held to be a public law of which every body is to take notice; because whatever concerns the Prince concerns the King, and whatever concerns the King concerns every subject in England (*a*). " So a grant from the King to the Prince does not make an alienation from the Crown, for the land continues parcel of the Crown (*b*)."

With respect to the remainder of the royal family, only those related within certain degrees to the Sovereign have any particular precedence; and even those nearly related, and within such degrees, have, it appears, independently of their general privileges as Peers and Peeresses, no other particularity attending them, but their right to such precedence, and are substantially in the same situation, entitled to the same rights, and subject to the same liabilities, as other subjects are (*c*). Their precedence is founded on the statute 31 H. 8. c. 10. which enacts, that no person, except the King's children, shall presume to sit or have place at the side of the cloth of estate in the Parliament chamber; and that certain great officers therein named shall have precedence above all Dukes, except only such as shall happen to be the King's son, brother, uncle, nephew (which Sir Edward Coke (*d*) explains to signify grandson or *nepos*), or brother's or sister's son. Therefore after these degrees are past, Peers or others of the blood royal, are entitled to no place or precedence except what belongs to them by their personal rank or dignity (*e*).

Of course all the children of the King, though born abroad, are deemed natural born subjects: but whether or not this would be the case if their father was not King at the time of their birth may be doubtful (*f*). The statute 25 Edw. 3. st. 2. after reciting " because that some people be in doubt whether children born in parts beyond the sea, out of the ligeance of

(*a*) 8 Co. R. 28. Fortesc. R. 411.

(*b*) Com. Dig. Roy G. cites Palmer's R. 89. See ante, 203.

(*c*) They are usually exempted from liability to pay tolls, &c. by particular statutes; but it does not appear that

they have any common law right to such exemptions.

(*d*) 4 Inst. 362.

(*e*) 1 Bla. Com. 225.

(*f*) See 1 Chitty on Com. 114. ch. 5. of subjects, aliens, &c.

England, should not be able to demand ' any inheritance' within the same ligeance or not, &c.' declares that the law of the Crown of England is and always hath been such, that the children of the Kings of England in whatsoever parts they be born, in England or elsewhere, be able and ought to bear the inheritance after the death of their ancestors": which may perhaps be a legislative declaration of the law, not only as to the inheritance of the Crown, but also to other inheritances. However this may be, it seems to be clear at common law, that the King's children may inherit lands in England, wherever such children were born, and though they may in law be deemed aliens. In the 17 Edw. 3. the archbishop of Canterbury came into Parliament and demanded " *si les enfans notre sen' le roy* born beyond the sea should inherit in England, because born out of the King's dominions and aliens:" and all the parliament agreed, let them be born where they would, they should inherit (*a*). Without any doubt the alienage if any of the eldest son would become extinct on his succeeding to the Crown on the death of his ancestor.

The exact extent of the right of the Crown to regulate the education and marriages of the royal family underwent considerable discussion in 1717, that is, on the commencement of the reign of Geo. I. (*b*). That sovereign proposed to the twelve judges the following question: " whether the education, and the care of the persons of his Majesty's grandchildren then in England, and of Prince Frederick, eldest son of his Royal Highness the Prince of Wales, when his Majesty should think fit to cause him to come into England, and the ordering the place of their abode, and appointing their governors, governesses and other instructors, attendants and servants, and the care and approbation of their marriages, when grown up, belonged of right to his Majesty, as king of the realm or not? Whereupon ten of the judges were of opinion in the affirmative; relying principally on historical instances of the exercise of this prerogative in the case of marriages of the royal family, and on principles of policy and necessity, that this prerogative should exist in the King even in derogation of the rights of the father of the King's grandchildren: and they considered

(*a*) Cotton, 38. Fortesc. R. 420. So a Queen dowager is entitled to dower, though an alien born. Ante, 403.

(*b*) See Fortesc. R. 401, &c.

7

that

that the King's right to superintend the education of his children and grandchildren, was a necessary consequence of his prerogative with respect to their marriages. The other two judges entertained different sentiments: they relied principally on the undoubted and admitted common law exclusive right of the father to regulate the education of his children in ordinary cases; they contended that the judges' minds ought not to be biassed by considerations of political inconvenience; and insisted that no legal authorities were to be found in support of this prerogative. But they admitted that the care and approbation of the royal grandchildren belonged to the King by virtue of his prerogative, not however exclusive of the prince their father, but only concurrently with him. There can indeed be no doubt whatever from immemorial usage, which is evidence of and constitutes common law, that the royal consent and approbation should be obtained previous to any marriage with the royal family. And in 1772 (*a*), the judges concurred in opinion that the King's care and approbation of such marriages extended to the presumptive heir of the Crown, though to what other branches of the royal family the same did extend they did not find precisely determined. " The most frequent instances of the Crown's interposition go no further," observes Sir W. Blackstone (*b*), "than nephews and nieces, but examples are not wanting of its reaching to more distant collaterals."

It will be observed, that at common law the royal consent was in no instance necessary to the validity of a marriage with one of the royal family; though the parties subjected themselves to severe punishment for this high contempt of the royal prerogative (*c*). This defect was supplied by the act "for the better regulating the future marriages of the royal family," (12 G. 3. c. 11.), by which, (after reciting that " marriages in the royal family are of the highest importance to the state; and that therefore the Kings of this realm have even been entrusted with the care and approbation thereof);" no descendant of the body of G. 2. (other than the issue of princesses married into foreign families), is capable of contracting ma-

(*a*) Lords' Journ. 28th Feb. 1772. 1 Bla. Com. 225.

(*b*) 1 Com. 225, 6.

(*c*) The statute of 28 Hen. 8. c. 18 which made it high treason for any man to contract marriage with the King's children or reputed children, his sisters or aunts *ex parte paternâ*, or the children of his brethren or sisters, was repealed by 1 Ed. 6. c. 12.

trimony,

trimony, without the previous consent of the King, signified under the great seal; and any marriage contracted without such consent is void. Provided that such of the said descendants as are above the age of twenty-five years, may, after a twelvemonth's notice, given to the King's privy council, contract and solemnize marriage without the consent of the Crown; unless both houses of Parliament shall, before the expiration of the said year, expressly declare their disapprobation of such intended marriage. And all persons solemnizing, assisting, or being present at any such prohibited marriage, shall incur the penalties of the statute of *præmunire.*

To assist the King in his legislative and executive functions, his Majesty is provided with several councils, as 1. the High Court of Parliament. 2. The Peers of the realm. 3. His Judges. 4. The Privy Council (*a*).

1. It is most probable that *Parliaments* (*b*) were originally called together solely for the purpose of advice with the King, on matters of state, without any pretensions on their part to a definite right of interference, till they gradually became a distinct and independent feature, and a substantive part, of the constitution. At all events, however, Parliament, even at the present day, are constitutionally, and in point of fact the first grand council of the King, and this necessarily so in matters of legislation. Acts of Parliament are made, as is now always expressed therein, by the King " by and with the *advice* and consent of the Lords and Commons." And it is usual to lay before Parliament for its discussion and consideration, such affairs and occurrences as are of weighty importance to the state ; though such matters may fall peculiarly and exclusively within the department of the executive authorities.

2. The *Peers* of the realm owe their titles entirely to the Crown, as the fountain of honours and dignities. They are the antient Barons, or great men or captains, under the feudal or military system; and now, as then, are appointed 1. *ad consulendum ;* 2. *Ad defendendum, regem* (*c*). It is indeed not only the duty, but (so far is that duty carried in law) the right of Peers to demand an audience of the King, that they may sub-

---

(*a*) Co. Litt. 110, a.   1 Bla. C. 227.   country, Com. Dig. Roy H.
ch. 5. See as to *Custos Regni* appointed   (*b*) Ante, 67.
during the King's absence from the   (*c*) See 1 Bla. Com. 227.

                                                                mit

mit to his Majesty their sentiments and suggestions on state matters (*a*). This is a duty which the Sovereign himself, by raising his subject to so high an honour as Peerage, has enjoined him to perform. Indeed so great a right has the King to the services and advice of all his subjects, that it is highly penal to refuse to accept a degree of nobility when proffered by the Crown (*b*).

To protect the King, (rather than the Peer,) the person of the latter is not subject to civil process of arrest (*c*), even when no Parliament is sitting, because their advice and assistance is at all times due to the King. And members of the House of Commons (*d*) are also protected (*e*), not only during the actual sitting of Parliament, but for a convenient time, sufficient to enable them to come from and return to any part of the kingdom, before the first meeting, and after the final dissolution of it ; and also for forty days (*f*) after every prorogation, and before the next appointed meeting, which is now in effect as long as the Parliament exists, it being seldom prorogued for more than fourscore days at a time (*g*).

3. The *Judges* are another council or source of advice for the King, on questions of law (*h*). Indeed in such questions this is the chief council for the King; and it is also their duty to attend the House of Lords when required to inform them what the law is on any given question (*i*).

4. The *Privy Council*, usually called " the Council," is the last, but the most effective and important council of the King. This is a body of such Peers, or private subjects, as the King particularly selects and honours with his peculiar confidence.

(*a*) 4 Inst. 53. 1 Bla. 228.

(*b*) Ante, 19.

(*c*) Finch L. 355. 1 Ventr. 298. So of peeresses whether by birth or marriage. 6 Co. 52. Styles, R. 252. Tidd. 6th ed. 198, 9 ; 5th ed. 192, 3. So of Irish and Scotch peers; Tidd *ubi supra :* though they do not sit in Parliament. Fortescue R. 165. This privilege does not extend to criminal process, or to attachments for contempts of court. 1 Wils. 332. 1 Burr. 631. Imp. K. B. 8th ed. 118. Tidd 6th ed. 199. It seems that servants of peers are not privileged, ibid. 10 G. 3. c. 50. 5 T. R. 687.

(*d*) 10 G. 3. c. 50. 2 Str. 985. Tidd 5th ed. 193. ; 6th ed. 199.

(*e*) That is as to civil process ; the privilege not extending to treason, felony or breach of the peace. 2 Wils. 159.

(*f*) 2 Lev. 72. 1 Chan. Cas. 221. S. C. but see 1 Sid. 29.

(*g*) 1 Bla. Com. 165. Imp. K. B. 8th ed. 118. 7 T. R. 448.

(*h*) 14 Edw. 3. c. 5. 1 Inst. 110. 3 Inst. 125. 1 Bla. Com. 229.

(*i*) 4 Inst. 50. See Fortescue's R. 384, &c.

Their

Their *number* (a) depends on the royal pleasure; they may be *appointed* merely by the royal nomination, without any particular ceremony or instrument; on taking the oaths for security of the government, and the test for the security of the church: and their *qualifications* have not been made the subject of legal definition, except by the statute 12 and 13 W. 3. c. 2. by which persons born out of the dominions of the Crown of England, unless born of English parents, even though naturalized by Parliament, are rendered unable to be of the Privy Council. Their *official existence* depends also entirely on the King's will; the whole or one of the members may be immediately removed: though to obviate the common law inconvenience of the demise of the Crown operating as a dissolution of this assembly, the statute 6 Ann. c. 7. s. 8. prolongs its continuance for six months after the royal demise, unless sooner determined by the successor.

The *duty* of a Privy Counsellor appears, says Sir Wm. Blackstone (b), from the oath of office (c), which consists of seven articles:—1. To advise the King according to the best of his cunning and discretion. 2. To advise for the King's honor and good of the public, without partiality through affection, love, meed, doubt, or dread. 3. To keep the King's counsel secret. 4. To avoid corruption. 5. To help and strengthen the execution of what shall be there resolved. 6. To withstand all persons who would attempt the contrary. And, lastly, in general, 7. To observe, keep, and do all that a good and true counsellor ought to do to his sovereign lord.

The privy council have also in certain cases a judicial appellate jurisdiction, and the powers of Magistrates.

1. The original and exclusive jurisdiction in cases relating to boundaries between provinces in the plantations, the domi-

---

(a) Mr. Christian remarks, (1 Bla. Com. 230, note 1.), that no inconvenience arises from the extension of their numbers, as those only attend who are especially summoned for that particular occasion, upon which their advice and assistance are required. The cabinet council, as it is called, consists of those ministers of state who are more immediately honoured with his Majesty's confidence, and who are summoned to consult upon the important and arduous discharge of the executive authority: their number and selection depend only on the King's pleasure; and each member of that council receives a summons or message for every attendance.

(b) 1 Com. 230. And see Com. Dig. tit. Roy. E. 2. An attempt to bribe a Privy Counsellor is an indictable offence. 4 Burr. 2494.

(c) 4 Inst 54.

nion, or proprietary government therein, is vested in the King in council (a). They possess judicial power through the King in all cases in which an appeal in the *dernier resort* lies to the King (b). So in Admiralty causes (c), being matters which arise out of the jurisdiction of the realm (d). And they have also jurisdiction in matters of idiotcy and lunacy (e). The judicial authority of the council is usually exercised in a committee of the whole privy council, who hear the allegations and proofs, and make their report to the King in council, and the decision rests with his Majesty (f). But the King in council cannot decree *in personam* in England (g). And it is expressly declared and enacted, by the statute 16 Car. 1. c. 10. s. 5. that neither the King, nor the privy council have any jurisdiction or power to take cognizance of any matter of property, real or personal, belonging to subjects of this kingdom.

2. The privy counsellors have whilst in council the power, by warrant, to commit offenders to safe custody, to take their trials for high offences against the government (h). And secretaries of state also may, (but not by general warrants,) cause a party accused of high treason to be arrested (i). But none of these officers can punish, they can only inquire; and the statute 16 Car. 1. c. 10. gives a *habeas corpus*, as if the party were committed by an ordinary justice of the peace.

Privy counsellors have also precedence and ranks as such (k); and the statutes 3 Hen. 8. c. 14., and 9 Ann. c. 16., were passed to protect them against conspiracies of the King's menial servants to kill them, which are felonies; and any attempt to kill them in the execution of their office, which is a capital offence.

(a) Ante, 28, 9 : 30, 1; 38, 9.

(b) Ibid.

(c) But now it seems the Privy Council disclaim all jurisdiction in Admiralty causes, leaving them to the Admiralty Courts, and have refused to hear any appeals in such cases, from the West Indies. See 3 Price, R. 110.

(d) 1 Bla. Com. 231.

(e) Ibid.

(f) Ibid. 231, 2.

(g) 1 Ves. sen. 447.

(h) 1 Bla. Com. 231. Com. Dig. Roy. E. 5. 2 Wilson, 151, 283. 7 Term R. 742. 1 Chitty, Crim. L. 26, 34, 107.

(i) Ibid. 2 Wils. 288.

(k) 1 Bla. Com. 405.

INDEX.

A.

ABATEMENT.

Page

Action by king and subject, may abate as to latter only   246
Extent does not abate by death of defendant   . 275, 280
Death of one of two crown defendants   .   . 276

ABEYANCE.

Of a title—Prerogative as to   .   ,   . 114, 15, 16

ABJURATION.

Oaths of, form of   16

ABUSE (of Office).

Forfeiture of office by   85

ACCOMPLICES.

(See *Pardon.*) 93, 4, 5, 100

ACCOUNT.

With crown—*distringas ad computandum* not necessary:
extent lies   269

ACQUITTANCE.

King not obliged to offer subject   378

ACT OF PARLIAMENT.

Prerogative as to assenting or dissenting to   . . 74

ACT OF PARLIAMENT.

Page

Prerogative copyright in 239
What binds crown—(See *Statutes.*)

ACTIONS.

What actions king may maintain . . . 245
May sue where he pleases . . . ibid.
King and subject joining in an action . 245, 6
May abate for subject and stand as to king . . 246
King cannot be sued by action, and why ? . 339, 40

ADMIRALTY,

King bound by judicial sale in Admiralty Court—(See
   Courts.—Offices.) 226

AFFIDAVIT.

To obtain extent, &c.—(See *Extents.*) . . . 322
Requisite to obtain *ne exeat regno* 22

ALDERMAN.

King may exempt a person from being elected . 20

ALDERNEY, Isle of.

Prerogative as to . . , ... 28

ALLEGIANCE.

(See *Natural-born subjects.—Aliens.*) . . . 13, 14
Nature of, and why, and how due ? . . 12, 15, 16
Not transferrable . . . 15
Due from inhabitants of conquered countries . . 13
Due from aliens here, and why ? . . . 12, 13
Not from alien enemy invading . . ibid.
Whether King can nullify . . . ibid.
Local, temporary 16
Oaths of,
   At common law . . ibid.
   Why required ? . . . . ibid.

ALLEGIANCE.

Page

Oaths of,

Form of 16
By whom to be administered . . .
Two justices of the peace . . . 17
By any one appointed by the privy council . ibid.
Or by commissioner under great seal . . ibid.
To be taken by every person admitted into any public
office, &c. . . . . . ibid.
To be administered to members of the Universities
the age of 18 years . . . . ibid.
Also to preacher and teachers of separate congregations ibid.
Refusal to take it to be certified to the next quarter-ses-
sions . . . . . . ibid.
Refusal to take disqualifies for holding any office, &c. 18

ALIENATIONS.

Though voluntary by crown debtor before crown lien
good 298

ALIENS.

Who are ?—(See *Natural-born subjects.*) . . 13
Owe allegiance, when—(See *Allegiance.*) . . 12, 13
Naturalization of.—(See *Naturalization.*) . . 14, 15
Prerogative on their purchasing or holding lands 229, 30
Granting the lands to their relations, &c. . . 235
Cannot take lands by descent.—(Vide *Escheat.*) . 228, 9
Inquisition when necessary to entitle King to his lands 249
Pardon of, under what words . . . 100
Alien may come into the country without licence, but
semble Crown may order them out . . 49
King may prevent ingress or egress of enemies and how 48, 9
Allowing them to come here . . . ibid.
Right of Crown to debts due to alien enemy . . 43
Alien, King cannot hinder the building of ships of war
in this country for 50

ALIEN ACT.

Page

For what purpose passed 49

ALMANACKS.

Crown has no prerogative copyright in . . . 240

AMBASSADORS.

King sends and receives 40
Appointment of them . . ibid.
Licences or passports from to enemy . . . 48, 9

AMENDMENT.

King may amend at any time 334

AMERCIAMENT.

King cannot be amerced 374

AMOVEAS MANUS.

Judgment of for subject—(See *Judgment.*) . 348, 9, &c.

ANNE'S, Queen, bounty 66

ANNUITY.

When King may grant 389

APPEAL.

To King in Council from his foreign territories—(See
Privy Council.) 28, 9
But foreign Court must first give some judgment . 29
King cannot direct re-hearing . . . . ibid.
To King as head of church, and how granted . 55, &c.

APPEAL. (Ecclesiastical)

Page

How determined 57

Does not lie from a local visitor, nor in cases of a temporal nature 55

Where King concerned, party may appeal to spiritual prelates, &c. within fifteen days after sentence—(See *Delegates.*) 56, 7

From places exempt, must be made immediately to King in Chancery 57

APPEARING and claiming on extents—(See *Extents Resisting.*) . . . . 358, &c.

APPROVEMENT.

What it is, and old doctrine of . . . 93, 4

APPROVER.

Who is an, and doctrine of approvement . . ibid.

ARCHBISHOP (See *Church—Bishop—Temporalities.*)

Appointment of, how, and by whom . . . 57, 8
Archbishopricks of King's foundation . . . 59
His power to grant dispensations 53

ARMS AND AMMUNITION.

King may prohibit exportation of . . . 49

ARMY.

Prerogative as to 45, 6
King cannot compel subject to enlist, or go out of the country 46, 7

ARREST.

Of course King never subject to 374
What King's servants protected, and when, &c. . 374, 5, 6

ARREST (*continued*).

Page

In royal presence, within verge of palaces, &c. not allowed, but defendant not discharged . . . 376
King in person cannot arrest 377
Privilege of Peers and Members of Parliament . 408, 9

ASSAULT.

By King, no redress 339, 40

ASSIGNMENT.

In trust for creditors, how it binds Crown . . 285

ATTAINDER.

When inquisition necessary for King as to the forfeiture
—(See *Forfeiture.*) 249

ATTORNEY-GENERAL.

Party in every cause for King 244
Confession by, when binds Crown . . . 370

ATTRIBUTES.

Of King 5

AUDITA QUERELA.

Does not lie against King 372

B.

BAIL.

Not to be taken under extents . . . 281

BANK of England 127

BANKRUPT.

Page

Not to be released on extent 284
May be arrested by Crown, though under examination ibid.
Goods bound by extent how far, &c. . . 286
If assignment not inrolled before *fiat* for extent, Crown
    may claim lands 300

BANKRUPTCY.

Statutes of, do not bind Crown . . . 366

BARGAIN AND SALE.

King cannot convey by 378

BARON AND FEME.

(See *Husband and Wife.*)

BARONY.

Origin of the title of—(See *Peerage.*) . . . 108

BARRISTERS.

Promotion of 118

BASTARDS.

(Vide *Escheat.*) 228

BATTERY.

By King, no redress 340

BEACONS.

(See *Light-houses.*) 175, 6

BENEFICES.

(See *Church.*) 59

BERWICK UPON TWEED.

Page

Prerogative in 27

BISHOP (See *Church—Archbishop*.)

How and by whom appointed 57, 8
Bishoprick of King's foundation . . . 59
No inquisition necessary to entitle King to temporalities
vacated, *aliter* forfeited . . . 249, 50

BODY OF CROWN DEBTOR.

Prerogative as to . . . . . 282, &c.

BONA VACANTIA.

Prerogative as to 135, 6

BONDS.

To King, in what form, and their force, &c. . 265, 6

BOOKS.

If no known author, not in King—(See *Copyright*.) . 241

BOROUGH COURTS 120

BOROUGH JUSTICES.

Exclusive Jurisdiction . . . . ibid.

BOROUGH, ENGLISH.

Custom of, binds Crown 380

BOUNDARIES.

Page

Of the prerogative 7, 8

C.

CANONS.

(See *Convocations.*) 51, 2
How and by whom made . . . . ibid.
When good 52
Do not bind laity . . . . . ibid.

CATTLE.

Strangers when liable for Crown debt . . 287, 8

CHAMBERLAIN. (Great)

Office of, how inheritable 81

CHANCELLOR, LORD.

How and by whom appointed 78
Vice-Chancellor . . . . . ibid.
Holds office during King's pleasure . . . 82

CHAPEL. (Free)

King may erect, &c. with exemption , . . 63
King and subject join in foundation, who founder . 53
By whom visitable . . . . . ibid.

CHARITIES.

Prerogative as to, as *parens patriæ* . . . 161
In chancellor from Crown, how far . . , ibid.
Crown appropriating general gift to a particular cha-
rity 161, 2

CHARITABLE FOUNDATIONS,

Page

Or CORPORATIONS 129

CHASE. (Free)

Prerogative as to 140

CHESTER.

Earl of, Prince of Wales is, and nature of title . 403, 4

CHILDREN. (King's)

(See *Prince of Wales.*) . . . . . ibid.
Eldest daughter, how protected . . . 403
The other children no peculiar rights, &c. . . ibid.
Precedence and rank of the royal children . . 405
Whether alienage may exist, and how it can affect . 405, 6
Prerogative as to their marriages and education . 406, 7, 8

CHOSES IN ACTION.

Due to enemy, King's right to 43
Forfeiture of 223
King may grant and take when 387, 8
Matter of record not necessary to vest . . 390, 1
Rights of grantee . . . . ibid. 399

CHURCH.

Of the King as head of, or supremacy of Crown : Usur-
pations of popes 50, 51
Ecclesiastical laws, by whom and how made, &c. . 51, &c.
King head of ecclesiastics, and their laws; reforms abuses,
&c. in 1, 53
Form of prayer for royal family, and on public occasions,
given by King 54
Prerogative as *dernier resort* in ecclesiastical causes 55, &c.
King patron paramount of benefices . . . 59
As such fills vacant dignities and benefices, when and
how . . . . . ibid. 64

CHURCH (*continued*).

Page

Presents to benefices on temporalities of archbishop, &c.
being in his hands 59, 61
Church not full till induction, against Crown   .   . 59
King presents to benefices vacant by promotion, though
other patron.—Prerogative herein   .   .   . 60
The patron loses his benefices by promotion, King may
enable him to retain, and herein of a *commendam re-
tinere*, and a *commendam capere* and nature thereof   60, 1
How prerogative presentation affects an advowson in
common, there being several patrons   .   . 61, 2
Where King has a private interest and a prerogative
right   62
The maxim *nullum tempus*, as to prerogative presenta-
tions   .   .   .   . ibid.
Neglect of King to present as patron within six months   ibid.
When King's presentation lost through usurpation   . ibid.
King may revoke his presentation when   .   .   . 63
Deans how elected   .   .   .   .   . ibid.
King erecting free chapel—(See *Chapel, free.*)   . ibid.
Temporalities of archbishop, &c. King seized of and pre-
rogative therein—(See *Temporalities.*)   .   . 64
King as supreme head of, hath right to publication of
liturgies, bibles, &c.   240
Subject building   63

CINQUE PORTS 119, 20

COIN.

(See *Money.*)   .   .   .   .   .   . 196 to 199

COLONIES.

Obtained by conquest or treaty, or peopling them when
found uninhabited   29
Prerogative over conquered or ceded territory   .   . ibid.
This prerogative subordinate to Parliament   .   . ibid.
King cannot break charter granted to people conquered,
&c.   .   .   .   . ibid. &c.

COLONIES (*continued*).

                                                        Page

Promise of charter, how it affects prerogative   . 32, &c.

Till laws thereof changed, what prevail   .   .   .   30

Uninhabited country, when peopled by Englishmen,
     what laws and prerogative prevail   .   .   .   ibid.

Colonies, three sorts :—

     1. Provincial establishments ;

     2. Proprietary governments ;

     3. Charter governments ;

         Nature of each 30, 31

Form of government in, in general   .   .   . 31, 2

Laws in, void, if contrary to English statutes respect-
     ing them   .   .   .   .   ibid.

Taxing them King alone cannot; only parliament or
     act of assembly 31, 2, 4

Primâ facie, English common law does not prevail in,
     but by charter does in almost all of them   .   .   32

When English statutes bind them   .   .   . 32, 3

Colonial charter cannot be violated by King   .   .   ibid.

Prerogative is governed by charter to colonies, otherwise
     criterion is English common law   .   .   ibid. &c.

King's various rights in colonies on this ground ; as to
     colonial courts of justice ; empowering town to send
     representatives ; entering *nol. pros.* presenting to be-
     nefices in ; right to mines ; escheats, &c. &c.   .   33

Courts of justice in, emanate from King   .   .   ibid.

Cannot make laws unless power from Crown   .   .   ibid.

Restrictions on the right and exceeding the limits al-
     lowed   .   .   .   .   .   .   ibid.

King when may alter the constitution of them   .   ibid. &c.

Different modes of granting them a constitution   .   34

Colonial governments in general have 1. governor ; 2. co-
     lonial council ; 3. representative assembly ; nature and
     powers of each   .   .   .   .   .   ibid.

Governor,

     Has in general kingly authority, but mere servant
     of his sovereign, list of his respective powers   . 34, 5, 6

     What prerogatives King may depute to governor   .   ibid.

     Right to assent to act of assembly, grantable by King   74

COLONIES (*continued*).

Page

Governor,

His acts, under what seal ; and how commission determined, and its effect on other officers . . 35

Colonial assemblies,

How different from Parliament 36, 7

Their powers and force of their acts . . 31, 2, 6, 7

Differences between them and Parliament, as to King's
assent to their acts 37

Effect of demise of Crown on . . . . ibid.

Sovereignty of King not weakened by termination of
charter—prerogative thereon—King may accept
surrender of 37, 8

Taking away the charter on absolute necessity, &c. . ibid.

Re-conquering territory, former charter rights revive ibid.

Proprietors may vary boundaries between themselves—
cannot dismember to bind Crown . . . ibid.

Question as to boundaries, &c. for King in Council . 38, 9

But Chancery has jurisdiction, when . . . ibid.

COMMERCE.—(See *Patents—Marts and Fairs—Coin.*)

Protection of an object of law 162

So of domestic trade 176, 7

Lex Mercatoria 162

Foreign commerce, how regulated . . . 162, 3

Statutes as to, bind Crown 163

King how far arbiter of, cannot in general restrain freedom of importation or exportation, &c. . 163 to 170

Treaties as to . . . . . 166, 7 ; 170

King appoints consuls 170

Gives liberty to enemy to import, when and how ? 170, 1

Licence to subject to trade with enemy, prerogative as
to 171, 2

The like by order in council 172

King makes new declarations of contraband . . ibid.

King's dominion over the seas—(See *Seas.*)

Prerogative as to Ports, Beacons and Light-houses—(See
those titles.) . . . . . 174 to 176

COMMISSION.

Page

New, judicial, and other Commissions, not warranted
by precedent, bad 77
Special, on extraordinary emergencies . . ibid.
To take recognizances, grantable by Crown . . ibid.
To inquire of and find simple contract debts of Crown,
&c.—(See *Extents*.) . . . . . 266, &c.
Of Review,
King may grant after sentence of delegates . . 56

COMMON. (Tenants in)—(See *Joint-tenants*.)

King and subject may be . . . 210, 11—242
Cattle of one whether liable for Crown debt due from
the other 288

COMMON, (Right of)

Not liable to escheat 233
How protected against extent—(See *Inquisition*.)

COMMONS.

Degrees of common people, prerogative as to . 116, 7, 8

COMPOUNDING,

Qui tam action, King how protected . . . 335

CONFESSION.

By Attorney-General, when binds Crown . . 370

CONQUEST.

Prerogative over conquered country, and how it may
be affected . . . . . 29, &c.
Charter, &c. to conquered country, effect of . . 32

CONSTABLE. (High)

Page

Office of, how inheritable 81

CONSTABLE.

King may exempt a person from serving . . 20

CONSULS.

Appointment of 40

CONTEMPT.

Seizure of lands for not returning to this kingdom on
being recalled 24
Inquisition necessary to entitle King to freehold forfeited for 250

CONTINGENCY.

King may grant 388

CONTRABAND OF WAR.

What is and prerogative as to . . . 172, 3

CONVEYANCE.

By King, how it may be 378, 9

CONVOCATIONS, ECCLESIASTICAL.

What they are, how and by whom assembled . 51, 2
Their jurisdiction ; and canons, when good and how far
binding 52, 3
Subject entirely to Crown 52

COPYHOLD.

Escheats to lord of manor . . . 232, 3
Copyhold lands not taken under extent . . 297
King cannot be a copyholder . . . 378

COPYHOLD (*continued*).

                                                                Page
    Suspension of whilst King holds   .   .   .   378
    Surrender of to King as lord, according to custom, good   391

COPYRIGHT (Prerogative.)

    On introduction of printing, general and exclusive
       right assumed by Crown, but finally limited, &c.   238, 9
    But King necessarily has a certain prerogative copyright   239
    As executive magistrate, a copyright in public ordi-
       nances, acts of parliament, proclamations, orders in
       council, &c.   .   .   .   .   .   ibid.
    As head of church, publishes liturgies, forms of prayer,
       bibles, &c.   240
    How far if notes, &c.   .   .   .   .   .   ibid.
    Whether a right by purchase to copies of certain law
       books, &c.   .   .   .   .   .   ibid.
    Not in almanacks   .   .   .   .   .   ibid.
    King cannot restrain press, no general right   240, 1
    If no certain author, books common   .   .   241
    Nature of prerogative copyright continues after publi-
       cation   .   .   .   .   .   .   ibid.

CORNWALL.

    Duke of, title in King's eldest son, and nature of it, &c.   404

CORODY.

    What it is, and King's right thereto   .   .   65

CORONERS.

    How and by whom appointed   .   .   .   79

CORONER'S INQUEST.

    An inquisition to entitle King   .   .   .   259

CORPORATIONS.

    Object and use of 120, 1
    Definition of   121

CORPORATIONS (*continued*).

	Page
Aggregate and sole	121, 2
Ecclesiastical and lay	122
Lay Corporations, civil or eleemosynary . .	ibid.
Various public corporations for sciences, &c. . .	ibid.
King alone can constitute .	122, 3
Common-law corporations without prerogative	123
Corporations by prescription . . .	ibid.
King's express assent by charter . . .	ibid.
Charter, what words sufficient, and what will constitute a corporation	123, 4
Usual functions and peculiar properties of corporations, need not be expressly granted . . .	124
Crown cannot compel a body to accept, or a subject to become a member	ibid.
When a prescriptive corporation, though charter contain words of creation	ibid.
Majority of town to be incorporated must accept charter	ibid.
Charter may be accepted by majority of part, though there be not a majority of whole, when . . .	ibid.
What sufficient acceptance of charter . .	125
Whether corporation may accept part only of a charter	ibid.
Old corporation may refuse new charter *in toto* .	ibid.
Charter should give name of corporation, but name by implication	126
King may mould them; when may alter rules and when not	ibid.
King cannot furnish them with powers, &c. inconsistent with law	127
King may grant the prerogative of creating to a subject, law and doctrine thereon . .	127, 8, 9
Statute corporations	129
Usually created by King	127
Corporations cannot make a sub-corporation . .	129
King when and how visitor of	130, 1
King cannot destroy corporation . .	119, 125, 132
King may take back charter by surrender inrolled .	132

CORPORATIONS *(continued)*.

Page

When dissolved by destruction of part, and prerogative
   as to revival, &c. 132

When by misuser or abuser, but not by omission to
   choose officers 132, 3

King's licence as to lands in mortmain . . . 131

Attainder of head of, how corporation affected as to forfeiture 218

Private goods of members not liable for fine on corporation 287

CORRUPTION, (Of blood.)

When it applies . . . . . 230, &c.

Consequence of.—*(See Escheat.)* . . 231, 2, &c.

Effect of pardon as to 103

COSTS.

General rule King neither pays nor takes . . 310

Exceptions—(See *Extents.*) . . . 310, 11

Not on *scire facias* to repeal Crown grants, &c. . 331

On *quo warranto* 338

COUNCIL.

Appeal to King in—(See *Appeal.*) . . 28, 9

COUNCILS OF KING.

1. Parliament. 2. Peers. 3. The Judges. 4. Privy
   Council . . . . . 408, &c.

Peers a right to counsel King . . . 408, 9

Peers therefore protected from arrest . . 409

Judges advise King on questions of law . ibid.

Privy Council—(See *Privy Council.*) . ibid. &c.

COUNTIES

Corporate 120

Palatine 119, 20

COURTS (Public Judicial).—(See *Offices.*)

Page

King alone can constitute 75

King cannot change their course of proceeding or their jurisdiction 76

Cannot be granted in a new way . . . . ibid.

King may appoint any number of ordinary Courts, with usual jurisdiction 77

New commissions not warranted by usage, bad—(See *Commissioners.*) . . . . . ibid.

Cannot vest ecclesiastical jurisdiction in lay person, and *vice versâ* 76

Officers in—(See *Judges. Officers.*) . . . 78

Chancellor . . . . . . ibid.

Of Wards and Liveries 268

King may sue in what Court he pleases, though out of their ordinary jurisdiction 244

Profits arising from, part of revenue . . . 236

Of what these consist . . . . . ibid.

Grants of them restrained . . . 236, 7

COVENANT (to stand seised).

King cannot convey by 378

CROWN—(See *King—Prerogatives, &c. &c.*)

Demise (not death) of King . . . 11

Descent of—(See *Descent.*) . . . 9

CROWN LANDS.

(See *Lands.*) . . . . . 202, &c.

CUSTOM.

As to person and goods does not bind King . . 377

Aliter as to lands, as borough English, gavelkind custom, &c. 380

CUSTOM—(*continued*).

Page

Of London as to pledgees' peculiar right to hold goods, does not bind Crown   .   .   .   285

CUSTOMS—(See *Revenue.*)

King's goods not liable to pay   .   .   .   377

D.

DAMAGES.

For King for injuries to his lands   .   .   334
Against King, petition the remedy   .   .   341, 344, 5

DEANS,

How elected   63

DEBT TO, AND FROM, CROWN.

When of record *per se*   .   .   .   .   .   265, &c.
Bonds to King, in what forms, &c.   .   .   .   ibid.
Simple contract debts   .   .   .   266, &c.
Remedies to recover—(See *Remedies for King.--Extents.*)
Due to Crown debtor, Crown may take, &c.—(See *Extents in second degree.*)   .   .   .   303, &c.
Information of debt for King   .   .   .   335
Due from King, petition *de droit* the remedy   .   341, 4, 5
King's personalty, when liable for his debts   .   242, 3

DECEIT.

On obtaining Crown Grants—(See *Grants.*)   .   396, &c.

DECLARATION—(See *Pleading.*)

When King may waive his, and declare *de novo*   .   334

DELEGATES (Ecclesiastical.)

Page

Appeal to in ecclesiastical causes.—Origin of their
power 55
Who may be, and their power . . . 55, 6, 7
King may grant commission of review after their sen-
tence 56
Suit before them does not abate by death of either of the
parties . . . . ibid.
If they exceed their authority may be prohibited by
courts of law . . . . . ibid.
No appeal from them to house of lords . . ibid.

DEMESNE LANDS.

(See *Lands*) . 202, &c.

DEMISE OF CROWN. 11

DEMURRER.

(See *Pleadings.*) . . 368, 9, &c.

DENIZATION, and DENIZEN.

(See *Naturalization.*) 14
Prerogative of King alone . . . . ibid.
Effect of, and how granted . . . . ibid.
Prerogative of, cannot be delegated . . . ibid.
Denization not presumptively obtained by King grant-
ing lands but grant void 393
As to denizens purchasing lands . . . 229

DEODANDS.

What are and former object of, and prerogative herein 153
Rule *omnia quæ movent ad mortem sunt deodanda,* and
decisions on . . , . . 153, 4
Death within what time necessary to give title to . 154

DEODANDS (*continued*).

Page

Alienation, &c. not to affect Crown . . . ibid.
Finding of death by the article necessary . . ibid.
By whom found and of the inquisition . . 154, 5
This prerogative discountenanced, and how . . 155

DERNIER RESORT.—(See *Church—Appeal.*)

Of King as, in ecclesiastical causes . . . 55

DESCENT, OF CROWN.

Rules in general, same as in private property . . 9
Exceptions 10

DIEM CLAUSIT EXTREMUM.

(See *Extent.*) . . . . . 328, &c.

DISPENSATIONS.

From the laws, antient exercise of the power . . 95
Of statutes, taken away , . . . ibid.
Of common law, in general void, a distinction . 95, 6
King may grant from ecclesiastical laws . . 53, 4
As to commercial dispensations—(See *Church.*)

DISTRESS.

(See *Replevin.—Rents.*) 208, 9
Prerogative as to, for Crown rents . . 208, &c.
King may at common law without attornment . 208
For all rents, and on all lands of tenant, though holden
of another lord when 208, 9
In highway 209
Grantee of Crown lands, his rights as to . . ibid.
On goods seized on extent bad . . . 281
For rent, how far extent operates against . . 287

DISTRESS (*continued*).

Page

    On Crown lands bad   376

    Damage feasant, not on Crown cattle   .   .   .   ibid.

DOWER.

    Not to be taken under extent when   .   .   287, 300

    And widow protected   309

DROIT OF CROWN.

    Ship taken as reprisals without King's authority   .   41

DUKE.

    Origin of the title—(See *Peerage.*)   .   .   .   108

DUTIES.

    Of King and subject   7

E.

EARLS.

    Origin of the title—(See *Peerage.*)   .   .   .   108

EAST INDIA COMPANY.   127

ECCLESIASTICAL LAW.—(See *Church.*)

    Of what compounded   51

    By whom and how made, and to whom subject   .   51, 2, 3

    King dispenses with   .   .   .   .   .   ibid.

ECCLESIASTICAL COURT.

    The Chancellor may issue *ne exeat regno* against defend-
        ant in that Court for alimony   .   .   .   22

ECCLESIASTICS.

Page

Subject to what authority 53

EDUCATION.

Of the royal children, &c.—Prerogative as to 406, 7

EJECTMENT.

Action of, at the suit of the King . . . 245

EMBARGO.

The King may lay on general embargo on sudden emergencies and necessity . . . 21, 50, 164, 5

ENEMY.—(See *Aliens.*)

Trading with—Prerogative as to dispensing with commercial disabilities as to . . . 170 to 173

ENTRY.

For King into land when necessary . . . 251, 2

ERROR.

Lies on judgment on extent against Crown, and how, &c. 373
Effect of writ of . . . . . ibid.
Restitution after . . . . . . ibid.

ESCHEATS.

Arise out of feudal system, and nature of . . 226
Difference between escheat and forfeiture . . ibid.
Lands escheat to lord of the seignory, or person of
whom held 227
Primâ facie King is lord when . . . . ibid.
Copyhold escheats to lord of manor . . 227, 232, 3
Is either for default of heir, or crime of tenant . 227
Default of heir in general 227, 8
So if a monster or bastard only . . ibid.

ESCHEATS (*continued*).

Page

So if an alien child only 228, 9

Prerogative as to lands holden by aliens . . ibid.

Escheat on corruption of blood for a crime . . 230

Now only holds on attainder of treason, petit treason
and murder, and heir, &c. in other cases may enter 230

In treason forfeiture applies, and lands go to King,
though another lord 230, 1

On attainder though lands escheat to another lord, King
entitled to his year, day and waste . . . ibid.

Corruption of blood by attainder—operation on after acquired property 231

And affects the posterity of offender, through whom
they cannot claim 231, 2

Aliter collateral issue . . . . . ibid.

Or where not necessary to trace through offender . ibid.

May inherit through one parent, though other attainted 232

What lands and tenements subject to escheat . . 232, 3

Even King claims by escheat on same rules as subject ibid.

If a tenant to perform services no escheat, as if *cestui que*
trust or mortgagor be attainted, &c. . . . ibid.

But Chancery will not decree foreclosure against Crown 234

Escheat of trust lands or mortgaged lands, on death of
trustee or mortgagee—Equitable claims how they
affect Crown 234

Pardon will not prevent vested escheat to lord . . ibid.

Effect of pardon on subsequent property, corruption of
blood only removed by Parliament . . . ibid.

In general, no inquisition or office necessary . 234, 249

Crown should immediately enter . . . 234

Liberal practice of Crown to grant to relatives, &c.
lands escheated 235, 6

Grant of lands when they shall escheat bad . . 389

ESQUIRES.

How created 118

ESTATES. (See *Lands, Crown.*)

Tail in King—(See *Tail, Estates.*) 206

ESTOPPELS.

Page

Not against, though for, King 381

ESTRAYS.

What are 151
Primâ facie in King, but generally in lords of manors, &c. ibid.
What necessary to vest property in King . . ibid.
When and how title to may be defeated . . . ibid.
King's goods cannot be estrays 152
How to be used by King . . . . ibid.
Payment by owner on reclaiming . . . . ibid.

EXCHEQUER (Court of).

King's revenue court 244
Where Crown interests involved, suits even *inter alios*,
    removeable into Exchequer . . . . ibid.
King may maintain any species of suit therein . ibid.
General seal day, &c. therein 359

EXCISE

Lien on goods for duties 293

EXECUTION.

In criminal cases, as to King pardoning part of it . 96
On extents, &c.—(See *Judgment.*) . . . 373
How if monies recovered on petition *de droit* . . 348, 9
As to lands, only judgment for subject, and this suffi-
    cient—(See *Judgment.*)

EXECUTIVE MAGISTRATE.

King's power as in general—must consider the laws . 2
His power kept separate from legislative authority, and
    why . . . . ibid.
Must have a share in legislation 2, 3
General nature and extent of King's rights as . . 3, 6, 7
Executive power why in single hand . . . 3

EXECUTIVE MAGISTRATE (*continued*).

Page

As such, Crown has right of promulgating to the people
all acts of state and government, and has copyright
in Acts of Parliament 239

EXECUTORS.

Must first pay Crown debt—when may pay debt in
equal degree, &c.—cannot retain against Crown—
(See *Extent.*) 329, 30
Goods of testator not taken under extent . . 287
Nor executor's goods for deceased's debts, unless assets ibid.
King may be, but prerogative thereon . . . 379

EXEMPTIONS.

From serving in public offices, King may in general
grant 20, 118
King cannot exempt where it would affect public jus-
tice, &c. . . . . . . ibid.
Grants of, how construed 21
From impress 48
From liability to be arrested—(See *Protection—Servants.*) 118
From laws—(See *Dispensations.*) . . . 95, 6
Discharge from future liabilities, when good . . 388, 9

EXPORTATION.—(See *Commerce.*)

King cannot in general restrain . . . 163 to 170
Licence, &c. to trade with enemy . . . 170 to 173

EXTENTS.

Extents in general.—A high prerogative remedy . 262
Statutable origin 263
Extents have the energy of statutes merchant, &c. 263, 4
Different kinds and descriptions of, and against whom . 264
Not in foreign dominions of King unless laws there al-
low it 34
In the 2d, 3d, &c. degree 264

EXTENTS IN CHIEF

Page

1. *Commission to find debts and inquisition thereon, and of debts due to Crown* . . . 265

No execution till debt of record . . . ibid.

What are debts of record for King . . . ibid.

Obligations and specialties to King, when and in what form, &c. 265, 6

Debts due from tax collectors . . . 266

Not simple contract debts . . . ibid. &c.

Against simple contract debtors to the Crown . ibid.

Debt must first be recorded by commission . . 266, 7

Nature and form of commission to find debts . . 267

Baron's authority for it necessary . . . . ibid.

As to notice to defendant of executing the commission ibid.

What evidence of the debt before the commissioners 267, 8

Witnesses disobeying, &c. 268

Inquisition must be openly taken, right of strangers to contest before commissioners, &c. . . . ibid.

Mode of finding debts, inquisition must be precise and decisive, what sufficient certainty and rules hereon 269

How to object if otherwise . . . . ibid.

What debts to Crown may be found by inquisition, general rule any suable debt . . . . ibid.

Monies on account . . . . . . ibid.

Monies received as King's money—When a man to be deemed a receiver of Crown monies, no constructive receipt, &c. Bill for the money not due . . 270

Bonds, bills of exchange and promissory notes, but must in general be due 270, 1

Balance between partners 271

Melius inquirendum if finding dissatisfactory—(See *Melius inquirendum*.) . . . . . ibid.

2. *Scire facias to justify the extent.*

In general necessary on record or inquisition to bring defendant into court, and why . . . ibid.

Not if insolvency 271, 2

On immediate extent—(See *Sect. 4, post.*) . 277, &c.

Not necessary to revive suits of King . . 271, 2

EXTENTS IN CHIEF (*continued*).

Page

On bonds for performance of covenants . . 272
Nature and form, and requisites, &c. of the *scire facias* ibid.
When sued out and tested . . . . ibid.
Warning defendant, and rule to appear, &c. post. 272, 3
Sheriff return . . . . . ibid.
Effect of non-appearance, judgment thereon . . 273

3. *The form, teste, issuing and return of.*
Form of,
Recites, inquisition or record debt, sheriff to enter and
take . . . . ibid.
Sheriff to summon witnesses 276
Proviso not to sell . . . . . . ibid.
Conclusion of . . . . . ibid.
Extent on bond does not state breach . . . 274

Teste of,
May be in vacation but not before fiat . . . ibid.
By whom tested, signed, sealed . . . ibid.

Issuing of,
Out of equity side of exchequer 274
In vacation 275
Several, when and how . . . . . . ibid.
After defendant's death . . . . ibid.
Another, first set aside . . . . ibid.
On old inquisition and *fiat* 276

Return of,
In term ; a general return . . . 274, 5
No term to intervene 275
Death of one of defendants 276
Filing return . . . . . . ibid.
False . . . . ibid.

4. *Immediate extent, when it may issue; Affidavit to*
obtain it, and fiat *thereon* 277
Immediate extent, i. e. without *scire facias*, founded
on statute of Hen. 8. . . . . . ibid.
Issues at discretion of court, how . . . 278

EXTENTS IN CHIEF (*continued*).

Page

In vacation before return day though after return of
commission 277, 8

Affidavit of danger 278
Must swear positively to debt when sufficient . . ibid.
Must state danger of debt being lost, and bad circum-
stances of defendant, and reason why, &c. . 278, 9
Application to set aside affidavit, &c. . . . 279
Before whom sworn . . . . . ibid.

Fiat of baron, &c.
How obtained, &c. 279, 80

5. *Execution of, in general* 280
Clause of *non omittas* . . . . ibid.
Sheriff's power under it, may break outer door ; not
to execute it on Sunday . . . . ibid.
What he may take, all property debts and person at
once . . . . . . ibid.
Notwithstanding death . . . . ibid.
Taking all goods, though more than sufficient . 280, 1
May take lands though goods sufficient . . 281
Defendant not bailable . . . . ibid.
Sheriff must not sell . . . . ibid.
Seizure of lands and debts nominal . . . 281
Keeping specialties . . . . . . ibid.
How writs take place *inter se*, concurring with extent
in aid 281, 2

What may be taken.
Body.
By common law and statute may be taken, but not
usual 282
King may protect his debtor by writ of protection,
but subject may still sue to execution and have
it if he undertake for King's debt : obsolete, but
exists still ; instances 282, 3
Writ of protection to subject for one year he serving King, &c. 284

EXTENTS IN CHIEF (*continued*).

Page

Subject may hold body with King, but latter chooses
custody, &c. 284

Defendant though bankrupt or insolvent liable notwithstanding to King . . . ibid.

Goods and sums of money . . . **284**

What defendant had at the teste or *fiat* is bound 284, 5

King not bound by statute of frauds . . ibid.

All goods though in trustees' hands but must leave
necessaries, &c. 285

King not bound by sale in market or custom of
London as to pledge . . . . ibid.

When stranger claims a *property* in the goods . 285

  As assignee in trust for creditors . . ibid.

  As pawnee, bailee, demisee, &c. . . 285, 6

  As assignee of Bankrupt . . . 286

Joint term of husband since deceased and wife 286, 7

Dower not taken under extent . . . 287

Partnership goods only defendant's share . . ibid.

Against several separate goods . . . ibid.

Where stranger claims *interest* without property . 287

  As goods distrained . . . . ibid.

  Landlord, year's rent . . . ibid.

  As executor . . . . . ibid.

  As member of corporation . . . ibid.

Cattle of stranger or tenant in common in King's
debtor's lands 287, 8

Generally prevails against subjects *fieri facias*,
though prior seizure (but not sale) under the
fieri facias 288

If subject's judgment prior to commencement of
Crown process, and subject's seizure before extent, which is to be preferred . . 289 to 292

Special finding better if doubt . . 292, 3

Court will protect officers if fair doubts whether
goods liable and how 293

Lien on excise goods . . . . ibid.

Taxes to be paid before execution of subject satisfied ibid.

EXTENTS IN CHIEF (*continued*).

Page

Lands.

May be seized though goods sufficient . . 293

Time from which lands (generally) bound . . ibid·

By bond made like record within statute
Henry 8. . . . . 293, 4

By other bonds and specialties . . 294

By simple contract debts . . . ibid.

By statute debts from certain Crown officers,
receivers, collectors, &c. . . . ibid.

From time of entering into their office . 294, 5

Other officers and private persons, lands not
within that statute from whence bound 295, 6

Time when simple contract is a debt of record . 296

May seize equitable titles as an equity of redemption—(See *Mortgage.*) . . . ibid.

May take an estate in trust for defendant . 296, 7

Rents service, &c. . . . 297

Tithes of lay impropriators . . . ibid.

Not tithes of beneficed clerk—(See *levari
facias.*) . . . . . . ibid.

Copyhold lands . . . . ibid.

Term for years . . . . ibid.

When stranger claims interest and property in them 298

Alienation by defendant if made after time whence
lands bound, bad . . . . ibid.

Aliter if made before . . . . ibid.

Term to attend inheritance . . . ibid.

Fee simple lands followed after the death of the
Crown debtor . . . . . ibid.

And estates tail by statute which only relates to
certain Crown debts . . . 298, 9

Effect of alienation by issue in tail before Crown
process on ancestor's debt . . . 299

Charging heir if executors have assets and feoffee
if heir have 300

When cannot follow estates tail after death . 299

Alienee of fee simple lands . . . 299, 300

EXTENTS IN CHIEF (*continued*).

Page

Surviving joint-tenant not liable for deceased's
Crown debt **300**

Wife's jointure and dower . . . . ibid.

If assignment of bankrupt lands be not enrolled
before fiat—(See *Bankrupt.*) . . . ibid.

Extent operates notwithstanding a subject's judgment, if not a sale under the judgment before
extent, when, &c. . . . **300 to 303**

Mere agreement by defendant for sale of land, or
equitable mortgage, does not bind Crown . **303**

6. *Of seizing debts and credits, and herein of*
Extents in Chief in Second Degree.

Jury to find debts, &c. due to defendant—seizure nominal, but entitles King to process against debtor to
his debtor . . . . . . ibid.

Semble King may for his own benefit proceed against
debtors to his debtor, &c. *in infinitum* . . ibid.

Whether debts to Crown debtor, &c. are bound from
fiat . . . . . ibid. to 305

Payment of debt to Crown debtor after *fiat*, but before
caption under inquisition **304**

Whether inquisition must state that the money is due to
Crown debtor . . . . . ibid.

What may be taken under it . . . **305**

Simple contract and other debts for which
Crown might have extent against its immediate debtor . . . . ibid.

No process for Crown against debtor to Crown debtor
till debt due or if outstanding bill . . . ibid.

If debt defendant could not alien . . . ibid.

When debts seized are due to Crown debtor and another,
whether Crown takes all . . . ibid. 306

Sheriff cannot compel payment seizure nominal only ibid.

Mode of proceeding for debts due to Crown debtors by
scire facias or immediate extent as against immediate
Crown debtor **306, 7**

If small debts seized, they may be collected and paid, &c. **306**

EXTENTS IN CHIEF in Second Degree (*continued*).

Page

Immediate extent against person to whom receiver-general has paid over 306

Process against debtor to Crown debtor before extent finding them is returnable . . . ˙ 306, 7

7. *Venditioni exponas.—Order for sale of lands.*

Sale of goods under *venditioni exponas* . 307

No motion for *venditioni exponas*, but defendant entitled to notice of sale . . . . . ibid.

If sheriff cannot sell at appraised price . . ibid.

Sheriff may move for allowance extra poundage . 307

Lands sold by motion of attorney-general under statute, how, &c. . . . . . . ibid. 8

Discretion of court as to sale of lands ; not allowed, if goods sufficient 309

Lands sold only to amount of debt . . . ibid.

Costs and expenses of Crown on sale of lands—(See *Costs.*) 308, 9, 11

Court protects mortgagee and claim of dower, &c. and how 309

8. *Costs.*

General rule, Crown neither pays nor takes . . 310

Exceptions, specialties made records by 33 Hen. 8. . ibid.

When lands sold by virtue of 25 Geo. 3. . . 311

Defendant applying to pay debt not to pay costs if his goods sufficient on sale of which Crown has no costs ibid.

Collectors of taxes liable to costs on extents . . ibid.

Bill may be taxed, motion to refund . . . ibid.

9. *Poundage.*

By common law 312

By statute . . . . . ibid. to 314

Payable out of sum levied and defendant not liable, otherwise if a penalty, or Crown entitled to its costs, &c. 314, 15

When the debt is paid after the *venditioni exponas* . 315

Apportionment of poundage to different sheriffs . ibid.

EXTENTS IN CHIEF in Second Degree (*continued*).

Page

Where extents into two counties and debt paid to one
sheriff 316

Sheriff may retain poundage, but must return whole
money . . . . . . ibid.

As to sheriff getting reward for extraordinary service ibid.

EXTENTS IN AID.

1. *In general.—Course of proceeding.*

Nature and origin of—Is the prerogative process used
in King's name for his debtor's benefit against debtor of latter 317

Mode and preliminary forms on issuing extent against
debtors of Crown debtor . . . 317, 18

To whom proceeds to be paid . . . ibid.

2. *To what degrees debts may be seized on.*

To the fourth degree and what so considered . 318

3. *What Crown debtor may issue it* . . 318 *to* 320

Common law hardships redressed by late statute . ibid.

Taken away in general from Crown debtor and restrained
to collectors of revenue bound by bond, &c. . 319, 20

4. *For sum may issue, affidavit, and* fiat . . 320

To issue only for amount due from Crown debtor issuing
it to Crown 320, 21

Sum to be stated in *fiat,* indorsed on writ . . ibid.

Affidavit for it 321

Difference between and for extent in chief . ibid.

1. That debt due to Crown from its debtor . 322

2 and 3. Debt to Crown debtor and likely to be
lost . . . . . . ibid.

4 and 5. That debt to Crown debtor was originally
debt due to him and has not been otherwise put
in suit 323, 4

6. That prosecutor less able to pay King 324

How to obtain *fiat* for extent in aid . . 324, 5

Proceedings, commission, &c. . . . ibid.

EXTENTS IN AID (*continued*).

Page

5. *Form of.—What taken.—Motions.—Pleadings.—*
Costs.—Poundage, &c. 325
    Form of 325, 273, 4
  What may be taken 325
    Body, goods, lands, simple contract or specialty debts
      and monies 326
    Personalty from whence bound . . . ibid.
    Land from whence bound . . . ibid.
    Discharge of body . . . . ibid.
    When more levied than was due . 327
  Motions to set it aside, &c. 326
    No equitable relief on ground that Crown debtor
      has assets without resorting to the writ, &c. ibid. 28
  Pleadings 327
    (See post, title *Extents resisting.*)
    Any defence which would hold as against defend-
      ant's creditor, i. e. Crown debtor, instances . ibid.
    Bill not due—set off—statute of limitations—bank-
      ruptcy, &c. 327, 8
  Costs 310, 328
  Poundage . . . . ibid.

EXTENT AFTER DEATH OF CROWN DEBTOR.

Diem clausit extremum 328
  Sheriff's duty under . . . . ibid.
  Substantially similar to other extents . . ibid.
  Form of . . . . . ibid.
  On what founded 328, 9
  It may issue immediately on death though no exe-
    cutor, &c. 329
  Must have died indebted, and debt must be of record ibid.
  Duty of executor in administering assets as to Crown
    debt, must pay Crown first, cannot retain against. ibid.
  Payment of equal debt to a subject before notice of
    Crown debt, funeral expenses, &c. . . 329, 30

EXTENTS (*continued*).

Page

Resisting.

i. e. traversing inquisition or office. A statutable remedy
for subject—(See *Traverse of Office.*) . . 358

1st. No *locus standi* in court against Crown without subject *claiming property* . . . . ibid.

On return of inquisition, rule for subject to appear and
claim—form of when given, &c. . . . 359

Appearing and claiming, when and how . 359, 60

Claiming a lease of the lands *pendente lite* . . ibid.

Who may appear and claim—defendant and stranger,
having interests, &c. 360, 1

Different parties, &c. claiming; prerogative of making
them interplead 361

2dly. *Motions* to set aside extents, &c. When and how
made, and notice thereof 362

May move to set aside for irregularity, &c. proceedings
not on face of record . . . . ibid.

When motions should be made, waiving irregularity . 363, 4

Must apply on irregularities not on face of proceedings 363

Setting aside partially. New writ . . . 364

Moving to lay out money levied in funds, &c. *pendente lite* ibid.

Moving to pay the money into court, when and on what
terms 364, 5

Defendant cannot dispute debt on affidavits . . ibid.

Motion to refund on excessive levy . . . 365

3dly. *Pleadings* on extents; four day rule to plead;
further time . . . . . ibid.

Pleas : 1. by defendant or his representative ; or, 2. by
strangers—(See *Pleadings.*) . . . 365, &c.

No ruling to reply, but court will enforce replication,
&c. 368, 9

(As to replication, rejoinder, &c. see *Pleadings.*)

4thly. *Venire* to try; Where King likes; issues on extents
at Westminster 370

Notice of trial 371

On Crown delaying to proceed . . ibid.

Crown tries where it pleases . . . ibid.

If distinct issues . . . . ibid.

EXTENTS (*continued*).

Page

Resisting.

Verdict, &c. 371

Postea. Rule for judgment; pleading matter after verdict 371, 2

5thly. Judgment on—(and see *Judgment.*) . . 372, 3

6thly. Execution,

In general 373

Restitution . . . . . . ibid.

7thly. Error,

Lies; and no *scire facias* . . . . ibid.

If reversal, &c. . . . . . ibid.

EXTRAORDINARY REVENUE OF THE CROWN . 237

What are the chief parts of— (See *Revenue.*) . . 238

F.

FAIRS.

(See *Marts and Fairs.*) . . . . 193, &c.

FAMILY (Royal).

Queen, Prince, children of King—(See *those titles.*) 401, &c.

After the Queen, the Prince and his consort, rest of

royal family no peculiar rights, &c. . . . 405

King's prerogative as to superintending their marriages

and education; and to what degrees, &c. . 406, 7, 8

FASTS.

King may by proclamation appoint days of . . 54

FELONIES.

General Pardon of—(See *Pardon.—Forfeitures.*) . 100

FELONS' GOODS.

Not by prescription in subject . . 147, 8

FEUDAL SYSTEM . . . . . 211, &c.

FIAT,

Baron's on extents—(See *Extents.*)

FICTIONS OF LAW.

Page

Do not bind Crown 381

FIERI FACIAS.

Extent, how it operates against—(See *Extents.*) . 288, &c.

FINES.

On offenders, &c. go to King, when . . . 236
Go to Crown *instanter*, and may be levied on *levari*
facias, though sentence be also imprisonment for cer-
tain period, and further till fine paid . . 260
Grants of them restrained 236, 7
Before conviction bad 385
When remitted, Attorney-General makes entry . . 260
Remedy to recover . . . . . ibid.
On *Quo Warranto* 337

FINE by King,

Should be by render, not writ of covenant . 340

FIRST FRUITS 66

FISHERIES and FISH—(See *Seas.*)

Freedom of public right as to ; and King cannot restrain 142, 3
Private *prescriptive* right in branch of sea good, but re-
strained as to *jura publica* . . . . ibid.
Private fishery 143, 4
King no general property in fish . . . 144
Only whales and sturgeons ; and prerogative as to these 144, 5

FLEET.

Prerogative as to 46, 7
(And see *Pressing.*)

FOREIGN STATES.

Prerogative in general as to 6
Prerogative as to, why in King alone . . . 39
Licence to reside therein 24
Subject not obliged to go to 21

FOREIGN STATES (continued).

Page

King may compel his subjects to return—(See *Ne exeat Regno.*) . . . . . 21 & 24

Consequences of not returning from, King's interest and fraudulent assignment, &c. 24, 25

Contempt for not returning 24

FORESTS.

What are ; prerogative as to ; grant of ; and rights of grantee . . . . . 137 to 140

FORFEITURES FOR OFFENCES.

Ground of inflicting ; necessary, especially in treason ; disabilities extending to posterity when unjust 213, 4, 5

Difference between, and escheats . . 215, 6

What forfeited for treason, and what not . . 216, 7, 8

Interest taken by King, and effect on inferior rights of others 218, 9

Petit treason and felony ;

What forfeited for ; chattels interests, profits of land and goods . . . . . 219, &c.

Year, day and waste . . . . . ibid.

Corruption of blood and forfeiture of lands after death abolished, except in treason, petit treason and murder 220, 1

Forfeitures of realty not vested till *attainder* . . 221

Rights of Crown on outlawry . . . ibid.

Of lands, has relation back to time of offence, so as to avoid, &c. ; how as to *mesne* profits—(See *Mesne Profits.*) . . . . . . ibid.

Time of offence, what to be deemed . . ibid.

Of goods generally and for what offences . 222, 3

Of choses in action 223

Where another interested with the offender . . ibid.

Goods forfeited on *conviction* . . . 224

Of goods, no relation back unless fraud . . ibid.

Restraints on offenders aliening goods, &c. to defeat Crown 224, 5

King's pardon of the offence will not prevent escheat to subject 225

FORFEITURES FOR OFFENCES (*continued*).

Page

Of offices—(See *Offices*.) . . . . 85 to 88

Against revenue laws; vest instantly . . . 226

But this prerogative right may be lost by a judicial sale

in Admiralty of same article as a *derelict* . . 226

Of lands purchased, &c. by alien . . . 229

Grant of forfeited lands by King to relatives . . 235, 6

Grants of before judgment bad 385

King's grant cannot create a forfeiture . . ibid.

FORTIFICATIONS.

The King may enter on lands of subjects to make them,

when 49

FORTS.

Prerogative as to making 45, 49

FRANCHISES.

What are; definition and list of . . . 118, 9

Formerly too many granted 119

King alone fountain of . . . . . ibid.

Cannot destroy them when vested . . 119, 125, 132

By prescription, what evidence of . . . 138

How they pass, by what words, &c.—(See *Grants.*) . 392

FRANKPLEDGE 120

FRAUDULENT CONVEYANCE.

To defeat King on forfeiture . . . 225

FRAUD.

Statute of, whether Crown bound by . . 285 & 366

FREE CHAPELS.

(See *Chapel.*)

FREE CHASE.

Prerogative as to . . . 140

King cannot make over subject's land without assent ibid.

FREE WARREN.

Page

What it is; franchise of; and prerogative as to . 141, 2

Not liable to escheat 233

G.

GAME.

Whether King has sole property in . . 134 to 137

King cannot make over subject's land without assent . 140

GAOLER.

Grant of office of, in fee 82

GAOLS.

Property of King in general 103

By whom governed . . . . . ibid.

King cannot grant custody of offenders to private person ibid.

Making new ones . . . . . ibid.

GAVELKIND.

Custom of, binds Crown 380

The lands subject to do not escheat, though they are

forfeitable for treason 233

GENERALISSIMO.

King is 44, 5

(See *War and Peace.*) 25

GERMAN TERRITORIES.

Prerogative in 32

GIBRALTAR.

Prerogative therein 29

GOODS.

Page

Of King

Cannot be wrecks 150

Estrays—(And see *Distress, &c.*) . . . 152

General nature of property in—(See *Personalty.*) 241, 2, 3

Chattel interests of King may go in succession . 208

Of Crown debtor, how far liable on extents, &c.—(See
Extents.) . . . . . 284, &c.

GOVERNMENTS.

Origin and different forms of, &c. . . . 1

English government 2

GOVERNOR.

Of colonies,
His powers, &c.—(See *Colonies.*) . . 34, 5, 6

GRAND SERJEANTRY.

Tenure by 81

GRANTS FROM KING.

1. *What good, &c.*

Not high prerogatives; as assenting to statutes, pardoning, making officers, &c. &c. . . . 384, 5

Bad if they cause failure of justice, &c. as general
exemptions from civil liability, &c. &c. . . 385

Bad grants of forfeitures, &c. *in futuro* . . ibid.

Bad if create a forfeiture, or tax, subject and instances 385, 6

Grants of toll when good . . . 386

Bad if contrary to common, or statute, law . ibid.

Of *letters of marque* . . . 40

Courts and offices . . . . 75, &c.

Franchises . . . 118 to 155

Crown lands and possession —(See *those Titles.*) 263, &c.

Crown copyright . . . 338 to 341

Protections . . . 282 to 284

Lands seized under offices . . 253, &c.

GRANTS FROM KING (*continued*).

Page

Revenue, grants of, restrained . . . 387

Choses in action assignable by and to Crown, when;
and prerogative herein . . . 387, 8

King may grant contingency or mere possibility, and
exemption from future liability, when—(See *Exemptions.*) 388, 9

Not an annuity, when 389

King cannot grant to stranger lands seized and
claimed by him till after office found and returned 253, &c.

But the subject claiming is on certain terms entitled
to a lease or grant of the lands in dispute . 255, &c.

2. *Grants from and to King, how effected.*

By record only in general as to realty . . 389, 90

How letters patent obtained and ceremony . . 390

When record not necessary to transfer from Crown 390, 1

In general Crown takes by record only; when otherwise 391

3. *Construction of—uncertainties, misrecitals, deceit, &c.*

General rule of construction . . 391, 2

General grant does not pass royal franchises, &c. . 392

What not under word "appurtenances" . . ibid.

Shall not operate to two purposes not expressed; shall
not operate presumptively, and instances . . 393

A liberal interpretation . . . ibid.

Especially if grant be ' by royal grace, &c.' . . 394

Or for valuable consideration . . . ibid.

If capable of constructions and one void . . ibid.

Uncertainty, avoids, and instances . . 394, 5

Aliter if capable of being reduced to certainty . 395

Rules as to necessity of noticing existing interests, &c.
in granting reversion . . . 396, 7

Mistaken conclusion as to King's title, or as to unimportant consideration, &c. how it affects grant 397

Misrecital as to thing for King's benefit, or real consideration, its effect . . . 397, 8

Difference whose misrecital . . . 397

GRANTS FROM KING (*continued*).

Page

    King misinformed not deceived   .   . 398
    Other rules, &c.   .   .   . 397, 8, 9

4. *Rights, &c. of grantee.*
    Not peculiar, except of *chose in action*, &c. . . 399

5. *Avoiding royal grants.*
    The remedy—(See *Scire facias to repeal, &c.*) . 400
    King in general bound by, and when otherwise
                119, 125, 132, 400
    Void or injurious to subject, *scire facias* to repeal 330, 1

GUERNSEY (Isle of.)

    Prerogative in   28
    Whether extent in   34

GUNPOWDER.

    King's prerogative right in   49

H.

HAVENS.

    (See *Ports and Havens.*) 174, 5

HEIR.

    How far liable for ancestor's Crown debts . 298, 99, 300

HIGHWAY.

    King may distrain in—(See *Lands.*)   .   .   . 209

HONOURS.

    (See *Peerage.*)   107
    Cannot legally refuse any, if offered by the King . 319

HOUSES OF PARLIAMENT.

    (See *Parliament.*)   67

HUSBAND AND WIFE.—(See *Queen.*)

Page

Attainder of husband, prerogative as to forfeiture, how
it affects wife 217, 18
Joint term of cannot be taken by King after husband's
death 286, 7

I.

IDIOTS (See *Lunatics.*)

Who are, and prerogative as to care of, as *parens patriæ* 157
Difference between them and lunatics . . 159
Statute of Ed. 2. 157
Generally, but not necessarily, in Chancellor through
Crown 158
Chancellor's power from Crown . . . ibid.
Jurisdiction though idiot or his property abroad . 158
Guardian of, nature of his interests and rights . 158, 9
King avoids his acts, &c. 160

IMPORTATION.

King cannot in general restrain—(See *Gunpowder.*) 163 to 170
Licence, &c. to trade with enemy . . 170 to 173

INFANCY.

Of King, no disability, when 376

INFANTS.

Prerogative as to, as *parens patriæ* . . 155 to 157
In chancellor from Crown 155, 6
Appointment of guardians for . . . 156, 7
Chancellor protects infants' interests and rights, and
when 157
Will assist guardians in their rights . . . ibid.

INFORMATION.

Prerogative remedy in nature of civil action . . 332
1. Of *intrusion*; 2. of *debt*; 3. in *rem* . . ibid.
Of intrusion—(See *Intrusion.*) . . 332 to 335

INFORMATION (*continued*).

Page

Of debt in nature of Crown action ; remedy on revenue
forfeiture ; compounding it, &c.　.　.　.　335

In *rem* to recover goods themselves as derelict, &c.　.　ibid.

What title or interest subject must shew　.　.　334

What objection waived by attorney-general not demurring　.　.　.　.　.　ibid.

Cannot plead double　.　.　.　.　ibid.

Crown may reply, traverse several matters in plea, &c.—
(See *Pleading*.)　.　.　.　.　ibid.

When King may waive count and declare *de novo*　.　ibid.

In nature of *quo warranto*　.　.　.　337

INHERITANCE. (See *Descent*.)

INJURIES.

By King to the person, no redress　.　.　340

Aliter to property—(See *Remedies*.)　.　.　ibid.

INQUESTS OF OFFICE.

(See *Inquisition*.)　.　.　.　.　216, &c.

INQUISITION.

A prerogative remedy for King; nature and object of　246, 7

Consequence of not having (when necessary for King)
before seizure of property　.　.　.　247

Old *inquisitio post mortem* under military tenures　247, 8

General object of inquiry as to lands　.　.　248

Not in general necessary when King's title appears
already of record　.　.　.　248, 9

Or equally notorious　.　.　.　.　249

Or possession or freehold cast on King; as descent in remainder ; escheat ; temporalities of bishops vacated ;
devised lands ; alien's lands, &c.　.　.　249, 50

Not on attainder of treason　.　.　.　249

General rule when entry by subject necessary, inquisition for King is so　.　.　.　.　249, 50

When necessary on clause of re-entry in Crown lease　250

INQUISITION (*continued*).

Page

Necessary for lands of idiots, &c. year day and waste,
temporalities, &c. forfeited for contempt, enemy's
choses in action 250
Actual seizure, or *scire facias*, when also necessary 250, 1, 2, 3
Some matter of record also necessary to divest estate in
King 253
When otherwise . . . . ibid.
Restraints on Crown grants to strangers, of lands seized
and claimed by King, before inquisition found and re-
turned; and when such restraints hold, &c. . 253, 4, 5
The defendant, claimant or traverser against King en-
titled to a grant or lease, and on what terms, &c. . 255, 6
Prerogative as to mesne or intermediate profits and is-
sues 257
Requisites of inquisition as to finding of whom lands,
holden, &c. 258
If finding not satisfactory, King may have a *melius in-
quirendum*, when, &c.—(See *Melius inq.*) 258, 9
General rule, inquisition not necessary for King claim-
ing personalty 259
Coroner's jury, an inquisition for this purpose . ibid.
Escheators where to sit, and as to return of inquisition ibid. 60
To find Crown debts under commission for extent 265, &c.
Nature of and proceedings on such commission, &c.—
(See *Extents*.)
Setting aside partially, &c.; and fresh writ thereon 364
Subject traversing or disputing them—(See *Traverse of
Office—Extents, resisting.*) . . 356, &c.
Persons holding copyhold terms, &c. and having rents,
commons, fees and profits *apprendre* in lands claimed
by Crown; protected though their interests not found
under inquisition . . . 351, 2

INSOLVENT.

Not to be released on extent . . 284
Extent against—(See *Extent.*)
Statutes relating to do not bind Crown . 366

INSURRECTION.

Page

In case of, King may command subject's assistance   18, 49

INTERPLEADER.

Where conflicting claims against Crown prerogative as
to parties interpleading   361

INTRUSION.

Information of intrusion, in nature of action for trespass 332, 3
Form of   332
In what Court and county   . . . 333
The general issue when improper   . . . ibid.
Aliter by statute   . . . . ibid.
Judgment and damages in   . . . 334, 5
Stranger not bound by the judgment   . . 335

INVASION.

King may command personal services of his subjects   18, 49

IRREGULARITIES.

In extents, &c.—(See *Extents, Resisting*.)   . . 362, &c.

IRELAND.

What laws and prerogative in   . . . 27, 8
Statutes when bind   27

ISSUE.

King waiving his 369, 70

J.

JERSEY (Isle of.)

Prerogative in   28

JEWELS OF CROWN.

Are heir looms, &c.   . . . 238
Whether King may grant them   . . ibid.

JOINT TENANTS.

King and subject cannot be   . . . 210, 11
King and a subject as to personalty when   . 241, 2

JOINTURE.

Page

Wife's jointure not liable to Crown debts when   .   300

JUDGES.

Chief, and others, how and by whom appointed   .   76, 8
Hold during good behaviour   .   .   .   82, 3
Do not lose their situation by demise of Crown   .   83
How removed   .   .   .   .   .   ibid.
Legal advisers of King, &c.   .   .   .   409

JUDGMENT.

Court to give *ex officio* for King, where his title appears
   though *inter alios* 244, 372
On extents, rule for   .   .   .   371, 2
Necessary to have award of *amoveas manus* and why   372, 3
For subject to recover lands is *amoveas manus* or *ouster*
   le main   .   .   .   .   348, 9, &c.
Without it lands remain in King, it puts King out   ibid.
Alone sufficient to enable subject to take possession   ibid. 50
Ouster le main to King's patentee of the lands   .   .   349
Amoveas manus where several recover   .   .   350
If subject misuse the *amoveas manus*, King may reseize,
   when and how   .   .   .   .   ibid. 1
Judgment for subject always general reservation of
   King's right   348

JURE POSTLIMINII.

Former charter rights revive on King reconquering a
   colony, &c.   38

JURY.

Persons cannot refuse to serve on   .   .   .   19
King may exempt a person from serving on   .   .   20

JUSTICE.

King, fountain of 6, 75
King cannot now personally administer   .   .   75, 6
Courts of—(See *Courts.*)   .   .   .   75, &c.

JUSTICES OF THE PEACE.

Page

By whom appointed 79
How and when their authority may be determined . 80
As to exclusive jurisdiction of borough justices . 120, 7
May administer oaths of allegiance . 17

K.

KING.

(See *Executive Magistrate—Legislative Authority—Parliament—Prerogative—Remedies for—&c.*)
Attributes of 5
  Perfection . . . . . ibid.
  Perpetuity . . . . . ibid.
Who is (See *Descent of Crown.*) . . . 9
De facto and *de jure* . . . 10, 11
Titular 11
Who may exercise prerogatives—(See *Prerogatives.*) 9, &c.
Cannot transfer Crown 12
Resignation of . . . . . ibid.
As *parens patriæ*—(See *Parens Patriæ.*) . . 155
Privileges and incapacities of—(See *those Titles.*)
A sole corporation 122
  So as to lands—(See *Lands.*) . . . 208
His personal property when subject to his will and debts 242, 3

KING'S BENCH (Court of).—(See *Courts.*)

As to its visitatorial power 131
Will bail offenders when they have legal right to pardon 95
Will put off trial of offenders where they have equitable claim to royal mercy . . . ibid.

KING'S EVIDENCE.

Where admissible; not *entitled* to pardon . . ibid.

KNIGHTS.

Knighthood offered by King cannot be legally refused 19

KNIGHTS (*continued*).

Page

Degrees of and how created . . . 116, 7, 8

L.

LACHES.

(See *nullum tempus, &c.*) 379, 80

LANCASTER (Duchy of.)

Crown lands in 206
Distress in 209

LANDLORD.

Claim for rent how affected by extent . . 287

LANDS, CROWN.

Antiently extensive 202, 3
How reduced 203
Interference of parliament and statute of Ann . ibid.
Restraints on transferring; when cannot be granted; for
    what period and how . . . 203, 4, 5
Crown lease . . . . . ibid.
What lessee must be bound to observe . . 204
Private lands of King, when grantable, devisable, &c. ibid.
When taxable 204, 5
Primâ facie, King takes *jure coronæ* . . 205
Descend as and with Crown—(See *Descent.*) . 205
When not 206
When King takes and holds in private capacity . ibid.
Lands under seas; *maritima incrementa*; derelict; shores;
    &c.—(See *Seqs.*) . . . 206 to 209
King sole corporation as to; takes chattels in succession;
    fee without ‘ heirs’ or ‘ successors’ . . 208
Distress for rent due to—(See *Distress.*) . ibid. 9
Rents out of—(See *Rent.*) . . ibid. 300
Land to King and subject; how King takes . 210
Cannot be joint tenants, but may tenants in common ibid. 11
Conveyance by Crown in fee, restraining alienation
    386, note (*h*)

LANDS.

Page

From what time liable to Crown debts, and what interests and titles Crown may take—(See *Extents.*) . 293, &c.

How far liable to extent against subjects' judgment, &c. (See *Extents.*) . . . . 300, &c.

Sale of on Extents—(See *Extents.*) . . 307, &c.

Forfeiture of—(See *Forfeiture.*)

Grants of lands claimed by Crown restrained . 253, 4

King's estate is how divested . . . 253

Remedy to recover against Crown—(See *Remedies against Crown.*)

LAWS.

Administration of, not by King personally . . 263

LEASE AND RELEASE.

King cannot convey by 378

LEASES FROM CROWN.

(See *Lands—Rents—Distresses.*) . . . 203, 4

As to demand before entry 210

Inquisition when necessary before Crown can act under clause of re-entry on non-payment of rent . 250, 55

Of lands seized and claimed by Crown, should be to subject claiming, &c. on what terms . . 255, &c.

LEET COURT 120

LEGISLATIVE AUTHORITY—(See *Parliament—Colonies.*)

Kept separate from executive and why . . 2

King necessarily has share in legislation . . ibid.

Nature of King's legislative authority . . 3

LETTERS PATENT.

Ceremonies in obtaining—(See *Grants—Patents.*) 389, 90

LEVARI FACIAS.

To recover fines for misdemeanors—(See *Fines.*) . 260

On indictment for not repairing . . . ibid.

LEVARI FACIAS (*continued*).

	Page
On an outlawry	261
Taking stranger's cattle, &c. . .	261, 287, 8
Against beneficed clerk for his lands instead of extent	297
Sheriff entitled to poundage on, for Crown debts .	312

LEX MERCATORIA.

| (See *Commerce.*) . . . . . | 162 |

LICENCE.

To subject to remain abroad, whether revocable, &c.	24
To enemy to come here . . .	48, 9
To trade with enemy	171, 2

LIEN.

| Of Crown on exciseable goods . . . | 293 |
| Equitable, does not hold against extent . . | 303 |

LIGHT-HOUSES.

| Prerogative as to erection of, and where, &c. . | 175, 6 |
| By Trinity-House . . . . | 176 |

LIMITATIONS.

| Statute of, does not bind Crown . . . | 366 |
| Does not affect dignities . . . . | 116 |

LORD CHANCELLOR—(See *Chancellor.*)

| How he holds his office . . . . | 82 |

LUNATICS—(See *Idiots.*)

Prerogative as to, as *parens patriæ* . .	159, 60
In Chancellor from Crown and how . .	ibid.
Difference between and idiots . . .	159
Crown interest in lunatic's property . . .	ibid.
Mad-houses by statutes	ibid.
Inquisition finding lunacy, and how . .	160
Whether necessary . . .	ibid. 250

LUNATICS (*continued*).

Page

Who appointed to mind 160
Care of property, and allowance for lunatic . . ibid.
Abuse of a contempt . . . ibid.
His acts avoided by King, how, and relation back . ibid.
Death of, effect on guardianship, &c. . . . ibid.

M.

MALA PRAXIS.

Crown may pardon 92

MAN (Isle of.)

Prerogative in 28

MANDAMUS.

Prerogative remedy to compel public officer to perform
his duty, &c. 338, 9

MANIFESTATION OF RIGHT.

(See *Monstrans de droit.*) . . . 352

MANSLAUGHTER.

On conviction of, King may pardon burning in hand 90

MARITIMA INCREMENTA.

In King—(See *Seas.*) 206, 7

MARKETS AND FAIRS.

(See *Marts and Fairs.*)

MARKET OVERT.

King not bound by sale in . . . 195, and 285
A shop cannot be made 194

MARQUE AND REPRISALS.

General right to make reprisals . . . 40
Why King alone can grant . . . 40, 1
Prerogative if reprisals without King's authority . 41
Powers under to what restrained . . . ibid.

MARQUE AND REPRISALS (*continued*).

Page

Effect of power under 41

Ancient form of granting . . . 41, 2

Grant of by admiralty 42

How vacated . . . . ibid.

King's right to release prize . . . ibid.

MARQUESSES.

Origin of the title—(See *Peerage*.) . . . 108

MARRIAGES. (Royal.)

Prerogative as to regulating marriages of royal family,
and to what extent, &c. . . . 406, &c.

Act relating to 407, 8

MARTS AND FAIRS.

Use of and why King alone grants, &c. . . . 193

When and how subject may have . . . ibid.

King alone judge where to be held . . . ibid.

If charters do not state where . . . 193, 4

If injurious to an antient mart, &c. . . 194

When owner of latter barred . . . ibid.

Market overt, a shop cannot be made . . ibid.

King not bound by sale in market overt . 195 and 285

General grant, what grantee takes and what not 194, 5

Not toll in general . . . . ibid.

Toll to be reasonable; grant of, how, and when, made 195

Forfeiture of, or liability to be seized, for taking unreasonable toll 195, 6

Or by not duly holding them . . . 196

MAXIMS.

King never dies 5

King can do no wrong . . . 5, 339, 40

Nullum tempus occurrit Regi . . 379, 80

MELIUS INQUIRENDUM.

Or second inquiry when insufficient finding; lies for
King, when, &c. . . . 258, 9

After inquisition under commission on extent . 271

MEMBERS OF PARLIAMENT.—(See *Parliament.*)

Page

    Privilege from arrest   409

MERCHANTS.

    Foreign—(See *Aliens.*)
    Coming here   49

MESNE PROFITS.

    Peculiar prerogative of King as to intermediate profits
        of lands to which he is entitled   .   .   .   257

MILITARY TENURES.

    (See *Feudal System.*)   .   .   .   .   211, &c.

MILITIA.

    King's power over   45

MINES.—(See *Money.*)

    Gold and silver, prerogative as to   .   .   .   145
    Prerogative where only part gold or silver   .   .   145, 6
    When may be in subject   ,   .   .   146

MINISTERS.

    Responsibility of King's   8

MONEY.—(See *Mines.*)

    Prerogative as to   196
    Foreign Money   .   .   .   .   ibid.
    And proclamation legitimating it   .   .   .   198
    Materials of 196, 7
    Stamping or impression of   .   .   .   197
    Denomination or value   .   .   .   ibid.
    Changing weight or alloy   .   .   .   197, 8
    Sums of money of Crown debtor may be taken on ex-
        tent   284

MONOPOLIES.

    Void and why—(See *Patents.*)   .   .   .   176, 7

MONSTRANS DE DROIT.

	Page
A statutable remedy against King . . .	352
To remedy hardships on petition . . .	341
When may be brought	352, 3
General form of	353
In general proper remedy where subject confesses King's claim but avoids it . .	353
When otherwise	ibid.
Subject must shew, and rely, on his own title	ibid.
Lies though King entitled by double matter of record	353, 4
Proceedings upon	352, 4
Judgment on . . .	354
Whether subject on is to be deemed a plaintiff or defendant . . .	354, 5, 6
Nonsuit on	354

MORTGAGE.

Under extent may take equity of redemption . .	296
Mortgagee protected on extent against mortgagor, &c. ibid. and 309, 360, 1	
Before Crown lien good	298
Equitable, not good against extent . .	303
Attainder of mortgagor, its effect .	217
Effect of escheat, &c. of mortgaged lands .	233, 4

MORTMAIN.

Licence of King necessary to enable corporation to hold lands in	131

MOTIONS.

To set aside extents to pay money, &c. upon—(See *Extents, resisting.*) . .	362, &c.

MURDER.

King may pardon, observing certain peculiar forms	91, 99, 100

N.

NATURAL BORN SUBJECTS.

Page

(See *Aliens.*) 13
Who are 13, 14

NATURALIZATION.

King cannot'effect it ; and how it may be done . . 14

NE EXEAT REGNO.

General right of subject to remain here . . 21
And to go abroad ; but King's power to restrain it, and
to recal ; and by what means . . . 21
Origin of *ne exeat regno* as a state writ ; and by whom
granted, &c. 21, 2
May be issued by the Chancellor at the request of the
Secretary of State 21
Gradually Chancery process to secure private debt . 22
Only equity debt 22, 3
Must be a bill filed 22
Affidavit of debt, &c. to ground it ; and requisites of
affidavit 22, 3
Defendant must give security, &c. and how . . 23
Under what seal, &c. and how directed . . 23, 4

NEUTRALS.

Assisting enemy with articles contraband of war . 173

NEW SOUTH WALES.

Governor of, may by commission under great seal, remit whole or part of term for which offenders transported 90

NOBILITY.

(See *Peerage.*) 107

NOLLE PROSEQUI.

Page

By Attorney-general . . . , . 245

In colonies 33

NON OBSTANTES.

(See *Dispensations.*) 95, 6

NONSUIT.

King can never be 24, 5

NON USER (of office).

Office how forfeited by 86

NUISANCE.

As to power of King to pardon . . . 91

NULLUM TEMPUS OCCURRIT REGI.

Instances 379, 80

When 60 years bars King 380

Prescription bars King . . . . ibid.

O.

OATHS.

(See *Allegiance.—Supremacy—Abjuration—Offices.*)

OCCUPANCY.

Prerogative as to . . . . 135 to 137

OFFICE,

Or inquisition, or inquest of office, to entitle the King
to lands, &c.—(See *Inquisition.*) . . . 246, &c.

OFFICERS, (Public.)—(See *Offices.*)

Must take oath of allegiance . . . 17

OFFICERS, (Public.) (*continued*).

Page

Refusing to take oath of allegiance disabled to sue, &c.   18

Judicial—(See *Courts.*)

    Appointed by King   76

    Chancellor and judges   .   .   .   78

Ministerial, public

    Named by Crown   80

Crown debtors holding public offices ; their liabilities to

    King, and from whence their hands are bound   270, 294, 5

OFFICES, (Public.)—(See *Officers.*)

    Judicial—(See *Courts.*)

    Ministerial, public.

       What new public ministerial offices are good and what

          not 80, 1

    Oaths to be taken by persons admitted into   .   . 16, 17

    King may compel his subjects to serve in   .   18, 19

    When King may exempt from serving in   .   . 20

    Not compelled to serve if refusal of oaths be conscientious 19

    Crown cannot create new offices with new fees, or annex

       new fees to old offices, this only by Act of Parliament   81

    Honorary offices   .   .   .   .   ibid.

    On granting offices sub-offices cannot be reserved to King ibid.

    Must be granted according to immemorial mode of so

       doing 81, 2

    When grantable in fee   .   .   .   82

    Judicial offices not grantable in fee, in reversion, or for

       years ; when and why   .   .   .   82

    Aliter ministerial offices   .   .   .   ibid.

    Grantable at will   .   .   .   .   ibid.

    How altered as to judicial offices   .   .   ibid.

    Such generally holden during good behaviour   .   82, 3

    Demise of Crown, effect on offices   .   . 83

    Offices when grantable to two persons   .   .   ibid.

    Mental or other incapacity, when disables party to hold

       public office 83, 4

    When no objection, and how obviated   .   . 84, 5

    Grant of, under what seal, &c. and what words   .   ibid.

OFFICES, (Public.) (*continued*).

Page

Lost or vacated by, 1. Misconduct; 2. Acceptance of
incompatible office; 3. By determination of subject-
matter of office 85

Implied condition to execute duly . . . ibid.

Abusing an office . . . . . . ibid.

Non user of offices vacates them when . . . 86

Refusal to perform duties of, when a forfeiture . ibid.

When these forfeitures bind others, and whom . . 86, 7

On forfeiture, what step necessary to oust officer . 87

King nominates to, on illegal sale of &c. creating forfeiture, without inquisition 259

Lost by acceptance of another incompatible office; and
instances 87, 8

Lost by destruction of subject-matter, of office, and instances 88

Pardon of illegal sale, &c. of does not enable party to
hold 92, 3

ORDERS IN COUNCIL 172

ORDINARY.

King may grant exemption from visitation and jurisdiction of 53

OUSTER LE MAIN.

Judgment of, for subject—(See *Judgment.*) . 348, 9, &c.

OUTLAWRY.

Forfeiture of realty on 221

Of personalty 223

Proceeds to plaintiff in civil action . . . 261

Petition to recover monies received by Crown on reversal of 345

OXFORD, (Chancellor of.)

His power as to making corporation . . . 128

P.

PALACES.

Page

No judicial process executed in, &c. . . . 376

PALATINATE.

Not now grantable 77

PARDONS.

General considerations as to policy and expediency of
pardoning offenders 88, 9
Why in King alone 89
An incommunicable prerogative, except in colonies 90
King may authorize Governor, &c. abroad, to remit
sentence of transportation . . . ibid.
General rule as to instances in which right to pardon holds ibid.
Not in private wrongs and rights . . ibid., &c.
Not to prevent escheat, vested in lord . . 234
Not on attachment for not paying money, &c. . 90
Not sureties of peace for benefit of private person 91
When of penalty given to common informer . ibid.
Of murder, rape, &c. . . . ibid.
Of common nuisances · . . . ibid.
When of suits, &c. in ecclesiastical courts . . 92
Not for illegally sending subject abroad . ibid.
Not pleadable in bar of impeachment by House of Commons ibid.
Of simonist or illegal sale of office; but does not enable
either to hoid . . . . ibid.
When party entitled to party
Approvers 93
Offenders discovering others . . . 94
On killing accidentally . . . ibid.
If promised a pardon . . . ibid.
Persons admitted to be King's evidence not *entitled* to pardon 95
If entitled to pardon, bailed to get it . . ibid.
As to dispensations or *non obstantes*—(See *Dispensations.*) ibid.
On pardoning King may annex condition—breach of 96
Partial exercise of this prerogative—remitting part of
sentence 96, 7

PARDONS (*continued*).

	Page
How granted, under what seal . . .	98
Under sign manual . . .	ibid.
At the Assizes or Old Bailey . . .	ibid.
Pleading a pardon . . .	98, 9
Omission to plead it	99
Charter of—statement of facts and requisites therein	99, 100
How to be drawn in treason, murder or rape .	ibid.
Construction of charter of pardons . .	100
Pardon of principal, or of several, or generally, how it enures ibid.	
Pardoning the act, pardons consequences, when	100, 101
On pardoning, sureties may be taken, and how, but not usual	101
Effect of pardon	102
Offender's property not restored unless clause of restitution 102	
Its effect as to corruption of blood—(And See *Forfeitures*.)	103
No implied pardon by Crown grant of lands to felon, but grant void	393

PARENS PATRIÆ.

King's prerogative as	155

1. Infants—(See *Infants*.)
2. Idiots—(See *Idiots*.)
3. Lunatics—(See *Lunatics*.)
4. As to charities—(See *Charities*.)

PARISH OFFICERS.

If elected, obliged to serve . . .	19

PARK KEEPER.

Grant of office of, in fee	82
Office of, how lost	84, 85

PARKS.

Franchise of and prerogative as to . .	140, 141

PARLIAMENT.

King's legislative authority—(See *Legislative Authority*.)

King head of	3

PARLIAMENT (*continued*).

Page

Legally bound to serve in either House, if qualified, when
elected 19
King cannot exempt from serving in . . . 20
King's prerogative over Parliament . . 67
Whether King may increase number of members . ibid.
King alone can summon, and why . . . 68
How often to be held . . . . ibid.
Each Lord entitled to be summoned --must attend . 69
How called together, proceedings as to election of mem-
bers of lower House ; fresh election in case of death, &c. ibid.
Writs of summonses ; requisites . . . 70
Cannot commence without King, in person, or by repre-
sentation . . . . . ibid.
King cannot adjourn 71
King prorogues and how . . . . ibid.
Effect of prorogation . . . . . ibid.
Session of, how ended 72
Dissolution of . . . . ibid.
Internally independent of Crown . . . 73
But King may be present . . . 73, 4
Proxy in Lords 74
Act of,—King's assent or dissent—this prerogative not
grantable, except in colonies—how exercised . 74, 5
Act of, may originate with King . . . 75
King when bound by—(See *Statutes.*)
Speakers of Lords and Commons how appointed . 74
As one of King's Councils 408

P ARTNERS.

King and subject cannot be 241
May seize partnership goods under extent against one :
how much liable 287

PATENTS.

Monopolies void—but even at common law patents just
and good, and why 177, 8
Ground of under St. of Jac. . . . 178
1. *The Invention.*
What in general subject of patent . . 178

PATENTS (*continued*).

Page

Comment on words ' new manufactures' . 178, 9
Novelty indispensable 179
What novelty sufficient; new effect, though old materials ibid.
Addition or improvement . . . ibid.
How to have patent for improvement . 180, 184, 5
Mere principle not sufficient, when . . 180
When contrary to law in general . . . 181
Liberal construction . . . . ibid.

2. *The Inventor.*
Who is, within the Act 182

3. *Specification.*
What it is and ground of requiring it . . 182, 3
Care in drawing it 183
General rule as to precision, and knowledge imparted ibid.
Bad if ambiguous or can mislead—instances of 184, 5
Or it be too diffuse . . . . ibid.
Or if false in statement as to process, &c.—instances 185, 6
Must give public most beneficial and least expensive
    mode of using invention, when . . 186, 7
No model or drawing necessary, but references when
    bad; complete *per se* 187
Bad if denomination of invention in patent and spe-
    cification differ—and instances . . 187, 8
When inrolled 188

4. *How obtained* 188, 9
Caveat 189, 191
If vested in five persons 191

5. *Remedies, and when infringed and evidence, &c.* 191, 2
6. *Vacating the patent* 193

PAWN.

Goods pawned, whether may be taken under extent, &c. 285, 6

PEACE.

(See *War and Peace.*) . . . . 43, &c.

PEERAGE AND PEERS.

The King only fountain of, and why . . 107, 8

PEERAGE AND PEERS (*continued*).

Page

Different titles or degrees of nobility, and antiquity of 108

Formerly territorial, now personal . . 108, 9

Creation of—1. By writ. 2. By patent—prescriptive
peerage 109

Creation by writ, how . . . . ibíd.

Creation by writ, King may restrain descent of, the title 110

Otherwise descends to lineal heirs, male and female . ibid.

Summons to call up eldest son of Peer, effect of, if in
father's title, &c. . . . . ibid.

Creation of by patent 111

When title complete . . . . ibid.

Restraining descent, &c. in the patent . . ibid.

Term, or interest, which may be granted in a dignity ibid.

Marriage of Peer, his wife takes title, &c. How loses it
by marrying again 111, 12

Peeress in her own right, marrying, effect on the title ibid.

Scotch Peer taking English Peerage, and *vice versa* 112

Precedence among Peers, grant of, &c. . . 112, 13

Title of cannot be legally refused . . 113

Cannot be lost, transferred, or surrendered, nor can
King deprive subject of his title . . 113, 14

Barony by writ, whether extinguished by taking a grant
of the barony 114

Barony whether extinguished by earldom . . ibid.

Dignity or title when in abeyance, nature of, and prerogative herein . . . 114, 5, 6

Dignities not affected by statute of limitations, or time 116

Peer disturbed in his title, remedy . . . ibid.

Counsellors of King . . . 408, 9

Cannot be arrested . . . 409

PENALTIES.

In *qui tam* action, King how protected as to compounding 335

King cannot apply contrary to directions of statute . 386

PERFECTION.

Of King 5

PERPETUITY.

Page

Of King 5

PERSONALTY.—(See *Goods.*)

Nature of King's interest in with subject . . 241, 2
Of King, devise of, &c. 242, 3

PETITION (*De Droit.*)

Origin, common-law remedy for subject . . 340
Exclusively against King, not Queen, &c. . 340, 1
Now better remedies for subject, but still applicable 341
For lands, chattels, debts, damages, or restitution on
reversal of outlawry, &c. . . . 341, 4, 5
General rule, lies where no *monstrans de droit* or tra-
verse 342
Instances 342, 3
If King put another subject in possession common-law
remedy lies 343
How drawn; must state King's titles . . 345
In what Court 345, 6
Must proceed according to prayer of, and King's in-
dorsement, &c. 346, 7
Scire facias, if the King has granted the land over . 347
Writs of search . . . 345, 7, 8
Pleadings—(See *Pleadings.*) . . . 348
Judgment on for lands—(See *Judgment.*) . 348, 9
When King may reseize if subject misuse his judgment 350, 1
Execution if money recovered . . . 348, 9
Suppliant nonsuited, fresh petition . . 349
After failure on demurrer on extents . . 368
On reversal of judgment for Crown, to recover monies 373

PHYSICIANS.

College of 127
Visitor of 131

PIRATES.

Goods seized by, may be detained by Crown . . 151

PLANTATIONS.

Page

Prerogative in—(See *Colonies.*) . . . 29

PLEADINGS.

On Extents, &c.

By whom . . . . . 365, &c.

Statute of Hen. 8. allowing party to plead any defence
in law or equity 366

In general as to subject-matter of defence, pleadings
same as between subject and subject . . ibid.

But defendant cannot plead defences given by statutes
by which Crown not bound—(*See Statutes.*) . ibid.

Pleading general issue *non est factum, non indebitatus,*
&c. . . . . . . ibid.

Defendant against whom extent issues does not claim
property, merely disputes debt . . 367

How his assignees, &c. plead . . . ibid.

Where extent not against immediate Crown debtor,
but against debtor of Crown debtor, &c. the latter
may plead any defence he has to debt, as against
his immediate debtor . . . ibid.

Instances, &c. . . . . . ibid.

Cannot plead double, but may plead, &c. separately
to distinct parts . . . . ibid.

Equitable defences, what allowed, and how brought
forward 368

Strangers claiming cannot dispute Crown debt . ibid.

Demurrer to inquisition . . . ibid.

No rule on Crown to reply . . . 368

But Court will enforce replication in reasonable time ibid.

Crown need not notice plea, but may re-assert its own
title 369

As to Crown replying double . . . ibid.

King may traverse all facts in plea . . ibid.

Need not maintain all his titles . . . ibid.

As to estoppel . . . . . ibid.

When Crown may waive issue . . 369, 70

Defendant cannot waive his plea, &c. . . ibid.

PLEADINGS (*continued*).

Page

On Extents, &c. (*continued*).

Crown waiving objections by not demurring . . 370

Replication a departure from inquisition . . ibid.

Attorney-General confessing the plea when binds
Crown, &c. . . . . . ibid.

Signing replication . . . . . ibid.

Rule to rejoin . . . . . ibid.

On information of intrusion—(See *Intrusion.*) . 333, 4

POOR'S RATES.

King not liable 376, 7

POPERY.

Usurpations of, by what statute destroyed . . 50, 1

POPISH RECUSANT.

Adjudged such by refusal to take oath of allegiance . 18

PORTS AND HAVENS.

Definition of by Lord Hale 174

Prerogative as to erecting, and where . . 174, 5

Claims by lord of county palatine, by owner of other
ports, and by subjects in general . ibid.

Nuisances as to 174

Duties for going to 175

POSSESSION OF KING.

Nature of in law and deed . . . 251, 2

As to entry and seizure—(*See Inquisitions.*) . . ibid.

POSSIBILITY.

King may grant 388

POUNDAGE.

On extents . . . . . . 312, &c.

PRAYERS.

For Royal Family, alteration of 54

PREFERMENTS (Ecclesiastical).

Page

Disposal of belongs to King—(*See Church.*) . . 57

PREROGATIVE.—(*See Analysis.*)

Definition of 4
Grounds of its existence . . . . ibid.
Prerogatives in general 6
Boundaries of 7
Restraints of 8
Who entitled to exercise—(*See Descent of Crown.*) . 9
    King *de facto* 10
    When King *de jure* cannot exercise them . 11
    Titular King cannot . . . . . ibid.
    Roman Catholic King cannot . . . 12
    Regent may . . . . . ibid.
Where exerciseable 25
    General principle, how far it extends to foreign
    British dominions 26
    In Wales—(*See Wales.*) . . . ibid.
    In Scotland—(*See Scotland.*) . . 27
    In Berwick-upon-Tweed . . . . ibid.
    In Ireland—(*See Ireland.*) . . . ibid.
    In Isle of Man—(*See Isle of Man.*) . . 28
    In Guernsey, Guernsey-Sark, Alderney, &c. . ibid.
    In German territories 32
    In conquered country, and how may be
    affected . . . 29, 30, 32, &c.
    In uninhabited country, discovered and peopled by
    Englishmen 30
    In the colonies or plantations.—(*See Colonies.*) 30, &c.
Of the King, as it relates to independent states and
    foreign matters—(*See Foreign States.*) . 39
As to war—(*See War and Peace.*) . . . 43
As to Houses of Parliament—(*See Parliament.*) . 67
As to dignities—(*See Peerage.*) . . 107, &c.
Copyright—(*See Copyright.*) . . . 238, &c.
As to *bona vacantia* 135, 6

PRESCRIPTION.

Good against Crown 380

PRESSING.

                                          Page

Prerogative right to impress 47
Only seamen . . . . . ibid.
Not landman, and what other persons are not liable . ibid.
Common-law exemptions 48
Prerogative and other grants of exemption . . ibid.

PRINCE OF WALES.

The title and that of Earl of Chester, origin of, do not
    necessarily enure to eldest son . . . 403
But King's eldest son, by inheritance and without grant,
    is Duke of Cornwall 404
Nature of latter title, and Duke's right . . ibid.
No other peculiar privileges over the other children . ibid.
Prince's dignity somewhat royal . . 404, 5
Acts relating to him public . . . 405
Grant of Crown lands to him whether an alienation . ibid.
His consort, high treason to conspire her death, &c. . 403
Petition *de droit* not proper remedy against . . 341

PRINTING.

Crown no general power as to—(*See Copyright.*) 238, 9, 10

PRIVILEGES.

King, fountain of, &c.—(*See Franchises—Peerage*) 107, 118, 119
Of King—(See *Incapacities.*)
    Cannot be amerced or arrested 374
    Which of his servants cannot be arrested, &c. . 374 to 376
    No arrest in royal presence, or verge of palaces, &c. . 376
    No distress on Crown lands . . . ibid.
    Nonage of King not a disability . . . ibid.
    Goods not liable to taxes, tolls, rates, &c. . . 376, 7
    And cannot be waifs, &c. or distrained, *damage feasant* 377
    As to tithes . . . . . ibid.
    Not bound to offer acquittance . . . 378
    As to Crown lands—(See *Lands.*) . 203, 209 to 211
    May be trustee, &c. or executor . . 378, 9
    Nullum tempus occurrit regi—(See *Nullum, &c.*) . 379
        Instances of 379, 80

PRIVILEGES (*continued*).

Page

But prescription good against King . 380
Now Crown limited to 60 years , . . ibid.
Not bound by relations or fictions of law or estoppels 381
If rights of King and subject concur, those of former
preferred . . . . . ibid.
Takes whole as joint tenant when . . 241, 2
As to judicial remedies, &c.—(See *Remedies for Crown—
Extents.*) 245

PRIVY COUNCIL.

Nature of it 409
Their number, qualifications, duty, &c. . 410
Their appellate jurisdiction in colonial and admiralty
causes, &c. 410, 11
Their power to cause oath of allegiance to be admi-
nistered 17
Power over state offenders . . . 411
Protection of . . . . ibid.

PRIVY PURSE.

Personalty of King, devise and will of it : liable to his
debts, &c.—(See *Revenue.*) . . . 241, 2

PRIZE.

Right of Crown to release when . . . 42

PROCLAMATIONS.

Object, and former use of, and how restrained . 104
General principle when good, only to inforce existing
law or promulgate what within King's discretion ibid.
Only can be by King ; when a subject punishable for
making 104, 5
Prerogative copyright in . . . 239
What King may do by in general . . 104, 5
Commanding subject to return from abroad . 21
Appointing fasts, &c. . . . 54

PROCLAMATIONS (*continued*).

Page

Not good if restrains where by law no restraint allowed,
though *pro bono publico* 104, 6
How made 106, 7
Disobedience to, *per se*, an offence . . . 107

PROPERTY.

Nature of Crown property as to personalty with a subject—(See *Lands.*) . . . 241, 2

PROTECTION.

Duty of King to protect his subjects . . 7
Prerogative of Crown as to protecting its debtors 282, 3
Not to prevent subject from suing Crown debtor to ex-
ecution and to have it if subject will satisfy Crown, &c. 283
Instances of granting . . . . ibid.
To Crown debtor abroad and serving King . . 284

PURCHASES OF LANDS.

From and by Crown—(See *Lands, Crown.*) . 203 to 206

PURLIEU.

What is, and prerogative as to . . . 139, 40

PURVEYANCE AND PRE-EMPTION . . . 213

Q.

QUARE IMPEDIT.

King may maintain in B. R. . . . 244, 5
Against King, must be by petition . . . 345

QUEEN.

Either Queen reigning in her own right; Queen consort; or Queen dowager . . . 401
1. Queen regent just as King, though married; and her
husband her subject 401; 11
2. Queen consort in general like a *feme sole* and why 401

QUEEN (*continued*).

Page

Queen Consort.

Separate property and courts, may devise and take, &c.
sue and be sued alone, &c.   .   .   . 401, 2
Petition *de droit* not the proper remedy against   .   341
High treason to compass death, or violate Queen consort   402
In general subject to all laws; but does not pay toll, &c.
but servants may be arrested, &c.   .   . ibid.
Ancient *aurum reginæ*, share of whales   .   . ibid. 3
3. Queen dowager no longer high treason, &c.   . 403
As to her marrying, &c. and dower   .   . ibid.

QUI TAM ACTION.

Compounding it, King how protected   .   .   334
When King may pardon—(See *Pardon*.)

QUO WARRANTO.

Prerogative remedy against usurper of a franchise or
public trust, &c.   336
When it lies   .   .   .   .   . ibid.
Lies though King could not hold the usurped franchise
or office 336, 7
Judgment for subject   337
Judgment for King   .   .   .   . ibid.
Capiatur for fine   .   .   .   .   . ibid.
How information in nature of *quo warranto*, object of,
and proceedings thereon   .   .   . ibid. 8

R.

RAPE.

King may pardon, observing certain peculiar forms 91, 99, 100

RECALLING subject from abroad   .   .   . 24, 5

RECEIPT.

King not obliged to offer   378

RECEIVERS OF CROWN MONIES.

Who are, and their peculiar liability to Crown   .   270
Time from which their lands, &c. are bound   . 294, 5

RECORD.

Page

When King's debts are of   .   .   .   265, &c.

Matter of, in general necessary to transfer from and to
    Crown; when otherwise—(See *Grants.*)   .   389, 90. 91

Matter of, in general necessary to divest King of estate   253

RECOVERY.

As to King being barred by, and suffering a   .   .   379

REFUSAL (of office.)

To execute office when a forfeiture   .   .   .   86

REGENT.

Appointment of a   12

RELATIONS OF LAW.

Do not bind King   381

RELIGION (See *Church*)

King cannot alter in this country or any other parts of
    his dominions   51

REM.

(Vide *Information* in).   335

REMEDIES FOR KING.

May waive prerogative remedies   .   .   .   244, 5

King may sue in what Court he pleases   .   .   .   ibid.

Suits involving his Majesty's interests, though he be not
    a party, removable into Exchequer   .   .   ibid.

Entitled to judgment, if his title incidentally appear
    inter alios 244, 372

To be made a party where concerned   .   .   244

Why provided with extraordinary remedies   .   .   ibid.

List of remedies :

    1. By Action; 2. By Inquisition, and of Extents,
    diem clausit extremum ; 3. By *Scire facias* to repeal,
    &c.; 4. By Information; 5. By *Quo Warranto* ;
    8. By *Mandamus*—(See *those titles.*)   .   .   245

REMEDIES AGAINST KING.

Page

In general . 339

   No action maintainable against King . . . ibid.
   1. Petition ; 2. *Monstrans de droit ;* 3. Traverse of
   office—(See *those titles.*) . . . 340
   None for personal injury by King . . . ibid.

RENTS.

(See *Lands—Distress.*) . . . . 208, &c.
King may reserve out of incorporeal inheritances . 209
And to stranger, but not to removable officer, when . ibid.
King need not demand previous to re-entry, when, but
   grantee must 210, 211
Landlord not entitled to year's rent under extent . 287
Rents, what Crown may take under extents . . 297

RENT CHARGE.

Not liable to escheat 233

REPLEVIN.

On Crown distress or seizure . . . 209, 10

REPLICATION OF CROWN.

(See *Pleadings.*) 368, 9

REPRIEVE.

Meaning of, &c. . . . . . ibid.
By whom granted . . . . . ibid.
How granted . . . . . . ibid.

RESIGNATION OF CROWN. 12

RESTITUTION.

On extents 373
After writ of error . . . . . ibid.

RESTRAINTS.

On prerogative 8

REVENUE.

Page

Utility of large revenue, but not if burthensome   199, 200
Why in King 200
1. ordinary; or, 2. extraordinary . . . ibid.
Nature of 'antient revenue; modern different, and in
   what respect . . . . . ibid.
Latter preferable 201
Civil list, extent of . . . . ibid.
Only civil list properly revenue of Crown, rest of public 201, 2
Temporalities, Corodies, Tithes of extra-parochial places,
   First Fruits, and Tenths—(See *those titles.*)
Profits from demesne lands—(See *Lands.*) . 202, &c.
From profits of courts of justice, fines, &c. . . 236
Grants of these profits restrained . . 236, 7
Forfeitures—(See *that title.*) . . . 213, &c.
Franchises—(See *that title.*)
Extraordinary;
   Nature of, since new system of finance . 237, 8
Chief parts of extraordinary revenue . . . 238
Pecuniary forfeitures sued for by information of debt, &c. 335
Ships, &c. forfeited, information in *rem* . . ibid.
King's rights as to part of penalty in *qui tam* action . ibid.
Personalty of King; devise of, &c. . . 241, 2, 3
Suits respecting may be removed into Exchequer . 244

REVERSION.
Grant of by King, what necessary . . . 396

REVOLUTIONS.
How they eventually terminate in England . . ibid.

RIGHT, (Writ of.)
For King in B. R. 244
Petition of right—(See *Petition.*)

RIVERS.
Prerogative in—(See *Seas.*) . . 142, 173, 206, 7, 8

ROMAN CATHOLIC
King, cannot reign 12

ROYAL FAMILY.

Page

(See *Family Royal.*) . . . . 401, &c.

Prayers for how alterable 54

S.

SAFE CONDUCT.

Letters of 48

SALTPETRE.

King has prerogative right in . . . 49

SARK (Isle of.)

Prerogative in 28

SCIRE FACIAS.

To justify issuing of extent—(See *Extents.*) . 271, &c.

In general unnecessary to revive proceedings in case of
the Crown 272, 373

To repeal grants—General rule when King's grants may
be avoided on 330

    Subject to have this remedy, when, and how . 331

    Where brought, and how obtained . . ibid.

    Summons, &c. thereon, no costs . . ibid.

Necessary for King as to lands claimed by him, when 252, 3

Necessary on forfeiture of office . . . 87

For King after judgment for the subject on subsequent
matter being discovered . . . 257, 8

Against subject on fresh title accruing to King after recovery against his Majesty . . . 357

Against King's patentee on petition . . . 347

SCOTLAND.

Union with England, and prerogative in . . 26, 7

Statutes when bind . . . . ibid.

SEALS.

King's 390

Seal days in Exchequer . . . 359

492   INDEX.

SEARCH (Writs of.)

Page

    On petition *de droit* . . . 345, 7, 8

SEAS.

    Sovereignty of King over what seas . . 142, 173
    Does not restrain *jura publica*—(See *Fisheries and Fish—*
      and *Commerce.*) . . . . ibid.
    Lands under, property of King, how far . ibid. 206, 7
    Maritima incrementa, or lands arising in sea, in King ibid.
    So of lands *derelict,* or deserted, prerogative herein . 207
    So of shores of seas and rivers . . ibid. 208
    Subjects claim therein . . . . ibid.
    Nuisance, &c. in seas, restrained by King . . 173
    Crown provides against inundations, &c. . . ibid.
    Ports, beacons and light-houses—(See *these titles.*) 174 to 176

SECRETARIES OF STATE.

    Power as to state delinquents . . . 411

SEIZURE.

    For King when necessary besides office . . 251, &c.

SENESCHAL OF ENGLAND.

    Office of, how inheritable . . . 82

SERJEANT AT LAW.

    By whom created 118
    A lawyer may be punished for not accepting that degree 19

SERVANTS.

    Of King what, protected when, &c. . . 374, 5, 6
    Of King cannot justify under his illegal command
                              340 note (*b*), 342
    Of Queen may be arrested . . . 402

SERVICES.

    King how far entitled to personal assistance of his sub-
      jects—(See *War.*) 18, 21

SET-OFF.

Page

Statute of, does not bind Crown . . . 366
When it may . .' 368 and note (c)

SHERIFFS.

By whom, and how, appointed . . . 78, 9
How long in office 79
Grant of Shrievalty in fee . . . 82
If appointed cannot refuse to act . . . 19
His duty and powers on extents, his poundage, &c.—
(See *Extents.*) . ' . . . 280, 285, &c.
His poundage, &c. on extents . . 312, &c.

SHIPS OF WAR.

King cannot prohibit the building of for alien *ami* in this
country 50

SHORES OF SEAS AND RIVERS.

Prerogative in—(See *Seas.*) . . . 173, 207, 8

SIMONY.

In case of, King shall present without inquisition . 259
Pardon of offence does not enable simonist to hold 92, 3

SOCIETY.

Origin of 1

SOLICITOR-GENERAL.

Acts if no attorney-general 370

STANNARIES. 146
Courts 119, 20

STATUTES (See *Dispensations.*)

When bind Wales, Scotland, Ireland . . 26, 7
When bind the colonies 31, 2, 3
King may take benefit of, though not bound unless named 382
Exceptions if for public good, justice, against fraud, &c. ibid.
Instances . . . . . ibid.
King must take new statutable right as given ibid. 383
No strictness of construction against subject . . 383

STATUTES (*còntinued*).

Page

Acts abridging Crown interests and remedies do not
bind 383
Instances 383, 366
Acts to ease Crown of duties do not bind though sole
right given elsewhere . . . 383, 4

STEWARDS (High).
Office of, how inheritable 81

STURGEONS.
Prerogative as to 144

SUCCESSOR.
Takes Crown at once 11

SUFFERANCE (Tenant by.)
Cannot be against King 380

SUPERSTITIOUS USES.
King's appointment of gift . . . 161, 2

SUPREMACY.
Of King—(See *Church*.) 50

SWANS.
Prerogative as to; when subject may possess . . 144

T.

TAIL ESTATES.
Do not escheat, though they are forfeitable for treason 233
How far liable under extent, after death of Crown debtor,
when—(See *Extents*.) . . . 298, &c.
King may bar; how 379

TAXES.
King cannot tax even English colony; without assent of
Parliament, or representative assembly 34, 202

TAXES (*continued*).

Page

King's grant cannot create 385, 6
King's lands, when subject to . . . 204, 5
King's goods, not subject to . . . 376, 7
Collector liable to costs under extent . . . 311
Debt due from tax collectors, of record, &c. . . 266
Collector's lands, from whence bound . . . 294, 5
Must be paid before subject's execution . . 293

TEMPORALITIES.

Of archbishops, &c.
    Prerogative as to . . . 64
Revenue of 65
Subject cannot have this prerogative . . . ibid.
Of bishops,
    Seized for bishop's offence 65
Inquisition when necessary for King as to . . 249, 50

TENANT.

King cannot be, when 378
Tenants of King—(See *Lands, &c.*)
In common, King and subject may be . . 210, 11
Joint, cannot be . . . . ibid.
Joint, the survivor not liable for Crown debts—(See
    Extents.) 300

TENTHS 66

TENURE.

By grand serjeanty 81

TERM OF YEARS.

Seizure of under extent . . . 297, 8

TITHES (Extraparochial.)

King entitled to 65
King may be liable, but generally not so, and how 377
Grantee liable . . . . ibid.
What tithes Crown may take on extents . . 297

TOLLS.

Page
In market or fair—(See *Marts and Fairs.*) . 194, 5, 6
When King may exempt from . . . 195
King's goods not subject to . . . 195, 376, 7
Queen does not pay 402
Rest of royal family do . . . 405 and note (*c*)

TORTS.

By King to the person, no redress, *aliter* if to property 340

TRADE.

(See *Commerce.*)

TRANSPORTATION.

Law of, on what founded 102
How part of sentence remitted by governor . . 90
Effect of, as amounting to effect of a pardon . . 102

TRAVERSE OF OFFICE.

That is, subject disputing King's claim on inquisition, and
setting up a right 356
At common law, a contracted remedy . . ibid.
How enlarged by statute . . . . ibid.
When may be done . . . . ibid.
Subject must shew his own legal title; possession insuffi-
cient; and must answer King's title . . 356, 7
Must traverse all, and which, of King's titles . . 357
Effect of a fresh title accruing to Crown . . ibid.
Traverser whether to be considered a plaintiff or de-
fendant 354
Judgment on—(See *Judgment.*) . . . 347
Granting the lands to the traverser *pendente lite* . 253
Protection to persons holding terms in, and having rents,
&c. out of the lands in dispute . . . 340
How to traverse and plead, &c.—(See *Extents—Plead-
ings—&c.*) . . . . 358, &c.

TREASON. (See *Allegiance.*)
What forfeited for—(See *Forfeitures.*) . . 216, 7, 8
No inquisition necessary to entitle King to forfeiture 249
Form of pardon of . . . 91, 99

TREASURE.

Page

And jewels of crown, nature of . . . 238

TREASURE TROVE.

What is 152, 3
Prerogative as to . . . . . ibid.
Concealing treasure found 153

TREASURER.

Treasurer's lands liable from time of entering on office.
—(See *Extents—Receiver.*) 294

TREATIES.

As to trade, binding on subjects . . . 166, 7, 170
As to war and peace—(See *War and Peace.*)

TRESPASS.

Information of intrusion, remedy for trespass to Crown
lands—(See *Intrusion.*) 332
Action of trespass *quare clausum fregit* by King . 245

TRIAL.

King may try where he pleases 370, 1
Notice of 371
Remedy if Crown delays . . . ibid.

TRUST ESTATE.

May under extent take estate held in trust for defendant 290

TRUSTEE.

Of lands, King may be, but not compellable to execute
the trusts 378
His lands whether forfeited . . . 217
Attainder of, its effect . . . 233, 4

U.

UNCERTAINTY.

Page

    In Crown grants, when avoids it—(See *Grants.*) . 394, 5

UNINHABITED COUNTRY.

    Prerogative on English peopling it . . . 30

UNION.

    Of England and Scotland 26, 7
    Great Britain and Ireland 27, 8

USE.

    King cannot be seized to an . . . 378

USURY 366, 7

V.

VENDITIONI EXPONAS.

    On extents—(See *Extents.*) 307

VENUE.

    King may lay where he pleases . . . 333

VICE-CHANCELLOR.

    Holds office during good behaviour . . 82

VISCOUNTS.

    Origin of the title—(See *Peerage.*) . . . 108

VISITOR.

    Of corporations, King's prerogative . . 130, 1

W.

WAIFS.

Page

What are 146, 7

Belong to Crown; and why; without office, but must
    be seized for King 147

No waif if not thrown away; or if goods of foreign
    merchant 146, 7

Owner entitled to restitution; when . . 147

May be prescriptively in subject; but not *bona felonum*
    or *fugitivorum* 147, 8

WAIVING.

King waiving his declaration . . . 334

His issue 369, 70

WALES.

Conquest of, &c. and prerogative therein . . 26

What laws hold therein . . . . ibid.

Prince of—(See *Prince of Wales.*) . . 403, &c.

WAR AND PEACE.

King has exclusive right to make . . . 43, 4

Partial exercise of, by King . . . 43

Truce or capitulation . . . . ibid.

Impliedly, at peace . . . . ibid.

When actual declaration of war necessary . . 44

War prerogative incident to right of making war; King
    conductor of . . . . ibid.

General nature of war prerogative . . . 50

King generalissimo 45, 25

Alone makes forts, &c. and where . . 45, 9

Militia; power of King as to 45

Army; prerogative as to 45, 6

King cannot compel subject to enlist, or to leave realm
    to fight . . . . . ibid. 18, 21

Fleet 46

Pressing—(See *Pressing.*) . . . 47, &c.

Preventing egress and ingress of aliens—(See *Aliens.*) 48, &c.

WAR AND PEACE (*continued*).

Page

King cannot hinder building ships of war here for alien
ami 50

Contraband of war; King may prohibit—(See *Contraband of War*.) 172, 3

Prerogative as to dispensing with commercial disabilities
as to enemy . . . . 170 to 173

WARREN.

Free 141, 2

WEIGHTS AND MEASURES · 196

WHALES.

Prerogative as to; when subject may possess it . 144

WILL.

Devise of King's personalty; and requisites of his will 242, 3

WITNESS.

King cannot be in criminal cases . . . 377
Semb. otherwise in civil suits; and how . . 377, 8

WRECKS.

Different species of 148
In King; and why 148, 9
Prerogative as to; and when King entitled; and when
not 149, 50
Law less severe than formerly; in what respects . 149
In King, without seizure or office . . 150
Owner entitled to restitution; when; and within what
time 149, 50
Goods of King not to be treated as wrecks . . 150
How to be used by King . . . . ibid.

Y.

YEAR DAY AND WASTE.

Prerogative as to 219, 20
Inquisition for King necessary 250

G. WOODFALL, PRINTER, ANGEL-COURT, SKINNER STREET, LONDON.

www.ingramcontent.com/pod-product-compliance
Lightning Source LLC
Chambersburg PA
CBHW030633270326
41929CB00007B/52